Student Mastery Guide

INTERMEDIATE

ACCOUNTING

FIFTH EDITION

JOHN CUMMING
Miami University

CLAYTON A. HOCK
Miami University

LANNY G. CHASTEEN

RICHARD E. FLAHERTY

MELVIN C. O'CONNOR

McGraw-Hill, Inc.
New York   St. Louis   San Francisco   Auckland   Bogotá
Caracas   Lisbon   London   Madrid   Mexico City
Milan   Montreal   New Delhi   San Juan
Singapore   Sydney   Tokyo   Toronto

Intermediate Accounting
Student Mastery Guide

3 4 5 6 7 8 9 0 SEM SEM 9 0 9 8 7 6

ISBN 0-07-011193-6

This book was set in Times Roman by Pat McCarney.
The editors were Judy Howarth, Alan Sachs, and Linda Richmond;
the production supervisor was Richard A. Ausburn.
The cover was designed by Joseph A. Piliero.
Semline, Inc., was printer and binder.

CONTENTS

PREFACE:
TO THE INSTRUCTOR

The *Student Mastery Guide* is a component crucial to the supplementary package that accompanies *Intermediate Accounting*, Fifth Edition, by Lanny G. Chasteen, Richard E. Flaherty, and Melvin C. O'Connor. As you know, many students find this course's material quite difficult and need additional textual aids to help them grasp the more conceptual issues presented in the intermediate accounting curriculum. The *Student Mastery Guide* provides just such a device, as it not only helps students focus on the key topics but also provides a well-organized and comprehensive summary of the chapter material, accompanying drills (with answers), and a unique section that clarifies many misconceptions students may have about the techniques, concepts, and issues presented in each chapter.

The first section in each chapter, "Chapter Objectives," lists those areas that students should thoroughly study to ensure their efficient, on-target review of the corresponding chapter material. These points are expanded upon in the "Chapter Review," which provides an extensive, detailed summary with explanations to bring the issues into an application context. Next, the "Self-Study Learning" section tests students by using key terms and concepts, true-false and multiple choice questions, and extended problems. These questions and problems help students to focus further on the key issues outlined in the "Chapter Objectives" and "Chapter Review" sections, as each is directly related to the chapter's major topics. "Common Errors," a section that should prove particularly useful in studying for examinations, is designed to clear up the areas that are most frequently misunderstood by students. This section covers several points. It begins by stating a common misconception that students have. It then goes on to specify the corresponding "right" principle or concept and gives the rationale for the correct concept or procedure, helping set students on the right track in comprehending the theory or technique involved. Finally, the "Answers" section is provided as a key to the "Self-Study Learning" section and allows students to gauge whether they have successfully completed the drills and what topic areas may require further study. Each false answer to the true-false questions includes an explanation of why that answer if false, and fully worked-through solutions to the extended problems are provided.

We believe that this focused approach to the concepts and procedures in *Intermediate Accounting* will allow students more confidence in their mastery of the material. They will know that they not only have reviewed the key issues of the text chapter but also have seen how well they can apply their new knowledge and have had the opportunity to rid themselves of the misconceptions that they could easily adopt. We feel that their successful completion of the *Guide*'s materials will result in equally successful performance in examinations and improved clarity of comprehension of your course material.

John Cumming
Clayton A. Hock

TO THE STUDENT

The *Student Mastery Guide* is designed to be used in conjunction with *Intermediate Accounting,* Fifth Edition, by Lanny G. Chasteen, Richard E. Flaherty, and Melvin C. O'Connor.

Closely coordinated with the corresponding text chapter, each chapter of the *Student Mastery Guide* contains the following sections:

- A "Chapter Objectives" section that identifies what you should know after reading and studying the corresponding text chapter.
- A "Chapter Review" section that provides a well-organized and comprehensive summary of the financial accounting and reporting principles discussed in the corresponding text chapter, including detailed descriptions of the journal entries and illustrated worksheets.
- A "Self-Study Learning" section that contains key terms and concepts, true-false and multiple choice questions, and extended problems designed to enable you to evaluate and improve your mastery of the significant concepts and principles presented in the corresponding text chapter. The key terms and concepts questions focus on financial accounting terminology, the true-false and multiple choice questions cover both the conceptual and the practical aspects of financial accounting, and the extended problems concentrate on the technical and numerical applications of financial accounting and reporting principles.
- A unique "Common Errors" section that identifies errors that students frequently make in the application of the concepts and principles presented in the corresponding text chapter. Each incorrect statement is followed by a corrected statement and an explanation of the correct accounting concept or practice.
- An "Answers" section that provides the answers to the key terms and concepts, true-false and multiple choice questions, and extended problems contained in that chapter of the *Guide,* so that you may measure the extent of your mastery of the material presented in the corresponding text chapter and identify those subject areas that you need to study further in preparation for examinations. Each false answer to the true-false questions includes an explanation of why that answer is false, and the solutions to the extended problems contain explanations of how the related amounts are calculated.

We hope the *Guide* contributes to your mastery of intermediate accounting and to your success in the course. However, remember that the *Guide* should be used as a supplement to, rather than a substitute for, the textbook.

We wish to express our appreciation to those who assisted us in the preparation of the *Student Mastery Guide,* including Judy Howarth, Alan Sachs, and Linda Richmond as editors; the authors of the textbook as reviewers; and our families for their support and encouragement.

John Cumming
Clayton A. Hock

1 FINANCIAL ACCOUNTING AND REPORTING: AN INTRODUCTION AND HISTORICAL DEVELOPMENT

CHAPTER OBJECTIVES

After reading Chapter 1 and completing the questions, cases, exercises, and problems from the text chapter, you should be able to:

1. Explain the nature of accounting and differentiate between financial and managerial accounting.
2. Understand the perceived relationships among the organized securities markets, investors, and published financial accounting information.
3. Distinguish between direct and indirect users of financial accounting information.
4. Understand the interrelationship between the economic environment and financial accounting and reporting.
5. Define generally accepted accounting principles (GAAP).
6. Understand the implications of ethical behavior facing the accounting profession.
7. Distinguish among the various sources of information available for investors and creditors to use in decision making.
8. Trace the development of financial accounting and reporting through the pre-formal-theory era, the problem-solving era, and the conceptual-framework era.
9. Understand the organizational structure and standard-setting process of the Financial Accounting Standards Board (FASB), and know the four types of pronouncements it issues.
10. Understand the political nature of accounting standard setting.
11. Identify the impact of the various groups that influence financial accounting and reporting theory and practice.
12. Appreciate the varied development of international accounting practices, and know the major setters of international accounting standards.

CHAPTER REVIEW

Introduction

1. Most new accounting students view accounting as a relatively recent phenomenon that is inexorably tied to debits and credits. The opposite is in fact true. Accounting has had a rich and interesting history that can be traced over several centuries, and it is certainly much more than debits and credits. This chapter focuses on the development of the accounting profession and the evolution of GAAP, that is, generally accepted accounting principles. More specifically, this chapter review discusses the nature of accounting, the economic environment and accounting, the nature and content of financial accounting and reporting, the historical development of financial accounting and reporting, and other influences on financial accounting and reporting.

The Nature of Accounting

2. Quite simply, accounting is utilitarian; that is, it is a means to an end. The means is a process that identifies, measures, and communicates financial information about an economic entity. The end is to

1

enable people who are interested in the entity to make informed financial decisions about it. In fact, some people refer to accounting as a measurement-communication activity.

3. The major fields of accounting are identified by the primary users of the information. *Financial accounting* provides information to individuals external to the entity, such as investors and creditors. *Managerial accounting* provides information to individuals internal to the entity, such as managers. Thus, accounting is not self-serving; rather, it functions to aid people not directly involved in the accounting process by providing relevant information to assist them in their decision-making process.

The Economic Environment and the Role of Accounting

4. Accounting as practiced in the United States has developed in response to an economic environment that may be described as a developed free market monetary-exchange economy. Unlike a barter economy, in which goods and services are exchanged, our economy uses money as the basis for exchange. Decisions of users of financial accounting and reporting information involve the allocation of their present and expected money resources.

5. The primary external users of financial accounting information are those individuals, such as owners and creditors, who supply the capital resources needed to carry on the activities of business entities, particularly corporations. These users can buy and sell their securities on organized securities markets, such as the New York Stock Exchange. Although many factors affect the market price of a company's securities, a primary factor is the cash flows generated by the company's earnings and other operating activities. Owners and creditors, in effect, entrust their resources to a company's management and want to be able to assess how management has fulfilled its stewardship role. Specifically, owners and creditors are concerned about the return *on* their investment in the form of either dividends (owners) or interest (creditors) and the return *of* their investment in the form of either the market price of stock (owners) or the principal of the debt (creditors).

6. Because owners and creditors are not usually close to a company's activities, they rely on published accounting information as a primary source of their information about the company. Research indicates that the securities markets assimilate accounting information efficiently, that is, quickly and without bias. This means that no investor can expect to use published accounting information to earn abnormal or above-average returns on security investments. Moreover, investors can be reasonably assured that published accounting information helps prevent people with access to unpublished information from earning a greater or abnormal return by trading on such inside information.

7. In addition to serving the resource-allocation decisions of investors and creditors, accounting and reporting information is used in activities such as wage negotiations, bonus distributions, and pension funding.

8. Other environmental factors that affect financial accounting and reporting are the taxation, spending, borrowing, and regulatory activities of governmental agencies and regulatory bodies. Many of these bodies use financial accounting and reporting information in planning and evaluating their programs.

9. U.S. financial accounting and reporting practices evolved in response to the U.S. legal, economic, and social environment. Because each country has its own unique environment, its accounting and reporting practices developed differently. For example, in countries where capital is provided by banks, financial accounting focuses on credit protection. Though an understanding of these differences is important, the emphasis here is on U.S. financial accounting and reporting.

10. Users. All users of accounting information have an economic interest in the reporting entity. Such users as present and potential owners, creditors, employees, and managers are said to have a *direct* economic interest in the entity; other users, such as financial analysts, securities exchanges, and regulatory authorities, have an *indirect* interest. In general, those with an indirect interest advise, represent, or otherwise influence those who have or contemplate having a direct interest. All users, however, share a common need fulfilled by financial accounting and reporting information: to receive unbiased financial information that will assist them in making decisions concerning the efficient allocation of scarce resources.

11. As accounting serves various users within the economic environment, the users' needs and the economic environment directly affect the development of financial accounting and reporting practices. Unfortunately, users' needs and the environment constantly change, and with them accounting and reporting practices. This fact is evidenced, for example, by the accounting profession's response to the growth in pension plans and changes in the rate of inflation. Each of these phenomena has been addressed by a comprehensive pronouncement setting accounting and reporting guidelines.

12. Similarly, the increase in international business has resulted in accounting standards for transactions denominated in a currency other than the U.S. dollar and translation to U.S. dollars of financial statements denominated in a foreign currency. In addition to these accounting practice issues, the globalization of financial markets has raised interest in international accounting standards for financial reporting. Since 1973 the International Accounting Standards

Committee (IASC), the recognized international accounting standard setter, has issued about 30 standards that essentially allow for alternatives that are currently accepted in developed countries.

13. Attention has recently been directed to the effects of financial accounting and reporting on the behavior of both users and preparers of financial accounting reports. Some people contend that the accounting practices used in the preparation of financial reports may at times have an *economic consequence* on the users of the accounting information. A heated debate, for example, took place over the accounting standards for the reporting of oil and gas exploration, troubled debt restructuring, and postretirement benefits other than pensions.

14. Because of possible economic consequences, critics challenge the FASB on two of its recent positions: (*a*) equity and debt investments and (*b*) executive stock compensation. *Statement No. 115* changes the way equity and debt investments are reported on a company's balance sheet from original cost to fair value (often referred to as "mark-to-market" accounting, covered in Chapters 13 and 14). Prior to *Statement No. 115*, companies were allowed to disclose debt investments at cost, which often overstated their true value. Opponents to fair value reporting contend that requiring companies, particularly banks, to disclose their loan portfolios at fair value will affect the way they conduct their business. The FASB proposes that executive stock compensation plans, including stock options, be valued at their fair value and expensed in determining periodic income. Opponents to this FASB proposal state that companies will either alter or eliminate their use of stock compensation plans because of the added expense recognition. Accounting for stock options is covered in Chapter 18. Moreover, some argue that U.S. corporations are put at a competitive disadvantage in the global environment because of the economic consequences of U.S. accounting practices, such as accrual of certain retirement benefits rather than the cash-basis approach used by most countries. The organizations responsible for establishing accounting and reporting standards, such as the FASB and the Securities and Exchange Commission (SEC), are now paying closer attention to the economic consequences of their pronouncements. Thus, accounting must be responsive to its environment and to users' needs, but at the same time standard-setting bodies should be aware of the economic consequences of their financial accounting and reporting standards on those whom accounting is to serve.

The Nature and Content of Financial Accounting and Reporting

15. GAAP. Financial accounting and reporting are by their nature an art, not an exact science. Profes-

sional judgment must be exercised in the preparation of financial statements and of the supplementary information that is put together for external users under generally accepted accounting principles. Professional judgment is required, for example, in calculating depreciation expense for an accounting period. Because accounting reports are intended for decision-making purposes, it is essential that users have assurances that the reports are credible and not biased or prepared in accordance with some idiosyncratic accounting system of the preparer's devising. These assurances are provided by the conventions, rules, and procedures of financial accounting and reporting that must be followed in the preparation of external reports—GAAP. Presently, the FASB is the designated authoritative body to establish generally accepted accounting principles. Because these standards do change over time, at any given moment they represent a consensus among accountants as to the practices that are then accepted.

16. One of the major tenets of the independent auditor's (CPA's) unqualified opinion states that a company's financial statements are in conformity to GAAP. To assist the auditor, the American Institute of Certified Public Accountants' (AICPA's) Auditing Standards Board issued *Statement on Auditing Standards No. 69*, which identifies five hierarchical categories or sources of GAAP for (*a*) nongovernmental entities and (*b*) state and local governments. The categories for nongovernmental entities range from *FASB Statements* and *APB Opinions* (the highest level) to FASB *Concepts Statements* and accounting textbooks (the lowest level).

17. Ethics in financial accounting. The guidance GAAP provides in the preparation of financial statements is not a substitute for ethical behavior of those who prepare or audit financial statements. Examples of perceived unethical business behavior abound—from insider trading to questionable practices by savings and loan institutions. Ethical dilemmas do not escape either public (independent auditors) or management (preparers of financial statements) accountants. Users of financial statements rely on the integrity of the statements, and it is incumbent upon the accountant to make sure that accounting data are measured and communicated fairly and without bias. Accountants must make decisions about the proper application of GAAP and the utilization of information that is not publicly available. In such circumstances, given the values of society, the accountant must make an ethical assessment of what is right or wrong. Thus, besides having technical competence, accountants must act ethically to enhance the credibility of financial statements and further the public good.

18. Information sources. Accounting reports provide only one source (albeit an important one) of information to investors and creditors. The table on the following page presents an example of each type of information available to users.

Examples of Five Types of Information Used by Investors and Creditors in Decision Making

---

(A)	(B)	(C)	(D)	(E)
Financial statements	Notes to financial statements	Supplementary information	Other means of financial reporting	Other information
Income statement	Accounting policies	Effects of changing price	Special reports requested, e.g., by bank	News releases

---

Source: Adapted from "Recognition and Measurement in Financial Statements of Business Enterprises," *Statement of Financial Accounting Concepts No. 5* (Stamford, Conn.: FASB, 1984), p. 5. Copyright by Financial Accounting Standards Board, 401 Merritt 7, P.O. Box 5116, Norwalk, Connecticut, 06856-5116, U.S.A. Reprinted with permission. Copies of the complete document are available from the FASB.

19. All types of information except Type *E* constitute financial reporting. The information of Types *A* through *C* constitutes general purpose external financial reporting and is of concern to the FASB, the organization that currently establishes GAAP. Only Types *A* and *B* information, however, are subject to an audit by an independent certified public accountant (CPA). The financial statements required under GAAP, whose preparation and dissemination is the responsibility of the reporting entity's management, are (*a*) the balance sheet or statement of financial position, (*b*) the income statement or statement of earnings, (*c*) the statement of owners' (or stockholders') equity, and (*d*) the statement of cash flows. All financial statements are formal representations of an entity's accounting records, that is, the accounts and their dollar amounts. It should be emphasized that all the financial statements articulate (are interrelated) and that the information contained in the notes to the financial statements is based on the same underlying economic data. Type *D* information is provided by management outside the formal financial statements and notes. This information may be disseminated widely, such as the letter to the stockholders found in the annual report, or prepared at the request of a particular user, such as a bank or governmental regulatory agency. Type *E* information represents all information from sources other than the financial reporting system, such as stock market newsletters, analysts' advice, and even rumor. Individually and collectively, the purpose of each type of information is to supply relevant information to external users about a company's ability to generate positive net cash flows from operating activities.

The Historical Development of Financial Accounting and Reporting

20. Financial accounting and reporting have gone through three distinct periods in their development.

In each period financial accounting and reporting practices responded largely to the needs of the institutional and professional organizations dominant at the time.

21. Pre-formal-theory era. Evidence exists that accounting practices were in use as far back as the days of the Roman Empire. It was not until 1494, however, that the first book on double-entry bookkeeping appeared. Nearly 300 years later, with the coming of the Industrial Revolution, the first real need for financial accounting and reporting information developed. From the Industrial Revolution to the early 1900s, business became steadily more complex, with increased capital requirements. To meet these capital requirements, the corporate form of business flourished, and with it the need to provide financial information to an increasing number of shareholders and large-scale creditors. Financial accounting and reporting were also influenced during this period by the growth in railroads and the taxing of business income.

22. Accounting practices during this era were determined by individual accountants in response to the circumstances they encountered. Even though accounting attained the status of a profession, no professional group existed to establish accounting practices.

23. Problem-solving era. Partly because of the stock market crash of 1929, the previous era's laissez-faire attitude toward accounting practices received severe criticism. In 1930 the foremost professional organization in the field, the American Institute of Accountants (AIA; later renamed the American Institute of Certified Public Accountants, or AICPA), explicitly recognized investors' and creditors' needs for accounting information and established a committee formally to address accounting issues and procedures. This shift in focus from management and creditors to investors and stockholders was furthered by the regulations of the Securities Act of 1933 and the Securities Exchange Act of 1934.

24. The Securities Act of 1933 set accounting and reporting requirements for companies issuing a particular security for the first time. The Securities Exchange Act of 1934 established periodic accounting and reporting requirements for companies whose stock was listed on organized stock exchanges and created the Securities and Exchange Commission, which was empowered to administer both securities acts and to ensure "full and fair" disclosure by prescribing accounting procedures and the form and content of financial reports filed with the SEC.

25. Five commissioners constitute the SEC, which is organized into separate offices and divisions. Two of the most important ones for accountants are (*a*) the Office of the Chief Accountant, which is responsible for all accounting and auditing matters associated with the various acts, and (*b*) the Division of Corporation Finance, which reviews all filed registration statements and reports for compliance with SEC regulations and GAAP. The SEC has authority only over business enterprises that are required to file with it; all others are not obligated to adhere to SEC regulations. Although the SEC delegated its responsibility for setting accounting procedures to the private sector in 1938 (and to the Financial Accounting Standards Board in 1973), it directly influences financial accounting and reporting practices through *Regulation S-X, Regulation S-K, Accounting Series Releases (ASRs), Financial Reporting Releases (FRRs), Accounting and Auditing Enforcement Releases (AAERs),* and *Staff Accounting Bulletins (SABs).*

26. From 1938 to 1959, the Committee on Accounting Procedure (CAP) was the AICPA's appointed accounting standard-setting body. During its tenure the CAP issued 51 *Accounting Research Bulletins (ARBs)* on specific accounting and reporting problems.

27. The Accounting Principles Board (APB) replaced the CAP in 1959 and continued to issue accounting standards through June 1973. The APB unsuccessfully tried to avoid the greatest weakness of the CAP: failure to develop a theoretical framework for financial accounting and reporting. Although the APB attempted to focus on theory, it succumbed to the temptation to resolve individual accounting and reporting problems at the expense of a theoretical framework. The APB issued 31 *Opinions,* which set GAAP, and four *Statements,* which were informative documents but did not establish GAAP.

28. Both the work and the structure of the APB were criticized. Charges leveled against it were that it was too large (18 to 21 members), that all of its members served on a part-time basis, that it met infrequently, and that it was unduly influenced by clients and CPA firms. In 1971 the AICPA responded by forming the Study Group on Establishment of Accounting Principles to investigate the organization and operation of the APB. The Study Group's recom-

mendations led to the ultimate demise of the APB and the formation of the FASB.

29. During this era the private sector, through the AICPA, established itself as the leader in determining GAAP. A significant development toward this end was the AICPA's adoption of Rule 203 of the *Code of Professional Ethics of the AICPA,* which states, in effect, that members may not express an opinion that financial statements are in conformity with GAAP if they contain any material departures from official pronouncements of the AICPA's designated rule-making body, that is, *ARBs, Opinions,* and now *FASB Statements of Financial Accounting Standards.*

30. Conceptual framework era. The present era started in 1973 with the founding of the FASB. The FASB was created when the Study Group on Establishment of Accounting Principles, an AICPA committee, recommended that the FASB replace the APB as the professional private sector standard-setting organization. The FASB is an independent, autonomous board of seven full-time paid members with varied professional backgrounds. Although the FASB is independent of the AICPA, the Accounting Standards Executive Committee (AcSEC) is the AICPA's senior technical committee and provides advice to the FASB on technical items. In general, the FASB has addressed pressing issues in a timely and expedient manner but at the same time has worked steadily on a theoretical foundation for accounting: the conceptual framework project.

31. An elaborate organization supports the FASB's activities. The Financial Accounting Foundation's responsibilities include (*a*) appointing the members of the FASB, (*b*) securing and managing the FASB's funds, and (*c*) overseeing the FASB's activities. Besides the Financial Accounting Standards Advisory Council's (FASAC) consulting role to the FASB, the FASB's Emerging Issues Task Force (EITF) serves the FASB by identifying emerging issues and, at times, resolving them.

32. Four official pronouncements are issued by the FASB:

   a. *Statements of Financial Accounting Standards (SFASs)* are considered to constitute GAAP.
   b. *Interpretations* clarify, explain, or elaborate on existing *SFASs* (and *ARBs* and *Opinions* that are still effective) and are also considered GAAP.
   c. *Technical Bulletins* provide assistance in applying other *SFASs, ARBs,* and *Opinions.*
   d. *Statements of Financial Accounting Concepts (SFACs)* relate to the conceptual framework project and do not constitute GAAP.

33. The FASB's output of pronouncements has been prolific. The Board cannot be accused, however, of railroading its pronouncements. Each *SFAS* and *SFAC* follows a nine-step process that ensures ample time for public reaction, discussion, and input to the FASB before a final pronouncement is issued.

34. The FASB has made steady progress on its conceptual framework project. It represents a "constitution, a coherent system of interrelated objectives and fundamentals that can lead to consistent standards and that prescribe the nature, functions, and limits of financial accounting and reporting." This is an ambitious and important project because it provides the theoretical foundation for future *SFASs*.

Standard Setting Is a Political Process

35. Those responsible for setting accounting standards, currently the FASB, operate in an environment accented by "politics" in groups both public, such as the SEC, and private, such as corporate lobbyists, vie for support of their position or interest on a particular accounting issue. It should be remembered that the SEC delegated its authority to establish accounting and reporting standards to the private sector; it did not relinquish its enforcement power. Consequently, the SEC still maintains influence on standard setting. In addition, in order for the standard setters to set "generally accepted" standards, they must earn and retain the support of their general constituency, the preparers and users of financial accounting information. The evolution of the accounting practices for the investment tax credit (ITC) provides a notable case on the delicate relationship between the private sector standard-setting body, the SEC, and the general constituency.

36. In 1962 the APB issued *Opinion No. 2* requiring firms to use the deferral method of accounting for the ITC. Rather than following the standard, companies criticized it. In response to this criticism, the SEC "encouraged" the APB to permit an alternative accounting treatment, the flow-through method. In 1964 the APB issued *Opinion No. 4*, which permitted both ITC accounting methods. Thus the APB in its infancy came under political pressure and was forced to modify an accounting standard. Although incidents like this are not common, it does illustrate the significant influence of the SEC on the setting of accounting standards.

37. More recently in the early 1990s, the FASB's issuance of *Statement No. 115* was influenced on several fronts. For instance, there was pressure from the SEC to use market value accounting for certain financial instruments. Other groups, such as the Federal Reserve Board staff, were opposed to market value accounting. In its deliberations, the FASB must balance all pressures exerted on its standard-setting role, not only those of the SEC.

38. In an environment with such diverse influences, accounting policy making is a political as well as a technical process. That is, the FASB weighs the political considerations and the technical and theoretical aspects of an accounting issue in order to ensure that the standard or policy it adopts is acceptable to a majority of the interested parties and serves the public interest.

Other Groups Influencing Accounting

39. Over the years the development of financial accounting and reporting has rested primarily with the SEC, CAP, APB, and FASB. During this time, however, other private sector and public sector organizations have had either a direct or a subtle influence on the evolution of accounting and reporting practices. Important private sector groups include the American Accounting Association (AAA), most of whose members are accounting academicians interested in the conceptual basis of accounting; the Institute of Management Accountants (IMA), most of whose members are practicing accountants concerned primarily with managerial accounting issues; and the Financial Executives Institute (FEI), most of whose members are corporate executives interested in the development of financial accounting and reporting standards. Public sector influences come from the Internal Revenue Service (IRS), a federal agency that at times has had its tax law adopted as GAAP.

40. A much broader type of influence is that created by the U.S. Congress and pressure groups. After probing the structure and operations of the accounting profession in the late 1970s, two congressional subcommittees agreed that accounting and reporting standards should be set in the private sector, but they also gave notice of congressional concern and intent to watch the accounting profession closely. As a follow-up to the earlier investigations, the Dingell Committee (1985) held hearings on the SEC's effectiveness in overseeing the accounting profession. Moreover, in 1985 a multiorganizational-sponsored commission, the National Commission on Fraudulent Financial Reporting (or Treadway Commission), was established in response to a growing concern about perceived fraudulent financial reporting practices. After much deliberation the Treadway Commission made specific recommendations for CPAs, the SEC and other regulatory bodies, and accounting educators that were designed to reduce the incidence of and heighten awareness of the risks of fraudulent reporting.

International Standard Setting

41. The double-entry bookkeeping system provides a common heritage for most countries' accounting procedures. As indicated previously, not all countries have developed the same accounting standards, nor do they follow U.S.-established GAAP. There are, however, two important international accounting standard-setting groups. First, the International Accounting Standards Committee (IASC), founded in 1973, has a membership of professional accounting bodies from approximately 75 countries. The objectives of the IASC are to (*a*) formulate, publish, and promote accounting standards for worldwide acceptance, and (*b*) work toward harmonization of accounting standards and financial statement presentation. The IASC sets international accounting standards following a due process procedure similar to that of the FASB. The IASC's standards, however, have no legal power or authority, and hence compliance is strictly voluntary. IASC standards are generally consistent with those of the FASB. IASC standards were criticized for permitting several acceptable accounting treatments for a particular accounting transaction. A major effort by the IASC to narrow existing accounting alternatives resulted in eliminating accounting alternatives for 22 accounting issues.

42. Second, the European Community (EC), or European Economic Community (EEC), founded in 1957, establishes "Directives" that must be adhered to by each of the 12 EC countries. These Directives must become "law" within each EC country. Two Directives designed to harmonize accounting and reporting are the Fourth Directive (form and content of financial statements) and the Seventh Directive (consolidated financial statements). These Directives are not always consistent with U.S. GAAP but must be followed by non-EC countries that want to do business there.

Self-Study Learning

Key Terms and Concepts

Provide the appropriate term or terms to complete each of the following statements:

1. _*Accounting*_ is a measurement-communication activity.

2. _*Managerial*_ provides information to decision makers internal to the company, whereas _*Financial*_ provides information to users external to the company.

3. _*Financial Reporting*_ (~~GAAP~~) encompasses financial statements, notes to financial statements, and supplementary information that are required to be published externally under GAAP.

4. Financial accounting and reporting conventions, rules, and procedures that a company must use in preparing external financial statements constitute _*GAAP*_.

5. The American Institute of Accountants was renamed the _*AICPA*_.

6. Established by the Securities Exchange Act of 1934, the _*SEC*_ has the authority to prescribe accounting procedures.

7. In 1938 the _*CAP*_ was created to develop financial accounting and reporting principles and practices; it was succeeded in 1959 by the _*APB*_.

8. Financial accounting and reporting standards are currently established by the _*FASB*_.

9. As new financial accounting and reporting standards are developed, they are issued in an official pronouncement called a(n) _*SFAS*_.

10. International accounting standards are set by the _*IASC*_.

True-False

Indicate by circling the appropriate response whether each of the following statements is true (T) or false (F):

(T) F 1. Accounting is a service activity.

T (F) 2. Managerial accounting provides information to investors, creditors, and governmental agencies.

T (F) 3. On the whole, investors who base their investment decisions on published accounting information can expect to earn above-average returns on their security investments.

(T) F 4. Financial accounting information is used by governmental agencies and commissions to assist them in policy making.

(T) F 5. Accounting information is used by various groups to make decisions about the allocation of resources.

T (F) 6. Once established, financial accounting and reporting practices remain constant.

(T) F 7. Estimates, assumptions, and professional judgments are necessary in financial accounting and reporting.

(T) F 8. Standards or principles of financial accounting and reporting contribute to the credibility and usefulness of financial information.

T (F) 9. An accounting practice that is established as GAAP has received the unreserved approval of all accountants.

(T) F 10. Only financial statements and accompanying notes are subject to a CPA's audit.

(T) F 11. General purpose external financial reporting information includes financial statements, notes, and supplementary disclosures.

T (F) 12. Before the Industrial Revolution, accounting served primarily external users.

T (F) 13. Accounting became recognized as a profession during the problem-solving era.

T (F) 14. The SEC administers only the Securities Exchange Act of 1934.

T (F) 15. The SEC is a private sector organization that currently sets accounting standards that constitute GAAP.

(T) F 16. The Committee on Accounting Procedure (CAP) basically focused on solving specific accounting and reporting problems.

T (F) 17. Both the *Opinions* and the *Statements* issued by the Accounting Principles Board (APB) established GAAP.

(T) F 18. Accounting standards of the pre-formal-theory era were substandard in comparison with GAAP today.

T (F) 19. Standards issued by the IASC are enforceable by the IASC.

(T) F 20. Before either a *Statement of Financial Accounting Standards* or a *Statement of Financial Accounting Concepts* is issued, it is subjected to a process of formal public exposure and deliberation.

Multiple Choice

Select the best response to each of the following items, and circle the corresponding letter:

1. When publicly available accounting information is assimilated by the market, securities markets are said to be efficient:

   a. Slowly and with bias.
   b. Slowly and without bias.
   c. Quickly and with bias.
   d. Quickly and without bias.

2. Select the one user group listed that is not considered to have a direct economic interest in the reporting entity.

   a. Financial analysts.
   b. Employees.
   c. Creditors.
   d. Managers.

3. Which of the following financial statements is *not* required under GAAP?

   a. Income statement.
   b. Statement of changes in liabilities.
   c. Balance sheet.
   d. Statement of cash flows.

4. Authoritative pronouncements of the Accounting Principles Board that established GAAP were:

   a. *Opinions.*
   b. *Accounting Series Releases.*
   c. *Statements.*
   d. *Technical Bulletins.*

5. Which of the following institutional factors did not influence the development of accounting during the pre-formal-theory era?

   a. Taxation.
   b. Governmental intervention through the SEC.
   c. The growth of railroads.
   d. The Industrial Revolution.

6. Criticism of the APB's activities centered on its:

   a. Failure to develop a theoretical framework.
   b. Emphasis on solving specific accounting and reporting issues as they arose.
   c. Lack of supportive research for its *Opinions.*
   d. All of the above.

7. Enforcement of *FASB Statements of Financial Accounting Standards* and effective *Opinions* and *Accounting Research Bulletins* is achieved through:

   a. The prestige of the AICPA.
   b. The prestige of the FASB.
   c. The delegation of authority to set accounting standards to the FASB by the SEC.
   d. Rule 203 of the *Code of Professional Ethics of the AICPA.*

8. The FASB issues several official pronouncements. Which pronouncements are considered to be GAAP?

   a. *Statements of Financial Accounting Standards.*
   b. *Interpretations.*
   c. *Technical Bulletins.*
   d. Both a and b.

9. Which of the following groups did *not* have the authority to issue pronouncements that constituted GAAP?

   a. The Accounting Principles Board.
   b. The Committee on Accounting Procedure.
   c. The Internal Revenue Service.
   d. The Financial Accounting Standards Board.

10. Several groups influence the development of financial accounting and reporting at a practical level. Which group's influence is felt more at the conceptual level?

    a. The Financial Executives Institute.
    b. The American Accounting Association.
    c. The Internal Revenue Service.
    d. The Institute of Management Accountants.

Extended Problems

1. An investor is interested in acquiring shares of a company's stock but wants to learn more about the company before making a decision.

REQUIRED

List and discuss the types of information that are publicly available to the potential investor.

2. Three eras of accounting have been identified, in each of which particular events occurred that were significant to the development of accounting and reporting standards.

REQUIRED

In outline form, identify the three major eras of accounting development, and under each identify (*a*) key events that affected accounting during the era and (*b*) the accounting standard-setting process during the era.

COMMON ERRORS

The first statement in each of the "common errors" listed here is *incorrect*. Each incorrect statement is followed by a corrected statement and an explanation.

1. Accounting is concerned only with the measurement of financial information. *Wrong*

Accounting is concerned with both the measurement and communication of financial information. *Right*

Measurement of financial information is only part of the accounting process. Accountants do spend considerable time and effort trying to measure properly the economic effect of transactions on a company, but the measurement aspect is only half of the accounting process. The information measured must be communicated before it can help users to make decisions. Accordingly, the accountant is also responsible for communicating the information to users in an understandable and unbiased manner. Thus accounting has been described as a measurement-communication system, a description that emphasizes the two aspects of the accounting process.

2. Financial accounting and reporting practices are influenced by but have no influence on the economic environment. *Wrong*

Financial accounting and reporting practices are influenced by the economic environment and also affect the environment. *Right*

It has long been acknowledged that the economic environment directly influences the development of financial accounting and reporting practices. Recently, however, evidence has suggested that a particular accounting practice can influence the economic behavior of both the preparer company and the user. Now those responsible for establishing accounting practices not only must be responsive to the economic environment but also must consider the economic consequences of the proposed accounting practice.

3. Accountants do not have ethical situations arise in the course of their work. *Wrong*

Accountants continually face ethical situations in the course of their work. *Right*

All accountants confront ethical situations—situations requiring a decision between right and wrong, not necessarily legal or illegal. Management accountants in the preparation of an income statement, for example, must choose an accounting method that reflects the economic substance of an event, not a method that would make the entity's management look good. Similarly, an external or public accountant when performing an audit must not succumb to management's pressure to accept a questionable application of GAAP.

Accountants face many ethical dilemmas, and they must develop a sense of ethical professional behavior. The accounting profession rests on maintaining its credibility to the public and serving the public good. Making ethical choices consistent with the morals of society and understanding one's own values are essential to professionalism.

4. The SEC can only recommend accounting and reporting standards to the accounting profession. *Wrong*

The SEC possesses legal authority to set accounting practices and reporting requirements. *Right*

Although the SEC permits the accounting profession to take the lead in developing accounting and reporting standards, it has the legal right to assume

this role through powers given to it by the Securities Exchange Act of 1934. At present, the SEC acts in an advisory capacity, but at any time it can reclaim the role now played by the private sector (FASB) and establish accounting procedures and reporting requirements.

5. *FASB Statements of Financial Accounting Standards* (*SFAS*s) and *Statements of Financial Accounting Concepts* (*SFAC*s) establish GAAP. *Wrong*

Only *FASB Statements of Financial Accounting Standards* establish GAAP. *Right*

The FASB is actively issuing both *SFAS*s and *SFAC*s, but only the former establish GAAP. *SFAS*s deal with accounting practice and must be followed when financial statements are prepared in accordance with GAAP. *SFAC*s focus on the conceptual framework project and do not set GAAP. Although the two forms of statements appear to be fundamentally different, they are nevertheless closely related. The FASB intends to use the *SFAC*s as a theoretical basis for establishing GAAP, that is, for developing new *SFAS*s and reviewing previously issued ones.

6. The development of financial accounting and reporting is based solely on the technical and theoretical influences of the AICPA, FASB, and SEC. *Wrong*

The development of financial accounting and reporting is based on the technical and theoretical influences of the AICPA, FASB, and SEC and on the political influences of other groups. *Right*

It may appear that financial accounting and reporting have been developed by professional accounting technocrats in the AICPA, FASB, and SEC. Those responsible for establishing accounting principles and practices constantly receive advice and opinions from many groups and individuals while they deliberate an accounting issue. Such professional organizations as the AAA, IMA, and FEI often express their views on an issue. Similarly, pressure groups selectively lobby for an accounting standard to be established in their interests. Through committee investigations the U.S. Congress expresses its opinion of the accounting profession, formulates policies to guide the accounting profession in setting standards, and even attempts to prescribe what those standards should be. Because accounting and reporting must be generally accepted, the standard setters must compromise to satisfy as many groups as possible. Thus the development of financial accounting and reporting practices may best be described as a technical *and* political process.

ANSWERS

Key Terms and Concepts

1. accounting
2. managerial accounting, financial accounting
3. financial reporting
4. generally accepted accounting principles (GAAP)
5. American Institute of Certified Public Accountants (AICPA)
6. Securities and Exchange Commission (SEC)
7. Committee on Accounting Procedure (CAP), Accounting Principles Board (APB)
8. Financial Accounting Standards Board (FASB)
9. *Statement of Financial Accounting Standards*
10. International Accounting Standards Committee (IASC)

True-False

1. T
2. F   Managerial accounting provides information to decision makers inside the entity, such as managers. Investors, creditors, and governmental agencies are external to the company and receive their information from financial accounting disclosures.
3. F   Research has determined that securities markets are "efficient" with respect to published accounting information. The efficient market assimilates the published accounting information rapidly and in an unbiased manner, so that an investor is prevented from using the published accounting information to earn an abnormal or above-average return.
4. T
5. T
6. F   As the economic environment and needs of users change, accounting and reporting practices also change in order to continue to provide information in the new environment and be responsive to users' needs.
7. T
8. T
9. F   Generally accepted accounting principles represent only a consensus among accountants.
10. T
11. T
12. F   Internal users were the primary users of accounting information before the Industrial Revolution because businesses were small and did not depend on large-scale credit. Thus there was no need to prepare accounting information for external users.
13. F   Accounting became a recognized profession during the pre-formal-theory era.

14. F   The SEC was established by the Securities Exchange Act of 1934. The SEC administers this act along with the Securities Act of 1933 and several others.
15. F   The SEC is the public sector regulatory agency that has the authority to set accounting standards, but it has delegated its authority to the private sector.
16. T
17. F   Only *APB Opinions* established GAAP. *APB Statements* were informative documents issued to aid interested parties' understanding of accounting issues.
18. T
19. F   The IASC can issue accounting standards, but it has no enforcement authority. Countries voluntarily accept and follow IASC standards.
20. T

Multiple Choice

1.	d	6.	d
2.	a	7.	d
3.	b	8.	d
4.	a	9.	c
5.	b	10.	b

Extended Problems

1. Five types of information are available to the potential investor. Four of them have as their source the financial reporting system of the reporting entity. This information is generally contained in the published annual report. The fifth type is from sources other than the entity's financial reporting system.

a. The most common type of information is perhaps that in the *financial statements*. Under GAAP four financial statements are required: the balance sheet, the income statement, the statement of owners' (or stockholders') equity, and the statement of cash flows. The financial statements are subject to an audit by a CPA.

b. Another common type of information is that contained in the *notes to financial statements (and parenthetical disclosure)*. These disclosures enhance or further explain the information reported in the financial statements. For example, a typical note would contain information describing a company's primary accounting policies, such as the depreciation or inventory method used, or an explanation of a lease arrangement. This information is also subject to the CPA's audit.

c. Another type of information is referred to as *supplementary information*. This information is required by the FASB or SEC but is not subject to a CPA's audit. The FASB has required selected companies, for example, to disclose as supplementary information data concerning oil and gas reserves on their financial statements.

d. *Other financial information* is often provided by management. For example, the letter to the stockholders and the management discussion and analysis provide means for management to disclose other financial information about the company. This information, however, is not audited by a CPA. Furthermore, additional information is usually made available when requested. Normally a request for special information is honored if it is made by a specific user for a stated purpose. A bank, for example, may request information to help it decide whether to grant credit.

e. *Other information* is often available to an investor from such sources as the financial press, stock market newsletters, and analysts.

An investor should use all publicly available information. To limit sources of information to one or two types is often to exclude important information that could affect the investor's decision.

2. I. Pre-formal-theory era.
   A. Significant events.
      1. The first book on double-entry bookkeeping appeared in the late fifteenth century.
      2. The Industrial Revolution caused the need for financial accounting and reporting information.
      3. The growth of railroads influenced accounting practices.
      4. The taxing of business income influenced accounting practices.
   B. Accounting standard-setting process.
      1. Largely determined by individual accountants in response to situations they encountered.
      2. No professional group designated to set accounting practices.

II. Problem-solving era.
   A. Significant events.
      1. The laissez-faire attitudes toward accounting practices of the previous period were criticized.
      2. The AIA recognized the needs of investors and creditors for accounting information.
      3. Government intervention.
         a). Securities Act of 1933.
         b). Securities Exchange Act of 1934 (creation of Securities and Exchange Commission, or SEC).
      4. The way the APB established GAAP was criticized.
   B. Accounting standard-setting process—the private sector assumes the leadership role.
      1. The Committee on Accounting Procedure (CAP), 1938–1959, issued *Accounting Research Bulletins* on specific accounting problems which established GAAP.
      2. The Accounting Principles Board (APB), 1959–1973, issued *Opinions* on specific accounting problems which constituted GAAP.
      3. The AICPA adopted Rule 203 of the *Code of Professional Ethics of the AICPA,* which states that members can express an opinion that financial statements are presented in conformity with GAAP only if the statements contain no material departures from official pronouncements of the AICPA's designated rule-making body (currently the FASB).

III. Conceptual framework era.
   A. Significant events.
      1. The Financial Accounting Standards Board (FASB) was created.
      2. Congressional hearings were held on the accounting profession.
   B. Accounting standard-setting process.
      1. The FASB issues pronouncements on practical accounting problems.
         a). *Statements of Financial Accounting Standards,* constituting GAAP.
         b). *Interpretations,* also considered GAAP.
         c). *Technical Bulletins.*
      2. The FASB issues *Statements of Financial Accounting Concepts* on the theoretical aspects of accounting (the conceptual framework project).

2 FINANCIAL ACCOUNTING AND REPORTING: A THEORETICAL STRUCTURE

CHAPTER OBJECTIVES

After reading Chapter 2 and completing the questions, cases, exercises, and problems from the text chapter, you should be able to:

1. Understand the environmental assumptions of financial accounting theory.
2. Recognize the limits of financial accounting and reporting.
3. Discuss the objectives of financial reporting, the qualitative characteristics of useful financial information, and the elements of financial statements established by the FASB's conceptual framework project.
4. Distinguish between accrual accounting and cash-basis accounting.

5. Identify the various points of revenue realization.
6. Apply the matching principle and expense recognition guidelines.
7. Differentiate among the three capital maintenance concepts: units of money, units of general purchasing power, and physical units.
8. Differentiate among the five alternative attributes or valuation methods: historical cost, current replacement cost, current exit value, expected exit value, and present value of expected cash flows.
9. Understand the purpose of disclosure and the means of achieving it.

CHAPTER REVIEW

Introduction

1. Financial accounting and reporting are more than measurement and communication practices. Underlying these practices is a theoretical structure, or set of broad principles. The study of financial accounting theory provides a basis for analyzing existing and future accounting issues and for developing new financial accounting and reporting standards.

2. Unfortunately, accountants do not agree as to the best accounting theory. Financial accounting and reporting practices are currently based on a combination of several theories. There is general agreement, however, on much of the theoretical structure of accounting. The following sections of the chapter review will consider the environmental assumptions of accounting, the FASB's conceptual framework project, the conventional and alternative financial accounting reporting systems for recognition and measurement, and disclosure methods.

Environmental Assumptions

3. The *environmental assumptions* provide a foundation for the structure of financial accounting

theory and explain the methods of financial information disclosure. The four environmental assumptions are discussed in the remainder of this section.

4. Accounting entity assumption. An *accounting entity* is a specifically identified unit whose financial information accountants account for and report. Once identified, the accounting entity establishes boundaries, or limits, for the information that is included in the financial statements. An accounting entity does not always correspond to a legal entity. The former identifies the unit for accounting and reporting purposes, whereas the latter identifies a unit for legal purposes.

5. Periodicity assumption. Since the users of financial information make resource allocation decisions continually, they need to receive information about an entity in which they are interested on a regular basis. Accountants therefore impose *periodicity* on the entity; that is, the economic activities of an accounting entity are divided or segmented into artificial time periods for financial reporting purposes. Most accounting entities publish financial reports annually and quarterly.

6. Going concern assumption. An accounting entity is assumed to be a *going concern*. That is, unless evidence exists to the contrary, it is assumed that the entity will continue to operate indefinitely, or at least long enough to carry out existing plans, commitments, and contracts. Even though most entities actually will not exist indefinitely, accountants assume that they will unless there is evidence of imminent failure. When circumstances do not support the going concern assumption in regard to a particular entity, the liquidation basis of accounting is appropriate.

7. Monetary assumption. Since economic exchanges are conducted in terms of dollars, accountants also use the dollar as their unit of measure. The *monetary assumption* assumes that the number of dollars or dollar equivalents (in noncash transactions) should be the measure of and basis for reporting the results of the economic activities of the accounting entity. Implicit in the assumption is the premise that the dollar is a stable unit of measure. The dollar is, of course, an unstable unit of measure, a fact that is particularly evident in periods of inflation or deflation. As the rate of inflation increases, the purchasing power of the dollar decreases, thus causing instability in the measuring unit and, in time, misleading financial statements. *FASB Statement No. 89* encourages but does not require that the impact of changing prices on selected companies be part of supplementary disclosures while the monetary assumption is maintained in the primary financial statements.

The Conceptual Framework Project

8. Financial reporting is not perfect; it has limitations. Currently, financial reporting restricts the accounting data set to information that is measured in units of money. Measurements made in different periods, however, may not result in comparable units of money. For example, the dollar amounts of two purchases of land may not be comparable because of the differing purchasing power of the dollar in the two periods land was purchased. Also, because of the nature of accounting practices, most dollar amounts reported are usually approximated, not exact. Furthermore, accounting information is basically historical, whereas users normally prefer future data such as forecasts of earnings. Working within and acknowledging these limitations, the FASB has developed a conceptual framework for financial accounting and reporting.

9. In developing the conceptual framework for financial accounting and reporting, the FASB has followed the deductive approach to theory formulation. The FASB has established, in part, (*a*) the objectives of financial reporting, (*b*) the qualitative characteristics of useful accounting information, and (*c*) the element of financial statements. An official pronouncement on each of the three completed phases of the conceptual framework has been issued: *Statements of Concepts No. 1, 2,* and *6,* respectively. The remainder of this section will review the conclusions of these documents.

10. Objectives of financial reporting. As the first step in establishing the conceptual framework, the FASB enumerated three basic objectives of financial reporting:

a. Financial reporting should provide information that present and potential investors, creditors, and others may use to make rational investment, credit, and similar decisions. The emphasis is on providing information useful for decision making. Since investors and creditors usually do not have access to other financial information and therefore rely on financial statements, they are regarded as the primary users of financial statements. This objective implies a responsibility on the part of both the preparer and the user of the reports. The former must prepare comprehensible financial reports, whereas the latter must understand the business environment and be willing to study the reports with reasonable diligence.

b. Financial information should provide information to help investors assess the amounts, timing, and uncertainty of future cash flows from dividends and redemption of securities, and it should provide information to help creditors assess the proceeds of loans. Although the focus is on the assessment of cash flows to the user, they are directly related to the reporting enterprise's cash flows. Therefore, financial reporting should provide information that will help users to assess the amounts, timing, and uncertainty of the enterprise's future cash flows.

c. Financial reporting should provide information about the enterprise's economic resources (sources of future cash flows) and its obligations to sacrifice economic resources to others and owners' equity (sources of future cash outflows). Information should also be disclosed about the effects of transactions, events, and circumstances of earnings and other activities that cause changes in resources and claims to those resources. In other words, information about enterprise operations or earnings should be presented. In fact, the FASB asserts that the "primary focus" of financial reporting is on "earnings and its components."

11. In summary, the FASB established objectives that focus on the common interests of various users: an enterprise's ability to generate positive or favorable cash flows.

12. Qualitative characteristics of useful accounting information. According to the objectives of financial reporting, financial reports are to provide information that is decision-useful; that is, they are to help the user to make a decision. To accomplish this objective, the FASB next established a hierarchy of qualities or characteristics of accounting information that make it useful for decision making.

13. The qualitative characteristics rest on the premise that, as prescribed in the objectives, accounting information is to be decision-useful to the users of the information. Understandability, a user-specific quality is the first identified quality. *Understandability* means that in order for the information to be useful in decision making, the user must be able to understand it. The ability to understand information, however, may depend on the user's willingness to make a special effort, such as to engage in additional study.

14. Designated as primary decision-specific qualities of useful accounting information are *relevance* and *reliability*. The accounting information is *relevant* if it is capable of making a difference in the user's decisions; that is, it will either confirm or change the user's expectations. Relevance consists of three components: (*a*) *predictive value:* the information will improve the user's ability to predict; (*b*) *feedback value:* the information will improve the user's ability to cor-

rect or confirm earlier expectations; and (*c*) *timeliness:* the information must be available to users at the time when it can be useful to them.

15. The reported information is *reliable* if a user can depend on or have confidence in it because the accounting measures represent what they purport to represent, are reasonably free from error and bias, and can be verified. For information to be reliable, it must possess two qualities. First, it must have *representational faithfulness*: there must be agreement between the accounting measure or description and the economic phenomenon it is supposed to measure or describe. Second, it must have *verifiability* (objectivity): it yields results that would be substantially duplicated by independent accountants who measured the same economic event by the same measurement method. Representational faithfulness is concerned with the measurement technique (does it measure what it purports to measure?), whereas verifiability is concerned with the accuracy of the application of the measurement technique.

16. For accounting information to be decision-useful, it must possess both relevance and reliability. Often the two are at odds. Information that is very reliable, for example, may be irrelevant for decision-making purposes. Thus a trade-off between the two primary decision-specific qualities must often be made.

17. Two secondary qualities of accounting information are *neutrality* and *comparability*. Accounting information is *neutral* if it is unbiased or evenhanded; it will not bias a decision maker. It is *comparable* if a user can compare it with similar information from other enterprises or from the same firm over time. *Interfirm comparability* is achieved when different entities use the same accounting procedure to record similar economic events; *interperiod comparability*, or *consistency,* requires the application of the same accounting procedures over time. Consistency is very important in financial reporting. Any time a company changes an accounting procedure, the company must make adequate disclosures, including a statement explaining why the new procedure is preferable to the old one.

18. The primary and secondary qualities may be modified in response to a cost-benefit analysis or materiality considerations. Gathering and communicating accounting information entail costs. Accordingly, when accountants consider making a disclosure, they must consider also an analysis of *information benefits versus information costs*. Simply, the benefit derived from the disclosure must exceed the costs of its preparation. Unfortunately, the measurement of the benefit from accounting information, as with that of any public good, is a very subjective process. Although difficult to determine with reasonable precision, the benefits and costs of accounting information should be evaluated to the extent possible.

19. Accounting information is *material* if it is likely to have a significant effect on a user's decision. The concept of *materiality* implies that GAAP should be applied in accounting for and reporting material items. One should not assume that immaterial items can be omitted, but such items should be handled cost effectively. The materiality of an item depends on its relative dollar amount, relative nature, or a combination of both. Each situation must be considered independently to determine whether it is material.

20. In summary, the qualitative characteristics described influence the definition, measurement, and reporting of the elements of financial statements.

21. Internationally, the IASC has issued its own *Framework for the Preparation and Presentation of Financial Statements,* which closely parallels the FASB's qualitative characteristics. The IASC's *Framework,* however, makes comparability equal to relevance and reliability. Furthermore, it adds two other qualitative characteristics: (*a*) *substance over form* refers to accounting for a transaction's substance, not its legal form, and (*b*) *prudence* refers to exercising caution in measurement. For example, measurement of assets and revenues (liabilities and expenses) should not be overstated (understated).

22. Elements of financial statements. *Elements of financial statements* are the building blocks, or basic categories, of financial statements. The elements of the balance sheet are assets, liabilities, and equity, whereas revenues, expenses, gains, losses, and net income or loss are the elements of the income statement. These components of financial statements are financial representations of an entity's economic resources (assets), its claim to or interest in the resources (liabilities and equity, respectively), and the effect of transactions or other economic events that result in changes in the resources and claims (revenues, expenses, gains and losses).

23. Once definitions of the elements are in place, they provide guidance for a decision as to the way a particular transaction or event should be reported in the financial statements. Each of the elements will be defined in the following paragraphs.

24. *Assets* are probable future economic benefits obtained or controlled by a particular entity as a result of a past transaction or event. The definition contains three key characteristics: (*a*) the asset has future economic benefit or service potential (positive cash flows), (*b*) the future benefits are controlled by a

particular entity, and (*c*) the asset is the result of a past transaction.

25. *Liabilities* are probable future sacrifices of economic benefits arising from a particular entity's present obligations to transfer assets or to provide services to other entities in the future as a result of a past transaction or event. A liability has three characteristics: (*a*) the entity has to satisfy the obligation by sacrificing an asset (usually cash) or rendering a service, (*b*) the obligation is of a particular entity, and (*c*) the obligation arose from a past transaction.

26. *Equity* (also called stockholders' equity or owners' equity) is the residual interest in the assets of an entity that remains after its liabilities have been deducted. Measurement of equity is dependent on the measurement of assets and liabilities: Equity = Assets − Liabilities. Two common equity or capital transactions are *investments by owners* (purchase of capital stock by stockholders) and *distributions to owners* (distribution of a cash dividend to stockholders).

27. *Revenues* (also called entity accomplishments) are inflows of assets or settlements of liabilities, or a combination of both, during a period as a result of the delivery or production of goods, the rendering of services, or other earnings activities that constitute an entity's ongoing major or primary operations. To be considered revenue, the activity must be a primary and continuing earnings operation.

28. *Expenses* (also called entity efforts) are outflows of assets or the incurrence of liabilities, or a combination of both, during a period resulting from the delivery or production of goods, the rendering of services, or other earnings activities that constitute an entity's major or primary operations. Expenses are incurred to generate revenue.

29. *Gains* and *losses* are increases and decreases, respectively, in equity or net assets resulting from the peripheral or incidental transactions of an entity. It should be noted that revenues and expenses relate to the primary or ongoing operations of an entity, whereas gains and losses relate to the entity's incidental or peripheral activities. Further revenues and expenses are *gross* inflows and outflows to the entity, whereas gains and losses are *net* inflows and outflows, respectively.

30. *Net income* or *net loss* (or *earnings*) is the change in equity or net assets of an entity during the period resulting from transactions and other economic events that result in revenues, expenses, gains, and losses. Net income or net loss reflects the results of all transactions that change equity except for capital transactions, and certain other changes in net assets. In *Statement of Concepts No. 5,* the FASB suggests yet another measure, *comprehensive income,* to reflect changes in net assets other than equity transactions. Essentially, the FASB has transferred certain gains and losses from the computation of earnings to that of comprehensive income in such a way that the statements complement each other:

+ Revenues	Earnings
– Expenses	+/– Cumulative accounting adjustments*
+ Gains	
– Losses	+/– Other nonowner changes in equity†
= **Earnings**	**Comprehensive Income**

*For example, cumulative effect of changes in accounting principle.
†For example, foreign currency translation adjustments.

It should be remembered that *SFAC*s do not constitute GAAP. Therefore, these statements as presented are only proposed by the FASB and are not required.

31. The elements constitute the basic financial statements prepared by an enterprise. The basic statements and their respective elements and purposes are summarized in the following table:

Elements and Purposes of Financial Statements

FINANCIAL STATEMENT	ELEMENTS	PURPOSE
Balance sheet	Assets, liabilities, and equity	To show status of each element at end of accounting period
Income statement	Revenues, expenses, gains, losses, and resulting net income or loss	To show results of operations during accounting period
Statement of changes in owners' equity	Capital transactions affecting owners' equity	To show changes in owners' equity during accounting period
Statement of cash flows		To show cash flows from operations and other investing and financing activities during an accounting period

Economic Events and Elements

32. An *economic event,* which may be either external to the entity or internal, is an occurrence, or happening, that has a consequence to the entity. A *transaction* is an external event that involves the transfer of something of value from one entity to another. When an entity both receives *and* sacrifices something of value, the transaction is called an *exchange* or *reciprocal transfer.* If an entity either receives or sacrifices something of value, the transaction is called a *nonreciprocal transfer.*

33. Significantly, all events or transactions recognized as part of the accounting data set have a dual effect on the financial statement elements. Only those events that can be identified with an accounting entity and quantified in dollars are recorded and reported in the financial statements. Each recognized event or transaction affects at least two elements, by increasing or decreasing either or both. We see here the basis for double-entry bookkeeping.

Elements—Their Recognition and Measurement

34. Two problems remain with respect to the financial statement elements: when to recognize them and how to measure them. Certain principles have evolved for recognition and measurement of the elements. Some of these principles are related to the conventional system (GAAP), and others are related to alternatives to the conventional system.

The Fundamental Recognition Principle

35. Recognition is the process of formally recording the financial effects of a transaction or an event and incorporating it as an element in the financial statements. Recognition includes the initial recording of an element and subsequent changes in it. *Statement of Concepts No. 5* delineates four recognition criteria (subject to the cost-benefit and materiality tests) to determine whether an item should be recognized in the accounting records:

a. The item meets the *definition* of an element of financial statements.
b. The item has an attribute that *can be measured* reliably.
c. Information about the item is *relevant,* that is, capable of making a difference in users' decisions.
d. Information about the item is *reliable*; that is, it is representationally faithful, verifiable, and neutral.

Note that all four criteria relate to other parts of the conceptual framework. Furthermore, it should be noted that the attribute of an item measured is normally its financial attribute, such as historical exchange price, because that attribute is more useful for decision making.

Principles Underlying the Conventional System

36. Accrual accounting. The earnings process is continuous, and for many companies it covers more than one accounting period. At issue is determining the method of reporting to users on a timely basis the effect of the cash consequences of revenue and expense transactions. One method, *accrual accounting*, focuses on transactions and other economic events that have cash consequences rather than transactions that involve only cash receipts or disbursements. Revenues are reported when they are earned and the amount and timing of the revenue can be reasonably estimated. Expenses are matched with revenue when they are incurred to calculate net income or loss. Another method, *cash-basis accounting*, reports revenues and expenses when cash is received and disbursed, respectively.

37. It should be noted that accrual and cash-basis accounting will result in the same net income or loss over the life of the entity (or time of a particular earnings activity), but the two methods will probably result in different net income or loss figures for a particular reporting period. The difference is in the timing of the recognition of net income or loss, not in the total amount recognized.

38. Accrual accounting reports cash consequences of revenue and expense transactions when the cash flows can be estimated with reasonable confidence. Cash flows may precede or follow the related earnings activity. A *prepayment* arises if the cash outflow precedes the incurrence of the expense, whereas a cash inflow from a revenue activity before it is earned is called *unearned revenue*. If the earnings activity precedes the cash flow, an *accrual* arises. An earned but not yet collected revenue is called an *accrued revenue*, and an incurred but not yet paid expense is called an *accrued expense*. The recognition of prepayments, unearned revenues, and accruals under accrual accounting better reflects the financial statement elements than cash-basis accounting.

39. Historical cost (historical exchange price) principle. According to the *historical cost (historical exchange price) principle,* assets and liabilities are initially recorded at the exchange price established, or cost incurred at the time a transaction takes place. At the time the transaction is initially recorded, the cost and fair value of an asset are conceptually the same. After that time, however, the cost is usually not adjusted to keep the recorded amount equal to the asset's fair value. An exception is the writing

down of some asset values to market value. The historical cost principle is criticized by those who believe that historical cost values are irrelevant for decision making and would prefer a basis for measurement that would be perhaps less reliable but more relevant.

40. Revenue realization principle. Two terms often associated with revenue are *realization* and *recognition*. *Realization* refers to when revenue (or *gain*) should be recognized and reported in the income statement. *Recognition* is the act of recording revenue in the books and reporting it in the financial statements. Two criteria have been set to determine when revenue should be recognized: (*a*) when the amount and timing of revenue to be received are reasonably determinable and (*b*) when the earnings process is complete or virtually complete. These criteria are more operational than the four fundamental recognition criteria previously listed. In effect, the two criteria set conditions that must be met before the revenue can be recognized (recorded): (*a*) the expected cash flows from the transaction must be objectively determinable and (*b*) the critical event or events that cause the revenue to be "earned" must have occurred.

41. Although the earnings process is continuous, it is possible to identify a point during the process that represents the critical event that triggers revenue realization. This point is similar for manufacturing, merchandising, and service companies. Most revenue is realized at the point of sale, but points before and after the point of sale may also be used. The four points at which revenue is normally realized during the earnings process are summarized as follows:

a. At *point of sale.* For most companies the critical event is either the transfer of a product's title to a buyer or the performance or provision of a service (for example, renting of a building). These events are commonly referred to as the point of sale.

b. During *production.* Production is the critical event, and revenue may be recognized before the sale and delivery of the item being produced. To realize revenue during production, a contract price must be fixed or determinable, total production costs must be reasonably estimable, and costs incurred during the period or percentage of production completed must be known or estimable. This method is used most often by contractors working on long-term construction projects that span two or more accounting periods. If the three criteria are met, the *percentage-of-completion* method is appropriate. Otherwise the *completed-contract* method should be used.

c. At *completion of production.* When a product has a ready market at a known market price and immaterial marketing costs, the revenue may be realized when the product is completed. The critical event is the completion of production at a time before the sale. When precious minerals (gold or silver) are mined or agricultural commodities (wheat or beans) are harvested, the production is complete and revenue may be realized.

    d. During *cash collection.* Even though a credit sale has occurred, collection of the receivable is not guaranteed. If no reasonable estimation of uncollectible accounts can be made, the collection of cash becomes the critical event. The *installment method* recognizes revenue as a proportion of each dollar collected, whereas the *cost-recovery method* recognizes revenue only after sufficient cash has been collected to recover the cost of the item sold.

42. Matching principle. According to the *matching principle,* revenues generated (in accordance with the realization principle) and expenses incurred in generating those revenues should be reported in the same income statement. Expenses are matched with revenues in accordance with three general guidelines: (*a*) *association of cause and effect* applies to costs that have a direct relationship with the revenue generated and are recognized during the period when the revenue is recognized (cost of goods sold or sales commissions, for example); (*b*) *systematic and rational allocation* applies to costs that are more easily associated with a period benefited than with specific revenues (the depreciation expense of a long-lived asset, for example); (*c*) *immediate recognition* applies to those costs that have no discernible future benefit and are recognized as expenses immediately (such as advertising or supervisory salaries).

43. Measuring unit or capital maintenance concept. Closely related to the monetary assumption previously discussed is the *capital maintenance concept,* which states that the net assets or investments of an entity must be maintained or recovered through revenues before the entity has earnings. In other words, earnings result when the price received for a good or service is sufficient for the company to recover its invested costs in the good or service and to have a balance or income remaining.

44. Modifications of basic principles and concepts. In certain circumstances the recognition and measurement principles must be modified. The inherent risk and uncertainty of business are recognized by the conservative manner in which accountants select among accounting alternatives. *Conservatism* is manifested when two or more accounting alternatives appear to be equally capable of fulfilling financial reporting objectives; in such circumstances the alternative that has the least favorable impact on net income and financial position is chosen. In addition, because of the distinctive nature of many industries, the member companies often follow *special industry accounting or reporting practices* unique to that industry.

Alternative Capital Maintenance Concepts

45. The choice of a capital maintenance concept influences the amount of the revenue or cash inflow that represents return *of* capital (cost recovery) and return *on* capital (income or earnings). Three concepts of capital maintenance exist, and each has its own concept of earnings.

    a. *Units of money.* Under the units of money (or nominal dollar) concept, income arises if the revenue earned is more than the number of dollars invested in the asset sold. The conventional accounting system adheres to this capital maintenance concept.

    b. *Units of general purchasing power.* Because a unit of money (the dollar in the United States) loses general purchasing power during periods of inflation and gains general purchasing power during periods of deflation, some people contend that the correct capital maintenance concept is units of general purchasing power. Under this concept, income arises if a company's revenues are greater than the general purchasing power equivalent of its investment. When the measuring unit is in general price-level adjusted dollars rather than nominal dollars, this capital maintenance concept is referred to as *constant dollar accounting.*

    c. *Physical units.* Rather than base the capital maintenance concept on the unit of measure or dollar, the physical units concept focuses on the current cost of the item sold. Income arises only if a company's revenues are greater than the current or replacement cost of the item sold.

Alternative Asset and Liability Valuation Methods

46. Methods of measuring or valuing an asset or liability can be based on five alternative attributes (the last four are often referred to as current value methods):

    a. *Historical cost* is the price paid for an asset or the cost incurred for a liability.

    b. *Current replacement cost* is the amount of cash that would have to be paid currently to acquire an existing or equivalent asset or the amount that would have to be received in order to incur an equivalent liability.

    c. *Current exit value* is the amount of cash that would be received currently if an asset were sold or the amount that would be paid if a liability were settled under conditions of an orderly liquidation.

d. *Expected exit value* is the nondiscounted cash flows associated with the expected sale or conversion of an asset or settlement of a liability at some future date.

e. *Present value of expected cash flows* is similar to expected exit value except that the cash flows are discounted at an appropriate rate of interest.

47. Another current value alternative, *fair value*, has received support as an asset/liability valuation alternative to historical cost. It appears in two recent FASB pronouncements, *Statement No. 107* and *Statement No. 115*. For example, the FASB states the "fair value" of financial instruments may be their quoted market price (current exit value) or quoted market price of similar financial instruments. Fair value accounting for investments is covered in Chapters 13 and 14.

48. Each of these valuation methods is used in the conventional system of accounting based on GAAP. Accordingly, the conventional system of accounting may be characterized as a *modified historical cost system*.

49. In order to determine periodic income, both a capital maintenance concept and an attribute or valuation method must be chosen. The specific selection and combination of these two factors will affect the reported income for the period.

Disclosure

50. Accountants must not only measure economic events and transactions but also communicate to interested parties or disclose through the financial statements the results of their measurements. *Disclosure* means that the published financial statements and related notes must include any economic information related to the accounting entity that is signifi-

cant enough to affect the decisions of an informed and prudent user. The entity's various accounts and account balances are fully reported, with clarifying parenthetical comments, explanatory footnotes, and supplementary information.

51. Disclosures in financial statements and notes enhance users' decisions and increase the relevance and reliability of accounting information. The FASB states four purposes of disclosure:

a. To describe and provide additional information concerning recognized items of financial statements, for example, a footnote explaining the inventory account in greater detail.

b. To describe and provide information about items not recognized on the financial statements, for example, information about accounting policies or subsequent events.

c. To provide information to assist users assess both recognized and unrecognized items, for example, information that expands a single point estimate, such as information about an entity's debt.

d. To provide information while an accounting issue is being studied, for example, the FASB-required disclosure about financial instruments before it issued a comprehensive *SFAS* on financial instruments.

52. Disclosure is necessary for U.S. markets to operate effectively. Disclosure is now even more critical with the emergence of global capital markets and differing accounting standards among countries. Companies may need to expand their disclosure to assist those making "international" capital resource-allocation decisions.

53. At present, financial statements provide a wealth of information, but much more could be disclosed. Some disclosure issues that currently confront the accounting profession are the means of distinguishing between recurring and nonrecurring earnings, the provision of additional segment information, the provision of information about a company's liquidity, and the display of earnings or income data.

SELF-STUDY LEARNING

Key Terms and Concepts

Provide the appropriate term or terms to complete each of the following statements:

1. _____Environ Assumption____ provide a foundation for the structure of financial accounting theory and explain the methods of financial information disclosure.

2. Verifiability and representational faithfulness are two qualities of ___RELIABILITY___.

3. _____*Assets*_____ are probable future economic benefits obtained or controlled by a particular entity as a result of a past transaction or event.

4. As proposed by the FASB, _____*Comprehensive Inc*_____ equals earnings plus or minus cumulative accounting adjustments and/or other nonowner changes in equity.

5. A(n) _____*Transactions*_____ is an external event that involves the transfer of something of value from one entity to another.

6. The method of accounting that focuses on transactions and other economic events that have cash consequences is called the _____*Accrual Basis*_____ of accounting.

7. _____*Realization*_____ refers to the timing of revenue (or gain) or the determination of the point at which revenue should be recognized and reported.

8. Two methods of accounting for long-term construction contracts are _____*% of Compltn*_____ and _____*Compltd - Contract*_____

9. The _____*Capital Maint.*_____ concept states that net assets or investments of an entity must be maintained, or recovered through revenue, before the entity has earnings.

10. The _____*Curr. Rpl Cost*_____ of an asset is the amount of cash that would have to be paid to acquire the asset currently.

True-False

Indicate by circling the appropriate response whether each of the following statements is true (T) or false (F):

T (F) 1. It is always assumed that a company is a going concern.

T (F) 2. The time period assumption implies that financial statements are prepared once a year.

(T) F 3. Financial information should provide information to help users assess the amount, timing, and uncertainty of future cash flows.

(T) F 4. Information is reliable if a user can depend on or have confidence in it.

T (F) 5. When the benefits of accounting information are evaluated in light of the costs entailed in producing it, the benefits and costs are easily quantified in dollars.

(T) F 6. Elements are the building blocks, or categories, of financial statements.

T (F) 7. Assets are probable future economic benefits obtained or controlled by a particular entity.

T (F) 8. For an item to be classified as an expense, it must be an outflow of an asset or the incurrence of a liability, or a combination of both, resulting from the entity's major or ongoing earnings activity.

(T) F 9. Net income or net loss is composed of all transactions and events that change equity.

T (F) 10. A balance sheet shows the status of each of its elements at the end of an accounting period.

(T) F 11. A transaction that involves both receiving and sacrificing something of value is referred to as an exchange or reciprocal transfer.

T F 12. Accrual accounting reports revenues and expenses only when cash is received and paid, respectively.

T (F) 13. Revenue should be recognized when the amount and timing of the revenue to be received are reasonably determinable.

(T) F 14. Under the installment method of revenue realization, revenue is recognized at the time when cash is collected.

T F 15. Risk and uncertainty in the business environment are handled, in part, by the modifying principle of conservatism.

T **F** 16. When an asset is sold, earnings under the physical units capital maintenance concept arise if the revenue earned is more than the nominal dollars invested in the asset sold.

T **F** 17. Although several asset and liability valuation methods exist, GAAP requires that the historical cost attribute be measured.

T F 18. The current replacement cost of an asset is the amount of cash that would have to be paid currently to acquire an equivalent asset.

T F 19. To measure periodic earnings, a company must select both a capital maintenance concept and a valuation method.

T **F** 20. Disclosure is achieved solely through the preparation of detailed footnotes.

Multiple Choice

Select the best response for each of the following items, and circle the corresponding letter:

1. Contemporary financial reporting has limitations. Which of the following is *not* deemed to be a limitation?

    a. Accounting measures all items in units of money.
    b. Accounting information is historical.
    c. Accounting reports are prepared periodically.
    d. Accounting measurements are approximations.

2. As established by the FASB, the objectives of financial reporting are to provide information:

    a. For managers as the primary users of the financial statements.
    b. Limited to enterprise financial resources.
    c. For making only investment decisions.
    d. To help users assess future cash flows.

3. Relevance has three components. Identify the characteristic listed here that is *not* a component of relevance.

    a. Feedback value.
    b. Verifiability.
    c. Predictive value.
    d. Timeliness.

4. Which of the following statements does *not* apply to a liability?

    a. The entity is obligated to transfer cash or other assets or to provide services at some future time.
    b. The obligation is of a particular entity.
    c. Future economic benefits are controlled by a particular entity.
    d. The obligation arose from a past transaction or event.

5. Accounting for the substance of a transaction over its legal form is basic to accounting. The qualitative characteristic "substance over form" is part of the conceptual framework of the:

	FASB	IASC
a.	Yes	Yes
b.	Yes	No
c.	No	Yes
d.	No	No

6. The financial statement that shows the effects of capital transactions during an accounting period is commonly referred to as the:

    a. Balance sheet.
    b. Income statement.
    c. Statement of changes in owners' equity.
    d. Statement of cash flows.

7. Revenue may be realized at several points during the earnings process. When is the earliest point at which revenue from the mining of precious metals could be realized?

    a. During production (extraction of metal or ore).
    b. Completion of production (metal separated or extracted from ore).
    c. Point of sale of metal.
    d. Collection of cash on account from sale of metal.

8. Guidelines exist for the matching of expenses with revenue. Which of the following is *not* one of the general guidelines?

    a. Cost recovery.
    b. Association of cause and effect.
    c. Systematic and rational allocation.
    d. Immediate recognition.

9. Capital may be maintained in terms of:

    a. Units of money.
    b. Units of general purchasing power.
    c. Physical units.
    d. All of the above.

10. When the current value of an asset or a liability is measured, several alternative measurements are available. Which of the following attributes does *not* measure current value?

   a. Current replacement cost.
   b. Current exit value.
   c. Expected exit value.
   d. Discounted historical cost.

Extended Problems

1. At a meeting of corporate executives, one executive states that accounting is all technique or practice and no theory. An accountant at the meeting defends the practice of accounting by pointing out the existence of some basic environmental assumptions supporting accounting practice and the FASB's attempt to develop a conceptual framework for financial accounting and reporting.

REQUIRED

Prepare a reasonably detailed outline for the accountant to use as he or she further develops his or her defense of accounting.

2. Income measurement is very important in financial accounting. Conceptually, an income measurement system will continue to center on a capital maintenance concept and an asset-liability measurement or valuation method. Until recently, however, accountants have followed fairly strictly what has been called the conventional system. Only now is income measurement being discussed in relation to alternative systems.

REQUIRED

Discuss the conventional system as it is practiced today (include revenue realization and expense recognition) and the alternative methods that are being considered for the measurement of capital maintenance, assets, and liabilities.

3. A realtor acquired a parcel of land for $5,000 on January 1, 1995. The land was sold September 1, 1995, for $7,000. For the first eight months of 1995, the general level of prices increased 25 percent, and the realtor could acquire a similar parcel of land on September 1, 1995, for $7,200.

REQUIRED

Calculate earnings for the realtor on the sale of land assuming the following capital maintenance concepts:

   a. Units of money.
   b. Units of general purchasing power (as of September 1, 1995).
   c. Physical units.

COMMON ERRORS

The first statement in each of the "common errors" listed here is *incorrect*. Each incorrect statement is followed by a corrected statement and an explanation.

1. *Statement of Concepts No. 1* states that financial reporting should provide useful information only to present and potential investors. *Wrong*
Statement of Concepts No. 1 states that financial reporting should provide useful information to present and potential investors, creditors, and others. *Right*
In *Statement of Concepts No. 1,* the FASB explicitly includes present and potential investors, creditors, and others as primary users of financial reports. The information provided in financial reports is useful to these several user groups because they are all interested in making rational investment, credit, and similar decisions concerning the reporting entity. Rather than focus on one group, such as investors, the FASB expanded the audience of financial reports beyond the reporting entity's stockholders.

2. The materiality of an item depends on its relative dollar amount. *Wrong*
The materiality of an item depends on its relative dollar amount, relative nature, or a combination of both. *Right*
Materiality is an accounting term often used but seldom explicitly defined. If an item's materiality could be determined solely on its relative dollar amount, determining materiality would be easy. This is not the case, however, and professional judgment must also be used in assessing the relative nature of the item.
The dollar amount of an item is an important measure of the item's materiality. But often the nature of an item is *more* important. A theft of only $100 involving collusion between two employees is material, for example, because of the nature of the item (collusion in the theft of company assets), not necessarily because of the dollar amount ($100). Thus

materiality decisions must be based on an item's relative dollar amount, its nature, or both.

3. Revenues and gains represent an increase in an entity's net assets as a result of its major or ongoing operations. *Wrong*

Revenues represent an increase in a company's net assets as a result of its major or ongoing operations; gains represent an increase in net assets as a result of the company's peripheral or incidental transactions. *Right*

Both revenues and gains do result in an increase in net assets, but an important distinction between them is the way they are derived. Revenues come from the delivery or production of goods, the rendering of services, or other activities that constitute the *primary* operations of the entity. Gains, on the other hand, arise from the entity's *peripheral* or incidental transactions. A taxi company, for example, earns revenue from the fees it charges its customers for the service it renders. If the company sold one of its taxis for more than the vehicle's book value, a gain would be recorded.

4. The use of the cash-basis method of accounting and of the accrual method will result in different amounts of total income (or loss) over the life of an entity. *Wrong*

The use of the cash-basis method of accounting and of the accrual method will result in the same amount of total income (or loss) over the life of an entity. *Right*

During the life of an entity the periodic income (or loss) reported under the cash-basis method of accounting will probably differ from that reported under the accrual method—and differ significantly at times. The difference is not permanent, however; by the end of the life of the entity, the total income or loss will be the same under both methods. The difference is in the timing of the recognition of income or loss, not in the total amount recognized. The difference occurs because the accrual method often recognizes revenues or expenses before (accruals) or after (deferrals or prepayments) cash receipts or disbursements.

5. Under the capital maintenance concept, earnings arise if the revenue from the sale or disposal of a good or service is equal to the cost of the good or service sold or disposed of. *Wrong*

Under the capital maintenance concept, earnings arise if the revenue from the sale or disposal of a good or service is greater than the cost of the good or service sold or disposed of. *Right*

The concept of capital maintenance focuses on maintaining an entity's net assets or investments. After the net assets or investments are maintained, earnings arise. Therefore, in order for earnings to arise, the revenue received from the sale of an asset or the rendering of a service must exceed the amount of investment. That portion of revenue that recovers the cost is said to be a return *of* capital (or capital maintenance); the amount of revenue in excess of cost is referred to as a return *on* capital (or earnings).

6. When a company prepares and publishes financial statements and related notes, disclosure is achieved if the statements and notes present all economic information about the firm. *Wrong*

When a company prepares and publishes financial statements and related notes, disclosure is achieved if the statements and notes present any significant information that would affect the decisions of an informed and prudent user. *Right*

Disclosure may appear to imply that the financial statements and related notes provide all the information about the reporting company. *Disclosure* in this sense, however, is impossible and probably would be unnecessary even if it could be achieved. *Disclosure* relates to the user of the data and the user's decision-making process. Accountants try to provide only the economic information that could affect the informed and prudent user's decisions.

Even though accountants prepare financial statements that comply with the notion of disclosure, there are still many areas in which the disclosure of items or transactions could be improved. More or different information might be provided concerning a company's liquidity, for example, than is currently contained in the financial statements. Thus disclosure is a relative concept and is constantly changing to meet the needs of financial statement users.

ANSWERS

Key Terms and Concepts

1. environmental assumptions
2. reliability
3. assets
4. comprehensive income
5. transaction
6. accrual basis
7. realization
8. percentage-of-completion method, completed-contract method
9. capital maintenance
10. current replacement cost

True-False

1. F   It is true that accountants assume that an entity will continue to operate indefinitely. If there is evidence to the contrary, however, accountants will not adhere to the going concern assumption but will use the liquidation basis of accounting.

2. F   The assumption of periodicity refers to the artificial segmentation of the life of an entity into reporting periods of any length, not just an annual reporting period. Most companies publish financial statements at least quarterly as well as annually.

3. T

4. T

5. F   Unfortunately, it is usually rather difficult to quantify the benefits of accounting information in any unit, let alone in dollars. The preparation costs are much easier to quantify in dollars. The measurement of the benefits of accounting information, like that of any public good, is a very subjective process.

6. T

7. F   Assets are probable future economic benefits obtained or controlled by a particular entity as a result of a past transaction or event.

8. T

9. F   Net income or net loss is composed of only those transactions and events that change equity and are classified as revenue, gain, expense, or loss. Capital transactions, such as issuance of stock or distribution of dividends, change equity but are not components of income.

10. T

11. T

12. F   Accrual accounting may report revenues and expenses when cash is received and paid, but they may also be reported when economic events have cash consequences. It is the cash basis of accounting that reports revenues and expenses at the time of cash receipt and disbursement.

13. F   Revenue should be recognized when the amount and timing of revenue to be received are reasonably determinable and when the earnings process is complete or virtually complete.

14. T

15. T

16. F   Under the physical units capital maintenance concept, earnings arise only if the revenue received is greater than the current cost of the asset sold.

17. F   Historical cost is the primary valuation method applied to assets and liabilities, but other valuation methods are also used. Lower-of-cost-or-market valuation, for example, is used for inventories. The "historical cost system" is really a modified historical cost system.

18. T

19. T

20. F   Disclosure is achieved partly through the preparation of detailed footnotes. Other methods used to achieve disclosure are the reporting of the various accounts and account balances, the use of clarifying parenthetical comments, and the presentation of supplementary information.

Multiple Choice

1. c	6. c
2. d	7. b
3. b	8. a
4. c	9. d
5. c	10. d

Extended Problems

1. I.   Environmental assumptions—to provide a foundation for financial accounting theory and financial disclosure.
   A.   Accounting entity assumption—the unit of accountability or unit for which accountants account and prepare financial reports is specifically identified.
   B.   Going concern assumption—the accounting entity is assumed to continue to operate indefinitely unless there is evidence to the contrary.
   C.   Periodicity assumption—the life of the accounting entity is artificially segmented into time periods so that financial statements may reflect the progress of the entity.
   D.   Monetary assumption—the dollar is the unit of measure for recording and reporting on the transactions and events of the entity.

   II.   Conceptual framework.
   A.   Objectives of financial reporting.
      1. The stated objectives identify present and potential stockholders, creditors, and others as the primary users of financial information.
         a) Users need the information to make investment and credit decisions.
         b) The users have a responsibility to study the information.
      2. The stated objectives establish the primary use to which the financial information will be put: to help users

assess the amount, timing, and uncertainty of future cash flows.
   a) Cash flows to owners (creditors) are future distributions of dividends (interest) and redemption of securities (maturity value of debt).
   b) Users may more easily assess their future cash flows if information about the reporting entity's cash flows is made available.
3. The stated objectives identify the type of information that should be disclosed in financial reports.
   a) The enterprise's resources, obligations, and owners' equity.
   b) The effects of transactions, events, and circumstances resulting from earnings activities.
B. Qualitative characteristics of useful accounting information.
   1. Focus on user and information—user must *understand* the information if it is to be *decision-useful*.
   2. Primary decision-specific qualities.
      a) *Relevance.* Reported information will make a difference in the user's decisions.
         (i) Components: *predictive value, feedback value, timeliness.*
      b) *Reliability.* User can have confidence in reported information if it reports what it purports to report.
         (i) Components: *representational faithfulness, verifiability.*
   3. Secondary qualities.
      a) *Neutrality.* Information must be evenhanded or unbiased.
      b) *Comparability.* Information is more useful if a user can compare it with information from other companies or from the same company over time.
   4. Additional considerations.
      a) *Benefits vs. costs.* The benefits derived from information should exceed the cost of its preparation.
      b) *Materiality.* The information that could affect a user's decision should be disclosed.
C. Elements of financial statements—the building blocks of financial statements.
   1. *Assets:* future economic benefits controlled by an enterprise as a result of a past transaction or event.
   2. *Liabilities:* future sacrifices of economic benefits owed by a particular enterprise as a result of a past transaction or event.

3. *Equity (owners' equity):* residual interest in an enterprise (Equity = Assets – Liabilities).
4. *Revenues:* inflows of assets or settlement of liabilities, or a combination of both, as a result of the primary operations of the enterprise.
5. *Expenses:* outflows of assets or incurrence of liabilities, or a combination of both, as a result of the primary operations of the enterprise.
6. *Gains (losses):* increases (decreases) in equity or net assets as a result of peripheral activities of the enterprise.
7. *Net income* or *net loss:* the change in the equity of an enterprise caused by revenues, expenses, gains, and losses. *Statement of Concepts No. 5* refines this traditional concept of income. It proposes a similar but slightly more narrow definition and labels it *earnings.* Furthermore, the FASB suggests a new concept, *comprehensive income:* Earnings +/– Cumulative accounting adjustments +/– Other nonowner changes in equity = Comprehensive income.
D. Recognition criteria—determining when an item should be recorded.
   1. The item meets the definition of an element.
   2. The item has an attribute to measure with reliability.
   3. Information about the item is relevant to the user.
   4. Information about the item is reliable.
2. The conventional system is based on the accrual accounting concept, which measures revenues and expenses when transactions or other events have a cash consequence (immediate or potential), not when cash is received or disbursed. Revenues are recognized in the accounts when it has been determined that the revenue is realized. Expenses are matched with the revenue to determine net income or loss for the period.

   The two established criteria for revenue realization are (*a*) that the amount and timing of revenue to be received are reasonably determinable and (*b*) that the earnings process is complete or virtually complete. Because the earnings process is continuous, revenue is realized in practice at several points during the earnings process. Most revenue, however, is realized at the point of sale; the other realization points are used under special circumstances.

   Revenue may be realized before the point of sale, that is, during production or at the completion of production. On certain long-term construction projects, for example, revenue may be realized during the construction period in accordance with the percentage-of-completion method if the contract price is fixed or determinable and if period and total costs are reasonably known or estimable. In earnings activities involving commodities and precious metals, revenue may be realized when the production (harvesting or mining, respectively) is completed. If the collection of the receivable from a sale under the installment method is very uncertain, revenue may be realized after the point of sale, when cash is collected.

Expenses are matched with the realized revenues according to three general guidelines. First, *cause-and-effect association* applies to expenses, such as cost of goods, that have a direct relation to the revenue. Second, *systematic and rational allocation* applies to those costs, such as depreciation, that are more easily associated with the period benefited than with revenue. Third, *immediate recognition* applies to costs, such as officers' salaries or obsolete inventory, that have no discernible future benefit.

The conventional system has received criticism, however. Increased emphasis is being placed on the capital maintenance concept and alternative valuation methods. *Capital maintenance* means that earnings arise only if the revenue from the sale of an item exceeds its cost. In other words, the revenue received permits recovery of the cost (or maintenance of the capital) of the item sold; the amount remaining is earnings. Capital may be maintained in units of money or of general purchasing power if the revenue exceeds the nominal or general purchasing power equivalent of the item sold, respectively. Under the physical units concept of capital maintenance, earnings arise if the revenue exceeds the current cost of the item sold.

In order to measure an asset or a liability, a valuation method or attribute to be measured must be selected. The proposed alternative asset attributes and methods of measurement are summarized as follows:

a. *Historical cost:* exchange price of asset.
b. *Current replacement cost:* amount required to attain an equivalent asset currently.
c. *Current exit value:* amount that would be received if an asset were sold in an orderly liquidation.
d. *Expected exit value:* nondiscounted net cash flows to be received from an asset in the future.
e. *Present value of expected cash flows:* discounted net cash flows to be received from an asset in the future.

It should be noted that liabilities are also measured under each of these alternatives.

To determine periodic income, a capital maintenance concept and a valuation method must be selected. Under the conventional system, the unit of money capital maintenance concept and the historical cost measurement method are used.

3. Calculation of earnings under alternative capital maintenance concepts:

	UNITS OF MONEY	UNITS OF GENERAL PURCHASING POWER	PHYSICAL UNITS
Revenue	$7,000	$7,000	$7,000
Cost of land sold	−5,000	−6,250*	−7,200
Earnings (Loss)	$2,000	$ 750	$ (200)

*$5,000 × 1.25 = $6,250.

3 THE ACCOUNTING PROCESS: A REVIEW

CHAPTER OBJECTIVES

After reading Chapter 3 and completing the questions, cases, exercises, and problems from the text chapter, you should be able to:

1. Describe the data input to the accounting system.
2. Know and understand the effects of transactions on the accounting equation.
3. Know the basic rules for debits and credits to accounts.
4. Differentiate between real and nominal accounts.
5. Discuss the importance to the accounting process of source documents and of data analysis.
6. Understand the use of the various journals to record transactions.
7. Understand the use of ledgers in the posting process.
8. Understand the purpose of a trial balance.

9. Identify and prepare the four types of adjusting entries (prepayments, accruals, estimated items, and inventory adjustments).
10. Identify the basic financial statements (income statement, balance sheet, statement of retained earnings, and statement of cash flows).
11. Prepare closing entries, and understand the use of the income summary account.
12. Identify the adjusting entries that could be reversed, and know how to prepare the appropriate reversing entries.
13. Differentiate between the accounting and equity accounts of the various forms of business organization.
14. Understand the relationships between cash flow and accrual income.

CHAPTER REVIEW

The Accounting Process

1. Chapters 1 and 2 focus on the historical development and theoretical framework of financial accounting. They emphasize that financial accounting exists to help investors, creditors, and others to make decisions about the reporting entity. This chapter addresses the process of capturing, processing, summarizing, and reporting economic events that are reported in the financial statements used by the decision makers.

More specifically, the type of events captured by the accounting system (data input), the accounting equation, and the accounting process are the primary topics of this chapter. In addition, equity accounting will be discussed briefly.

2. It should be noted that the accounting process applies to enterprises of all types and sizes. The degree of complexity and volume of data handled by a particular accounting system will depend on the type and size of the company, but the fundamentals of the accounting process remain the same.

Data Input to the Accounting System

3. Essentially, the basic data input to the accounting system is an economic event: an occurrence or happening that has a consequence to an entity. Of all the economic events that affect an entity, only those that meet the four recognition criteria listed in Chapter 2 are captured and reported by the accounting system.

The Accounting Equation

4. Each economic event and transaction that is captured as part of the accounting data affects the basic accounting equation: Assets = Liabilities + Equity. The elements of the equation are defined in Chapter 2. Whether a transaction is a capital, an asset and liability, or a revenue and expense transaction, the equation always remains in balance after the effects of the transaction are recorded.

5. The equity element of the equation is often split into *contributed capital,* which represents the investments by shareholders, and *retained earnings,* which represents the accumulated earnings (Revenues – Expenses + Gains – Losses) of the corporation less any *dividends* or distributions to stockholders. The change in retained earnings over an accounting period is caused by the net income or loss from operations and dividend distributions and is expressed as follows: Beginning retained earnings + (–) Net income (Net loss) – Dividends = Ending retained earnings.

6. Accounts and the accounting equation. As previously stated, each captured transaction causes changes in two or more financial statement elements. An *account* is used to accumulate the effects of transactions and other economic events on each financial statement element. An account is described as a T-account because increases and decreases in the account are recorded in the form of a *T*, with increases on one side and decreases on the other. The left side of the account is called the *debit* side and the right side, the *credit* side. Debits increase an asset, expense, or loss account, whereas credits to such an account reduce it. In contrast, credits increase a liability, equity (shareholders' equity and retained earnings), revenue, or gain account, whereas debits reduce it. An account's normal balance is usually found on the side (that is, debit or credit) that increases the account and is determined by the difference between the debit and credit entries in the account.

7. The rules for debits and credits and the positioning or ordering of the elements of the accounting equation provide a sound basis for the double-entry accounting system. Each transaction affects at least two accounts, with one account being debited and another credited. After the effects of the transaction on the elements are analyzed and the appropriate debit or debits and credit or credits recorded, the accounting equation remains in balance.

8. *Real,* or *permanent,* accounts are accounts for balance sheet items. These accounts represent an ongoing record for the balance sheet items. *Nominal,* or *temporary,* accounts are accounts for income statement items. As these accounts accumulate amounts related to earnings activities during an accounting period, they are closed—that is, the accounts are reduced to a zero balance—at the end of each accounting period.

The Accounting Process, or Cycle

9. The preparation of an entity's financial statements at the end of an accounting period represents the end, and most visible and familiar part, of the accounting process, or cycle. The *accounting process* consists of the procedures used to collect, process, and report the economic events that affect an entity during an accounting period. The accounting process has not escaped the computer revolution. Computer software, called *general ledger packages,* has changed the way accounting data are handled and stored, but it has not changed the concepts underlying the accounting process. The steps presented in the remainder of this section apply to both pen-and-paper and computerized accounting processes.

10. Data collection. The first step in the accounting process is the collection of evidence that an economic event that affects the entity has occurred and should become part of the accounting data. A *source document* usually provides such evidence. A source document may be internally generated, such as a sales invoice from a credit sale, or externally generated, such as a note contract from a creditor.

11. Analyzing data. The next step is to analyze the data collected about the economic events and determine the effects of the individual events on the financial statement elements. This analysis determines how an event will enter the accounting system. It is during this step that accounting theory may be applied. The realization principle, for example, helps in the analysis of a revenue transaction.

12. Recording in a journal. After the data about economic events are collected and analyzed, the transactions are recorded or journalized in a *journal* or book of original entry that provides a chronological record of the entity's transactions and other economic events that have occurred. When only one journal is used, it is called a *general journal.* The general journal usually consists of columns for the dates of transactions, the titles of accounts that are debited and credited, explanations of the transactions, posting references (used in the next step of the accounting process), and the dollar amounts of the debits and credits.

13. A *special journal* is used to record each set of similar economic events. Because similar transactions are recorded in a special journal, speed and efficiency are usually increased. The most frequently used special journals are the *cash receipts journal*, for all transactions involving cash receipts; the *cash disbursements journal*, for all transactions involving cash disbursement; the *sales journal*, for all credit sales; and the *purchases journal*, for all purchases of merchandise on account. Firms that use special journals still must maintain a general journal for those transactions that cannot be recorded in one of the special journals.

14. Posting to the ledger. As previously explained, an account accumulates the effects of transactions and other events on each financial statement element. Thus far in the accounting process, each transaction has been listed chronologically in the journal, but the individual accounts have been unaffected. Step 4 of the accounting process involves the transfer or *posting* of the amounts recorded in the journal to the accounts in the ledger. The *ledger* is a composite of all accounts.

15. When an amount is posted from the journal to an account in the ledger, the account number is entered into the posting reference, or folio, column of the journal. As a cross-reference, the specific journal and the page number in the journal are entered into the account.

16. The *general ledger* consists of all the entity's accounts. Because the general ledger does not often contain sufficient detail about the composition of an account balance, the entity may maintain a *subsidiary ledger* to provide such detail. Subsidiary ledgers are maintained for accounts such as accounts receivable, accounts payable, and plant and equipment. The sum of the account balances in a subsidiary ledger should equal the balance in the related general ledger account, referred to as a *controlling account*. It should be noted that subsidiary accounts also require posting.

17. Preparing an unadjusted trial balance. At the end of an accounting period, after all the entries have been posted, an *unadjusted trial balance*, a listing of every account in the general ledger and its balance, is prepared. An unadjusted trial balance verifies the accuracy of the debits and credits posted to the ledger accounts; it does not verify that all transactions have been recorded or, if so, whether they have been journalized and posted to the proper accounts. The unadjusted trial balance also facilitates the preparation of the necessary adjusting entries.

18. Preparing adjusting entries. The next step in the accounting process is the preparation of adjusting entries. *Adjusting entries* record some internal transactions that have occurred but have not been recorded. These entries are necessary under accrual accounting to recognize revenues and expenses for a period and to reflect properly assets and liabilities at the end of an accounting period. An adjusting entry may be classified as one of four types: prepayments and unearned items, accruals, estimated items, and inventory adjustments.

19. *Prepayments and unearned items,* the first type of adjusting entry, represent a situation in which the cash flow precedes the earnings activities. Prepayments, which apply to both expenses and revenues, have been recorded and necessitate allocation between asset and expense accounts (prepaid expenses) or between liability and revenue accounts (unearned revenues) at the end of the accounting period.

20. When a company acquires future economic benefits, as by paying for supplies or by making rental payments in advance, it acquires a *prepaid expense* or asset that must be expensed as the benefit or asset is consumed or as it expires. The adjusting entry to allocate the cost between the expense (expired portion of the cost) and asset (unexpired portion of the cost) depends on how the initial entry was recorded. If the initial expenditure was debited to an expense account, the adjusting entry requires a debit to an asset account and a credit to the expense account in order to transfer the portion of the expenditure that has future economic benefit to an asset account. If the initial transaction was debited to an asset account, the adjusting entry requires a debit to an expense account and a credit to the asset account in order to transfer the portion of the expenditure that has no future benefit to an expense account. Regardless of the method followed, the adjusting entry results in proper expense recognition and asset valuation for the period.

21. *Unearned revenues* arise when a company receives payment for goods or services to be distributed or rendered at some future time, as when it receives rent payments in advance. As in the case of prepaid expense adjusting entries, the method of recording the initial transaction determines the proper adjusting entry. If a revenue account was initially credited, the adjusting entry is a debit to the revenue account and a credit to an unearned revenue (liability) account for the amount of revenue that has not yet been earned. If the initial transaction was credited to an unearned revenue account, the adjustment is a debit to the unearned revenue account and a credit to a revenue account for the amount of revenue that has been earned during the period. Under either method, the adjusting entry results in proper recognition of revenues and proper measurement and disclosure of liabilities (unearned revenues).

22. *Accruals,* the second type of adjusting entry, represent situations in which earnings activities precede the related cash flows. The internal transaction that caused the accrual has occurred but has not been recorded. Accordingly, the adjusting entry for a revenue accrual, such as interest earned on a note receivable but not collected, is recorded by a debit to a receivable account and a credit to a revenue account for the amount of the earned but unrecorded revenue. An expense accrual, such as salaries incurred but not paid, is recorded by a debit to an expense account and a credit to a liability account for the amount of the incurred but unrecorded expense. It should be noted that all accrual adjusting entries affect either asset and revenue accounts or liability and expense accounts.

23. *Estimated items,* the third type of adjusting entry, are expenses that must be estimated and recorded at the end of the accounting period in order to match the expense with revenue for that period. Two such items are depreciation expense and uncollectible accounts expense. *Depreciation expense* is the estimated cost of the services of a long-lived asset that have been consumed or that have expired in the earnings process during the period. Depreciation is the systematic and rational allocation of an asset's cost (less salvage value, if any) over its estimated useful economic life. The adjusting entry to record depreciation is a debit to depreciation expense and credit to accumulated depreciation for the estimated amount of depreciation expense. The accumulated depreciation account is a contra asset or asset valuation account, and its balance is deducted from the related asset's cost on the balance sheet.

24. *Uncollectible accounts expense,* or *bad debts expense,* is the estimated amount of credit sales that will be uncollectible. Recognition of uncollectible accounts expense matches the cost of those credit sales that ultimately will be uncollectible with the revenue in the period the sale is made. To prepare the adjusting entry, uncollectible accounts expense is debited and allowance for uncollectible accounts is credited for the estimated amount of the uncollectible receivables. The latter account is also a contra account, and its balance is deducted from accounts receivable on the balance sheet.

25. *Inventory adjustments,* the fourth type of adjusting entry, are made in order that the inventory account on the balance sheet and cost of goods sold on the income statement will be properly stated. Assuming a periodic inventory system in which purchases and related costs are recorded in temporary accounts, the cost of the ending inventory is determined by a physical count of the inventory on hand at the end of the period, and cost of goods sold is calculated by the following formula: Beginning inventory + Net purchases − Ending inventory = Cost of goods sold. Adjusting entries are made (*a*) to close beginning inventory (debit cost of goods sold and credit inventory for the amount of the beginning inventory), (*b*) to establish ending inventory in the accounts (debit inventory and credit cost of goods sold for the amount of ending inventory), and (*c*) to transfer net purchases to cost of goods sold (debit cost of goods sold and credit purchases for the amount of purchases; other accounts related to purchases, such as transportation in, must be individually closed to cost of goods sold).

26. Technically, no adjusting entries are necessary if the perpetual inventory system is used. The perpetual inventory system records all purchases and related costs in the inventory account and reduces the inventory account for the cost of goods sold when a sale is made. Thus the balances of the inventory account and the cost of goods sold account should be current and correct at all times during and at the end of an accounting period.

27. As an alternative, adjustments may be made to inventory and cost of goods sold when closing entries are prepared during another step in the accounting process.

28. Several generalizations about adjusting entries should be mentioned. First, adjusting entries are an integral part of the accounting cycle. They are made to record those events that affect the earnings activities during an accounting period but have not yet been recorded. Second, adjusting entries provide data necessary for proper matching of revenues and expenses on the income statement and measurement of assets and liabilities on the balance sheet, resulting in financial statements that are reliable, representationally faithful, and thus more useful to decision makers. Third, and related to the second, every adjusting entry affects a real (balance sheet) account and a nominal (income statement) account.

29. Preparing an adjusted trial balance. An *adjusted trial balance* lists all ledger accounts and their balances after the adjusting entries have been posted. Like an unadjusted trial balance, an adjusted trial balance tests the equality of debits and credits of the listed accounts but does not verify that all transactions have been properly recorded and posted. It also facilitates the next step of the accounting cycle, preparation of the financial statements.

30. Preparing the financial statements. Four primary financial statements are prepared at the end of each accounting period: income statement, balance sheet, statement of retained earnings, and statement of cash flows. Each of the statements will be briefly discussed in the following paragraphs.

31. The *income statement* presents a summary of a company's earnings activities during an accounting period. This statement matches the revenues earned and the expenses incurred to generate the revenues over a particular period of time. In addition, gains and losses from nonoperating activities appear on the income statement. If revenues exceed expenses, the company has net income or has earned a profit. Conversely, if expenses exceed revenues, the company has sustained a net loss. Further details of the income statement are presented in Chapter 4.

32. The *balance sheet,* or *statement of financial position,* presents a company's financial position at a point in time, usually the end of an accounting period. Assets and liabilities are classified as current or noncurrent. Such assets as cash, accounts receivable, and inventory are classified as current because they are expected to be converted into cash or consumed within one year or during the course of the company's operating cycle, whichever is longer. Similarly, such liabilities as accounts payable are considered current if they will require the use of a current asset to discharge the debt or will be discharged within one year. Assets such as building and fixtures, whose benefits will be received over several years, are classified as noncurrent under descriptive headings, such as land and equipment and intangibles. Liabilities to be paid after one year, such as a note payable due four years after the balance sheet date, are classified as noncurrent. The balance sheet is discussed further in Chapter 5.

33. The *statement of retained earnings* reconciles the beginning and ending balances of retained earnings. Net income is normally added to (or net loss is subtracted from) the beginning balance of retained earnings, and dividends (distributions to owners) are deducted to determine the ending balance of retained earnings. Since dividends are a distribution of accumulated earnings to owners, they appear as a deduction on the retained earnings statement, not as an expense on the income statement. Chapters 4 and 18 expand on the discussion of the statement of retained earnings and dividends.

34. The *statement of cash flows* discloses cash inflows and outflows generated by and applied as a result of a company's operating, investing, and financing activities during an accounting period. This statement is explained more fully in Chapters 6 and 21.

35. Preparing closing entries. In the course of an accounting period, revenues and expenses have been accumulated in nominal accounts in order to determine net income or loss during that period. *Closing entries* reduce all nominal account balances to zero so that they can accumulate the revenues and expenses of the next accounting period. Through the closing process, the net income or loss is transferred to owners' equity. Specifically, (*a*) all nominal accounts with a credit balance (for example, sales) are individually debited and a new nominal account, income summary, is credited for the total amount of the debits; (*b*) income summary is debited for the total amount of all nominal accounts with debit balances (for example, cost of goods sold and salaries expense) which are individually credited; and (*c*) if income summary has a credit balance (net income), the income summary account is debited and retained earnings is credited for the amount of net income. If, however, the income summary account has a debit balance (net loss), retained earnings is debited and income summary is credited for the amount of the net loss.

36. Preparing a postclosing trial balance. The last step in the accounting cycle is the preparation of a postclosing trial balance. This trial balance, like the others, lists all accounts and their balances

(only real accounts have a balance after the closing entries are posted) and tests the accuracy of the debits and credits. The accounting process, or cycle, is now ready to begin again. The real accounts are carried forward to the next accounting period, whereas the nominal accounts with their zero balances are ready to accumulate the results of the earnings activities during the next period.

37. Reversing entries. *Reversing entries* are entries made at the beginning of the next accounting period to reverse certain adjusting entries made at the end of the immediately preceding period. Reversing entries are *optional* and are made to simplify the recording of some transactions in the next accounting period. Not all adjusting entries are reversed—only those that increase an asset or liability account. Of the various adjusting entries studied, only prepayments and unearned items that were originally recorded in nominal accounts and accruals need to be reversed. If, for example, a company's accounting policy is to record all prepayments as expenses and then to transfer the unused portion to an asset account with an adjusting entry, a reversing entry can be made to reestablish the unused portion as an expense: debit the expense account and credit the asset account for the amount of the adjusting entry. When subsequent acquisitions are made, they will be debited to the expense account. During the next accounting period, the expense account will thus contain all relevant data pertaining to that expenditure item, rather than have a portion of it as an asset (from the last period's adjusting entry) and the balance as an expense (from the current period's acquisitions).

38. When an expenditure is originally entered in an asset account and the adjusting entry transfers the expired portion to an expense account, no reversal is needed, because subsequent acquisitions will be debited to the asset account, which already contains unexpired costs from the previous period. Therefore, all amounts related to the type of expenditure are in only one account, the asset account, until the accounts are adjusted at the end of the accounting period. Similar reasoning applies to unearned revenue items.

39. All accrual adjustments should be reversed if reversing entries are used. As accrual adjustments pertain to items of revenue that are earned or of expense incurred before the related cash flow, reversing entries simplify the accounting procedures at the time of the future cash flow. If revenue such as interest on a note receivable is accrued at the end of an accounting period, for example, a receivable is established and the revenue is recognized in the period in which the adjusting entry is made. The reversing entry debits the revenue account and credits the receivable account for the amount of the accrued revenue. Subsequently, when the next interest payment is received, the entire amount is debited to cash and credited to the revenue account. It does not matter whether the amount of cash received is equal to or greater than the amount accrued, because the total amount of the interest credited to the revenue account will be offset by the amount of the accrual debited to the revenue account from the reversing entry. The net balance in the revenue account, if any, represents revenue during the period in which the cash is received. This procedure is simpler than allocating the cash collected between the accrued revenue (the receivable account) and revenue for the current period (the revenue account).

Accounting for Owners' Equity

40. The steps in the accounting cycle apply to all types of business organizations: sole proprietorships, partnerships, and corporations. The accounts constituting owners' equity, however, differ. A sole proprietor or a partner has a *capital,* or *owner's equity, account* established, which is usually named for the individual. Assume, for example, that Robert Snyder is the owner of his own business. The capital account for his business would be called R. Snyder, capital. This account is credited to record all of Snyder's investments and to close the income summary account when a profit is earned and is debited if a loss is sustained. When an owner withdraws assets for personal use, a nominal, or *drawing, account* is debited for the fair value of the assets withdrawn. The drawing account accumulates all drawings made during an accounting period and is closed to the capital account at the end of the accounting period. To close Robert Snyder's drawing account, debit R. Snyder, capital, and credit R. Snyder, drawing, for the amount accumulated in the drawing account during the period.

41. Unlike a partnership, a corporation does not maintain an individual ledger account for each of its owners (its stockholders). When a corporation issues shares of stock to its shareholders for cash, the cash account is debited for the issue price of the stock; the common stock account is credited with an amount equal to the par value of the stock, if any; and contributed capital in excess of par is credited with the difference between the issue price and par value of the stock. Distributions to owners as cash dividends are debited to dividends declared, a nominal account, and credited to cash for the amount of the dividend. As previously explained, dividends are a reduction of retained earnings and are thus subsequently closed to retained earnings (*not* to income summary) by a debit to retained earnings and a credit to dividends declared for the amount accumulated in the dividends declared account.

Cash-Basis vs. Accrual Accounting

42. GAAP requires financial statements to be prepared on an accrual basis. However, as Chapter 2 discussed, cash-basis accounting is used by some entities.

Often accountants must convert a cash-basis income statement to an accrual statement. The text illustrates 11 typical adjustments for converting from a cash flow income to an accrual income. These may be summarized as follows:

a. Cash received (collected) from customers is considered income (sales) and must be adjusted for changes in customer receivables. For example, if receivables increase during the period, the amount of the increase must be added to the amount of cash sales to determine the total accrual income (both cash and credit sales) for the period.

b. Cash payments for inventory, supplies, salaries, or utilities affect cost of goods sold, supplies expense, salaries expense, or utilities expense, respectively, and usually need to be adjusted to reflect the appropriate accrual amount. For example, cash paid for inventory during the period that is not sold should not be considered as cost of goods sold (an expense) until the inventory is sold in a future period. Accordingly, the cash paid for inventory and not sold must be deducted from the total amount paid for inventory to determine accrual cost of goods sold. Similarly, the amount of cash paid to suppliers during the current period for inventory that was acquired in a previous period must be deducted from the total cash paid for inventory to determine accrual cost of goods sold for the current period.

c. Some items, such as depreciation expense, uncollectible accounts, and accrued interest payable, need to be recognized for accrual-basis income. Since these are noncash expenses, they must be included in determining accrual-basis income. For example, depreciation expense does not require a cash payment and would not be considered an expense in determining cash-basis income. It must be recognized, however, for accrual-basis income.

43. When a statement of cash flows is prepared, it is often necessary to convert an accrual-basis income amount to a cash-basis or cash flow income. This requires an analysis similar to that above except that the changes are reversed. To illustrate, the increase in accounts receivable during the period must be deducted from the amount of accrual-basis sales to determine cash flow from sales (customers). The statement of cash flows is discussed in Chapters 6 and 21.

Appendix: The Use of a Worksheet

44. The preparation of a worksheet is an optional step in the accounting process, but worksheets have several advantages. They facilitate the making of adjusting entries and the preparation of financial statements and permit the preparation of interim financial statements without the need to close the books.

45. As illustrated in the text, a typical worksheet consists of 10 columns—five pairs of debit and credit columns, hence the name 10-column worksheet. The five pairs of columns (in order from left to right) and a brief explanation of their purpose follow: (*a*) The first pair of columns is for a *trial balance*. The figures for the trial balance can be transferred from an independently prepared trial balance or may be prepared directly from the ledger. (*b*) The *adjustments* columns are for recording the adjusting entries for the period. Each entry should be keyed or identified in the columns for easy reference. If an account is needed for an adjusting entry that does not appear in the trial balance, it is added at the bottom of the worksheet. (*c*) The *adjusted trial balance* columns contain all the account balances after the effects of the adjusting entries. Each account in the adjustments columns will be extended to either of the next two pairs of columns (the financial statement columns). The adjusted trial balance columns are often omitted, so that the worksheet has only eight columns. (*d*) The *income statement* columns contain all the accounts that appear in the income statement. All nominal accounts with a credit balance, such as revenues and contra purchase accounts, are extended to the credit column; whereas those accounts with a debit balance, such as expenses and contra sales accounts, are extended to the debit column. Elaboration of cost of goods sold, taxes, and recognition of net income or loss are considered later. (*e*) The *balance sheet* columns contain all real account balances that will appear in the balance sheet. Real accounts with a debit balance are extended to the debit column; those with a credit balance, to the credit column. It should be remembered that when the worksheet is completed, each pair of debit and credit columns should balance.

46. The amount of net income or loss is determined by totaling the income statement debit and credit columns on the worksheet. If credits (basically revenue items) exceed debits (basically expense items), a profit has been earned. Conversely, if debits exceed credits, a loss has been sustained. Net income, if it is indicated, is transferred to the balance sheet by entering net income (the amount by which the credits exceed the debits) in the debit column of the income statement columns and extending it to the credit

column of the balance sheet columns. After the amount of net income has been recorded, the income statement columns are equal and the balance sheet columns are equal.

47. When taxes are levied on earnings, an additional adjusting entry is required: debit income tax expense and credit income tax payable for an amount equal to earnings before tax times the tax rate. This entry is entered in the proper accounts in the *adjustments* columns and extended to the financial statements. That is, the income tax expense is extended to the debit column of the income statement columns, and income tax payable is extended to the credit column of the balance sheet columns. The addition of income tax expense as a debit reduces the amount of excess credits in the income statement columns to an amount equal to earnings after tax, or net income. As before, the amount of net income is entered in the debit column of the income statement columns and the credit column of the balance sheet columns.

48. Since all adjusting entries are recorded on the worksheet, they can be formally journalized from the worksheet and then posted. In addition, the financial statements can be prepared directly from the income statement and balance sheet columns of the worksheet. Moreover, the closing entries can be prepared from the income statement columns. Accounts that appear in the debit column will be individually credited for their balance, and income summary will be debited for an amount equal to the sum of the credits. All accounts that appear in the credit column will be individually debited for their balance, and income summary will be credited with an amount equal to the sum of the debits. Net income or loss is then closed to owners' equity.

49. A common modification of the 10-column worksheet involves the addition of two columns for retained earnings between the income statement and balance sheet columns. Instead of being extended to the balance sheet columns, the beginning balances in retained earnings and dividends are extended to the credit and debit columns, respectively, of retained earnings. Net income or loss is also extended to the credit or debit column of retained earnings. The amount needed to balance the retained earnings columns (usually entered in the debit column) represents the ending balance in the retained earnings account and is extended to a balance sheet column (usually to the credit column).

SELF-STUDY LEARNING   Items marked with an asterisk (*) refer to the Appendix.

Key Terms and Concepts

Provide the appropriate term or terms to complete each of the following statements:

1. A(n) _Econ Event_ is an occurrence, or a happening, that has a consequence to an entity.

2. The effects of transactions and other economic events on each element of the financial statements are accumulated in a(n) _Account_.

3. Balance sheet accounts are referred to as _Real_, or _Permanent_, accounts, whereas income statement accounts are called _Nominal_, or _Temporary_, accounts.

4. The _Acct'g Cycle_ consists of the procedures used to collect, process, and report economic events that affect an entity during an accounting period.

5. Transactions are initially recorded or journalized in a(n) _Journal_ and then posted to the _Ledger_.

6. _Accruals_ represent situations in which earnings activities precede the related cash flows.

7. _Closing_ entries reduce all income statement or nominal accounts to zero.

8. _Reversing_ entries are prepared at the beginning of an accounting period but are not required.

9. Investments by a sole proprietor are posted to the _Capital_ account, whereas the proprietor's withdrawal of assets for personal use are posted to the _Drawing_ account.

*10. An optional step in the accounting process is the preparation of a(n) _Worksheet_, which facilitates the making of adjusted entries and the preparation of financial statements.

True-False

Indicate by circling the appropriate response whether each of the following statements is true (T) or false (F):

T (F) 1. Economic events that can be identified as affecting the accounting entity are captured and reported.

T (F) 2. Dividends are distributions to stockholders and normally represent a return of their investment.

T (F) 3. A debit increases a real account.

(T) F 4. Nominal accounts are accounts for income statement elements.

T (F) 5. The only evidence that an economic event that affects the entity has occurred is supplied by internally generated source documents.

(T) F 6. Books of original entry are commonly referred to as journals.

T F 7. The general ledger contains a company's real and nominal accounts.

 F 8. *Posting* refers to the transferring of amounts recorded in the journal to the accounts in the ledger.

T 9. The fact that the unadjusted trial balance is in balance indicates that all transactions have been properly posted.

T F 10. Some transactions and internal events that have occurred but have not previously been recorded are recorded by means of adjusting entries.

T F 11. When the cash flow precedes the earnings activity, an accrual arises.

 F 12. Prepaid expenses represent benefits received to be expensed in the future.

T F 13. Accrual adjusting entries depend on the way the original entry in regard to the item that requires the accrual was recorded.

 F 14. Estimated item adjusting entries record expenses that must be estimated at the end of the accounting period to achieve a proper matching of revenues and expenses.

 F 15. When a perpetual inventory system is used, no inventory adjusting entries are normally required at the end of an accounting period.

 F 16. An adjusted trial balance lists all real and nominal accounts and their balances after adjusting entries have been posted.

 F 17. The current-noncurrent classification applies to both asset and liability accounts on the balance sheet.

T F 18. The closing of an expense account requires a debit to the expense account and a credit to income summary for an amount equal to the balance in the expense account.

T F 19. The income summary account is a real account used in the closing process.

 F *20. Preparation of a worksheet is an optional step in the accounting process.

Multiple Choice

Select the best response for each of the following items, and circle the corresponding letter:

1. An account's normal balance is usually:

   a. The debit side.
   b. The credit side.
   c. The side that increases the account.
   d. The side that decreases the account.

2. Which of the following transactions would be recorded in a special cash disbursements journal?

   a. Issuance of stock for cash.
   b. Declaration of cash dividend.
   c. Payment of a court settlement.
   d. Receipt of proceeds from the sale of an asset.

3. The adjusting entry for a prepaid expense originally recorded with a debit to an asset account would include:

   a. A debit to the expense account and a credit to cash.
   b. A debit to the asset account and a credit to the expense account.
   c. A debit to the asset account and a credit to cash.
   d. A debit to the expense account and a credit to the asset account.

4. The accumulated depreciation account is:

   a. A contra asset.
   b. A liability.
   c. An asset.
   d. An expense.

5. When a periodic inventory system is used, the inventory adjusting entries do all but which of the following?

   a. Close purchases to the inventory account.
   b. Close beginning inventory.
   c. Establish ending inventory.
   d. Transfer purchases to cost of goods sold.

6. All adjusting entries affect:

   a. Two real accounts.
   b. Two nominal accounts.
   c. One real and one nominal account.
   d. One real account or one nominal account and income summary.

7. A financial statement is headed by the reporting company's name, the name of the statement, and the date. The date of which of the following

financial statements represents one particular point in time?

a. Balance sheet.
b. Income statement.
c. Statement of retained earnings.
d. Statement of cash flows.

8. Each form of business organization uses a different account to record equity transactions. Which of the following pairs of accounts, the first used by a sole proprietorship and the second by a corporation, are not equivalent?

a. Capital, common stock.
b. Drawings, dividends.
c. Capital, retained earnings.
d. Excess capital, contributed capital in excess of par.

*9. When a worksheet is prepared, the credit column of the income statement contains the amount extended from the:

a. Sales account.
b. Purchases account.
c. Income taxes payable account.
d. All of the above.

*10. On a typical 10-column worksheet:

a. The first set of debit and credit columns is used for the adjusting entries.
b. Real accounts in the adjusted trial balance are extended to the income statement columns.
c. The balance of the income tax expense account appears only in the debit column of the income statement.
d. The net income amount is extended to the credit column of the balance sheet.

Extended Problem

Designer Fads Company, a local retail clothing store, was established April 1, 1995. The company issued 6,000 shares of $10 par value common stock (30,000 shares authorized); acquired inventory, supplies, and fixtures; borrowed $20,000 on a five-year 12 percent note (interest payable each March 31); secured a one-year property insurance policy; and rented its store space for one year. The accountant for Designer Fads then compiled the following trial balance as of April 1, 1995:

DESIGNER FADS COMPANY
TRIAL BALANCE
APRIL 1, 1995

Cash	$ 17,000	
Inventory	35,000	
Supplies	1,200	
Prepaid rent	12,000	
Fixtures	66,000	
Accounts payable		$ 25,000
Note payable		20,000
Common stock		60,000
Contributed capital in excess of par		28,000
Insurance expense	1,800	
	$133,000	$133,000

During the next three months, the accountant assembled the following data concerning Designer Fads' activities during the quarter. (*Note:* Whereas most data represent single transactions, some data have been accumulated.)

Apr. 11 Paid salaries to salesclerks, $400.
Apr. 30 Sold clothing totaling $18,000 ($12,000 cash sales plus $6,000 on credit).
May 10 Paid $20,000 of accounts payable balance.
May 13 Paid salaries to salesclerks, $1,700.
May 20 Purchased additional clothing on account from Shirts to Skirts, Inc., $26,000. (Debit purchases account.)
May 21 Collected $4,800 of credit sales from customers.
May 25 Returned goods to Shirts to Skirts, Inc., because of poor quality and received credit for the goods, $900.
May 31 Sold merchandise totaling $27,000 ($15,000 cash sales plus $12,000 credit sales).
June 2 Paid utility bills for April and May totaling $600.
June 3 Paid balance due Shirts to Skirts, Inc.
June 10 Purchased clothing on account from Stitches Co., $29,340.
June 10 Paid freight charges on clothing from Stitches Co., $100.
June 10 Paid salaries to salesclerks, $1,900.
June 15 Paid $7,840 toward amount owed Stitches Co.
June 18 Issued 1,500 additional shares of common stock for $16 per share.
June 20 Collected $11,300 on account from customers.
June 21 Received a letter from creditor requesting payment for $5,000 balance due since April 1, 1995.
June 28 Paid balance due Stitches Co.

June 30   Sold merchandise totaling $31,000 ($20,000 cash sales plus $11,000 credit sales).

June 30   Declared a quarterly dividend of $.50 per share on stock outstanding on June 30, 1995.

Additional data gathered that are pertinent to adjusting entries for the quarter are:

a. Accrued salaries for salesclerks, $1,200.
b. Depreciation on fixtures, $1,600.
c. Uncollected accounts are estimated to be 3 percent of credit sales.
d. $1,500 of the cash sales recorded on June 30 were gift certificates redeemable between July 1 and August 15, 1995.
e. Utility bills for services during June, $250.
f. Supplies on hand June 30, 1995, $840.
g. Income tax rate is 40 percent.

Note: Inventory on hand June 30, 1995, totaled $38,000.

REQUIRED

On the basis of the data for Designer Fads Company:

a. Prepare entries in general journal form to record the transactions for the quarter ended June 30, 1995.
b. Set up T-accounts, and post the entries to the T-accounts. Indicate that an account has been posted by placing a check mark in the reference, or folio, column of the journal.
*c. Prepare a trial balance, and enter it on a 10-column worksheet with columns for a trial balance, adjustments, an adjusted trial balance, an income statement, and a balance sheet.
*d. Complete the worksheet.
e. Prepare a quarterly income statement, a statement of retained earnings, and a balance sheet.
f. Journalize and post the adjusting entries. In the ledger accounts (T-accounts), indicate the adjusting entries with an *A*.
g. Journalize and post the closing entries. In the ledger accounts (T-accounts), indicate the closing entries with a *C*.
h. Prepare a postclosing trial balance.

COMMON ERRORS

The first statement in each of the "common errors" listed here is *incorrect*. Each incorrect statement is followed by a corrected statement and an explanation.

1. The accounting equation remains in balance only if the recorded transaction affects balance sheet accounts. *Wrong*

The accounting equation remains in balance if the recorded transaction affects only balance sheet accounts or balance sheet and income statement accounts. *Right*

Although the accounting equation (Assets = Liabilities + Equity) appears to imply only balance sheet accounts, equity is composed, in part, of the entity's undistributed accumulated earnings (Revenues – Expenses + Gains – Losses). The results of operations appear in the balance sheet as part of equity: capital for a sole proprietorship or partnership and retained earnings for a corporation. Although earnings transactions are recorded in income statement (nominal) accounts, their net effect is transferred to equity through the closing process. Therefore, transactions that affect income statement accounts as well as transactions that affect balance sheet accounts can be analyzed by their effect on the accounting equation. Moreover, both types of transaction maintain the equality of the fundamental accounting equation.

2. When special journals are used, a general journal is not necessary. *Wrong*

When special journals are used, a general journal is still maintained. *Right*

Special journals, such as cash receipts, cash disbursements, sales, and purchases journals, have a rather narrow use. Each is used to record transactions of a specific type. All receipts of cash, for example, are recorded in the cash receipts journal. Some transactions, however, do not fit neatly in one of the special journals and must be entered in the general journal. Special journals provide efficiencies in the recording process, but they cannot handle all transactions. Therefore, a general journal must be maintained in conjunction with any special journals that are used.

3. The purpose of preparing adjusting entries for prepaid and unearned items is to achieve proper recognition of revenues or expenses. *Wrong*

The purposes of preparing adjusting entries for prepaid items are to achieve proper recognition of revenues or expenses and proper valuation of liabilities or assets. *Right*

Prepayments and unearned items are transactions in which the cash flow precedes the earnings (revenue or expense) activity. As the transaction had to be recorded initially as a revenue or an expense or as an asset or a liability (that is, unearned revenue), it must be adjusted at the end of the accounting period. The adjusting entry allocates the prepayment between earned revenue (expired cost or expense) on the income statement and unearned revenue or liability (unexpired cost or asset) on the balance sheet. Thus the adjusting entry results in proper recognition of revenue or expense *and* proper valuation of the liability or asset.

4. To prepare closing entries is to reduce to zero all nominal and real accounts. *Wrong*

To prepare closing entries is to reduce to zero only nominal accounts. *Right*

An important distinction between real and nominal accounts is that real accounts remain open and are carried forward from period to period, whereas nominal accounts are closed at the end of each period. As nominal accounts (revenues and expenses) are accumulated for a period of time (usually a year) so that periodic earnings may be determined, the objective of closing entries is to reduce nominal or temporary accounts to zero so that they are ready to receive the recorded earnings activities of the next period. The net amount of the nominal accounts for the period—that is, net income or loss—is closed to an equity account, such as retained earnings in a corporation. In effect, after the closing entries are recorded and posted to the ledger, the net amount of the nominal accounts is carried forward to the next period in owners' equity, but the individual nominal accounts have a zero balance.

5. Reversing entries are an integral or required step in the accounting process. *Wrong*

Reversing entries are an optional step in the accounting process. *Right*

Preparation of reversing entries is the last step in the accounting cycle and is normally done at the beginning of the next accounting period. Such entries reverse certain adjusting entries (those that increase an asset or liability account) made at the end of the immediately preceding period. It is important to remember, however, that reversing entries are *optional*, not required. Even though reversing entries simplify the recording of some transactions in the next accounting period, the accounting cycle could begin without the preparation of reversing entries.

6. Dividends paid to stockholders represent an expense of doing business and are deducted as an expense in the income statement. *Wrong*

Dividends paid to stockholders represent a distribution to owners and as such are not treated as an expense on the income statement. *Right*

A very common mistake is to include dividends as an expense on the income statement. Because they are distributions to owners, dividends belong instead on the statement of retained earnings. The dividends declared account is a nominal account, but unlike other nominal accounts that are closed to the income summary account, the dividends declared account is closed directly to the retained earnings account. Dividends are, in effect, a distribution of earnings, not a determinant of net income.

7. When converting a cash-basis income statement to an accrual income statement, only income statements accounts affected by cash need to be considered. *Wrong*

When converting a cash-basis income statement to an accrual income statement, income statement accounts affected by cash and not affected by cash need to be considered. *Right*

Obviously, those accounts affected directly by cash may need to be adjusted when converting from a cash-basis income statement to an accrual-basis income statement. For example, on a cash-basis income statement, the nominal account interest revenue will only be credited for amounts of cash actually received from interest during the period. Consequently, the interest revenue account needs to be adjusted for the net increase or decrease in the interest receivable account during the period to arrive at interest revenue on an accrual basis.

Other accounts, such as depreciation expense, would not normally be found on a cash-basis income statement because no cash is expended. Depreciation expense, however, must be included in an accrual-basis income statement. Thus, "noncash" accounts also need to be considered when converting from a cash-basis to an accrual-basis income statement.

ANSWERS
Items marked with an asterisk (*) refer to the Appendix.

Key Terms and Concepts

1. economic event
2. account
3. real, permanent, nominal, temporary
4. accounting process (or cycle)
5. journal, ledger
6. accruals
7. closing
8. reversing
9. capital, drawing
*10. worksheet

True-False

1. F Economic events that are captured and reported by an entity must be not only identified with the entity but also quantified in dollars. An event such as an increase in the market price of a company's stock is identified with the company, but there is no way to quantify in dollars its direct effect on the company. Thus the market increase is not captured and reported.

2. F Dividends are a distribution to stockholders as a return on their investment. Dividends are declared only if retained earnings has a positive, or credit, balance which indicates net undistributed earnings. Therefore, dividends represent a return *on* the stockholders' investment, not a return *of* their investment.

3. F Of the real accounts, only assets are increased by a debit; liabilities and owners' equity are decreased by a debit.

4. T

5. F Evidence that an economic event that affects an entity has occurred is supplied by source documents generated both internally (for example, a sales receipt) and externally (for example, debt contract with a lender).

6. T

7. T

8. T

9. F An unadjusted trial balance that is in balance verifies only the accuracy of debits and credits posted to the ledger accounts. A credit to the sales account in the journal, for example, could be posted as a credit to the interest revenue account in the ledger. This posting error would not be detected in the unadjusted trial balance, as the posting was a credit. It should be noted that the total debits and credits would be equal, but the composition of the accounts would not be correct (that is, the sales and interest revenue accounts would be incorrectly stated).

10. T

11. F When the cash flow precedes the earnings activity, a *prepayment* and *unearned items* occurs.

12. T

13. F Accrual adjusting entries are prepared for earnings activities that have occurred but have not previously been recorded. Accordingly, there is no initial entry to refer to.

14. T

15. T

16. T

17. T

18. F The purpose of closing the expense account is to reduce its balance to zero. As an expense normally has a debit balance, the closing entry would be a debit to income summary and a credit to the expense account for an amount equal to the balance (debit) in the expense account.

19. F The income summary account is a nominal account used in the closing process. After all income statement (nominal) accounts are closed to income summary, the balance in income summary is closed to owners' equity.

*20. T

Multiple Choice

1.	c	6.	c
2.	c	7.	a
3.	d	8.	d
4.	a	*9.	a
5.	a	*10.	d

Extended Problem

a, f, g. Journal entries:
1995

Apr. 11	Salary expense		√	400	
	Cash		√		400
	To record payment of salaries.				
30	Cash		√	12,000	
	Accounts receivable		√	6,000	
	Sales		√		18,000
	To record sales for April.				

May 10	Accounts payable	√	20,000	
	Cash	√		20,000
	To record payment to creditor.			
13	Salary expense	√	1,700	
	Cash	√		1,700
	To record payment of salaries.			
20	Purchases	√	26,000	
	Accounts payable	√		26,000
	To record purchase of merchandise on account.			
21	Cash	√	4,800	
	Accounts receivable	√		4,800
	To record collections from customers.			
25	Accounts payable	√	900	
	Purchase returns	√		900
	To record return of defective merchandise.			
31	Cash	√	15,000	
	Accounts receivable	√	12,000	
	Sales	√		27,000
	To record sales for May.			
June 2	Utilities expense	√	600	
	Cash	√		600
	To record payment of utility bills.			
3	Accounts payable ($26,000 – $900)	√	25,100	
	Cash	√		25,100
	To record payment of account due Shirts to Skirts, Inc.			
10	Purchases	√	29,340	
	Accounts payable	√		29,340
	To record purchase of merchandise on account.			
10	Transportation in	√	100	
	Cash	√		100
	To record payment for transportation charges on goods purchased.			
10	Salary expense	√	1,900	
	Cash	√		1,900
	To record payment of salaries.			
15	Accounts payable	√	7,840	
	Cash	√		7,840
	To record partial payment.			
18	Cash (1,500 shares × $16)	√	24,000	
	Common stock (1,500 shares × $10)	√		15,000
	Contributed capital in excess of par	√		9,000
	To record issuance of capital stock.			
20	Cash	√	11,300	
	Accounts receivable	√		11,300
	To record collections from customers.			
Note:	No entry should be made for receipt of letter from creditor. This event does not affect a financial statement element.			
28	Accounts payable ($29,340 – $7,840)	√	21,500	
	Cash	√		21,500
	To record payment to settle account with Stitches Co.			
30	Cash	√	20,000	
	Accounts receivable	√	11,000	
	Sales	√		31,000
	To record sales for June.			
30	Dividends declared (7,500 shares × $.50)	√	3,750	
	Dividend payable	√		3,750

To record declaration of dividend.

Adjusting entries:

June 30	Salary expense	√	1,200	
	Salary payable	√		1,200
	To record accrued salaries.			
30	Depreciation expense	√	1,600	
	Accumulated depreciation	√		1,600
	To record depreciation expense.			
30	Uncollectible accounts expense	√	870	
	Allowance for uncollectible accounts ($29,000 × 3%)	√		870
	To record provision for uncollectible accounts.			
30	Sales	√	1,500	
	Unearned revenue	√		1,500
	To record gift certificate revenue as unearned revenue.			
30	Utilities expense	√	250	
	Utilities payable	√		250
	To record accrual of utilities expense.			
30	Supplies expense ($1,200 – $840)	√	360	
	Supplies	√		360
	To record consumption of supplies.			
30	Interest expense ($20,000 × 12% × 3/12)	√	600	
	Interest payable	√		600
	To record accrual of interest on note payable.			
30	Prepaid insurance ($1,800 × 9/12)	√	1,350	
	Insurance expense	√		1,350
	To record unexpired portion of insurance as an asset.			
30	Rent expense ($12,000 × 3/12)	√	3,000	
	Prepaid rent	√		3,000
	To record rent expense.			
30	Cost of goods sold	√	35,000	
	Inventory	√		35,000
	To transfer beginning inventory balance to cost of goods sold.			
30	Cost of goods sold	√	54,540	
	Purchase returns	√	900	
	Purchases	√		55,340
	Transportation in	√		100
	To transfer net cost of purchases to cost of goods sold.			
30	Inventory	√	38,000	
	Cost of goods sold	√		38,000
	To record ending inventory.			
30	Income tax expense	√	4,012	
	Income tax payable	√		4,012
	To record income tax on earnings.			

Closing entries:

June 30	Sales	√	74,500	
	Income summary	√		74,500
	To close all nominal accounts with credit balances.			
30	Income summary	√	68,482	
	Cost of goods sold	√		51,540
	Salary expense	√		5,200
	Depreciation expense	√		1,600
	Utilities expense	√		850
	Insurance expense	√		450
	Uncollectible accounts expense	√		870
	Interest expense	√		600
	Rent expense	√		3,000

Supplies expense	√		360
Income tax expense	√		4,012

To close all nominal accounts with debit balances.

30	Income summary	√	6,018	
	Retained earnings	√		6,018

To close net income to retained earnings.

30	Retained earnings	√	3,750	
	Dividends declared	√		3,750

To close dividends to retained earnings.

b, f, g. T-accounts and posting:

Cash

4/1	17,000	400	4/11
4/30	12,000	20,000	5/10
5/21	4,800	1,700	5/13
5/31	15,000	600	6/2
6/18	24,000	25,100	6/3
6/20	11,300	100	6/10
6/30	20,000	1,900	6/10
		7,840	6/15
		21,500	6/28
Bal.	24,960		

Accounts receivable

4/30	6,000	4,800	4/21
5/31	12,000	11,300	6/20
6/30	11,000		
Bal.	12,900		

Inventory

4/1	35,000	35,000	A
A	38,000		
Bal.	38,000		

Supplies

4/1	1,200	360	A
Bal.	840		

Prepaid rent

4/1	12,000	3,000	A
Bal.	9,000		

Prepaid insurance

A	1,350		

Fixtures

4/1	66,000		

Accumulated depreciation

		1,600	A

Allowance for uncollectible accounts

		870	A

Accounts payable

5/10	20,000	25,000	4/1
5/25	900	26,000	5/20
6/3	25,100	29,340	6/10
6/15	7,840		
6/28	21,500		
		5,000	Bal.

Salary payable

		1,200	A

Utilities payable

		250	A

Dividend payable

		3,750	6/30

Income tax payable

		4,012	A

Interest payable

		600	A

Unearned revenue

		1,500	A

Note payable

		20,000	4/1

Common stock

		60,000	4/1
		15,000	6/18
		75,000	Bal.

Contributed capital in excess of par

		28,000	4/1
		9,000	6/18
		37,000	Bal.

Retained earnings

C	3,750	6,018	C
		2,268	Bal.

Dividends declared

6/30	3,750	3,750	C

Income summary

C	68,482	74,500	C
C	6,018		
	74,500	74,500	

Sales

		18,000	4/30
		27,000	5/31
		31,000	6/30
A	1,500	76,000	
C	74,500		
	76,000	76,000	

Purchases

5/20	26,000		
6/10	29,340	55,340	A
	55,340	55,340	

Transportation in

6/10	100	100	A

Cost of goods sold

A	35,000	38,000	A
A	54,540	51,540	C
	89,540	89,540	

Purchase returns

A	900	900	5/25

Salary expense

4/11	400		
5/13	1,700		
6/10	1,900		
A	1,200	5,200	C
	5,200	5,200	

Utilities expense

6/2	600		
A	250	850	C
	850	850	

Depreciation expense

A	1,600	1,600	C

Income tax expense

A	4,012	4,012	C

Insurance expense

4/1	1,800	1,350	A
		450	C
	1,800	1,800	

Interest expense

A	600	600	C

Uncollectible accounts expense

A	870	870	C

Rent expense

A	3,000	3,000	C

Supplies expense

A	360	360	C

*c, *d. Worksheet:

DESIGNER FADS COMPANY
WORKSHEET
FOR QUARTER ENDING JUNE 30, 1995

	TRIAL BALANCE DR	TRIAL BALANCE CR	ADJUSTMENTS DR	ADJUSTMENTS CR	ADJUSTED TRIAL BALANCE DR	ADJUSTED TRIAL BALANCE CR	INCOME STATEMENT DR	INCOME STATEMENT CR	BALANCE SHEET DR	BALANCE SHEET CR
Cash	24,960				24,960				24,960	
Accounts receivable	12,900				12,900				12,900	
Inventory	35,000		(l) 38,000	(j) 35,000	38,000				38,000	
Supplies...................	1,200			(f) 360	840				840	
Prepaid rent..............	12,000			(i) 3,000	9,000				9,000	
Fixtures	66,000				66,000				66,000	
Accounts payable		5,000				5,000				5,000
Dividend payable........		3,750				3,750				3,750
Note payable		20,000				20,000				20,000
Common stock		75,000				75,000				75,000
Contributed capital in excess of par		37,000				37,000				37,000
Retained earnings										
Dividends declared.......	3,750				3,750				3,750	
Sales		76,000	(d) 1,500			74,500		74,500		
Purchases	55,340			(k)55,340						
Transportation in	100			(k) 100						
Purchase returns..........		900	(k) 900							
Salary expense...........	4,000		(a) 1,200		5,200		5,200			
Utilities expense	600		(e) 250		850		850			
Insurance expense.......	1,800			(h) 1,350	450		450			
	217,650	217,650								
Cost of goods sold......			(j) 35,000 (k) 51,540	(l)38,000	51,540		51,540			
Salary payable				(a) 1,200		1,200				1,200
Depreciation expense...			(b) 1,600		1,600		1,600			
Accumulated depreciation				(b) 1,600		1,600				1,600
Uncollectible accounts expense			(c) 870		870		870			
Allowance for uncollectible accounts.........				(c) 870		870				870
Unearned revenue........				(d) 1,500		1,500				1,500
Utilities payable........				(e) 250		250				250
Interest expense..........			(g) 600		600		600			
Interest payable..........				(g) 600		600				600
Prepaid insurance........			(h) 1,350		1,350				1,350	
Rent expense.............			(i) 3,000		3,000		3,000			
Supplies expense........			(f) 360		360		360			
			139,170	139,170	221,270	221,270	64,470	74,500		
Income tax expense			4,012				4,012			
Income tax payable				4,012						4,012
Net income							6,018			6,018
							74,500	74,500	156,800	156,800

e. Income statement:

DESIGNER FADS COMPANY
INCOME STATEMENT
FOR QUARTER ENDING JUNE 30, 1995

Sales		$74,500
Cost of goods sold		51,540
Gross margin		$22,960
Other expenses		
Salary	$5,200	
Depreciation	1,600	
Utilities	850	
Insurance	450	
Uncollectible accounts	870	
Interest	600	
Rent	3,000	
Supplies	360	
Total other expenses		12,930
Income before income tax		$10,030
Tax expense		4,012
Net income		$ 6,018

e. Statement of retained earnings:

DESIGNER FADS COMPANY
STATEMENT OF RETAINED EARNINGS
FOR QUARTER ENDING JUNE 30, 1995

Retained earnings, April 1, 1995	$ -0-
Net income for quarter	6,018
	6,018
Dividends	3,750
Retained earnings, June 30, 1995	$2,268

e. Balance sheet:

DESIGNER FADS COMPANY
BALANCE SHEET
JUNE 30, 1995

ASSETS

Current assets		
Cash		$24,960
Accounts receivable	$12,900	
Less: Allowance for uncollectible accounts	(870)	12,030
Inventory		38,000
Supplies		840
Prepaid rent		9,000
Prepaid insurance		1,350
Total current assets		$86,180
Plant and equipment fixtures	$66,000	
Less: Accumulated depreciation	(1,600)	64,400
Total assets		$150,580

LIABILITIES AND STOCKHOLDERS' EQUITY

Current liabilities		
Accounts payable	$ 5,000	
Salary payable	1,200	
Utilities payable	250	
Dividend payable	3,750	
Interest payable	600	
Income tax payable	4,012	
Unearned revenue	1,500	
Total current liabilities	$16,312	
Long-term liabilities		
Note payable (due 2000)	20,000	
Total liabilities		$ 36,312
Stockholders' equity		
Common stock ($10 par, 30,000 shares authorized, 7,500 shares issued)	$75,000	
Contributed capital in excess of par	37,000	
Retained earnings	2,268	
Total stockholders' equity		114,268
Total liabilities and stockholders' equity		$150,580

h. Postclosing trial balance:

DESIGNER FADS COMPANY
POSTCLOSING TRIAL BALANCE
JUNE 30, 1995

ACCOUNTS	DEBIT	CREDIT
Cash	$ 24,960	
Accounts receivable.......................	12,900	
Allowance for uncollectible accounts		$ 870
Inventory	38,000	
Supplies.....................................	840	
Prepaid rent	9,000	
Prepaid insurance.........................	1,350	
Fixtures.....................................	66,000	
Accumulated depreciation		1,600
Accounts payable.........................		5,000
Salary payable............................		1,200
Utilities payable...........................		250
Dividend payable..........................		3,750
Interest payable		600
Income tax payable.......................		4,012
Unearned revenue.........................		1,500
Note payable...............................		20,000
Common stock.............................		75,000
Contributed capital in excess of par..		37,000
Retained earnings........................		2,268
	$153,050	$153,050

4 THE INCOME STATEMENT AND STATEMENT OF RETAINED EARNINGS

CHAPTER OBJECTIVES

After reading Chapter 4 and completing the questions, cases, exercises, and problems from the text chapter, you should be able to:

1. Differentiate between the net assets approach and the transactions approach to the determination of net income.
2. Understand the meaning and purpose of disaggregation of income tax.
3. Identify a discontinued segment or operation of a business entity, and prepare the related income statement disclosures.

4. Identify an extraordinary item, and prepare the related income statement disclosures.
5. Distinguish a change in accounting principle and a change in accounting estimate.
6. Understand the importance of the earnings per share (EPS) figure, and know what EPS disclosures are required.
7. Appreciate the issues confronting the FASB in its attempt to develop a format for the reporting of earnings activities.
8. Prepare a combined statement of income and retained earnings.

CHAPTER REVIEW

Introduction

1. Users often base many of their investment, credit, and other decisions on information contained in the financial statements published by an enterprise, particularly the income statement. An *income statement* reports the net income or net loss from operating activities. Its preparation can easily become very complex because of the various activities a company engages in and the number of requirements in regard to reporting and disclosure. The two basic issues

of the income statement are the determination of net income—the *measurement issue*—and the reporting of income information—the *format issue*.

2. This chapter review includes an examination of the theory underlying the measurement of accounting income and focuses on the format issue: the presentation of the components of income determination. Related income disclosures of earnings per share (EPS) are briefly reviewed. A discussion of the statement of retained earnings concludes the chapter.

The Theory of Income Measurement

3. As Chapter 2 explained, in order for income to be measured or determined, an asset and liability measurement attribute and a capital maintenance concept must be selected. To review, for income determination GAAP specifies historical cost as the primary attribute to be measured and nominal dollars as the basic capital maintenance concept. GAAP further refines income measurement with the accrual accounting principles. The realization principle and the matching principle state that revenues and expenses are recognized when resources and obligations change as a result of the entity's earnings activities. Two equivalent definitions of income based on these theoretical constructs lead to two approaches to the measurement of net income. The remainder of this section focuses on the two definitions of and approaches to calculating net income.

4. First, net income or net loss is the change in equity or net assets resulting from transactions and other economic events related to an entity's operating activities, both primary and peripheral. In other words, net income is equal to the change in net assets (assets less liabilities) exclusive of equity or capital transactions, such as investments by owners and distributions to owners, between two points in time. This approach is referred to as the *net assets approach.* An increase or a decrease in net assets represents a net income or loss for the period. If capital transactions took place during the period, however, the change in net assets must be adjusted to eliminate the effect of these transactions on the change in net assets. Because an investment by owners increases net assets and a distribution to owners decreases them, but neither is related to the entity's earnings activities, the investment must be deducted from the change in net assets and the distribution added to determine net income or loss for the period. This approach is faulted because it provides little information for decision making. All earnings activities are lumped together in one number, with no information disclosed as to why or how the net income or loss was derived.

5. Second, Net income = Revenues – Expenses + Gains – Losses. This is the traditional method of determining income and is referred to as the *transaction approach.* Because the component transactions and events of the period related to the primary earnings activities (revenues and expenses) and peripheral activities (gains and losses) are disclosed, this approach provides better information for decision making.

The Format Issue

6. Specific requirements for the reporting of earnings information are found in *APB Opinion*

No. 30 and other authoritative pronouncements. Requirements for the disclosure of the following items will be discussed in the remainder of this section: disaggregation of income tax, income from continuing operations, discontinued operations, extraordinary items, changes in accounting principle, and earnings per share.

7. **Disaggregation of income tax.** The income tax effect of an item is important in the assessment of the item's net effect on income. If a company had a nonrecurring gain, for example, the gain would be taxed, and thus the amount of gain recognized would be reduced. The procedure of having the income tax reported with the item to which the tax is related is called *disaggregation of income tax.* The nonrecurring gain would be reported on the income statement at an amount equal to the gain less the applicable income tax, or simply *net of tax.* Disaggregation of income tax applies only to four components on the income statement and one item on the statement of retained earnings. These special items are discussed later in the chapter review.

8. Disaggregation of income tax procedures are used to prevent the special item and its income tax effect from distorting the earnings from regular or continuing operations. It should be remembered that all regular revenues and expenses are reported at their gross amounts and one income tax amount is applied to their net amount.

9. **Income from continuing operations.** Two basic approaches to the reporting of the various income statement elements that constitute income from continuing operations have developed in practice: the single-step approach and the multiple-step approach. The *single-step approach,* which is the simpler of the two, matches total revenues and gains with total expenses and losses. The *multiple-step approach* matches the elements in such a way that several subtotals are derived before net income or net loss is determined. Cost of goods sold, for example, is deducted from sales to yield *gross profit on sales,* and general selling and administrative expenses are then deducted to yield *operating profit.* The particular types of other revenues, expenses, gains, and losses a company may have influence the types and number of other subtotals presented in the income statement. Both approaches are acceptable, but once an approach is selected, it must be used consistently, so that the information contained in the income statement will be useful to users. The next three items to be discussed must be reported separately, regardless of the approach used to determine income from continuing operations.

10. **Discontinued operations.** *APB Opinion No. 30* requires that when a company decides to discontinue an existing segment of its business, the operating results and the gain or loss on the disposal of the discontinued segment must be separ-

ated from the earnings of the continuing operations. A *discontinued segment of operation* is an entity's separate major line of business or class of customer that has been sold, abandoned, spun off, or otherwise disposed of or, if still operating, is the subject of a formal plan for disposal. The discontinued operation's assets, operating results, and activities must be clearly distinguishable both physically and operationally from those of the company's other operations.

11. Two dates are critical to the accounting for and reporting of discontinued operations. The *measurement date* is the date on which management commits itself to the disposal of the segment. The *disposal date* is the date of the actual disposal of the discontinued segment by sale, abandonment, or spinoff. Earnings of the discontinued segment before the measurement date must be disclosed separately (net of applicable income tax) in the income statement under the major heading "Discontinued operations." In addition, earnings during the phase-out period—between the date of measurement and the date of disposal—and the gain or loss on the disposal of the segment are combined and disclosed net of applicable income tax in a second line under "Discontinued operations." The phase-out earnings and the gain or loss on the disposal are estimated on the measurement date. If the measurement date and disposal date occur in the same accounting period, any profit or loss from the phase-out operations and gain or loss on disposal would be realized during the period. On the other hand, if the measurement and disposal dates are in different accounting periods, a portion of the phase-out operation's profit or loss (from the measurement date to the end of the accounting period) would be realized. The remainder of the estimated profit or loss (from the end of the accounting period to the disposal date), as well as the estimated disposal gain or loss, assuming that it occurs when the segment is disposed of, would be unrealized. An unrealized net loss (combined estimate of phase-out operations and disposal) would be recorded. An unrealized net gain would be recognized only to the extent of any realized losses from the date of measurement to the end of the accounting period. The remainder of the gain would be recognized as it is realized in the following period. Further disclosures, such as the identity of the discontinued segment, expected disposal date, and description of the discontinued segment's remaining assets and liabilities, are made in the related footnotes.

12. Extraordinary items. An event or a transaction that qualifies as an extraordinary item receives special disclosure in the income statement. Specifically, it is disclosed net of applicable income tax after income from continuing operations or, if appropriate, income from discontinued operations.

Extraordinary items are not part of the on-going operations, and this method of disclosure highlights their uniqueness to users of the financial statements.

13. *APB Opinion No. 30* established two criteria that must be met before an item can be classified as extraordinary:

a. *Unusual nature.* The underlying event or transactions should possess a high degree of abnormality and be of a type clearly unrelated to, or only incidentally related to, the ordinary and typical activities of the entity.

b. *Infrequency of occurrence.* The underlying event or transaction should also be of a type that would not reasonably be expected to recur in the foreseeable future.

It is important to note that both criteria take into consideration the *environment* in which the entity operates. The environmental factors include the enterprise's industry, its geographic location, and the extent of governmental regulation of its operations. Thus what may be extraordinary for one entity may not be extraordinary for another because of environmental differences. Given the differences in geographic environments, for example, damage from a tidal wave would be considered extraordinary in a desert community but not in a seacoast town.

14. *Opinion No. 30* specifically lists events that do not qualify as extraordinary items because they may be expected to recur regularly: events such as write-down of accounts receivable, gains or losses on disposal of a segment of a business, and adjustment of long-term contract accruals. These same items, however, may be extraordinary if they are the direct result of a major casualty loss, such as a loss attributable to an earthquake, expropriation, or prohibition under a new law or regulation. Again, the key determinant appears to be the environment in which the entity operates.

15. Although the number of items expected to meet both criteria for an extraordinary item is small, any material gain or loss in the extinguishment of debt is always reported as extraordinary. This reporting has evolved in practice because the FASB desires that this gain or loss receive special disclosure, not because it meets the established criteria.

16. When an event or a transaction meets *one but not both* of the established criteria for extraordinary items, the item is reported at its gross amount as a separately listed component of income from continuing operations. This manner of disclosure enables a reader of the financial statements to make a better assessment of the item's nature and its impact on earnings.

17. A recent disclosure issue related to the proper reporting of "restructuring charges," charges incurred in consolidation and/or abandonment of operations, was settled by the SEC. To provide guidance in reporting, the SEC issued *Staff Accounting Bulletin No. 67,* which requires that restructuring charges be presented in the income statement as a component of income from continuing operations and be disclosed separately, if material. These charges do not meet the criteria for discontinued operations or extraordinary items.

18. The extraordinary item classification used in U.S. GAAP is much more restrictive than in most other countries. For example, British accounting standards permit a transaction that would be classified as part of continuing operations under U.S. GAAP to be disclosed as extraordinary if it is not expected to recur regularly. On the other hand, British standards require a disposal of a segment to be disclosed as an extraordinary item. Users of international financial statements must be aware of disclosure differences such as these.

19. Changes in Accounting Principle. Companies try to use an accounting principle consistently from period to period. There are situations however, when a company makes a *change in accounting principle* from the one used in prior periods. *Opinion No. 20* requires that the cumulative effect of the accounting change, that is, the difference between the carrying value of an affected asset or liability under the previously used accounting principle, be reported in the income statement net of applicable taxes in the period of the change in principle. This is referred to as the *current period approach.* This approach also requires that (*a*) the new accounting principle be used in the period of change and (*b*) pro forma disclosures be made, that is, disclosure of comparative net incomes and earnings per share figures for all prior periods presented as if the new accounting principle had been used in those prior periods.

20. To illustrate the current period approach, assume that a company changes its depreciation method for a particular asset. If the amount of depreciation using the new depreciation method for all periods since the asset was acquired is less than the amount under the previously used depreciation method, the entry to record the change in depreciation methods would be a debit to accumulated depreciation and a credit to cumulative effect of change in accounting principle for the amount of the cumulative effect.

21. Accountants are required to make many estimates, such as the estimated life or salvage value of an asset. As circumstances change or additional information is acquired, it may be necessary, for example, to change the estimate of an asset's useful life. A *change in accounting estimate* occurs when new information is obtained. Changes in accounting estimate must be accounted for *prospectively* in the current and, perhaps, future periods with no changes made to prior periods' financial statements.

To illustrate this treatment, assume that the straight-line depreciation method is used for a depreciable asset and its estimated useful life has increased from its original estimate. In the period the change in estimate is made, the book value of the asset is divided by the remaining estimated new life of the asset to determine depreciation expense for this and future periods. Accounting changes and changes in accounting estimates are covered in Chapter 19.

22. Earnings per share. *Earnings per share,* or EPS, is a popular measure of a company's performance. Although the calculation of EPS is conceptually easy (earnings divided by the number of common shares outstanding), in practice, it is often very involved. Because of the complexity of some companies' capital structure and the importance attached to the EPS figure, the APB issued *Opinion No. 15* to establish reporting and computational guidelines for EPS. If a firm has a capital structure that includes securities, such as convertible debt or stock options, which permit the holder to acquire shares of common stock, the company is required to provide a dual disclosure of EPS. The company must present both *primary EPS* and *fully diluted EPS* data. Chapter 20 discusses the detailed EPS computational guidelines. The table that follows depicts the bottom portion of an income statement and indicates the required and optional EPS disclosures.

Reporting the Results of Operations
TYPICAL INCOME STATEMENT FORMAT

Results of continuing operations (including unusual or infrequently occurring items)		$xx
Provision for income tax (on continuing operations)		xx
Income from continuing operations		xx*
Discontinued operations:		
Income (loss) from operations of discontinued segment (net of tax)	+/−$x	
Loss on disposal of segment including income (loss) from operations during phase-out period (net of tax)	x	x†
Income before extraordinary items and cumulative effect of accounting changes:		$xx*
Extraordinary items (listed separately)		
Extraordinary gain or loss (net of tax)		+/−x†
Cumulative effect of change in accounting principle:		
Change in accounting principle (net of tax)		+/−x*
Net income (loss)		$xx*

*Required EPS figure on these amounts.
†Optional EPS data because it could be calculated by means of the other EPS figures disclosed.
Note: Adequate disclosure would have to be made for each of the special items above as required by the applicable official pronouncement.

Additional Income Reporting Issues

23. Previous paragraphs have presented a rather definitive format for the reporting of earnings activities. Unfortunately, the present format is criticized as inadequate and too inconsistent in the reporting of some events to meet the information needs of users. As part of its conceptual framework project, the FASB is currently addressing this issue in order (*a*) to improve the information displayed so that users may realistically assess cash flows and (*b*) to increase the credibility of the income statement prepared by the reporting entity.

24. A part of the FASB's earnings reporting project focuses on the components of income, their behavior, and their effects on users' decisions. Data on some components of income, such as sales and operating expenses, are regular and stable over time and are useful in attempts to predict cash flows. In addition to the traditional historical data, however, the FASB is considering the inclusion of other historical data, such as information on volume and selling price, to improve users' predictions. Conversely, such income components as extraordinary items are irregular and highly volatile, yet they, too, must be meaningfully disclosed. The outcome of the FASB's earnings reporting project is unknown, but it is hoped that it will improve the display of income information. As previously discussed, the FASB has suggested statements of earnings and comprehensive income in *Statement of Concepts No. 5*. These statements, however, do not drastically change present reporting requirements and are probably part of the evolution of earnings disclosure. It may be assumed that the income statement, related notes, and supplementary information will all continue to be used to report the components of income.

Statement of Retained Earnings

25. A *statement of retained earnings*, a reconciliation of the retained earnings account, normally is presented with a company's income statement, balance sheet, and statement of cash flows. The basic format of the statement of retained earnings is simple: Retained earnings (beginning of period) +/- Net income/loss for the period – Dividends = Retained earnings (end of period).

26. The only other item that can appear on the statement of retained earnings is a *prior period adjustment*. *Statement No. 16* lists two prior period adjustments: (*a*) the correction of an error related to prior periods and (*b*) the realization of the income tax benefit of preacquisition operating loss carryforwards of purchased subsidiaries. Prior period adjustments are reported as an addition to or subtraction from the beginning balance of retained earnings in the year they are recognized.

27. A *combined statement of income and retained earnings* consists of all items that affect income (or loss), prior period adjustments, and dividends for the accounting period. This statement has the advantage of combining in one statement the information in the income statement and in the statement of retained earnings. Net income can easily become buried, however, because it is not the "bottom line" of the combined statement. A company earning a profit would typically first make the usual income statement display. Dividends would then be deducted from net income to determine the net addition to retained earnings, which is (normally) added to the beginning retained earnings balance to determine the ending balance in retained earnings and the bottom line of the statement.

SELF-STUDY LEARNING

Key Terms and Concepts

Provide the appropriate term or terms to complete each of the following statements:

1. Two theoretical approaches to income determination are the ___NET ASSETS___ approach and the ___TRANSACTIONS___ approach.

2. When the income tax effect of an item is reported with the item, the procedure is called ___DISALC OF INC TAX___

3. The ___SINGLE___ -step income statement lists all revenues and gains and matches them with all expenses and losses.

4. The date of _____MEASUREMENT_____ is the date that a company's management commits itself to the disposal of an operating segment of the company's business.

5. Earnings of a discontinued operating segment after the measurement date and up to the date of disposal are referred to as earnings during the _____PHASE-OUT_____ period.

6. To be reported as an extraordinary item, an event or transaction must be both _____UNUSUAL_____ and _____INFREQUENT_____.

7. _____EPS_____ is a popular measure of a company's earnings performance for a period.

8. A change in accounting estimate is accounted for using the _____PROSPECTIVE_____ method.

9. The _____STMT OF RET EARN_____ is a reconciliation of the retained earnings account.

10. _____PRIOR PERIOD ADJ_____ are reported directly as an adjustment to the beginning balance of retained earnings.

True-False

Indicate by circling the appropriate response whether each of the following statements is true (T) or false (F):

T (F) 1. When the net assets approach is used, investments by owners are added to the change in net assets to determine income.

(T) F 2. The transaction approach to income determination provides information about the components of income.

T (F) 3. When disaggregation of income tax expense procedures are used, the income tax effect of each element in the income statement is separately disclosed.

(T) F 4. In the determination of income from continuing operations, the single-step and multiple-step approaches normally result in the same net income amount.

T (F) 5. To qualify as a discontinued segment, or operation, of a business, the segment must be identified as a major line of business and sold to another party.

(T) F 6. When a segment of a business is disposed of, the measurement date is the date when management decides to dispose of the segment and its operations.

T (F) 7. For an event to be an extraordinary item, it must either be unusual in nature or occur infrequently.

T (F) 8. A gain or loss arising from the early extinguishment of long-term debt is not considered an extraordinary item because firms frequently retire long-term debt before its maturity.

T (F) 9. The definition of *extraordinary items* is consistent internationally.

(T) F 10. An example of a change in accounting principle is the change from the straight-line to the sum-of-the-years'-digits depreciation method.

(T) F 11. The cumulative effect of a change in accounting principle is disclosed as the last item on the income statement, net of applicable income tax.

T (F) 12. A change in the estimated useful life of an asset for depreciation purposes is considered a change in accounting principle.

13. A change in the method of applying an accounting principle, for example changing depreciation methods, is a change in accounting principle.

 14. A change in accounting estimate is accounted for prospectively.

 15. Companies with complex capital structures are often required to disclose figures on primary and fully diluted earnings per share.

 16. Earnings per share is a measure of a company's earnings performance that is found by dividing earnings by the number of shares of common stock outstanding.

 17. When a statement of retained earnings is prepared, only net income is normally added to (or net loss subtracted from) the beginning balance of retained earnings to derive the ending balance of retained earnings.

 18. Prior period adjustments are reported as additions to (or subtractions from) the beginning balance of retained earnings on the statement of retained earnings.

 19. All components of the income statement can be considered regular and stable over time.

 20. In a combined statement of income and retained earnings, the bottom line is net income (or net loss).

Multiple Choice

Select the best response for each of the following items, and circle the corresponding letter:

1. Which one of the following statements is *true* about net income determined according to the net assets approach?

   a. Dividends paid are included in net income.
   b. Detail of income activity is easily discernible.
   c. An increase in net assets always indicates a profit for the period.
   d. Primary and peripheral operating activities are grouped together.

2. If the measurement date and the end of the accounting period coincide, the estimated operating earnings during the phase-out period and the estimated gain on or loss from the disposal of a discontinued segment are reported:

   a. Separately in income from continuing operations.
   b. After income from continuing operations, separately.
   c. After income from continuing operations, if a net loss is indicated, and net of applicable income tax.
   d. After income from continuing operations, if a net gain is indicated, and net of applicable income tax.

3. Of the following transactions and events, the one that qualifies as an extraordinary item is:

   a. A material gain from early extinguishment of debt.
   b. A write-down of accounts receivable.
   c. A loss from disposal of the assets of a discontinued segment.
   d. Restructuring charges.

4. When a change in accounting principle occurs in the current period:

   a. The cumulative effect of the change is treated as an adjustment to retained earnings.
   b. Prior period financial statements are restated to reflect the new principle.
   c. The old principle is applied in the current period.
   d. The new principle is applied in the current period.

5. Relative to a fixed asset, which of the following is considered a change in accounting estimate?

   a. Selection of the initial depreciation method to be used.
   b. Change in the depreciation method used after several years of use.
   c. Change in the estimated salvage value after several years of use.
   d. Failure to take depreciation on the asset in one year.

6. The proper order to disclose these four selected items appearing on the income statement is:

	Results of Continuing Operations	Cumulative Effect of Accounting Change	Discontinued Segment	Extraordinary Item
a.	1	2	3	4
b.	1	4	2	3
c.	3	2	1	4
d.	4	3	2	1

7. Earnings per share (EPS) calculations are required for selected income statement items. Which of the following terms does *not* require EPS disclosure?

   a. Income from continuing operations.
   b. Provision for income tax.
   c. Income from extraordinary items.
   d. Net income.

8. An event that would be disclosed as a prior period adjustment is:

   a. Dividends paid to stockholders.
   b. A change from the depreciation method used in prior periods to a new method during the current period.
   c. Correction of a mathematical error in the calculation of estimated bad debts in a prior period.
   d. Selection of a new revenue recognition method.

9. In what order would a statement of retained earnings disclose the three items listed?

	Dividends	Net Income/ Loss	Prior Period Adjustment
a.	1	2	3
b.	1	3	2
c.	2	1	3
d.	3	2	1

10. When a combined statement of income and retained earnings is prepared, dividends distributed to owners should be:

   a. Combined with operating expenses.
   b. Reported before extraordinary items.
   c. Deducted from net income.
   d. Deducted from income from continuing operations.

Extended Problem

Since its inception on January 3, 1994, Nittany Corporation has operated in two different lines of business—sporting goods and home appliances. The bookkeeper has assembled selected information related to the operations of the two lines of business for December 31, 1994, and December 31, 1995. (See the following table.)

	SPORTING GOODS		HOME APPLIANCES	
	1995	1994	1995	1994
Sales	$130,000	$110,000	$35,000	$48,000
Cost of goods sold	69,000	52,000	24,000	30,000
Salary expense	32,500	28,000	18,250	14,000
Depreciation expense	1,600	4,000	900	900
Rent expense	2,800	-0-	1,000	1,000
Utilities expense	2,000	1,600	850	500
Safety warning cost	-0-	4,500	-0-	-0-

In addition, the bookkeeper provides the following information about Nittany Corporation's activities during the past two years:

a. At the start of 1995, Nittany Corporation decided to change the method used to depreciate its sporting goods division's fixtures for both financial reporting and tax purposes. It formerly used an accelerated method; the straight-line method would now be used. The $1,600 depreciation expense for 1995 represents the straight-line amount that also would have applied in 1994 if the straight-line method had been used in 1994.

b. Because of rising costs and an operating loss in the home appliance division, a decision was reached on December 29, 1995, to sell the home appliance inventory, fixtures, and other related assets. It is believed that an arrangement can be completed by April 1, 1996, to sell the assets related to the home appliance division. It is estimated that the sale would result in a pretax loss of $14,000. Until the sale is completed, Nittany Corporation plans to continue to operate the division at an estimated pretax loss of $1,500.

c. The federal government enacted legislation that required Nittany Corporation to provide a safety warning on some items in inventory on October 1, 1994. This law caused Nittany to incur a one-time tax-deductible cost of $4,500.

d. Nittany Corporation paid three years' rent in advance in 1994 and made the following entry to record the payment:

Prepaid rent.................	7,200	
Cash......................		7,200

It was discovered in February 1995 that no adjustment had been made to recognize the rent expense of $1,400 for the sporting goods division in 1994. The bookkeeper corrected the error by doubling the 1995 rent expense for the sporting goods division. *Note:* This procedure for handling the error is *incorrect.* The correct entries would have been as follows:

Retained earnings..........	1,400	
Prepaid rent.............		1,400
Tax liability*..............	560	
Tax effect of prior		
period adjustment...		560

*This account could be "tax refund" if an amended tax return were filed immediately.

Assuming that the proper correcting entry is made, future income statements should have a rent expense of $1,400 for 1994 and 1995.

e. Nittany Corporation earned $6,000 in 1994 from its portfolio of investments. Early in 1995 the portfolio was sold at a gain of $9,500. More securities will probably be acquired in 1996.

f. Dividends paid to stockholders totaled $4,000 in 1994 and $5,500 in 1995 (2,000 shares outstanding).

g. The applicable income tax rate on all items for 1994 and 1995 is 40 percent.

REQUIRED

a. Without considering the information applicable to 1995—that is, the change in depreciation method, the decision to discontinue the home appliance division, and the error in rent expense—prepare an income statement for the year ended December 31, 1994, using the single-step approach, including earnings per share disclosure.

b. Prepare comparative income statements for the years ending December 31, 1994, and December 31, 1995, using the multiple-step approach, including earnings per share disclosure.

c. Prepare a statement of retained earnings for the year ending December 31, 1995. (Assume that the balance in retained earnings as of January 1, 1995, is $12,500.)

COMMON ERRORS

The first statement in each of the "common errors" listed here is *incorrect.* Each incorrect statement is followed by a corrected statement and an explanation.

1. Income determined under the net assets approach will differ from that determined under the transaction approach. *Wrong*

Income determined under the net assets approach will be the same as that determined under the transaction approach. *Right*

The two methods of determining income are indeed different, but they will result in the same earnings figure. Both approaches attempt to measure the effects of operating activities. The net assets approach measures income by comparing the net assets of a firm at the beginning and end of an accounting period. If the change in net assets (with the effects of capital transactions eliminated) is positive, net income is indicated; a negative change

indicates a loss. The transactions approach matches revenues and gains with expenses and losses to determine net income or net loss. This approach focuses on the individual transactions of the earnings process. Thus the approaches differ, but both the net assets and transaction approaches measure the results of earnings activities to determine an identical net income or net loss amount.

2. The significant date in accounting for a discontinued operating segment is the date of disposal. *Wrong*

The significant dates in accounting for a discontinued operating segment are the date of measurement and the date of disposal. *Right*

Since the date of disposal is the date that the segment is actually disposed, whether by sale, spin-off, or abandonment, it may be the most important date to the company disposing the segment. From an accounting perspective, however, the date of measurement is, perhaps, more important. The date of measurement is not only the date management commits itself to dispose the segment, but it also provides a cutoff date for accounting disclosures.

The results of operations for the period or periods up to the date of measurement, that is, (a) the portion of the current reporting period up to the measurement date and (b) all other prior periods presented for comparative purposes, are disclosed net of tax on a separate line under the heading "Discontinued operations." Future operating results of the segment, if any, are considered as part of the phase-out operations and are included with the gain or loss on the disposal of the segment. The two combined amounts are reported, net of tax, on a second separate line under the heading "Discontinued operations." Thus, from an accounting perspective, both the dates of measurement *and* disposal are important for preparing proper accounting disclosures for a discontinued operating segment.

3. If an event or a transaction qualifies as an extraordinary item for one company, it will qualify as an extraordinary item for any other company. *Wrong*

An event or a transaction that qualifies as an extraordinary item for one company may not qualify as an extraordinary item for another company. *Right*

When the two characteristics of an extraordinary item (unusual nature and infrequency of occurrence) are considered, the environment of the company must also be taken into account. Environmental considerations include the company's industry, its geographic location, and the extent of governmental intervention. What may be an extraordinary item for one company may not necessarily be extraordinary for another, given the environments of the two companies. When geographic environments are considered, for example, damage from a freeze in late May would be considered extraordinary for a fruit grower in southern California but not for a farmer in northern Michigan. Thus before an event or a transaction can be deemed extraordinary, the environment of the entity must be considered.

It should also be noted that some transactions, such as material gains and losses on extinguishment of debt, are always treated as extraordinary items, if material. Although these items do not meet the criteria for an extraordinary item, they are handled as such because official pronouncements by the APB or FASB have stated that they should be considered as extraordinary items.

4. A transaction or an event that either is unusual in nature or occurs infrequently is reported as a separate amount in income from continuing operations, net of applicable income tax. *Wrong*

A transaction or an event that either is unusual in nature or occurs infrequently is reported as a separate amount in income from continuing operations. *Right*

The APB issued *Opinion No. 30* in an attempt to curb abusive reporting practices. Prior to its issuance, management had considerably more flexibility in determining how and where certain transactions or events were to be disclosed. It is usually to management's advantage to consider some events, particularly events that result in a loss, as an extraordinary item. Disclosing an item as extraordinary implies that the event was beyond the control of management. The intent of *Opinion No. 30* was to severely limit the kinds and number of extraordinary items. It set two criteria that an item had to meet to qualify as extraordinary: (a) unusual in nature *and* (b) infrequent in occurrence. If an item meets both criteria, then it receives special reporting treatment, including net of tax disclosure.

Items that meet only one of the two criteria may receive special treatment, such as line item disclosure on the income statement in income from continuing operations or inclusion with other items under another account title. Under either disclosure, the amount of the item is reported at its gross amount, not net of tax. Therefore, items that are unusual in nature *or* occur infrequently, may be given special disclosure on the face of the income statement, but it is not the same as that of an extraordinary item.

5. Users and the FASB accept without challenge the income statement as it has evolved and is currently prepared. *Wrong*

Users continue to criticize the income statement as it is currently prepared, and the FASB is reviewing the form and content of the income statement. *Right*

As evidenced by the various required disclosures on the income statement, it has evolved into a rather complex and, it is hoped, informative statement. Nevertheless, users continue to criticize the income statement as inadequate and inconsistent, as in the reporting of unusual events and transactions. The FASB is addressing these criticisms in its earnings reporting project. The project is focusing on the components of income, their behavior, and their effects on users' decisions. It should be noted that *FASB Statement of Concepts No. 5* perhaps provides an insight into the direction the FASB might take in income disclosure. The FASB has distinguished between the components of earnings and comprehensive income.

ANSWERS

Key Terms and Concepts

1. net assets, transactions
2. disaggregation of income tax
3. single
4. measurement
5. phase-out
6. unusual in nature, infrequent in occurrence
7. earnings per share (EPS)
8. prospective
9. statement of retained earnings
10. prior period adjustments

True-False

1. F Investments by owners were originally added to equity and thus increased the change in net assets between two successive periods. Since an investment is not an earnings activity, the amount of the owners' investment must be *deducted* from the change in net assets to determine income for the period.
2. T
3. F Procedures for the disaggregation of income tax permit the tax effect of selected items (discontinued operations, extraordinary items, and cumulative effect of a change in accounting principle) on the income statement to be reported with the item. Regular revenues and expenses are disclosed at their gross amount, and only one tax amount is applied to their net amount.
4. T
5. F A discontinued segment may be a major line of business or a class of customer that has been or will be sold, abandoned, spun off, or otherwise disposed of.
6. T
7. F To qualify as an extraordinary item, an event must both be unusual in nature *and* occur infrequently.
8. F Though firms often retire long-term debt before its maturity resulting in a gain or loss on the retirement, the gain or loss *is* nevertheless considered extraordinary. It is obvious that this transaction does not meet the criteria established for extraordinary items. The FASB made an exception for these gains and losses and allows them to be classified as extraordinary even though they do not meet the criteria established for extraordinary items.

9. F There is no common or standard world-wide definition of *extraordinary item*. The U.S. definition is more restrictive than the British definition, for example. U.S. users of international financial statements are cautioned that a word that may appear just like a U.S. word does not necessarily mean that the definitions of the word are the same.

10. T
11. T
12. F A change in the estimated useful life of an asset is a change in an accounting estimate, not an accounting principle. Changes in accounting estimate arise when more and/or newer information is available upon which to base the accounting estimate, for example, the estimated salvage value of an asset. This is not the same as changing an accounting principle.

13. T
14. T
15. T
16. T
17. F Net income for a period is normally added to (or net loss subtracted from) the beginning balance of retained earnings. Two other items—prior period adjustments and dividends—however, may also affect retained earnings. Thus, to determine the ending balance of retained earnings, the beginning balance must be adjusted for (*a*) any prior period adjustments (net of applicable income tax), (*b*) net income (or net loss) for the period, and (*c*) dividends during the period.

18. T
19. F Some components of income are regular and stable over time, but certainly not all income components are. Extraordinary items and effects of changes in accounting principle, for example, are considered irregular and highly volatile.
20. F The last line in a combined statement of income and retained earnings is the ending balance of retained earnings. Because the net income figure is not the last line, some people contend that this statement may be misleading or confusing to the user.

Multiple Choice

1.	d	6.	b
2.	c	7.	b
3.	a	8.	c
4.	d	9.	d
5.	c	10.	c

Extended Problem

a. Income statement for the year ended December 31, 1994, under the single-step approach:

Nittany Corporation
INCOME STATEMENT
FOR THE YEAR ENDED DECEMBER 31, 1994

Revenues		
Net sales ($110,000 + $48,000)		$158,000
Investment revenue		6,000
Total revenues		$164,000
Expenses		
Cost of goods sold ($52,000 + $30,000)	$82,000	
Salary ($28,000 + $14,000)	42,000	
Depreciation ($4,000 + $900)	4,900	
Rent	1,000	
Utilities ($1,600 + $500)	2,100	
Income tax	12,800	
Total expenses		144,800
Income from continuing operations and before extraordinary charge		$ 19,200
Extraordinary charge—cost of meeting government regulation (net of applicable tax of $1,800)		2,700
Net income		$ 16,500
Earnings per common share		
Continuing operations ($19,200/2,000 shares)		$9.60
Extraordinary charge ($2,700/2,000 shares)		1.35
Net income ($16,500/2,000 shares)		$8.25

b. Comparative income statements for the years ended December 31, 1994, and December 31, 1995, under the multiple-step approach (excluding pro forma disclosures for change in accounting principle):

Nittany Corporation
COMPARATIVE INCOME STATEMENTS
FOR THE YEARS ENDED DECEMBER 31, 1994, AND DECEMBER 31, 1995

	December 31	
	1995	**1994**
Sales	$130,000	$110,000
Cost of goods sold	(69,000)	(52,000)
Gross profit	$ 61,000	$ 58,000
Operating expenses (see Schedule 1)	(37,500)	(35,000)
Operating profit	$ 23,500	$ 23,000
Other income and expense		
Investment revenue	-0-	6,000
Gain on sale of investments	9,500	-0-
Earnings before tax	$ 33,000	$ 29,000
Income tax expense	(13,200)	(11,600)
Income from continuing operations	$ 19,800	$ 17,400
Discontinued operations		
Income (loss) from operations of discontinued home appliance division (less applicable income tax effects of $4,000 and $640) (see Schedule 2)	(6,000)	960
Loss on disposal of home appliance division, including provision of $1,500 for operating losses during phase-out period (less applicable income tax savings of $6,200) (see Schedule 3)	(9,300)	-0-
Income before extraordinary charge and cumulative effect of change in accounting principle	$ 4,500	$ 18,360
Extraordinary charge—cost of meeting government regulation (net of applicable income tax of $1,800)	-0-	(2,700)
Cumulative effect of change in accounting principle (net of applicable income tax of $960) (see Schedule 4)	1,440	-0-
Net income	$ 5,940	$ 15,660
Income per common share[a]		
Continuing operations	$ 9.90	$ 8.70
Discontinued operations		
Home appliance division	$ (3.00)	$.48
Loss on disposal of division and phase-out operations	(4.65) (7.65)	-0- .48
Income before extraordinary item and cumulative effect of accounting change	$ 2.25	$ 9.18
Extraordinary charge	-0-	(1.35)
Cumulative effect of accounting change	.72	-0-
Net income	$ 2.97	$ 7.83

[a]Including optional earnings per share computations.

SCHEDULE 1
OPERATING EXPENSES

	1995	1994
Salary expense	$32,500	$28,000
Depreciation expense	1,600	4,000
Rent expense	1,400[a]	1,400[a]
Utilities expense	2,000	1,600
Total operating expenses	$37,500	$35,000

[a]In order for each year's income statement to be correct, the $1,400 rent expense applicable to each year must be disclosed in the proper year.

SCHEDULE 2
INCOME FROM DISCONTINUED OPERATION

		December 31	
		1995	1994
Sales		$35,000	$48,000
Cost of goods sold		(24,000)	(30,000)
Gross profit		$11,000	$18,000
Operating expenses			
Salary	$18,250		$14,000
Depreciation	900		900
Rent	1,000		1,000
Utilities	850 (21,000)		500 (16,400)
Income (loss) before tax		$(10,000)	$ 1,600
Tax expense (savings)		(4,000)	640
Net income (loss)		$ (6,000)	$ 960

SCHEDULE 3		**SCHEDULE 4**	
LOSS ON DISPOSAL OF DIVISION		**CUMULATIVE EFFECT OF ACCOUNTING CHANGE**	
Estimated operating loss	$ 1,500	Depreciation under accelerated method	
Estimated loss on disposal of assets	14,000	for 1994	$4,000
	$15,500	Depreciation if straight-line method used	
Tax benefit	(6,200)	in 1994	1,600
Net loss	$ 9,300	Cumulative effect of change	$2,400
		Income tax effect	960
		Cumulative effect of change, net of tax	$1,440

c.   Statement of retained earnings for the year ended December 31, 1995:

Nittany Corporation
STATEMENT OF RETAINED EARNINGS
FOR THE YEAR ENDED DECEMBER 31, 1995

Retained earnings, 1/1/95	$12,500*
Prior period adjustment	
Correction of error in recording of rent expense in 1994, net of applicable income tax of $560	(840)
Retained earnings, 1/1/95, adjusted	$11,660
Net income	5,940
	$17,600
Dividends paid on common stock	(5,500)
Retained earnings, 12/31/95	$12,100

*1994 earnings	$16,500
1994 dividends	(4,000)
	$12,500

5 THE BALANCE SHEET (STATEMENT OF FINANCIAL POSITION)

CHAPTER OBJECTIVES

After reading Chapter 5 and completing the questions, cases, exercises, and problems from the text chapter, you should be able to:

1. Understand the nature and limitations of the balance sheet.
2. Differentiate between the account form and the report form of the balance sheet.
3. List and define the major classifications of the balance sheet.
4. Identify and know the valuation methods for the various items that constitute assets and liabilities.

5. Describe the essential characteristics of contingencies.
6. Differentiate between contributed capital and retained earnings.
7. Distinguish the decision concerning the placement of information from the decision concerning the display of information.
8. Explain the various types of notes and supplementary information usually included with published financial statements.

CHAPTER REVIEW

Introduction

1. Chapter 4 implied that the income statement is the primary or most important of the financial statements on which users base their decisions. With the subtle shift in users' needs from information related to earnings to information related to cash flow, the balance sheet has taken on added importance. This chapter focuses on (a) the uses, classifications, and valuations of the balance sheet; (b) the notes and supplementary information related to the financial statements; and (c) the techniques of financial statement analysis (see the Appendix).

The Balance Sheet

2. **Uses of the balance sheet.** The *balance sheet* is a summary of assets, liabilities, and owners' equity accounts and their balances at a specific date. A balance sheet prepared at the end of an accounting period represents an entity's resources (assets), the claims to those assets (liabilities), and the interests in those assets (owners' equity) after all earnings and other activities have been recorded according to generally accepted accounting principles. In addition, the balance sheet at the end of a period is the base with which the entity starts the next accounting period.

to demand repayment for more than one year (or operating cycle, if longer) from the balance sheet date.

22. Obligations that are scheduled to mature within one year (or operating cycle, if longer) are generally classified as current liabilities. *Statement No. 6,* however, requires that short-term obligations arising from transactions outside the normal course of business, including the current portion of a long-term debt, be reported in the noncurrent liabilities section of the balance sheet if there is both an intent and a demonstrated ability to refinance the obligations on a long-term basis. The ability to *refinance short-term obligation on a long-term basis* can be demonstrated either (*a*) by the issuance of long-term debt of capital stock during the period between the balance sheet date and the date the financial statements are issued for the purpose of using the proceeds to settle the short-term obligation when it is due or (*b*) by the existence of a financing agreement, entered into before the financial statements are issued, that clearly permits refinancing of the short-term obligation on a long-term basis. The amount reclassified from current to noncurrent liabilities should not exceed the proceeds obtained from long-term debt or capital stock that is used to settle the short-term obligation or the minimum amount available for refinancing under a financing agreement.

23. Noncurrent assets. *Noncurrent assets* are those that are not expected to be converted into cash or consumed during one year or during the operating cycle, whichever is longer.

24. *Investments* and *special-purpose funds* are noncurrent nonoperating assets. These assets generate future cash flows, but over an extended period of time. Investments in capital stock of other companies, for example, result in dividends and stock appreciation. Similarly, funds for a special purpose, such as acquisition of an asset, are invested and earn a return before the fund is expended for its designated purpose. Investments and funds are generally disclosed on the balance sheet after current assets and are reported at their historical cost. Exceptions to this valuation are discussed in future chapters.

25. *Property, plant, and equipment* (also called *fixed assets* or *plant assets*) represents physical property currently being used by the entity to generate cash flows from operations that are expected to continue for several periods. This category typically includes land, land improvements, buildings, machinery, and furniture. Property, plant, and equipment accounts are normally maintained at historical cost. The cost of assets in the form of plant, equipment, and property other than land is periodically and systematically allocated to an expense account over the period benefited by the asset. This cost allocation process is called *depreci-*

ation and is designed to match the cost of the depreciated asset with the benefits derived in the form of operating cash flows. For balance sheet disclosure, depreciable assets are reported at cost less accumulated depreciation up to the balance sheet date.

26. *Intangible assets* are assets that lack tangible substance. Their value is derived from the rights and privileges they convey to their owner. Intangible assets such as patents, copyrights, franchises, and goodwill are recorded at cost. The cost of an intangible asset, like that of property, plant, and equipment, is periodically and systematically allocated as an expense to the periods benefited. When this process is applied to an intangible, it is called *amortization.* The maximum period over which an intangible asset can be amortized is 40 years. Intangibles are reported on the balance sheet at cost less accumulated amortization.

27. *Other assets* is a category for assets that do not fit into one of the other classifications. Examples of other assets are organizational costs (costs associated with beginning a business) and idle equipment. Because of the special nature of these assets, they normally require description in greater detail in the footnotes to the financial statements.

28. Long-term liabilities. In contrast to current liabilities, *long-term liabilities* are obligations that mature in *more than* one year or the entity's operating cycle, whichever is longer. Such long-term liabilities as long-term notes, bonds, deferred taxes, pension obligations, and lease obligations require extensive disclosure to enable users to understand fully the effects of the obligation on the entity. Disclosure of a long-term bond, for example, includes the terms of repayment, interest payments, and conversion features, if any. Long-term liabilities are reported at the present value of the future amounts to be paid.

29. Contingencies. A *loss* or *gain contingency* exists if, at the balance sheet date, certain conditions or circumstances are present that will not be resolved until the occurrence or nonoccurrence of some future event. A *loss contingency,* such as uncollectible receivables, is a possible reduction in an entity's future net cash flows. There are three possible accounting treatments for a loss contingency: (*a*) accrual and disclosure of the estimated loss, if it is probable that a loss has been incurred and the amount is reasonably determinable; (*b*) disclosure but no accrual of the potential loss; and (*c*) neither accrual nor disclosure. A *gain contingency,* such as litigation against another firm for patent infringement, is a possible increase in an entity's future net cash flows. Gain contingencies are normally not accrued; they are recognized when realized. Contingencies are covered more extensively in Chapter 8.

30. Owners' (stockholders') equity. The classifications and types of asset and liability accounts are the same for all forms of business organizations. Ownership equity accounts, however, vary according to the type of business enterprise. The owner of a sole proprietorship and each partner of a partnership have separate owners' equity accounts. On the other hand, the complexity of corporations and the regulations that apply to them require that the two primary sources of or claims to corporate assets be disclosed separately: contributed capital and retained earnings.

31. *Contributed capital* represents the owners' contributions to the corporation and shareholders' investments in its stock. *Legal capital,* which is defined by individual state laws, usually refers to the portion of contributed capital that is equal to the par or stated value (an arbitrarily stipulated amount assigned to each share of stock) of all shares issued and outstanding. *Additional paid-in capital* is the excess of resources received by the corporation over the par or stated value of the shares issued. A separate account is maintained for each class of stock a corporation has outstanding. Thus the ownership equity section of the balance sheet of a corporation that has several classes of stock outstanding can become complex.

32. *Retained earnings* consists of the net accumulated reinvested earnings of a corporation. Retained earnings is increased by net income and decreased by a net loss and dividends. In addition, prior period adjustments can either increase or decrease retained earnings. *Statement No. 16* narrowed the number of allowable items that could qualify as prior period adjustments to two: (*a*) the correction of an error in the financial statements of a prior period and (*b*) adjustments that result from realization of income tax benefits of preacquisition operating loss carryforwards of purchased subsidiaries. As stated in Chapter 4, prior period adjustments are reported as increases or decreases to the beginning balance of retained earnings. Issues relating to the second type of prior period adjustment are covered in Chapter 17.

33. A *statement of stockholders' equity* is another statement often prepared by companies. This statement reconciles changes in balances of the major components of stockholders' equity. Additional disclosures that are required for each class of stock include the number of shares authorized, issued, and held in the treasury and certain characteristics of each class of stock, such as par or stated value and dividend rate. The disclosures may be in the financial statements or their notes.

34. Unclassified balance sheet. Not all companies prepare balance sheets according to the prescribed classification schemes discussed. These companies, in industries such as banking, insur-

ance, and utilities, prepare their balance sheets in accordance with regulatory requirements. Regulators seldom consider the needs of users when they specify the required disclosure for financial statements. Consequently, financial statements prepared under regulatory specifications generally do not provide information as useful to users as those prepared under generally accepted accounting principles.

Notes and Supplementary Information

35. A company provides financial statements as a primary means of communicating with people who are interested in its financial affairs. Other means of supplying information to users are also available. Two of the most common are notes to the financial statements and supplementary information. When these means are used, management must decide the appropriate *placement* of information—that is, which of the alternatives should be selected to report the information—and the appropriate *display* of information—that is, the amount of detail to be reported and the manner of presentation.

36. Two general guidelines in regard to the placement of information may be followed. First, information that meets the definition of an element of the financial statements and other recognition criteria as described in Chapter 2 should be disclosed in the main body of the financial statements. Further explanation of items in the financial statements should be included in the notes. Supplementary information may provide a different perspective on the information provided in the financial statements. The balance sheet, for example, may simply disclose the balance in the plant and equipment account. The notes can provide a more detailed listing of the various plant and equipment assets, and the supplementary information can contain information about the assets' current value. Second, the notes and supplementary information options offer management an opportunity to supply different levels of detail. Normally, supplementary information is unaudited. It supplies greater detail than notes and is usually helpful to a limited number of users for special analysis. The remainder of this section discusses several typical disclosures made in the notes and supplementary information: long-term commitments; property, plant, and equipment; accounting policies; and subsequent events.

37. Special disclosures are normally made for *long-term commitments* or obligations, such as notes, bonds, and leases. Such disclosures are often made in the form of supporting schedules and notes and include the amounts of the obligations, their due dates and interest rates, and other pertinent information about the obligations that will help the user to assess future cash flows.

38. Schedules are also prepared to disclose additional information about the *property, plant, and equipment* account listed in the balance sheet. Since the account usually consists of several categories of assets, such as land, buildings, machinery, and leasehold improvements, supporting schedules detail the categories used. Additional disclosures are made about the depreciation methods used and accumulated depreciation. Information about property, plant, and equipment permits the user to assess potential cash flows from the assets and potential cash outflows for the assets' eventual replacements.

39. U.S. companies must disclose as an integral part of their financial statements a summary of significant *accounting policies,* that is, the specific accounting principles and methods of applying them that management used to prepare the financial statements. Most foreign countries also require disclosure of accounting policies. *APB Opinion No. 22* recommends that a disclosure headed "Summary of Significant Accounting Policies" lead the note section of the financial statements. This disclosure was deemed necessary because management often adopts one of several acceptable accounting alternatives, and users' understanding of the financial statements is enhanced if they know which accounting principles and methods of applying them were used. Although this disclosure should not duplicate those found in other parts of the financial statements, a typical accounting policy disclosure includes mainly verbal descriptions, where applicable, of items such as the company's consolidation basis, depreciation methods, inventory pricing, amortization of intangibles, and foreign currency translation practices.

40. Sometimes *poststatement* or *subsequent events*—events that occur between the statement date and the date of issuance of the financial statements—are required to be either accrued or disclosed (in effect, retroactively) in order to ensure that the financial statements will not be misleading or present inaccurate cash flow signals. Subsequent events are of two types and require different accounting treatments. First, events such as the default of a significant receivable held at the statement date but defaulted before the statements are issued should be accrued because this information about the subsequent event constitutes additional evidence about conditions existing at the statement date. Second, events that affect the company but that had not occurred at the statement date, such as the acquisition of a new plant site, need to be disclosed only in a footnote or schedule. Other subsequent events, such as the introduction of a new product after the statement date, do not require

adjustment or disclosure in the financial statements. Events of this nature are hard to quantify and are best presented by other means, for example, in management's letter to the stockholders.

Appendix: Analysis of Financial Statements

41. *Market efficiency* is the relationship between security prices and information reported in published financial statements. When security prices fully reflect financial statement information, the securities market is efficient. In such circumstances, it can be argued that investors should invest in a portfolio on the basis of risk, rather than attempt to discover undervalued or overvalued securities. Nevertheless, analysis of financial statements is important to investors in evaluating non-publicly traded companies and relative risk to creditors and to financial analysts.

42. Analysis of a company's financial report should include, as a minimum, consideration of (*a*) the auditor's report, which, among other things, indicates whether the financial statements present fairly the company's financial position and results of operations in accordance with generally accepted accounting principles; (*b*) the notes to the financial statements, especially the description of significant accounting policies; and (*c*) the financial statements. Two techniques that are often used to analyze the information reported in financial statements are percentage analysis and ratio analysis. These techniques are designed to identify trends and significant relationships in a company's financial data.

43. Percentage analysis. *Percentage analysis* is a technique in which the amounts reported in the financial statements are expressed as a percentage of a designated base. Two methods of applying percentage analysis are horizontal analysis and vertical analysis. Under *horizontal analysis,* the amounts reported in the financial statements are expressed as a percentage of the corresponding amounts as of a designated base period. Horizontal analysis may be applied by expressing financial data from two or more accounting periods as a percentage of a single designated base period or by expressing financial data in each succeeding period as a percentage of the immediately preceding period. This technique is especially useful in identifying the trends and relative changes in financial data over time or from period to period. Under *vertical analysis,* the amounts reported in a particular financial statement are expressed as a percentage of a designated amount within that financial statement. Each amount reported on the income statement may be expressed as a percentage of net sales, for example, and each amount reported on the balance sheet may be expressed as a percentage of total assets. This technique is especially useful in identifying the relative size of the amounts reported in the financial statements.

44. Ratio analysis. *Ratio analysis* is a technique in which two or more amounts reported in the financial statements are expressed as a ratio to identify significant relationships concerning a company's liquidity, asset activity or turnover, leverage, and profitability.

45. The ratios that generally are applied to analyze a company's liquidity are the current ratio, quick ratio, and defensive interval ratio. These *liquidity ratios* are especially useful in evaluating a company's ability to pay its short-term obligations. The *current ratio* (also called the *working capital ratio*) is current assets divided by current liabilities. This ratio is a measure of a company's ability to pay its short-term obligations from current assets. The *quick ratio* (also called the *acid-test ratio*) is cash, short-term marketable securities, and net short-term receivables divided by current liabilities. This ratio is a measure of a company's ability to pay its short-term obligations from liquid current assets. Inventory, prepaid items, and other nonliquid current assets are excluded from the numerator of this ratio, as these assets may not be readily available for the payment of short-term obligations. The *defensive interval ratio* is cash, short-term marketable securities, and net short-term receivables (also called *defensive assets*) divided by average daily operating expenditures (cost of goods sold, selling and administrative expenses, and other ordinary expenses exclusive of any noncash expenses, such as depreciation and deferred taxes, divided by 365 days). This ratio is a measure of the length of time a company could continue its daily operations by using liquid assets only.

46. The ratios that normally are applied to analyze a company's asset activity or turnover are the inventory turnover ratio, accounts receivable turnover ratio, and total assets turnover ratio. These *activity,* or *turnover, ratios* are especially useful in evaluating the effectiveness with which a company uses its assets. The *inventory turnover ratio* is cost of goods sold divided by average inventory for the period (beginning inventory plus ending inventory divided by 2). This ratio is a measure of the rate at which inventories are sold. A low inventory turnover ratio may be indicative of sluggish sales or excessive inventories; a high ratio generally is desirable, but it may be indicative of possible "stockout" problems. The *accounts receivable turnover ratio* is net sales divided by average net accounts receivable for the period (beginning net accounts receivable plus ending net accounts receivable divided by 2). This ratio is a measure of the rate at which accounts receivable are collected. A low accounts receivable turnover ratio may be indicative of a need to adopt a more stringent credit policy; a high ratio generally is desirable, but it may be indicative of possible lost sales resulting from an excessively stringent credit policy. The *total assets turnover ratio* is net sales divided by average total assets for the period (beginning total assets plus ending total assets divided by 2). This ratio is a measure of a company's efficiency in using its total assets.

47. The ratios that typically are applied to analyze a company's financial leverage are the total liabilities to total assets ratio and the times interest earned ratio. These *leverage ratios* are especially useful in evaluating a company's ability to meet both short-term and long-term obligations. These ratios also are useful in evaluating the riskiness of a company from the perspective of both stockholders and long-term creditors. The *total liabilities to total assets ratio* is total liabilities divided by total assets. This ratio is a measure of a company's ability to absorb losses and reduction of assets without impairing the claims of the creditors. Accordingly, a low total liabilities to total assets ratio is desirable, especially from the perspective of the creditors. A low ratio also may be indicative of financial flexibility in the event that a company wishes to issue debt in the future. The *times interest earned ratio* is ordinary income before taxes and interest expense divided by interest expense. This ratio is a measure of a company's ability to pay annual interest from ordinary income. A high times interest earned ratio generally is preferred. This ratio may be modified to include other fixed expenses, such as lease payments and pension payments, in the denominator and as adjustments to ordinary income in the numerator. This modified ratio (called the *fixed expenses* or *fixed charges coverage ratio*) is a measure of a company's ability to pay all its fixed annual expenses from ordinary income.

48. *Profitability ratios* are especially useful in analyzing the efficiency of a company's operating activities. Long-term creditors are interested in the profitability of a company because debt and the related interest are paid primarily from assets generated by profitable operations. Present and potential stockholders also are interested in a company's profitability because both dividends and market value appreciations of stock depend on future profitability. The *profit margin on sales* is net income divided by net sales. This ratio is a measure of the return generated by each dollar of sales. The *net operating margin* is operating income (net sales minus cost of goods sold and operating expenses) divided by net sales. This ratio is a better measure of the efficiency of a company in producing and selling its products than the profit margin on sales, because nonoperating items are excluded. The *return on total assets* is net income (or net income plus interest expense multiplied by 1 minus the tax rate) divided by average total assets for the period (beginning total assets plus ending total assets divided by 2). This ratio is a better measure of profitability than either profit margin on sales or net operating margin, as it is a measure of the effectiveness with which a company is using its assets to generate income. The *return on stockholders' equity* is income applicable to common stockholders (net income minus preferred dividends) divided by average common stockholders' equity for the period (beginning common stockholders' equity plus ending common stockholders' equity divided by 2). This ratio is a measure of the return to common stockholders. When the return on stockholders' equity exceeds the return on total assets, the trading on the equity by the company may be favorable to the common stockholders. *Trading on the equity* (also called the use of *financial leverage*) is the practice of borrowing money at fixed interest rates or issuing preferred stock with fixed dividend rates with the expectation of generating a return on the invested assets that exceeds the interest or preferred dividends paid. *Earnings per share* is a measure of profitability on the basis of the amount of earnings per share of common stock. When no potentially dilutive securities are outstanding, earnings per share is net income minus preferred dividends divided by the weighted average number of shares of common stock outstanding during the period. When potentially dilutive securities are outstanding, two earnings per share figures, called primary and fully diluted earnings per share, may be reported. Chapter 20 contains a detailed discussion of earnings per share. The *price-earnings ratio* is the market price per common share divided by earnings per share. The trend of this ratio is an indicator of the long-term growth potential of a company. An increasing price-earnings ratio may be indicative of investors' expectations of favorable growth potential; a decreasing ratio may be indicative of investors' doubt about growth potential. The *dividend yield* is dividends per common share divided by the

market price per common share. This ratio plus the percentage change in the market price of the common stock during the period is a measure of the total return to common stockholders during the period. The *dividend payout ratio* is cash dividends on common stock divided by income applicable to common stockholders (net income minus preferred dividends). This ratio may be indicative of a company's dividend policy and its plans for internal growth. The *book value per share* is common stockholders' equity (total stockholders' equity minus preferred stockholders' claims) divided by the number of common shares outstanding at the end of the period. Even though this ratio often is quoted or reported, it normally is not a good measure of the economic or market value of a common share, since the numerator is based on historical cost amounts rather than current market values. The *DuPont method* is a system of combining financial ratios in an interrelated series used to evaluate the basic components that affect return on investment.

49. Time series and cross-section analysis. The percentages and ratios derived from an analysis of a company's financial statements may be evaluated further by means of time series analysis and cross-section analysis. *Time series analysis* is an evaluation of the change (increase or decrease) in the financial data of a company over time. This technique is especially useful in identifying trends and in forming expectations about the future. *Cross-section* (or *comparative*) *analysis* is a comparison of the financial data of the company with the corresponding data of other companies for the same period of time. This technique is especially useful in evaluating the financial strength and profitability of a company relative to other companies in the same industry. Its usefulness, however, may be limited by several factors. A company may not operate in a single identifiable industry. Industry averages also may not be an appropriate standard for comparison, particularly if the entire industry is economically depressed. And differences in accounting procedures, size, and economies of scale may affect the comparability of the financial data.

SELF-STUDY LEARNING   Items marked with an asterisk (*) refer to the Appendix.

Key Terms and Concepts

Provide the appropriate term or terms to complete each of the following statements:

1. A(n) __BS_____ summarizes a company's assets, liabilities, and owners' equity accounts and their balances at a specific date.

2. _____LIQUIDITY_____ refers to the amount of time expected to elapse before an asset is converted into cash or before a liability is paid.

3. The basic balance sheet formats are the _ACCT FORM_ and the _REPORT FORM_.

4. Current assets are listed on the balance sheet in order of their _LIQUIDITY_.

5. Working capital is equal to _CURRENT ASSETS_ less _CURRENT LIAB_.

6. The systematic and rational process of allocating the cost of property, plant, and equipment assets to expense is referred to as _DEPR_; the same process applied to intangible assets is called _AMORT_.

7. An existing condition, situation, or set of circumstances involving uncertainty as to possible gain or loss to an enterprise that will ultimately be resolved when one or more future events occur or fail to occur is defined as a(n) _CONTINGENCY_.

8. The amount received from a shareholder in excess of the par or stated value of the shares issued by a corporation is called _ADDIT PAID IN CAPITAL_.

9. _RET EARN_ is increased by net income and decreased by a net loss and dividends.

10. A(n) _SSE_ reconciles changes in balances of the major components of stockholders' equity.

11. *Opinion No. 22* requires that a company disclose in its published financial statements a summary of its significant _ACCTG POLICIES_.

12. A(n) _SUBSEQUENT EVENT_ occurs between the statement date and the date of issuance of the financial statements.

*13. Two techniques are often used to analyze the information contained in financial statements: _% ANAL_, in which the amounts reported in the financial statements are expressed as a percentage of a designated base; and _RATIO ANAL_, in which two or more amounts reported in the financial statements are expressed as a ratio.

*14. There are two methods of applying percentage analysis: _HORIZ ANAL_, by which the amounts reported in the financial statements are expressed as a percentage of the corresponding amounts as of a designated base period; and _VERT ANAL_, by which the amounts reported in a particular financial statement are expressed as a percentage of a designated amount within that financial statement.

*15. Two techniques are often used to evaluate the percentages and ratios calculated from an analysis of financial statements: _TIME-SERIES_, by which the changes in the financial data of a company are evaluated over time; and _COMPARATIVE_, by which the financial data of a company are compared with the corresponding financial data of other companies for the same period of time.

True-False

Indicate by circling the appropriate response whether each of the following statements is true (T) or false (F):

T **(F)** 1. A balance sheet is prepared for a period of time.

T **(F)** 2. Generally accepted accounting principles permit all resources to be recorded at amounts relevant for decision making.

(T) F 3. In the account form of the balance sheet, all assets are listed on the left side; liabilities and owners' equity account are listed on the right.

(T) F 4. Trading securities held as an investment are classified as a current asset if it is the intent to sell them in the near future.

T **(F)** 5. Available-for-sale securities are reported at their amortized cost.

T **(F)** 6. Short-term receivables are disclosed on the balance sheet at their face value.

(T) F 7. Trade receivables are short-term receivables that arise from credit sales of a company's goods or services.

T **(F)** 8. For balance sheet purposes, all inventories are valued at historical cost.

(T) F 9. A prepaid expense arises if the payment precedes the receipt of a benefit or service expected to be realized within one year or the normal operating cycle, whichever is longer.

T **(F)** 10. The current ratio is computed by dividing current assets by total liabilities.

T **(F)** 11. The current portion of long-term obligations always should be reclassified as a current liability.

(T) F 12. Long-term obligations that are callable by the creditor because of the debtor's violation of a provision of the debt agreement at the balance sheet date generally must be classified as current liabilities.

T **(F)** 13. A short-term obligation arising from a transaction outside the normal course of business should be reported as a noncurrent liability if there is an intent to refinance the obligation on a long-term basis.

T **(F)** 14. When a short-term obligation is refinanced on a long-term basis by the issuance of capital stock between the balance sheet date and the date the financial statements are issued, the short-term obligation should be excluded from current liabilities and reported in the stockholders' equity section of the balance sheet.

(T) F 15. When the refinancing of a short-term obligation on a long-term basis is consummated between the balance sheet date and the date the financial statements are issued, the amount reclassified from current liabilities to non-current liabilities should not exceed the proceeds obtained from the issuance of the long-term debt or capital stock.

T **(F)** 16. Depreciable assets are reported on the balance sheet at cost.

(T) F 17. The value of intangible assets is derived from the rights and privileges they convey to their owner.

T **(F)** 18. Contributed capital and legal capital usually are equal in dollar amount.

T **(F)** 19. Retained earnings is increased only by net income or profit from operations.

(T) F 20. The correction of an error in the financial statements of a prior period is reported as a prior period adjustment.

(T) F 21. If information meets the definition of a financial statement element and satisfies the recognition criteria, it should be disclosed in the main body of the financial statements.

(T) F 22. Normally, the greatest amount of detail about a particular account or transaction is provided in the supplementary information section of the financial statements.

T **(F)** 23. The APB recommended that the disclosure on accounting policy,

"Summary of Significant Accounting Policies," be placed at the end of the notes to the financial statements.

(T) F 24. The United States and most foreign countries require disclosure of accounting policies.

(T) F 25. Certain subsequent events are either accrued or disclosed in the financial statements to ensure that the financial statements will not be misleading.

(T) F *26. The current ratio and quick ratio are useful in evaluating a company's ability to pay its short-term obligations.

T (F) *27. The times interest earned ratio is useful in evaluating the length of time a company could continue its daily operations by using liquid assets only.

(T) F *28. A low inventory turnover ratio may be indicative of sluggish sales or excessive inventories.

T (F) *29. The net operating margin is a better measure of profitability than the return on total assets, since non-operating items are excluded.

(T) F *30. The trend of the price-earnings ratio may be indicative of the investors' expectations of the growth potential of a company.

Multiple Choice

Select the best response for each of the following items, and circle the corresponding letter:

1. A balance sheet prepared using the account form would have:

   a. Noncurrent assets before current assets.
   (b.) Assets on the left side and liabilities and owners' equity on the right side.
   c. Current assets and current liabilities on the right side and noncurrent assets, noncurrent liabilities, and owners' equity on the left side.
   d. Liabilities and owners' equity on the left side and assets on the right side.

2. The normal operating cycle is:

   a. One year.
   b. Usually the same for all companies.

(c.) The period of time between the acquisition of inventory and its conversion to cash.
   d. The useful life of a fixed asset.

3. Which of the following short-term investment securities should be reported at their fair value?

	Trading	Available-for-Sale	Held-to-Maturity
a.	No	No	No
b.	No	Yes	Yes
(c.)	Yes	Yes	No
d.	Yes	Yes	Yes

4. On a merchandising company's balance sheet, inventory is normally classified as:

   a. Raw materials inventory.
   (b.) Finished goods inventory.
   c. Work-in-process inventory.
   d. All of the above.

5. The working capital ratio, a liquidity measure, is defined as:

   a. The sum of all current liabilities.
   b. Current assets less current liabilities.
   (c.) Current assets divided by current liabilities.
   d. Current assets plus current liabilities.

6. The current portion of a long-term obligation should be reclassified as a current liability when the amount currently due will be settled:

   (a.) By the use of existing current assets or by the creation of another current liability.
   b. By the use of noncurrent assets.
   c. By the issuance of capital stock.
   d. By the use of proceeds obtained from the issuance of long-term debt or capital stock between the balance sheet date and the date the financial statements are issued.

7. Which of the following does *not* constitute evidence of an ability to refinance a short-term obligation on a long-term basis?

   a. The issuance of long-term debt during the period between the balance sheet date and the date the financial statements are issued for the purpose of using the proceeds to settle the short-term obligation when it is due.
   b. The issuance of capital stock during the period between the balance sheet date and the date the financial statements are issued for the purpose of using the proceeds to settle the short-term obligation when it is due.
   (c.) The issuance of long-term debt or capital stock during the period between the balance sheet date and the date the financial statements are issued for the purpose of replen-

ishing current assets that were used previously to settle the short-term obligation when it was due.

   d. The existence of a financing agreement, entered into before the financial statements are issued, that clearly permits refinancing of the short-term obligation on a long-term basis.

8. Obligations that are callable by the creditor should be classified by the debtor as current liabilities under several circumstances. Which of the following is *not* such a circumstance?

   a. The obligations, by their terms, are or will be due on demand within one year (or operating cycle, if longer) from the balance sheet date.

   b. The obligations are due in five years, but the creditor has the right to call them in two years.

   c. The obligations are long-term but are or will be callable by the creditor because of the debtor's violation of a provision of the debt agreement at the balance sheet date.

   d. The obligations are long-term but are or will be callable by the creditor because it is not probable that the debtor's violation will be corrected within a specified grace period.

9. Which of the following assets would *not* be amortized?

   a. Plant fixture.
   b. Patent.
   c. Copyright.
   d. Goodwill.

10. Certain events or transactions affect retained earnings. For the following events or transactions, which one will *not* have the effect given?

	EVENT OR TRANSACTION	EFFECT ON RETAINED EARNINGS
a.	Prior period adjustment	Increase only
b.	Dividend distribution	Decrease only
c.	Operating profit	Increase only
d.	Operating loss	Decrease only

11. Which of the four accounts listed would be reconciled in a statement of stockholders' equity?

	Additional Paid-in-Capital	Common Stock	Investments	Retained Earnings
a.	No	Yes	Yes	No
b.	Yes	Yes	Yes	No
c.	Yes	Yes	No	Yes
d.	Yes	Yes	Yes	Yes

12. In preparing its financial statements, a company discovered items that it considered to be subsequent events. Which of the following items should *not* be accrued or disclosed in the footnotes?

   a. Payment of litigation initiated in the prior period.
   b. Default of a major customer.
   c. Issuance of a large long-term debt.
   d. New governmental regulation that might affect the company.

*13. Which of the following ratios is *not* affected by the purchase of inventory on short-term credit at the end of the accounting period?

   a. Current ratio.
   b. Quick ratio.
   c. Defensive interval ratio.
   d. Inventory turnover ratio.

*14. Which of the following ratios is useful in evaluating the riskiness of a company from the perspective of both stockholders and long-term creditors?

   a. Total liabilities to total assets ratio.
   b. Book value per share.
   c. Accounts receivable turnover ratio.
   d. Price-earnings ratio.

*15. Which of the following ratios is useful in evaluating the effectiveness with which a company is using its assets to generate income?

   a. Total assets turnover ratio.
   b. Return on total assets.
   c. Return on stockholders' equity.
   d. Profit margin on sales.

EXTENDED PROBLEMS

Items marked with an asterisk (*) refer to the Appendix.

1. An adjusted December 31, 1995, trial balance for Adviser Corporation appears below. Additional information that is not yet reflected in this adjusted trial balance includes:

   a. The trading securities were acquired on December 30, 1995, and are being held with the intent to sell them early in 1996. The market value has not changed since their acquisition.

   b. The noncurrent investment is an investment in Landon Co. bonds carried at their amortized cost.

   c. On January 10, 1996, an agreement was reached with the bank to refinance $15,000 of the note payable. This amount is due January 10, 1999.

REQUIRED

Prepare a balance sheet in good form for Adviser Corporation as of December 31, 1995.

	1995 DEBIT	1995 CREDIT
Cash	$ 45,000	
Accounts receivable	62,000	
Inventory	26,000	
Trading securities	45,000	
Investments (noncurrent)	87,000	
Machinery	194,000	
Copyrights	71,000	
Accumulated depreciation (machinery)		$ 54,000
Accumulated amortization (copyrights)		60,000
Accounts payable		28,000
Wages payable		3,000
Note payable (due 1996)		25,000
Common stock ($10 par)		140,000
Additional paid-in capital		165,000
Retained earnings		34,000
Sales		210,000
Investment revenue		15,000
Cost of goods sold	96,000	
Wages expense	65,000	
Depreciation expense (machinery)	18,000	
Amortization expense (copyrights)	7,000	
Rent expense	15,000	
Interest expense	3,000	
	$734,000	$734,000

*2. Presented here are the financial statements of OITAR Corporation for the years ended December 31, 1995, and December 31, 1994.

OITAR Corporation

BALANCE SHEET
AS OF DECEMBER 31, 1995, AND DECEMBER 31, 1994

	1995	1994
Cash	$ 15,700	$ 8,600
Trading securities	9,300	6,400
Accounts receivable, net	85,000	65,000
Inventory	90,000	70,000
Total current assets	$200,000	$150,000
Land	50,000	50,000
Building and equipment	400,000	400,000
Less: Accumulated depreciation	(150,000)	(120,000)
Total assets	$500,000	$480,000
Accounts payable	$ 87,500	$ 76,500
Accrued liabilities	12,500	10,400
Total current liabilities	$100,000	$ 86,900
Deferred tax liability	20,000	16,000
Bonds payable (12% stated rate)	100,000	100,000
Total liabilities	$220,000	$202,900
8% preferred stock, $100 par (issued and outstanding, 350 shares; aggregate liquidation value, $38,500)	35,000	35,000
Common stock, $5 par (issued and outstanding, 10,000 shares; market price per share, $16 and $14, respectively)	50,000	50,000
Contributed capital in excess of par—common	100,000	100,000
Retained earnings	95,000	92,100
Total liabilities and stockholders' equity	$500,000	$480,000

OITAR Corporation

INCOME STATEMENT
FOR THE YEARS ENDED DECEMBER 31, 1995, AND DECEMBER 31, 1994

	1995	1994
Net sales	$600,000	$500,000
Interest revenue	1,000	1,000
Total revenue	$601,000	$501,000
Cost of goods sold	$360,000	$280,000
Administrative expenses	104,000	96,000
Selling expenses	65,000	58,000
Depreciation expense	30,000	30,000
Interest expense	12,000	12,000
Total expenses	$571,000	$476,000
Income before taxes	$ 30,000	$ 25,000
Income taxes		
Currently payable	8,000	7,000
Deferred	4,000	3,000
Net income	$ 18,000	$ 15,000
Earnings per common share	$ 1.52	$ 1.22

OITAR Corporation

STATEMENT OF RETAINED EARNINGS
FOR THE YEARS ENDED DECEMBER 31, 1995, AND DECEMBER 31, 1994

	1995	1994
Retained earnings, beginning	$ 92,100	$ 92,200
Net income	18,000	15,000
Dividends		
Preferred ($8.00 per share)	(2,800)	(2,800)
Common ($1.23 per share)	(12,300)	(12,300)
Retained earnings, ending	$ 95,000	$ 92,100

REQUIRED

Calculate the following ratios for OITAR Corporation for the year ended December 31, 1995. Where necessary, round to the nearest tenth of a percent.

a. Current ratio.
b. Quick ratio.
c. Defensive interval ratio.
d. Inventory turnover ratio.
e. Accounts receivable turnover ratio.
f. Total assets turnover ratio.
g. Total liabilities to total assets ratio.
h. Times interest earned ratio.
i. Profit margin on sales.
j. Net operating margin.
k. Return on total assets.
l. Return on stockholders' equity.
m. Price-earnings ratio.
n. Dividend yield.
o. Dividend payout ratio.
p. Book value per share.

COMMON ERRORS

The first statement in each of the "common errors" listed here is *incorrect*. Each incorrect statement is followed by a corrected statement and an explanation.

1. *Liquidity* and *financial flexibility* refer to the same concept of cash analysis. *Wrong*
Liquidity and *financial flexibility* refer to different concepts of cash analysis. *Right*
Users' desire for information related to cash flow appears to be increasing. To meet this desire, the FASB has included among the objectives of financial reporting that of providing information to help the user assess the amount, timing, and uncertainty of future cash flows. In addition, the FASB has recently embarked on a project that focuses on the flow and liquidity of funds. *Liquidity* refers to the amount of time expected to elapse before an asset is converted into cash or before a liability is paid. *Financial flexibility* refers to a company's ability to alter cash flows by responding to unexpected needs and opportunities. Thus, although both liquidity and financial flexibility are related to cash flow analysis, they are different concepts. Important information about a company's liquidity and financial flexibility may be obtained by studying the company's balance sheet and statement of cash flows.

2. Current assets are those that can reasonably be expected to be converted to cash or consumed during one year. *Wrong*
Current assets are assets that can reasonably be expected to be converted to cash or consumed within one year or during the normal operating cycle, whichever is longer. *Right*
For many companies, current assets are those that can reasonably be expected to be converted to cash or consumed *during one year*. Because financial statements are usually prepared annually, the one-year guideline is convenient and logical. To increase comparability among companies in different industries, however, the definition of current assets is broadened to encompass the operating cycle concept, that is, the time between the acquisi-

tion of inventory and its conversion back to cash. A bakery should turn over its inventory nearly every day, for example, but a company that makes fine wine should allow its inventory to age for several years. In order for both the bakery and the winery to report inventory as a current asset, the definition of current assets must necessarily be broader than the one-year guideline, which by itself is too limiting. Therefore, a current asset is any asset that can reasonably be expected to be converted to cash or consumed within one year *or* during the normal operating cycle, *whichever is longer.*

3. At a particular balance sheet date, all assets are reported at their historical cost. *Wrong*

At a particular balance sheet date, some assets are reported at historical cost, whereas others are reported at other values. *Right*

The initial valuation of all assets is historical cost, but that valuation is not always maintained until the asset is written off the balance sheet. GAAP requires different valuations for some assets after their acquisition. Accounts receivable, for example, are reported at their net realizable value, and land at its fair value if its value has significantly and permanently declined below its cost. Thus the balance sheet reports assets at several valuations; historical cost is only one of those valuations.

4. Obligations that are due within one year always should be reported as current liabilities. *Wrong*

Although obligations that are due within one year generally should be reported as current liabilities, such obligations should be reported as noncurrent liabilities when their settlement will not require the use of existing current assets or the creation of other current liabilities. *Right*

Accounting Research Bulletin No. 43 defines current liabilities as obligations whose settlement is reasonably expected to require the use of existing current assets or the creation of other current liabilities. As current assets are defined as cash and other assets that are reasonably expected to be realized in cash or sold or consumed within one year, obligations that are due within one year generally should be reported as current liabilities. Such obligations, however, should be reported as noncurrent liabilities when their settlement will not require the use of existing current assets or the creation of other current liabilities. Such circumstances include the use of noncurrent assets, such as a sinking fund, to settle short-term obligations and the refinancing of short-term obligations on a long-term basis, either by the use of the proceeds obtained from the issuance of long-term debt or capital stock

between the balance sheet date and the date the financial statements are issued to settle the obligation or by a financing agreement entered into before the financial statements are issued that clearly permits refinancing of the obligation on a long-term basis.

5. Short-term obligations that are refinanced on a long-term basis should not be reported as liabilities. *Wrong*

Short-term obligations that are refinanced on a long-term basis should be excluded from current liabilities and reported in the noncurrent liabilities section of the balance sheet. *Right*

A short-term obligation that has been refinanced on a long-term basis is still an obligation as of the balance sheet date, and thus it should be reported as a liability. However, because a short-term obligation that has been refinanced on a long-term basis will not require the use of existing current assets or the creation of other current liabilities, it should be excluded from current liabilities and reported in the noncurrent liabilities section of the balance sheet.

6. Like asset and liability accounts, owners' equity accounts are the same for all forms of business enterprise. *Wrong*

Unlike asset and liability accounts, owners' equity accounts vary from one form of business enterprise to another. *Right*

The measurement and disclosure of asset and liability accounts are the same for all forms of business organization. Owners' equity accounts, however, vary in accordance with the form of the business enterprise. In a sole proprietorship, the proprietor's investments and withdrawals and the results of operations are all reflected in a single owner's equity account. Each partner in a partnership has a separate equity account to reflect his or her investments, withdrawals, and share of partnership profits and losses. In a corporation, owners' equity consists of separate accounts for contributed capital (assets contributed by shareholders) and retained earnings (accumulated undistributed earnings). In addition, the ownership equity section of a corporate balance sheet is usually much more complex than that of a sole proprietorship or partnership.

7. When management decides the placement of information and the display of information, it is making the same disclosure decision. *Wrong*

When management decides the placement of information and the display of information, it is making different disclosure decisions. *Right*

One of management's most important responsibilities is to provide information to users. When management has financial information to disclose, it must make two separate but related decisions. It must decide (*a*) where the information should be reported (main body of financial statements or notes and supplementary information sections) and (*b*) the amount of detail to be reported and the manner of presentation. Both decisions relate to the financial disclosure package and must be based on the need to provide users with complete and comprehensible information.

8. A high current ratio is desirable. *Wrong*

A high current ratio is generally but not necessarily desirable. *Right*

The current ratio is current assets divided by current liabilities. This ratio is a measure of a company's ability to pay its short-term obligations by using current assets. A high current ratio generally is desirable, especially from the perspective of short-term creditors. A current ratio that is too high, however, may be undesirable from the perspective of stockholders, because excessive amounts of current assets such as cash, accounts receivable, and inventory might yield higher returns to the company if they were invested elsewhere.

9. The profit margin on sales is the best indicator of profitability. *Wrong*

The return on total assets is a better indicator of profitability than the profit margin on sales. *Right*

The profit margin on sales is net income divided by net sales. This ratio is a measure of the return generated by each dollar of sales. The total assets turnover ratio is net sales divided by average total assets for the period. This ratio is a measure of the efficiency with which a company uses its assets. The return on total assets is net income divided by average total assets during the period. Stated somewhat differently, the return on total assets (net income divided by average total assets) is the profit margin on sales (net income divided by net sales) multiplied by the total assets turnover ratio (net sales divided by average total assets). As this relationship shows, the return on total assets is a measure of the effectiveness with which a company uses its assets to generate income. For this reason, the return on total assets is a better indicator of profitability than the profit margin on sales.

ANSWERS   Items marked with an asterisk (*) refer to the Appendix.

Key Terms and Concepts

1. balance sheet
2. liquidity
3. account form, report form
4. liquidity
5. current assets, current liabilities
6. depreciation, amortization
7. contingency
8. additional paid-in capital
9. retained earnings
10. statement of stockholders' equity
11. accounting policies
12. subsequent event (or poststatement event)
*13. percentage analysis, ratio analysis
*14. horizontal analysis, vertical analysis
*15. time series analysis; cross-section, or comparative, analysis

True-False

1. F   Unlike the income statement, which does represent net income earned or loss incurred during an accounting period, the balance sheet represents the company's situation at a specific point in time, not over a period of time.

2. F   The balance sheet is criticized because generally accepted accounting principles prohibit the recognition of some resources, such as management ability, and the recording of the fair value of assets, which is believed to be more relevant for decision making than historical cost.

3. T

4. T

5. F   Available-for-sale securities are reported at their fair value, not amortized cost. *Statement No. 115* requires that both trading and available-for-sale securities be reported at their fair value. Held-to-maturity securities (debt securities) are reported at their amortized cost.

6. F   Short-term receivables should be disclosed at their *net realizable value,* that is, the amount of cash expected to be collected after allowances for uncollectible accounts, discounts, and so forth. The face value of short-term receivables is disclosed, but from their face value the various allowances must be deducted to determine their net realizable value.

7. T

8. F   Most inventories are valued at their historical cost, but in some situations inventory

is valued at its net realizable value or lower-of-cost-or-market value.

9. T

10. F The *current* ratio is calculated by dividing *current* assets by *current* liabilities, not total liabilities. The working capital ratio is an indicator of liquidity and should, therefore, be calculated with *current* monetary assets and liabilities.

11. F The current portion of a long-term obligation should be reclassified as a current liability, except when the amount currently due will not require the use of existing current assets or the creation of other current liabilities. Specifically, the current portion of a long-term obligation should not be reclassified as a current liability in three circumstances: (*a*) the amount currently due will be settled by the use of noncurrent assets, such as a sinking fund; (*b*) the amount currently due will be settled by the issuance of capital stock; and (*c*) the amount currently due will be refinanced on a long-term basis, as specified in *Statement No. 6*.

12. T

13. F A short-term obligation arising from a transaction outside the normal course of business should be reported as a noncurrent liability only if there is both an intent and a demonstrated ability to refinance the obligation on a long-term basis.

14. F When a short-term obligation is refinanced on a long-term basis by the issuance of capital stock between the balance sheet date and the date the financial statements are issued, the short-term obligation should be excluded from current liabilities and reported in the noncurrent liabilities section of the balance sheet.

15. T

16. F Depreciable assets are reported on the balance sheet at cost less accumulated depreciation up to the date of the balance sheet.

17. T

18. F Contributed capital is equal to the total amount contributed by owners, whereas legal capital is normally equal to the amount of par or stated value, an arbitrary amount assigned to each share of stock. As most companies issue stock in an amount greater than par or stated value, the dollar amount of contributed capital is normally greater than that of legal capital.

19. F Recognition of net income or profit from operations is the primary means to increase retained earnings, but on occasion retained earnings is also increased by some prior period adjustments.

20. T
21. T
22. T
23. F On the contrary, the APB recommended that the "Summary of Significant Accounting Policies" *precede* the other notes.

24. T
25. T
*26. T
*27. F The times interest earned ratio is useful in evaluating a company's ability to pay annual interest from ordinary income. The defensive interval ratio is useful in evaluating a company's ability to continue its daily operations by using liquid assets only.

*28. T
*29. F The net operating margin excludes non-operating items. For this reason, the net operating margin is a better measure of the efficiency with which a company is producing and selling its product than the profit margin on sales. But the return on total assets is a better measure of profitability than either profit margin on sales or net operating margin, because it is a measure of the effectiveness with which a company is using its assets to generate income.

*30. T

Multiple Choice

1.	b	9.	a
2.	c	10.	a
3.	c	11.	c
4.	b	12.	d
5.	c	*13.	c
6.	a	*14.	a
7.	c	*15.	b
8.	b		

Extended Problems

1. Adviser Corporation's balance sheet:

Adviser Corporation
BALANCE SHEET
DECEMBER 31, 1995

ASSETS

Current assets
Cash	$ 45,000	
Accounts receivable	62,000	
Inventory	26,000	
Trading securities	45,000	$178,000

Investments and funds
Investments (noncurrent)..... 87,000

Property, plant, and equipment
Machinery	$194,000	
Less accumulated depreciation	54,000	140,000

Intangible assets
Copyrights	$ 71,000	
Less accumulated amortization	60,000	11,000

Total assets......................... $416,000

LIABILITIES AND OWNERS' EQUITY

Current liabilities
Account payable	$ 28,000	
Wages payable	3,000	
Note payable	10,000	$ 41,000

Long-term liabilities
Note payable (due 1999)...... 15,000

Owners' equity
Common stock ($10 par)	$140,000	
Additional paid-in capital	165,000	
Retained earnings	55,000	360,000

Total liabilities and owners'
equity............................. $416,000

*2. Calculation of financial ratios:

a. Current ratio: 2.0.

$$\frac{\text{Current assets (\$200,000)}}{\text{Current liabilities (\$100,000)}} = 2.0$$

b. Quick ratio: 1.1.

$$\frac{\text{Cash (\$15,700) + Trading securities (\$9,300) + Net accounts receivable (\$85,000)}}{\text{Current liabilities (\$100,000)}} = 1.1$$

c. Defensive interval ratio: 73.1 days.

$$\frac{\text{Cash (\$15,700) + Trading securities (\$9,300) + Net accounts receivable (\$85,000)}}{\begin{array}{c}\text{[Cost of goods sold (\$360,000) + Administrative expenses (\$104,000) +}\\ \text{Selling expenses (\$65,000) + Interest expense (\$12,000) +}\\ \text{Income taxes exclusive of deferred taxes (\$8,000)]} \div 365 \text{ days}\end{array}} = 73.1$$

d. Inventory turnover ratio: 4.5 times per year, or every 81.1 days.

$$\frac{\text{Cost of goods sold (\$360,000)}}{\text{[Beginning inventory (\$70,000) + Ending inventory (\$90,000)]} \div 2} = 4.5$$

e. Accounts receivable turnover ratio: 8.0 times per year, or every 45.6 days.

$$\frac{\text{Net sales (\$600,000)}}{\text{[Beginning net accounts receivable (\$65,000) + Ending net accounts receivable (\$85,000)]} \div 2} = 8.0$$

f. Total assets turnover ratio: 1.2 times per year, or every 304.2 days.

$$\frac{\text{Net sales (\$600,000)}}{[\text{Beginning total assets (\$480,000)} + \text{Ending total assets (\$500,000)}] \div 2} = 1.2$$

g. Total liabilities to total assets ratio: .44.

$$\frac{\text{Total liabilities (\$220,000)}}{\text{Total assets (\$500,000)}} = .44$$

h. Times interest earned ratio: 3.5 times.

$$\frac{\text{Income before taxes (\$30,000)} + \text{Interest expense (\$12,000)}}{\text{Interest expense (\$12,000)}} = 3.5$$

i. Profit margin on sales: .03.

$$\frac{\text{Net income (\$18,000)}}{\text{Net sales (\$600,000)}} = .03$$

j. Net operating margin: .068.

$$\frac{\substack{\text{Net sales (\$600,000)} - [\text{Cost of goods sold (\$360,000)} + \text{Administrative expenses (\$104,000)} + \\ \text{Selling expenses (\$65,000)} + \text{Depreciation expense (\$30,000)}]}}{\text{Net sales (\$600,000)}} = .068$$

k. Return on total assets: .037 or .051.

$$\frac{\text{Net income (\$18,000)}}{[\text{Beginning total assets (\$480,000)} + \text{Ending total assets (\$500,000)}] \div 2} = .037$$

or alternatively

$$\frac{\text{Net income (\$18,000)} + \text{Interest expense (\$12,000)} \times [1 - \text{Tax rate (.40)}]}{[\text{Beginning total assets (\$480,000)} + \text{Ending total assets (\$500,000)}] \div 2} = .051$$

l. Return on stockholders' equity: .062.

$$\frac{\text{Net income (\$18,000)} - \text{Preferred dividends (\$2,800)}}{\substack{[\text{Beginning common stockholders' equity (\$242,100)} + \\ \text{Ending common stockholders' equity (\$245,000)}] \div 2}} = .062$$

m. Price-earnings ratio: 10.5.

$$\frac{\text{Market price per common share (\$16.00)}}{\text{Earnings per common share (\$1.52)}} = 10.5$$

n. Dividend yield: .077.

$$\frac{\text{Dividends per common share (\$1.23)}}{\text{Market price per common share (\$16.00)}} = .077$$

o. Dividend payout ratio: .809.

$$\frac{\text{Common cash dividends (\$12,300)}}{\text{Net income (\$18,000)} - \text{Preferred dividends (\$2,800)}} = .809$$

p. Book value per share: $24.15.

$$\frac{\text{Total stockholders' equity (\$280,000)} - \text{Preferred stockholders' claims (\$38,500, liquidation value)}}{\text{Number of common shares (10,000)}} = \$24.15$$

6 THE STATEMENT OF CASH FLOWS

After reading Chapter 6 and completing the questions, cases, exercises, and problems from the text chapter, you should be able to:

1. Describe the historical background and usefulness of the statement of cash flows.
2. Distinguish a company's operating activities, investing activities, and financing activities.
3. Determine the transactions and other events that caused inflows or outflows of cash during the period by analyzing any available income statement data, any additional information provided,

and the changes in noncash balance sheet accounts.
4. Calculate cash flows from operating activities during the period under both the direct approach and the indirect approach.
5. Prepare a statement of cash flows, at a principles level, in accordance with the standards specified by *Statement No. 95*.
6. Prepare a supplementary schedule to disclose investing and financing activities not involving cash flows.

CHAPTER REVIEW

Introduction

1. The *statement of cash flows* is a financial statement that complements the income statement, balance sheet, and other disclosures by providing information about the cash inflows and the cash outflows during the accounting period from *operating activities, investing activities,* and *financing activities.* The information provided in the statement about the cash flows resulting from these activities helps users to assess a company's present and future cash flows. The historical background, usefulness, and preparation of the statement of cash flows, at a principles level, are described in this

chapter review. The statement of cash flows is also discussed in Chapter 21 to illustrate the effects of intermediate-level transactions and the use of a worksheet.

Historical Background

2. Statement of changes in financial position. Most companies began to include a funds flow statement in their annual reports during the 1960s, and in 1971 the APB issued *Opinion No. 19* to require a funds flow statement titled "The Statement of Changes in Financial Position." *Opinion No. 19* also contained guidelines regarding the form and content of the statement of changes in financial position.

3. Statement of cash flows. Since *Opinion No. 19* was issued, the significance of information about a company's cash flows has increasingly been recognized. Indeed, in *Statement of Concepts No. 5,* the FASB stated that a full set of financial statements should report the cash flows for the period. Moreover, certain problems were identified with the application of *Opinion No. 19* in practice, including the ambiguity of terms such as *funds,* the lack of comparability arising from diversity in the focus of the statement of changes in financial position (cash, cash and cash equivalents, net current monetary assets, or working capital), differences in formats of the statement (sources and uses format or activity format), variations in classification of funds flows, and the reporting of net changes in amounts of assets and liabilities rather than funds flows.

4. As a result of the increasing importance placed on cash flow information and in an attempt to reduce variations in practice, in 1987 the FASB issued *Statement No. 95.* This *Statement,* as amended by *Statements No. 102* and *104,* supersedes *Opinion No. 19* and requires, as a primary financial statement, a statement of cash flows instead of the statement of changes in financial position whenever financial statements purporting to present both financial position (balance sheet) and results of operations (statement of income and retained earnings) are issued.

5. Most multinational corporations report some type of funds or cash flow statement, often on a voluntary basis. A funds or cash flow statement, however, is not required in all countries. The International Accounting Standards Committee, though, has issued *International Accounting Standard 7* (revised), titled "Cash Flow Statements."

Overview

6. Activity format. *Statement No. 95* states that the primary purpose of the statement of cash flows is to provide information about a company's cash receipts and cash payments during a period. It states further that cash receipts and cash payments must be classified in the statement of cash flows by operating, investing, and financing activities. Under this reporting format (called an *activity format*), the statement of cash flows consists of three sections—operating, investing, and financing—each reporting the cash receipts, cash payments, and net cash provided or used by that activity during the period. The aggregate effect of the net cash provided or used by these activities should equal the net increase or decrease in cash and cash equivalents during the period. This net amount must be reported at the

bottom of the statement of cash flows as an addition to or deduction from the beginning cash and cash equivalents balance to reconcile to the ending balance.

7. Cash and cash equivalents. *Statement No. 95* states that cash purchases and sales of *cash equivalents* (defined as short-term highly liquid investments that are readily convertible to known amounts of cash generally within original maturities of three months or less, such as treasury bills, commercial paper, and money-market funds) should not be reported in the statement of cash flows, because such activities are part of a company's cash management rather than its operating, investing, and financing activities. Instead, if there are cash equivalents, the net increase or decrease in cash and cash equivalents in the period must be reported as one amount in the reconciliation of the beginning and ending cash and cash equivalents balances at the bottom of the statement. Thus, in such circumstances, the statement of cash flows should report those transactions and other events that caused cash and cash equivalents to increase or decrease during the period.

Usefulness

8. The statement of cash flows reports useful information about the following company activities and characteristics:

a. **Cash provided or used by operating activities.** Net income or loss reported in the income statement is useful in evaluating a company's operating performance for a period. Many revenues and expenses that are included in the determination of net income or loss, however, result from accruals and cost allocations that do not affect cash during that period. The statement of cash flows provides useful information about the cash inflows and cash outflows related to a company's operating activities during the period.

b. **Cash provided or used by investing activities.** The statement of cash flows reports useful information about a company's investing activities, such as the amount of cash used to modernize, expand, or replace plant assets or the amount of cash provided by the sale of long-term investments during the period.

c. **Cash provided or used by financing activities.** The statement of cash flows reports useful information about a company's financing activities, such as the amount of cash provided or used by the issuance or retirement of long-term debt or equity securities during the period.

d. **The "quality" of earnings.** The statement of cash flows reports information that may be useful in evaluating the quality of earnings, which refers to the correlation between income and cash flows. Under this view, the quality of earnings is assessed by comparing the net income or loss, as reported in the income statement, with the net cash provided or used by operating activities, as reported in the statement of cash flows.

e. **Evaluation of solvency, liquidity, and financial flexibility.** The statement of cash flows reports information that is useful in evaluating a company's ability to pay its maturing debt (*solvency*); its ability to generate cash for specific purposes (*liquidity*); and its ability to adapt during a period of financial adversity, to obtain financing, to liquidate assets for cash, and to modify operations to increase short-term cash inflows (*financial flexibility*).

Thus the statement of cash flows complements the income statement by disclosing the amount of cash provided or used by a company's operating activities. It also complements the balance sheet by disclosing the cash transactions that cause changes in a company's assets, liabilities, and stockholders' equity.

9. The statement of cash flows satisfies many of the qualitative characteristics discussed in Chapter 2. In addition to *relevance,* which underlies the five uses just discussed, the information reported in the statement of cash flows is *reliable,* enhances *comparability* among companies, and is readily *understandable.*

Preparation

10. The procedures for preparing the statement of cash flows involve the following steps:

a. Calculating, as a "control number," the net increase or decrease in cash and cash equivalents during the accounting period.

b. Determining the specific transactions and other events that caused inflows or outflows of cash during the period by analyzing any available income statement data, any additional information provided, and the changes in *noncash* balance sheet accounts that have not been explained or reconciled by the other analyses.

c. Preparing the statement of cash flows for the period on the basis of the preceding analyses

and in accordance with the standards specified by *Statement No. 95.*

Of these steps, it is particularly important to remember that the change in each noncash balance sheet account ultimately should be analyzed and reconciled, since the net change (increase or decrease) in the cash account must equal the net change (increase or decrease) in the noncash accounts.

11. Cash flows from operating activities. *Operating activities* are all transactions and other events that are not investing or financing activities. Operating activities generally involve producing and delivering goods and providing services. Cash flows from operating activities are generally the cash effects of transactions and other events that are included in the determination of net income. Cash inflows from operating activities include cash receipts from sales of goods or services and from returns on loans and other debt securities for interest and on equity securities for dividends. Cash outflows for operating activities include cash payments to suppliers for goods and services, to employees for services, to creditors for interest, and to governmental authorities for taxes. *Statement No. 95* requires that *cash flows from operating activities* during the period be disclosed in the statement of cash flows. Furthermore, although it permits cash flows from operating activities to be determined and reported by either a direct approach or an indirect approach, *Statement No. 95* encourages companies to report cash flows from operating activities by the direct approach within the statement of cash flows and to disclose a reconciliation of net income and net cash provided by operating activities by the indirect approach in a supplementary schedule to the statement.

12. Under the *direct approach,* net cash provided by operating activities is determined and reported as the difference between the operating cash receipts and the operating cash payments during the period. To apply this approach, the revenues and expenses reported on the accrual-basis income statement are analyzed individually to determine their effects on cash during the period, in essence, to convert the accrual-basis amounts to a cash basis. There are three possible situations. First, the effect of the revenue or expense on cash during the period may equal the accrual-basis amount, and thus the accrual-basis amount is included in the determination of net cash provided by operating activities. Revenues that represent cash receipts and expenses that represent cash payments during the period exemplify this situation. Second, the effect of the revenue or expense on cash during the period may differ from the accrual-basis amount, and thus the accrual-basis amount, adjusted to a cash basis, is included in the determination of net cash provided by operating activities. The net changes in noncash accounts that are related to the company's operating activities, for example, are added to or deducted from the corresponding revenues and expenses to convert the accrual-basis amounts to a cash basis. The more common adjustments include the following: (*a*) an increase or a decrease in accounts receivables related to sales of merchandise is deducted from or added to the related sales revenue reported on the income statement because the amount of cash collections from customers during the period is less or greater than the sales revenue, (*b*) an increase or a decrease in unearned sales revenue is added to or deducted from the related sales revenue reported on the income statement because the amount of cash collections from customers during the period is greater or less than the sales revenue, (*c*) an increase or a decrease in inventory is added to or deducted from cost of goods sold reported on the income statement because the amount of purchases from merchandise suppliers during the period is greater or less than the cost of goods sold, (*d*) an increase or a decrease in payables related to purchases of merchandise is deducted from or added to cost of goods sold reported on the income statement because the amount of cash payments to merchandise suppliers during the period is less or greater than the purchases, (*e*) an increase or a decrease in a liability is deducted from or added to the related expense reported on the income statement because the amount of cash payments during the period is less or greater than the expense, and (*f*) an increase or a decrease in a prepaid expense is added to or deducted from the related expense reported on the income statement because the amount of cash payments during the period is greater or less than the expense. Third, the revenue or expense may have no effect on cash during the period or may not be related to operating activities, and thus the accrual-basis amount is excluded from the determination of net cash provided by operating activities. Depreciation expense is a good example of this situation.

13. Under the *indirect approach,* net cash provided by operating activities is determined and reported by adjusting net income for the effects of all deferrals and accruals of operating cash flows and for the effects of all items whose cash effects are investing or financing cash flows, in essence, to convert the accrual-basis net income to a cash basis. The net changes in noncash accounts that are related to the company's operating activities, for example, are added to or deducted from net income. The more common adjustments include the following: (*a*) an increase or a decrease in receivables related to sales of merchandise is deducted from or added to net income because the related sales revenue reported on the income statement is greater or less than the amount of cash collections from customers during

the period, (*b*) an increase or a decrease in unearned sales revenue is added to or deducted from net income because the related sales revenue reported on the income statement is less or greater than the amount of cash collections from customers during the period, (*c*) an increase or a decrease in inventory is deducted from or added to net income because cost of goods sold reported on the income statement is less or greater than purchases during the period, (*d*) an increase or a decrease in payables related to purchases of merchandise is added to or deducted from net income because purchases are greater or less than the amount of cash payments to merchandise suppliers during the period, (*e*) an increase or a decrease in a liability is added to or deducted from net income because the related expense reported on the income statement is greater or less than the amount of cash payments during the period, and (*f*) an increase or a decrease in a prepaid expense is deducted from or added to net income because the related expense reported on the income statement is less or greater than the amount of cash payments during the period. As another example, depreciation expense is added to net income because it decreases net income but does not result in an outflow of cash during the period.

14. Cash flows from investing and financing activities. *Investing activities* include lending money and collecting amounts loaned and purchasing and selling debt or equity securities and property, plant, and equipment and other productive assets. Cash inflows from investing activities are receipts from collections or sales of loans and of debt securities of other companies (other than cash equivalents and trading securities); receipts from sales or returns of investments in equity securities of other companies (other than trading securities); and receipts from sales of property, plant, and equipment and other productive assets. Cash outflows for investing activities are disbursements for loans made by the company; payments to acquire debt securities of other companies (other than cash equivalents and trading securities); payments to acquire equity securities of other companies (other than trading securities); and payments to acquire property, plant, and equipment and other productive assets. *Financing activities* include obtaining resources from owners and providing them with a return on their investment (through dividends) and a return of their investment, borrowing money and repaying amounts borrowed, and obtaining and paying for other resources obtained from creditors on long-term credit. Cash inflows from financing activities are proceeds from issuance of equity securities; proceeds from issuance of bonds, mortgages, and notes; and proceeds from other short-term or long-term borrowing. Cash outflows for financing activities are payments of dividends or other distributions to owners (including outlays to acquire the company's equity securities), repayments of amounts borrowed, and other principal payments to creditors who have extended long-term credit. *Statement No. 95* requires that the gross amounts of cash inflows and cash outflows resulting from investing and financing activities be reported separately in the corresponding section of the statement of cash flows. For example, outlays for acquisitions and proceeds from sales of property, plant, and equipment must be reported separately in the cash flows from investing activities section of the statement; proceeds from borrowings and outlays for repayments of debt must be reported separately in the cash flows from financing activities section; and proceeds from issuing and outlays to acquire the company's equity securities must be reported separately in the cash flows from financing activities section.

15. The occurrence of some investing activities and financing activities may be determined directly by analyzing any additional information provided. For example, information provided may indicate that equity securities were acquired and formally retired and plant assets were sold during the period. As described earlier, the outlays to acquire the equity securities should be presented in the cash flows from financing activities section of the statement, and the proceeds from the sale of the plant assets should be presented in the cash flows from investing activities section. Additionally, under the direct approach, the gain or loss on the sale of the plant assets should be excluded from the determination of net cash provided by operating activities, since it neither measures the cash provided or used by the sale nor relates to operating activities. Similarly, under the indirect approach, the gain or loss on the sale of the plant assets should be deducted from or added to net income to determine net cash provided by operating activities for the same two reasons just cited.

16. Finally, the change in each noncash balance sheet account should be analyzed and reconciled to determine that all transactions and other events that affect cash during the period have been identified. The changes in most noncash accounts should already be reconciled as a result of the analyses of the available income statement data and any additional information provided. Information about the causes of the changes in some noncash accounts, however, may not be provided. In these circumstances, it may be necessary to make an inference about the types of transactions that caused the unexplained changes in noncash accounts. Income statement data and additional information may indicate, for example, that plant assets were sold during the period, yet an analysis of the change in the plant assets account may indicate that the account decreased by an amount less than the book value of the assets sold, or perhaps even increased. In either case, it can be inferred that the unexplained reconciling difference represents outlays for the purchase of plant assets, which should be presented in the cash flows from investing activities section of the statement.

17. Noncash investing and financing activities. *Statement No. 95* requires that investing and financing activities not involving cash receipts or cash payments in the period be disclosed separately in either a narrative or a supplementary schedule to the statement of cash flows, so that information is provided about all investing and financing activities. It requires further that the cash and noncash aspects of transactions involving similar items be clearly identified. Noncash investing and financing activities include the acquisition of plant assets by the issuance of short-term or long-term debt or equity securities, the retirement of long-term debt by the issuance of equity securities or other long-term debt or by the transferral of noncash assets, the conversion of long-term debt into equity securities, and the conversion of preferred stock into common stock.

SELF-STUDY LEARNING

Key Terms and Concepts

Provide the appropriate term or terms to complete each of the following statements:

1. *APB Opinion No. 19* required companies to report a funds flow statement titled a(n) ___STATEMENT OF ∆ IN FINANCIAL POSITION___

2. The basic financial statement that provides information about the cash inflows and cash outflows resulting from various activities of the company during the accounting period is called the ___STATEMENT OF CASH FLOWS___

3. Short-term, highly liquid investments that are readily convertible to known amounts of cash, such as treasury bills, commercial paper, and money-market funds, are called ___CASH EQUIVALENTS___.

4. ___OPERATING___ activities generally involve producing and delivering goods and providing services.

5. ___INVESTING___ activities include lending money and collecting amounts loaned and purchasing and selling debt or equity securities and property, plant, and equipment and other productive assets.

6. ___FINANCING___ activities include obtaining resources from owners and providing them with a return on their investment (through dividends) and a return of their investment, borrowing money and repaying amounts borrowed, and obtaining and paying for other resources obtained from creditors on long-term credit.

7. To prepare the statement of cash flows, the transactions and other events that caused inflows or outflows of cash during the accounting period are determined by analyzing three types of data: ___ANY AVAILABLE___ _____, and ___AIN NONCASH BALANCE SHEET___

8. The net amount of funds generated by earnings activities during the period that is reported in the statement of cash flows is commonly referred to as ___NET CASH PROVIDED BY OPER___

9. Under the ___DIRECT___ approach, net cash provided by operating activities is determined and reported as the difference between the operating cash receipts and the operating cash payments during the period.

10. Under the ___INDIRECT___ approach, net cash provided by operating activities is determined and reported by adjusting net income to remove the effects of all deferrals of past operating cash flows and all accruals of expected future operating cash flows and the effects of all items whose cash effects are investing or financing cash flows.

True-False

Indicate by circling the appropriate response whether each of the following statements is true (T) or false (F):

T (F) 1. The primary purpose of the statement of cash flows is to provide information about the investing and financing activities of a company during a period.

(T) F 2. Cash receipts and cash payments must be classified in the statement of cash flows by operating, investing, and financing activities.

T (F) 3. Payments of accounts payable arising from acquisitions of inventory should be reported in the statement of cash flows as cash outflows for financing activities.

T (F) 4. Payments of dividends on the company's equity securities should be included in the determination of net cash provided by operating activities.

T (F) 5. Payments to creditors for interest should be reported in the statement of cash flows as cash outflows for financing activities.

(T) F 6. Proceeds from the issuance of the company's equity securities should be reported in the statement of cash flows as cash inflows from financing activities.

(T) F 7. Receipts from sale of property, plant, and equipment should be reported in the statement of cash flows as cash inflows from investing activities.

(T) F 8. Depreciation expense is excluded from the determination of net cash provided by operating activities under the direct approach and is added to net income to determine net cash provided by operating activities under the indirect approach, because it decreases net income but has no effect on cash during the period.

T (F) 9. When net cash provided by operating activities is determined by the direct approach, an increase in salaries payable should be added to salaries expense.

T Ⓕ 10. When the direct approach is used to determine net cash provided by operating activities, a decrease in inventory should be deducted from cost of goods sold, since the amount purchased during the period is less than the cost of goods sold reported on the income statement.

T Ⓕ 11. Under the direct approach of determining net cash provided by operating activities, an increase in unearned sales revenue should be deducted from sales revenue.

T Ⓕ 12. When net cash provided by operating activities is determined by the indirect approach, an increase in accounts payable should be deducted from net income.

T Ⓕ 13. Companies are encouraged to determine and report cash flows from operating activities within the body of the statement of cash flows by the indirect approach.

Ⓣ F 14. In preparing a statement of cash flows, the changes in each noncash balance sheet account should be analyzed and reconciled to determine that all transactions and other events that affect cash during the period have been identified.

Ⓣ F 15. Proceeds from the issuance and outlays for the repayment of long-term debt should be reported separately in the cash flows from financing activities section of the statement of cash flows.

T Ⓕ 16. Acquisition of plant assets by issuing equity securities should be reported in the statement of cash flows as both an investing activity and a financing activity.

Ⓣ F 17. Information about investing and financing activities not involving cash receipts or cash payments in the period should be disclosed separately in either a narrative or a supplementary schedule to the statement of cash flows.

Ⓣ F 18. Proceeds from the issuance of short-term notes payable arising from nonoperating activities should be reported in the statement of cash flows as cash inflows from financing activities.

Ⓣ F 19. The net increase or decrease in cash and cash equivalents during the period should be reported at the bottom of the statement of cash flows as an addition to or deduction from the beginning balance to reconcile to the ending balance.

T Ⓕ 20. U.S. companies are required to report a statement of cash flows whenever they issue either a balance sheet or a statement of income and retained earnings.

Multiple Choice

Select the best response for each of the following items, and circle the corresponding letter:

1. Which of the following cash flows should *not* be included in the determination of net cash provided by operating activities?

   a. Receipts from returns on loans for interest and on equity securities for dividends.
   Ⓑ Payments of dividends.
   c. Payments to suppliers for goods and services.
   d. Payments to governmental authorities for taxes.

2. Which of the following amounts should be excluded from the determination of net cash provided by operating activities under the direct approach?

   a. Interest revenue from short-term, highly liquid investments.
   b. Salaries expense minus net increase in salaries payable.
   Ⓒ Depreciation expense.
   d. Interest expense.

3. Which of the following should be deducted from the sales revenue reported on the income statement to determine the amount of cash collections from customers during the period?

   a. An increase in accounts receivable.
   b. A decrease in unearned sales revenue.
   Ⓒ Both a and b.
   d. Neither a nor b.

4. When net cash provided by operating activities is determined and reported under the indirect approach, the deductions from net income should include:

   a. A decrease in accounts receivable.
   Ⓑ Gains on sales of property, plant, and equipment.
   c. An increase in short-term bank loans.
   d. Depreciation expense.

5. The sale of a plant asset at a gain should be reported in the statement of cash flows as follows:

   a. The book value of the asset sold should be reported in the cash flows from the investing activities section.

b. The book value of the asset sold should be reported in the cash flows from investing activities section and the gain on the sale should be reported as part of net cash provided by operating activities.
c. The proceeds from the sale should be reported in the cash flows from investing activities section.
d. The proceeds from the sale should be reported in the cash flows from investing activities section, and the gain on the sale should be reported as a part of net cash provided by operating activities.

6. Which of the following cash outflows should be reported in the statement of cash flows as cash outflows for investing activities?

a. Payments to acquire property, plant, and equipment.
b. Payments to acquire debt securities of other companies as short-term, highly liquid investments that are considered to be cash equivalents.
c. Payments of dividends.
d. Repayments of amounts borrowed.

7. Which of the following cash inflows should be reported in the statement of cash flows as cash inflows from financing activities?

a. Receipts from collections of loans.
b. Receipts from sale of debt or equity securities of other companies.
c. Proceeds from the issuance of equity securities.
d. Receipts from sale of property, plant, and equipment.

8. The proceeds from the issuance and the outlays for the acquisition of the company's equity securities should be reported in the statement of cash flows as follows:

a. A net increase in the equity securities should be reported in the cash flows from financing activities section.
b. A net decrease in the equity securities should be reported in the cash flows from investing activities section.
c. The proceeds from the issuance and the outlays for the acquisition of the equity securities should be reported separately in the cash flows from financing activities section.
d. The proceeds from the issuance of the equity securities should be reported in the cash flows from financing activities section, and the outlays for the acquisition of the equity securities should be reported in the cash flows from investing activities section.

9. Noncash investing and financing activities should be:

a. Reported in the body of the statement of cash flows.
b. Reported in either a narrative or supplementary schedule to the statement of cash flows.
c. Both a and b.
d. Neither a nor b.

10. Cash receipts from sales and cash payments for purchases of short-term, highly liquid investments that are considered to be cash equivalents should be reported in the statement of cash flows as follows:

a. The net increase or decrease in the short-term, highly liquid investments should be reported as part of the net increase or decrease in cash and cash equivalents in the period.
b. The net increase or decrease in the short-term, highly liquid investments should be included in the determination of cash provided by operating activities.
c. The net increase or decrease in the short-term, highly liquid investments should be reported in the cash flows from investing activities section.
d. The cash receipts from sales and the cash payments for purchases of short-term, highly liquid investments should be reported separately in the cash flows from investing activities section.

Extended Problem

Presented here are an income statement, comparative balance sheets, and additional information for SOC Company.

SOC Company
INCOME STATEMENT
FOR THE YEAR ENDED DECEMBER 31, 1995

Sales	$590,000
Gain on sale of equipment	5,000
	$595,000
Cost of goods sold	$400,000
Depreciation expense	40,000
Other operating expenses	95,000
Interest expense	10,000
	$545,000
Income before income taxes	$ 50,000
Income taxes	20,000
Net income	$ 30,000

SOC Company
BALANCE SHEET
AS OF DECEMBER 31, 1995, AND DECEMBER 31, 1994

	DECEMBER 31, 1995	DECEMBER 31, 1994
Cash	$ 32,000	$ 15,000
Accounts receivable	72,000	80,000
Inventories	148,000	135,000
Prepaid expenses	11,000	10,000
Total current assets	$ 263,000	$ 240,000
Land	$ 92,000	$ 80,000
Plant and equipment	440,000	400,000
Accumulated depreciation	(150,000)	(120,000)
	$ 382,000	$ 360,000
Total assets	$ 645,000	$ 600,000
Accounts payable	$ 130,000	$ 110,000
Salaries payable	2,000	5,000
Short-term note payable	40,000	10,000
Unearned sales revenue	18,000	20,000
Total current liabilities	$ 190,000	$ 145,000
Long-term debt (10%)	50,000	100,000
Total liabilities	$ 240,000	$ 245,000
Common stock ($10 par)	$ 290,000	$ 260,000
Contributed capital in excess of par—common	36,000	30,000
Retained earnings	79,000	65,000
Total stockholders' equity	$ 405,000	$ 355,000
Total liabilities and stockholders' equity	$ 645,000	$ 600,000

Additional information for the year ended December 31, 1995:

a. Land with a fair value of $12,000 was acquired by issuing 1,000 shares of common stock.
b. Equipment with an original cost of $20,000 and accumulated depreciation of $10,000 was sold for $15,000, and equipment was purchased for $60,000.
c. A six-month note payable was issued to a bank on December 31, 1995, for $40,000, and a one-year note payable was repaid to a bank on January 1, 1995, at $10,000.
d. $50,000 of the long-term debt was repaid on December 31, 1995.
e. 2,000 shares of common stock were issued for $24,000.

f. Cash dividends of $16,000 were declared and paid.

REQUIRED

a. Prepare a schedule that reconciles the income statement and net cash provided by operating activities for 1995 by the direct approach.
b. Prepare a schedule that reconciles net income and net cash provided by operating activities for 1995 by the indirect approach.
c. Prepare a statement of cash flows for 1995, reporting cash flows from operating activities by the direct approach and noncash investing and financing activities in a supplementary schedule.

COMMON ERRORS

The first statement in each "common error" listed here is *incorrect*. Each incorrect statement is followed by a corrected statement and an explanation.

1. The net changes in noncash balance sheet accounts that are related to investing and financing activities may be reported in the statement of cash flows. *Wrong*

The cash receipts and cash payments from investing and financing transactions that caused the changes in noncash balance sheet accounts should be reported separately in the statement of cash flows. *Right*

The change in a noncash balance sheet account may result from more than one type of transaction during the period. A company, for example, may both purchase and sell plant assets during the same period. Since these two transactions are different investing activities, the outlays for the purchase and the proceeds from the sale of plant assets must be reported separately in the cash flows from investing activities section of the statement. As a general rule, the proceeds and outlays related to the investing and financing transactions that caused the net changes in noncash accounts must be reported separately, rather than as net amounts, in the statement.

2. When a plant asset is sold during the period, the book value of the asset should be reported in the cash flows from investing activities section of the statement of cash flows. *Wrong*

When a plant asset is sold during the period, the proceeds from the sale should be reported in the cash flows from investing activities section of the statement of cash flows, and the gain or loss on the sale should be either excluded from the determination of net cash provided by operating activities, under the direct approach, or deducted from or added to net income to determine net cash provided by operating activities, under the indirect approach. *Right*

The proceeds from the sale of a plant asset should be reported in the cash flows from investing activities section of the statement of cash flows because this represents the amount of cash that was provided by the transaction. Additionally, since the gain or loss on the sale neither relates to operating activities nor measures the cash that was provided or used by the transaction, it should be either (*a*) excluded from the determination of net cash provided by operating activities, under the direct approach, or (*b*) deducted from or added to net income to determine net cash provided by operating activities, under the indirect approach.

3. All investing and financing transactions may be reported in the statement of cash flows. *Wrong*

Only investing and financing transactions that affect cash should be reported in the statement of cash flows; investing and financing transactions that do not affect cash should be reported in either a narrative or a supplementary schedule to the statement. *Right*

Some investing and financing transactions do not affect cash. Such transactions include the acquisition of plant assets by the issuance of short-term or long-term debt or equity securities, the retirement of long-term debt by the issuance of other long-term debt or equity securities or by the transferral of noncash assets, the conversion of long-term debt into equity securities, and the conversion of preferred stock into common stock. Since the primary purpose of the statement of cash flows is to provide information about the cash receipts and cash payments of a company during a period, such investing and financing transactions should not be reported in the body of the statement. Investing and financing transactions not involving cash receipts and cash payments in the period, however, should be disclosed in either a narrative or a supplementary schedule, so that the statement and related disclosures provide a comprehensive summary of the company's cash and noncash investing and financing activities during the period.

4. Cash purchases and sales of short-term, highly liquid investments that are considered to be cash equivalents should be reported separately in the cash flows from investing activities section of the state-ment of cash flows. *Wrong*

Cash purchases and sales of short-term, highly liquid investments that are considered to be cash equivalents should not be reported in the statement of cash flows; instead, the net increase or decrease in such temporary investments of idle cash should be reported as part of the net increase or decrease in cash and cash equivalents in the period. *Right*

Cash purchases and sales of short-term, highly liquid investments that are considered to be cash equivalents should not be reported in the statement of cash flows, because such activities are part of a company's cash management rather than its operating, investing, and financial activities. Instead, if there are cash equivalents, the cash and cash equivalents balances at the beginning and the end of the period should be aggregated and the net increase or decrease in the aggregate balance should be reported as one amount in the reconciliation of the beginning and ending cash and cash equivalents balances at the bottom of the statement.

ANSWERS

Key Terms and Concepts

1. statement of changes in financial position
2. statement of cash flows
3. cash equivalents
4. operating
5. investing
6. financing
7. any available income statement data, any additional information provided, the changes in noncash balance sheet accounts
8. net cash provided by operating activities
9. direct
10. indirect

True-False

1. F The primary purpose of the statement of cash flows is to provide information about the cash receipts and cash payments of a company during a period. A secondary purpose is to provide information about the investing and financing activities of the company during the period.
2. T
3. F Most repayments of amounts borrowed are financing activities. Payments of accounts payable arising from acquisitions of inventory, however, are operating activities that should be included in the determination of net cash provided by operating activities.
4. F Payments of dividends on the company's equity securities should be reported in the statement of cash flows as cash outflows for financing activities.
5. F Cash flows from operating activities are generally the cash effects of transactions and other events that are included in the determination of net income. Thus payments to creditors for interest should be included in the determination of net cash provided by operating activities.
6. T
7. T
8. T
9. F When net cash provided by operating activities is determined by the direct approach, an increase in salaries payable should be deducted from salaries expense, because it increases salaries expense but has no effect on cash during the period.
10. T

11. F Under the direct approach of determining net cash provided by operating activities, an increase in unearned sales revenue should be added to sales revenue because the cash collections from customers are greater than sales revenue earned during the period.
12. F When net cash provided by operating activities is determined by the indirect approach, an increase in accounts payable should be added to net income because the cash payments to merchandise supplies are less than the purchases during the period.
13. F Companies are encouraged to determine and report cash flows from operating activities within the body of the statement of cash flows by the direct approach instead of the indirect approach.
14. T
15. T
16. F Acquisition of plant assets by issuing equity securities is a noncash investing and financing activity that should be disclosed in either a narrative or a supplementary schedule to the statement of cash flows.
17. T
18. T
19. T
20. F U.S. companies are required to report a statement of cash flows whenever they issue both a balance sheet and a statement of income and retained earnings.

Multiple Choice

1. b	6. a
2. c	7. c
3. c	8. c
4. b	9. b
5. c	10. a

Extended Problem

a. Reconciliation of income statement and net cash provided by operating activities by the direct approach:

	ACCRUAL BASIS	ADJUSTMENTS AND EXCLUSIONS	CASH BASIS
Sales..	$590,000	$ { 8,000 / (2,000) }	$596,000
Gain on sale of equipment............................	5,000	(5,000)	-0-
Cost of goods sold.......................................	(400,000)	{ (13,000) / 20,000 }	(393,000)
Depreciation expense....................................	(40,000)	40,000	-0-
Other operating expenses..............................	(95,000)	{ (1,000) / (3,000) }	(99,000)
Interest expense...	(10,000)	-0-	(10,000)
Income taxes..	(20,000)	-0-	(20,000)
Net income..	$ 30,000		
Net cash provided by operating activities......................			$ 74,000

The decrease in accounts receivable ($8,000) is added to sales because the cash collections from customers are greater than the sales during the period. The decrease in unearned sales revenue ($2,000) is deducted from sales because the cash collections from customers are less than sales during the period. The gain on the sale of equipment ($5,000) is excluded because it neither measures the cash provided by the sale nor relates to operations. The increase in inventories ($13,000) is added to cost of goods sold because the purchases are greater than the cost of goods sold during the period. The increase in accounts payable ($20,000) is deducted from cost of goods sold because the cash payments to suppliers are less than the purchases during the period. Depreciation expense ($40,000) is excluded because it does not require an outlay of cash during the period. The increase in prepaid expenses ($1,000) is added to other operating expenses because the cash payments are greater than the expense during the period. The decrease in salaries payable ($3,000) is added to other operating expenses because the cash payments to employees are greater than the salaries expense during the period.

b. Reconciliation of net income and net cash provided by operating activities by the indirect approach:

Net income	$ 30,000
Adjustments to reconcile net income to net cash provided by operating activities:	
Gain on sale of equipment..	(5,000)
Depreciation expense	40,000
Decrease in accounts receivable..	8,000
Increase in inventories...	(13,000)
Increase in prepaid expenses..	(1,000)
Increase in accounts payable...	20,000
Decrease in salaries payable	(3,000)
Decrease in unearned sales revenue	(2,000)
Net cash provided by operating activities..	$ 74,000

c. Statement of cash flows and supplementary schedule for noncash investing and financing activities:

SOC Company
STATEMENT OF CASH FLOWS
FOR THE YEAR ENDED DECEMBER 31, 1995

Cash flows from operating activities:		
Cash received from customers	$ 596,000	
Cash paid to suppliers of merchandise	(393,000)	
Cash paid to employees and other suppliers	(99,000)	
Interest paid	(10,000)	
Income taxes paid	(20,000)	
Net cash provided by operating activities		$ 74,000
Cash flows from investing activities:		
Purchase of equipment	$ (60,000)	
Sale of equipment	15,000	
Net cash used by investing activities		(45,000)
Cash flows from financing activities:		
Issuance of common stock	$ 24,000	
Dividends paid	(16,000)	
Issuance of short-term note payable	40,000	
Repayment of short-term note payable	(10,000)	
Repayment of long-term debt	(50,000)	
Net cash provided by financing activities		(12,000)
Net increase in cash		$ 17,000
Cash at beginning of year		15,000
Cash at end of year		$ 32,000
Supplementary schedule of noncash investing and financing activities:		
Purchase of land by issuing common stock		$ 12,000

7 REVENUE RECOGNITION AND INCOME DETERMINATION

CHAPTER OBJECTIVES

After reading Chapter 7 and completing the questions, cases, exercises, and problems from the text chapter, you should be able to:

1. Understand the nature of revenue and the earnings process.
2. Define *recognition* and know the basic revenue recognition criteria.
3. Account for revenue recognized at the point of sale and its related problems.
4. Know the circumstances in which the percentage-of-completion method and the completed-contract method of accounting for long-term construction contracts are applicable, and understand how each method is applied.

5. Understand the basic accounting issues involved in the recognition of revenue from products that require aging.
6. Identify situations in which revenue should be recognized when production is complete, and know how to account for it.
7. Know when the installment sales method and cost-recovery method of revenue recognition are appropriate and the basic accounting under each method.
8. Describe the accounting issues and practices related to revenue recognition in selected specialized industries, such as service industries, franchises, and real estate.

CHAPTER REVIEW

Introduction

1. Revenue recognition and income determination are two of the most important areas of accounting, yet both are controversial. As Chapters 2 and 4 discuss, the income statement provides valuable information to users about future cash flows. Under traditional accrual accounting, income is determined by matching expenses against revenues, which are recognized according to the realization principle. Accrual accounting signals future cash flows more reliably than cash-basis accounting, but the numerous concepts underlying it are sometimes abused.

2. Revenue recognition is most often associated with the producing and/or selling of a product. An increasing number of companies, however, are engaging in an expanding array of services, for example, accounting and computer services, entertainment, health care, and recreation. A company that renders a service must recognize revenue from its service transactions. The basic issues of revenue recognition apply to service companies as well as manufacturing and merchandising companies. This

chapter reviews basic revenue recognition and income determination concepts, discusses revenue recognition at selected points in the earnings process, and considers special applications of the revenue recognition concepts. Consignment transactions are discussed in the Appendix.

Revenue Concepts

3. *Revenue* is the increase in net assets (assets less liabilities, or owners' equity) from the delivery or production of goods, the rendering of services, or other activities that constitute a company's major or primary operations. Revenue is measured at the fair value or cash equivalent price of the assets received. *Recognition* refers to the *timing* of revenue. In other words, recognition determines when revenue should be recognized (recorded) and reported in the income statement.

4. Conceptually, revenue is earned continuously during the entire earnings process. Moreover, during the earnings process, value (in the form of time, place, and form utility) is added to the cost of the productive inputs. The time diagram at the bottom of this page is representative of the earnings process for some but not all companies.

5. In practice, various units of a product are at various points in the earnings process at any one point in time. As one unit of product is completed, for example, another unit may be sold. Also, costs associated with the generation of revenue are not all the same. Some costs, such as cost of goods sold, benefit only one period, whereas others, such as the cost of depreciable assets, benefit several periods.

6. As previously stated, revenue could theoretically be recognized at any point during the earnings process. The realization concept helps the accountant to decide when revenue should be recognized. *Realization* refers, conceptually, to the occurrence of an event or events that reduce to an acceptable level the uncertainty about the effects of an earnings activity on net cash flow. Practically, revenue is recognized and reported in the income statement when (*a*) the amount and timing of revenue to be received are reasonably determinable, that is, the expected cash inflows (revenues) can objectively be determined; and (*b*) the earnings process is complete or virtually complete, that is, the expected cash outflows (expenses) are completed or known.

7. **Revenue recognition at point of sale.** The realization criteria are met at the point of sale for most manufacturing and merchandising firms. If the merchandise is exchanged for cash or a short-term receivable, there is little or no uncertainty about the amount or timing of revenue. Also, the earnings process is completed, since the merchandise is transferred to the buyer and the company has no further obligations to the buyer. In some situations, however, other factors arise to complicate revenue recognition at the point of sale. These factors are addressed in the following paragraphs.

8. *Credit sales* should be recorded net of any trade and sales discounts and at the present value of the amount of cash to be received, if the cash inflows are to be received over an extended period of time, that is, over one year. In addition, provision for uncollectible accounts receivable should be made in order (*a*) to reduce revenue for any sales estimated to be uncollectible and (*b*) to reduce accounts receivable to the amount expected to be collectible (or to their net realizable value). The estimation of uncollectible accounts receivable is discussed at length in Chapter 8.

9. To achieve proper matching of revenue and expense, accrual accounting requires the accrual or recognition of any estimable costs that may be incurred after the point of sale. These costs should be recorded at the time of the sale or at the end of the accounting period in which the sale is made. To account for a *cost incurred after the point of sale,* such as a multiperiod warranty on a product sold, (*a*) debit expense (warranty expense, for example) and credit estimated expense obligation for an amount equal to the estimated amount of the cost to be incurred, and (*b*) debit estimated expense obligation and credit cash (or another appropriate asset account) for the actual amount of the cost incurred when the company fulfills its obligation (as by providing service on a warranty).

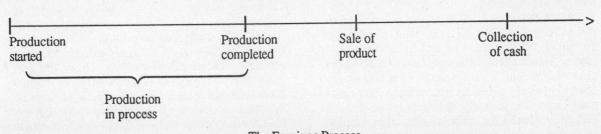

The Earnings Process

10. Customers often have *return privileges,* which permit them to return goods purchased in exchange for a refund, credit applied to the amounts owed on other purchases, or other goods or merchandise. The accounting issue is one of recognition of the returns and possible returns so that the reported revenue will more accurately measure the ultimate inflow of cash. The various alternatives of accounting for sales returns are discussed in the remainder of this section.

11. A company whose returns are infrequent, small in dollar amount, and close to the point of sale need only recognize the returns as they occur with an entry of a debit to sales returns and a credit to accounts receivable (or to cash if the goods were paid for) for the amount of the sales price of the goods returned. No accruals are necessary.

12. When returns are expected to be material in amount and to extend over a substantial period of time, an allowance for the expected sales returns should be established at the time of the sale or at the end of the period in which the sale is made. Assuming a perpetual inventory system and the allowance method for sales returns, recording a sale would require two entries: (*a*) debit accounts receivable and credit sales for the amount of the sale, and (*b*) debit cost of goods sold and credit inventory for the cost of the inventory sold. When goods are returned during the period, debit sales returns and credit accounts receivable for the sales price of the goods returned and debit inventory and credit cost of goods sold for the cost of the merchandise returned. At the end of the accounting period, adjusting entries must be made to provide for the expected return of merchandise: (*a*) debit sales returns and credit allowance for sales returns for the sales price of the merchandise sold in the current period but estimated to be returned, and (*b*) debit inventory and credit cost of goods sold for the cost of the merchandise estimated to be returned. If the periodic inventory system is used, cost of goods sold will automatically be adjusted for goods returned during the period of sale in the physical count of inventory. For goods expected to be returned after the period of sale, an additional entry would have to be made: debit inventory and credit cost of goods sold for an amount equal to the cost of the goods expected to be returned.

13. *Statement No. 48* stipulates that when the risk of returns is great, revenue (sales) should not be initially recognized. The FASB listed the following circumstances: (*a*) the lack of a fixed or determinable sales price, (*b*) the purchaser's lack of obligation to pay the seller if the merchandise cannot be sold or is stolen or damaged, (*c*) an obligation on the part of the seller to assist the purchaser in product resale, and (*d*) an inability to make a reasonable estimate of future returns. Under such circumstances, cash received from the customer should be treated as a deposit or unearned revenue until the two revenue recognition criteria are met.

14. Similar to manufacturing and retail firms, service companies can earn revenue at the point of sale. That is, revenue is recognized when the service is performed. This occurs in situations when the service is a single act or of a short-term nature.

15. Revenue recognition during production. Long-term projects, such as the construction of an office tower, an ocean liner, or a shopping complex, typically require several accounting periods to be completed. In addition, some service transactions may be of a long-term nature. Other products, such as timber and aged wine, must mature over time that spans several accounting periods. At issue is whether revenue and income should be recognized during the production process. This section discusses this issue in detail in regard to construction contracts and only briefly in regard to products that require several accounting periods to age or complete.

16. *Long-term construction contracts* can be accounted for by two acceptable methods: the percentage-of-completion method and the completed-contract method. The *percentage-of-completion method* is appropriate for construction contracts and production processes that extend over more than one accounting period and meet the following criteria: (*a*) the total contract price is known or determinable, (*b*) the total cost of the project is reasonably estimable, and (*c*) the current period's cost or percentage of completion is known or reasonably estimable. When these conditions exist, the revenue criteria are considered to be met, and revenue is recognized during the construction process.

17. Under the percentage-of-completion method, the contract price is compared with estimated total construction costs to determine the total estimated income from the project. It should be noted that estimated project income can vary over time as estimated construction costs change from original projections. At the end of each accounting period, the portion of estimated project income applicable to the period (assuming a profit) is found by multiplying the estimated project income by an estimated (contract) percentage of completion and subtracting any income recognized on the project in prior periods.

18. The estimated percentage of completion may be determined on the basis of costs or some physical measure of completion. Under the cost basis, the percentage of completion is determined by dividing the total actual costs incurred to date by the total up-to-date estimated construction costs. Construction costs include the costs of materials actually used in the construction (not materials purchased to be used in the future), labor, and overhead. When a physical measure, such as labor hours, is used, the percentage of completion is calculated by dividing actual physical units to date by estimated total physical units for the project.

19. Several new accounts are used to record the transactions related to the construction contract. *Construction in progress,* an inventory account, is debited for all costs incurred in the construction project. This account is also used in the periodic recognition of income: debit (*a*) construction in progress for the amount of profit earned for the period and (*b*) construction expenses for the amount of cost recognized that period and credit construction revenue for an amount equal to the two debits. Thus the balance in the construction-in-progress account equals the actual costs incurred plus income recognized to date. Assuming a profit on the project, the balance in the construction-in-progress account will equal the contract price [Total cost + Total income = Contract price (Revenue)] at the completion of the project.

20. Normally the contractor periodically bills the customer for a portion of the contract price until the entire contract price is billed. To record the billings, debit accounts receivable and credit *billings on construction contract* for the amount of the periodic billing. The construction-in-progress account (which usually has a debit balance) and the billings on construction contract account (which usually has a credit balance) are reported on the balance sheet as offsets. Since the contractor's operating cycle is the length of the construction period, the net amount is reported as a *current asset* on the balance sheet if the debits exceed the credits and as a *current liability* if the credits exceed the debits.

21. The *completed-contract method* is used for long-term construction contracts when the conditions for use of the percentage-of-completion method—that is, known contract price and reasonable estimation of costs and completion—are not met. Thus the methods are *not alternatives* for the same set of circumstances. The completed-contract method is used if the conditions do not allow the percentage-of-completion method.

22. Under the completed-contract method, income is recognized when the contract is completed. Usually this is also the time of the sale, since the purchaser normally receives title to the property at this time. The accounting entries for the completed-contract method are identical to those for the percentage-of-completion method *except* that no income is recognized during the construction period because all income is recognized when the project is completed. For proper balance sheet reporting, the balances in the construction-in-progress account and the billings on construction contract account are offset in the manner previously described.

23. When the construction project is completed, the related construction accounts must be closed. Under the percentage-of-completion method, the balances in the construction-in-progress account and the billings on construction contract account are equal. The accounts are closed by a debit to billings on construction contract and a credit to construction-in-progress for an amount equal to the contract price. Under the completed-contract method, in contrast, only costs have been debited to the construction-in-progress account and the total contract price credited to billings on construction contract. The difference between the two account balances represents income, which is recognized when the accounts are closed by debits to billings on construction contract for the contract price and construction expenses for an amount equal to the total costs incurred and by credits to construction in progress for the total costs incurred and construction revenue for the amount of the contract price.

24. Occasionally, a loss is incurred on a long-term contract. Losses should be *immediately recognized* regardless of the accounting method used. A loss peculiar to the percentage-of-completion method occurs when a profit is estimated for the project but changes in estimated costs cause too much profit to be recognized in an early period with a resultant loss in a later period. The loss is recognized by a debit to construction expenses for an amount equal to the costs incurred that period and credits to (*a*) construction-in-progress for the amount of loss to be recognized and (*b*) construction revenue for the difference between costs incurred that period and the amount of the recognized loss.

25. Another type of loss, one that occurs under both construction accounting methods, arises when total estimated costs exceed the contract price, resulting in a net loss on the contract. The entry to record the loss under the percentage-of-completion method would be a debit to construction expenses for an amount equal to the costs incurred that period and credits to (*a*) construction-in-progress for the amount of loss to be recognized and (*b*) construction revenue for the difference between the costs incurred that period and the amount of the recognized loss. Under the completed-contract method, the entry would be a debit to loss on long-term contract and a credit to construction in progress for an amount equal to the estimated loss (estimated total costs minus contract price). Each method results in the recognition of the loss when it is first indicated, which is consistent with the concept of conservatism.

26. Service companies that have obligations to perform over several periods, such as a health club, often recognize income using the *proportional-performance method* (similar to the percentage-of-completion method). On the other hand, some

service companies may perform many acts, but it is not until the final act that the earnings process is completed. For these companies, the *completed-performance method* (similar to the completed-contract method) is appropriate. Under this method, revenue is not recognized and costs are deferred until the service is completed. Upon completion, revenue is recognized and the deferred costs are matched with it to determine income.

27. Products that require continuous aging. Products such as timber and wine require time to mature or age properly. As such products become older, they increase in value, or, more technically, there is an *accretion* in value. So many uncertainties usually surround the product and its ultimate sale that income is not recognized on an accretion basis. Income can be recognized in accordance with the percentage-of-completion method if the following conditions are met: (*a*) a contract was entered into by a customer for a specific product before the aging process started, (*b*) future costs are reasonably estimable, and (*c*) the seller has no future obligations once the product is delivered.

28. Revenue recognition at completion of product. Revenue from such products as commodities (wheat, corn, beans, and so forth) and precious metals is recognized when the production is completed. When the grain is harvested or the metal mined, for example, the production process is completed. Recognition of revenue before the sale is justified in these cases for the following reasons: (*a*) the product is sold in a market at a reasonably assured selling price, (*b*) selling and distribution costs are insignificant and reasonably estimable, and (*c*) production (or completion of production) is deemed to be the critical event in the earnings process.

29. The accounting entries to recognize revenue at the completion of production are similar to those made when revenue is recognized at the point of sale, with one exception. The following additional entry is necessary to recognize revenue and expenses associated with the completed but unsold inventory: cost of goods sold is debited for the actual costs incurred to produce the product, inventory is debited for the product's *net realizable value* or *expected exit value* (sales price less estimated selling and distribution costs), selling expense is debited for the estimated selling costs, and revenue is credited for the anticipated sales price. When the inventory item is sold in a subsequent period (assuming all estimations become actual figures), accounts receivable is debited for the sales price of the product, inventory is credited for its net realizable value, and cash is credited for the amount of selling costs paid. It should be noted that once the product is sold, net income will be the same under both the sales and completion-of-production

methods. Because of the early recognition under the completion-of-production method, the only difference is the *timing* of net income, not the amount.

30. Revenue recognition during cash collection. When sales are made on credit and uncollectible accounts can be reasonably estimated, revenue is normally recognized at the point of sale because the net cash flow is reasonably certain. If, however, the net cash flow is uncertain, revenue should not be recognized until the cash is actually collected. Future cash flow may be uncertain, for example, if no basis exists for estimating uncollectible accounts. In this and similar situations, revenue should be recognized after the sale in accordance with either the installment method or the cost-recovery method.

31. The *installment method* is appropriate when the receivable is collected over a long period of time and there is no reasonable basis for estimating uncollectible accounts. Not every sale made on an installment or deferred payment basis, however, is appropriate for the installment method of revenue recognition—only those sales on which the company cannot estimate uncollectible accounts.

32. Under the installment method, the amount of gross profit (sales less cost of goods sold) on the sale is deferred and recognized as cash is collected. The amount of cash collected is multiplied by the gross profit percentage (gross profit divided by sales) to determine the gross profit recognized. Thus a portion (gross profit percentage) of each dollar collected represents gross profit, whereas the remainder represents cost recovery. It should be realized that various products have different gross profit rates and that a product's rate may change over time. Accordingly, adequate accounting records must be kept by product and by year.

33. General journal entries to record an installment sale (assuming perpetual inventory) are initially the same as those for a sale recorded at the point of sale, with the following exceptions: (*a*) *accounts receivable* is debited and *sales* is credited for the amount of the sale, and (*b*) *cost of goods sold* is debited and inventory is credited for the cost of merchandise sold on the installment basis. At the end of the period, (*a*) sales is debited for the amount of the installment sales for the period, *cost of goods sold* is credited for the cost of merchandise sold during the period, and *deferred gross profit* is credited for the amount of gross profit on the installment sales for the period; and (*b*) deferred gross profit is debited and *realized gross profit* is credited for the amount of gross profit calculated to be recognized from cash collections on installment sales during the period (cash collected times gross profit percentage), if any.

34. The realized gross profit account is disclosed on the income statement, whereas the deferred gross profit account (a contra asset account) is deducted from the accounts receivable account on the balance sheet. Accounts receivable are classified as current assets if their collection will occur within one year or during the operating cycle, whichever is longer; otherwise they are classified as noncurrent assets.

35. Two complications can arise when the installment method is used. First, the gross profit percentage usually varies from product to product and from year to year. This requires that accounting records be maintained for sales with different gross profit rates. Second, interest may be charged on long-term installment receivables. The effective interest method should be used to recognize periodic interest per installment payment.

36. Since uncollectible accounts receivable cannot be estimated, default on an accounts receivable usually results in a loss or gain equal to the difference between the fair value of the repossessed merchandise, if it is repossessed, and the net accounts receivable (accounts receivable balance due less any related unrecognized deferred gross profit). To record the repossession of merchandise and to write off the related receivable, debit *inventory of repossessed merchandise* for the fair value of the merchandise repossessed, debit deferred gross profit for the balance in that account related to the defaulted installment sale, and credit accounts receivable for the uncollected balance that is defaulted; the entry is balanced by a debit to *loss on repossession* (or a credit to *gain on repossession*).

37. In the *cost-recovery method,* income on credit sales is recognized only after sufficient cash has been received to recover the cost of merchandise sold. Once the cost has been recovered, every dollar subsequently collected is reported as income in the period in which it is collected. This method is used when the profitability of a venture or contract is highly uncertain.

38. If a service transaction is performed on account and no estimate of the receivables' uncollectibility can be made, the cost-recovery method should be used to recognize income for the service activity.

39. Although both the installment method and the cost-recovery method delay recognition of income until cash is received, the installment method is more popular. It is also generally accepted for tax purposes, whereas the cost-recovery method is not. Theoretically, the cost-recovery method is better because it appears to consider the fact that the methods of delaying recognition of income were devised, in part, because the collectibility of the receivable was uncertain. Given this uncertainty, it appears that better cash flow signals are given if income is recognized only after the cost has been recovered (cost-recovery method) rather than proportionately as cash is received (installment method).

Summary of Revenue Recognition Methods

40. Income may thus be recognized at any of several points in time. Although the point of sale most often meets the revenue recognition criteria, points before and after the point of sale are also acceptable in certain circumstances. It should be noted that regardless of the method used to recognize income, the total amount of revenue recognized does not vary; only the timing of the revenue recognition varies according to the method used.

41. The revenue recognition concepts also apply to gains and losses. A gain is usually recognized only when an exchange takes place. A loss, however, is sometimes recognized before an exchange involving an item occurs. If the market value of marketable securities is lower than their cost, for example, the loss is recognized even though the securities have not been disposed of.

Special Application of Revenue Recognition Concepts

42. Because of unique circumstances, some companies and several industries have had specialized accounting standards for revenue and income recognition promulgated by the accounting profession. This section provides an overview of selected revenue recognition practices.

43. Franchises. A *franchise* is an arrangement whereby the *franchisee* (buyer) receives from the *franchisor* (seller) the right to use the franchisor's name and sell its product or service in return for an *initial fee* related to the sale of the franchise and services performed and a *continuing periodic fee* for services provided on a continuing basis. Franchises are popular in the fast-food, motel, and auto rental businesses. Typical services provided by the franchisor include site selection, employee training, recordkeeping help, and advertising.

44. Since the franchisor receives continuing periodic fees (usually based on a percentage of the franchisee's sales), each such fee received represents revenue in the period in which it is received. The recognition of revenue from the initial fee, however, is more complicated. This fee often involves a series of services to be performed by the franchisor over an extended period of time, and the collectibility of the receivable associated with the initial fee is usually uncertain. *Statement No. 45* establishes the following two criteria for recognition of the initial fee: (*a*) the franchisor has substantially performed the services promised the franchisee, and

(b) the collectibility of the initial franchise fee is reasonably assured. These criteria are designed to prevent the once common practice of recording the entire initial fee when the contract is signed even if few or no services have been performed. This practice is referred to as "front-ending" the franchise income.

45. Typically, the initial franchise fee is paid by means of a small down payment with the balance in periodic installments. The credit portion of the entry to record the initial franchise fee varies with circumstances. If the revenue recognition criteria are met, for example, the franchisor records the agreement by debiting cash for the amount of the down payment, debiting *receivable from franchisee* for the balance due (installment payments), and crediting *franchise fee revenue* for the entire amount of the initial franchisee fee. If the revenue recognition criteria are not satisfied, however, *unearned franchise fee* is credited and recognized as revenue as the criteria are satisfied. If the services are performed but there is no basis for estimating the uncollectible receivable, *deferred franchise fee* is credited for the amount of the receivable. As cash is collected, either the installment sales method or the cost-recovery method can be used to recognize the franchise revenue. Since the continuing franchise fee accrues after the franchisee starts operations and is based on actual sales, it is recorded by a debit to cash (or accounts receivable) and a credit to service revenue for the calculated amount of the continuing fee.

46. Real estate. *Real estate sales* are characterized by relatively small down payments, an extended period to pay the balance due (and often uncertainty about the collectibility of the extended payments), and obligations of the seller to perform services after the sale. Because most real estate sales do not meet the revenue recognition criteria, revenue is not recognized until the services are performed, and even then the installment sales or cost-recovery method may be appropriate. Before revenue is recognized, all cash collections should be recorded as deposits or unearned revenue.

47. Retail sales of undeveloped land are similar to real estate sales except that the volume is greater, the down payment is smaller, the seller has more services to perform, the contract is usually unenforceable, and the purchaser may receive refund privileges. The FASB has established detailed guidelines to determine when revenue from retail land sales should be recognized. Basically, the accounting for cash collected before the revenue criteria are met and for revenue recognized after they are met is similar to that for real estate sales.

48. Barter transactions. In increasing numbers companies are engaging in *barter transactions*. These transactions involve exchanges of goods and/or services, so that revenue is received in the form of nonfinancial assets or of services rather than cash. Although no specific guidelines for barter transactions exist, it appears that revenue from a barter transaction could be recognized and measured at the exchange price established in the transaction (called the trading unit). Further guidelines will probably be forthcoming if the popularity of barter transactions continues.

49. Other industries that have had detailed revenue recognition standards established are insurance, record and music, cable television, and motion picture.

50. In summary, special economic and environmental circumstances have caused the accounting profession to issue specific standards that modify the basic revenue recognition criteria for some companies and industries. Nevertheless, all revenue recognition standards are designed to recognize revenue and income when uncertainty about the net cash flow effects of the service transaction or transactions has been reduced to an acceptable level.

Appendix

51. Appendix 7-1 discusses revenue recognition of consignment sales.

52. Consignment sales. *Consignment sales* involve two primary parties: a *consignor* (manufacturer or distributor), who transfers goods but retains the title to them, and a *consignee* (dealer), who sells the goods for a commission. The two principal parties have unique accounting and revenue recognition problems. The consignor, for example, does not recognize revenue until the consignee remits the proceeds from the sale of the consigned goods (less the consignee's commission). The consignor recognizes consignment revenue by debiting cash for the amount of the proceeds received, debiting commission expense for the amount of the agreed-upon commission, and crediting consignment sales for the total amount of the sale price charged by the consignee. The consignor must also reclassify inventory out on consignment in an *inventory on consignment* account and charge the cost of consigned goods sold to the *cost of consignment sales* account.

53. As the consignee sells the goods held on consignment, revenue equal to the stipulated commission is recognized. When consignment goods are sold, the consignee debits cash (or accounts receivable) for the sales price, credits *commission revenue* for the calculated amount of the commission, and credits *payable to consignor* for the amount to be remitted to the consignor. The amount in the payable to consignor account is periodically remitted to the consignor.

SELF-STUDY LEARNING   Items marked with an asterisk (*) refer to the Appendix.

Key Terms and Concepts

Provide the appropriate term or terms to complete each of the following statements:

1. Increases in net assets from the delivery or production of goods, the rendering of services, or other activities that constitute a company's major or primary operations are called ___REVENUE___.

2. *Recognition* refers to the ___TIMING___ of revenue.

3. Income from a long-term construction contract is recognized periodically if the ___% OF COMPLETION___ method is used.

4. Costs incurred in a long-term construction contract are charged to an inventory account called ___CONSTR IN PROGRESS___

5. When revenue is recognized at the completion of the production process, inventory is recorded at its ___NET REL'Z VALUE___ or ___EXPECTED EXIT VALUE___

6. ___ACCRETION___ refers to the increase in value of a product over time.

7. Both the ___INSTALLMENT SALES___ and ___COST RECOVERY___ methods of revenue recognition delay the recognition of revenue until cash is collected.

8. When a franchise agreement is reached, the ___FRANCHISOR___ provides services for and receives payment from the ___FRANCHISEE___.

9. ___BARTER TRANSACTION___ involve exchanges of goods and/or services.

*10. Under a consignment arrangement, the ___CONSIGNEE___ sells the consigned goods and receives revenue in the form of a(n) ___COMMISSION___.

True-False

Indicate by circling the appropriate response whether each of the following statements is true (T) or false (F):

 (T) F   1. Accrual accounting traditionally determines income by matching expenses against revenue recognized according to the realization principle.

T (F)   2. Revenue is measured at the cost of the assets received.

T (F)   3. If a sale is recorded at the point of sale, the expense related to fulfillment of a warranty on the product should normally be expensed in the period when the warranty is satisfied.

T (F)   4. To determine the income for the third year of a five-year construction contract under the percentage-of-completion method, estimated total net income is multiplied by the estimated percentage of completion.

(T) F   5. Under the percentage-of-completion method, the construction-in-progress account is debited for costs incurred and for earned income related to the construction contract.

(T) F   6. The billings on construction contract account normally has a credit balance.

T (F)   7. If costs rise to such an extent as to indicate a projected net loss on a long-term construction contract, the loss is recognized immediately under the percentage-of-completion method but not under the completed-contract method.

(T) F   8. Even though some products increase in value over time, income is usually not recognized on an accretion basis.

T F 9. A company will earn the same income if it recognizes revenue when the product is completed as it will if it recognizes revenue from the sale of the same product at the point of sale.

T F 10. The installment method of accounting for sales transactions focuses on the collection of cash as the critical event in revenue recognition.

T F 11. When a sale is accounted for by the installment method, each cash receipt represents revenue.

T F 12. If merchandise sold on an installment sales basis is repossessed, it should be recorded in inventory at its original cost.

T F 13. The cost-recovery method recognizes income equal to the amount of each cash receipt.

T F 14. The revenue recognition principles apply to gains and losses, and accordingly gains and losses are recognized only when an exchange takes place.

T F 15. A company that renders a service recognizes revenue from service fees at points during the earnings process very similar to the points of revenue recognition for a manufacturing or merchandising company.

T F 16. Franchise agreements generally provide a franchisor with two revenue streams, the initial franchise fee and a continuing periodic fee.

T F 17. The continuing franchise fee is usually recognized periodically as service revenue.

T F 18. Most real estate sales meet the criteria for revenue recognition at the time of sale.

T F *19. When a consignor transfers (consigns) goods to a consignee, title to the goods is transferred to the consignee.

T F *20. When a consignor receives notice that goods on consignment have been sold, cost of goods sold is recorded by a debit to cost of consignment sales and a credit to inventory for the amount of the cost of consigned merchandise sold.

Multiple Choice

Select the best response for each of the following items, and circle the corresponding letter:

1. Revenue may be earned at several points during the earnings process. Most companies recognize revenue:

   a. During the production process.
   b. At the completion of the production process.
   c. At the point of sale.
   d. When cash is collected.

2. In which of the following situations is the percentage-of-completion method for long-term construction contracts *not* appropriate?

   a. The total contract price is known or determinable.
   b. The total contract costs are unknown.
   c. The total contract costs are reasonably estimable.
   d. The cost or percentage of completion applicable to the current period is known or reasonably estimable.

3. If the balance in the construction-in-progress account is less than the balance in the billings on construction contract account, the net amount is reported on the balance sheet as:

   a. A current asset.
   b. A current liability.
   c. A noncurrent asset.
   d. A noncurrent liability.

4. Determine which of the following alternatives correctly states when income from long-term construction contracts is recognized—that is, periodically or at completion of project—under the two accounting methods shown.

PERCENTAGE-OF-COMPLETION METHOD	COMPLETED-CONTRACT METHOD
a. Periodically	Periodically
b. Periodically	At completion
c. At completion	Periodically
d. At completion	At completion

5. If revenue is recognized immediately when the production process is completed and selling costs are estimable, revenue should be recognized equal to:

   a. The anticipated sales price of the completed product.
   b. Net realizable value.
   c. Expected exit value.
   d. The anticipated sales price plus estimated selling costs.

6. The deferred gross profit account is properly disclosed on the balance sheet as:

   a. A deferred credit.
   b. Unearned revenue.
   c. A current asset.
   d. A contra asset to the installment receivables account.

7. The receivable account from an installment sale may be classified as:

   a. Both a current asset and a noncurrent asset.
   b. A current asset only.
   c. A noncurrent asset only.
   d. Neither a current asset nor a noncurrent asset.

8. What is the appropriate revenue recognition method for a company that provides a service to its client in several distinct phases?

   a. Specific performance method.
   b. Proportional performance method.
   c. Completed performance method.
   d. Collection method.

9. When a franchise agreement is entered into, several accounts may be credited for the initial franchise fee. Which of the following accounts would *not* be credited?

   a. Franchise fee revenue.
   b. Unearned franchise fee.
   c. Accrued franchise fee revenue.
   d. Deferred franchise fee.

*10. The consignor normally recognizes revenue when:

   a. Production of the product is completed.
   b. Consigned goods are delivered to the consignee.
   c. Consigned goods are sold by the consignee.
   d. The consignee remits the proceeds from the sale of consigned goods.

Extended Problem

Meridian Agribusiness, Inc., is an agricultural company engaged in growing wheat for sale in the commodity market and corn to be used, in part, in a special corn-blend bread that the company bakes and sells on consignment. When the corn-blend bread became popular in the local area, Meridian began to franchise its baking operations in several midwestern states. It is Meridian's policy to authorize two new franchises each year at a cost of $40,000,

payable 25 percent down with the balance due December 31 of the year operations commence. A 5.5 percent continuing franchise fee is assessed on the gross sales of each franchisee. In a separate contract, Meridian agrees to construct the necessary corn storage building, operating facility, and assembly line for the making of the corn-blend bread. The buildings take approximately 13 months to construct, and the assembly line takes about 4 months.

Information concerning Meridian's operations for fiscal year 1995 appears as follows:

a. Costs and distribution of the wheat and corn crops for the year are summarized here:

	WHEAT	CORN
Beginning inventory, 1/1/95	a	a
Costs of planting and harvesting	$57,000	$43,200
Bushels harvested	30,000	18,000
Bushels sold	20,000	15,000
Bushels used for baking	-0-	3,000
Market price per bushel[b]	$2.80	$3.40
Selling costs per bushel[b]	0.25	0.30

[a]Immaterial in quantity and dollar value.
[b]Stable amount for 1995 and the near future.

b. In keeping with its franchise policy, Meridian sold two $40,000 franchises (No. 11 and No. 12) on February 1. The amount due was sure to be collected. Franchises No. 9 and No. 10 commenced operations during the year and on December 31 paid the balance due on their franchises. Meridian completed the remaining 30 percent of the services due franchises No. 9 and No. 10 and performed 65 percent of the services due No. 11 and No. 12 during 1995. By the end of the year the franchises had gross sales totaling $2.4 million and paid 75 percent of the 5.5 percent continuing periodic fee due Meridian.

c. Meridian's construction activity is summarized on page 106.

d. Meridian divided a tract of unused farmland into parcels of various sizes to be sold. On May 1, 1995, it sold one parcel that cost $38,400 for $60,000 (10 percent down and the balance due in four installments every six months, starting November 1, 1995) to a land developer who hopes to develop the land for a recreational park. Because of some concern about an access road being built by the state, the collectibility of the receivable is very uncertain. Accordingly, the installment method is used for this transaction.

STORAGE BUILDING AND OPERATING FACILITY

	FRANCHISE			
	NO. 9	NO. 10	NO. 11	NO. 12
Contract price..	$350,000	$350,000	$360,000	$360,000
Costs incurred, 1994	210,000	240,000	-0-	-0-
Estimated costs to complete, 12/31/94..............	90,000	60,000	-0-	-0-
Costs incurred, 1995	110,000	60,000	232,500	304,000
Estimated costs to complete, 12/31/95..............	-0-	-0-	77,500	76,000
Billings, 1994..	200,000	200,000	-0-	-0-
Collections, 1994...	145,000	170,000	-0-	-0-
Billings, 1995..	150,000	150,000	-0-	-0-
Collections, 1995...	190,000	180,000	270,000	290,000
Date completed [estimated]...............................	2/95	5/95	200,000	210,000
			[3/96]	[4/96]

ASSEMBLY LINE

	NO. 9	NO. 10	NO. 11	NO. 12
Contract price..	$ 55,000	$ 55,000	$ 61,500	$ 61,500
Costs incurred, 1994	40,000	10,000	-0-	-0-
Estimated costs to complete, 12/31/94..............	-0-	32,500	-0-	-0-
Costs incurred, 1995	-0-	31,000	47,000	25,600
Estimated costs to complete, 12/31/95..............	-0-	-0-	-0-	38,400
Billings, 1994..	45,000	20,000	-0-	-0-
Collections, 1994...	17,000	20,000	-0-	-0-
Billings, 1995..	10,000	35,000	61,500	18,000
Collections, 1995...	28,000	35,000	52,000	16,250
Date completed [estimated]...............................	12/94	3/95	12/95	[2/96]

e. Meridian baked and consigned to various grocery stores 100,000 loaves of corn-blend bread that cost $.70 a loaf to make and $.10 per loaf to distribute. The stores sell the bread for $1.20 per loaf and are entitled to a 15 percent commission per loaf. Meridian received remittances for 97,000 loaves of corn-blend bread in 1995.

REQUIRED

a. Assuming that income from the wheat is recognized at the completion of production—that is, when it is harvested—and from corn when it is sold, prepare a partial income statement for the year ended December 31, 1995, for the two crops (assuming the 3,000 bushels of corn used in baking are in inventory), and calculate the value of the ending inventory of wheat and corn on December 31, 1995.

b. Prepare journal entries to record the sale of the new franchises, collection of cash from the initial franchise fees, and recognition of revenue from the initial franchise fees and the continuing franchisees' fees.

c. Assuming the percentage-of-completion method, prepare:
   (1). A schedule to determine the amount of recognized income or loss per construction

contract for the storage and facilities buildings as of December 31, 1995.
   (2). All journal entries for the year 1995 for construction on contracts No. 10 and No. 12.
   (3). Illustrative balance sheet (as of December 31, 1995) disclosures related to construction contracts No. 10 and No. 12.

d. Assuming the completed-contract method, prepare:
   (1). A schedule to determine the amount of recognized income or loss per construction contract for the assembly lines as of December 31, 1995.
   (2). All journal entries for the year 1995 for construction related to franchises No. 10 and No. 12.
   (3). Illustrative balance sheet (as of December 31, 1995) disclosures related to construction contracts No. 11 and No. 12.

e. Prepare all journal entries related to the sale of land for 1995, and illustrate proper balance sheet disclosure for the receivable from the sale of the land.

*f. Prepare entries to record the distribution of the corn-blend bread to the consignees and the recognition of revenues and related costs at the end of 1995.

COMMON ERRORS

The first statement in each of the "common errors" listed here is *incorrect*. Each incorrect statement is followed by a corrected statement and an explanation.

1. Revenue is recognized when either the amount and timing of revenue to be received are reasonably determinable or the earnings process is complete or virtually complete. *Wrong*

Revenue is recognized when both the amount and timing of revenue to be received are reasonably determinable and the earnings process is complete or virtually complete. *Right*

It is important to remember that in most situations *both* criteria should be met before revenue is recognized. The two criteria focus on different aspects of revenue recognition. The first is concerned with the determination of the expected cash inflows (revenues). The second is concerned with the determination of the expected cash outflows (expenses) or obligations the seller may experience in the earnings process. Both revenues and expenses are needed to determine income. Therefore, revenue should not be recognized until the cash inflows are determinable and the cash outflows are complete or virtually complete.

2. Either the percentage-of-completion method or the completed-contract method may be used to account for any long-term construction contract. *Wrong*

If certain criteria are met, the percentage-of-completion method must be used to account for a long-term construction contract. Otherwise the completed-contract method should be used. *Right*

Accounting for long-term construction contracts is somewhat unusual in that alternative accounting methods cannot be applied in any situation, as they may be in inventory costing, for example. Three criteria have been set: (*a*) a known or determinable contract price, (*b*) a reasonably estimable total cost, and (*c*) known or reasonably estimable total costs or percentage of completion for the current period. If the criteria are met, the percentage-of-completion method must be used. When the criteria are not met, the completed-contract method is used. Thus the two methods of accounting for long-term construction contracts are *not alternatives* for the same set of circumstances.

3. The installment method of accounting is used to record all installment sales. *Wrong*

The installment method of accounting should be used only when the collectibility of future cash flows from installment sales is uncertain. *Right*

Installment sales should not be confused with the installment method of accounting. An installment sale is simply any credit sale that will be paid in several payments or installments. The installment method of accounting is reserved for those situations in which there is considerable uncertainty about the collectibility of the future cash flows from installment sales. When collection is uncertain, the proper practice is to defer the gross profit on the sale and recognize it only as cash is received. This method prevents early recognition of income (gross profit) when the related cash flow is in doubt.

4. In a given situation, a company can recognize more total revenue and income by using one method of revenue recognition rather than another method. *Wrong*

In any given situation, a company will recognize the same total revenue and income regardless of the method of revenue recognition selected. *Right*

At first glance it might appear that one method of revenue recognition will result in more revenue and income than another method. This is an illusion. If a credit sale is recognized at the point of sale, for example, all revenue is recorded immediately. If the same sale were accounted for by the installment method, much less income, if any, would be recognized at the time of the sale. As cash is subsequently collected, no additional revenue will be recognized under the point of sale method, but a portion of each cash receipt will be recorded as income under the installment method. After all cash has been received from the sale, the total amounts of income under both methods will be identical. Selection of one method of revenue recognition over another will change only the *timing* of revenue and income, not the total amount.

5. Initial franchise fee revenue is recognized when the franchise agreement is signed. *Wrong*

Initial franchise fee revenue is recognized only after the franchisor's services are substantially performed and collection of the fee is reasonably assured. *Right*

Until *Statement No. 45*, many franchisors inflated their profit by recognizing the entire initial franchise fee as revenue upon the signing of the franchise agreement. After several early years of dramatic earnings, some of these franchisors watched as their large profits were later reduced considerably. The franchisor usually is required to provide certain services, such as helping in site selection or training, and incurs costs to perform these services. Since the franchise revenue was recognized in a period preceding the incurrence of some of the related costs, the franchisor had little, if any, revenue to match with these costs. In addition, franchisors discovered that, after signing, many franchisees were unable to make payments on their initial fee and had to be written off the franchisor's books as a bad debt. Hence many franchisors had lower profits or even losses within several years of the large profits. To prevent this practice of "front-ending" income and the resulting earnings effects, the FASB established rather restrictive revenue recognition guidelines for the initial franchise fee.

FASB Statement No. 45 requires that (a) the franchisor has substantially performed the services promised the franchisee and (b) the collectibility of the franchise fee is reasonably assured before the initial franchise fee revenue is recognized. These criteria are normally met at the time the franchisee commences operations or later. The effect of the revenue recognition guidelines is to *delay* revenue recognition, not to permit immediate recognition upon the signing of the franchise agreement. It should be noted that *Statement No. 45* permits immediate recognition of the continuing periodic fee.

6. Revenue recognition concepts vary widely between service companies and manufacturing or retailing companies. *Wrong*

Revenue recognition concepts are similar between service companies and manufacturing and retailing companies. *Right*

Manufacturing and retail companies usually have a tangible product to sell, whereas service companies normally have an intangible product (service). Service companies nevertheless recognize revenue at the same points in the earnings process as manufacturing and retail firms. The names given to service company revenue realization may differ from those of manufacturing and retail firms, but their underlying concepts are the same. For example, a

service company may provide services over an extended period of time and recognize income using the proportional-performance method, that is, in a manner similar to the percentage-of-completion method. Moreover, service companies also recognize revenue when (a) services are performed using the point-of-sale method, (b) an extended service obligation is completed using the completed-performance method (completed-contract method), or (c) collectibility of the related receivable is uncertain under the cost-recovery method. Thus manufacturing, retail, and service companies recognize revenue using the same basic revenue realization concepts.

7. A consignee's commission revenue on the sale of goods on consignment is equal to the consignor's profit on the sale. *Wrong*

A consignee's commission revenue on the sale of goods on consignment usually does not equal the consignor's profit on the sale. *Right*

Although both the consignee and the consignor record the same sale transactions, the amount and timing of their revenue recognition differ. The consignee's commission revenue is earned when goods held on consignment are sold and is normally equal to the sale price of the goods times a predetermined commission percentage. Upon receipt of the consignee's periodic remittance of cash (sale price less the earned commission), the consignor records (a) the cash received, (b) an expense (commission) equal to the amount of the commission withheld by the consignee, and (c) consignment sales equal to the selling price of the goods sold. Thus the consignor measures income by matching the consignment sale revenue with the commission expense and cost of consignment goods sold. The amount of the consignee's consignment commission revenue is an expense to the consignor, and only coincidentally would the consignee's commission revenue equal the profit of the consignor.

ANSWERS　Items marked with an asterisk (*) refer to the Appendix.

Key Terms and Concepts

1. revenue
2. timing
3. percentage-of-completion
4. construction in progress
5. net realizable value, expected exit value
6. accretion
7. installment sales, cost-recovery
8. franchisor, franchisee
9. barter transactions
*10. consignee, commission

True-False

1. T
2. F　Technically, revenue is measured at the fair value or cash equivalent price of the assets received. At times the cost of an asset and its fair value may be the same, but it is better to use the term *fair value* or *cash equivalent price* to designate the measure of revenue.
3. F　Accrual accounting requires that to achieve proper matching of revenues and expenses,

all estimable costs should be accrued at the time of the sale or at the end of the period in which the sale is made. Warranty costs are usually estimable and therefore should be recognized in the period when the sale is made. The expense should not be recognized when the warranty is fulfilled, since fulfillment may occur in a period other than that of the sale.

4. F If estimated net income is multiplied by the estimated percentage of completion, the result is the amount of income for the first three years of the project. From this amount there must be deducted the net income recognized for the first two years to determine income for the third year.

5. T

6. T

7. F If a loss is indicated on a long-term construction contract, the loss is recognized immediately under both the percentage-of-completion and completed-contract methods.

8. T

9. T

10. T

11. F Under the installment method, each cash receipt represents part recovery of cost and part profit.

12. F Repossessed merchandise should be recorded at its fair value, since it is unlikely that its value is the same as its original cost. The repossessed merchandise may be damaged or may even have appreciated in value; neither eventuality would be reflected in the original cost.

13. F The cost-recovery method recognizes income equal to the amount of cash received *only after* the cost of the merchandise has been recovered through cash receipts.

14. F Gains are usually recognized at the time of a transaction. Losses and some gains, however, are sometimes recognized before a transaction has occurred, as in the valuation of marketable securities at their market value.

15. T

16. T

17. T

18. F Most real estate sales do *not* meet the criteria for revenue recognition at the time of sale, because the seller usually has services to perform after the sale, and often there is uncertainty about the collectibility of the receivable from the sale.

*19. F The consignee acts as an agent for the consignor and, therefore, does not receive title to the goods received. The title remains with the consignor.

*20. F For good control, the consignor should reclassify inventory out on consignment to the inventory on consignment account. Therefore, to record cost of goods sold, the inventory on consignment account should be credited, not the inventory account.

Multiple Choice

1.	c	6.	d
2.	b	7.	a
3.	b	8.	b
4.	b	9.	c
5.	a	*10.	d

Extended Problem

a. Partial income statement for the year ended December 31, 1995, including wheat and corn operations:

Meridian Agribusiness, Inc.
PARTIAL INCOME STATEMENT
FOR THE YEAR ENDED DECEMBER 31, 1995

	WHEAT	CORN		
Revenues				
Wheat (30,000 bu. × $2.80)			$84,000	
Corn (15,000 bu. × $3.40)			51,000	$135,000
Expenses				
Planting and harvesting	$57,000	$36,000[a]		
Selling	7,500[b]	4,500[c]		
Total expenses	$64,500	$40,500		105,000
Net income				$ 30,000

[a]$43,200 + 18,000 bu. = $2.40/bu. × 15,000 bu. = $36,000.

[b]$.25/bu. × 30,000 bu. = $7,500.

[c]$.30/bu. × 15,000 bu. = $4,500.

Inventory valuation for wheat and corn as of December 31, 1995.

Wheat (at net realizable value): 10,000 bu. × ($2.80 – $.25) = $25,500.
Corn (at cost): 3,000 bu. × $2.40/bu. = $7,200.

b. Journal entries related to initial franchise fees and franchise revenue:

Feb. 1	Cash [2 × ($40,000 × 25%)]...	20,000	
	Receivable from franchisees...	60,000	
	Unearned franchise revenue (2 × $40,000)..		80,000
Dec. 31	Cash [2 × ($40,000 – $10,000)]..	60,000	
	Receivable from franchisees..		60,000
	Unearned franchise fee	76,000[a]	
	Franchise fee revenue...		76,000[a]
	Cash ($2,400,000 × 5.5% × 75%)	99,000	
	Accounts receivable	33,000	
	Service revenue ($2,400,000 × 5.5%)..		132,000

[a] No. 9 & No. 10 [2 × (30% × $40,000)] = $24,000
  No. 11 & No. 12 [2 × (65% × $40,000)] = <u>52,000</u>
                                      $76,000

c. (1). Schedule of income on construction of storage and facilities buildings:

**Schedule to Determine Income or Loss from
Construction Projects (Percentage-of-Completion Method)**
DECEMBER 31, 1995

	NO. 9	NO. 10	NO. 11	NO. 12
1. Contract price..	$350,000	$350,000	$360,000	$360,000
2. Construction costs to date...........................	320,000	300,000	232,500	304,000
3. Estimated costs to complete	-0-	-0-	77,500	76,000
4. Total construction costs (2 + 3)....................	320,000	300,000	310,000	380,000
5. Estimated income (loss)(1 – 4)....................	$ 30,000	$ 50,000	$ 50,000	$ (20,000)
6. Estimated percentage of completion to date (2 ÷ 4)............	100%	100%	75%	80%
7. Income (loss) recognized to date (5 × 6)...........	$ 30,000	$ 50,000	$ 37,500	$ (20,000)[a]
8. Income recognized in 1994	35,000[b]	40,000[b]	-0-	-0-
9. Income (loss) recognized in 1995 (7 – 8).........	$ (5,000)	$ 10,000	$ 37,500	$ (20,000)

[a] Entire loss is recognized in year loss is estimated.

	NO. 9	NO. 10
[b]1. Contract price.............................	$ 350,000	$ 350,000
2. Costs incurred, 1994................................	210,000	240,000
3. Estimated costs to complete...........................	90,000	60,000
4. Total construction costs (2 + 3)	300,000	300,000
5. Estimated income (1 – 4)	50,000	50,000
6. Estimated percentage of completion (2 ÷ 4).........	70%	80%
7. Income recognized to date (5 × 6)...................	35,000	40,000
8. Income recognized in prior year.......................	-0-	-0-
9. Income recognized in 1994 (7 – 8)	$ 35,000	$ 40,000

(2). Journal entries for construction on No. 10 and No. 12:

	NO. 10		NO. 12	
Construction-in-progress	60,000		304,000	
Materials, cash, etc.		60,000		304,000
Accounts receivable	150,000		290,000	
Billings on construction contract		150,000		290,000
Cash	180,000		210,000	
Accounts receivable		180,000		210,000
Construction-in-progress	10,000		No entry	
Construction expenses	60,000		No entry	
Construction revenue		70,000		No entry
Construction expenses	No entry		304,000	
Construction-in-progress		No entry		20,000
Construction revenue		No entry		284,000
Billings on construction contract	350,000		No entry	
Construction-in-progress		350,000		No entry

(3). Balance sheet disclosure for construction on No. 10 and No. 12:

	NO. 10	NO. 12
Current assets		
Accounts receivable	-0-	$ 80,000
Current liabilities		
Billings on construction contracts	-0-	$ 290,000
Less: Construction-in-progress	-0-	(284,000)[a]
		$ 6,000

[a]$304,000 − $20,000 = $284,000.

d. (1). Schedule of income on assembly lines:

Schedule to Determine Income or Loss from
Construction Projects (Completed-Contract Method)
DECEMBER 31, 1995

	NO. 10	NO. 11	NO. 12
1. Contract price	$55,000	$61,500	$ 61,500
2. Construction costs, 1994	10,000	-0-	-0-
3. Construction costs, 1995	31,000	47,000	25,600
4. Estimated costs to complete	-0-	-0-	38,400
5. Total construction costs (2 + 3 + 4)	$41,000	$47,000	$64,000
6. Income (loss) recognized, 1995 (1 − 5)	$14,000	$14,500	$ (2,500)[a]

[a]Even though this contract is *not* completed, the loss on the contract is recognized when it is first estimated.

(2). Journal entries related to No. 10 and No. 12:

	NO. 10		NO. 12	
Construction-in-progress	31,000		25,600	
Materials, cash, etc.		31,000		25,600
Accounts receivable	35,000		18,000	
Billings on construction contract		35,000		18,000
Cash	35,000		16,250	
Accounts receivable		35,000		16,250
Loss on construction contract	No entry		2,500	
Construction-in-progress		No entry		2,500
Billings	55,000		No entry	
Construction-in-progress		41,000		No entry
Income on construction contract		14,000		No entry

(3). Balance sheet disclosure as of December 31, 1995, for No. 11 and No. 12:

	NO. 11	NO. 12
Current assets		
Accounts receivable	$9,500	$ 1,750
Inventories		
Construction-in-progress	-0-	$23,100[a]
Less: Billings on construction contract	-0-	18,000
		$ 5,100

[a]$25,600 – $2,500 = $23,100.

e. Journal entries to record sale of land and collection of first installment due:

May 1	Cash ($60,000 × 10%)	6,000	
	Accounts receivable	54,000	
	Sales		60,000
	Cost of goods sold	38,400	
	Land (inventory)		38,400
Nov. 1	Cash ($54,000 ÷ 4)	13,500	
	Accounts receivable		13,500
Dec. 31	Sales	60,000	
	Cost of goods sold		38,400
	Deferred gross profit on installment sales		21,600
	Deferred gross profit on installment sales	7,020[a]	
	Realized gross profit on installment sales		7,020[a]

[a]$21,600 ÷ $60,000 = 36%; 36% × ($6,000 + $13,500) = $7,020.

Balance sheet disclosure on installment receivable as of December 31, 1995:

Accounts receivable ($54,000 – $13,500)	$40,500
Deferred gross profit on installment sales ($21,600 – $7,020)	14,580
Accounts receivable (net)	$25,920

*f. Journal entries to record consignment activities:

Inventory on consignment	70,000	
Inventory (100,000 × $.70)		70,000
Inventory on consignment	10,000	
Cash (100,000 × $.10)		10,000
Cash	98,940	
Commission expense ($116,400 × 15%)	17,460	
Consignment sales (97,000 × $1.20)		116,400
Cost of consignment sales [97,000 × ($.70 + $.10)]	77,600	
Inventory on consignment		77,600

8 CASH, CURRENT RECEIVABLES AND LIABILITIES, AND CONTINGENCIES

CHAPTER OBJECTIVES

After reading Chapter 8 and completing the questions, cases, exercises, and problems from the text chapter, you should be able to:

1. Understand the nature of cash.
2. Prepare a reconciliation of cash balances.
3. Understand the nature of and accounting for trade discounts, sales discounts, and sales returns.
4. Determine the amount of uncollectible accounts under the accrual (allowance) approach.
5. Apply the effective interest method of amortization.
6. Differentiate between and account for a short-term interest-bearing note and a noninterest-bearing note.
7. Distinguish and account for the various methods of securing immediate cash from receivables: discounting, assigning, and factoring.
8. Describe the essential characteristics of liabilities.

9. Distinguish between current, or short-term, liabilities and noncurrent, or long-term, liabilities.
10. Prepare the journal entries required to account for current obligations (called determinable current liabilities) whose existence and amount due are known with certainty, including trade accounts payable, current notes payable, dividends payable, sales taxes payable, payroll-related taxes payable, compensated employee absences, property taxes payable, and prepayments and deposits by customers.
11. Prepare the journal entries required to account for current obligations (called current liabilities dependent on operating results) whose amount due, and perhaps existence, can be determined with certainty once operating results for the annual accounting period are known, including income taxes payable and bonuses payable.
12. Define contingency and understand the accounting and reporting of loss and gain contingencies.

CHAPTER REVIEW

Introduction

1. This is the first of several chapters that focus on individual components of the financial statements. Specifically, this chapter covers short-term monetary assets, liabilities, and contingencies. Monetary assets (liabilities) include money and claims to receive (obligations to pay) a sum of money, the amount of which is fixed or determin-able without reference to future prices of specific goods or services. Examples of monetary assets are cash, accounts receivable, and notes receivable. Examples of monetary liabilities are accounts payable, notes payable, accrued liabilities, and bonuses payable.

2. Investors, creditors, and others are interested in the amount, timing, and uncertainty of a company's future cash flows. In addition, these users are concerned about a company's liquidity. Management must also continually be aware of its liquidity position, which indicates the ease with which an asset can be converted into cash. A company's liquidity also provides an indication of its ability to pay obligations as they become due. The accounting for cash and other short-term monetary assets and liabilities is designed to assist users in assessing a company's liquidity.

Cash

3. *Cash* is a medium of exchange used to purchase goods and services and to discharge obligations. Cash consists, in part, of U.S. currency and coins, money orders, personal checks, petty cash, and demand deposits. Although such items as certificates of deposit and postdated checks appear to be cash, they are excluded from the accountant's definition of cash because they are not readily available for the acquisition of goods or the liquidation of debt.

4. Petty cash. Although good accounting systems usually require that all disbursements be properly authorized and paid by check, situations arise when the amount of the disbursement is immaterial and it would be inconvenient to process a check. In these situations the payment is made in cash from the *petty cash fund*. To achieve the greatest control, the petty cash fund is maintained at a fixed amount. Such a fund is called an *imprest* petty cash fund.

5. The petty cash fund is established by transferring from cash a fixed amount to petty cash: petty cash is debited and cash is credited for the fixed amount of the petty cash fund. When petty cash is disbursed, the petty cash fund cashier normally completes a voucher that indicates the amount and purpose of the payment. At all times the petty cash fund cashier should have vouchers or cash on hand totaling the fixed amount of the fund.

6. Periodically, the petty cash fund needs to be replenished. At this time the vouchers for similar purposes, such as delivery charges or postage, are totaled and debited to the proper expense accounts, and cash is credited. Notice that petty cash is not affected when the petty cash fund is replenished. The only time the petty cash account is affected is when the fund is established or the amount of the fund is increased (by debits) or when the fund is liquidated or the amount of the fund is decreased (by credits). If the amount of the vouchers and petty cash on hand is less than the fixed amount established for the fund, the difference is debited to cash short when the fund is replenished; if the amount of vouchers and petty cash on hand is more than the fixed amount established, the difference is credited to cash over.

7. Bank reconciliation. One of the most common controls over cash is the bank reconciliation. The bank reconciliation provides the opportunity for the firm to compare its cash account balance with a balance determined by an external source, the bank. Theoretically, if no errors were made by either the bank or the company, the bank balance and cash account balance should be equal. The book and bank balances, however, will seldom be equal at the end of an accounting period. The difference can usually be traced to the time lag that occurs between the time a transaction is recorded on one set of records (the company's, for example) and the time it is entered in the other records (the bank's, for example). The form of the reconciliation is relatively simple, as shown in the following table:

Bank Reconciliation

Balance per bank	$xx
+/– adjustments for transactions recorded by the company but not by the bank..........	x
+/– corrections for errors made by the bank affecting the company's account..............	x
Corrected cash balance................................	$xx
Balance per books.....................................	$xx
+/– adjustments for transactions recorded by the bank but not by the company..........	x
+/– corrections for errors made by the company affecting cash..........................	x
Corrected cash balance..............................	$xx

8. Typical adjustments that appear on the reconciliation that affect the bank balance are outstanding checks (deductions) and deposits in transit (additions). Typical adjustments that appear on the reconciliation of the book balance are bank service charges, return of NSF (not sufficient funds) checks (deductions), and collection of money for the company by the bank (additions). For financial reporting purposes, the company's cash balance is adjusted to equal the corrected cash balance figure determined in the bank reconciliation. The adjusting entry is required for all items appearing on the book reconciliation to adjust the book balance to the corrected cash balance. The company need make no entry for items on the reconciliation of the bank balance, since these items have previously been recorded by the company.

9. Appendix 8-1 describes an alternative form of reconciliation called a comprehensive reconciliation or a proof of cash. Besides reconciling the ending book and bank balances, this form also reconciles the beginning cash balance and all cash receipts and disbursements during the period.

10. Cash disclosures. Cash is properly disclosed on the balance sheet as a current asset. If a company has written checks in excess of its checking account balance, the *overdraft* should be reported as a current liability. Cash designated for a specific purpose is normally reported as an investment. Any restrictions on cash should also be disclosed. A company and its bank, for example, often establish a *compensating balance,* a portion of a loan from the bank to the company that must remain on deposit during the period of the loan. Because of these restrictions, special disclosures are required to indicate the nature and amount of the compensating balance.

Receivables

11. *Receivables* are *monetary assets*—that is, they represent claims to receive fixed amounts of cash—and arise when a company sells its goods, renders a service, or lends money that is to be repaid in cash in the future. Receivables should be valued at their present value, but many short-term receivables are often reported at their face amount or at net realizable value. The most common receivables are accounts receivable and notes receivable.

12. *Accounts receivable* or *trade receivables* arise from the sale of goods and services on credit. The accountant must determine (*a*) the amount due on receivables, (*b*) when receivables should be recorded, and (*c*) the recognition of potential uncollectible accounts. Each of these items is discussed in the remainder of this section.

13. Amount due on accounts receivable. Accounts receivable are recorded as an asset at the time the revenue from a sales transaction is recognized. The *amount due* on receivables is theoretically equal to the current cash equivalent exchange price as a result of the sales transaction. Thus the amount due is the amount recorded initially as the receivable and the amount of revenue in the transaction.

14. The initial amount of the receivable is normally the list price of the item sold or the list price less a trade discount. *Trade discounts* are special discounts offered the buyer and are never recorded in the accounts. *Sales* or *cash discounts* are offered to customers for early payment and are often expressed as "$x\%/D_1$, net D_2," where x percent is the discount allowed if the customer pays within D_1 days, and "net D_2" means that if the amount is not collected within the discount period, the entire amount is due in D_2 days.

15. When there is a sales discount offered, the sales transaction normally is recorded at the net amount of the sale (sales price less sales discount) by debiting accounts receivable and crediting sales for the net sales price or the "cash equivalent price" at the date of the sale. If the remittance is received before the discount period expires, the company

receives the net sales amount. If, however, the discount period lapses before payment is received, cash is debited for the gross amount of the sale, accounts receivable is credited for the net amount of the sale, and interest revenue is credited for the amount of the discount. Sales discounts that have lapsed at the end of an accounting period should be accrued by a debit to accounts receivable and a credit to interest revenue for the amount of lapsed discounts.

16. In certain situations customers are allowed to return all or a portion of the goods purchased. *Sales returns* can be handled in any one of three ways (which are discussed in Chapter 7): (*a*) they are recorded as they occur if the number of returns is small and the dollar amount immaterial, (*b*) the allowance method is used if returns are material and an estimate of the returns can be made, and (*c*) the sale is not recorded until after the return period has expired if the risk of return is great.

17. Interest on accounts receivable. In some sales, such as those made under an installment or deferred payment plan, the receivable extends over several months or even years. Sales of this type either implicitly or explicitly contain an interest factor, because the seller is in effect financing the purchase for the buyer. In other words, the total payments made by the buyer will exceed the "cash purchase price" because of the interest factor. Assume, for example, that a company sold an appliance on an extended payment plan. The company would record the sale by debiting accounts receivable and crediting sales for the present value of the receivable or the cash equivalent exchange value of the item sold. Part of each subsequent receipt is interest. The *effective interest method* should be used to determine the portion of each subsequent remittance that represents interest and the portion that reduces the receivable balance. Each future receipt is recorded by a debit to cash for the amount of cash received, a credit to interest revenue for the amount of interest earned (interest percentage multiplied by receivable balance at the beginning of the period), and a credit to accounts receivable for the amount of cash collected less the interest revenue recognized. It should be observed that the receivable balance decreases after each periodic collection (the amount of receivable decrease equals the amount of cash received minus the interest earned), and consequently, the amount of interest earned also decreases each period.

18. Recognition of accounts receivable as an asset. Receivables should be recognized when revenue is recognized from an exchange transaction; that is, when (*a*) the earnings process is complete or virtually complete and (*b*) the amount and timing of cash to be received can be reasonably estimated. Like revenue, receivables are usually recognized at the point of sale but may be recognized at points in the earnings process before and after the point of sale. These various revenue recognition points are discussed in Chapter 7.

19. Estimating uncollectible accounts receivable. For various reasons, not all trade receivables initially recorded will be collected. For a better matching of revenues and expenses, a company should estimate uncollectible accounts expense (or bad debts expense) and record it in the period in which the sales are made if (*a*) it is highly probable that some accounts will prove uncollectible and (*b*) the dollar amount of the uncollectible accounts can be reasonably estimated. The method of accounting for uncollectible receivables is the allowance or accrual method.

20. Under the *allowance* or *accrual method,* uncollectible accounts are estimated at the end of each accounting period and recognized as an expense on the income statement (uncollectible accounts expense) and as a contra account (allowance for uncollectible accounts) to accounts receivable on the balance sheet. The estimated uncollectible accounts are recorded by a debit to uncollectible accounts expense and a credit to allowance for uncollectible accounts for the amount estimated. The amount of uncollectible receivables may be estimated as a percentage of sales or as a percentage of ending accounts receivable, or the accounts receivable may be aged.

21. When uncollectible accounts are estimated as a *percentage of credit sales,* the focus is on the income statement and the matching of uncollectible accounts expense with sales for the period. This method is often called the *income statement approach.* The amount charged to the expense account is equal to the amount of credit sales multiplied by the estimated uncollectible accounts percentage (based on historical trends or data). When the *percentage of ending accounts receivable* or *aging of accounts receivable* method is used, the focus is on the balance sheet and on the valuation of the receivables at their net realizable value. These methods are often referred to as the *balance sheet approaches.* The amount of uncollectible accounts expense recognized is equal to the amount needed to bring the allowance account to the desired balance in order to value the receivables. If it is estimated that a certain percentage of the ending receivables will be uncollectible, for example, the desired balance in the allowance account is equal to the ending receivable balance multiplied by the estimated percentage. Similarly, the aging method determines the desired balance in the allowance account by applying various estimated uncollectible percentages to the receivables classified by the number of days they have been outstanding—for example, less than 30 days, 30 to 60 days, and so on. Once the desired balance is known, the amount

of uncollectible accounts expense can be found by referring to the allowance account balance and determining how much the account needs to be (normally) credited to attain the desired balance.

22. When one of the allowance methods is used, an uncollectible account receivable is written off by a debit to allowance for uncollectible accounts and a credit to accounts receivable for the amount of the uncollectible receivable. It should be noted that the write-off of an account does not affect the balance sheet, since both the receivable and allowance accounts are reduced by the same amount.

23. In summary, accounts receivable are recognized following the realization concept and measured initially at their current cash equivalent exchange price. Subsequently, accounts receivable may be reduced by allowances for returns and for uncollectible accounts resulting in a balance sheet valuation equal to their net realizable value.

Short-Term Notes

24. A *note receivable* (*payable*) is a more formal contractual agreement than an account receivable (payable) stating that a specified amount of cash will be received (paid) in the future. Notes arise through sale or lending transactions and may or may not be interest-bearing. The maker of the note agrees to pay the payee the principal and interest, if the note bears interest, in one payment at maturity. Short-term notes mature in one year or less and are dis-cussed in this chapter. Notes maturing in more than one year are covered in Chapter 14.

25. Interest on short-term notes. An interest-bearing short-term note has (*a*) a stated interest rate approximating the market rate of interest for notes of similar risk and (*b*) a maturity value or amount due at maturity equal to the principal amount plus interest. A noninterest-bearing, short-term note has (*a*) no stated interest rate and (*b*) a maturity value equal to the amount of the principal or face value.

26. Interest on short-term notes is calculated as follows: Interest = Principal × Interest rate per year × Time (portion of a year). For example, the calculation of interest on a 3-month, $R\%$, $\$P$ note would be $I = \$P \times R\% \times 3/12$. If a noninterest-bearing note is issued in a loan situation, the amount of cash exchanged at the inception of the note is normally less than the principal or maturity value of the note. The lender usually deducts an amount from the maturity value. This deducted amount is calculated in a manner identical with that of calculating interest on an interest-bearing note. Thus, the amount of cash exchanged at the inception of the note is the principal amount minus the calculated interest.

27. Accounting for short-term notes. To record a short-term interest-bearing note, the debtor would debit cash and credit notes payable for the face amount of the note. At maturity, the debtor would debit notes payable for the face amount of the note and interest expense for the amount of the calculated interest and credit cash for the maturity value of the note (principal plus interest). To record a noninterest-bearing note, a creditor would debit notes receivable and credit cash for an amount equal to the principal amount minus the interest. At maturity, the creditor would debit cash for the maturity value of the note and credit interest revenue for the interest on the note and notes receivable for an amount equal to the principal minus the interest. Whether an interest-bearing or noninterest-bearing note is outstanding, interest must be accrued if the accounting period ends before the note matures. The debtor (creditor) must accrue interest expense (revenue) for the amount of interest accrued, since the note was issued to the end of the accounting period.

Securing Immediate Cash from Receivables

28. Since receivables represent the probable receipt of cash in the future, their ultimate liquidity depends on a future collection. A company has several options, however, in its efforts to secure immediate cash from its receivables. The most common methods are pledging or assignment of receivables, factoring accounts receivable, and discounting notes receivable.

29. Pledging or assignment of receivables. A company may use accounts receivable as collateral for a loan by informally *pledging* its receivables, or it may enter into a more formal *assignment agreement.* When receivables are pledged, they simply serve as security for a loan from a bank. When receivables are assigned, the assignor enters into a loan agreement with the assignee that stipulates that money collected (which is usually paid to the assignee) from the assigned receivables will be used specifically to settle the loan and pay the interest on it. Normally, the assignee requires that more receivables be assigned than the face value of the loan. Moreover, the assignee deducts a finance charge from the face value of the loan and charges periodic (usually monthly) interest on the unpaid loan balance. To record the loan and assignment of receivables, the assignor (*a*) debits cash for the proceeds from the loan (the face value of the loan less the finance charge), debits finance fee for the amount of the finance charge, credits payable to assignee for the face value of the loan; and (*b*) debits accounts receivable assigned and credits accounts receivable for the amount of the receivables assigned as security for the loan. As assigned receivables are collected, the cash is used to reduce the loan and pay any interest that may have accrued on the loan. For purposes of balance sheet disclosure, the payable to assignee account is offset against the accounts receivable assigned account. The net amount of the offset is labeled "equity in assigned receivables."

30. Factoring receivables. Accounts receivable may be sold or *factored* to a financial institution (factor), which usually pays less than the face value of the receivables. The factor usually charges a factoring fee and interest to compensate for the waiting period before the receivables are collected. Customers are normally notified of the factoring arrangement and make payments to the factor.

31. Receivables factored *without recourse*—that is, all risks associated with the receivables are shifted to the factor—are treated as a *sale* of the receivables. A sale is appropriate because (*a*) ownership risks and benefits are shifted from the transferor to the transferee (the factor) and (*b*) the net cash flow effects of the factoring arrangement are known at the date of the transfer. To record the sale of receivables, the transferor debits cash for the amount of the receivables sold less the factoring fee and interest, if any; the allowance for uncollectible accounts for the estimated amount accrued as uncollectible on the factored receivables; and, normally, the loss on the sale of receivables for the difference between the *net* receivables surrendered and cash received. The transferor then credits accounts receivable for the amount of receivables sold.

32. Receivables factored *with recourse*—that is, the transferor "makes good" on any uncollectible receivables—may be treated as a sale or borrowing. Factoring arrangements with recourse are normally recorded as a sale if the net cash flow effects can be reasonably estimated. *Statement No. 77* stipulates three conditions that must *all* be met if the transferor is to record the transfer as a sale: (*a*) the transferor surrenders control of the economic benefits associated with the receivables; (*b*) the transferor can reasonably estimate its obligations to the transferee under the recourse provisions; and (*c*) the transferee cannot require the transferor to repurchase the receivables, except in accordance with the recourse provisions. The entry to record the transfer of receivables with recourse as a sale is similar to that illustrated for a sale without recourse with two exceptions: (*a*) the debit to cash is reduced by the amount that the transferee holds back (an amount to provide for reductions in the amounts collected); and (*b*) an additional debit is required to an account, *due from the transferee,* for the amount of the "hold-back" less any estimated accrued uncollectibles and sales discounts related to the factored receivables.

33. In situations where all three conditions are not met, the transfer is treated as a borrowing and a liability is recorded. To record a transfer of receivables as a borrowing, the transferor debits cash for the amount of the factored receivables less the factoring fee, interest, and any hold-back due from the transferee for the amount of the hold-back, and interest expense for the amount of receivables factored less the cash received and the amount due the transferee. The transferor also credits payable to the transferee for the amount of the receivables factored. The interest expense should be amortized over the life of the loan. As the transferee makes collections, the transferor should debit payable to the transferee and credit accounts receivable for the amount collected. After all receivables have been collected or otherwise accounted for, for example, written off as uncollectible, the transferor would debit cash for the amount received from the transferee that represents collections over the amount needed to satisfy the loan, payable to the transferee for the balance in the account, and credit due from the transferee for the amount of the hold-back, assuming none was needed to satisfy the factoring agreement.

34. Discounting notes receivable. A company may sell or *discount* notes receivable to a third party (usually a bank) in order to receive cash immediately. If the notes are sold *with recourse,* the company remains contingently liable to the third party for payment of the maturity value of the note if the debtor defaults. When the notes are sold *without recourse,* the company has no further obligation to the third party.

35. When a note is discounted at the bank, the *proceeds,* or amount of cash received from the bank, are equal to the maturity value of the note (the face amount plus the total interest on the note, if any) less the *discount* or finance charge levied by the bank, which is usually expressed as a percentage of the note's maturity value [Maturity value × Discount percentage × (Days to maturity ÷ 360)]. The receipt of the proceeds is normally recorded by a debit to cash for the amount of the proceeds, a credit to notes receivable discounted for the face value of the note, and to balance the entry, a debit to interest expense if the amount of the proceeds is less than the face value of the note or a credit to interest revenue if the amount of the proceeds is more than the face value of the note. The notes receivable discounted account is a contra asset account to the notes receivable account. If the notes are discounted with recourse, the contingent liability must be disclosed. When the note that is discounted is paid by the debtor, notes receivable discounted is debited and notes receivable is credited

for the face amount of the note. If the debtor defaults on the note and the company has to pay the bank, the company debits receivable from customer for the maturity value of the note, debits notes receivable discounted for the face value of the note, credits notes receivable for the face value of the note, and credits cash for the maturity value of the note.

Liabilities

36. *Liabilities* are defined as probable future sacrifices of economic benefits arising from present obligations of a particular entity to transfer assets or provide services to other entities in the future as a result of past transactions or events. A liability has three essential conditions: (*a*) a present duty or responsibility to one or more other entities is expected to be settled by transfer of assets or provision of services in the future, (*b*) the duty or responsibility obligates a particular entity, and (*c*) the transaction or event that caused the entity to be obligated has already occurred.

37. Liabilities normally are reported on the balance sheet in two subcategories, current, or short-term, liabilities and noncurrent, or long-term, liabilities. *Current liabilities* are obligations that are expected to be settled by the use of existing resources classified as current assets or by the creation of other current liabilities. *Noncurrent liabilities* are all obligations that are not current liabilities.

38. *Monetary liabilities* are obligations to pay a sum of money that is fixed or determinable without reference to future prices of specific goods or services, whereas *nonmonetary liabilities* are obligations to transfer nonmonetary assets or to provide services. Most liabilities, whether current or noncurrent, are monetary liabilities.

39. Liabilities theoretically should be valued at the present value of the assets or services that must be transferred in the future to settle the obligation. Because the due dates usually are within very short periods of time, however, it has become customary to record most current liabilities at their future payment amounts (or face amounts) rather than at their present values.

40. Current liabilities usually are presented as the first group of items in the liabilities section of the balance sheet. Secured liabilities, and the assets pledged as collateral for those liabilities, should be disclosed. Current liabilities should not be offset against current assets that may be used to settle the obligations.

41. Determinable current liabilities. *Determinable current liabilities* are current obligations that are known with certainty to exist as of the balance sheet date and whose amounts are known with certainty or can be estimated with reasonable certainty. The existence, amounts, and due dates of most determinable current liabilities are specified by written or implied contracts. Determinable current liabilities include trade accounts payable, current notes payable, the current portion of long-term obligations, obligations callable by creditors, dividends payable, collections for third parties, accrued liabilities, and prepayment and deposits by customers.

42. Trade accounts payable. Obligations that arise from the purchase of goods, supplies, and services from other entities on open account are known as *trade accounts payable,* or simply *accounts payable.* Accounts payable should be recognized when legal title to the goods or supplies passes or when the services are received. Furthermore, accounts payable may be recorded at the gross amount due or net of any available purchase discounts, either directly by a credit to accounts payable for the net amount due or indirectly by a credit to accounts payable for the gross amount due and a debit to a contra account, such as allowance for purchase discounts, for the amount of the available purchase discount.

43. Current notes payable. Current obligations for which there are written promissory notes specifying a face amount and due date are known as *current notes payable.* The note may or may not specify an interest rate to be applied to the face amount. Current notes payable include trade notes payable and short-term notes payable. *Trade notes payable* are current notes that typically are issued to suppliers when the terms of payment specify a period longer than normal for trade accounts payable. It is a generally accepted practice to record trade notes payable at their face amounts. *Short-term notes payable* are current notes that often are issued in exchange for cash or for special purposes, such as the purchase of equipment on short-term credit. Short-term notes payable should be recorded at their face amounts, and any excess of the face amount over the present value of the note should be debited to discount on notes payable, a contra account, which should be amortized as an adjustment of interest over the term of the note. Alternatively, short-term notes payable may be recorded at their present value. The present value of a note issued solely for cash is equal to the amount of cash received; the present value of a note issued for noncash assets is equal to the fair value of the noncash assets or the discounted present value of the note, whichever is more clearly determinable. Chapter 14 contains a more detailed discussion of the accounting for and reporting of notes payable.

44. Dividends payable. *Dividends payable* are obligations that arise when the board of directors declares its intent to distribute cash or other assets to shareholders in the future in proportion to their ownership interest. Dividends payable should be recorded on the dividend declaration date at the amount of cash or the fair value of the noncash assets that will be distributed. Stock dividends distributable should not be reported as a liability, since stock dividends require the issuance of additional shares of stock rather than the distribution of assets. Chapter 18 contains a more detailed discussion of accounting for and reporting of dividends.

45. Collections for third parties. *Collections for third parties* are obligations that arise from the withholding or collection of assets (usually cash) from one party for the purpose of remitting those assets to a third party to comply with governmental or contractual requirements. Two such obligations are the collection of sales taxes from customers and the withholding of payroll-related taxes, insurance premiums, union dues, and other authorized amounts from employees' wages.

46. Companies often collect *sales taxes* or other taxes from customers and remit the taxes to local and/or state governments. When sales taxes are collected from customers, revenue is credited for the selling price of the goods sold or services rendered and sales taxes payable is credited for the selling price of the goods or services multiplied by the sales tax rate. Cash or accounts receivable is debited for the amount of the revenue plus the sales tax.

47. The *payroll-related taxes* that the employer is required to withhold from employees' wages are the employees' share of FICA (Federal Insurance Contribution Act) taxes and federal, state, and local income taxes on their wages. The amounts required to be withheld are specified by governmental regulations. Because the employer is required to remit the payroll-related taxes to the governmental taxing units, the journal entry to record the payroll should include (*a*) a debit to wages expense for the total amount earned by employees during the period, (*b*) credits to the appropriate payroll taxes payable accounts (such as employee FICA taxes payable and federal, state, and local income taxes payable) for the amounts withheld from employees' wages during the period, and (*c*) a credit to cash or to wages payable for the residual amount payable to employees during the period. Later, when the employer remits to the governmental taxing units the amounts withheld from employees' wages, the appropriate payroll taxes payable accounts should be debited and cash should be credited for the amount remitted.

48. Accrued liabilities. *Accrued liabilities* are obligations that arise in conjunction with expenses that have been incurred but not yet paid as of the end of the accounting period. Most accrued liabilities are recognized by adjusting journal entries recorded at the end of the accounting period. Wages earned by employees but not yet paid as of the end of the accounting period, for example, are accrued by a debit to wages expense and a credit to wages payable. Other accrued liabilities include compensated employee absences, payroll taxes payable, and property taxes payable.

49. *Compensated absences* are employee absences, such as vacation, illness, and holidays, for which it is expected that employees will be paid by the employer. An employer must accrue a liability for employees' rights to receive compensation for future absences if all the following conditions are met: (*a*) the obligation is attributable to services already rendered by the employees, (*b*) the obligation is related to rights that either are not contingent on the employees' future services (called vested rights) or can be accumulated over time by the employees, (*c*) payment of the compensation for future absences is probable, and (*d*) the amount of the compensation that will be paid for future absences can be reasonably estimated. When these conditions are met, the employer should record an adjusting entry in the year in which the rights to receive compensation for future absences are earned by the employees by a debit to an expense account (such as wages expense) and a credit to a liability account (such as vacation wages payable) for the estimated amount of the earned compensation that will be paid for future absences. An employer, however, is not required to accrue a liability for employees' rights to receive sick pay benefits that must be paid to employees only for absences due to illness.

50. The most common *employer payroll-related taxes* are FICA taxes and federal and state unemployment taxes. Both the employer and the employees are required to contribute FICA taxes, whereas only the employer is required to contribute unemployment taxes. The employees' share of FICA taxes is recorded as a liability by the employer when the amounts are withheld from their wages. The employer's share of FICA taxes and the federal and state unemployment taxes are accrued by a debit to payroll taxes expense and credits to the appropriate payroll taxes payable accounts (such as employer FICA taxes payable, federal unemployment taxes payable, and state unemployment taxes payable) for the amounts due on employees' wages for the period as specified by various governmental regulations. Later, when the employer remits the accrued amounts to the governmental taxing units, the appropriate payroll taxes payable accounts should be debited and cash should be credited for the amount remitted.

51. *Property taxes* based on the assessed value of real and personal property are levied and collected by local governmental units to finance their opera-

tions. There are two generally accepted methods of accounting for property taxes. Both methods recognize property taxes as an expense over the fiscal year of the governmental taxing unit. The methods differ, however, in the way in which the liability for property taxes is recognized. Under one method, deferred property tax expense is debited and property taxes payable is credited on the date the property taxes become a legal claim against the taxed property (called the *lien date*) for the total amount of the annual property taxes. Subsequently, as the property taxes are paid to the governmental taxing unit, property taxes payable is debited and cash is credited for the amount paid. Coincidentally, property tax expense is debited and deferred property tax expense is credited monthly over the fiscal year of the governmental taxing unit for a twelfth (1/12) of the total annual property taxes. Under the other method, the total amount of the annual property taxes is not recognized as a liability on the lien date. Instead, until a property tax payment is remitted to the taxing unit, property taxes are accrued monthly over the fiscal year of the governmental taxing unit by a debit to property tax expense and a credit to property taxes payable for a twelfth (1/12) of the total annual property taxes. Later, upon the remittance of a property tax payment to the governmental taxing unit, (*a*) property taxes payable is debited, but only to the extent of the balance in the account, if any; (*b*) deferred property tax expense is debited for any excess of the amount paid over the cumulative amount accrued previously; and (*c*) cash is credited for the amount paid. Thereafter, property tax expense is debited and deferred property tax expense is credited monthly for a twelfth (1/12) of the total annual property taxes until the deferred balance is fully amortized, before the property taxes payable account is credited.

52. Prepayments and deposits from customers. *Prepayments from customers* are obligations that arise from payments that are received for the future delivery of goods or services. Upon the receipt of such advance payments, a nonmonetary liability (often called unearned revenue or revenue collected in advance) should be recorded at the amount of cash received. Later, when the goods or services are delivered to the customer, the liability should be reduced and revenue should be recognized to the extent that it has been earned.

53. *Deposits from customers* are obligations that arise from payments that are received to guarantee performance of a contract, to guarantee return of property, or to guarantee against damage of property. Upon the receipt of such deposits, a nonmonetary liability (such as liability for returnable deposits) should be recorded at the amount of cash received. Later, when the property is returned or the contract is completed, the liability should be reduced as the deposit is returned to the customer. Any unclaimed deposits should be recognized as miscellaneous revenue (such as revenue from unclaimed deposits).

54. Current liabilities dependent on operating results. *Current liabilities dependent on operating results* are current obligations that cannot be known with certainty until the end of the annual accounting period. The amounts, and perhaps even the existence, of these obligations can be determined with certainty only when operating results for the annual period are known. Current liabilities dependent on operating results include income taxes payable and bonuses payable.

55. Income taxes payable. *Income taxes payable* are current obligations that arise as a result of taxes assessed by governmental units on the taxable income of corporations. Sole proprietorships and partnerships do not report income taxes payable because proprietors and partners are taxed individually for their share of the business entity's taxable income. The corporate income tax generally is due by the fifteenth day of the third calendar month following the end of the tax year. Most corporations, however, are required to pay income taxes in advance in the form of an estimated tax that is due in four equal installments during the tax year. The installment payments of estimated tax may be debited to a prepaid income tax account. And later, at the end of the annual accounting period, the journal entry to record income taxes may include (*a*) a debit to income tax expense; (*b*) a credit to prepaid income tax to the extent of the balance in the account, if any; and (*c*) either a credit to income taxes payable or a debit to income taxes refund receivable for the difference between the income taxes for the year and the estimated tax payments. Chapter 17 contains a detailed discussion of accounting for and reporting of income taxes.

56. Bonuses payable. *Bonuses payable* are current obligations that normally arise from contractual arrangements with key employees providing for the payment of additional compensation beyond their basic wages or salaries. Such bonuses may be based on revenue earned, on output produced, or on income. Bonuses are recorded by a debit to bonus expense and a credit to bonus payable for the amount of the bonus due. When the bonus is based on revenue earned or on output produced, the amount of bonus due is determined by multiplying the specified bonus rate by the revenue or output subject to the bonus. When the bonus is based on income, the amount of bonus due may be determined by means of an equation that mathematically describes the bonus plan. Typical equations, where B denotes the amount of bonus due, b denotes the specified bonus rate, I denotes income before bonus expense and income taxes, T denotes income taxes, and t denotes the tax rate, include (*a*) $B = bI$, if the bonus is based on income before bonus expense and income taxes; (*b*) $B = b(I - B)$, if the bonus is based on income after bonus expense but before income taxes; (*c*) $B = b(I - T)$ with $T = t(I - B)$, if the bonus is based on income after income taxes but before the bonus expense; and (*d*) $B = b(I - B - T)$ with $T = t(I - B)$, if the bonus is based on income after bonus expense and income taxes.

Contingencies

57. Contingencies. A *contingency* is defined as an existing condition, situation, or set of circumstances involving uncertainty as to possible gain (called a gain contingency) or loss (called a loss contingency) to an enterprise that will ultimately be resolved when one or more future events occur or fail to occur.

58. A *loss contingency* exists when the resolution of the uncertainty may confirm the loss or impairment of an asset or the incurrence of a liability. Typical loss contingencies include the collectibility of receivables; obligations related to product warranties and product defects; the risk of loss of or damage to property by fire, explosion, or other hazards; pending or threatened litigation; actual or possible claims or assessments; guarantees of the indebtedness of other; and agreements to repurchase receivables that have been sold.

59. There are three methods of accounting for and reporting loss contingencies under U.S. GAAP: (*a*) *accrual* of an estimated loss from the contingency; (*b*) *disclosure,* but not accrual, of the loss contingency; and (*c*) *neither accrual nor disclosure* of the loss contingency. The method of accounting and reporting required by a loss contingency depends in part on the likelihood that one or more future events will confirm the impairment of an asset or the incurrence of a liability. The FASB has identified three levels of likelihood concerning the resolution of loss contingencies: (*a*) *probable*—the future event or events are likely to occur; (*b*) *reasonably possible*—the chance that the future event or events will occur is more than remote but less than probable, and (*c*) *remote*—the chance that the future event or events will occur is slight.

60. U.S. GAAP requires that an estimated loss from a contingency be accrued by a charge to income if both of the following conditions are met: (*a*) Information available before issuance of the financial statements indicates that it is *probable* that an asset had been impaired or a liability had been incurred by the date of the financial statements. It is implicit in this condition that it must be *probable* that one or more future events will confirm the fact of the loss. (*b*) The amount of loss can be reasonably estimated. When both of these conditions are met, the circumstances surrounding the accrued loss contingency ordinarily should be disclosed in the notes accompanying the financial statements. Also, if there is a reasonable possibility of loss in excess of the amount accrued, the additional possible loss must be disclosed. Furthermore, if only a range of loss can be reasonably estimated, the minimum amount in the range must be accrued by a charge to income and the difference between the minimum amount and the maximum amount in the range must be disclosed. Loss contingencies that generally should be accrued include estimated uncollectible receivables, guarantees and product warranties, premium obligations, and litigation claims under specified circumstances. Specifically, a loss contingency resulting from *threatened litigation* (lawsuit not yet filed), *pending litigation* (lawsuit filed but not settled), a *claim,* or an *assessment* should be accrued by a charge to income only if the two criteria for accrual for a loss contingency are met. Since it is often difficult to estimate the amount of settlement in a pending lawsuit, most companies disclose litigation contingencies through a footnote.

61. A loss contingency that fails to meet either or both of the two conditions for accrual should not be accrued, but it should be disclosed in the financial statements if there is at least a reasonable possibility that a loss may have been incurred or if a remote loss contingency has the characteristics of a guarantee. Loss contingencies with the characteristics of guarantees include direct or indirect guarantees of the indebtedness of others, obligations of commercial banks under "standby letters of credit," and guarantees to repurchase receivables. The disclosures required for reasonably possible loss contingencies are the nature of the contingency and either an estimate of the possible loss or range of loss or a statement that such an estimate cannot be made. The disclosures required for remote loss contingencies with the characteristics of guarantees are the amount of the guarantee and, if estimable, the amounts that are expected to be recoverable from outside parties. No disclosures are required for loss contingencies related to unasserted claims or assessments, unless it is probable that a claim will be asserted and there is a reasonable possibility that the outcome will be unfavorable. Finally, when an asset has been impaired or a liability has been incurred after the date of the financial statements, or if there is at least a reasonable possibility of such an impairment or liability after that date, the disclosures required for reasonably possible loss contingencies may be necessary so that the financial statements will not be misleading. Such loss contingencies should not be accrued, however, as no asset was impaired or liability was incurred by the date of the financial statements.

62. General or unspecified business risks, such as strikes, wars, and recessions, do not meet the two conditions for accrual of loss contingencies. Thus possible losses from such risks should not be accrued and are not required to be disclosed under U.S. GAAP. Other countries, however, allow accrual for losses from general risks, with no specific contingency, to "smooth" periodic income by adjusting the amount for general risk "reserves."

63. A *gain contingency* exists when the resolution of the uncertainty may confirm the acquisition of an asset or the reduction of a liability. Typical gain contingencies include claims against others for patent infringement, upward price redetermination, and claims for reimbursement under condemnation proceedings. *ARB No. 50* contains two guidelines regarding such contingencies: (*a*) gain contingencies usually should not be accrued (recognized) until they are realized, and (*b*) material gain contingencies should be given adequate disclosure, provided that care is exercised to avoid misleading implications as to the likelihood of realization.

Appendix: Comprehensive Cash Reconciliation

64. Appendix 8-1 illustrates the mechanics of a *comprehensive cash reconciliation,* or *proof of cash.* The comprehensive cash reconciliation reconciles the company's and the bank's beginning and ending cash balances *and* receipts and disbursements for the period.

65. The comprehensive cash reconciliation requires a more complex schedule than the one for the traditional bank reconciliation discussed in the body of the text. The schedule illustrated on page 123 consists of four columns:

   a. Column 1—a bank reconciliation for the beginning of the period.
   b. Column 2—receipts for the period.
   c. Column 3—disbursements for the period.
   d. Column 4—a bank reconciliation for the end of the period.

It should be noted that the accounting period normally covered is one month.

66. The first and last columns are similar to a bank reconciliation; that is, corrected cash balances are determined from the ending cash balance per bank (per bank statement) and ending cash balance per books (per cash account). The differentiating feature of the comprehensive cash reconciliation is the middle columns for cash receipts and disbursements for the period. These columns begin with the amount for cash receipts and

Comprehensive Cash Reconciliation

	BEGINNING OF PERIOD RECONCILIATION	PERIOD RECEIPTS	PERIOD DISBURSEMENTS	END OF PERIOD RECONCILIATION
Balance per bank	$ xx	$ xx	$ xx	$ xx
Add:				
Deduct:				
Corrected bank balance	$ xx	$ xx	$ xx	$ xx
Balance per books	$ xx	$ xx	$ xx	$ xx
Add:				
Deduct:				
Corrected book balance	$ xx	$ xx	$ xx	$ xx

disbursements as recognized by the bank and on the books for the period and are "adjusted" to the "corrected" receipts and disbursements for the period. Thus the comprehensive cash reconciliation reconciles the balances per books with the bank statement for the beginning and ending balances for the period *and* the cash receipts and disbursements for the period.

67. To illustrate the basic techniques for a comprehensive cash reconciliation, three common items will be considered:

a. *Deposits in transit.* A deposit in transit at the beginning of the period must be added to column 1 under "Balance per bank" and deducted from the bank receipts for the period in column 2 because the deposit was actually a receipt for the prior period but was recognized by the bank at the beginning of the current period. A deposit in transit at the end of the period must be added to the bank receipts in column 2 and to the bank balance in column 4 since the deposit is a deposit for the current period, even though it will not be recorded by the bank until the following period.

b. *Outstanding checks.* Checks outstanding at the beginning of the period must be deducted from the beginning of the period reconciliation in column 1 and deducted from the disbursements per bank in column 3 because it is assumed that the checks cleared the bank in the current period and were included

(incorrectly) in the disbursements for the current period. Checks outstanding at the end of the period are added to the bank disbursements in column 3 and deducted from the end of the period bank balance in column 4 because these checks represent disbursements for the current period but will not be recognized by the bank until the following period.

c. *Service charges.* Service charges levied by the bank are normally not known until the bank statement is received. They are usually recognized by the company in the period after the bank makes the charges. Since last period's charges would have been recognized in the current period, they must be deducted from the beginning balance per books in column 1 and the book disbursements in column 3. The current period's bank charges should be added to the book disbursements in column 3 and deducted from the ending book balance in column 4 because the bank charges are a disbursement of the current period but not yet recognized by the company.

68. In addition, other items, such as NSF (not sufficient funds) checks, errors by the bank and/or company, and proceeds from collections, appear on the comprehensive cash reconciliation. It should be remembered that each item is usually entered into two of the four columns, that is, (*a*) beginning reconciliation and receipts or disbursements columns, or (*b*) receipts or disbursement and ending reconciliation columns.

Key Terms and Concepts

Provide the appropriate term or terms to complete each of the following statements:

1. A(n) ___MONETARY___ asset is an asset that is money or a claim to receive a sum of money, the amount of which is fixed or determinable without reference to future prices of specific goods or services.

2. ___CASH___ is a medium of exchange that is freely available for the purchase of goods and services and for the discharge of obligations.

3. A(n) ___PETTY CASH___ is used for small, immaterial expenditures.

4. A(n) ___BANK RECONCILIATION___ compares a company's ending cash balance with the bank statement balance and adjusts the balances to a "correct" cash balance.

5. When a company permits a buyer the option of paying its account early at a reduced amount, the company extends a(n) ___SALES OR CASH___ DISCOUNT.

6. The ___EFFECTIVE INTEREST___ method of amortization recognizes interest revenue on a receivable at an equal rate (percentage) each period.

7. When the length of time a receivable has been outstanding is taken into consideration in the process of estimating uncollectible accounts, the method is called ___AGING OF ACCTS RCV___

8. A company that discounts a note at a bank ___W/ RECOURSE___ remains contingently liable if the maker defaults on the note.

9. Accounts receivable that are used as collateral for a loan and whose proceeds are used to retire the loan are said to be ___ASSIGNED___.

10. Probable future sacrifices of economic benefits arising from the present obligations of a particular entity to transfer assets or provide services to other entities in the future as a result of past transactions or events are defined as ___LIABILITIES___.

11. Liabilities normally are reported on the balance sheet in two subcategories: ___CURRENT & LT LIABILITIES___, which are obligations that typically are expected to be settled by the use of existing resources classified as current assets, and ___LT LIABS___, which include all other obligations.

12. Obligations that arise in conjunction with expenses that have been incurred but not yet paid as of the end of the accounting period are called ___ACCRUED LIABS___.

13. Employee absences, such as vacations, illnesses, and holidays, for which it is expected that employees will be paid by the employer are called ___COMPENSATED ABSENCES___

14. The date that property taxes become a legal claim against the taxed property is called the ___LIEN DATE___.

15. A(n) ___CONTINGENCY___ is an existing condition, situation, or set of circumstances involving uncertainty as to possible gain or loss to an enterprise that will ultimately be resolved when one or more future events occur or fail to occur.

True-False

Indicate by circling the appropriate response whether each of the following statements is true (T) or false (F):

(T) F 1. Cash normally includes U.S. currency and coin, demand deposits, and money orders.

(T) F 2. Postdated checks are properly classified as receivables.

T (F) 3. When a petty cash fund is reimbursed, petty cash should be credited.

T (F) 4. An imprest petty cash fund is maintained with a variable amount as its balance.

(T) F 5. A bank reconciliation verifies the company's cash balance with the independent records maintained by the company's bank.

T (F) 6. After preparation of the bank reconciliation and the required entry to adjust and correct the cash account, the cash balance should equal the ending balance on the bank statement.

T (F) 7. When a bank reconciliation is prepared, deposits in transit should be added to the "Balance per books."

(T) F 8. The exchange price determined for a credit sale transaction theoretically represents the amount to be recognized as the receivable and sales revenue.

T (F) 9. Trade discounts are recorded in the accounting records at the time they are granted to the buyer.

(T) F 10. Companies offer sales discounts in an effort to reduce the time between the sale and collection of the receivable.

(T) F 11. When a seller offers a sales discount, accounts receivable and sales are usually recorded at the net sales price.

T (F) 12. Under the effective interest method, an equal amount of interest is recognized with each period's payment.

T (F) 13. Estimation of uncollectible accounts expense by the aging method requires that the balance before adjustment in allowance for uncollectible accounts be ignored.

T (F) 14. If the amount of credit and cash sales varies considerably from year to year, the uncollectible accounts expense should be based on total sales when the percentage of sales method is used.

(T) F 15. Notes receivable should be valued at the present value of future cash flows to be received.

(T) F 16. Interest on a short-term, interest-bearing note is normally recognized when the note is settled.

(T) F 17. Although liabilities theoretically should be valued at the present value of the assets or services that must be transferred in the future to settle the obligation, current liabilities customarily are recorded at their face amounts, since the due dates are within short periods of time.

(T) F 18. Trade accounts payable are monetary liabilities, whereas unearned revenues are nonmonetary liabilities.

T (F) 19. Current liabilities may be offset against current assets that can be used to settle the obligations.

(T) F 20. Dividends payable should not be recognized until a dividend is formally declared by the board of directors.

(T) F 21. Sales taxes payable are recognized at the time of the sale.

(T) F 22. Although both the employer and employees are required to contribute FICA taxes, the employer should recognize a liability for the employees' share as well as for its own share of the taxes.

(T) F 23. An employee may, but is not required to, accrue a liability for employees' rights to receive sick pay benefits that must be paid to employees only for absences due to illness.

(T) F 24. Prepayments and deposits by customers represent liabilities, because such transactions create obligations to deliver goods or services or to refund the amounts received.

T (F) 25. A loss involving pending or threatened litigation should be accrued by a charge to income if it is probable that the outcome will be unfavorable and the amount of loss can be reasonably estimated, even though the cause for action occurred after the date of the financial statements.

T F 26. When a loss contingency is not accrued but there is at least a reasonable
possibility that a loss may have been
incurred, the financial statements
should disclose the nature of the contingency and an estimate of the possible loss or range of loss or a statement that such an estimate cannot be
made.

T F 27. Possible losses from general or
unspecified business risks may be
accrued by a charge to income under
U.S. GAAP.

T F 28. Material gain contingencies may be
disclosed in the financial statements,
but care should be exercised to avoid
misleading implications as to the
likelihood of realization.

T F 29. An estimated loss from a contingency
may be accrued only by recognizing
an increase in a liability.

T F *30. A comprehensive cash reconciliation
reconciles only the beginning and ending balances of the cash account with
the bank statement.

Multiple Choice

Select the best response for each of the following
items, and circle the corresponding letter:

1. Which of the following statements concerning
an imprest petty cash fund is false?

    a. It provides fixed accountability over the
    amount of the fund.
    b. It requires that vouchers be prepared to sup-
    port each petty cash disbursement.
    c. It should be replenished at the end of an
    accounting period.
    d. It usually requires authorization by the
    treasurer before funds can be disbursed.

2. When the "Balance per bank" section is reconciled:

    a. Bank service charges are deducted.
    b. Outstanding checks are deducted.
    c. Deposits in transit are deducted.
    d. Proceeds from a note collected by the bank
    are added.

3. If a seller grants a sales discount but it is not
taken by the buyer, at the time of payment the

seller would credit which account for the
amount of the discount?

    a. Cash.
    b. Sales revenue.
    c. Sales discounts.
    d. Interest revenue.

4. A company that emphasizes the matching of
revenues and expenses would select which of
the following methods to determine uncollectible accounts expense?

    a. Percentage of sales.
    b. Aging of accounts receivable.
    c. Percentage of ending accounts receivable.
    d. Either b or c.

5. When an account receivable is written off by
the allowance method:

    a. Total current assets decrease.
    b. Uncollectible accounts expense increases.
    c. Accounts receivable increase.
    d. Accounts receivable (net) are unaffected.

6. When the effective interest method is used to
determine interest on a receivable issued at a
discount, the amount of periodic interest revenue recognized:

    a. Varies randomly each period.
    b. Remains constant each period.
    c. Increases each period.
    d. Decreases each period.

7. If a company discounted a note receivable with
a bank and the debtor defaults on the note, the
company should debit:

    a. Accounts receivable for the face value of the
    note.
    b. Cash for the maturity value of the note.
    c. Loss on notes discounted for the face value
    of the note.
    d. Accounts receivable for the maturity value
    of the note.

8. Which of the following transactions would not
allow a company to secure immediate cash?

    a. Factoring of receivables.
    b. Discounting of notes receivable.
    c. Assignment of receivables.
    d. Aging of receivables.

9. Which of the following is not an essential
characteristic of a liability?

a. There is a present duty or responsibility to one or more other entities that is expected to be settled by transfer of assets or provision of services in the future.

b. The duty or responsibility to transfer assets or provide services in the future can be traced to a legally enforceable claim, such as one specified in a contract.

c. The duty or responsibility obligates a particular entity.

d. The transaction or event that caused the entity to be obligated has already occurred.

10. When the total property tax obligation is *not* recognized as a liability on the lien date, the monthly journal entry to recognize property taxes as an expense equally over the fiscal year of the governmental taxing unit should include a credit to:

a. Deferred property tax expense.

b. Property taxes payable.

c. Either deferred property tax expense, if there is a balance in the account, or property taxes payable, if there is no balance in the deferred property tax expense account.

d. Cash.

11. Which of the following is the equation that mathematically describes a bonus plan specifying that the bonus is based on 10 percent of income after bonus expense but before income taxes, where I denotes income before bonuses and income taxes, B denotes the bonus, and T denotes income taxes?

a. $B = .10I$.

b. $B = .10(I - B)$.

c. $B = .10(I - T)$.

d. $B = .10(I - B - T)$.

12. An estimated loss from a contingency should be accrued by a charge to income if the amount of loss can be reasonably estimated and if:

a. It is at least reasonably possible that an asset was impaired or a liability was incurred after the date of the financial statements but before the financial statements are issued.

b. It is probable that an asset was impaired or a liability was incurred after the date of the

financial statements but before the financial statements are issued.

c. It is at least reasonably possible that an asset had been impaired or a liability had been incurred by the date of the financial statements.

d. It is probable that an asset had been impaired or a liability had been incurred by the date of the financial statements.

13. When it is probable that an asset had been impaired or a liability had been incurred by the date of the financial statements but only a range of loss can be reasonably estimated:

a. The maximum amount in the range should be accrued by a charge to income.

b. The average amount in the range should be accrued by a charge to income.

c. The minimum amount in the range should be accrued by a charge to income.

d. No loss should be accrued by a charge to income.

14. A loss contingency must be disclosed in the financial statements except when:

a. A loss has been accrued by a charge to income and it is at least reasonably possible that an additional loss in excess of the amount accrued may have been incurred.

b. There is at least a reasonable possibility that a loss may have been incurred by the date of the financial statements.

c. The loss contingency has the characteristics of a guarantee even though the possibility of loss may be remote.

d. A loss was incurred, or there is at least a reasonable possibility that a loss was incurred, after the date of the financial statements.

*15. When a proof of cash bank reconciliation is prepared, which one of the following would *not* be a column heading?

a. Revenues for period.

b. Receipts for period.

c. Disbursements for period.

d. Beginning of period reconciliation.

Extended Problems

1. Data pertaining to cash transactions for the month ended June 30, as recorded by WWEZ Company and its bank, Last City Bank, are as follows:

	LAST CITY BANK		WWEZ CO.	
	May 31	June 30	May 31	June 30
Balance	$1,047	$ 725	$1,110	$ 570
Receipts	-0-	3,500	-0-	3,270
Disbursements	-0-	3,822	-0-	3,810
Other data:				
Bank service charges	18	20		
Outstanding checks			145	160
Deposits in transit			190	70

Other data as of June 30 are as follows:

a. Quarterly safe-deposit box charge, charged to WWEZ's account in June, $25.
b. Collection of note for WWEZ by Last City Bank, $50.
c. During June, Last City Bank recorded a deposit of $210 as $120.
d. WWEZ Company collected $150 from a customer but failed to record the cash sale; however, the money was properly deposited with the bank on the day the money was collected.

REQUIRED

a. Prepare a bank reconciliation for WWEZ Company for the month ended June 30.
b. Prepare the proper general journal entry to adjust the cash account.
*c. Prepare a comprehensive cash reconciliation for June 30 assuming that adjusting entries were not made at the end of May.

2. Selected account balances of Edition Corporation appear here as of December 31, 1995.

	DEBIT	CREDIT
Cash	$ 90,000	
Petty cash	800	
Accounts receivable	320,000	
Accounts receivable assigned	28,000	
Allowance for sales returns		$ 17,000
Allowance for uncollectible accounts		500
Notes payable (secured by accounts receivable assigned)		20,000
Sales		900,000
Sales discounts	21,000	

During 1996 Edition Corporation entered into the following transactions:

a. Edition Corporation collected $15,000 of the assigned accounts receivable and remitted that amount to reduce its outstanding note and $200 for interest to its bank, Troy City National Bank.
b. It was determined that $3,000 of the assigned accounts receivable were worthless. They were written off by the allowance method and were replaced by $3,000 of new accounts receivable.
c. $7,000 of assigned accounts receivable were collected, and the company's note, including a $50 interest charge, was settled with Troy City National Bank.
d. Edition sold without recourse $85,000 of its accounts receivable to Pine Factors. Pine Factors charged a factoring fee of 11 percent plus interest of $2,500. Edition had estimated $1,700 of the factored receivables to be uncollectible.
e. Edition factored with recourse $100,000 of its receivables (with a related allowance for uncollectible accounts of $2,200) to DI Factoring. DI Factoring charges a 3 percent factoring fee, interest of $3,400, and is permitted to hold back $9,000 to allow for reductions in the amounts collected. This transaction qualifies as a sale of receivables.

REQUIRED

a. Prepare the appropriate adjusting entry as of December 31, 1995, to record uncollectible accounts. It is assumed that uncollectible accounts will equal 3 percent of the year-end nonassigned balance of accounts receivable.

b. The vouchers in the petty cash drawer were as follows: office supplies, $100; delivery charges, $150; miscellaneous, $25; and an IOU, $5. Petty cash on hand amounted to $510. Prepare the proper entry to record the reimbursement of the petty cash fund on December 31, 1995.

c. Prepare the entry to reduce the petty cash fund permanently to $500.

d. Illustrate in good form the current asset section of the December 31, 1995, balance sheet after the preceding adjustments.

e. Prepare the proper journal entries to record the 1996 transactions.

3. Selected transactions and other data concerning the activities of Liabi Company for the year ended December 31, 1995, are presented as follows. The company was formed on January 1, 1995, to merchandise a single product.

a. On January 9, 1995, the company received merchandise that was purchased at a cost of $20,000, terms 2/10, n/30. Full payment for the merchandise was remitted to the supplier on January 18, 1995. The company uses the periodic system of accounting for inventory and the net method of accounting for purchase discounts.

b. On January 1, 1995, the lien date, the company received a property tax bill of $6,000 from a local governmental taxing unit for the fiscal year July 1, 1995, to June 30, 1996. The property tax bill was paid in two equal installments, on September 1, 1995, and December 1, 1995. The company follows the policy of accruing the property taxes monthly over the fiscal year of the governmental unit instead of recognizing the total property tax obligation on the lien date.

c. The company pays its employees their wages on the last day of each month. Total wages for the month of August were $50,000, with $42,000 subject to the 7.65 percent FICA tax and $5,000 subject to unemployment taxes of 5.4 percent by the state and .8 percent by the federal government after credit for the state unemployment taxes. Federal, state, and local income taxes of $9,500 were withheld from employee wages.

d. On September 2, 1995, the company received a $500 advance from a customer to be applied against the purchase price of a delivery scheduled for October 15, 1995. The order was shipped on the scheduled delivery date, and the customer was sent an invoice of $4,500 for the balance due. The sale was not subject to sales taxes, as the customer is located in another state.

e. On December 31, 1995, the company borrowed cash from a local bank in exchange for a 12 percent $50,000 discounted note due in 90 days. The money was borrowed to finance the acquisition of two new trucks.

f. The company has a bonus plan under which its president is to receive a bonus of 10 percent of income after income taxes, but before deduction of bonus expense. The bonus is payable on the 15th of the third month after the end of the year. The income tax rate is 40 percent, and the bonus is deductible for income tax purposes. Income before bonus and income taxes was $260,000 for the year ended December 31, 1995.

g. The company hired 15 hourly employees on the date it was formed, January 1, 1995, at a wage rate of $9 per hour for a 40-hour week. In addition, each hourly employee is to receive two weeks (80 hours) of vested vacation wages for each full year of employment, with no paid vacation to be taken until after one full year. All 15 hourly employees still are employed by the company as of December 31, 1995.

REQUIRED

a. Prepare the journal entries required to record the preceding transactions and events for the year ended December 31, 1995, and prepare any adjusting journal entries required as of December 31, 1995.

b. Assume that the company's 15 hourly employees were paid their vacation wages at the end of April 1996, when the wage rate is $10 per hour. All the vacation wages were subject to the 7.65 percent FICA tax, and $2,500 was withheld for federal, state, and local income taxes. Prepare the journal entry required to record the payment of vacation wages.

COMMON ERRORS

The first statement in each of the "common errors" listed here is *incorrect*. Each incorrect statement is followed by a corrected statement and an explanation.

1. Cash is a medium of exchange that can be used to acquire goods and services and discharge debts. *Wrong*

Cash is a medium of exchange that is freely available for the acquisition of goods and services and the discharging of debts. *Right*

To be considered cash, an item must be freely available to be used at management's discretion. Any restriction of a fund's use prevents it from being freely available, and thus it cannot be considered cash. It is tempting to include common monetary items such as certificates of deposit as cash, but they are not freely available without the incurrence of a severe penalty for early withdrawal.

2. The balance of a company's cash account and the checking account's bank statement balance are always equal. *Wrong*

The balances of the cash account and checking account are seldom equal. *Right*

Even though the cash account balance and the bank statement balance theoretically reflect the same transactions, there is almost always a time lag between the time a transaction is recorded by the company and the time it is recorded by the bank, and vice versa. A company may have recorded a deposit at the end of an accounting period, for example, but it is unlikely to be entered by the bank until the next period. Therefore, at any one time the two balances will not reflect the same transactions, nor will they be in balance. In order to determine the correct cash balance, a bank reconciliation is prepared.

3. When an uncollectible account receivable is written off by the allowance method, net receivables are reduced. *Wrong*

When an uncollectible account receivable is written off by the allowance method, there is no effect on net receivables. *Right*

The write-off of an uncollectible account reduces both accounts receivable and the allowance for uncollectible accounts by the amount of the bad debt, so that there is no change in net receivables. Net receivables are reduced when the adjustment providing for uncollectible accounts is made.

4. A note payable secured by assigned accounts receivable is a liability on the balance sheet. *Wrong*

A note payable secured by assigned accounts receivable is deducted from the balance of the assigned accounts receivable. *Right*

This is one of the few instances in which a liability can be offset against an asset. The proceeds from the assigned receivables are specifically designated to be used to retire the note, and proper balance sheet disclosure requires that the note be deducted from the assigned receivables. As it is customary to assign receivables of greater value than the amount of the note, the resulting difference is a debit balance and labeled equity in assigned receivables.

5. Since the transferor receives cash from the transferee when accounts receivable are factored, the transaction is always treated as a sale. *Wrong*

Since the transferor receives cash from the transferee when accounts receivable are factored, the transaction may be treated as a sale or a borrowing. *Right*

All transfers of receivables to a factor *without recourse* are treated as a sale because ownership risks and benefits are transferred to the factor (transferee) and the net cash flow effects of the transfer are known at the date of the transfer. Transfers of receivables *with recourse,* however, may be treated as a sale *or* as a borrowing with a liability being recorded. If a company transfers receivables with recourse and the net cash flow effects can be determined, the transfer is still recorded as a sale. Three conditions must be met for a transfer with recourse to qualify as a sale: (*a*) the transferor surrenders control of receivables, (*b*) the transferor can estimate obligations to the transferee, and (*c*) the transferee cannot make the transferor repurchase receivables, except as under recourse agreement.

When receivables are transferred with recourse but the three conditions are not met, the transaction is in substance a borrowing and a liability is created. The difference in handling is tied to the probability of knowing the net cash flows and is, perhaps, best illustrated by the credit portion of the entry to record the transfer. When the cash consequences can be estimated, a sale is made and accounts receivable is credited, indicating the surrender or sale of an asset (receivables) for cash. On the other hand, if the net cash effects cannot be estimated, the transferor is borrowing cash as evidenced by the credit to a liability, due to the transferee or factor. Hopefully, the transferee will collect enough from the receivables to satisfy the debt.

Although many transfers of receivables to a factor are treated as a sale, there are cases when the net cash flow effects are uncertain and the transfer must be recorded as a borrowing, not a sale.

6. When sales taxes are included in sales revenue, the amount of sales taxes collected from customers during the period can be determined by multiplying the amount recorded in the sales revenue account by the sales tax rate. *Wrong*

When sales taxes are included in sales revenue, the amount of sales taxes collected from customers during the period can be determined by subtracting from the amount recorded in the sales revenue account an amount equal to the sales revenue divided by 1 plus the sales tax rate. *Right*

Under one method of accounting for sales taxes, the total proceeds including the sales taxes are credited originally to sales revenue, and at the end of the accounting period an adjusting journal entry is recorded to debit sales revenue and credit sales taxes payable for the amount of sales taxes collected from customers during the period. Because the amount recorded in the sales revenue account is equal to the selling price of the goods or services plus the sales taxes on the selling price, the amount of sales taxes collected from customers during the period can be determined by subtracting from the amount recorded in the sales revenue account an amount equal to the sales revenue divided by 1 plus the sales tax rate.

7. When the total property tax obligation is not recognized as a liability on the lien date, property taxes should be recognized monthly over the fiscal year of the governmental taxing unit by a debit to property tax expense and a credit to property taxes payable for a twelfth of the total annual property taxes. *Wrong*

When the total property tax obligation is not recognized as a liability on the lien date, property taxes should be recognized monthly over the fiscal year of the governmental taxing unit by a debit to property tax expense and a credit to either property taxes payable or deferred property tax expense for a twelfth of the total annual property taxes. *Right*

Property taxes normally are paid to the governmental taxing unit in two equal installments, with the first installment due either before or after the beginning of the taxing unit's fiscal year. When the total property tax obligation is not recognized as a liability on the lien date and the first property tax payment is remitted after the beginning of the taxing unit's fiscal year, property taxes should be accrued monthly over the fiscal year of the governmental taxing unit, until the first property tax payment is made, by a debit to property tax expense and a credit to property taxes payable for a twelfth (1/12) of the total annual property taxes. Later, when the first property tax payment is remitted, (a) property taxes payable should be debited to the extent of the balance in the account, (b) deferred property tax expense should be debited for the excess of the amount paid over the cumulative amount accrued previously, and (c) cash should be credited for the amount paid. Thereafter, property tax expense should be debited and deferred property tax expense should be credited monthly for a twelfth (1/12) of the total annual property taxes until the deferred balance is fully amortized, before property taxes payable is credited. When the total property tax obligation is not recognized as a liability on the lien date and the first property tax payment is remitted before the beginning of the taxing unit's fiscal year, deferred property tax expense should be debited and cash should be credited for the amount of the first property tax payment. Thereafter, property taxes should be amortized monthly over the fiscal year of the governmental taxing unit by a debit to property tax expense and a credit to deferred property tax expense for a twelfth (1/12) of the total annual property taxes until the deferred balance is fully amortized, before property taxes payable is credited. Thus when the total property tax obligation is not recognized as a liability on the lien date, the journal entry to recognize property taxes as an expense over the fiscal year of the governmental taxing unit should include either a credit to deferred property tax expense, if there is a balance in the account, or a credit to property taxes payable, if there is no balance in the deferred property tax expense account.

8. A loss contingency resulting from litigation, a claim, or an assessment should not be accrued, since disclosure of such an accrual in the financial statements could weaken the entity's position in the dispute. *Wrong*

A loss contingency resulting from litigation, a claim, or an assessment should be accrued if the two conditions for the accrual of such contingencies are met. *Right*

A loss contingency resulting from litigation, a claim, or an assessment must be accrued by a charge to income if the following conditions are met: (a) the cause of the litigation, claim, or assessment occurred by the date of the financial statements; (b) it is probable that the outcome will be unfavorable; and (c) the amount of loss can be reasonably estimated. In addition, disclosure of the nature of the accrual and, in some circumstances, the amount of the accrual may be necessary so that the financial statements will not be misleading. Thus when a loss contingency resulting from litigation, a claim, or an assessment is accrued, the nature and amount of the accrual may be, but are not required to be, disclosed in the financial statements. For this reason, accrual of such a loss contingency will not necessarily weaken the entity's position in the dispute.

ANSWERS

Items marked with an asterisk (*) refer to the Appendix.

Key Terms and Concepts

1. monetary
2. cash
3. petty cash fund
4. bank reconciliation
5. sales or cash discount
6. effective interest
7. aging of accounts receivable
8. with recourse
9. assigned
10. liabilities
11. current (or short-term) liabilities, noncurrent (or long-term) liabilities
12. accrued liabilities
13. compensated absences
14. lien date
15. contingency

True-False

1. T
2. T
3. F   When a petty cash fund is reimbursed, the credit is to cash, not to petty cash. One of the purposes of reimbursing the petty cash fund is to replace the cash previously disbursed by the petty cash fund trustee; thus the credit to cash "resupplies" the petty cash fund with cash. Petty cash is credited only when the fund is to be permanently reduced or closed.
4. F   The purpose of an imprest petty cash fund is to have fixed accountability; therefore, there is a known, or fixed, not variable, balance maintained for the petty cash fund.
5. T
6. F   A bank reconciliation is prepared to determine the "correct" cash balance. After the proper adjusting entry is made, the cash balance should equal the "corrected" cash balance.
7. F   Deposits in transit have previously been recorded by the company, and adding them to "Balance per books" would be a double counting of the deposits. Deposits in transit are correctly added to the "Balance per bank," since they do not appear on the bank statement.
8. T
9. F   Trade discounts are set by the seller to establish the sale price and are never recorded.
10. T

11. T
12. F   When the effective interest method is used, interest is recognized at an equal rate (percentage), not an equal dollar amount each period.
13. F   The aging of accounts receivable method focuses on valuation of the receivables. After the receivables are analyzed and the amount of uncollectibles is estimated, the ending balance in allowance for uncollectible accounts must equal the amount estimated to be uncollectible. Therefore, to adjust the allowance account to the desired amount, the balance in the account must be considered; otherwise the proper valuation would not be achieved.
14. F   Estimation of uncollectible accounts expense on the basis of total sales is appropriate only if the percentage can be adjusted for the portion of cash sales in total sales. When the proportion of cash and credit sales varies considerably, it is hard to estimate a reasonable percentage to apply to total sales. In the situation presented, it would be best if just credit sales were used.
15. T
16. T
17. T
18. T
19. F   Current liabilities should not be offset against current assets that may be used to settle the obligations.
20. T
21. T
22. T
23. T
24. T
25. F   A loss involving pending or threatened litigation should be accrued by a charge to income only if three conditions are met: (a) the cause for action occurred by the date of the financial statements, (b) it is probable that the outcome will be unfavorable, and (c) the amount of loss can be reasonably estimated.
26. T
27. F   General or unspecified business risks do not meet the two conditions specified by U.S. GAAP for the accrual of loss contingencies. Accordingly, possible losses from such risks should not be accrued by a charge to income.
28. T

29. F   Some estimated losses from contingencies (for example, product warranties) are accrued by recognizing an increase in a liability, whereas other (for example, estimated uncollectible receivables) are accrued by recognizing a decrease in the book value of an asset.

*30. F   A comprehensive cash reconciliation does reconcile the beginning and ending cash balances with the bank statement, similar to a typical bank reconciliation. In addition, the comprehensive cash reconciliation reconciles receipts and disbursements for the period with the bank statement.

Multiple Choice

1. d	9. b
2. b	10. c
3. d	11. b
4. a	12. d
5. d	13. c
6. c	14. d
7. d	*15. a
8. d	

Extended Problems

1. a. Bank reconciliation for June 30:

WWEZ Company
BANK RECONCILIATION
JUNE 30

Balance per bank...........................		$725
Add: Deposits in transit...............	$ 70	
Deposit error ($210 – $120)...	90	160
		$885
Deduct: Outstanding checks.............		(160)
Corrected cash balance...................		$725
Balance per books		$570
Add: Collection of note by bank	$ 50	
Unrecorded cash sale.............	150	200
		$770
Deduct: Bank service charge..........	$ 20	
Safe-deposit box charge	25	(45)
Corrected cash balance...................		$725

b. Journal entry to adjust cash account:

Cash	155	
Bank service charge expense ($20 + $25)	45	
Note receivable.........................		50
Sales revenue		150

*c.   Comprehensive cash reconciliation for June 30:

WWEZ Company
COMPREHENSIVE CASH RECONCILIATION
JUNE 30

	MAY 31 RECONCILIATION	JUNE RECEIPTS	JUNE DISBURSEMENTS	JUNE 30 RECONCILIATION
Balance per bank	$1,047	$3,500	$3,822	$725
Add:				
Deposits in transit 5/31	190	(190)		
Deposits in transit 6/30		70		70
Deposit error		90		90
Deduct:				
Outstanding checks 5/31	(145)		(145)	
Outstanding checks 6/30			160	(160)
Corrected bank balance	$1,092	$3,470	$3,837	$725
Balance per books	$1,110	$3,270	$3,810	$570
Add:				
Collection of note		50		50
Unrecorded sale		150		150
Deduct:				
Service charge				
May	(18)		(18)	
June			20	(20)
Safe-deposit box charge			25	(25)
Corrected book balance	$1,092	$3,470	$3,837	$725

2. a. Year-end adjusting entry:

Uncollectible accounts expense...... 9,100
  Allowance for uncollectible
    accounts (3% × $320,000
    = $9,600 − $500)............... 9,100

b. Entry to reimburse petty cash fund:

Office supply expense................. 100
Delivery expense........................ 150
Miscellaneous expense................ 25
Accounts receivable.................... 5
Cash short............................. 10[a]
  Cash...................................... 290

[a]Petty cash fund $800
Total vouchers + IOU   (280)
Expected cash on hand   520
Actual cash on hand   (510)
Cash short $ 10

c. Entry to reduce petty cash fund:

Cash ($800 − $500) 300
  Petty cash 300

d. Partial balance sheet disclosure:

Edition Corporation
PARTIAL BALANCE SHEET
DECEMBER 31, 1995

Current assets:
  Cash ($90,000 + $300 − $290).. $ 90,010
  Petty cash ($800 − $300).........   500
  Accounts receivable............... $320,000
  Allowance for uncollectible
    accounts ($500 − $9,100)..... (9,600)
  Allowance for sales returns....... (17,000)
  Net accounts receivable........... 293,400
  Accounts receivable assigned.... $ 28,000
  Note payable....................... (20,000)
  Equity in receivables assigned... 8,000
  Total current assets................ $391,910

e. Journal entries for 1996 transactions:

Cash...................................... 15,000
  Accounts receivable assigned.... 15,000
Note payable........................... 15,000
Interest expense....................... 200
  Cash...................................... 15,200

Allowance for uncollectible
  accounts................................ 3,000
  Accounts receivable assigned...... 3,000
Accounts receivable assigned......... 3,000
  Accounts receivable.................. 3,000
Cash...................................... 7,000
  Accounts receivable assigned...... 7,000
Notes payable ($20,000 − $15,000) 5,000
Interest expense......................... 50
  Cash...................................... 5,050
Accounts receivable ($28,000 −
  $15,000 − $7,000)................... 6,000
  Accounts receivable assigned...... 6,000
Cash [$85,000 − ($85,000 × .11)
  − $2,500]............................. 73,150
Allowance for uncollectible accounts 1,700
Loss on sale of receivables............ 10,150
  Accounts receivable.................. 85,000
Cash [$100,000 − ($100,000 × .03)
  − $3,400 − $9,000]................... 84,600
Allowance for uncollectible accounts. 2,200
Due to DI Factoring ($9,000 −
  $2,200)................................ 6,800
Loss on sale of receivables............. 6,400
  Accounts receivable.................. 100,000

3. a. Journal entries for the year ended December 31, 1995:

Trade accounts payable:
1/9/95   Purchases [$20,000 − ($20,000 × 2%)] 19,600
      Accounts payable 19,600
1/18/95 Accounts payable 19,600
      Cash 19,600

Property taxes:

7/31/95	Property tax expense ($6,000 ÷ 12)..	500	
	Property taxes payable...		500
8/31/95	Property tax expense ($6,000 ÷ 12)..	500	
	Property taxes payable		500
9/1/95	Property taxes payable ($500 × 2)...	1,000	
	Deferred property tax expense ($3,000 − $1,000)...................................	2,000	
	Cash ($6,000 ÷ 2)...		3,000
9/30/95	Property tax expense ($6,000 ÷ 12)..	500	
	Deferred property tax expense..		500
10/31/95	Property tax expense ($6,000 ÷ 12)..	500	
	Deferred property tax expense...		500
11/30/95	Property tax expense ($6,000 ÷ 12)..	500	
	Deferred property tax expense...		500
12/1/95	Deferred property tax expense...	3,000	
	Cash ($6,000 ÷ 2)...		3,000
12/31/95	Property tax expense ($6,000 ÷ 12)..	500	
	Deferred property tax expense...		500

Payroll-related taxes:

8/31/95	Wages expense	50,000	
	Federal, state, and local income taxes payable..............................		9,500
	Employee FICA taxes payable ($42,000 × 7.65%).............................		3,213
	Cash ($50,000 − $9,500 − $3,213)...		37,287
8/31/95	Payroll taxes expense ($3,213 + $40 + $270).........................	3,523	
	Employer FICA taxes payable ($42,000 × 7.65%).............................		3,213
	FUTA taxes payable ($5,000 × .8%).........................		40
	State unemployment taxes payable ($5,000 × 5.4%)...........................		270

Prepayment by customer:

9/2/95	Cash	500	
	Unearned revenue..		500
10/15/95	Accounts receivable...	4,500	
	Unearned revenue..	500	
	Sales revenue ($4,500 + $500)...		5,000

Short-term note payable:

12/31/95	Cash ($50,000 − $1,500).......................................	48,500	
	Discount on notes payable ($50,000 × 12% × 90/360)........................	1,500	
	Notes payable...		50,000

Bonus:

12/31/95	Bonus expense..	16,250	
	Bonus payable..		16,250[a]

[a]The amount of bonus due (B) is determined by solving the following equation, where the income taxes (T) are equal to .40 ($260,000 − B): $B = .10($260,000 − T)$ or $B = .10[$260,000 − .40($260,000 − B)]$.

Vacation wages:

12/31/95	Wages expense ($9 × 80 × 15)..	10,800	
	Vacation wages payable...		10,800

b. Journal entry to record payment of vacation wages.[a]

4/30/96	Vacation wages payable ($9 × 80 × 15)..	10,800	
	Wages expense ($12,000 − $10,800).................................	1,200	
	Federal, state, and local income taxes payable.............................		2,500
	Employee FICA taxes payable ($12,000 × 7.65%).............................		918
	Cash ($12,000 − $2,500 − $918)...		8,582

[a]The gross amount of vacation wages based on the current wage rate is $10 × 80 hours × 15 employees, or $12,000.

9

INVENTORY VALUATION: DETERMINING COST AND USING COST FLOW ASSUMPTIONS

After reading Chapter 9 and completing the questions, cases, exercises, and problems from the text chapter, you should be able to:

1. Define the major inventory classifications for merchandising and manufacturing companies.
2. Differentiate between the periodic and perpetual inventory systems.
3. Calculate cost of goods sold under the periodic inventory system.
4. Identify the units that should be included in inventory.
5. Distinguish between inventory or product costs and period costs.

6. Distinguish between the absorption costing and direct or variable costing methods for assigning manufacturing costs to a product.
7. List and apply the four traditional inventory cost flow assumptions, that is, specific identification, average cost, FIFO (first in, first out) and unit LIFO (last in, first out), and pooled LIFO.
8. Understand the major advantages and disadvantages of the various cost flow assumptions.
9. Understand the basic procedures for and application of the dollar-value LIFO inventory method.
10. Know the required disclosures for inventory.

CHAPTER REVIEW

Introduction

1. One of the most significant items, in dollar amount, for many manufacturing and merchandising enterprises is inventory. Inventory on hand at the end of an accounting period is often one of the largest assets on the balance sheet, and inventory sold during the period is represented by one of the major expenses, cost of goods sold, on the income statement. *Inventory* (or *stock* in some countries) is a tangible asset either (*a*) intended for resale in the ordinary course of business, (*b*) in the process of being produced for sale, or (*c*) to be used currently in the production of goods to be sold. What constitutes inventory varies from company to company

and depends on the nature of the company's operations. Inventory is reported on the balance sheet as a current asset because it will be converted to cash (sold) or consumed (used in production) within one year or the operating cycle, whichever is longer.

2. This chapter review discusses in depth the major classifications of inventory, inventory systems, inventoriable items, and costs and cost flow assumptions. The disclosure requirements for inventory and the LIFO-related issues are then addressed.

Classification of Inventory

3. A *merchandising* company, which buys goods ready for resale, normally has one general class of inventory, merchandise inventory. The merchandise inventory account usually represents several types of inventory. A jewelry store, for example, might have items such as rings, watches, pins, and necklaces in its merchandise inventory account. The cost of merchandise inventory is normally the purchase price plus costs incurred to ready the inventory for resale.

4. A *manufacturing* company, which produces goods for resale, has three types of inventory, which are related to the stages of production:

   a. *Raw material inventory* consists of goods and materials that ultimately become part of the manufactured product but have not yet entered the production process. The purchase price of the inventory and costs incurred to get the materials into place for use in production are reported as the cost of the raw material inventory.

   b. *Work-in-process inventory* consists of units of product that have been started in the production process but have not yet been finished. The cost of raw materials, direct labor (labor applied directly to the product), and manufacturing overhead (such incidental production costs as depreciation and utilities) are reported as the cost of work-in-process inventory.

   c. *Finished goods inventory* consists of units that have been completed and are available for sale at the end of the accounting period. The costs of raw materials, direct labor, and manufacturing overhead incurred to produce the completed product are reported as cost of finished goods inventory.

5. The flow of inventory costs for a merchandising company is relatively simple: Inventory is increased when goods are acquired and decreased when goods are sold by transferring the cost of merchandise sold to an expense account. To record these events, debit merchandise inventory and credit cash or accounts payable for the cost of the inventory acquired, and debit cost of goods sold and credit merchandise inventory for the cost of the inventory sold.

6. Because a manufacturing company has more inventory accounts than a merchandising company, the flow of costs for a manufacturing company is more complex. The purchase of raw materials is recorded by a debit to raw materials inventory and a credit to cash or accounts payable for the cost of the materials acquired. As the materials are placed in production, the cost of the materials is transferred to work in process: Work-in-process inventory is debited, and raw materials inventory is credited for the cost of the materials transferred to production. In addition, the direct labor costs and manufacturing overhead incurred in the production process are charged to the work-in-process inventory account. When units in production are completed, the total cost of the units finished is transferred to finished goods: Finished goods inventory is debited, and work-in-process inventory is credited for the cost of the units completed and transferred. As units of finished inventory are sold, the cost of the units sold is transferred to an expense account: Cost of goods sold is debited, and finished goods inventory is credited for the cost of units sold.

7. In addition to the types of inventory described for merchandising and manufacturing companies, some companies have an inventory of supplies to be used in the production process.

Inventory Accounting Systems

8. Two inventory accounting systems are used to determine the amount of inventory on hand at the end of an accounting period and the cost of inventory sold during the period: the periodic inventory system and the perpetual inventory system.

9. Periodic inventory system. The *periodic inventory system,* which is appropriate for companies with a large variety of low-cost inventory items, requires a physical count of inventory to determine the amount of inventory on hand at a particular point in time and a calculation to determine cost of goods sold. As inventory is acquired during the period, it is recorded in a temporary account, not the inventory account, by a debit to purchases and a credit to cash or to accounts payable for an amount equal to the cost of the goods acquired. When inventory is sold, the only entry is a debit to cash or to accounts receivable and a credit to sales for the selling price of the inventory sold. Thus during the accounting period, the balance in the inventory account remains as it was at the beginning of the period; no adjustments are made to reflect either the purchases or sales of inventory during the period.

10. At the end of an accounting period, a physical count of inventory must be made to determine the quantity of inventory on hand. After the cost of ending inventory is determined, cost of goods sold is calculated as follows:

Beginning inventory	$x
+ Net purchases	x
Goods available for sale	$x
− Ending inventory	x
Cost of goods sold	$x

This calculation makes it apparent that cost of goods sold depends on the determination of ending inventory and is therefore a *residual* amount. Also inherent in the computation is the assumption that any goods not in the ending inventory must have been sold. This assumption does not always reflect the true situation. Goods could have been pilfered, for example, or removed from inventory because of damage. Nevertheless, the cost of these unsold units is buried in cost of goods sold.

11. In order to record ending inventory and cost of goods sold under the periodic inventory system, debit inventory for the dollar amount of ending inventory determined by the physical count, debit cost of goods sold for the residual amount calculated, credit inventory for the amount of beginning inventory, and credit purchases for the amount of the acquisitions made during the period. The cost of goods sold account must be closed to the income summary account as part of the closing process.

12. Perpetual inventory system. The *perpetual inventory system,* which is appropriate for companies with high-cost inventory (the use of the computer now makes this method practical for nearly any type of inventory), provides a *continuous record* of the balances in the inventory and cost of goods sold accounts. When inventory is acquired, the inventory account is debited for the cost of goods acquired, and when it is sold, the inventory account is credited for the cost of the inventory sold. In addition, the entry to reduce inventory when a sale is made also records the cost of the inventory sold as an expense: Cost of goods sold is debited, and inventory is credited for the cost of the inventory sold. Thus a running record of both inventory and cost of goods sold is maintained under the perpetual inventory system.

13. Even under the perpetual inventory system, a periodic physical count of inventory is required in order to determine whether the inventory on hand agrees with the amount reported under the perpetual inventory system. When the amount of inventory determined by the physical count differs from the perpetual inventory records, the inventory account should be adjusted to agree with the physical count. If the physical count is greater or smaller than the amount indicated by the perpetual records, the inventory account must be debited or credited and inventory overage or inventory shortage must be credited or debited for the amount of the indicated increase or decrease in inventory.

14. Because the perpetual inventory system maintains a continuous balance in the inventory and cost of goods sold accounts, it permits the preparation of interim reports without the need to make a physical inventory count, as under the periodic system. In addition, the running inventory balance provides management with more effective control over inventory. By comparing the inventory amount indicated by the physical count with the inventory account balance, management can deter-

mine whether inventory is over or short and can take any corrective action that may be needed.

Inventory—What to Include

15. In general, if a company has possession of goods and holds legal title to them, they are included in the inventory. In some situations, however, the general rule is not easy to apply. Factors to be considered in deciding to include an item in inventory are legal title, physical possession, contractual terms, industry practice, and the intentions of the parties involved. This section reviews some of the special inventory identification problems.

16. Goods in transit. As stated previously, when legal title is transferred to the buyer, the purchases should be recorded by the buyer. It is common practice to assume that the title passes when goods are received by the buyer. When inventory is in transit at the end of an accounting period, the shipping agreement determines whether title has effectively passed. When goods are shipped "f.o.b. (free on board) shipping point," the title is transferred to the buyer when the seller delivers the goods to the shipping agent. Because the buyer assumes title as the goods are shipped, all shipping-related costs, such as insurance and transportation costs, are expenses to the buyer, and the goods should be included in the *buyer's* inventory.

17. When goods are shipped "f.o.b. destination," title passes to the buyer when the goods are delivered to the destination point by the shipping agent. Until the goods reach the destination, the seller retains title to them and includes them in inventory. Transportation costs are an expense of the seller.

18. Consigned goods. Chapter 7 describes a *consignment* as a transaction in which the consignor ships goods to a consignee, who attempts to sell the goods for the consignor for a commission. Legal title to the goods consigned to the consignee remains with the consignor. Therefore, inventory on consignment should be included in the *consignor's* inventory at an amount equal to the cost of the goods plus transportation costs to ship them to the consignee.

19. Sales on approval. When goods are shipped to potential customers "on approval," the buyer has the option either to keep the goods and pay for them or to return them to the seller. Goods sent on approval should be included in the *seller's* inventory until payment is received from the buyer.

20. Product financing arrangements. A product financing arrangement is a transaction in which a company "sells" inventory items and at the same time agrees to repurchase those items or substantially identical items from the buyer at a specified price over a specified future period. *Statement No. 49* requires that items sold under certain product financing arrangements be considered inventory of the seller and that the obligation to repurchase items from the buyer be considered a liability. Even though legal title may pass to the buyer, the risks of ownership remain with the seller, and, therefore, no sale should be recorded.

21. Conditional sales. When merchandise sold is subject to a high rate of return by the buyer, as in the case of records or books, the sale is called a *conditional sale*. If a reasonable estimate of the expected returns can be made, *Statement No. 48* requires that the inventory be excluded from the seller's inventory and an estimated sales returns and allowances account be established. Otherwise, the seller must include the goods in inventory until they cannot be returned by the buyer, that is, until the buyer sells the goods.

Inventory Errors and Their Effects

22. As the preceding sections have made clear, errors in the determination of inventory are inevitable. Inventory errors can affect beginning inventory, purchases, ending inventory, costs of goods sold, and/or retained earnings. Several points about inventory errors should be remembered: (*a*) inventory errors affect both the balance sheet and the income statement; (*b*) each error should be analyzed separately to determine its effects on the financial statements; (*c*) analysis of errors may be made easier if basic relationships are used, for example, Beginning inventory + Purchases – Ending inventory = Cost of goods sold; (*d*) some errors are self-correcting or *counterbalancing* over two accounting periods; and (*e*) the ending inventory of one period is the beginning inventory of the next period, so that errors in the ending inventory are carried forward to the next period. Errors and their correction are covered in Chapter 19.

Costs to Include in Inventory

23. Under the cost principle, the *cost of inventory*, or *product cost*, is the sum of all expenditures required to get inventory items into condition and location for sale. In other words, the purchase price of the inventory plus expenditures for freight in, handling, storage, insurance, and taxes (and material and labor used in manufactured inventory) are all included in the cost of inventory. An argument could be made that costs such as the expenses of the purchasing department should also be included in inventory costs. Because of the difficulty of allocating these costs and their immateriality, they are usually treated as *period costs*, or expenses of the period in which they are incurred.

24. Costs that are not directly related to acquisition or production of inventory, such as selling costs, are also treated as period costs. Similarly, interest on the financing of inventory is generally considered a period cost and is not capitalized as a cost of inventory. *Statement No. 34* prohibits the capitalization of interest for inventories that are routinely manufactured in large quantities on a repetitive basis.

25. The remainder of this section considers more specifically the costs and cost adjustments for inventories of purchased merchandise and manufactured goods.

26. Costs of purchased merchandise inventory. After a company has recorded the cost of inventory in accordance with the guidelines previously described, events and circumstances may cause adjustments in the original amount recorded. It is common practice to record such adjustments in a separate account rather than to adjust the purchases account (in a periodic inventory system) or the inventory account (in a perpetual inventory system) directly. Before these inventory adjustments are discussed, a special type of purchase situation is considered.

27. When a company acquires two or more types of inventory for a single or "basket" purchase price, the total purchase price is usually allocated to the various types of inventory by the *relative sales value method*. This technique allocates the total purchase price to each type of inventory in accordance with the ratio of the selling price of each item (number of units times sales price) to the total selling price of all items. To find the cost of one item (item *A*) of three (items *A*, *B*, and *C*) purchased for one "basket" price ($*xx*), for example, multiply $*xx* by the ratio of the selling price of item *A* to the sum of the selling price of items *A*, *B*, and *C*.

28. Sellers offer *purchase discounts* as an incentive to buyers to make prompt payment on purchases. The discount terms are usually stated in a form similar to the following: $x\%/D_1$, net D_2, where $x\%$ equals the discount percentage granted if the invoice is paid within D_1 days, or the discount period, and net D_2 means that the full invoice price is due within D_2 days. Normally, the net method is used to record a purchase discount.

29. The *net method* initially records purchases and accounts payable at the net invoice price. To record a subsequent payment either during or after the discount period, accounts payable must be debited for the net invoice price. If payment is made within the discount period, only a credit to cash for the net invoice price is recorded. If payment is made after the discount period, purchase discounts lost must also be debited for the amount of the discount lost and cash must be credited for the gross invoice price (net invoice plus discount lost). Discounts that have lapsed on unpaid invoices at year's end are accrued with a debit to purchase discounts lost and a credit to accounts payable for the amount of the purchase discounts that have lapsed by the end of the year. The purchase discounts lost account is usually disclosed as a financing expense or general operating expense on the income statement.

30. *Freight in on purchases,* or transportation cost, is theoretically an expenditure to be included in the cost of inventory, but for practical purposes it is often recorded in a special account, such as the freight in account. When a periodic inventory system is used, the freight in account is normally reflected in cost of goods sold, since it is added to purchases to determine goods available for sale from which ending inventory is subtracted. When the perpetual inventory system is used, the freight in account is usually added to cost of goods sold at the end of the accounting period. Conceptually, freight in should not be an adjustment to cost of goods sold; rather, it should be allocated between inventory (for that portion of the expenditure applicable to goods unsold at the end of the period) and cost of goods sold (for the balance).

31. *Purchase returns* represent goods returned to the seller for credit against existing accounts payable or future purchases. *Purchase allowances* arise when damaged or otherwise unsatisfactory goods are shipped by the seller and the buyer elects to receive an appropriate adjustment of the purchase price rather than return the goods. To record a purchase return (allowance) when the periodic inventory system is used, debit accounts payable and credit purchase returns (purchase allowances) for the amount of the adjustment. The purchase returns and purchase allowances accounts are contra accounts to the purchases account on the income statement and are closed at year's end. When a perpetual system is used, the inventory account is directly credited for the amount of the purchase return or allowance.

32. Manufactured inventory costs. Manufacturing companies normally have three types of inventory: raw materials, work-in-process, and finished goods. Raw materials are costed at the purchase price of the goods adjusted for discounts, returns and allowances, and freight in. Work-in-process and finished goods inventories entail three types of costs: (*a*) raw materials; (*b*) direct labor, that is, the outlay of money to employees who work expressly in the production process; and (*c*) manufacturing overhead, that is, all manufacturing costs other than those of raw materials and direct labor.

33. Manufacturing costs may be assigned to the product by two methods, absorption costing and direct or variable costing. Under *absorption costing,* all costs of manufacturing are assigned to the product, whether the costs vary with the volume of

production or are fixed. Under *direct,* or *variable, costing,* only those costs that vary directly with the volume of production are treated as product costs. Costs that are fixed, such as the fixed manufacturing overhead expenses, are considered period costs and expensed in the period in which they are incurred. Absorption costing must be used in the preparation of financial statements to conform with GAAP and for tax purposes. Direct costing is often used for internal managerial purposes.

Actual Cost Flows and Cost Flow Assumptions

34. At the end of an accounting period, costs of beginning inventory and goods purchased or manufactured constitute goods available for sale and must be assigned to the goods remaining on hand (ending inventory) and to the goods sold (cost of goods sold). Because the cost per unit of beginning inventory and the costs of subsequent purchases differ, a cost flow assumption must be selected to assign costs to either ending inventory or cost of goods sold. Several cost flows are discussed in this section: specific identification, average cost, FIFO, and LIFO.

35. Specific identification. The *specific identification* cost flow method traces the actual flow of costs. That is, the costs assigned to ending inventory are the costs of the actual units on hand, and the costs assigned to cost of goods sold are the actual costs of the units sold. This method is best suited to individual units of inventory that are relatively costly, easily distinguishable, and relatively few; otherwise the method is impractical to apply. Because this method allows management to select units that are sold, management could manipulate income by selling units of higher or lower cost. In practice, the specific identification method is not widely used. Instead, most firms employ one of the cost flow assumptions that are *not* based on the actual physical flow of goods through a company, but rather are based on an assumed cost flow.

36. Average cost. Under average cost, the cost of goods is allocated equally, or averaged, among the units of inventory. Two average cost methods are used: weighted average and moving average.

37. The *weighted average cost method,* which is used with the periodic inventory system, applies one average cost number to both ending inventory and cost of goods sold. The weighted average cost per unit is usually calculated at the end of the accounting period by dividing the total *cost* of goods available for sale (beginning inventory plus net purchases) during the period by the total *units* of goods available for sale during the period.

38. The *moving average cost method,* which is used with the perpetual inventory system, requires a new average unit cost to be calculated after each purchase, because cost of goods sold must be determined whenever goods are sold. The moving average unit cost is calculated by dividing the *cost* of inventory on hand plus the cost of the most recent purchase by the number of *units* on hand plus the number of units of the most recent purchase. The unit average cost must be recalculated after each purchase of new inventory if the purchase price per unit differs from the average cost per unit before the most recent purchase.

39. First in, first out (FIFO). Regardless of the actual physical flow of goods, FIFO assumes that the first costs in (acquired) are the first costs out (sold). Accordingly, the earliest inventory costs are assigned to the units sold as cost of goods sold, whereas the latest inventory acquisition costs are assigned to the units in ending inventory. FIFO can be used with either the periodic or the perpetual inventory system. The resulting amounts for cost of goods sold and ending inventory are identical under the two systems.

40. Last in, first out (LIFO). Regardless of the actual physical flow of goods, LIFO assumes that the last costs in (acquired) are the first costs out (sold). Thus the costs of the most recent purchases are the first costs assigned to the units sold as cost of goods sold, whereas the earliest inventory costs are the last costs assigned to the units as cost of goods sold unless the items remain in inventory. Like FIFO, LIFO can be applied to either the periodic or the perpetual inventory system; under LIFO, however, when prices change during the period, the amounts for cost of goods sold and ending inventory are not identical for the two inventory systems. This difference arises because LIFO periodic assumes sale of the latest purchases in the accounting period, whereas LIFO perpetual assumes sale of the most recent purchases as of the time of each sale.

41. Implicit in the LIFO method is the notion of *layers* of inventory. Layers are added in periods when purchases exceed sales and are reduced in reverse order in periods when sales exceed purchases. Once any part of a particular layer is reduced, it is never replaced.

42. In periods of changing prices, the amounts reported for cost of goods sold and ending inventory will depend on the inventory cost flow assumption selected. In periods of rising prices or costs, for example, FIFO yields a higher ending inventory ("recent" higher costs in inventory) and lower cost of goods sold ("older" lower costs expensed) than LIFO. Under an average cost method, the amounts of cost of goods sold and ending inventory will fall between those obtained under FIFO and LIFO.

43. Evaluation of cost flow assumptions. An advantage of FIFO is that its cost flow assumptions are considered to follow more closely the actual physical flow of goods. Therefore, it conforms to the physical flow of many inventory items. Also, FIFO is simple to use with either the periodic or the perpetual inventory system. FIFO is systematic and objective and less susceptible to manipulation by management than LIFO. As the most recent acquisition costs are assigned to ending inventory under FIFO, in periods of rising prices the ending inventory is reported at current costs. During periods of rising costs, however, cost of goods sold is assigned the earliest inventory costs, so that "old" (lower) costs are matched with "current" revenue on the income statement. Matching old costs with current revenues can cause reported earnings to be inflated by "inventory holding profit" (gains), the difference between the old inventory cost and its replacement cost. These inflated earnings in turn can send misleading cash flow signals to the users. This is perhaps the strongest criticism leveled against FIFO.

44. The major advantages of the LIFO cost flow assumption lie in its income effects. LIFO matches the most current cost incurred against revenue, which is particularly important during periods of rising prices. Thus LIFO reduces inventory holding profits and causes reported earnings to approximate the amount that is distributable to owners. In addition, from a management perspective the lower reported income that results from LIFO defers payment of income taxes. If a company uses LIFO for tax purposes, however, it must also use LIFO for external financial reporting purposes. When LIFO is used, a company may disclose what income would have been if another inventory method were used.

45. The United States is the only major country that permits the use of LIFO. Some countries (for example, Great Britain) do not allow LIFO to be used; whereas, countries that do permit LIFO for financial reporting purposes do not allow it for tax purposes.

46. Although LIFO results in some positive income statement effects, its effects on the balance sheet and subsequent profits on inventory sold are usually considered primary disadvantages. The amount reported on the balance sheet as inventory is usually the oldest acquisition costs. During periods of rising prices, the inventory cost reported is usually very low. If the low-valued LIFO inventory layers are ever liquidated, the result will be abnormally high profits and taxes, because very old and low costs are matched against current revenue. To avoid these high profits caused by a *temporary* liquidation of LIFO layers, some companies match the current inventory cost with revenue or next in, first out (NIFO) inventory accounting as follows:

(a) debit cost of goods sold for the current inventory cost; (b) credit inventory for the LIFO flow costs; and (c) credit an account, such as "excess of replacement cost over the LIFO cost of basic inventory temporarily liquidated," for the difference between the current replacement cost and the actual LIFO cost of the inventory sold. The latter account is disclosed as a current liability on the statement of financial position until the inventory is replaced. Furthermore, to minimize these high profits, management may make economically unsound inventory acquisition decisions. Management could, for example, acquire inventory at the end of a period when sales have exceeded purchases to avoid dipping into the lower-cost LIFO layers and pushing profits up. Conversely, management could delay inventory acquisition and increase profits by matching the older and lower inventory costs with the current revenue. Thus management could use the LIFO techniques to manipulate income.

47. The average cost procedures are easy to apply, objective, and less subject to manipulation than specific identification and LIFO. Under average cost, the amounts reported as cost of goods sold and ending inventory are usually between those obtained under FIFO and LIFO.

48. Problems with unit LIFO. The LIFO procedures explained can be called unit LIFO because they focus on individual units of inventory. When a company applies the unit LIFO approach, two problems may arise: (a) the keeping of detailed records for units and costs of inventory can be costly, and (b) liquidation of an early LIFO layer (usually with a low acquisition cost) could raise profits and taxes.

49. Pooled LIFO. Some of the problems with LIFO inventory can be overcome if similar units of inventory are grouped, or pooled, together before LIFO is applied. Under this approach all units in the beginning inventory pool are assumed to have been acquired at the average cost of the units in the pool. If in the second (or a subsequent) accounting period there is an increase in the ending inventory, the additional layer of inventory is added to the beginning pool (plus any previous layers from subsequent periods) at the average cost of all units purchased during the second (or subsequent) period. Decreases in inventory are costed at the LIFO average cost for each layer.

50. The use of the pooled LIFO approach reduces recordkeeping and minimizes the possibility that an early LIFO layer will be liquidated. Changes in style and inventory mix, however, will cause the composition of the inventory pool to change. This change normally requires the inventory pools to be redefined.

51. Dollar-value LIFO. The dollar-value LIFO method is a special procedure that applies the LIFO cost flow assumption while avoiding the problems of the unit LIFO or pooled LIFO approaches.

52. The dollar-value LIFO method does not require detailed records of individual inventory units and unit costs. Only unit quantities and costs at the end of each accounting period must be determined. Also, because dollar-value LIFO can be applied to larger inventory pools or groups of inventory rather than one type of inventory at a time, the problem of liquidating specific inventory types is reduced.

53. Assuming a single layer of beginning inventory, the basic procedure for calculating ending inventory under the dollar-value LIFO approach consists of three basic steps. First, the ending inventory is valued at the year-end acquisition cost. Second, any effects of changing prices during the period are removed from the dollar amount of ending inventory. Third, the adjusted year-end inventory dollar amount is compared with the beginning balance of inventory to determine whether there was a *physical* increase or decrease in inventory over the period. If an increase in inventory is indicated, a new layer based on the current period's costs is added to the cost of the beginning inventory; if a decrease in inventory is indicated, a portion of the beginning layer is deducted from the cost of the beginning inventory.

54. In practice, the basic approach to dollar-value LIFO is refined. The *base layer* represents the first year that dollar-value LIFO was adopted. Inventory at the beginning of the base year is called the *base inventory,* and the unit costs of the base inventory are the *base year costs.* An *inventory cost index* is used to state the ending inventory in terms of base year costs. The inventory cost index relates the end-of-period acquisition cost of a unit of inventory to the beginning-of-the-base-year acquisition cost of a unit of the same type of inventory. The cost index must be calculated internally or secured from an external source for each year following the adoption of dollar-value LIFO. Cost indexes are either (a) calculated internally using the double-extension method or the link-chain method or (b) determined from an externally published index, such as the Consumer Price Index. Appendix 9-1 describes the double-extension and link-chain methods to calculate a cost index.

55. Once the cost index for the end of an accounting period is known, the year-end inventory stated at the current year's costs is divided by the index to restate the inventory in base year costs. As both beginning and year-end inventories are stated in base year costs, the difference between them is a change in the quantity of units held from the beginning to the end of the period. If the change is an increase, the change is multiplied by the current cost index to determine the cost of the new LIFO layer and is added to the beginning inventory to yield the dollar-value LIFO year-end inventory. If the change is a decrease, the layer or layers that were decreased must be determined. The appropriate portions of the layers decreased are then multiplied by their respective indexes and subtracted from beginning inventory to yield the dollar-value LIFO year-end inventory.

Inventory Disclosure

56. The financial statements should disclose the basis of accounting used for inventory. In addition, if a change is made in inventory accounting, the nature of the change and the effect, if material, on income should be disclosed.

57. It is not uncommon for a company to use the LIFO inventory method for external reporting and tax purposes but to use another inventory method for internal purposes, for example, to calculate income for management and employee compensation plans and interim financial reporting. The inventory amount calculated under LIFO and another inventory method will generally not be the same. To adjust the inventory amount under a non-LIFO method to the LIFO amount, the allowance to reduce inventory to LIFO basis account is used. When the LIFO inventory cost (for external reporting and tax purposes) is less than the calculated amount on the balance sheet (for internal purposes), the valuation allowance account will be deducted from the reported inventory amount to report inventory at LIFO.

Appendix

58. The methods of calculating or obtaining the inventory cost index are discussed in Appendix 9-1.

The *double-extension method,* an internal cost index method, calculates the cost index by dividing the cost of a unit of ending inventory by the cost of that unit at the beginning of the base year. If there is more than one type of inventory in an inventory pool, the cost index is found by dividing the sum of the year-end quantities of the various items times their year-end cost by the sum of the year-end quantities of the various items times their base year cost.

59. Although conceptully straightforward, the double-extension method may be burdensome to apply if (*a*) a firm has many different items in inventory that require a calculated index or (*b*) technological changes over time make comparison of inventory units difficult. To minimize the first problem, the double-extension method may be applied to a sample group of inventory items. The sample group approach requires current year-end and base year inventory costs for only the sample, not all, inventory items. The same group index is applied to all inventory items.

60. The *link-chain method,* a less complex approach to calculate an internal cost index, requires two steps to calculate inventory cost indexes. First, the current year cost change index is calculated by using the double-extension method, that is, by dividing the end-of-year inventory at year-end costs by the end-of-year inventory at beginning-of-year costs. Second, the linked cost index for the year is calculated by multiplying the previous year's linked cost index by the current year's inventory cost change index. Most firms apply the link-chain method using the same group approach similar to and for the same reasons discussed for the double-extension method.

SELF-STUDY LEARNING   Items marked with an asterisk (*) refer to the Appendix.

Key Terms and Concepts

Provide the appropriate term or terms to complete each of the following statements:

1. For a manufacturing company, the _____ inventory represents units of product that have been started but not yet completed.

2. The _____ inventory system requires a physical count before cost of goods sold can be calculated.

3. Goods may be shipped either f.o.b. _____ or f.o.b. _____.

4. A(n) _____ is a transaction in which a company sells inventory items and at the same time agrees to repurchase those items or substantially identical items from the buyer at a specified price over a specified future period.

5. An expenditure that is related directly to inventory is called a(n) _____ cost.

6. When several similar types of inventory are acquired at a single or lump-sum amount, the _____ method is used to allocate the total acquisition price among the types of inventory.

7. If a company receives a purchase discount from a seller, the company uses the _____ method to record the purchase.

8. A method often used to assign manufacturing costs to a product for internal reporting purposes is the _____, or _____, costing method.

9. A company that follows the perpetual inventory system would use the _____ average cost inventory method.

10. Under the dollar-value LIFO cost assumption, a(n) _____ is used to state the ending inventory in terms of base year costs.

True-False

Indicate by circling the appropriate response whether each of the following statements is true (T) or false (F):

T   F   1. Inventory is normally reported on the balance sheet as a current asset.

T   F   2. The merchandise inventory account of a merchandising company is most similar to the raw materials inventory account of a manufacturing company.

T   F   3. The periodic inventory system requires that a physical count of inventory be made before ending inventory can be determined for a period.

T   F   4. Under the periodic inventory system, acquisitions of inventory are debited to the inventory account for the amount of the purchase price of the goods acquired.

T   F   5. The perpetual inventory system provides for a continuous record of the balance in the inventory account, but cost of goods sold must be calculated at the end of an accounting period.

T   F   6. When the amount of inventory determined by a physical count differs from the balance in the perpetual inventory account, the account balance is adjusted to the physical count.

T   F   7. Normally, if a company has possession of goods and holds the title to them, they are included in the company's inventory.

T   F   8. An uncorrected error in the determination of ending inventory for the current period will cause a misstatement in earnings for the current period, but next period's earnings will be correctly stated.

T   F   9. Costs directly associated with inventory are usually treated as product costs, whereas costs not directly related to inventory are treated as period costs.

T   F   10. If a purchase discount is offered, the goods purchased are recorded at their list price.

T   F   11. If the purchase discount period is past, the net method of accounting for purchase discounts accrues purchase discounts lost on unpaid invoices at year's end.

T   F   12. Manufacturing companies include only costs of raw materials and direct labor in work-in-process inventory.

T   F   13. Under absorption costing, both variable and fixed manufacturing costs are considered product costs.

T   F   14. Product costs are inventoriable costs, whereas period costs are treated as expenses in the period in which they are incurred.

T   F   15. The moving average cost per unit must be recalculated after every sale of merchandise.

T   F   16. If a LIFO inventory layer is depleted in one period, it can be replenished by an identical layer in the next period.

T F 17. In periods of rising prices, cost of goods sold under LIFO will be greater than under FIFO.

T F 18. The use of LIFO increases inventory holding profits during periods of rising prices.

T F 19. A company may use LIFO inventory procedures for tax purposes and another cost method for financial reporting purposes.

T F *20. The double-extension method of determining the cost index to be used in the dollar-value LIFO inventory method for a single type of inventory is calculated by dividing the year-end cost of a unit of ending inventory by the base year cost of that unit.

Multiple Choice

Select the best response for each of the following items, and circle the corresponding letter:

1. Inventory is a tangible asset:

    a. Intended for resale in the ordinary course of business.
    b. In the process of being produced for sale.
    c. To be used currently in the production of goods to be sold.
    d. All of the above.

2. When the periodic inventory system is used, the cost of goods sold calculation includes:

    a. Net purchases subtracted from beginning inventory.
    b. Ending inventory subtracted from goods available for sale.
    c. Net purchases added to ending inventory.
    d. Beginning inventory added to goods available for sale.

3. If at the end of an accounting period a company were identifying items to be included in inventory, it would include goods:

    a. Received that were shipped "f.o.b. shipping point."
    b. Held on consignment.
    c. Purchased on an approval basis at year's end.
    d. Purchased at year's end and shipped "f.o.b. destination."

4. If a company pays for a purchase on account after the discount period is over, under the net method it would record:

    a. A debit to purchase discounts lost.
    b. A debit to purchases.
    c. A credit to purchase discounts lost.
    d. A credit to purchases.

5. When net purchases are determined under a periodic inventory system:

    a. Purchase returns are added to the purchases account.
    b. Purchase allowances are added to the purchases account.
    c. Freight in is added to the purchases account.
    d. Purchase discounts are added to the purchases account.

6. When a company uses the weighted average inventory method, the company:

    a. Is also using the perpetual inventory method.
    b. Assigns the same unit costs to units sold and units still on hand at year's end.
    c. Calculates the weighted average cost by dividing the cost of units purchased by the number of units purchased during the period.
    d. Recalculates the weighted average cost after each acquisition of inventory.

7. When purchases exceed sales for the current year in a period of falling prices, profits reported under LIFO will be:

    a. Lower than profits reported under FIFO.
    b. Greater than profits reported under FIFO.
    c. Lower than profits reported under average cost.
    d. The same as profits reported under average cost.

8. When comparing FIFO with LIFO, which of these arguments is *incorrect?* (Assume rising prices.)

    a. The dollar amount reported as ending inventory under FIFO more closely approximates the current cost of inventory.
    b. The dollar amount reported as cost of goods sold under FIFO more closely approximates current cost of goods sold.
    c. FIFO is simpler to apply to both the periodic and the perpetual inventory systems.
    d. FIFO more closely follows the actual physical flow of many inventory items.

9. During periods of sustained rising prices, how will the liquidation of early LIFO layers affect a company's cost of goods sold, net income, and income tax liability?

	COST OF GOODS SOLD	NET INCOME	INCOME TAX LIABILITY
a.	Increase	Increase	Increase
b.	Increase	Increase	Decrease
c.	Decrease	Decrease	Increase
d.	Decrease	Increase	Increase

10. The dollar-value LIFO inventory method:

a. Is applicable to both the periodic and the perpetual inventory systems.
b. Ignores changing prices of inventory costs during the period.
c. Minimizes the effect of liquidating a specific type of inventory when it is applied to larger inventory pools.
d. Determines the change in inventory quantity by subtracting the current cost of ending inventory from the beginning inventory value.

Extended Problems

1. Crimson Jewelers sells both high-priced and costume jewelry and uses the FIFO perpetual and periodic systems, respectively, to maintain its inventories. Crimson Jewelers had $2,200 of costume jewelry on hand June 1. During June the company entered into the following transactions:

June 2 Purchased on account, terms 2%/10, net 30, 12 silver necklaces for $450 per necklace from Silver Distributors.
4 Returned one of the silver necklaces for credit because of a faulty clasp.
5 Purchased from Ross Jewelers on account, terms 2%/15, net 45, a box of costume jewelry (bracelets and rings) for $1,900.
6 Sold two silver necklaces for cash, $600 each.
7 Paid transportation charges of $60 on the costume jewelry.
10 Paid the amount due Silver Distributors.
12 Sold items of costume jewelry for $1,240 cash.
13 Sold three silver necklaces on account for $500 each during a special promotion.
15 Paid one-half of the amount due Ross Jewelers.
19 Purchased 15 men's quality watches for $280 per watch on account, terms 1%/10, net 30.
23 Sold 5 of the men's watches on account, $350 per watch.
25 Paid balance due Ross Jewelers.
29 Sold costume jewelry for $1,670 on account.

After a physical count and pricing of the costume jewelry, the inventory as of June 30 was $2,016.

REQUIRED

a. Prepare general journal entries relative to the transactions for Crimson Jewelers for the month of June and the accrual on June 30 of the lost discount on the June 19 purchase.
b. Calculate cost of goods sold for the costume jewelry for the month of June, and prepare the journal entry to record ending inventory and cost of goods sold.
c. Complete the following table to show the balances of the inventory and cost of goods sold accounts as of June 30.

	COSTUME JEWELRY	SILVER NECKLACES	MEN'S WATCHES
Inventory	$	$	$
Cost of goods sold			

2. During May, Warner Corporation made the following purchases and sales of a product that it sells at wholesale.

		UNITS	COST/UNIT
May 1	Inventory	100	$2.00
5	Purchase	300	2.40
12	Purchase	100	2.50
15	Sale	150	-0-
24	Purchase	200	2.45
28	Sale	300	-0-
30	Purchase	50	2.56

REQUIRED

Compute the cost of the ending inventory and cost of goods sold:

a. On a weighted average basis. (Carry unit amounts to three decimal places.)
b. On a moving average basis.
c. On a FIFO periodic basis.
d. On a FIFO perpetual basis.
e. On a LIFO periodic basis.
f. On a LIFO perpetual basis.

3. Harper, Inc., has applied the dollar-value LIFO method to its inventory since January 2, 1995, when its inventory was valued at $44,000. Based on current market prices, the value of its inventory at the end of 1995 and 1996 was $56,100 and $52,470, respectively.

REQUIRED

a. Assuming a cost index of 1.00 on January 1, 1995; 1.10 on December 31, 1995, and 1.06 on December 31, 1996, determine the cost of ending inventory for Harper as of December 31, 1995 and 1996, using the dollar-value LIFO inventory method.

b. Assuming that Harper had sales of $540,000 and net purchases of $328,000 during 1996 and using the dollar-value inventory method, determine gross profit for the year ended December 31, 1996.

*4. Storm, Inc., adopted the dollar-value LIFO method for its inventories on January 2, 1995. Storm's LIFO inventory pool at January 2, 1995, and the end of the fiscal years 1995 and 1996 are:

DATE	PRODUCT	NUMBER OF UNITS	COST PER UNIT	TOTAL COST
Jan. 1, 1995	UT	100	$7.00	$ 700
	OU	175	8.00	1,400
	BG	80	5.50	440
				$ 2,540

DATE	PRODUCT	NUMBER OF UNITS	COST PER UNIT	TOTAL COST
Dec. 31, 1995	UT	150	$7.60	$ 1,140
	OU	210	9.00	1,890
	BG	104	6.25	650
				$ 3,680
Dec. 31, 1996	UT	170	$10.00	$ 1,700
	OU	190	11.00	2,090
	BG	120	8.50	1,020
				$ 4,810

REQUIRED

a. Using the double-extension method, calculate the inventory cost indexes for 1995 and 1996. Round answers to three decimal places.

b. Using the link-chain method, calculate the cost change indexes *and* the cost change indexes linked to the base index for 1995 and 1996. Round answers to three decimal places.

COMMON ERRORS

The first statement of each of the "common errors" listed here is *incorrect*. Each incorrect statement is followed by a corrected statement and an explanation.

1. A physical inventory count is made only when the periodic inventory system, and not the perpetual system, is used. *Wrong*

A physical inventory count is made whether the periodic or perpetual inventory system is used. *Right*

Under the periodic inventory system a physical inventory count is *required* before ending inventory and cost of goods sold can be determined. Since a running record of inventory and cost of goods sold is maintained under the perpetual inventory system, a physical count is not needed to determine the ending inventory or cost of goods sold balances. A physical count is necessary, however, to verify that the amount in the inventory account is equal to the amount actually on hand. Inventory that is lost or pilfered, for example, would not normally have been deducted from the perpetual inventory record and could be determined only by comparing the inventory account balance with the amount established by the physical count. Although the basic purposes of a physical count differ under the two systems, a physical inventory count should be made when either the periodic or perpetual inventory system is used.

2. When external financial statements are prepared, either absorption costing or direct costing may be used to assign manufacturing costs to the product. *Wrong*

When external financial statements are prepared, only absorption costing may be used to assign manufacturing costs to the product. *Right*

Companies often use both absorption costing and direct costing when they assign manufacturing costs to a product, but GAAP requires that only absorption costing be used for external financial statements. Absorption costing assigns *all* manufacturing costs—that is, raw materials, direct labor, and variable and fixed manufacturing overhead—to the product as a product cost. Thus a unit manufactured during the period but unsold at the end of the period will be carried in inventory at an amount equal to all manufacturing costs associated with its manufacture. In contrast, direct costing treats all manufacturing costs as product costs *except* fixed manufacturing overhead, which is handled as a period cost and expensed immediately in the period in which it is incurred. Consequently, no portion of fixed manufacturing overhead is ever part of inventory. Direct costing is considered to be a good method for internal managerial purposes, but it cannot be used for external reporting purposes.

3. The flow of goods and the flow of costs refer to the same concept. *Wrong*

The flow of goods and the flow of costs refer to related but different concepts. *Right*

The flow of goods and the flow of costs both refer to inventory, but the similarity ends there. The flow of goods refers to the physical flow of the inventory into and out of the company. A retailer of produce is very concerned with physical flow, or turnover, of the produce on the stands. The flow of costs, however, refers to the manner or order in which the costs of inventory acquired are assigned to cost of goods sold or, in the case of goods purchased but unsold at the end of an accounting period, to ending inventory. Typical cost flow assumptions are specific identification, average cost, LIFO, and FIFO. Only the little used specific identification cost flow assumption is designed so that the actual cost of specific units flows with the unit; that is, if the unit is sold, its actual cost becomes cost of goods sold, and if the unit remains in inventory, its actual cost is carried as inventory. The other cost flow assumptions do not attempt to trace the physical flow of goods and their costs but rather trace the cost of goods acquired in a particular order. The LIFO cost flow assumption, for example, traces the *cost* of the last goods in (purchased) as the *cost* of the first goods out (sold), or cost of goods sold. This cost flow does not necessarily follow the physical flow of the goods.

4. The cost flow assumptions of average cost and FIFO, but not of LIFO, may be applied when either the periodic or perpetual inventory system is used. *Wrong*

The cost flow assumptions of average cost, FIFO, and LIFO may be applied when either the periodic or perpetual inventory system is used. *Right*

It may not be as easy to apply the various cost flow assumptions to the perpetual inventory system as it is to apply them to the periodic inventory system, and the results may not be the same, but those assumptions are applicable. The weighted average method is used with the periodic inventory system, for example, whereas the moving average method is used with the perpetual inventory

system. When prices are changing, the two average cost methods yield different average cost figures to be used to determine cost of goods sold and ending inventory. Similarly, LIFO can be applied to either inventory system, but its application to the perpetual inventory system is more tedious; and if prices are changing, it will yield different results for cost of goods sold and ending inventory from those it will yield when it is applied to the periodic inventory system. Under FIFO, however, the resulting amounts for cost of goods sold and ending inventory will be identical in the two inventory systems.

5. All inventory costing methods are subject to the same degree of manipulation by management. *Wrong*

All inventory costing methods are subject to manipulation by management, but to different degrees. *Right*

Any inventory costing method is susceptible to manipulation by management, but some are more susceptible than others. Under pressure to show increasing or at least steady profits each period, management can select an inventory costing method that permits a high degree of manipulation of profits. If the specific identification costing method is used, management can determine whether a low-cost or high-cost item is sold and thus raise or lower reported profits for the year. Similarly, by strategically timing the purchases of goods at the end of an accounting period, a manager can use LIFO to manipulate profits. If prices are rising, for example, profits can be lowered by purchasing goods at the end of the period and matching the newer and higher costs with revenue; if management wishes to raise reported profits, it need only refrain from purchasing high-priced goods at the end of the period. Manipulation is not so pronounced when either the average cost or FIFO costing method is used, since management has less opportunity to influence cost of goods sold. Nevertheless, all inventory costing assumptions are subject to manipulation.

6. If, under the dollar-value LIFO approach, a reduction in inventory is determined, the cost of ending inventory is calculated by subtracting the amount of the reduction multiplied by the current cost index from the beginning inventory. *Wrong*

If, under the dollar-value LIFO approach, a reduction in inventory is determined, the cost of ending inventory is calculated by subtracting the appropriate layers of inventory multiplied by their cost index from the beginning inventory. *Right*

When a reduction of inventory is determined under the dollar-value LIFO approach, it indicates that sales for the period exceeded purchases and that one or more previous LIFO layers were liquidated. The current cost index applies only to purchases of the current period. Accordingly, if inventory is reduced, previous layers of inventory are consumed and their cost indexes are relevant, not the current cost index, in the calculation of ending inventory.

ANSWERS
Items marked with an asterisk (*) refer to the Appendix.

Key Terms and Concepts

1. work-in-process
2. periodic
3. shipping point, destination
4. product financing arrangement
5. product
6. relative sales value
7. net
8. direct, variable
9. moving
10. cost index

True-False

1. T
2. F The merchandise inventory account is for goods that have been purchased and readied for resale. The raw materials inventory account consists of goods that will become part of a product but have not yet entered the production process. The finished goods inventory account, which consists of units completed and ready for sale, is most similar to the merchandise inventory account.
3. T
4. F Under the periodic system, all inventory acquired is debited to the purchases account. During the accounting period, the balance in the inventory account is the amount of beginning inventory, and it is adjusted only at the end of the period to record the ending balance for the period.
5. F The perpetual system also provides a continuous balance in the cost of goods sold account. Every time a sale is made, cost of goods sold is debited for the cost of the inventory sold. Thus there is a continuous, or running, balance of cost of goods sold; it need not be calculated.
6. T
7. T
8. F An error in ending inventory in one period will cause a misstatement in earnings for the current and next period if the error is not corrected. The error will counterbalance in the two years; that is, the current period will be overstated (or understated) and the next period's earnings will be understated (or overstated) by the same dollar amount.

Nevertheless, each period's earnings will be misstated.

9. T
10. F When a purchase discount is offered, purchases are recorded at their net amount, that is, list price minus purchase discount.
11. T
12. F Three cost elements constitute the work-in-process inventory account for a manufacturing company: raw materials, direct labor, and manufacturing overhead.
13. T
14. T
15. F The moving average cost per unit is recalculated after every purchase if the most recent purchase price differs from the average cost per unit before the most recent purchase. Units sold are costed at the same unit cost until a new purchase of goods is made and the moving average cost per unit is recalculated.
16. F Each layer of LIFO inventory represents the cost of units of inventory acquired at a particular time and price. Once a layer is depleted, it can never be replaced.
17. T
18. F When prices are rising, LIFO *reduces* the amount of inventory holding profits, the difference between the cost of the unit sold and the current cost of replacing the same unit. Since sales prices are usually current, the matching of an old cost with a current sales price will result in a larger profit than would occur if a current cost were matched against the current sales price. Because LIFO matches the newest cost of goods acquired with revenue, that cost most nearly reflects the current replacement cost of the unit sold, and thus inventory holding profit is reduced.
19. F If a company used LIFO inventory for tax purposes, it must use LIFO for financial reporting purposes. Since LIFO reduces taxable income (when prices are rising) and thus taxes payable, government regulation requires that if the advantages of tax saving are recognized by the company, it must also report the lower earnings in its financial statements. A company may disclose, however, what income would have been had another inventory method been used.
*20. T

Multiple Choice

1. d	6. b
2. b	7. b
3. a	8. b
4. a	9. d
5. c	10. c

Extended Problems

1. a. Journal entries to record the June transactions:

June 2	Inventory—silver necklaces	5,292	
	Accounts payable (12 × $450 × .98)		5,292
4	Accounts payable ($450 × .98)	441	
	Inventory—silver necklaces		441
5	Purchases ($1,900 × .98)	1,862	
	Accounts payable		1,862
6	Cash (2 × $600)	1,200	
	Sales		1,200
	Cost of goods sold ($450 × .98 × 2)	882	
	Inventory—silver necklaces		882
7	Freight in	60	
	Cash		60
10	Accounts payable	4,851	
	Cash ($5,292 − $441)		4,851
12	Cash	1,240	
	Sales		1,240
13	Accounts receivable ($500 × 3)	1,500	
	Sales		1,500
	Cost of goods sold ($450 × .98 × 3)	1,323	
	Inventory—silver necklaces		1,323
15	Accounts payable (.5 × $1,862)	931	
	Cash		931
19	Inventory—men's watches	4,158	
	Accounts payable (15 × $280 × .99)		4,158
23	Accounts receivable (5 × $350)	1,750	
	Sales		1,750
	Cost of goods sold (5 × $280 × .99)	1,386	
	Inventory—men's watches		1,386
25	Accounts payable ($1,862 − $931)	931	
	Purchase discounts lost ($950 × .02)	19	
	Cash		950
29	Accounts receivable	1,670	
	Sales		1,670
30	Purchase discounts lost	42	
	Accounts payable (15 × $280 × .01)		42

b. Calculation of cost of goods sold for costume jewelry:

Beginning inventory		$2,200
Purchases	$1,862	
Plus: Freight in	60	
Net purchases		1,922
Goods available for sale		$4,122
Less: Ending inventory		(2,016)
Cost of goods sold		$2,106

Entry to record ending inventory and cost of goods sold:

Inventory (ending)..	2,016	
Cost of goods sold...	2,106	
Inventory (beginning)..		2,200
Purchases		1,862
Freight in..		60

c. Completion of table:

	COSTUME JEWELRY	SILVER NECKLACES	MEN'S WATCHES
Inventory	$2,016	$2,646	$2,772
Cost of goods sold	2,106	2,205	1,386

Inventory—silver necklaces

6/2	5,292	441	6/4
		882	6/6
		1,323	6/13
		2,646	

Cost of goods sold

6/6	882	
6/13	1,323	
	2,205	

Inventory—men's watches

6/19	4,158	1,386	6/23
	2,772		

Cost of goods sold

6/23	1,386	

2. Computation of cost of ending inventory and cost of goods sold under various assumptions:
a. Weighted average:

	UNITS	COST/ UNIT	TOTAL COST
Inventory, May 1	100	$2.00	$ 200
Purchases			
May 5	300	2.40	720
12	100	2.50	250
24	200	2.45	490
30	50	2.56	128
Total (goods available for sale)	750		$1,788

Weighted average cost per unit = $1,788 ÷ 750 units
= $2.384

Units available for sale   750
Units sold (150 + 300)   (450)
Units in ending inventory   300

Ending inventory: 300 × $2.384 = $715.20

Cost of goods sold: 450 × $2.384 = $1,072.80

b. Moving average:

	UNITS	TOTAL COST	MOVING AVERAGE COST
Beginning inventory	100 @ $2.00	$ 200	$2.00
Purchase, 5/5	300 @ 2.40	720	
Inventory balance	400	920	2.30
Purchase, 5/12	100 @ 2.50	250	
Inventory balance	500	1,170	2.34
Sale, 5/15	(150) @ 2.34	(351)	
Inventory balance	350	819	
Purchase, 5/24	200 @ 2.45	490	
Inventory balance	550	1,309	2.38
Sale, 5/28	(300) @ 2.38	(714)	
Inventory balance	250	595	
Purchase, 5/30	50 @ 2.56	128	
Inventory balance	300	723	2.41

Ending inventory: 300 × $2.41 = $ 723

Cost of goods sold: 150 × $2.34 = $ 351
300 × $2.38 = 714
$1,065

c. FIFO periodic:

Ending inventory: 300 units (refer to part a)

50	units from May 30 purchase @ $2.56 =	$128
200	units from May 24 purchase @ $2.45 =	490
50	units from May 12 purchase @ $2.50 =	125
300	units	$743

Cost of goods sold:

150	units sold on May 15	100 @ $2.00 =	$ 200
		50 @ $2.40 =	120
300	units sold on May 28	250 @ $2.40 =	600
		50 @ $2.50 =	125
450	units		$1,045

or

Cost of goods available for sale (750 units)	$1,788
Less ending inventory (per above)	743
Cost of goods sold	$1,045

d. FIFO perpetual:

Cost of goods sold:

100	units from beginning inventory	@ $2.00	= $	200
300	units from May 5 purchase	@ $2.40	=	720
50	units from May 12 purchase	@ $2.50	=	125
450	units			$1,045

Ending inventory:

50	units from May 12 purchase	@ $2.50	= $	125
200	units from May 24 purchase	@ $2.45	=	490
50	units from May 30 purchase	@ $2.56	=	128
300	units			$ 743

or

Cost of goods available for sale (750 units)	$1,788
Less cost of goods sold (per above)	1,045
Ending inventory	$ 743

e. LIFO periodic:

Ending inventory:

100	units from beginning inventory	@ $2.00	=	$200
200	units from May 5 purchase	@ $2.40	=	480
300	units			$680

Cost of goods sold:

50	units from May 30 purchase	@ $2.56	= $	128
200	units from May 24 purchase	@ $2.45	=	490
100	units from May 12 purchase	@ $2.50	=	250
100	units from May 5 purchase	@ $2.40	=	240
450	units			$1,108

or

Cost of goods available for sale	$1,788
Ending inventory (per above)	680
Cost of goods sold	$1,108

f. LIFO perpetual:

DATE	TRANSACTION	COST OF PURCHASE	COST OF GOODS SOLD	CUMULATIVE BALANCE OF INVENTORY		
May 1	Beginning			100 @ $2.00	=	$ 200
May 5	Purchase	300 @ $2.40 = $720		100 @ $2.00 300 @ $2.40 }	=	$ 920
May 12	Purchase	100 @ $2.50 = $250		100 @ $2.00 300 @ $2.40 100 @ $2.50 }	=	$ 1,170
May 15	Sale		100 @ $2.50 50 @ $2.40 = $370	100 @ $2.00 250 @ $2.40 }	=	$ 800
May 24	Purchase	200 @ $2.45 = $490		100 @ $2.00 250 @ $1.40 200 @ $2.45 }	=	$ 1,290
May 28	Sale		200 @ $2.45 100 @ $2.40 = $730	100 @ $2.00 150 @ $2.40 }	=	$ 560
May 30	Purchase	50 @ $2.56 = $128		100 @ $2.00 150 @ $2.40 50 @ $2.56 }	=	$ 688

Cost of goods sold..	$1,100
Ending inventory	$688

3. a. Computation of the dollar-value LIFO cost of ending inventory as of December 31, 1995, and 1996:

1995

1/1 beginning inventory at base prices	$44,000
12/31 inventory converted to base prices:	
$56,100 ÷ 1.10 =..............................	51,000
Real increase in inventory	$ 7,000
Beginning inventory (base)......................	$44,000
New layer at current prices	
($7,000 × 1.10) (1995).......................	7,700
Ending inventory	$51,700

1996

1/1 beginning inventory at base prices	$51,000
12/31 inventory converted to base prices:	
$52,470 ÷ 1.06 =..............................	49,500
Real decrease in inventory	$ 1,500

Beginning inventory (base)......................	$44,000
1995 layer reduced to 1995 current prices:	
$7,000 − $1,500 = $5,500 × 1.10 (1995)	6,050
Ending inventory	$50,050

b. Calculation of gross profit for the year ended December 31, 1996:

Sales....................................		$540,000
Cost of goods sold		
Beginning inventory..........	$ 51,700	
Net purchases	328,000	
Goods available for sale	$379,700	
Ending inventory	50,050	
Cost of goods sold............		$329,650
Gross profit		$210,350

*4. a. Calculation of inventory cost indexes, using the double-extension method for 1995 and 1996:

1995

$$\frac{[(150 \times \$7.60) + (210 \times \$9) + (104 \times \$6.25)]}{[(150 \times \$7) + (210 \times \$8) + (104 \times \$5.50)]} = \frac{\$3,680}{\$3,302} = 1.114$$

1996

$$\frac{[(170 \times \$10) + (190 \times \$11) + (120 \times \$8.50)]}{[(170 \times \$7) + (190 \times \$8) + (120 \times \$5.50)]} = \frac{\$4,810}{\$3,370} = 1.427$$

b.   Calculation of inventory cost change indexes and cost change indexes linked to the base index for 1995 and 1996:

	<u>1995</u>	<u>1996</u>
Cost change index	$\frac{\$3,680}{\$3,302^a} = 1.114$	$\frac{\$4,810}{\$3,752^b} = 1.282$

[a][(150 x \$7) + (210 x \$8) + (104 x \$5.50)] = \$3,302
[b][(170 x \$7.60) + (190 x \$9) + (120 x \$6.25)] = \$3,752

	<u>1995</u>	<u>1996</u>
Cost change index linked to the base index	1.114 x 1 = 1.114	1.114 x 1.282 = 1.428

10 INVENTORY VALUATION: DEPARTURES FROM HISTORICAL COST AND METHODS OF ESTIMATING INVENTORY COST

CHAPTER OBJECTIVES

After reading Chapter 10 and completing the questions, cases, exercises, and problems from the text chapter, you should be able to:

1. Understand the rationale behind the lower-of-cost-or-market (LCM) inventory method.
2. Know the meaning of cost and market and the boundaries of market—that is, ceiling and floor—as they pertain to LCM.
3. Apply LCM to individual inventory items, groups of inventory items, or total inventory.
4. Differentiate between the two alternative approaches to record and report LCM.
5. Account for a firm purchase commitment at LCM.
6. Understand the basic valuation measurement technique and accounting issues related to the replacement cost, net realizable value, and standard cost inventory valuation methods.
7. Estimate ending inventory by the gross profit method.
8. Understand the general steps of the retail inventory method.
9. Understand the terminology associated with retail pricing, such as original cost, markup, and net markdowns.
10. Know how to handle freight in, purchase discounts, sales returns and allowances, employee discounts, and spoilage in the calculation of the cost to retail percentage.
11. Determine ending inventory by the variations of the retail method: average cost, lower of cost or market, and LIFO cost.
12. Calculate ending inventory by the dollar-value retail LIFO method.

CHAPTER REVIEW

Introduction

1. The inventory cost flow assumptions discussed in Chapter 9 (specific identification, average cost, FIFO, and LIFO) are all based on historical cost. There are times when an inventory valuation method other than a historical cost method is appropriate. If historical cost is no longer a reasonable basis to use, for example, or if it would be impossible to make a physical inventory count, then another inventory costing method must be used. This chapter discusses four inventory valuation bases that depart from historical cost (lower of cost or market, replacement cost, net realizable value, and standard cost) and three methods used to estimate inventory without the need for a physical inventory count (the gross profit, retail, and dollar-value retail LIFO methods).

Inventory Costing Methods— Departures from Historical Cost

2. Lower of cost or market. When the sale utility of inventory declines as a result of deterioration, obsolescence, price-level changes, or any other event that causes the value of the inventory to fall below its original cost, the decline in the inventory value should be recognized as a loss in the income statement and a reduction in the inventory value on the balance sheet. In other words, the inventory's revenue-producing ability has fallen below its original cost, and this loss must be recognized in the period of the loss. In such situations, U.S. generally accepted accounting principles require that the lower-of-cost-or-market (LCM) method be used to value the inventory. In addition, LCM is used worldwide.

3. When LCM is applied, *cost* means the inventory value calculated in accordance with one of the historical cost methods, such as specific identification, average cost, FIFO, or LIFO. *Market* means the replacement cost of the inventory. For a merchandising company, *replacement cost* refers to the price in the market where inventory is purchased; for a manufacturing company, it refers to the cost to produce the inventory, called the reproduction cost.

4. The market value used in LCM, however, has limits, or boundaries. The upper boundary, or *ceiling,* which the market value cannot exceed, is the net realizable value (NRV) of the inventory. NRV is equal to the estimated normal selling price less reasonably predictable costs of completion and disposal. The lower boundary, or *floor,* below which the market value cannot fall, is equal to the NRV less a normal profit margin (NPM). If the current replacement cost (RC) is greater than the NRV or ceiling, the designated market value to be used is the ceiling value. If, however, the RC is less than the floor (NRV–NPM), the designated market value to be used is the floor value. In all other cases, when the RC lies between the ceiling and the floor, the RC is the market value used.

5. To determine LCM, the historical cost of the inventory is compared with the appropriate market value, that is, RC, floor, or ceiling. If the cost is below market value, no adjustment to inventory is necessary, but if the market value is less than the cost, the inventory is reduced to market.

6. Generally, the replacement cost of an item of inventory bears a close relationship to the selling price of the item. That is, if the replacement cost goes up or down, the selling price will usually increase or decrease accordingly. Therefore, the cash flow potential of inventory (through a subsequent sale) normally declines as RC declines. This decline is recognized if the RC falls below the cost of the inventory. When the sales price and RC do not move together, the RC or market value may not be the proper value for the inventory.

7. The purpose of setting the ceiling and floor boundaries on the market value or RC is to avoid the use of RC when the normal gross profit relationship between RC and selling price fails to hold. Only under unusual circumstances would a company pay more than the net realizable value for an inventory item, for example, because the company could not realize a net cash inflow from the sale of the item at an amount that exceeds its NRV. Thus NRV serves as an appropriate ceiling for RC as a measure of utility. Similarly, under normal conditions the RC of an item would not usually be less than the NRV less a normal profit. Only in a special situation would a company pay less than the NRV less a normal profit margin to acquire new inventory. Thus NRV less a normal profit margin serves as an appropriate floor on replacement cost as a measure of inventory utility.

8. Application of LCM. When a company has several inventory items, it may apply LCM to individual items, groups of items, or the entire inventory. In any approach, the cost and market values of each item are determined. If the individual item approach is used, the LCM valuations of the individual items are added to determine the total inventory LCM value. If LCM is applied to groups of items, the lower-of-total-cost-or-total-market value of each inventory group is determined, and the amounts are added to determine the total inventory LCM value. Similarly, when LCM is applied to the total inventory, the sum of the costs of all inventory items is compared with the sum of the items' market value, and the lower of the two sums is the total inventory LCM value.

9. The approach a company elects to use in applying the LCM method can affect the LCM valuation. The lowest inventory valuation results when the individual item approach is applied, because the lower of cost or market is used for each item and the individual values are totaled to yield the LCM valuation for the entire inventory. When the group or total inventory approach is applied, the pooling of inventory items may cause items whose market is below cost to be offset by items whose market is above cost. Such offsetting reduces the LCM effect and increases the dollar amount of inventory. In practice, most companies apply LCM to individual items, because an item-by-item basis must be used for income tax purposes.

10. The use of LCM produces a very conservative balance sheet and income statement, particularly in a period when the market value falls below the cost of the inventory, because the recorded decline from cost to market is recognized in the income statement in the year of the market decline. In subsequent periods the new, lower inventory value is considered to be cost for future LCM valuations. Recovery of market value is ignored. When the inventory is subsequently sold, however, the lower inventory values are charged to cost of goods sold, causing income to be unconservatively higher.

11. Recording LCM. Two approaches may be used to account for and report inventory value when market is below cost: (*a*) the inventory account is reduced directly by the amount that market is below cost, and (*b*) reported inventory is reduced by using a contra inventory allowance account that is equal to the amount that market is below cost. The allowance to adjust inventory to market account is a contra inventory account and is deducted from the inventory account, so that inventory is reported at its LCM value on the balance sheet. At the beginning of the following accounting period, the inventory allowance account must be eliminated so that the beginning inventory balance is not overstated.

12. The reduction in market value below cost can be recognized in the income statement by charging the loss to (*a*) cost of goods sold or (*b*) a separate holding loss account. The disclosure of the inventory holding loss as an expense rather than its absorption in cost of goods sold is conceptually better, because the holding loss arises from the holding of inventory, not from the selling of inventory. Accordingly, the appropriate entry to record a reduction of inventory from cost to an LCM value is to debit inventory holding loss and credit inventory for the amount of the decline from cost to the LCM value.

13. Valuing firm purchase commitments at LCM. In certain situations, such as a projected price increase or shortage of an inventory item, a company may enter into a *firm purchase commitment,* a commitment that is noncancelable or virtually so, to purchase goods in the future from a supplier. LCM procedures must be applied to firm purchase commitments, just as if the goods were on hand. The accounting entries to reflect LCM depend on the timing of the contract.

14. If the contract is entered into and executed in the same accounting period when the current market price is equal to or greater than the contract price, the buyer would debit inventory and credit cash for the amount of the contract price of the inventory. (For purposes of the illustrations in this section, assume a cash purchase and the perpetual inventory system.) If the market price falls below the contract price when the goods are purchased, the decline below the contract price must be recognized: debit inventory for the current market value of the inventory, debit loss on purchase commitment for the difference between the contract and current market price of the inventory, and credit cash for the contract price of the inventory.

15. When the firm purchase commitment extends beyond one accounting period, adequate footnote disclosure of the terms and amount of the contract should be made. In addition, if the current market price of the inventory is below the contract price at year-end before the contract is executed, the decline in market value is recognized by a year-end adjusting entry: debit estimated loss on purchase commitment, and credit estimated liability on purchase commitment for the difference between the contract price and the current market value of the inventory. The estimated loss account is reported on the income statement, whereas the estimated liability account is normally disclosed as a current liability on the balance sheet.

16. When the purchase commitment is executed in a subsequent accounting period and the market price has either remained at the amount at year-end or has risen, the buyer debits inventory for the market value of the inventory at the time of the adjustment, debits estimated liability on purchase commitment for the amount of the year-end adjustment, and credits cash for the contract price of the inventory acquired. However, if the market value of the inventory declined from the date of adjustment, the buyer debits (*a*) inventory for the current market value of the inventory, (*b*) estimated liability on purchase commitment for the amount of the year-end adjustment, and (*c*) loss on purchase commitment for the difference between the market value at the year-end adjustment and the current market value of the inventory; and credits cash for the contract price of the inventory. Thus, consistent with the LCM rule, no recovery of market value for firm purchase commitments is recognized, although additional market declines are.

17. Some buyers *hedge* against price changes of a firm purchase commitment through a *futures contract,* whereby the buyer contracts to sell the same quantity of similar goods at a fixed price. Thus if the market price of the goods under the firm purchase commitment declines, the buyer offsets the loss on the purchase by selling similar goods at the fixed price under the futures contract. Under *Statement No. 80,* changes in the market value of a futures contract should be recognized as income in the period when they occur. If the futures contract is a hedge, then changes in the market value of the futures contract should be recognized as income when the price change effects of the related hedged items are recognized.

18. Replacement cost valuation. Some accountants believe that the measurement of inventory at its replacement cost or current cost provides better information for decision making and should be used for financial statement purposes. As discussed, the LCM procedure recognizes replacement cost when it is below cost, but GAAP does not permit recognition of replacement cost when it is above cost. Those who favor replacement cost valuation of inventory believe that if replacement cost properly reflects an inventory item's utility when it drops below cost, it should also be valid to use replacement cost when it reflects an increase in the item's utility by rising above cost.

19. Comprehensive replacement cost valuation of inventory would require holding gains and losses to be recognized each period in which replacement cost is above or below the replacement cost of the previous period. If replacement cost is higher at the end of the current period than it was at the end of the preceding period, a gain would have to be recognized before the inventory was actually sold. Although the comprehensive replacement cost valuation of inventory is not permitted in the primary financial statements, it may be reported in notes to the financial statements under the guidelines of *Statement No. 89.*

20. Some international accountants, notably the Dutch, advocate replacement cost for tangible assets. The Dutch, however, disclose inventory holding gains in stockholders' equity rather than in the income statement.

21. Net realizable value valuation. Net realizable value as defined for LCM is permitted for inventory valuation under GAAP if two conditions exist: (*a*) the inventory has a known and reasonably certain selling price, and (*b*) any costs of completion and selling of the inventory are known or are not material. When net realizable value is used for inventory valuation, revenue is recognized before the point of sale. This inventory valuation method is most often used for (*a*) inventories that are readily marketable, such as precious metals and minerals and some agricultural products, and (*b*) inventories from long-term construction contracts that are accounted for by the percentage-of-completion method. Accounting for these types of inventory items is discussed in Chapter 7.

22. Standard cost valuation. Many manufacturing companies maintain inventory at standard cost. Inventory at *standard cost* is costed at a predetermined amount for material, labor, and manufacturing overhead. Management analyzes the differences between standard and actual costs to help it control and manage inventory costs. Inventory may be reported at standard cost for financial statement purposes if the standard costs are periodically adjusted so that the inventory valuation approximates the valuation that would have resulted if a historical cost method, such as average cost or LIFO, had been used.

Inventory Estimation Methods

23. At times it is necessary to estimate the dollar amount of ending inventory. Under special circumstances, such as a flood or fire that destroys the inventory, an estimate of the inventory destroyed is required. In addition, inventory may be estimated periodically, as when it is not feasible to take a physical inventory at the time interim financial statements are prepared. The two inventory estimation methods discussed are the gross profit method and the retail method.

24. Gross profit method. Under the *gross profit,* or *gross margin, method* of estimating inventory, the sales price of goods sold during a period is converted to a cost basis and is then subtracted from the cost of goods available for sale (also stated on a cost basis) to yield an estimate of the cost of ending inventory. This method relies on the basic accounting relationships in the calculation of gross profit and assumes that all goods available for sale either are sold or remain in inventory. The gross profit percentage (gross profit divided by sales) used in the gross profit method is normally based on a historical relationship between gross profit and the selling price of the inventory.

25. The steps to take to estimate inventory by the gross profit method are as follows:

a. Estimate gross profit on goods sold (sales times estimated gross profit percentage).
b. Estimate cost of goods sold [sales less estimated gross profit (from step *a*)].
c. Determine cost of goods available for sale (beginning inventory plus net purchases).
d. Estimate ending inventory [goods available for sale (from step *c*) less estimated cost of goods sold (from step *b*)].

Most companies figure gross profit as a percentage of sales. Some companies, however, compute gross profit as a percentage of cost, which must be adjusted to a gross profit percentage of sales before the gross profit method can be used.

26. Although the concepts behind the gross profit method are easily understood and the computations simple, there are some concerns about the estimation technique. As evidenced by the steps outlined previously, the accuracy of the gross profit method is only as good as the gross profit percentage used. If the historical relationship used to determine the gross profit percentage is not relevant to the relationship between current selling price and cost, the resulting inventory estimation will be inaccurate. Similarly, if the inventory cost flow assumptions or inventory conditions that existed when the gross profit percentage was calculated have changed, the use of the gross profit percentage could yield inaccurate results. Also, since each inventory item usually has its own gross profit percentage based on the relationship between its cost and its selling price, the method is better applied to each type of inventory individually than to one "average" gross profit percentage derived from several types pooled together.

27. The gross profit method of estimating inventory is an acceptable technique, but, as explained, its accuracy is unreliable. Its use should be limited to situations in which the physical inventory cannot be counted or the other estimating technique cannot be used.

Retail Inventory Method— General Considerations

28. The primary advantage of the retail inventory method is that it uses the *current* relationship between cost and selling price to estimate inventory. Thus it results in more accurate estimations of ending inventory than the gross profit method, which is based on a *historical* gross profit percentage. The two methods are used in similar circumstances, but the retail inventory method can also be used by retail stores on a daily basis.

29. The more complex applications of the retail inventory estimation method will be discussed later; its basic steps are considered first. The four basic steps are as follows:

a. Determine the historical cost *and* retail (selling) price of goods available for sale (beginning inventory plus purchases).
b. Calculate the *cost to retail percentage* (goods available for sale at cost divided by goods available for sale at retail prices).
c. Estimate ending inventory at retail prices (goods available for sale at retail prices less sales for the period at retail prices).
d. Estimate ending inventory at cost by converting ending inventory at retail to cost [ending inventory at retail (from step *c*) times the cost to retail percentage (from step *b*)].

30. The retail method is most appropriate when retail prices are set by use of a consistent markup above acquisition cost. If several inventory items have different markup rates above cost, a separate cost to retail percentage should be computed for each inventory item.

31. In order to apply the retail inventory method, the terminology associated with retail pricing must be understood. The terms associated with changes in retail selling prices are as follows:

a. *Original cost:* costs required to get inventory into condition and location for sale.
b. *Initial, or original, selling price:* the price at which the inventory is initially sold.
c. *Original markup:* the difference between initial selling price and original cost.
d. *Markup:* increases in selling prices above the initial selling price.

e. *Markdown:* the amount a selling price is reduced below the initial selling price.
f. *Markup cancellation:* the amount a sales price previously raised above the initial selling price is subsequently lowered until the price is reduced to the level of the initial selling price.
g. *Markdown cancellation:* the amount a sales price previously reduced below the initial selling price is subsequently increased until the price is increased to the level of the initial selling price.
h. *Net markups:* markups less markup cancellations.
i. *Net markdowns:* markdowns less markdown cancellations.

32. In addition to the changes in selling price described earlier, other factors must be considered in the estimation of inventory under the retail inventory method. These factors affect the determination of the cost to retail percentage and hence estimated inventory at cost. Because the data on costs and retail prices are maintained in separate columns for computational purposes, as illustrated in the text, reference is made to the Cost and Retail columns.

33. *Freight in* should be an addition to purchases in the Cost column but not in the Retail column. Similarly, *purchase allowances* should be deducted from the Cost column but not from the Retail column. These factors are omitted from the Retail column because the initial selling price is set to cover such items. *Purchase returns* should be deducted from purchases in both the Cost and Retail columns; the goods available for sale are physically reduced, and thus both columns are affected. *Purchase discounts taken* (under the gross purchase method) should be deducted from purchases in the Cost column.

34. If sales are recorded at their gross amount, *sales returns and allowances,* but not sales discounts, should be deducted from sales in the Retail column. *Sales discounts* should be handled as an operating expense, not as an adjustment to sales for the period. When sales to employees are recorded net, *employee discounts* should be added to sales in the Retail column in order to determine total retail sales.

35. Since *normal spoilage* is relevant to the determination of the normal cost to retail percentage, it should be deducted in the Retail column *after* goods available for sale at retail have been determined. *Abnormal spoilage,* however, should be deducted in both the Cost and Retail columns *before* the cost to retail percentage is computed, because these goods are not available for sale.

Retail Inventory Method— Variations

36. The basic retail inventory method may be modified by shifting the components included in the computation of the cost to retail percentage. Variations of the retail inventory method include the average cost and LIFO cost flow assumptions and the lower-of-cost-or-market valuation method.

37. Average cost. An average cost of ending inventory results when the cost to retail percentage includes the cost and retail amounts of both beginning inventory and net purchases, adjusted for net markups and net markdowns. It should be noted that this approach is the one described in the general discussion of the retail inventory method. Since beginning inventory and purchases are combined and net markups and net markdowns are applied to all goods available for sale, the cost to retail percentage is an average percentage.

38. Lower of cost or market. When the cost to retail percentage is calculated exclusive of net markdowns, the resulting percentage is lower than that under the average retail approach because the denominator of the ratio is larger. Consequently, when the cost to retail percentage is applied to the ending inventory at retail, the cost of the inventory is lower than it would be under the average cost retail method. Net markdowns represent a loss in utility of the inventory on hand, and thus the merchandise should be reported at a figure below cost. If there are no net markdowns during a period, the merchandise has not declined in utility, and it should be reported at cost. Since GAAP requires that the lower of cost or market be applied to inventory valuation, the lower-of-cost-or-market retail method is commonly referred to as the *conventional retail inventory method.*

39. LIFO cost. To determine the estimated LIFO cost of ending inventory, the cost to retail percentage is calculated excluding the cost and retail

amounts of beginning inventory. When purchases exceed sales during a period, the LIFO cost flow assumes that ending inventory is composed of the beginning inventory layer or layers and an incremental layer (ending inventory at retail less beginning inventory at retail). The cost to retail percentage calculated for the current period is applied to the incremental layer, and the cost to retail percentages applicable to the beginning layers are applied to the beginning inventory to determine the LIFO retail cost of the ending inventory. If the inventory has decreased over a period, the layers constituting the beginning inventory are liquidated on the normal LIFO cost flow basis.

40. The table below presents the components of the cost to retail percentage used in the various retail inventory valuation methods. It should be noted that if a component is excluded from the computation of the cost to retail percentage, it is included in the determination of goods available for sale to complete the retail inventory procedure. Net markdowns, for example, are excluded from the lower-of-cost-or-market variation to determine the cost to retail percentage, but they are deducted after the computation of the percentage to figure goods available for sale.

Dollar-Value Retail LIFO Method

41. The retail LIFO method assumes that the retail selling price remains constant over time. This assumption is, of course, not true, and it can affect the results of the LIFO retail calculations. If during a period of inflation, for example, purchases exceed sales for the period, the apparent increase or incremental layer of inventory is partly the result of the change in the retail price level, not a *real* increase in the physical level of inventory. To adjust for the inflation effect, the ending retail inventory needs to be deflated by the amount of retail price increase—

Components of Cost to Retail Percentage
Used in Variations of Retail Inventory Method

RETAIL INVENTORY METHOD VARIATIONS	COST COMPONENTS		RETAIL COMPONENTS			
	BEGINNING INVENTORY	NET PURCHASES	BEGINNING INVENTORY	NET PURCHASES	NET MARKUPS	NET MARKDOWNS
Average	X	X	X	X	X	X
LCM (conventional method)	X	X	X	X	X	
LIFO		X		X	X	X

that is, inflation—in a manner similar to that used in the dollar-value approach discussed in Chapter 9. When the retail LIFO method is adjusted for changing retail prices, the technique is aptly referred to as the *dollar-value retail LIFO method.*

42. When the dollar-value retail LIFO method is applied, the cost to retail percentage and ending inventory at retail prices are determined in exactly the same way as under the retail LIFO method. The ending inventory at retail prices, however, must be restated in base retail prices (ending inventory at retail divided by retail price index) before it is compared with the beginning inventory expressed in base retail prices. Since both beginning and ending inventory at retail are expressed in base year retail prices, the increase or decrease in inventory during the period represents a *real* change in inventory. If an increase is found, the increase must be restated in current retail prices (amount of increase multiplied by current retail price index). If a decrease is

found, it is restated in terms of the retail price index for each year in which the layers now sold were originally added. After the increase or decrease has been restated to the appropriate retail price level, it is converted to a cost basis (amount of increase or decrease multiplied by appropriate cost to retail percentage). To determine the cost of the ending inventory to be used in preparation of the current financial statements, the cost of the increase or decrease is added to or deducted from beginning inventory stated at cost.

43. The procedure for the dollar-value retail LIFO method can be applied to successive years. It should be remembered, however, that each year has its own cost to retail percentage and retail price index that applies to that year's layer and must be maintained until the layer is liquidated. Also, ending inventory restated in base retail prices must be compared with the beginning inventory expressed in retail base year prices.

SELF-STUDY LEARNING

Key Terms and Concepts

Provide the appropriate term or terms to complete each of the following statements:

1. When the inventory on hand has declined in utility, it should be valued at the _____.

2. The upper limit for the market value used in the lower-of-cost-or-market inventory method is referred to as the _____, and the lower limit is referred to as the _____.

3. When LCM is used and the market value of inventory is below its cost, the difference can be charged to _____ or a contra inventory _____ account.

4. If a company has a firm _____ commitment, it can _____ against the effects of possible price decline by entering into a(n) _____ contract.

5. Inventory that is costed at a predetermined amount for material, labor, and manufacturing overhead is maintained at _____ cost.

6. An inventory estimation method based on the relationship of gross profit to sales is called the _____ method.

7. The retail inventory method of estimating inventory centers on the determination of the _____ percentage.

8. When the selling price is reduced below the initial selling price, the amount of the reduction is called a(n) _____.

9. The variation of the retail inventory method commonly referred to as the "conventional retail inventory method" is the _____ retail method.

10. The retail inventory method that takes into account changing retail prices is called the _____ method.

True-False

Indicate by circling the appropriate response whether each of the following statements is true (T) or false (F):

T F 1. The lower-of-cost-or-market inventory valuation method may be used if the market value of inventory on hand is less than its cost.

T F 2. The term *market* in the lower-of-cost-or-market (LCM) inventory method refers to the sales price of the inventory.

T F 3. A company can use the LCM inventory method only if it applies this technique to the total or entire inventory as one "pool" of inventory.

T F 4. LCM inventory is used only in the United States.

T F 5. If the market value of inventory is below cost, the inventory account will always be stated at market value.

T F 6. If the market price of goods under a firm purchase commitment rises above the firm purchase commitment price, the amount of the increase is recognized as a gain on purchase commitment.

T F 7. The replacement cost inventory valuation method recognizes an increase (gain) or a decrease (loss) in the utility of inventory as its replacement cost rises above or falls below its cost.

T F 8. The net realizable value (NRV) inventory valuation method values inventory at sales price less a normal profit.

T F 9. Management often uses the standard cost inventory valuation method to control and manage its inventory costs.

T F 10. The gross profit percentage used in the gross profit inventory estimation method is usually based on an estimate of the current or prevailing gross profit.

T F 11. If the gross profit method is used to estimate the ending inventory of several distinct items, it is normally best to use an individual gross profit percentage for each item rather than an average gross profit percentage.

T F 12. The retail inventory estimation method incorporates the current relationship between cost and selling price in its inventory estimation procedure.

T F 13. Detailed records of inventory and purchases should be maintained only at retail prices if the retail inventory method is used to estimate inventory.

T F 14. The retail inventory method requires ending inventory first to be determined at retail prices and then to be converted to a cost basis by multiplying the retail inventory amount by the gross profit percentage applicable to the inventory.

T F 15. Freight in charges should be added to purchases to determine goods available for sale on both a cost and a retail basis in order to calculate the cost to retail percentage.

T F 16. To determine ending inventory on a retail basis, sales, employee discounts, sales returns and allowances, and normal spoilage should be deducted from goods available for sale at retail prices.

T F 17. When the average retail inventory method is applied, the components of the retail portion of the cost to retail percentage include beginning inventory at retail, purchases at retail, net markups, and net markdowns.

T F 18. Net markdowns for a period indicate a loss in utility of the inventory and, accordingly, are excluded from the calculation of cost to retail percentage under the lower-of-cost-or-market retail method.

T F 19. Under the dollar-value retail LIFO inventory method, the price index used in calculating the cost to retail ratio is the retail price index.

T F 20. The cost to retail percentage for the dollar-value retail LIFO method includes net markups but excludes net markdowns.

Multiple Choice

Select the best response for each of the following items, and circle the corresponding letter:

1. When the lower-of-cost-or-market inventory method is applied, *market* can be:

   a. Replacement cost.
   b. Normal sales price minus cost of completion and disposal.
   c. Net realizable value minus normal profit.
   d. All of the above.

2. To maximize the effect of the lower-of-cost-or-market inventory valuation method, it should be applied to:

   a. Individual inventory items.
   b. Groups of similar inventory items.
   c. Groups of dissimilar inventory items.
   d. All inventory combined in one inventory pool.

3. When the market value of inventory is below cost, would the following accounts be debited or credited to recognize LCM?

	INVENTORY	COST OF GOODS	INVENTORY ALLOWANCE
a.	Credit	Credit	Credit
b.	Debit	Debit	Credit
c.	Credit	Debit	Credit
d.	Debit	Debit	Debit

4. Inventory may be reported at standard cost for financial statement purposes if:

   a. Actual inventory costs are less than standard inventory costs.
   b. Standard inventory costs are less than actual inventory costs.
   c. Standard inventory costs are periodically adjusted to approximate lower-of-cost-or-market inventory valuation.
   d. Standard inventory costs are periodically adjusted to approximately a historical cost inventory method.

5. Assuming that in some periods prices rise and in others they fall, which of the listed inventory methods would *not* be permitted under generally accepted accounting principles?

   a. Lower of cost or market.
   b. Replacement cost.
   c. Net realizable value.
   d. Standard cost.

6. In the gross profit method, ending inventory is estimated by subtracting:

   a. Beginning inventory from estimated cost of goods sold.
   b. Goods available for sale from sales.
   c. Estimated cost of goods sold from goods available for sale.
   d. Estimated cost of goods sold from sales.

7. A company that has a markdown cancellation has:

   a. Increased the sales price of an item that was previously reduced below its initial selling price.
   b. Decreased the sales price of an item that was previously raised above its initial selling price.
   c. Decreased the sales price of an item further below its initial selling price.
   d. Increased the sales price of an item after a previous markup.

8. When the cost to retail percentage is calculated under the lower-of-cost-or-market approach to the retail inventory method, which of the following items is included in both its cost and retail components?

   a. Net markups.
   b. Net markdowns.
   c. Freight in.
   d. Purchases.

9. If the LIFO retail inventory method is used, which of the following calculations should include net markups?

   a. Cost to retail percentage and cost of goods available for sale.
   b. Cost of goods available for sale only.
   c. Cost to retail percentage only.
   d. Neither cost to retail percentage nor cost of goods available for sale.

10. If at the end of the period there is a real increase in inventory when the dollar-value LIFO retail method is used to calculate the cost of the new LIFO layer, the amount of increase in inventory is:

   a. Multiplied by the current cost to retail percentage.
   b. Divided by the current price index.
   c. Multiplied by the current price index and then the current cost to retail percentage.
   d. Divided by the current price index and then multiplied by the current cost to retail percentage.

Extended Problems

1. Thunder Corporation sells a single product at $9 per unit with an estimated cost of disposal of $1 and a normal profit of $2 per unit. During 1995 Thunder Corporation sold 7,000 units. Because of varying demand, the current replacement cost of the inventory can fluctuate. Accordingly, Thunder entered into a firm purchase commitment on September 14, 1995, to acquire 2,000 units of inventory at $7.70 per unit. At December 31 the current market price of the inventory was $7.50 per unit. Thunder executed the contract on February 3, 1996, and March 18, 1996, by acquiring 1,500 and 500 units, respectively. The current market price of the inventory was $7.40 and $7.90 per unit on February 3 and March 18, respectively.

The following data were assembled on Thunder's inventory for 1995:

Beginning inventory (2,000 units)...... $10,000
Purchases (6,000 units).................... 42,000

REQUIRED

a. Assuming an average gross profit percentage of 25 percent on the sales price of the product, estimate the cost of ending inventory on December 31, 1995, using the gross profit method.
b. Complete the following table relative to Thunder Corporation's single product to determine the lower-of-cost-or-market inventory valuation per unit of inventory. Assume a constant cost of $6.50 per unit and the various replacement cost figures provided.

COST	REPLACE-MENT COST	CEILING	FLOOR	MARKET	LCM VALUE
$6.50	$8.50				
6.50	7.10				
6.50	5.75				
6.50	6.30				

c. Determine the dollar amount of ending inventory as of December 31, 1995, assuming the lower-of-FIFO-cost-or-market inventory valuation method and a replacement cost of $6.40 per unit.
d. Prepare all entries relative to the firm purchase commitment for the following dates: September 14 and December 31, 1995, and February 3 and March 18, 1996.

2. Great Midland Corporation adopted the retail inventory method on January 1, 1995, when its K-10 inventory had a cost of $15,600, a retail value of $20,000, and a retail selling price index of 1.00. The records of Great Midland Corporation reveal the following data relative to its K-10 inventory for the years 1995 and 1996.

	1995		1996	
	COST	RETAIL	COST	RETAIL
Purchases	$93,600	$117,000	$104,000	$129,000
Freight in	$ 7,000		$ 10,000	
Purchase returns	$ 3,000	$ 5,400		
Net markups		$ 8,500		$ 11,000
Markdowns		$ 13,000		$ 15,000
Markdown cancella-tions		$ 9,000		$ 8,000
Sales		$110,000		$125,000
Retail selling price index		1.05		1.11

REQUIRED

In all of the following computations, round all dollar amounts to the nearest dollar and all percentages to the nearest whole percent.

a. Calculate the cost of ending inventory as of December 31, 1995, assuming the following variations of the retail inventory method: average cost, lower of cost or market, LIFO, and dollar-value retail LIFO.
b. Prepare an income statement for December 31, 1996, through gross profit using the dollar-value retail LIFO inventory method. Assume that your answers to the dollar-value retail LIFO portion of part *a* were as follows: cost to retail percentage, 84 percent; ending inventory at dollar-value retail LIFO cost, $19,884.

COMMON ERRORS

The first statement in each of the "common errors" listed here is *incorrect*. Each incorrect statement is followed by a corrected statement and an explanation.

1. When cost and market are compared in the lower-of-cost-or-market (LCM) inventory method, market cannot be less than the ceiling or more than the floor. *Wrong*

When cost and market are compared in the lower-of-cost-or-market (LCM) inventory method, market cannot be greater than the ceiling or less than the floor. *Right*

The ceiling and floor in LCM are used as the upper limit and lower limit, respectively, of the market value to be compared with cost. It is assumed that the replacement cost and selling price of an inventory item move in the same direction. If the selling price goes up, it is assumed that the replacement cost also rises, and if the selling price falls, so does the replacement cost. If, however, the replacement cost and sales price do not rise or fall together, the use of replacement cost as the market value in LCM is suspect. When the sales price falls without a corresponding decrease in replacement cost, for example, the use of the higher replacement cost may not reflect the inventory item's true utility to the company. If the replacement cost is greater than the ceiling (sales price less costs of disposal, or net realizable value), the ceiling provides a more reasonable maximum amount that the company would normally pay to acquire more of the inventory. In other words, the company would not normally pay more for the inventory than it expects to recover through the sale of the inventory. Thus market or replacement cost cannot exceed the ceiling. A similar analysis illustrates why the market value cannot be less than the floor.

2. The use of the lower-of-cost-or-market inventory method will always cause conservative inventory valuation and reported earnings. *Wrong*

The use of the lower-of-cost-or-market inventory method will always cause conservative inventory valuation but not always conservative reported earnings. *Right*

The basic purpose of the lower-of-cost-or-market (LCM) inventory method is to recognize a decline in the utility of ending inventory (as measured by its market or replacement cost) in the period in which utility is lost. If the market value of the inventory is below its cost, the loss is recognized in the current period. Accordingly, the balance sheet will be conservative because the inventory will be valued at the *lower* market value, and the reported earnings will be conservative because of the recognized loss. In subsequent periods, however, earnings may be very unconservative if the anticipated loss in utility is not reflected in a lowering of the sales price of the inventory. If the selling price remains constant or rises, for example, earnings will be higher than normal as the lower cost of inventory is matched with sales. LCM causes conservative financial statements in the period in which the loss in utility is recognized, but not necessarily thereafter.

3. The net realizable value inventory valuation method determines only the valuation of inventory and of cost of goods sold. *Wrong*

The net realizable value inventory valuation method determines the valuation of inventory and of cost of goods sold and the recognition of revenue. *Right*

Inventory valuation methods are usually associated with the determination of the amounts of ending inventory and cost of goods sold. The net realizable inventory (NRV) method also affects the recognition of revenue. When the inventory has a known and reasonably certain selling price and the costs of completion and disposal are known or immaterial, the NRV method is the appropriate inventory valuation method to use. It should be recalled from Chapter 7 that when these two conditions are met, revenue can be recognized before the inventory is actually sold. Types of inventory that commonly meet the conditions include precious metals, some agricultural crops, and long-term construction contracts accounted for by the percentage-of-completion method. Thus use of the NRV inventory valuation method triggers revenue realization as well as providing a means to value inventory and to assign costs to cost of goods sold.

4. Most companies use the replacement cost inventory valuation method to prepare their primary financial statements. *Wrong*

Some companies use the replacement cost inventory valuation method as supplementary information disclosed in footnotes to the financial statements. *Right*

The use of replacement cost (RC) as an inventory valuation method is very controversial. Those who support its use believe that the RC of an inventory item reflects its true utility and should be allowed for financial statement purposes. Like the lower-of-cost-or-market method, RC requires the recognition of holding losses as well as *holding gains,* so that in effect revenue would be recognized before the point of sale. GAAP, however, does not permit the recognition of RC (and the gain) when the RC is above cost. So much pressure from financial statement users, the SEC, and others was put on the FASB that *Statement No. 33* was issued and modified by *Statement No. 89. Statement No. 89* permits RC disclosures in notes to the financial statements but still does not permit RC to be recognized in the primary statements. This is an interesting situation, since information that is deemed useful for decision making but is not permitted under GAAP is nevertheless disclosed in the notes to the financial statements.

5. The average retail inventory method is considered the conventional retail inventory method. *Wrong*

The lower-of-cost-or-market retail inventory method is considered to be the conventional retail inventory method. *Right*

Generally accepted accounting principles require that inventory be reported on the balance sheet at the lower of its cost or market value. Normally, then, a company is required to determine the cost of the inventory according to one of the cost assumptions, such as average cost or FIFO, and to compare that cost with the market value or replacement cost of the inventory (within the constraints of the ceiling and floor). The lower-of-cost-or-market (LCM) value is then reported on the balance sheet. The LCM retail inventory method closely approximates the LCM procedure. The general retail inventory procedure considers both net markups and net markdowns in the development of the cost to retail percentage and results in an average cost figure. To develop the cost to retail percentage for the LCM retail method, the general retail method is modified by excluding the net markdowns, which reflect a loss in the utility of the inventory. Consequently,

the cost to retail percentage will be lower than the cost to retail percentage computed in accordance with the average retail method, resulting in a lower cost of ending inventory—one that approximates the LCM inventory valuation.

6. During periods of changing prices, the retail inventory method that best accounts for the changing prices is the LIFO retail inventory method. *Wrong*

During periods of changing prices, the retail inventory method that best accounts for the changing prices is the dollar-value retail LIFO inventory method. *Right*

Particularly during periods of rising prices, the LIFO retail inventory method recognizes the price change better than the average or lower-of-cost-or-market method. But the best retail method to account for all price changes is the dollar-value retail LIFO method, since it explicitly adjusts for changing prices. The adjustment occurs when the effect of changing prices during the period is removed from the ending inventory at retail prices (ending inventory at retail prices divided by current retail selling price index). The effects of changing prices are removed before the ending inventory is compared with the beginning inventory to determine whether there has been a *real* increase or decrease in inventory during the period. If an increase occurs during the period, for example, the amount of the increase is multiplied by the retail selling price index for the period to state the increase in current prices. This restated increase is then multiplied by the current cost to retail percentage to determine the cost of the incremental layer. Therefore, when price changes must be considered, the dollar-value retail LIFO method should be used.

ANSWERS

Key Terms and Concepts

1. lower of cost or market
2. ceiling, floor
3. cost of goods sold, allowance
4. purchase, hedge, futures
5. standard
6. gross profit
7. cost to retail
8. markdown
9. lower-of-cost-or-market
10. dollar-value retail LIFO

True-False

1. F   Generally accepted accounting principles *requires* that the LCM procedure be applied if the market value of inventory has fallen below its cost.

2. F   *Market* in LCM refers to the replacement cost of the inventory. For merchandising companies, it refers to the price in the market where inventory is purchased; for manufacturing companies, it refers to the cost to produce the inventory.

3. F The LCM method may be applied to either individual inventory items, groups of inventory items, or the total inventory. In fact, most companies that apply the LCM method use the individual item approach because it is required for federal income tax purposes.

4. F LCM is required in the United States, but it is also followed in most other countries.

5. F The net inventory balance on the balance sheet will always be at market value, but not necessarily the inventory account. The inventory account can be reduced to market value directly, but it can also be reduced through the contra inventory allowance account.

6. F Price *increases* above the firm purchase commitment price are never recognized. Following the conservatism principle, only decreases from the firm purchase commitment price are recognized.

7. T

8. F The valuation of inventory under the NRV method is the same as the calculation of NRV when NRV is determined for the ceiling in LCM: estimated selling price less estimated cost to complete and dispose of the inventory.

9. T

10. F Unfortunately, the gross profit percentage is not a current percentage; rather, it is based on a historical relationship between gross profit and the selling price of inventory. This is one of the criticisms of the gross profit method: the pivotal percentage in the technique is based on a historical and not a current gross profit percentage. If the historical gross profit percentage differs from the current percentage, the estimation of ending inventory can be extremely inaccurate.

11. T

12. T

13. F Detailed records of inventory and purchases at retail should be maintained along with comparable records at cost. The cost to retail percentage used to convert ending inventory at retail to a cost basis is calculated each period by the use of data on both the cost *and* the retail prices of inventory and purchases.

14. F It is important to remember that each inventory estimation method has its own unique percentage to apply. The gross profit percentage pertains to the gross profit method. When the retail inventory method is used, the ending inventory stated in retail prices is multiplied by the *cost to retail percentage* to convert the retail inventory to a cost basis.

15. F Freight in charges are added only to purchases at cost, not to purchases at retail. The initial retail (selling) price of the purchases includes an amount for freight in, so to add it separately would be to count it twice. The freight in charges must be added to purchases at cost to determine the total acquisition cost of the purchases.

16. F Sales, employee discounts, and normal spoilage should be deducted from goods available for sale at retail to determine ending inventory at retail. But sales returns and allowances should not be deducted because they represent contra sales transactions, or transactions that reduce the actual sales for the period. Accordingly, they should be added to the figure for goods available for sale to determine ending inventory at retail prices.

17. T

18. T

19. T

20. F It should be noted that the cost to retail percentage calculation is the same for both the LIFO retail and dollar-value retail LIFO methods. Both net markups and net markdowns are included in the calculation of the cost to retail percentage.

Multiple Choice

1.	d	6.	c
2.	a	7.	a
3.	c	8.	d
4.	d	9.	a
5.	b	10.	c

Extended Problems

1. a. Estimated ending inventory calculated by the gross profit method:

Estimated gross profit:

Sales (7,000 units × $9).....................	$63,000
Times: Gross profit percentage.......... ×	.25
	$15,750

Estimated cost of goods sold:

Sales...	$63,000
Less: Estimated gross profit .... −	15,750
	$47,250

Goods available for sale:
Beginning inventory...................... $10,000
Plus: Purchases .... + 42,000
$52,000

Estimated ending inventory:
Goods available for sale.................. $52,000
Less: Estimated cost of goods sold..... − 47,250
$ 4,750

b. Determination of LCM value per unit:

COST	REPLACE-MENT COST	CEILING	FLOOR	MARKET	LCM VALUE
$6.50	$8.50	$8.00[a]	$6.00[b]	$8.00[c]	$6.50[c]
6.50	7.10	8.00	6.00	7.10[d]	6.50[d]
6.50	5.75	8.00	6.00	6.00[e]	6.00[e]
6.50	6.30	8.00	6.00	6.30[f]	6.30[f]

[a]Selling price ($9) − disposal costs ($1) = $8 (net realizable value).

[b]Net realizable value ($8) − normal profit ($2) = $6.

[c]Since RC is above the ceiling, the market value is the ceiling. Cost is lower than the market; therefore, cost is the LCM value.

[d]Since RC lies between the ceiling and the floor, the market value is RC. Cost is lower than the market; therefore, cost is the LCM value.

[e]Since RC is below the floor, the market value is the floor value. Cost is greater than the market value; therefore, the floor is the LCM value.

[f]Since RC lies between the ceiling and the floor, the market value is RC. Cost is greater than market; therefore, the market is the LCM value.

c. Determination of the lower-of-FIFO-cost-or-market ending inventory value:

FIFO inventory cost:
Units available (2,000 + 6,000) 8,000
Units sold...................................... 7,000
Units in ending inventory................... 1,000

1,000 units × $7 cost per unit = $7,000.

Market value of inventory:
Ceiling ($9 − $1).............................. $8
Floor ($8 − $2) $6

RC of $6.40 lies between the floor and the ceiling; therefore, the market value is $6,400 ($6.40 × 1,000 units).
LCM: $6,400 [$6,400 (market) is lower than $7,000 (cost)].

d. Entries for the firm purchase commitment:
1995
Sept. 14 No entry required to record signing of the firm purchase commitment contract.
Dec. 31 Estimated loss on purchase commitment .... 400[a]
Estimated liability on purchase commitment 400

[a][($7.70 − $7.50) × 2,000] = $400.

1996
Feb. 3 Inventory ($7.40 × 1,500) 11,100
Estimated liability on purchase commitment.......... 300[b]
Loss on purchase commitment.. 150[c]
Cash ($7.70 × 1,500).......... 11,550

[b][($7.70 − $7.50) × 1,500] = $300.
[c][($7.50 − $7.40) × 1,500] = $150.

Mar. 18 Inventory ($7.50 × 500) 3,750
Estimated liability on purchase commitment........ 100[d]
Cash ($7.70 × 500)........... 3,850

[d]($.20 × 500).

2. a. Computations of the cost of the December 31, 1995, ending inventory under various retail inventory methods:

AVERAGE COST RETAIL METHOD

	COST	RETAIL
Beginning inventory............	$ 15,600	$ 20,000
Purchases	93,600	117,000
Freight in............................	7,000	
Purchase returns	(3,000)	(5,400)
Net markups........................		8,500
Markdowns..........................		(13,000)
Markdown cancellations........		9,000
Goods available for sale........	$113,200	$136,100

Cost to retail percentage: $113,200 ÷ $136,100 = 83%.

Net sales .... (110,000)
Estimated ending inventory at retail......... $ 26,100

Estimated ending inventory at average cost:
$26,100 × 83% = $21,663.

LOWER-OF-COST-OR-MARKET RETAIL METHOD

	COST	RETAIL
Beginning inventory............	$ 15,600	$ 20,000
Purchases	93,600	117,000
Freight in............................	7,000	
Purchase returns	(3,000)	(5,400)
Net markups........................		8,500
	113,200	140,100

Cost to retail percentage: $113,200 ÷ $140,100 = 81%.

Markdowns		(13,000)
Markdown cancellations...........		9,000
Goods available for sale	$113,200	$136,100
Net sales		(110,000)
Estimated ending inventory at retail...........................		$ 26,100

Estimated ending inventory at lower cost or market: $26,100 × 81% = $21,141.

LIFO RETAIL METHOD

	COST	RETAIL
Purchases	$ 93,600	$117,000
Freight in...........................	7,000	
Purchase returns	(3,000)	(5,400)
Markups.............................		8,500
Markdowns.........................		(13,000)
Markdown cancellations........		9,000
	$ 97,600	$116,100

Cost to retail percentage: $97,600 ÷ $116,100 = 84%.

	COST	RETAIL
Beginning inventory...............	15,600	20,000
Goods available for sale	$113,200	$136,100
Net sales		(110,000)
Estimated ending inventory at retail...........................		$ 26,100

Estimated ending inventory at LIFO cost:

Ending inventory @ retail	$ 26,100
Beginning inventory @ retail..........	20,000
Increase in inventory (new layer)......	$ 6,100

Beginning inventory @ cost ($20,000 × 78%[a])..................... $ 15,600
Current layer ($6,100 × 84%).......... 5,124
Ending inventory @ LIFO cost......... $ 20,724

[a]$15,600 ÷ $20,000 = 78%.

DOLLAR-VALUE RETAIL LIFO METHOD

	COST	RETAIL
Purchases	$93,600	$117,000
Freight in............................	7,000	
Purchase returns	(3,000)	(5,400)
Markups..............................		8,500
Markdowns...........................		(13,000)
Markdown cancellations........		9,000
	$97,600	$116,100

Cost to retail percentage: $97,600 ÷ $116,100 = 84%.

	COST	RETAIL
Beginning inventory...............	15,600	20,000
Goods available for sale	$113,200	$136,100
Net sales		(110,000)
Estimated ending inventory at retail...........................		$ 26,100

Estimated ending inventory at dollar-value retail LIFO:

Ending inventory at base retail prices ($26,100 ÷ 1.05).........................	$ 24,857
Beginning inventory at base retail prices	(20,000)
Real increase in inventory at base retail prices	$ 4,857
Real increase in inventory stated in current retail prices ($4,857 × 1.05)..	$ 5,100
Real increase in inventory converted to current period cost ($5,100 × 84%)...	$ 4,284
Beginning inventory........................	15,600
Estimated inventory at dollar-value retail LIFO cost...........................	$ 19,884

b. Partial income statement assuming dollar-value retail LIFO:

Great Midland Corporation
INCOME STATEMENT
FOR THE YEAR ENDED DECEMBER 31, 1996

Sales........................			$125,000
Cost of goods sold:			
Beginning inventory........................		$ 19,884	
Purchases	$104,000		
Freight in........................	10,000	114,000	
Goods available for sale		$133,884	
Ending inventory (See Schedule A)........................		(25,482)	
Cost of goods sold........................			(108,402)
Gross profit			$ 16,598

SCHEDULE A
CALCULATON OF ENDING INVENTORY
DOLLAR-VALUE RETAIL LIFO

	COST	RETAIL
Purchases	$104,000	$129,000
Freight in...	10,000	
Net markups...		11,000
Markdowns...		(15,000)
Markdown cancellations..		8,000
	$114,000	$133,000

Cost to retail percentage: $114,000 ÷ $133,000 = 86%.

	COST	RETAIL
Beginning inventory...	19,884	26,100
Goods available for sale	$133,884	$159,100
Net sales		125,000
Estimated ending inventory at retail		$ 34,100

Estimated ending inventory at dollar-value retail LIFO:

Ending inventory at base retail prices ($34,100 ÷ 1.11).............................		$ 30,721
Beginning inventory at base retail prices.............................		24,857
Real increase in inventory at base retail prices		$ 5,864
Real increase stated in current retail prices ($5,864 × 1.11)		$ 6,509

Real increase in inventory in terms of relevant current costs:

1995 ($5,100 × 84%)...	$ 4,284	
1996 ($6,509) × 86%)..	5,598	
Base inventory	15,600	
	$ 25,482	

11

PLANT ASSETS AND INTANGIBLES: ACQUISITION AND SUBSEQUENT EXPENDITURES

CHAPTER OBJECTIVES

After reading Chapter 11 and completing the questions, cases, exercises, and problems from the text chapter, you should be able to:

1. Describe the nature and characteristics of plant assets, natural resources (wasting assets), and intangibles.
2. Prepare the journal entries required to account for capitalized costs associated with the acquisition of land, machinery and equipment, buildings, and self-constructed assets.
3. Distinguish among the four categories of costs associated with natural resources: acquisition costs; exploration costs; development costs, including the costs of both tangible assets and intangible development; and production costs.
4. Identify those circumstances when the costs associated with intangibles should be capitalized and amortized and those circumstances when such costs should be expensed.
5. Prepare the journal entries required to account for such specifically identifiable intangible assets as patents, copyrights, trademarks and trade names, franchises, lease prepayments and leasehold improvements, and other assets.
6. Define and identify research and development activities, and compute the amount of research and development costs that must be expensed in a year.
7. Prepare the journal entries required to account for the costs incurred in developing and producing computer software, both before and after technological feasibility has been established.
8. Prepare the journal entry required to record the acquisition of the net assets of another company.
9. Determine the recorded value of an asset acquired through issuance of stock, donation, a lump-sum purchase, or exchanges of nonmonetary assets.
10. Differentiate between capital and revenue expenditures.
11. Prepare the journal entries required to account for expenditures subsequent to the acquisition of plant assets and intangibles including the costs of repair and maintenance, additions, replacements and improvements, rearrangement and relocation, and litigation.

CHAPTER REVIEW

Introduction

1. Previous chapters have discussed accounting and reporting issues related to current assets, that is, cash, receivables, and inventory. Most companies also possess assets that are intended to be used in operations for an extended period of time rather than converted to cash or consumed in one year or the operating cycle, whichever is longer. Such assets are called plant assets and intangibles.

2. Long-lived, operating assets that have physical existence are commonly referred to as *property, plant, and equipment; fixed assets;* or *plant assets.* Long-lived, operating assets that do not have physi-

cal existence, such as a patent, are referred to as *intangible assets*. Both plant assets and intangible assets are identified by two characteristics:

a. *They are acquired or developed to be used in operations.* The benefits of plant assets and intangibles are to be derived from their use, not their resale. They are usually disposed of when their services have expired or are no longer needed.

b. *They provide benefits over several accounting periods.* The matching principle requires that costs be matched with revenue in the period benefited. It would be inappropriate to expense the cost of plant assets and intangible assets in the period in which they are acquired since their costs benefit more than one period. They are normally classified as noncurrent assets in the balance sheet, and the cost is expensed over the period benefited by one of the allocation processes discussed in Chapter 12.

3. The remainder of this chapter review describes the financial accounting and reporting principles for the valuation of plant assets and intangibles at acquisition and for expenditures subsequent to their acquisition. Chapter 12 continues the coverage of plant assets and intangibles with a discussion of accounting and reporting for their use and disposition.

Plant Assets

4. Most plant assets are acquired through an exchange transaction, although some are donated (a nonreciprocal transfer) or constructed by the company. Regardless of the specific means by which their service potential is acquired, plant assets should be recorded initially at their fair value or the fair value of the consideration sacrificed, whichever is more reasonably determinable. In most cases, cost is the best estimate of the asset's fair value at the acquisition date. This method of valuation is an application of the historical cost principle.

5. Internationally, Canada, Germany, and Japan also follow the historical cost principle in valuing plant assets. Other countries, such as the Netherlands and most English-speaking countries, however, allow periodic revaluation to current value (with disclosure of historical cost).

6. The remainder of this section discusses the application of the historical cost principle to plant assets. The historical cost principle requires that all necessary sacrifices made to obtain the asset's service potential and to place the asset in position for its intended use should be recorded (capitalized) in the asset account.

7. **Land.** The costs to be capitalized in the land account should include the purchase price, plus any closing costs, survey costs, earth-moving costs, unpaid taxes or mortgages assumed by the purchaser, and similar costs related to obtaining and readying the land for its intended use. If land is acquired with structures that must be removed before starting construction of a new building, the cost of their removal, net of any salvage value, should be charged to the land account. Similarly, costs incurred to make relatively permanent improvements in the land, such as landscaping, sewer installation, and special assessments for street lights and paving, should also be capitalized in the land account. A land improvement account, however, should be charged for improvements with limited lives, such as fences and parking lots, so the cost of the improvements can be depreciated over their useful lives.

8. Because plant assets are used in the operations of a company, land acquired for a nonoperating purpose (for example, for speculation) should be classified as an investment, rather than as a plant asset. Furthermore, some argue that property taxes on land held for speculation should be capitalized, as no revenues are being generated by the land. Others contend that for expediency such taxes should be expensed as they are incurred.

9. **Machinery and equipment.** Costs that should be capitalized in the machinery and equipment account or the furniture and fixtures account include the net invoice price; plus such items as freight charges; in-transit insurance cost; applicable taxes; the cost of special foundations or bases; and the costs of assembly, installation, and testing. Theoretically, if there is a cash discount offered, the invoice amount capitalized should be net of the discount and any discount lost should be recorded as a financing expense. However, due to materiality or practical considerations, many companies treat discounts lost as part of the asset cost.

10. **Buildings.** A building may be acquired by several means, such as purchase, construction by an outside contractor, or self-construction. The capitalized cost of a building purchased or constructed by an outside contractor should include the purchase or construction price and any additional costs incidental to the acquisition, such as attorneys' fees and building permits.

11. **Self-constructed assets.** The cost of self-constructed assets (buildings as well as machinery and equipment) should include all costs necessary to construct the asset and to get it in a position for its intended use. The company that constructs a plant asset may incur direct costs, indirect manufacturing costs, and interest costs. *Direct costs,* such as direct material, direct labor, and direct overhead costs, are capitalized in the asset account,

since they are incremental costs associated with or incurred because of the construction of the asset. In addition, *indirect manufacturing costs,* such as electricity, taxes on manufacturing facilities, factory supervisory and janitorial costs, and depreciation of manufacturing facilities may be allocated to the self-constructed asset. Specifically, there are three methods of accounting for these costs: (*a*) *direct costing approach,* which assigns none of the fixed manufacturing overhead to self-constructed assets; (*b*) *full costing approach,* which assigns the fixed manufacturing overhead to self-constructed assets on the same basis as these costs are charged to inventory; and (*c*) *opportunity cost approach,* which uses the direct costing approach unless the company is operating at full capacity, and then the profit that would have been earned had there been no construction project is allocated to the self-constructed asset. The full costing approach is used most often in practice because it follows historical cost principles similar to those applied to inventories. The direct costing approach is not acceptable under GAAP, and the opportunity cost approach is too subjective to be practical.

12. Interest during construction. Interest incurred during construction raises a unique accounting problem. While the asset is being constructed, it is not generating any revenue to match with the interest expense. Thus at issue is whether such interest cost should be considered a period cost or not.

13. The evolution of accounting for interest during construction is noteworthy in that practices have literally been reversed. Public utilities have traditionally capitalized interest during construction so that these costs can be included in the rate-making process. Nonregulated companies, on the other hand, did not capitalize such interest until the economic reversals of the early 1970s contracted profits. Companies saw the capitalization of interest during construction as one way to increase profits by reducing the immediate recognition of interest as an expense. The SEC in 1974 issued a moratorium prohibiting companies that had not previously capitalized interest during construction from adopting the practice. It appears that the SEC was concerned over the diversity of practices and the resultant lack of comparability of financial statements. After strong encouragement from the SEC, the FASB in 1979 finally issued *Statement No. 34,* which requires that interest cost be capitalized for all qualifying assets that require a period of time to get them ready for their intended use.

14. *Qualifying assets* that require interest to be capitalized are those assets that an entity constructs for its own use, such as machinery, and those constructed as discrete projects for sale or lease, such as real estate developments and ships. Excluded are routinely manufactured inventories, assets in use or ready for use, and assets that are not ready for or being prepared for the earnings process, such as vacant land being held for possible expansion.

15. The *amount of interest to be capitalized* is based on the concept of "avoidable interest," or interest that could have been avoided had the qualifying asset not been constructed. The avoidable interest is based on the company's actual interest cost and actual borrowings during the period. The amount of interest to be capitalized is the product of the actual expenditures for the qualifying asset during the period multiplied by the number of months outstanding (that is, the number of months the expenditures are outstanding over 12) multiplied by the appropriate interest rate. Furthermore, if a specific construction loan can be associated with the qualifying asset, the interest rate on the loan should be applied to the actual expenditures incurred for that qualifying asset. However, a weighted average interest rate on the company's other debts must be applied to the excess of the actual expenditures incurred over the specific borrowing if the specific borrowing is less than the actual total expenditures or if there is no specific borrowing. The sum of interest capitalized also cannot exceed the actual amount of interest incurred during the period. For financial reporting purposes, the amount of interest capitalized and the total amount of interest incurred during the period must be disclosed.

16. In practice, several complicating factors may arise. First, professional judgment is required to be certain that the weighted average interest rate of other debt reflects current borrowing costs. If the interest rate of an older debt is substantially different from current rates, that older rate should not be included in the weighted average calculation. Second, it should be remembered that the beginning balance in the construction account for each year after the first year of construction is the sum of the actual costs incurred plus capitalized interest. Third, any interest incurred during the period that is not capitalized must be recognized as interest expense for the period.

17. The *capitalization period* for interest on a qualifying asset begins and continues as long as (*a*) expenditures for the asset are being made, (*b*) activities necessary to prepare the asset for its intended use are in progress, *and* (*c*) interest cost is being incurred. The capitalization ends when the qualifying asset is substantially complete and ready for its intended use.

Natural Resources

18. *Natural resources* (also called *wasting assets*) are resources that are physically consumed (or depleted) in the production process and usually are replaced only by an act of nature. Typical wasting assets are timberland, oil and gas deposits, and mineral deposits.

19. The costs associated with natural resources may be classified in four categories: (*a*) *acquisition costs* that are incurred to acquire the property or property rights; (*b*) *exploration costs* that are incurred to determine the existence of recoverable natural resources; (*c*) *development costs* that are incurred to gain access to the recoverable natural resources, including both the *costs of tangible assets* necessary to extract the natural resources and *intangible development costs* for items such as the drilling of wells and the digging of shafts or tunnels; and (*d*) *production costs* that are incurred to extract the natural resources. Depending on the circumstances, acquisition, exploration, and intangible development costs (often called the *capitalized costs*) associated with recoverable natural resources should be recorded as an asset and allocated over the period estimated to be benefited, by a process called *depletion*. That is, all the costs incurred to acquire the property, to determine the existence of recoverable natural resources, and to prepare the property for extraction of the natural resources should be capitalized and subsequently allocated (depleted) over the future benefit period.

Intangible Assets

20. *Intangible assets* are operating resources that are expected to provide benefits for more than one year but lack physical substance. Because intangible assets are not physical in nature, the existence and timing of their future benefits are difficult to observe and verify. Typical intangible assets are patents, copyrights, trademarks, franchises, and goodwill.

21. Intangible assets may be classified on the basis of the following characteristics: (*a*) *identifiability*—specifically identifiable or not specifically identifiable, (*b*) *manner of acquisition*—purchased from others or developed internally, (*c*) *expected period of benefit*—useful life limited by economic factors or by legal or contractual restrictions or indefinite or indeterminate, and (*d*) *separability* (exchangeability) —rights transferable or salable or inseparable from the enterprise as a whole.

22. The accounting and reporting guidelines for intangible assets are contained in *Opinion No. 17*. These guidelines distinguish between intangible assets that are specifically identifiable and those that are not, and between intangible assets that are purchased from others and those that are developed internally. The principal guidelines are as follows:

a. *Specifically identifiable and purchased from others.* The costs of specifically identifiable intangible assets purchased from others must be recorded as an asset and amortized to expense over the period estimated to be benefited.

b. *Specifically identifiable and developed internally.* The costs incurred internally to develop specifically identifiable intangible assets may be either recorded as an asset and amortized to expense over the period estimated to be benefited or recorded as an expense as they are incurred. According to *Statement No. 2*, however, most research and development costs must be expensed as they are incurred.

c. *Not specifically identifiable and purchased from others.* The excess of the purchase price (cost) over the fair value of identifiable net assets acquired as a group from another entity must be recorded as an asset (called goodwill) and amortized to expense over the period estimated to be benefited.

d. *Not specifically identifiable and developed internally.* The costs incurred internally to develop intangible assets that are not specifically identifiable (such as a good reputation for quality products and services, good labor relations, and other elements of goodwill) must be recorded as an expense as they are incurred.

In addition, *Opinion No. 17* specifies that the capitalized costs of intangible assets should be amortized over a period not to exceed 40 years, and the method of amortization should be straight-line unless it can be demonstrated that another systematic method is more appropriate. The application of these guidelines to specific intangible assets is described in the remainder of this section.

23. Patents. A *patent,* granted by the U.S. Patent Office, conveys to the holder the exclusive right to use, manufacture, and sell a product or process for a period of 17 years. The costs incurred to purchase an existing patent should be recorded as an asset and amortized to expense over the benefit period. Research and development costs incurred to develop a new product or process that subsequently is patented, however, must be expensed as they are incurred.

24. Copyrights. A *copyright* is a grant by the federal government of the exclusive right to reproduce and sell an artistic or literary work. For individuals, a copyright is granted for the life of its creator plus 50 years; for companies, a copyright is granted for 75 years. The costs incurred to acquire a copyright should be recorded as an asset and amortized to expense over the benefit period.

25. Trademarks and trade names. *Trademarks* and *trade names* are words, symbols, or other devices that identify particular products. The right of exclusive use of a trademark under common law resides with the original user as long as it is used continuously. A trademark also may be registered with the U.S. Patent Office for renewable 20-year periods as long as it is used continuously. The costs incurred to acquire a trademark should be recorded as an asset and amortized to expense over the benefit period.

26. Franchises. A *franchise* is an agreement whereby one party (the franchisor) grants to another party (the franchisee) the exclusive right to market a product or service within a designated area. The initial franchise fee incurred to acquire a franchise should be recorded by the franchisee as an asset and amortized to expense over the benefit period. The franchisee should record the costs of periodic fees required under a franchise agreement, such as fees based on services received or periodic operating income, as an expense in the period in which they are incurred.

27. Lease prepayments and leasehold improvements. A *lease* is a contractual agreement whereby one party (the lessor) grants to another party (the lessee) the right to use specified property owned by the lessor for a specified period of time in exchange for periodic cash payments. A lump-sum *lease prepayment* made at the time the lease agreement is signed should be recorded by the lessee as an asset and amortized to lease expense over the benefit period. Likewise, because improvements made by the lessee to leased property usually revert to the lessor at the termination of the lease, the costs of *leasehold improvements* should be recorded by the lessee as an asset and amortized to lease expense over the benefit period.

28. Organization costs. *Organization costs* are expenditures such as legal fees, accounting fees, state fees and taxes, and promotional costs incurred in the formation of a company. Organization costs should be recorded as an asset and amortized to expense over the benefit period.

29. Other assets. *Other assets* or *deferred charges* include long-term prepayments (such as license fees, rent, insurance, and taxes), plant rearrangement or relocation costs, and the book value of idle plant assets. Such assets should be amortized to expense over the benefit period.

30. Research and development costs. *Research* is defined as planned search or critical investigation aimed at discovery of new knowledge with the hope that such knowledge will be useful in the development of a new product or service or a new process or technique, or will bring about a significant improvement in an existing product or process. *Development* is defined as the translation of research findings or other knowledge into a plan or design for a new product or process or for a significant improvement in an existing product or process, whether intended for sale or for use.

31. *Statement No. 2* requires that research and development costs be expensed as they are incurred. Two reasons underly this requirement: (*a*) normally the future benefits of specific research and development projects are highly uncertain, and (*b*) a demonstrated cause-and-effect relationship between research and development costs and specific future benefits is generally lacking.

32. *Statement No. 2* also specifies five elements of costs that should be identified with research and development activities: (*a*) costs of materials, equipment, or facilities acquired or constructed for research and development activities; (*b*) salaries, wages, and other related costs of personnel engaged in research and development activities; (*c*) costs of intangible assets purchased from others for use in research and development activities; (*d*) costs of services performed by others in connection with research and development activities; and (*e*) a reasonable allocation of indirect costs. These elements of costs must be expensed as research and development costs as they are incurred, except for elements *a* and *c* when the test of alternative future uses is met. Specifically, if the materials, equipment, or facilities or the purchased intangibles have alternative future uses (either in other research and development projects or otherwise), then the costs should be recorded as an asset and subsequently expensed as research and development costs as the materials are used, as the equipment or facilities are depreciated, or as the purchased intangibles are amortized. Conversely, if the materials, equipment, or facilities or the purchased intangibles are obtained for a specific research and development project and have no alternative future uses (and thus no separate economic value), then the costs must be expensed as research and development costs in the period when the materials, equipment, or facilities or the purchased intangibles are acquired.

33. Computer software costs. *Statement No. 86* requires that the costs incurred in developing computer software to be sold, leased, or otherwise marketed be expensed as research and development costs when they are incurred, until the technological feasibility of the product or process is established. Technological feasibility is deemed to be established when the company has completed all planning, designing, coding, and testing activities necessary to determine that a product can be produced to design specifications.

34. Once technological feasibility has been established, the costs incurred to produce product masters must be capitalized as an asset and subsequently amortized on a product-by-product basis.

The costs incurred to duplicate the software, documentation, and training materials from the product masters and to package the product physically for distribution must be capitalized as inventory cost and subsequently expensed as cost of goods sold when the sales revenue for the product is recognized. Maintenance and customer support costs must be expensed when the related revenue is recognized or when the costs are incurred, if earlier.

35. Goodwill. *Goodwill* consists of the favorable characteristics of a business enterprise that are intangible in nature, not separately identifiable, indeterminate in duration, and inseparable from the enterprise as a whole. Such favorable characteristics include a superior management team, effective advertising, a secret manufacturing process, good labor relations, an outstanding credit rating, high standing in the community, and a strategic location. Such characteristics increase the value of the company by increasing its earning power.

36. Goodwill can be recorded as an asset only if (*a*) a transaction (called a business combination) takes place whereby one company acquires the assets and assumes the liabilities of another company and (*b*) the purchase price (cost) exceeds the fair value of the identifiable net assets (assets less liabilities) acquired. That is, from the perspective of financial accounting and reporting, goodwill is the excess of cost over the fair value of identifiable net assets acquired as a group from another company. In contrast, costs incurred internally to develop, maintain, or restore goodwill must be expensed as they are incurred.

37. When a company acquires the net assets of another company, the acquiring company should (*a*) debit the individual tangible and identifiable intangible assets acquired at their fair values, (*b*) credit the individual liabilities assumed at their fair values, and (*c*) credit cash (and/or other consideration paid, such as capital stock or long-term debt) for the purchase price. Additionally, any excess of the purchase price (cost) over the fair value of the identifiable net assets acquired should be debited to goodwill and amortized to expense over the benefit period. Alternatively, any excess of the fair value of the identifiable net assets acquired over the cost (called *negative goodwill* or *badwill*) should be treated as a reduction of the amounts otherwise debited to the noncurrent assets (other than long-term investments in marketable securities) in proportion to their fair values. And if the amounts assignable to the noncurrent assets are reduced to zero, any remainder of the excess of the fair values over the cost should be credited to a deferred account and amortized to income in future periods.

Other Acquisition Valuation Issues

38. Issuance of stock. Capital stock may be issued to acquire a plant asset or an intangible asset. The asset should be recorded at the fair value of the stock or asset, whichever is more readily determinable. If the stock is actively traded on an organized stock exchange, the current market price of the stock is usually a good estimate of the asset's fair value. The par or stated value of the stock would only by coincidence reflect the stock's fair value. If no fair value of the stock can be determined, then the fair value of the asset should be determined by sales price or appraisal. Only when no other method can be used should the board of directors assign a value to the asset acquired. A value assigned by the board of directors normally would not be very objectively determined.

39. Donated assets. Unlike most transactions, which involve an exchange, *nonreciprocal transfers* involve either a receipt or a sacrifice but not both. Assets received through a nonreciprocal transfer never require a sacrifice. Companies sometimes receive donated assets, such as land or a building, from owners or local governments as an enticement to locate in a particular locality. Unless there are conditions attached to the donation that are not likely to be satisfied, the donated asset should be recorded at its fair value as determined by appraisal or current market activity. Recording the asset at cost is unrealistic in this situation, because the recipient incurred little or no cost to acquire the donated asset. For example, if land were donated, the nonreciprocal transfer is recorded by a debit to land and a credit to donated capital (a stockholders' equity account) for the fair value of the property received. A donated asset also should be depreciated, amortized, or depleted over its useful life. Some believe that a revenue account should be credited when a donated asset is received. This approach, however, has not gained acceptance in practice, as revenue is normally earned through use of an asset, not through its acquisition.

40. Lump-sum purchases. When several assets are acquired for a single exchange price, the transaction is referred to as a *lump-sum* or *basket purchase*. The total cost of the assets is normally allocated to the individual assets on the basis of their estimated fair values. Under this approach, the cost of one asset is determined by multiplying the total purchase price of all the assets by the ratio of the estimated fair value of that asset to the total fair value of all the assets acquired. Alternatively, if there is not a determinable fair value for one of the assets, then the assets that have such values are recorded at their fair values and the other asset is recorded at the remainder of the total cost.

41. Exchanges of nonmonetary assets.
Some plant assets are acquired in exchange for other assets in *nonmonetary exchanges. Opinion No. 29,* which contains guidelines for accounting for such exchanges, distinguishes between exchanges of dissimilar assets and exchanges of similar assets.

42. When *dissimilar assets* are exchanged—that is, assets that perform different functions for the entity—the asset received should be recorded at its fair value or the fair value of the asset surrendered, whichever is more clearly determinable, and a gain or loss should be recognized on the asset surrendered. If, for example, land with a book value less than its known fair value is exchanged for a patent (an exchange of dissimilar assets because each asset obviously performs a different function for the company), the transaction should be recorded by a debit to patent for the fair value of the land, a credit to land for its book value, and a credit to gain on exchange for the difference between the fair value and book value of the land. The gain or loss should be recognized in exchanges of dissimilar assets because the earnings process is culminated for the asset surrendered and a new earnings process starts for the asset received. If the fair values of the assets exchanged are not equivalent, cash or "boot" may be involved in the exchange. The recorded value of the asset received should be increased if boot is paid; it should be decreased if boot is received. However, when the fair value of neither the asset received nor the asset surrendered is determinable, the exchange should be recorded at the book value of the asset surrendered and no gain or loss should be recognized.

43. Exchanges of *similar assets*—that is, assets that are of the same general type or that perform the same function—generally do not result in the culmination of the earnings process. Such exchanges should be recorded at the book value of the asset surrendered. Exchanges of similar assets include exchanges of inventory items and exchanges of similar productive assets. These exchanges simply continue the earnings process of the old asset in the form of the new asset. When similar assets are exchanged, any losses (book value greater than fair value) should be recognized. However, when cash or boot is received in such exchanges, only a portion of a gain (book value less than fair value) should be recognized. The fair value used to determine whether there is a gain or loss may be the fair value of the asset surrendered or that of the asset received, whichever is more evident.

44. When similar assets are exchanged and a loss is indicated, the loss should be recognized at the time of the exchange and the new asset should be recorded at the fair value of the asset surrendered or received, whichever is used to determine the loss on the exchange. If a gain is indicated on the ex-

change of similar assets and boot is not involved or is paid, no gain should be recognized. The new asset is recorded at the book value of the asset surrendered plus the amount of cash paid, if any.

45. The recording of an exchange of similar assets when cash is received is more complex because two transactions have actually occurred: the exchange of the similar assets and a sale of a portion of the asset surrendered, as evidenced by the receipt of cash. If a loss is indicated on the exchange, the entire loss should be recognized. If a gain is indicated on the exchange, only the portion of·the gain that represents the sale should be recognized. The amount of the gain to be recognized should be determined by multiplying the entire gain by the ratio of the cash received to the total fair value received (cash plus fair value of the asset received). The asset received should be recorded at its fair value less the unrecognized portion of the gain (or at the book value of the asset surrendered less the portion of the book value converted to cash).

Expenditures Subsequent to Acquisition

46. Expenditures related to plant assets and intangibles subsequent to their acquisition may be either (*a*) charged to an asset account (or *capitalized*) or (*b*) charged to current operations (or *expensed*). Theoretically, if the expenditure materially enhances the asset's future service potential, it should be capitalized (*capital expenditure*); otherwise, the expenditure should be expensed or charged to current operations (*revenue expenditure*). Enhancement of future service potential may be evidenced by (*a*) an extension of the useful life of the asset, (*b*) an increase in the *quantity* of services provided by the asset, or (*c*) an increase in the *quality* of services provided by the asset. If an expenditure results in one or more of these effects, the expenditure should be capitalized and periodically recognized as an expense as the related asset is depreciated, amortized, or depleted. For expediency, however, many companies establish a dollar cutoff point, so that any expenditure under this point is automatically expensed because of immateriality. Expenditures above the cutoff point must be evaluated individually to determine their proper accounting treatment. The remainder of this section discusses several types of expenditures subsequent to acquisition and the recommended method of accounting for them.

47. Repair and maintenance. Expenditures made to maintain an asset's originally anticipated service potential or to keep the asset in normal operating condition, such as lubricating a machine or changing the oil in a delivery truck, do not enhance the asset's future service potential and thus should be expensed when they are incurred. Certain repair and maintenance expenditures are seasonal, such as those to service equipment while the company closes for vacation during the summer. For interim reporting purposes, annual repair costs that are reasonably estimated may be accrued each quarter by debiting repairs expense and crediting allowance for repairs for one-fourth of the estimated annual repair cost. Later, repair expenditures are recorded by debiting allowance for repairs and crediting cash for the amount of the actual repair costs. During the year, the allowance for repairs is reported as a contra asset, but at year-end, any balance in the allowance account should be closed to repairs expense. Other repair and maintenance expenditures, such as those to paint a building, may occur at infrequent intervals, but are predictable and can usually be reasonably estimated. Some contend that these expenditures benefit more periods than the one in which the expenditure is made and should be accrued each period by a debit to an expense account and a credit to a liability account. The credit portion of the entry, however, is not a liability because the "obligation" did not arise from a past transaction. Moreover, accruing amounts for activity to occur in the future, perhaps several years, is suspect. Accordingly, these costs should be expensed when they are incurred, unless the expenditure enhances future service potential, in which case the cost should be capitalized.

48. Additions. *Additions* are enlargements, expansions, or extensions of existing plant assets. These expenditures, plus any expenditures made to ready the present asset for the addition, enhance the future service potential of the asset, and should be capitalized. If the cost of the addition is an integral part of the existing asset, it should be depreciated over the shorter of the estimated life of the addition or the remaining life of the existing asset. Otherwise, the addition should be depreciated over its own useful life.

49. Replacements and improvements. Some expenditures are made to dispose of and replace a major component of an existing asset. If the new component merely maintains the operating capacity of the asset, it is referred to as a *replacement*. If the new component substantially enhances the operating capacity of the asset, it is referred to as an *improvement* or a *betterment*. Both replacements and improvements are considered capital expenditures. Three methods are used in practice to record them:

a. *Substitution.* This method is contingent on the ability to identify the cost and accumulated depreciation of the component of the asset being replaced. The cost and accumulated depreciation of the component are written off and a gain or loss on the disposal is recorded. The cost of the new component is then charged to the asset account. Although this method is conceptually sound, it is often difficult to identify the cost and accumulated depreciation of the old component.

b. *Capitalization of the new cost.* When the cost and accumulated depreciation of the old component cannot be determined, or when it is assumed that the book value of the old component is immaterial, the cost of the new component may be charged directly to the asset account without writing off any portion of the old component.

c. *Reduction of accumulated depreciation.* If the replacement or improvement extends the useful life of the asset, its cost may be charged to the asset's accumulated depreciation account. This method, in effect, recognizes a recapture of previously recorded depreciation.

It should be noted that each of these three alternatives increases the book value of the related asset either directly by a debit to the asset account or indirectly by a debit to the asset's accumulated depreciation account.

50. Rearrangement and relocation. When expenditures to rearrange machinery or equipment or to relocate plants or portions of plants are material and clearly benefit future periods, the cost should be capitalized as deferred rearrangement (relocation) costs and amortized over the estimated periods benefited. Otherwise, the costs should be expensed as they are incurred.

51. Litigation. Litigation costs incurred for a successful defense of an intangible asset, such as a patent, copyright, or trademark, against an infringement suit should be capitalized and amortized over the remaining life of the intangible asset. Conversely, costs incurred in an unsuccessful attempt to defend against an infringement suit should be expensed. In such circumstances, the recoverable value of the intangible asset also should be assessed to determine whether a partial or total write-down of the unamortized cost is required.

SELF-STUDY LEARNING

Key Terms and Concepts

Provide the appropriate term or terms to complete each of the following statements:

1. Plant assets should initially be recorded at their _____.

2. The cost of a self-constructed asset includes _____ costs, such as labor and material, and _____ costs, such as utility and depreciation expenses.

3. *Statement No. 34* required that _____ incurred during the construction of certain assets be capitalized.

4. Resources that are physically consumed in the production process and usually are replaced only by an act of nature are called _____.

5. The costs associated with natural resources may be classified in four categories: _____, that is, the costs incurred to acquire the property or property rights; _____, that is, the costs incurred to determine the existence of recoverable natural resources; _____, that is, the costs incurred to gain access to the recoverable natural resources; and _____, that is, the costs incurred to extract the natural resources.

6. Operating resources that are expected to provide benefits for more than one year but lack physical substance are called _____.

7. Typical intangible assets include _____, which are exclusive rights granted by the federal government to use, manufacture, and sell a product or process for a period of 17 years; _____, which are exclusive rights granted by the federal government to reproduce and sell an artistic or literary work for the life of its creator plus 50 years; _____, which are words, symbols, or other devices that identify particular products; and _____, which are exclusive rights granted by one party to another party to market a product or service within a designated area.

8. Planned search or critical investigation aimed at discovery of new knowledge with the hope that such knowledge will be useful in the development of a new product or process or will bring about a significant improvement in an existing product or process is defined as _____, whereas the translation of research findings or other knowledge into a plan or design for a new product or process or for a significant improvement in an existing product or process is defined as _____.

9. _____ is deemed to be established in connection with the development of computer software when a company has completed all planning, designing, coding, and testing activities necessary to determine that a product can be produced to design specifications.

10. The favorable characteristics of a business enterprise that are intangible in nature, not separately identifiable, indeterminate in duration, and inseparable from the enterprise as a whole are referred to collectively as

    _____.

11. An asset that is acquired through donation is an example of a(n) _____ transfer.

12. An exchange of dissimilar assets results in the _____ of the earnings process of the asset exchanged.

13. When an exchange of nonmonetary assets includes a payment of cash, the cash is referred to as

_____ .

14. _____ expenditures are capitalized, whereas _____ expenditures are expensed when they are incurred.

15. In order for an expenditure subsequent to the acquisition of an asset to be capitalized, it should either extend

the _____ of the asset or increase the _____ or

_____ of services provided by the asset.

True-False

Indicate by circling the appropriate response whether each of the following statements is true (T) or false (F):

T F 1. Plant assets and intangible assets are acquired to be either used in the company's operations or resold.

T F 2. Plant assets and intangible assets are initially recorded at the best estimate of their fair value.

T F 3. The cash or cash equivalent sacrificed to obtain a plant asset is generally the best evidence of the fair value of the asset acquired.

T F 4. When land is acquired with structures on it that must be removed before the land can be used, the cost of removing the structures should be included in the cost of the land.

T F 5. Property taxes on land that is being either used or held for speculation are usually expensed in the period in which they are incurred.

T F 6. When machinery and equipment are acquired, the total capitalized cost of the asset should include only the net invoice price.

T F 7. Direct costs incurred in the self-construction of a plant asset should be capitalized in the asset account.

T F 8. Traditionally, the capitalization of interest during construction has been an accepted practice by regulated and nonregulated companies.

T F 9. Under GAAP a company should capitalize interest during the construction of any asset.

T F 10. The costs of intangible assets purchased from others must be capitalized as an asset and amortized over the period estimated to be benefited, whereas the costs incurred internally to develop intangible assets must be expensed as they are incurred.

T F 11. The capitalized costs of intangible assets must be amortized even if the expected period of benefit is indefinite or indeterminate.

T F 12. The capitalized costs of intangible assets must be amortized over the longer of the period estimated to be benefited or 40 years.

T F 13. The costs incurred internally to develop a new product or process must be expensed as they are incurred, but the costs incurred to obtain a patent for a new product or process may be capitalized as an asset and amortized over the period estimated to be benefited.

T F 14. Costs incurred for the successful defense of a patent against an infringement suit should be expensed as they are incurred.

T F 15. The cost of an initial franchise fee should be recorded by the franchisee as an asset.

T F 16. The costs of equipment acquired or constructed for a particular research and development project must be expensed as they are incurred if the equipment cannot be used in other research and development projects or otherwise.

T F 17. The costs incurred internally in developing computer software must be expensed as research and development costs when they are incurred until technological feasibility is established for the product.

T F 18. Goodwill developed internally should be recorded at its estimated value.

T F 19. Goodwill may be recorded as an asset only if it is purchased as part of a transaction whereby one company acquires the assets and assumes the liabilities of another company.

T F 20. Goodwill should be recorded at the excess of the purchase price (cost) over the book value of the identifiable net assets acquired as a group from another company.

T F 21. The excess of the fair value of the identifiable net assets acquired from another company over the purchase price (cost) must be recorded as "negative goodwill."

T F 22. A good indicator of the fair value of capital stock issued to acquire a plant asset or intangible asset is the average market price of the stock over the past year.

T F 23. A donated asset should be recorded at the amount of cost incurred to acquire the asset.

T F 24. An exchange of dissimilar nonmonetary assets results in a recognized gain if the book value of the asset surrendered is greater than its fair value.

T F 25. If the earnings process of a plant asset culminates in an exchange of nonmonetary assets, the asset received is recorded at the book value of the asset surrendered.

T F 26. A loss occurs on the exchange of nonmonetary assets if the book value of the asset surrendered is greater than the fair value of the asset surrendered.

T F 27. Whenever the book value of an asset sacrificed in an exchange of nonmonetary assets is greater than its fair value, the entire loss should always be recognized.

T F 28. An expenditure subsequent to the acquisition of an asset that materially enhances the asset's service potential should be capitalized.

T F 29. For interim reporting purposes, annual repair costs that can be reasonably estimated may be accrued for each interim period.

T F 30. When an expenditure on a plant asset is identified as a replacement, it must be accounted for using the substitution method.

Multiple Choice

Select the best response for each of the following items, and circle the corresponding letter:

1. When compared with intangible assets, which of the following characteristics is true only for plant assets?
   a. They are physical objects.
   b. They are used in the operations of the company.
   c. They have no bodily substance.
   d. Their benefits are to be received over several accounting periods.

2. Theoretically, when a plant asset is acquired and the purchase discount is lost, the lost discount should be:
   a. Ignored.
   b. Charged to the asset account.
   c. Deferred in a separate account and written off over the life of the asset.
   d. Treated as a financing expense.

3. Most companies account for indirect manufacturing costs incurred during the self-construction of a plant asset by following:
   a. The direct costing approach.
   b. The full costing approach.
   c. The opportunity cost approach.
   d. The partial cost approach.

4. According to *Statement No. 34*, interest should be capitalized on qualifying assets as long as:
   a. Expenditures for the asset are being made.
   b. Activities to prepare the asset for its intended use are in progress.
   c. Interest cost is being incurred.
   d. All of the above.

5. The maximum amount of interest that should be capitalized in any period under *Statement No. 34* is:

   a. The actual interest incurred during the period on all company borrowings.
   b. The actual interest incurred during the period on a specific borrowing for the construction project.
   c. The amount computed by multiplying the total construction cost for the period by the weighed average interest rate for all outstanding debt.
   d. The amount computed by multiplying the actual construction cost for the period by the interest rate on the specific borrowing for the project.

6. The amount of interest to be capitalized on a qualifying asset for a period is based on:

   a. The balance in the qualifying asset account at the beginning of the period.
   b. The balance in the qualifying asset account at the end of the period.
   c. The total expenditures for the qualifying asset during the period.
   d. The average accumulated expenditures for the qualifying asset during the period.

7. The capitalized costs of recoverable natural resources should *not* include:

   a. The acquisition costs incurred to acquire the property or property rights.
   b. The exploration costs incurred to determine the existence of recoverable natural resources.
   c. The intangible development costs incurred to gain access to the natural resources.
   d. The production costs incurred to extract the natural resources.

8. Which of the following is *not* an authoritative guideline regarding the accounting for intangible assets?

   a. The costs of specifically identifiable intangible assets purchased from others must be recorded as an asset and amortized over the period estimated to be benefited.
   b. The costs incurred internally to develop specifically identifiable intangible assets must be expensed as they are incurred.
   c. The excess of the purchase price (cost) over the fair value of identifiable net assets acquired as a group from another company must be recorded as an asset and amortized over the period estimated to be benefited.
   d. The costs incurred internally to develop intangible assets that are not specifically identifiable must be expensed as they are incurred.

9. Research and development costs must be:

   a. Expensed as they are incurred.
   b. Capitalized and amortized over some arbitrary period.
   c. Either capitalized and amortized over some arbitrary period if specified conditions are met or expensed as they are incurred if the specified conditions for capitalization are not met.
   d. Capitalized in a special suspense account until existence of future benefits can be determined and then either amortized over the determined benefit period or written off as a loss if it is determined that there are no future benefits.

10. Which of the following costs associated with research and development activities should be capitalized and depreciated (or amortized) over the period estimated to be benefited?

    a. Indirect costs reasonably allocable to research and development projects.
    b. The cost of equipment acquired for a particular research and development project that cannot be used in other research and development projects or otherwise.
    c. The cost of a building constructed as a general laboratory facility for research and development projects.
    d. Consulting fees paid to outsiders for research and development projects.

11. As part of the journal entry to record the acquisition of the net assets of another company:

    a. The identifiable assets acquired should be recorded at their book values.
    b. The liabilities assumed should be recorded at their face values.
    c. Any excess of the purchase price (cost) over the fair value of the identifiable net assets acquired should be recorded as goodwill.
    d. Any excess of the fair value of the identifiable net assets acquired over the purchase price (cost) should be recorded as a gain.

12. When the cost of a lump-sum purchase of several assets is allocated among the assets acquired, the cost of one asset is determined by multiplying the lump-sum purchase cost by the ratio of:

    a. The cost of the asset to the fair value of the asset.
    b. The fair value of the asset to the lump-sum purchase cost.

c. The fair value of the asset to the total fair value of all the assets.

d. The fair value of all the assets to the fair value of the asset.

13. If a company exchanged a nonmonetary asset and paid a small sum of cash for a similar non-monetary asset with no impairment of value, the company should record the new asset at an amount equal to:

a. The fair value of the asset surrendered.

b. The book value of the asset surrendered plus the cash paid.

c. The book value of the asset surrendered less the cash paid.

d. The fair value of the asset received plus the cash paid.

14. Of the various types of expenditures made subsequent to the acquisition of a plant asset, which ones are normally considered capital expenditures?

	REPAIR AND MAINTENANCE	ADDITIONS	IMPROVE-MENTS	REARRANGE-MENT AND RELOCATION
a.	Yes	Yes	Yes	Yes
b.	No	No	Yes	Yes
c.	Yes	Yes	Yes	No
d.	No	Yes	Yes	Yes

15. Costs incurred to successfully defend a patent infringement case should be debited to:

a. Legal expense.

b. Patent.

c. Sales revenue.

d. Amortization expense.

Extended Problems

1. On January 1, 1995, selected plant asset account balances of Rodeo Company were as follows:

Machine A	$ 55,000
Accumulated depreciation, machine A.....	30,500
Machine B	163,000
Accumulated depreciation, machine B.....	70,000
Warehouse	100,000
Accumulated depreciation, warehouse.....	47,000
Land, site 1	84,500
Land, site 2	30,000

Additional information:

a. On January 2, 1995, machine B was sold for $105,000.

b. Additional warehouse space can be acquired in one of three ways:

(1). By purchase from Landsales Realty for $63,000.

(2). By exchange of land (site 2), with a fair value of $61,800, for the warehouse.

(3). By construction of the warehouse over a nine-month period (January through September) at a cost of $57,000 incurred as follows:

January 1	$ 6,000
February 1	4,500
April 1	13,500
May 31	9,000
August 1	21,600
September 30	2,400
	$57,000

A 10 percent two-year construction loan of $36,000 would be secured on January 2, 1995, to finance part of the warehouse construction. Other debt currently outstanding has a weighted average interest rate of 12 percent.

c. Machine A, with a current fair value of $33,300, is exchanged with $2,700 cash on January 2, 1995, for a similar machine owned by Zippo Company. Zippo paid $48,000 for its machine, which now has a book value of $29,600 and a fair value of $36,000.

REQUIRED

a. Prepare the journal entry required to record the sale of machine B.

b. Determine the recorded value of the new warehouse under each of the three alternatives in part *b*.

c. Prepare the journal entry required to record the exchange of similar machines on the books of both Rodeo Company and Zippo Company.

2. Data concerning selected transactions of IN Company for the year ended December 31, 1995, follow. IN Company uses the straight-line method to compute depreciation and amortization and amortizes intangible assets over their legal life.

a. On January 1, 1995, IN Company paid $24,000 for a patent that has a remaining legal life of 12 years. Later, on July 1, 1995, IN Company paid legal fees of $2,300 to defend the patent against an infringement suit. The defense was successful.

b. On January 1, 1995, IN Company acquired a franchise for an initial fee of $30,000, with

$10,000 payable immediately and the remaining $20,000 payable in two equal installments on December 31, 1995 and 1996, plus interest at 10 percent. In addition, IN Company is required to pay an annual franchise fee of $3,500 at the end of each year during the 20-year franchise term.

c. Near the end of 1995, IN Company began negotiations to acquire the net assets of Apt Company. As an initial step, IN Company obtained the following data concerning the identifiable net assets of Apt Company:

	BOOK VALUES	FAIR VALUES
Accounts receivable (net)	$ 60,000	$ 60,000
Inventory	100,000	110,000
Property, plant, and equipment (net)	400,000	420,000
Patents	-0-	20,000
Accounts payable	(110,000)	(110,000)
Total identifiable net assets	$450,000	$500,000

On December 31, 1995, IN paid $535,000 for the net assets of Apt Company.

d. During 1995, IN Company incurred the following costs in connection with a research and development project that is expected to be completed by the end of 1996.

Materials and supplies used in project	$ 8,000
Equipment, acquired 1/1/95, which cannot be used in future research and development projects or otherwise, with expected useful life of remaining term of project, no salvage value	10,000
Equipment, acquired 1/1/95, which can be used in future research and development	

projects, with expected useful life of 5 years, no salvage value	15,000
Salaries, wages, and other related personnel costs	30,000
Indirect costs reasonably allocable to project	4,000
Total costs	$67,000

e. During 1995, IN Company also incurred the following costs in developing and producing a computer software program: planning and designing, $30,000; coding, $120,000; testing, $50,000; and production of product masters, $15,000. The planning and designing, coding, and testing costs all were incurred before the technological feasibility of the product was established. The product masters were produced at the end of the year.

REQUIRED

a. Prepare the journal entries required to record the acquisition of the patent and the payment of the legal fees to defend the patent against the infringement suit, and compute the amount of patent amortization for 1995.
b. Prepare the journal entries required to record the acquisition of the franchise and the payment of the annual franchise fee.
c. Prepare the journal entry required to record the acquisition of Apt Company's net assets.
d. Compute the amount of the research and development project costs that must be expensed in 1995.
e. Compute the amount of the computer software costs that must be expensed as research and development costs in 1995.

COMMON ERRORS

The first statement in each of the "common errors" listed here is *incorrect*. Each incorrect statement is followed by a corrected statement and an explanation.

1. Plant assets and intangible assets are initially recorded using the fair value principle. *Wrong*
Plant assets and intangible assets are initially recorded using the historical cost principle. *Right*
Since most plant assets and intangible assets are recorded at their fair value at the time of acquisition, it would be easy to assume that plant assets are initially recorded using the fair value principle. It should be noted, however, that the fair value of an asset when acquired is also its historical cost. That is, under the historical cost principle an asset

is recorded at the fair value of the sacrifice or sacrifices made to obtain and ready the asset for its intended use. Thus at the date of acquisition the historic cost and fair value of an asset are usually identical. Nevertheless, assets are recorded under the historical cost principle, not the fair value principle.

2. The amount of interest capitalized on a qualifying self-constructed asset is based on a weighted average interest rate on all present borrowings and equity capital. *Wrong*
The amount of interest capitalized on a qualifying self-constructed asset is based on interest from specific borrowings for the construction project, if any, and on a weighted average interest rate on all present borrowings. *Right*

One of the controversial issues related to the capitalization of interest during construction is the type of interest and the interest rate to apply to the construction costs. Some accountants argue that all funds employed should be considered, and that both actual interest on debt and imputed interest on other funds or equity capital should be capitalized. Although this approach is conceptually appealing, it is difficult to determine a cost of equity capital, and there is no agreement on a satisfactory method for handling the credit side of the charge for the interest. Others argue that only interest that is actually incurred from specific borrowings for the construction project should be capitalized. The FASB elected to take a middle position by permitting the cost of interest on specific new borrowings and interest based on a weighted average rate of interest on all present borrowings (if their interest rates are not substantially different from current rates) to be capitalized. The weighted average interest rate is applied only if there are no new borrowings for the construction project or if the actual construction expenditures for the period exceed the specific construction borrowings. In no case should the amount of interest capitalized exceed the actual interest paid during the period.

3. The costs incurred internally to develop a new product or process that subsequently is patented may be capitalized as an intangible asset and amortized over the period estimated to be benefited. *Wrong*

The costs incurred internally to develop a new product or process that subsequently is patented must be expensed as they are incurred. *Right*

Research and development activities that result in a new product or process that subsequently is patented obviously provide future economic benefits. It therefore may be argued that these costs can be capitalized as an intangible asset and amortized over the period estimated to be benefited. However, in the period during which research and development costs are incurred, the company has no assurance that a particular project ultimately will result in a patentable product or process. Because of this uncertainty about the future benefits of individual projects, *Statement No. 2* requires that research and development costs be expensed as they are incurred. This requirement applies even if a research and development project results in a new product or process that subsequently is patented.

4. The costs of equipment or facilities that are acquired or constructed for a particular research and development project and that have no alternative future uses may be capitalized as a tangible asset and depreciated over the life of the project. *Wrong*

The costs of equipment or facilities that are acquired or constructed for a particular research and development project and that have no alternative future uses must be expensed as they are incurred. *Right*

Statement No. 2 requires that research and development costs be expensed as they are incurred because of the high degree of uncertainty about the future benefits of individual research and development projects. It requires further that if equipment or facilities that are acquired or constructed for a particular research and development project have no alternative future uses in other research and development projects or otherwise, the costs must be expensed in the period in which the equipment or facilities are acquired or constructed. The reasoning underlying this requirement is that such equipment or facilities have no separate economic values, and thus their costs should be expensed as they are incurred rather than capitalized and depreciated.

5. The costs of equipment or facilities that are acquired or constructed for research and development activities and that have alternative future uses may be expensed as they are incurred. *Wrong*

The costs of equipment or facilities that are acquired or constructed for research and development activities and that have alternative future uses must be capitalized as a tangible asset and depreciated over the period estimated to be benefited. *Right*

As stated earlier, *Statement No. 2* requires that research and development costs be expensed as they are incurred because of the high degree of uncertainty about the future benefits of individual research and development projects. If, however, equipment or facilities that are acquired or constructed for research and development activities have alternative future uses in other research and development projects or otherwise, the costs must be capitalized as a tangible asset and depreciated over the period estimated to be benefited. The reasoning underlying this requirement is that such equipment or facilities have separate economic values, and thus their costs should be capitalized and depreciated rather than expensed as they are incurred.

6. Goodwill should be recorded at the excess of the cost over the fair value of the recorded net assets acquired as a group from another company. *Wrong*

Goodwill should be recorded at the excess of the cost over the fair value of the identifiable (recorded and previously unrecorded) net assets acquired as a group from another company. *Right*

The costs incurred internally to develop intangible assets that are specifically identifiable may be expensed as they are incurred rather than recorded as an asset. Indeed, research and development costs incurred to develop a new product or process that subsequently is patented must be expensed as they are incurred. The identifiable net assets acquired as a group from another company, therefore, may include some identifiable intangible assets, such as patents or trademarks, that were not recorded as assets by the seller. Nonetheless, *Opinion No. 17* requires that the buyer record the individual tangible and identifiable intangible assets acquired and liabilities assumed at their fair values, whether or not the items were previously recorded by the seller. It requires further that the buyer record any excess of the cost over the fair value of these identifiable (recorded and previously unrecorded) net assets as goodwill. Thus when the net assets acquired include unrecorded patents that were developed internally by the seller, for example, the buyer must record the previously unrecorded patents as well as the other identifiable net assets acquired at their fair values. Additionally, the buyer must record goodwill at the excess of the cost over the sum of the fair values of the previously unrecorded patents and other identifiable net assets acquired.

7. Whenever debt or capital stock is exchanged for a plant asset, the plant asset should be recorded at the fair value of the debt or capital stock. *Wrong*

Whenever debt or capital stock is exchanged for a plant asset, the plant asset should be recorded at the fair value of the debt or capital stock or the fair value of the asset received, whichever is more readily determinable. *Right*

In some situations the fair value of the consideration given cannot be determined, and some other means must be used to place a value on the acquired asset. If, for example, capital stock that is not actively traded on a stock exchange is exchanged for the asset, there probably is no good way to determine its fair value. In this case the recorded amount of the acquired asset should be the fair value of the asset, if that is determinable. Similarly, if a non-interest-bearing note is exchanged for a plant asset, the asset should be recorded at its fair

value. Only when the fair value of neither the consideration given nor the asset received is determinable are other valuation techniques, such as appraisal, used. Although most acquired assets are valued at the fair value of the consideration given, the general guideline is to record the acquired asset at the fair value of the consideration given or that of the asset received, whichever is more readily determinable.

8. When a company exchanges a nonmonetary asset for a similar asset and receives cash, any gain or loss should be recognized. *Wrong*

When a company exchanges a nonmonetary asset for a similar asset and receives cash, a loss should be recognized, but only a portion of a gain should be recognized. *Right*

The exchange of similar nonmonetary assets is not the culmination of the earnings process, since the asset received performs the same function as the asset surrendered. Only the physical asset has changed, not its function. Accordingly, a gain—that is, the excess of the fair value of the asset surrendered over its book value—should not be recognized. A loss—that is, the excess of the book value of the asset surrendered over its fair value—should always be recognized, however, because the loss signals impairment of the asset's value. If cash is received in the exchange, a portion of the asset surrendered has been sold rather than exchanged. Moreover, the cash received is a monetary asset, or an asset dissimilar to the one surrendered. Thus two exchanges have actually occurred: the exchange of similar assets and the sale of a portion of the asset surrendered. Since the sale portion represents the culmination of the earnings process of part of the asset surrendered, a portion of the gain is recognized. The amount recognized may be determined by multiplying the total gain by the ratio of cash received to the total fair value of the consideration received (cash plus fair value of the asset received).

ANSWERS

Key Terms and Concepts

1. fair value, or cost
2. direct, indirect
3. interest
4. natural resources or wasting assets
5. acquisition costs, exploration costs, development costs, production costs
6. intangible assets
7. patents, copyrights, trademarks and trade names, franchises
8. research, development
9. technological feasibility
10. goodwill
11. nonreciprocal
12. culmination
13. boot
14. capital, revenue
15. useful life, quality, quantity

True-False

1. F Plant assets and intangible assets are acquired to be used in the company's operations. They may eventually be sold when their service potential has diminished or is no longer needed, but unlike inventory, they are not acquired to be resold.

2. T

3. T

4. T

5. F In such situations, many accountants probably expense the property tax assessment as a period cost on all land held. Other accountants, however, believe that land being held for speculation is not generating any revenue and therefore capitalize the property taxes. Property taxes on land being used should be expensed, but property taxes on land held for speculation may be either expensed or capitalized.

6. F The capitalized cost of machinery and equipment includes not only the net invoice price but also such other costs as freight in, in-transit insurance, applicable taxes, and the costs of installation and testing. In other words, all costs incurred to obtain and ready the asset for use are capitalized.

7. T

8. F Capitalization of interest during construction has been a common practice of regulated industries but not of nonregulated industries. Only during the early 1970s did nonregulated companies start to capitalize interest on construction, in an attempt to bolster their sagging profits. The SEC even issued a moratorium on the practice until the FASB could issue a pronouncement clarifying the diverse practices that had developed.

9. F *Statement No. 34* specifically limits the type of assets that are eligible to have interest capitalized during construction. Qualifying assets are those that a company constructs either for its own use or as discrete projects for sale. Assets that are not permitted to have interest capitalized are routinely manufactured inventories, assets in use or ready for use, and assets that are not ready for or being prepared for the earnings process.

10. F The costs of intangible assets purchased from others, whether specifically identifiable or not, must be capitalized as assets and amortized over the shorter of the period estimated to be benefited or 40 years. The costs incurred internally to develop intangible assets that are specifically iden-

tifiable may be either expensed as they are incurred or capitalized as an asset and amortized over the shorter of the period estimated to be benefited or 40 years. Research and development costs, however, must be expensed as they are incurred. Finally, the costs incurred internally to develop intangible assets that are not specifically identifiable must be expensed as they are incurred.

11. T

12. F The capitalized costs of intangible assets must be amortized over the shorter of the period estimated to be benefited or 40 years.

13. T

14. F Costs incurred in the successful defense of a patent against an infringement suit should be capitalized and amortized over the remaining life of the patent. In contrast, costs incurred in an unsuccessful attempt to defend against an infringement suit and perhaps the unamortized cost of the related patent should be expensed.

15. T

16. T

17. T

18. F The costs incurred internally to develop, maintain, or restore goodwill must be expensed as they are incurred. That is, goodwill developed internally cannot be recorded as an asset.

19. T

20. F Goodwill should be recorded at the excess of the purchase price (cost) over the fair value of the identifiable net assets acquired as a group from another company.

21. F The excess of the fair value of the identifiable net assets acquired from another company over the purchase price (called negative goodwill or badwill) must be treated as a reduction of the amounts otherwise assignable to the noncurrent assets (other than long-term investments in marketable securities) in proportion to their fair values. And if the amounts assignable to the noncurrent assets are reduced to zero, any remainder of the excess of fair values over the purchase price (cost) must be recorded as a deferred credit and amortized over a period not in excess of 40 years.

22. F The average market price may be better than the par or stated value of the stock, but it certainly is not a good indication of the fair value of the stock for purposes of determining the value at which to record the acquired asset. The asset should be recorded at the *current* fair value of the

stock, not at an average value for the year, which may easily be distorted by extremely high or low market values during the year. Moreover, the current market price reflects the fair value of the stock or amount sacrificed at the time of the transaction.

23. F   The costs incurred to acquire assets by donation are usually minimal and thus provide an unrealistic valuation. A donated asset should be recorded at its fair value as determined by appraisal or current market activity.

24. F   Gains are recognized when dissimilar monetary assets are exchanged. A gain, however, arises when the book value of the asset surrendered is *less than* its fair value.

25. F   After the earnings process of a plant asset has culminated, the bundle of future service potential provided by the asset is believed to be eliminated when it is exchanged for an asset with a dissimilar bundle of future service potential. Since the new asset performs a different function, the proper value of the new asset is the fair value of the asset surrendered, not its book value.

26. T
27. T
28. T
29. T
30. F   Perhaps ideally the substitution method, that is, writing off the cost and related accumulated depreciation of the old "replaced" component of the asset and capitalizing the cost of the replacement part, is the preferred method. At times, however, it may not be possible to determine the cost and/or accumulated depreciation of the replaced component, and the new cost should then be (*a*) capitalized directly to the asset account or (*b*) charged to the related accumulated depreciation account.

Multiple Choice

1. a	6. d	11. c
2. d	7. d	12. c
3. b	8. b	13. b
4. d	9. a	14. d
5. a	10. c	15. b

Extended Problems

1. a. Journal entry to record the sale of machine B:

Cash	105,000	
Accumulated depreciation, machine B	70,000	
Machine B..........................		163,000
Gain on sale of machine..........		12,000

b. Recorded value of the new warehouse under alternative means of acquisition:
   (1). If purchased: $63,000 cash paid for warehouse.
   (2). If land is exchanged: $61,800. This is an exchange of dissimilar assets, and a new asset is recorded at the fair value of the asset surrendered. A gain of $31,800 ($61,800 − $30,000) should be recognized on the land.
   (3). If self-constructed: $59,147.

Construction costs................		$57,000
Interest costs		
Construction loan $1,775		
Other debt 372		2,147[a]
		$59,147

[a]Expenditures and interest:

January 1	$ 6,000 × 9/12 × 10%	=	$	450
February 1	4,500 × 8/12 × 10%	=		300
April 1	13,500 × 6/12 × 10%	=		675
May 31	9,000 × 4/12 × 10%	=		300
August 1	3,000 × 2/12 × 10%	=		50
Construction loan	$36,000			$1,775
August 1	$18,600 × 2/12 ×12%	=		$372
September 30	2,400 × 0/12 × 12%	=		-0-
Other debt	$21,000			$372
Total	$57,000			$2,147

c. Journal entry to record exchange on Rodeo Company's books:

Machine (new)...........................	27,200	
Accumulated depreciation, machine A	30,500	
Machine A		55,000
Cash.....................................		2,700

Note: The $8,800 gain ($33,300 − $24,500) is ignored because this is an exchange of similar assets.

Journal entry to record exchange on Zippo Company's books:

Machine (new)..........................	27,380	
Accumulated depreciation (old)		
($48,000-$29,600)................	18,400	
Cash	2,700	
Machine (old)		48,000
Gain on exchange		480[a]

[a]This is an exchange of similar assets, and gains are usually ignored. Because cash is received, however, a partial gain is recognized.

Fair value of asset	$36,000
Book value of asset	29,600
Total gain......................................	$ 6,400

$$\text{Gain recognized} = \frac{\text{Cash}}{\text{Cash} + \text{FMV of asset received}} \times \text{Total gain}$$

$$= \frac{\$2,700}{\$2,700 + \$33,300} \times \$6,400$$

$$= \underline{\$480}$$

2. a. Journal entries related to patent:

1/1/95	Patent...............................	24,000	
	Cash...........................		24,000
7/1/95	Patent...............................	2,300	
	Cash...........................		2,300

Computation of amount of patent amortization:

Amortization of acquisition cost ($24,000 ÷ 12).................................	$2,000
Amortization of legal fees ($2,300 ÷ 11.5).	200
Total patent amortization for 1995	$2,200

b. Journal entries related to franchise:

1/1/95	Franchise ($10,000 + $20,000)................	30,000	
	Cash..		10,000
	Notes payable.................................		20,000
12/31/95	Franchise fee expense............................	3,500	
	Cash..		3,500

c. Journal entry to record acquisition of net assets:

12/31/95	Accounts receivable................................	60,000	
	Inventory..	110,000	
	Property, plant, and equipment	420,000	
	Patents..	20,000	
	Goodwill ($535,000 – $500,000)................	35,000	
	Accounts payable..............................		110,000
	Cash..		535,000

d. Computation of amount of research and development costs related to project:

Costs of materials and supplies used	$ 8,000
Cost of equipment that has no alternative future use in other research and development projects or otherwise..	10,000
Depreciation on equipment that has alternative future use in other research and development projects ($15,000 ÷5)	3,000
Salaries, wages, and other related personnel costs	30,000
Indirect costs reasonably allocable to project........................	4,000
Total research and development costs to be expensed in 1995........	$55,000

e. Computation of amount of research and development costs related to computer software:

Planning and designing costs	$ 30,000
Coding costs...	120,000
Testing costs..	50,000
Total computer software costs to be expensed as research and development costs in 1995	$200,000

12

PLANT ASSETS AND INTANGIBLES: DEPRECIATION, DEPLETION, AMORTIZATION, AND DISPOSITION

CHAPTER OBJECTIVES

After reading Chapter 12 and completing the questions, cases, exercises, and problems from the text chapter, you should be able to:

1. Describe the nature of depreciation, depletion, and amortization.
2. Identify the factors that affect depreciation—that is, depreciation base, useful life, and patterns of allocation—and understand their effects on depreciation.
3. Calculate depreciation by the basic methods, and recognize when each method is most applicable.
4. Calculate partial-year depreciation under the straight-line, sum-of-the-years'-digits, and double-declining-balance methods.
5. Calculate depletion on natural resources by the units-of-production (activity) method, and apportion depletion between units sold and units unsold for the purposes of financial statement reporting.
6. Determine the appropriate period over which to depreciate the costs of tangible assets associated with the exploration, development, or production of natural resources.
7. Distinguish between the successful efforts and full-cost methods of accounting for acquisition and exploration costs.
8. Describe and apply the requirements governing the amortization of the capitalized costs of intangible assets.
9. Describe when an impairment of value of plant assets and intangibles should be recognized.
10. Prepare the journal entry required to account for the disposal of plant assets, natural resources, and intangibles through voluntary means—that is, sale, abandonment, donation, and exchange—and by involuntary conversion.
11. Describe the general disclosure requirements for plant assets, natural resources, and intangible assets.

CHAPTER REVIEW

Introduction

1. Chapter 11 discussed accounting for the acquisition of and subsequent expenditures for plant assets, natural resources, and intangible assets. This chapter extends that discussion by describing the processes of depreciation, depletion, and amortization and the accounting for impairments of value and disposals of plant assets, natural resources, and intangible assets.

Nature of Depreciation, Depletion, and Amortization

2. *Depreciation* is a process of cost allocation rather than a means of valuation. The depreciation process allocates the cost of an asset to the periods benefited to match the asset's cost with the revenues generated by its use. Similarly, depletion and amortization are the processes of cost allocation for natural resources and intangible assets, respectively. Since the three cost allocation processes are identical, only depreciation is emphasized here.

3. When a plant asset is acquired, it is recorded at its cost, which normally represents the fair value of the asset at the date of acquisition. A plant asset is expected to provide benefits for several periods. Eventually, however, the benefits will expire even though the asset physically still exists; that is, it has not been physically consumed in the earnings process. Obviously, when the asset's service potential has expired, the amount initially recorded is no longer the fair value of the asset. An asset's estimated fair value at its disposal date is referred to as *salvage value* or *residual value*. Rather than recognizing the entire difference between the cost of the asset and its salvage value as a loss at the disposal date, the depreciation process periodically recognizes this difference—that is, the amount not expected to be recaptured when the asset is disposed of—as *depreciation expense*. Although the amount of depreciation expense can vary from period to period depending on the depreciation method used, the total amount of depreciation expense recognized on the asset is considered to be the cost of service potential used up over the life of the asset.

4. One common misconception about depreciation is that it is a source of funds. How depreciation could create funds is a mystery, since depreciation is a cost allocation process. Funds are expended to purchase an asset, but no funds are acquired through subsequent recognition of depreciation. Depreciation, however, creates a tax savings, because depreciation is tax-deductible. Thus depreciation "shields" revenues from being taxed and so "saves" tax payments, but this "saving" certainly is not a source of funds. In summary, depreciation is simply a process of cost allocation, *not* a valuation procedure or a source of funds.

Factors Affecting Depreciation

5. Depreciation expense is based on three factors which require estimates based on well-informed accounting judgment: depreciation base, useful life, and patterns of cost allocation.

6. Depreciation base. The *depreciation base* is the difference between the acquisition cost and the estimated net salvage value of an asset. The amount of salvage, or residual, value, however, is often very subjective, and its determination requires professional judgment. *Salvage value* represents the amount a company expects to recover from the asset at a future time, when it disposes of the asset. Moreover, if costs are expected to be incurred to dispose of an asset, they should be deducted from the estimated disposal proceeds to determine the net salvage value. In some cases, the expected proceeds and costs of disposal are likely to offset each other, and the estimated net salvage value is therefore zero. An asset, for example, may be used until it is virtually worthless and its scrap or salvage value nearly equals the costs incurred to dispose of the asset. When the estimated net salvage value is negative (that is, the estimated costs of disposal exceed the salvage value), the depreciable base should be increased by that amount.

7. Useful life. The *useful life* of a plant asset is the period of time during which the company expects to use the asset in the earnings process. An asset's useful life does not necessarily equal its physical life; its useful life, however, can never exceed its physical life. An asset's useful life is determined by physical and economic factors.

8. *Physical factors,* such as normal wear and tear from use of the asset and the passage of time, affect the useful life of an asset. Much of the normal wear and tear can be minimized through routine repair and maintenance expenditures. If such expenditures are not made, the physical factors can shorten the useful life of an asset considerably.

9. *Economic factors,* such as obsolescence, inadequacy, and changing economic conditions, often have a greater influence on the useful life of an asset than physical factors, especially in high technology industries. *Obsolescence* is the process by which an existing asset becomes outmoded as improved, more efficient substitutes become available. Unfortunately, an asset may become obsolete long before its ability to provide services has expired. In that case, a company would have to replace the old asset before its physical life was near its end. *Inadequacy* usually occurs because a company's operations have expanded beyond the capabilities of its present assets. The old assets may be replaced with larger assets even though the old assets still have years of productivity remaining. *Changing economic conditions,* such as inflation, energy crises, and changes in consumer tastes, may also shorten the useful life of an asset that otherwise is capable of producing for several more periods.

10. The 1986 Tax Reform Act, as amended, requires companies to use a modified accelerated cost recovery system (MACRS) for tax purposes. MACRS is based on classes of depreciable assets.

Each class of assets has its own prescribed life, with no consideration given to useful life or salvage value.

11. Patterns of cost allocation. Depreciation is affected by the pattern of cost allocation, or the depreciation method, used. According to GAAP, all depreciation methods must be systematic and rational.

Depreciation Methods

12. Depreciation is a process of allocating the acquisition cost of a plant asset. Theoretically, a company should select a depreciation method that reflects the decline in the asset's usefulness, as measured by the asset's ability to generate cash flows. Practically, companies most commonly use the depreciation methods discussed in this section.

13. Straight-line method. In the *straight-line method* of depreciation, depreciation expense is seen as a linear function of time. The amount of depreciation recognized on an asset in all accounting periods is equal. The depreciation expense per period is computed by dividing the *depreciation base* (acquisition cost less estimated net salvage value) by the estimated useful life of the asset. The depreciation rate per period can also be expressed as a percentage equal to depreciation expense per period divided by the depreciation base. At the end of the estimated useful life of the asset, the book value of the asset (cost less accumulated depreciation) is (theoretically) equal to the estimated salvage value.

14. The straight-line method is the simplest method to apply, which probably accounts for its popularity. Underlying the method is the assumption that approximately the same amount of the asset's service potential is used up each period. This method further implies an assumption that may not hold true: the net cash flows generated by the asset (revenue less maintenance costs) are equal in all periods. Nevertheless, the straight-line method provides a reasonable cost allocation pattern.

15. Production, or use, method. The *production, or use, method* of depreciation is based on an activity measure of the use of the asset being depreciated, such as miles driven (for trucks) or hours used (for machines). Depreciation expense for a period is equal to the actual measure of activity during the period multiplied by the depreciation rate per unit of activity (that is, acquisition cost less estimated net salvage value divided by the total estimated units of activity over the asset's use by the company).

16. The production or use depreciation method is a good method to use if (*a*) actual use of the depreciable asset varies substantially over time, (*b*) a reasonable activity measure exists that can be reliably estimated for the useful life of the asset, and (*c*) the decline in service potential is closely related to the extent of the asset's use. This method, however, requires detailed records of the actual use of the asset. As with the straight-line depreciation method, when the production or use method is used, the book value of the asset declines in a straight line, but in this case the decline in value is a function of activity rather than of time.

17. Accelerated depreciation methods. *Accelerated depreciation methods* are designed to provide higher ("accelerated") depreciation expense in the earlier years of an asset's useful life and lower depreciation expense in the later years. Until accelerated depreciation methods were permitted for income tax purposes in 1954, few companies adopted them for financial reporting purposes. Since then many companies have done so for external reporting, but the primary reason for adopting such methods is to defer tax payments. The higher depreciation expense in the early years lowers taxable income and thus tax payments in those years. Admittedly, taxes will increase in the later years as depreciation expense declines, but the present value of the total tax obligation is reduced. In addition to offering tax advantages, accelerated depreciation methods are theoretically justifiable. An asset is usually more productive and generates higher net cash flows in the earlier years than in the later years, when the asset is less efficient, maintenance costs increase, and net cash flows are reduced. Thus recognition of depreciation expense on an accelerated basis can be supported by theory, too.

18. *Sum-of-the-years'-digits* depreciation is one of the accelerated methods. Under this method, depreciation expense for a period is calculated by multiplying the asset's depreciation base by a fraction equal to the number of years of useful life remaining at the beginning of the year for which depreciation is being calculated divided by the sum of the numbers representing each year of useful life (or the sum of the years' digits). For computational efficiency, the following formula gives the sum of the years' digits or the denominator of the fraction: $n(n + 1) \div 2$, where n is the number of years of useful life. Since the depreciation base is constant each year but the numerator of the fraction decreases (from n to 1) each year, the result is a smaller or decreasing amount of depreciation expense each year.

19. Another accelerated method is the *declining balance method*. In general, under this method, depreciation expense for a period is calculated by multiplying the asset's book value, not the depreciation base, by a depreciation fraction or rate. A popular declining balance method is the *double-declining balance method,* which uses a depreciation rate equal to twice or double the straight-line rate (straight-line depreciation per year divided by the depreciation base). Because the asset's book value (cost minus accumulated depreciation) decreases each period and the depreciation rate is a constant amount, the amount of depreciation expense is largest in the first year and decreases each succeeding year. This method often requires an adjustment in the later years so that the asset is not depreciated below its estimated net salvage value. Normally, the book value of the asset is depreciated by the straight-line method starting in the year in which the double-declining balance method will depreciate the asset below its estimated net salvage value, and the straight-line method continues to be used during the remaining useful life of the asset. A more exact method that will depreciate the asset to its salvage value is called the *constant percent of declining balance method*. This method is complex and rarely used.

20. Group and composite methods. As a means to eliminate the clerical work associated with depreciating assets individually, many companies apply an average depreciation rate to a group of assets. The accounting method is the same under the *group depreciation method* (for similar assets) or the *composite depreciation method* (for dissimilar assets). The *average depreciation rate* is calculated when the group of assets is formed and is used throughout the life of the group unless new assets that have significantly different useful lives are added to the group. This rate is calculated by dividing the total of the straight-line depreciation amounts for the assets by the total acquisition cost of the group of assets. The *average composite life* of the group of assets is calculated by dividing the total depreciation base for the group of assets by the total of the straight-line depreciation amounts for all assets in the group. The depreciation expense for each period is determined by multiplying the group depreciation rate by the acquisition cost of the assets in use during the period. Since an individual record of depreciation is not maintained for each asset, it is assumed that the assets in the group are retired at their book values. The journal entry to record the sale of one machine of a group, for example, would include a debit to cash (or other asset) for the amount of the consideration received, a debit to accumulated depreciation for the difference between the cost of the machine sold and any consideration received, and a credit to machinery for the cost of the machine sold. No gain or loss is ever recognized; it is, in effect, buried in the accumulated depreciation account, under the assumption that over time the gains and losses for the group will offset one another.

Partial-Year Depreciation

21. It is quite unlikely that a company will always acquire or dispose of its plant assets at the beginning or end of its fiscal year. Depreciation policies must therefore be established for partial-year depreciation. Many companies adopt a policy of recording depreciation to the nearest month, which requires modifications in the application of the depreciation methods. Assuming that an asset is used for its total estimated useful life, the modifications of three selected depreciation methods are as follows:

a. Modification of the *straight-line method* is necessary only for the year of acquisition and year of disposal. To calculate depreciation expense for the year of acquisition, the annual depreciation expense must be multiplied by $\frac{n}{12}$, where n = the number of months the asset is used in the year of acquisition. Similarly, depreciation expense for the year of disposal is equal to the annual depreciation expense multiplied by $(12 - n) \div 12$, where n = the number of months the asset was used in the year of acquisition.

b. Since the *sum-of-the-years'-digits method* calculates a distinct depreciation expense for each year, a continuous modification of depreciation expense for each year is required. To determine depreciation expense in the year of acquisition, the first year's calculated depreciation expense is multiplied by $\frac{n}{12}$ where n = the number of months the asset is used in the year of acquisition. For each succeeding full year of use, depreciation expense is composed of two elements: (*a*) the remainder of the previous year's depreciation expense—that is, the previous year's calculated depreciation multiplied by $(12 - n) \div 12$, where n = the number of months of depreciation recognized from the previous period's calculated amount—and (*b*) a portion of the current year's calculated depreciation, that is, the current year's calculated depreciation expense multiplied by $\frac{n'}{12}$, where n' = the number of months applicable to the current year's depreciation. It should be noted that a total of 12 months' depreciation must be recognized each year in which a full year's depreciation is recorded, and that n and n' are always the same each year. In the last year of the asset's useful life, depreciation expense is equal to the last year's calculated depreciation expense multiplied by $(12 - n) \div 12$, where n = the number of months of depreciation recognized the previous year from the last year's calculated depreciation expense.

c. The only modifications of the *double-declining balance method* are made to calculate the first year's and later years' depreciation expense. In the year of acquisition only a portion of the first year's calculated depreciation is recognized as depreciation expense, that is, first full year's calculated depreciation expense multiplied by $\frac{n}{12}$, where n = the number of months the asset is used in the year of acquisition. In order not to depreciate the asset below its estimated net salvage value, the book value at the beginning of the year in which the double-declining balance method would depreciate the asset below its salvage value is depreciated by the straight-line method, and the straight-line method continues to be used during the remainder of the asset's useful life.

Alternatively, to simplify the process, some companies adopt a policy of recognizing one-half year's depreciation in both the year of acquisition and the year of disposal, whereas other companies record no depreciation in the year of acquisition and a full year's depreciation in the year of disposal.

Depletion of Natural Resources

22. Calculating depletion. *Depletion* is the process of allocating the capitalized costs of natural resources over the future benefit period. The *depletion base* of recoverable natural resources is the capitalized costs less the expected net residual value of the property. *Expected net residual value* is the amount that is estimated to be received at the time the property is sold less any estimated additional costs that may be required to restore the property to its previous state. Thus the expected net residual value may be positive or negative. If the expected net residual value is positive, it should be deducted from the capitalized costs to determine the depletion base. If the expected net residual value is negative, it should be added to the capitalized costs to determine the depletion base.

23. Depletion normally is computed by the units-of-production (activity) method on the basis of some physical measure of output, such as tons or barrels. Under this method, the depletion base is divided by the total number of units of natural resources expected to be recoverable from the property (often called the *estimated recoverable units*) to determine a depletion rate per unit. The depletion rate per unit then is multiplied by the actual number of units recovered during the period to determine the depletion for that period. Additionally, changes in the number of recoverable units estimated or in the net residual value expected should be accounted for prospectively by dividing the un-

amortized costs (less the revised expected net residual value) by the estimated remaining recoverable units to determine a revised depletion rate per unit.

24. Depletion may be recorded by crediting either the asset account directly or a contra asset account, accumulated depletion. Depletion and production costs associated with units sold should be included in the cost of goods sold reported on the income statement, whereas depletion and production costs associated with unsold units should be included in the cost of the inventory reported on the balance sheet. Finally, the unamortized costs (capitalized costs less accumulated depletion) of natural resources should be reported in the plant asset section of the balance sheet.

25. Costs of tangible assets. The costs of tangible assets associated with the exploration, development, or production of recoverable natural resources should be recorded as an asset and depreciated over the period estimated to be benefited. A tangible asset that can be moved from site to site should be depreciated over its useful life, whereas a tangible asset that cannot be moved should be depreciated over the shorter of its expected useful life or the expected life of the natural resources.

26. Acquisition and exploration costs. Acquisition and exploration costs, especially in the oil and gas industry, may not result in the discovery of recoverable natural resources. At the time the costs are incurred, however, it usually is not possible to determine whether a particular exploratory effort will be successful or unsuccessful. There are two methods of accounting for acquisition and exploration costs in such circumstances: the successful efforts method and the full-cost method.

27. Under the *successful efforts method,* acquisition and exploration costs initially are capitalized in a "suspense" asset account. If it is subsequently determined that the property does not contain recoverable natural resources (that is, the effort was unsuccessful), the acquisition and exploration costs initially capitalized are written off as an expense or loss. If it is determined that the property does contain recoverable natural resources (that is, the effort was successful), the capitalized acquisition and exploration costs plus the capitalized intangible development costs are allocated (depleted) over the estimated recoverable units. The principal argument for this method is that only costs that provide future economic benefits should be capitalized and carried forward as an asset to be allocated over the future benefit period.

28. Under the *full-cost method,* the acquisition and exploration costs incurred in both successful and unsuccessful efforts and the intangible development costs incurred in successful efforts are capitalized as an asset and allocated (depleted) over the estimated recoverable units from the successful efforts. The principal argument for this method is that costs of unsuccessful efforts are just as much a part of the cost of recoverable natural resources as are the costs of successful efforts, and thus all acquisition and exploration costs should be capitalized and allocated over the future benefit period.

29. In *Statement No. 19* the FASB concluded that acquisition and exploration costs incurred by oil and gas companies should be accounted for by the successful efforts method. After various sectors of the economy exerted pressure, however, the FASB suspended this requirement. Thus both the successful efforts method and the full-cost method are now acceptable.

30. Percentage (statutory) depletion. For tax purposes, the amount deducted from income for the depletion of oil, gas, and most minerals is the greater of cost depletion (computed as described earlier) or percentage depletion (also known as statutory depletion). Percentage depletion is computed by multiplying the gross income from the property for the period by a rate specified by the Internal Revenue Service. Because percentage depletion is based on gross income rather than on costs, the depletion amount deducted from income for tax purposes may over time exceed the capitalized cost of the property. Consequently, percentage depletion may give rise to a difference between taxable income and pretax financial income. The financial accounting implications of such differences are discussed in Chapter 17.

Amortization of Intangible Assets

31. *APB Opinion No. 17* specifies that the capitalized costs of intangible assets must be allocated to expense, through a process called *amortization,* over a period not to exceed 40 years. It states further that capitalized costs of intangible assets must be amortized by the straight-line method, unless another systematic method is clearly more appropriate, and changes in the estimated life of intangible assets must be accounted for prospectively by allocating the unamortized costs over the estimated remaining useful life. The amortization periods of specific intangible assets are as follows:

a. *Patents.* The shorter of the remaining legal life (17 years for a newly issued patent) or the estimated useful life of the patent.
b. *Copyrights.* The shorter of the estimated economic life of the copyright or 40 years.
c. *Trademarks and trade names.* The shorter of the estimated economic life of the trademark or trade name or 40 years.
d. *Franchises.* The shorter of the number of years specified in the franchise agreement, the estimated economic life of the franchise, or 40 years.

e. *Lease prepayments.* The shorter of the lease term or 40 years.
f. *Lease improvements.* The shorter of the remaining term of the lease, the estimated life of the improvement, or 40 years.
g. *Organization costs and other deferred charges.* The shorter of the estimated benefit period or 40 years.
h. *Goodwill.* The shorter of the estimated benefit period or 40 years.

Amortization of intangible assets may be credited directly to the asset account or to a contra asset account, accumulated amortization.

32. *Statement No. 86* specifies that capitalized computer software costs must be amortized on a product-by-product basis. It states further that the periodic amortization of the capitalized costs must be the greater of the amount computed using (*a*) the ratio of the current gross revenues from the product to the total of current and anticipated future gross revenues from the product or (*b*) the straight-line method over the estimated remaining economic life of the product.

Impairment of Value of Noncurrent Assets

33. Recently, some companies have adopted a practice of *partial write-downs* of assets that are still being used. Although there are no authoritative guidelines, possible solutions may be determined by considering the accounting treatment of related events and the specific issues of asset write-downs.

34. Most assets are carried at their book value (cost less accumulated depreciation). In cases where an asset's value declines significantly and permanently below its book value, the loss (book value minus *recoverable value*) is recognized in the period of the decline. For assets to be sold, recoverable value is defined as *net realizable value;* for assets to be used internally to generate cash flows, recoverable value is defined as *present value of net future cash flows.*

35. The major accounting issue is whether an impairment of value is "permanent" and hence should be recognized. Theoretically, when there is a high degree of certainty about the significance of an impairment and the amount of the write-down can be objectively determined, the write-down should be recognized. However, because of the subjectivity involved in determining when and how much to write down an asset, there is potential for management to "time" the recognition of the loss to its advantage. For example, if earnings are already depressed for a period, management may decide to absorb or bury the loss now so that future periods (hopefully profitable) will not be burdened with the loss or higher depreciation charges (if the asset was not written down).

36. Until an official standard is issued on asset impairments, management and auditors will have to evaluate each potential asset write-down separately. If the situation is such that a writing down will provide relevant and reliable future cash flow signals about the company, the write-down, either partial or total, should be recognized. Indeed, *Statement No. 86* specifies that, if the estimated net realizable value of the product is less than the unamortized cost of computer software as of a balance sheet date, the computer software must be written down to its net realizable value.

37. The FASB recently issued an *Exposure Draft* of a proposed *Statement* on accounting for impairments of long-lived assets, identifiable intangibles, and goodwill related to these assets. It would require that the book (carrying) value of an impaired asset be reduced to its fair value (less disposal cost) whenever the sum of the undiscounted expected future cash flows is less than the carrying value of the asset. In such circumstances, the asset's fair value would be measured by its market price or, if no market price is available, at the discounted expected future cash flows.

Disposition of Plant Assets, Natural Resources, and Intangible Assets

38. Companies dispose of plant assets, natural resources, and intangible assets, either voluntarily (through sale, abandonment, exchange, or donation) or involuntarily (through a disaster such as a fire or flood or by condemnation by a governmental body). Depreciation (depletion or amortization) on the asset must be recorded up to the date of disposal in order to update the asset's book value and to recognize the related expense for the period. To record the disposal of an asset, (*a*) the asset's cost and related accumulated depreciation balances must be written off; (*b*) the consideration received, if any, should be recorded; and (*c*) a gain or loss should be recognized for any difference between the consideration received and the book value of the asset. The gain or loss from disposal is normally part of income from continuing operations unless the criteria for an extraordinary item or of a disposal of a segment are satisfied.

39. **Sale.** Assets may be sold voluntarily before their service potential has completely expired. Because the asset possesses service potential, its fair value probably will not be equal to its book value. In such circumstances, cash should be debited for the amount of cash received, accumulated depreciation should be debited for the up-to-date balance of the account, the asset should be credited for its cost, and gain on sale should be credited for the difference between the consideration received (cash) and the book value of the asset (cost minus accumulated depreciation).

40. **Abandonment.** An asset that has no service potential should be written off as an "abandonment." If the cost of the asset exceeds the amount of its related accumulated depreciation, a loss should be recognized. This loss should be increased by any disposal cost incurred or decreased by any salvage value received for the asset.

41. **Donation.** Companies may donate plant assets, such as land or a building, to a local community for recreational facilities. Donation expense should be recorded at the fair value of the asset donated, and the asset should be removed from the company's books. The difference, if any, between the fair value and book value of the asset should be recognized as a gain or loss on donation, included in the results of operations from continuing operations.

42. **Involuntary conversion.** Involuntary conversion of plant assets, either through a catastrophe or by a governmental body's exercise of its right of eminent domain, are treated just like voluntary disposals of plant assets. That is, any consideration received, as from the proceeds of an insurance policy or a government payment, should be recorded at its fair value, the asset's cost and related accumulated depreciation balances should be written off, and a gain or loss, if any, should be recognized. Sometimes the proceeds from an involuntary conversion are reinvested or are intended to be reinvested in a similar asset. Some accountants claim that this situation is an exchange of similar nonmonetary assets, and, therefore, no gain or loss should be recognized. The FASB, however, ruled in *Interpretation No. 30* that such gains and losses should be fully recognized.

Financial Statement Disclosures

43. **Plant assets.** Because plant assets represent a significant resource for most companies, specific disclosure requirements for plant assets were established by the APB in *Opinion No. 12*. These disclosures provide data that help financial statement users to evaluate management's use of plant assets and their future cash flow potential. The historical cost information that must be disclosed in the financial statements or notes includes the following:

a. Depreciation expense for the period.
b. Balances of major classes of depreciable assets on the balance sheet date.
c. Accumulated depreciation, by major classes of assets or in total, on the balance sheet date.

d. A general description of the method or methods used to calculate depreciation with respect to the major classes of depreciable assets.

44. Natural resources. The disclosure requirements for natural resources are similar to those just described for plant assets. *Statement No. 69*, however, specifies that companies must disclose the method of accounting for costs incurred in oil and gas producing activities and the manner of disposing of any capitalized costs related to those activities. It states further that these companies must include supplementary, unaudited information about the following items in their annual reports:

a. Proven oil and gas reserves.

b. Capitalized costs related to oil and gas producing activities.
c. Costs incurred for property acquisition, exploration, and development activities.
d. Results of operations for oil and gas producing activities.
e. A standardized measure of discounted future net cash flows relating to proven oil and gas reserves.

45. Intangible assets. The method and period of amortization of intangible assets should be disclosed, generally as part of the accounting policies note to the financial statements, as well as any significant write-downs in the unamortized cost of intangible assets due to impairments of value.

SELF-STUDY LEARNING

Key Terms and Concepts

Provide the appropriate term or terms to complete each of the following statements:

1. The process of allocating the capitalized cost of a long-term asset over the period estimated to be benefited is called _____ when the asset is property, plant, or equipment; _____ when the asset is intangible; and _____ when the asset is recoverable natural resources.

2. The estimated fair value of a plant asset at the time of its disposal is referred to as its _____.

3. The _____ of a plant asset is the difference between the asset's cost and its estimated fair value at disposal.

4. Factors such as obsolescence and inadequacy, which affect the useful life of a plant asset, are referred to as _____ factors.

5. The _____ method of depreciation results in equal amounts of depreciation expense in all years in which the asset is depreciated.

6. _____ depreciation methods provide higher depreciation expense in the earlier years of the asset's useful life.

7. Under the _____ depreciation method, depreciation expense is calculated by multiplying the acquisition cost of the assets in use during the period by an average depreciation rate.

8. For tax purposes, the amount deducted from income for the depletion of oil, gas, and most minerals is the greater of _____ or _____.

9. When the value of a plant asset to be used in production is impaired, it should be written down to its _____.

10. Loss of a plant asset due to a fire or other catastrophe is an example of a(n) _____ conversion.

True-False

Indicate by circling the appropriate response whether each of the following statements is true (T) or false (F):

T F 1. At no time is the recorded cost of a plant asset equal to its fair value.

T F 2. The difference between the acquisition cost and salvage value of a plant asset usually is recognized as depreciation expense over the useful life of the asset.

T F 3. The depreciation base of a plant asset is an objectively determined amount.

T F 4. A plant asset's useful life and physical life are usually the same.

T F 5. The useful life of a plant asset may be affected by physical factors, such as normal wear and tear from use.

T F 6. Plant assets become obsolete when a company's operations have expanded beyond the capabilities of its present assets.

T F 7. Inflation and changing economic conditions have no effect on the estimated useful life of a plant asset.

T F 8. Straight-line depreciation expense per year is calculated by dividing the asset's depreciation base by its estimated useful life.

T F 9. Under the production or use depreciation method, depreciation expense increases in the periods when the asset's use increases.

T F 10. The numerator in the fraction used to calculate depreciation expense by the sum-of-the-years'-digits method is equal to the number of years the asset has been used.

T F 11. When the double-declining balance depreciation method is used, it is common to switch to the straight-line method in the year in which the double-declining balance method will depreciate the asset below its salvage value.

T F 12. When an average depreciation rate is applied to a group of similar assets, the depreciation method is referred to as the group depreciation method.

T F 13. The estimated additional costs that may be required to restore property to its previous state should be recorded as part of the capitalized costs of recoverable natural resources.

T F 14. The costs of tangible equipment acquired for the production of recoverable natural resources should be depreciated over the shorter of its estimated life or the estimated life of the natural resources, if the equipment cannot be moved from site to site.

T F 15. Under the full-cost method, exploration costs incurred for both successful and unsuccessful efforts are expensed as they are incurred.

T F 16. The capitalized costs of a patent must be amortized over its legal life of 17 years.

T F 17. When the proceeds from the involuntary conversion of an asset are reinvested in an asset similar to one that was involuntarily converted, no gain or loss is recognized on the involuntary conversion.

T F 18. When an asset is donated to a charity, for example, the amount of donation expense recognized should be equal to the fair value of the donated asset.

T F 19. Companies are required to disclose information about the depreciation method used, but not the amount of depreciation expense for the period.

T F 20. An asset acquired and used during the current year must be depreciated to the nearest month for the current year.

Multiple Choice

Select the best response for each of the following items, and circle the corresponding letter:

1. Depreciation:

   a. Is a process of valuing plant assets.
   b. Provides a tax savings, because depreciation is a tax-deductible expense.
   c. Is a source of cash.
   d. Allocates the salvage value of an asset over its useful life.

2. Under the straight-line depreciation method, depreciation expense:

   a. Is a linear function of time.
   b. Is a curvilinear function of time.
   c. Varies each period.
   d. Is rather complex to compute.

3. To apply the production or use depreciation method, the asset must possess several characteristics. Select the one characteristic listed that must *not* be met.

   a. A reasonable activity base exists.
   b. The actual use of the asset varies over time.
   c. The decline in service potential is closely related to the use of the asset.
   d. The service potential of the asset declines rapidly in the early years of its useful life.

4. When depreciation expense is computed by the sum-of-the-years'-digits method, the depreciation base is multiplied by a fraction. Over the life of the asset:

   a. Both the depreciation base and the fraction decrease.
   b. The depreciation base increases and the fraction remains constant.
   c. The depreciation base remains constant and the fraction decreases.
   d. The depreciation base remains constant and the fraction increases.

5. Under the group or composite depreciation method:

   a. A gain or loss on the disposal of an asset is buried in the accumulated depreciation account.
   b. Depreciation expense is equal to the average depreciation rate multiplied by the book value of the assets at the beginning of the period.
   c. The average depreciation rate must be recalculated each period.
   d. Detailed depreciation records must be maintained for each asset that is part of the group of assets.

6. When depreciation expense is computed for a partial year in the year of an asset's acquisition, the normal annual depreciation calculation must be adjusted. For each of the methods shown, must the calculation of depreciation expense for the second year also be adjusted? (Assume that the asset has a 15-year estimated useful life.)

	STRAIGHT-LINE METHOD	SUM-OF-THE-YEARS'-DIGITS METHOD	DOUBLE-DECLINING BALANCE METHOD
a.	Yes	Yes	No
b.	No	Yes	Yes
c.	No	No	Yes
d.	No	Yes	No

7. Depletion associated with the units unsold at the end of the accounting period should be:

   a. Reported as an expense on the income statement.
   b. Included in the cost of goods sold reported on the income statement.
   c. Included in the cost of the inventory reported on the balance sheet.
   d. Reported as a loss on the income statement.

8. Which of the following is *not* an authoritative guideline regarding the amortization of the capitalized costs of intangible assets?

   a. Intangible assets need not be amortized unless the expected period of benefit is limited by legal or contractual restrictions.
   b. Intangible assets must be amortized over a period not in excess of 40 years.
   c. Intangible assets must be amortized on a straight-line basis unless it can be demonstrated that another systematic method is more appropriate.
   d. None of the above.

9. Under the FASB's *Exposure Draft*, the amount of loss required to be recognized for an impairment of a long-lived asset for which no market price is available would be the excess of the book value over the fair value, measured at:

   a. Undiscounted expected future cash flows.
   b. Discounted expected future cash flows.
   c. Undiscounted acquisition cost.
   d. Discounted acquisition cost.

10. If the amount of cash received by the company in a voluntary conversion of an asset does not equal the asset's book value, the difference should:

    a. Be recognized only if a gain.
    b. Be recognized only if a loss.
    c. Be recognized if a gain or loss.
    d. Not be recognized.

Extended Problems

1. On January 1, 1995, Falcon Print Center acquired for $48,000 a new copy machine that has an estimated physical life of 10 years, but because of technological improvements, its useful life is only 4 years, with a salvage value estimated to be $6,000. Also acquired on January 1 were four similar typesetting displays. Data concerning the typesetting displays are as follows:

TYPESETTING DISPLAY	COST	SALVAGE VALUE	USEFUL LIFE
A-101	$1,500	$300	6
A-103	1,200	-0-	4
A-105	1,300	200	5
A-107	1,400	100	5

The income tax rate for all years is 40 percent.

REQUIRED

a. Prepare separate schedules to calculate depreciation expense for each of the years of the copy machine's estimated useful life under the straight-line, sum-of-the-years'-digits, and double-declining balance depreciation methods.

b. Assuming that the copy machine was acquired on September 1, 1995 (instead of January 1), and that the company recognizes depreciation to the nearest month, prepare separate schedules to calculate depreciation expense for each year the asset is to be used under the straight-line, sum-of-the-years'-digits, and double-declining balance methods.

c. Assuming that the group depreciation method is used by Falcon for the typesetting displays, prepare the journal entries required to record depreciation at the end of 1995 and the sale of typesetting display A-105 for $800 on January 1, 1996.

2. Data concerning selected transactions of NR Company for the year ended December 31, 1995, follow:

   a. On January 1, 1995, NR Company acquired for $300,000 a tract of land containing recoverable natural resources estimated by geological surveys at 100,000 tons. State laws require that the land be restored to its previous state after the natural resources have been extracted. NR Company estimates that the land will be sold for $90,000 after the company has incurred restoration costs of $60,000. During 1995, NR Company incurred $130,000 of intangible development costs to prepare the land for extraction of the natural resources. In addition, on July 1, 1995, NR Company paid $40,000 for equipment necessary to extract the natural resources. The equipment can be moved from site to site and has an estimated useful life of 10 years with an expected salvage value of $2,000. NR Company extracted 15,000 tons of the natural resources in 1995.

   b. On January 1, 1995, NR Company paid $24,000 for a patent that has a remaining legal life of 12 years and an estimated useful life of 6 years.

   c. During 1995, NR Company incurred costs in developing and producing a computer software program. After the technological feasibility of the product was established, the product masters were produced at the end of the year at a cost of $15,000. Estimated gross revenues from the product over its expected production period are $250,000, $175,000, and $75,000 for the next three years, respectively.

REQUIRED

a. Calculate the amount of depletion that should be recorded in 1995.

b. Prepare the journal entry required to record amortization of the patent for 1995.

c. Calculate the amount of the amortization of the capitalized computer software costs for 1996.

3. Among the assets on Odyssey Company's December 31, 1995, balance sheet were (a) a machine that cost $60,000, with a current book value and fair value of $36,000 and $40,000, respectively, and (b) a parcel of land that cost $84,000 with a current fair value of $100,000.

REQUIRED

a. Assuming that the machine was sold for $30,000 on January 1, 1996, prepare the journal entry required to record the sale.

b. The local city government exercised its right of eminent domain and acquired a portion of Odyssey's land (cost of $15,000) for a road. The city paid Odyssey $7,000 for the land. Prepare the journal entry required to record the involuntary conversion of the land.

COMMON ERRORS

The first statement in each of the "common errors" listed here is *incorrect*. Each incorrect statement is followed by a corrected statement and an explanation.

1. Stated as simply as possible, depreciation is a valuation process that provides a source of funds. *Wrong*

Stated simply, depreciation is a process of cost allocation. *Right*

One of the most misunderstood accounting concepts is depreciation. Many people believe that depreciation is a valuation procedure because they often loosely refer to their personal property, such as an automobile, as "depreciating" or losing value as time passes. In an accounting context, however, depreciation is a process of allocating the cost of an asset over its useful life. Theoretically, depreciation expense is matched with revenue generated, in part, by the asset's use. When accumulated depreciation is deducted from the cost of the related asset on the balance sheet, the result is the asset's book value. Perhaps the valuation notion comes from the use of the term *book value*. Nevertheless, book value represents only undepreciated cost, not a "current" or "market" value of the asset. Only by coincidence will the book value and market value of an asset be the same after the asset is initially recorded.

Another frequently misunderstood notion about depreciation is that it provides a source of funds. Funds are expended to acquire an asset and may be received from the disposal of the asset, but depreciation of and by itself is not a source of funds. Depreciation does provide a tax savings because depreciation is a tax-deductible expense. The tax savings effect of depreciation will reduce taxable income, but this reduction certainly does not qualify as a source of funds.

Although many otherwise knowledgeable people believe that depreciation is a valuation process that provides funds, they are simply incorrect. Depreciation is a process of cost allocation, nothing more or less.

2. Accelerated depreciation methods began to be used for financial reporting purposes to provide better information for decision making. *Wrong*

Accelerated depreciation methods began to be used for financial reporting purposes when these methods were permitted for income tax purposes. *Right*

Accelerated depreciation methods have always been considered systematic and rational and thus viable depreciation methods. Their use was very rare, however, until the IRS permitted them for tax purposes. If an accelerated method best reflects the expiration of an asset's service potential, then it should be used for financial reporting purposes. But a company often selects an accelerated method solely because of its income tax advantage: the higher depreciation charges in the earlier years of an asset's useful life reduce taxable income for those years, and thus reduce the present value of the company's total tax obligation. As it is easier to maintain only one depreciation schedule per asset, companies often elect the method that produces the best tax advantage, whether or not that cost allocation pattern coincides with the expiration of the asset. The popularity of the accelerated depreciation methods for financial reporting purposes is a classic example of how tax law influences the development of financial accounting practices.

3. Under the double-declining balance method, a year's depreciation expense is calculated by multiplying the depreciation base by twice the straight-line ratio. *Wrong*

Under the double-declining balance method, a year's depreciation expense is calculated by multiplying book value at beginning of year by twice the straight-line rate. *Right*

The double-declining balance method is one of the few depreciation methods that is *not* based on salvage value. (Note, however, that an asset cannot be depreciated below its salvage value.) Instead, this method bases periodic depreciation expense on the book value (cost minus accumulated depreciation) of the asset at the beginning of the period. Thus, because the book value, which becomes smaller each period as accumulated depreciation increases each year, is multiplied by the constant depreciation rate, the amount of depreciation each successive period declines.

4. Depletion associated with units recovered during the period should be reported as an expense on the income statement. *Wrong*

Depletion associated with units sold during the period should be included in the cost of goods sold reported on the income statement, whereas depletion associated with units unsold at the end of the period should be included in the cost of the inventory reported on the balance sheet. *Right*

Costs that can be associated with particular revenue on a direct cause-and-effect basis should be recognized (matched) as an expense in the same period in which the related revenue is recognized. Accordingly, depletion associated with units recovered during the period initially should be included as part of the cost of the recovered units. Later, in the period when the recovered units are sold, the depletion and production costs associated with the units sold should be reported as part of the cost of goods sold on the income statement. Conversely, the depletion and production costs associated with recovered units that are not yet sold at the end of the period should be reported as part of the cost of the inventory on the balance sheet.

5. The capitalized costs of intangible assets need not be amortized if the period estimated to be benefited is indefinite. *Wrong*

The capitalized costs of intangible assets must be amortized over the shorter of the period estimated to be benefited or 40 years. *Right*

Certain intangible assets, such as trade names and perpetual franchises, may provide economic benefits indefinitely. Because these intangible assets may have an unlimited life, it is sometimes argued that their capitalized costs need not be amortized. *Opinion No. 17,* however, requires that the capitalized costs of all intangible assets be amortized over the shorter of the period estimated to be benefited or 40 years. This requirement is based on the supposition that the value of all intangible assets disappears eventually.

ANSWERS

Key Terms and Concepts

1. depreciation, amortization, depletion
2. salvage or residual value
3. depreciation base
4. economic
5. straight-line
6. accelerated
7. group or composite
8. cost depletion, percentage (statutory) depletion
9. recoverable value or present value of net future cash flows
10. involuntary

True-False

1. F Normally the recorded cost of a plant asset is not equal to the current fair value of the asset. When a plant asset is first acquired, however, the cost of the asset and its fair value should be the same.
2. T
3. F The depreciation base of a plant asset is equal to the cost of the asset less its salvage value. The cost of the asset is normally objectively determined, but the salvage value is subjective. Determination of the salvage value requires professional judgment as to the future fair value of the asset at the time of its disposal. In addition, the salvage value may have to be adjusted for expected costs of disposal. Therefore, the depreciation base cannot be considered to be objectively determined.

4. F A plant asset's useful life is the period of time during which a company expects to use the asset in the earnings process. A plant asset's physical life is the period of time during which the asset is capable of functioning. Often the useful life is shorter (but never greater) than the physical life. A machine may be mechanically capable of producing, for example, but because of technological changes, its useful life may be cut short.
5. T
6. F *Obsolescence* occurs when a company's present assets become outmoded as new and improved substitutes become available. *Inadequacy* occurs when a company's operations expand beyond the capabilities of its present assets. Whether the assets become obsolete or inadequate, a company must normally replace assets before their physical lives are over.
7. F Inflation and changing economic conditions have an effect on the useful life of a plant asset because these factors affect consumers' behavior and thus their buying habits. If plant assets are used to produce a particular product, for example, and inflation rises rapidly, it could cut the demand for the product. If demand declines, the useful life of the plant assets probably will be affected.
8. T
9. T
10. F The numerator in the sum-of-the-years'-digits' fraction is equal to the number of years of the asset's useful life *remaining* at

the beginning of the year for which depreciation is being calculated. Thus, in the earlier years of an asset's useful life, more years remain, so that the numerator is higher and more depreciation is recognized than in later years.

11. T

12. T

13. F The estimated additional costs that may be required to restore property to its previous state should not be recorded as part of the capitalized costs of recoverable natural resources. Estimated restoration cost, however, should be deducted from the amount that is estimated to be received at the time the property is sold to determine the expected net residual value of the property. And, if positive (or negative), the expected net residual value should be deducted from (or added to) the capitalized costs to determine the depletion base.

14. T

15. F Under the full-cost method, exploration costs incurred for both successful and unsuccessful efforts are capitalized as an asset and amortized (depleted) over the estimated number of units recoverable from the successful efforts.

16. F The capitalized costs of a patent should be amortized over the shorter of its remaining legal life or its estimated useful life.

17. F Some claim that when the proceeds from an involuntary conversion are reinvested in similar assets, the exchange amounts to an exchange of similar nonmonetary assets and thus no gain or loss should be recognized. The FASB has ruled, however, that gains and losses from involuntary conversions should be fully recognized.

18. T

19. F All companies are required to disclose historical cost information about their plant assets, including information about (a) depreciation expense for the period, (b) asset balance or balances, (c) accumulated depreciation, and (d) depreciation method or methods used.

20. F An asset acquired and used during the year should be depreciated, but companies may adopt various policies for the depreciation of assets acquired in midyear. Some companies, for example, recognize one-half year's depreciation in the year of acquisition, whereas other companies record no depreciation for the partial period. A company may record depreciation to the nearest month, but this practice is not required.

Multiple Choice

1. b
2. a
3. d
4. c
5. a
6. d
7. c
8. a
9. b
10. c

Extended Problems

1. a. Depreciation expense schedules:

STRAIGHT-LINE METHOD

YEAR	DEPRECIATION BASE[a] ÷ USEFUL LIFE	DEPRECIATION EXPENSE
1	$42,000 ÷ 4 =	$10,500
2	42,000 ÷ 4 =	10,500
3	42,000 ÷ 4 =	10,500
4	42,000 ÷ 4 =	10,500
		$42,000

[a]$48,000 − $6,000 = $42,000.

SUM-OF-THE-YEARS'-DIGITS METHOD

YEAR	DEPRECIATION BASE[a] × FRACTION[b]	DEPRECIATION EXPENSE
1	$42,000 × 4/10 =	$16,800
2	42,000 × 3/10 =	12,600
3	42,000 × 2/10 =	8,400
4	42,000 × 1/10 =	4,200
		$42,000

[a]$48,000 − $6,000 = $42,000.
[b]$[n(n+1)] \div 2 = [4(4+1)] \div 2 = 20 \div 2 = 10$.

DOUBLE-DECLINING BALANCE METHOD

YEAR	BOOK VALUE × RATE[a]	DEPRECIATION EXPENSE
1	$48,000 × 50% =	$24,000
2	($48,000 − $24,000) × 50% =	12,000
3	($48,000 − $36,000) × 50% =	6,000
4	b	-0-
		$42,000

[a]$10,500 ÷ $42,000 = 25% × 2 = 50%.
[b]An asset cannot be depreciated below its salvage value. Therefore, no depreciation expense is recognized in year 4.

b. Depreciation expense schedules under the assumption that the asset was acquired on September 1, 1995.

STRAIGHT-LINE METHOD

YEAR	DEPRECIATION BASE[a] ÷ USEFUL LIFE	DEPRECIATION EXPENSE
1	($42,000 ÷ 4) × 4/12	$ 3,500
2	$42,000 ÷ 4	10,500
3	$42,000 ÷ 4	10,500
4	$42,000 ÷ 4	10,500
5	($42,000 ÷ 4) × 8/12	7,000
		$42,000

[a]$48,000 − $6,000 = $42,000.

SUM-OF-THE-YEARS'-DIGITS METHOD

YEAR	DEPRECIATION BASE[a] × FRACTION[b]	DEPRECIATION EXPENSE
1	$42,000 × 4/10 × 4/12	$ 5,600
2	($42,000 × 4/10 × 8/12)	
+	($42,000 × 3/10 × 4/12)	15,400
3	($42,000 × 3/10 × 8/12)	
+	($42,000 × 2/10 × 4/12)	11,200
4	($42,000 × 2/10 × 8/12)	
+	($42,000 × 1/10 × 4/12)	7,000
5	$42,000 × 1/10 × 8/12	2,800
		$42,000

[a]$48,000 − $6,000 = $42,000.
[b]$[n(n+1)] ÷ 2 = [4(4+1)] ÷ 2 = 20 ÷ 2 = 10.$

DOUBLE-DECLINING BALANCE METHOD

YEAR	BOOK VALUE × RATE[a]	DEPRECIATION EXPENSE
1	$48,000 × 50% × 4/12	$ 8,000
2	($48,000 − $8,000) × 50%	20,000
3	($48,000 − $28,000) × 50%	10,000
4[b]	($48,000 − $38,000 − $6,000) × 12/20	2,400
5[b]	($48,000 − $38,000 − $6,000) × 8/20	1,600
		$42,000

[a]$10,500 ÷ $42,000 = 25% × 2 = 50%.
[b]Because a full year's double-declining balance depreciation in year 4 would reduce the book value of the asset below its salvage value—that is, $10,000 × 50% = $5,000 and the book value would then be $48,000 − $43,000 = $5,000, which is less than the $6,000 estimated salvage value—the straight-line method is used for the remaining 20 months of the asset's life.

c. Journal entry to record depreciation of typesetting displays:

Depreciation expense ($5,400 × 18.1%) 977
    Accumulated depreciation 977

Journal entry to record the disposal of typesetting display A-105:

Cash 800
Accumulated depreciation 500
    Typesetting displays (A-105) 1,300

TYPESETTING DISPLAY	ACQUISITION COST	SALVAGE VALUE	DEPRECIATION BASE	USEFUL LIFE (YEARS)	STRAIGHT-LINE DEPRECIATION
A-101	$1,500	$300	$1,200	6	$200
A-103	1,200	-0-	1,200	4	300
A-105	1,300	200	1,100	5	220
A-107	1,400	100	1,300	5	260
	$5,400	$600	$4,800		$980

Average depreciation rate = $980 ÷ $5,400
    = 18.1%

2. a. Calculation of amount of depletion:

Capitalized costs
  Acquisition costs $300,000
  Intangible development costs 130,000 $430,000
Expected net residual value
  Estimated value of property .... $ 90,000
  Estimated restoration costs .... (60,000)   30,000
Depletion base $400,000
Depletion rate per ton [depletion base ($400,000) ÷ estimated recoverable units (100,000 tons)] $4.00
Amount of depletion for 1995 [number of units extracted in 1995 (15,000 tons) × depletion rate per ton ($4)] .... $ 60,000[a]

[a]Because the equipment can be moved from site to site, it should be depreciated separately over its estimated useful life of 10 years. The depreciation on the equipment for 1995 should be $1,900 [($40,000 − $2,000) ÷ 10 × 6/12].

b. Journal entry to record patent amortization:

Patent amortization expense ($24,000 + 6)	4,000	
Patent (or accumulated amortization on patent)		4,000

c. Calculation of amount of computer software amortization:

Amortization computed on the basis of ratio of current revenues to total of current and future revenues [$15,000 × ($250,000 + $500,000)]	$7,500
Amortization computed on straight-line basis ($15,000 + 3)	$5,000
Amortization of capitalized computer software costs ($15,000) for 1996 (larger of above two amounts)	$7,500

3. a. Journal entry to record the sale of the machine:

Cash	30,000	
Accumulated depreciation–machine	24,000	
Loss on sale of machine	6,000	
Machine		60,000

b. Journal entry to record the involuntary conver-sion of the land:

Cash	7,000	
Loss on disposal of land	8,000	
Land		15,000

13

FINANCIAL INSTRUMENTS: INVESTMENTS IN EQUITY SECURITIES

CHAPTER OBJECTIVES

After reading Chapter 13 and completing the questions, cases, exercises, and problems from the text chapter, you should be able to:

1. Define financial instruments, and differentiate the six types of fundamental financial instruments.
2. Explain what equity securities represent and the meaning of common stock ownership.
3. Determine the value of an investment in common stock when it is acquired.
4. Know when the cost method should be used to account for an investment in common stock and the related accounting entries.
5. Apply the fair value method of accounting for investments in equity securities.

6. Explain when the equity method of accounting for investments in common stock should be used, and apply the equity method.
7. Account for investments in preferred stock.
8. Understand the purpose of consolidated financial statements.
9. Account for stock rights and stock warrants.
10. Record stock splits and stock dividends on investments in stock.
11. Understand the purpose of and accounting for special-purpose funds.
12. Understand the nature of the cash surrender value of a life insurance policy, and prepare the related journal entries.

CHAPTER REVIEW

Introduction

1. The nature of financial instruments has changed dramatically over the past several years. The traditional equity securities (such as common stock) and debt securities (such as bonds) have become more complex. The changing economic environment, globalization of equity markets, deregulation of financial institutions, increased volatility in interest rates and credit, and technological advances in communication have led to some unique financial instruments. A few of these new instruments are baby bonds, bunny bonds, flip-flop notes, PERLs, and ZEBRAs. Perhaps the best known of

the new instruments are junk bonds. Many of these combine both equity and debt characteristics into one instrument.

2. Responding to pressures from regulators, the FASB recently issued a controversial *SFAS* that requires mark-to-market accounting for certian investments in equity and debt securities. This requirement was opposed vigorously by financial institutions. Chapters 13 and 14 study fair value accounting and the accounting and reporting requirements of *Statement No. 115*.

3. This chapter focuses on equity investment and discusses accounting for stock rights, stock warrants, special-purpose funds, and cash surrender value of life insurance. Chapter 14 addresses debt securities in depth. Before starting the discussion of investments, however, fundamental financial instruments are considered.

Fundamental Financial Instruments

4. The FASB defines a financial instrument as cash, evidence of an ownership interest in an entity, or a contract that both (*a*) imposes on Entity *A* a contractual obligation to either deliver cash or another financial instrument to Entity *B* or exchange financial instruments on potentially unfavorable terms with Entity *B* and (*b*) conveys to Entity *B* a contractual right to either receive cash or another financial instrument from Entity *A* or exchange other financial instruments on potentially favorable terms with Entity *A*. There are six fundamental financial instruments that satisfy the definition.

  a. *Unconditional receivables/(payables)* represent instruments to receive (pay) cash or another financial asset on demand or on or before a specified date (for example, accounts receivable or payable).
  b. *Conditional receivables/(payables)* are instruments for which the right to receive (pay) cash or another financial asset depends on an event beyond the control of either party (for example, term life insurance).
  c. *Forward contracts* represent an unconditional right (obligation) to exchange financial instruments (for example, forward exchange contract).
  d. *Options* are a right (obligation) to exchange other financial instruments on potentially favorable (unfavorable) terms that is conditional on an event within the control of one of the parties (for example, common stock option).
  e. Guarantees or other conditional exchanges are similar to options except that the conditional event is beyond the control of both parties (for example, loan guarantee).
  f. Equity instruments represent an ownership interest in an entity (for example, common and preferred stock).

5. Financial instruments should be recognized and measured consistent with the concepts discussed in Chapter 2.

Investments in Equity Securities

6. *Equity securities* represent ownership interest in an enterprise (for example, common, preferred, and other capital stock) or the right to acquire them,

as through warrants, rights, and call options, or to dispose of them, as through put options, at fixed or determinable prices. An equity security of another company is acquired for several reasons, including to gain control of another entity or to realize a gain when the market price of the security appreciates and the security is sold. The next sections discuss the valuation of equity securities at and followed by their acquisition.

Investments in Equity Securities—Valuation at Acquisition

7. Whether an equity security is acquired on an organized stock exchange (such as the New York Stock Exchange), or over the counter, from the issuing company, or from a current owner of the common stock, its valuation at acquisition should be governed by the historical cost principle: the investment is recorded at its fair value at the date of acquisition. If cash is paid for the security, the amount paid is considered its fair value. The cost of the security also includes broker's fees, taxes, and other miscellaneous costs incurred to acquire the investment.

8. If an investment is acquired in exchange for a nonmonetary item or items, it should be recorded at the fair value of the resource or resources sacrificed or at the fair value of the security received, whichever is more readily determinable. When the security acquired is actively traded on a stock exchange, the fair value of the security is normally used as the amount at which it is recorded. When the fair value of the acquired security is not readily determinable—if it is not listed on an exchange or actively traded on an over-the-counter market—the security is recorded at the fair value of the asset exchanged or surrendered. The principles explained in Chapter 11 concerning the exchange of dissimilar nonmonetary assets apply in these situations. That is, the earnings process of the surrendered asset has culminated, and the acquired security is recorded at the fair value of the asset surrendered, with a gain or loss recognized if the fair value of the asset surrendered is greater or less than its book value.

9. A company that issues a security may try to improve its marketability by including another security as a sweetener. Thus a company that acquires the security is in effect acquiring two securities for a single sum. Such a transaction is referred to as a *lump-sum*, or *basket, purchase*. The cost is allocated among the acquired securities on the basis of their relative fair values, as in the case of fixed assets acquired in a lump-sum transaction, discussed in Chapter 11. This technique may not be appropriate, however, in all circumstances. If the market value of only one of two acquired securities is known, for example, the security with the known market value is assigned its market value and the remainder of the total purchase price is assigned to the other security.

Investments in Equity Securities— Valuation Subsequent to Acquisition

10. As discussed previously, all investments in equity securities are initially recorded at their fair value. Depending on the investment characteristics, there are three accounting and reporting methods for equity investments *subsequent to acquisition:* (*a*) *fair value method* if an equity or debt security is a trading security; (*b*) *cost method* if an equity security is an available-for-sale security and its fair value is not determinable or *amortized cost method* (also referred to as the effective interest method) if a debt is a held-to-maturity security; and (*c*) *equity method* if an investor can exercise significant influence over the company issuing the equity security, that is, common stock. The fair value, cost, and equity accounting and reporting methods are discussed in this chapter; Chapter 14 covers the amortized cost method.

11. Fair value method. *Statement No. 115* requires that all equity securities be classified in one of two categories at the time of their acquisition: (*a*) *trading securities* for those bought and held principally for the purpose of selling them in the near term; and (*b*) *available-for-sale securities* for those not classified as trading securities. Another category, *held-to-maturity securities,* applies only to certain debt securities that will be held until the debt matures; this is covered in Chapter 14.

12. Equity securities that have a readily determinable fair value, for example, if their sales prices or bid-and-asked quotations are currently available, are to be "marked-to-market" on the statement of financial position. Any unrealized holding gains or losses for trading securities and available-for-sale securities are to be reported in the income statement and a separate component of stockholders' equity until realized, respectively. Included in earnings for both trading and available-for-sale securities are (*a*) dividends received and (*b*) realized gains and losses from their sale.

13. Reporting the fair value of an equity security is perceived by many as providing relevant and useful information for making decisions, evaluating a firm's investment strategies, assessing cash flows, and indicating solvency of financial institutions. Since trading securities are acquired with the intent of disposing of them in a short period, they may be viewed as operating assets and any unrealized holding gains and losses from holding them should be reported in earnings. Conversely, since available-for-sale securities are considered more like an investment, recognizing unrealized holding gains

and losses in earnings could cause earnings to fluctuate unrealistically. Accordingly, unrealized holding gains and losses on available-for-sale securities are reported as a separate component of owners' equity and deferred until the disposal of the security.

14. To record the cash purchase of an equity security classified as a trading security, debit investment and credit cash for the acquisition price of the investment. Receipt of dividends is recorded by debiting cash and crediting dividend revenue for the amount of the dividend received. If at the end of the current reporting period the fair value (FV_1) of the equity security has changed since the date of acquisition (FV_0) (or date of last valuation), the change in fair value must be recognized: (*a*) an increase by debiting investment and crediting unrealized holding gain for the amount of the increase in the market value ($FV_1 - FV_0$), and (*b*) a decrease by debiting unrealized holding loss and crediting investment for the amount of the decrease in fair value ($FV_0 - FV_1$). The unrealized holding gain (loss) is reported in the income statement. Assuming that the fair value of the equity security has risen to FV_2 and the security is sold at the current market price (FV_2), the entry to record the sale is a debit to cash for the amount of FV_2, and credits to investment for the market value of the stock at the end of the last reporting period (FV_1) and realized gain on sale of securities for the difference between FV_2 and FV_1.

15. The accounting for the purchase of an available-for-sale security and subsequent dividend receipt and market change or changes are accounted for exactly as described for a trading seucrity. The unrealized gain/loss account, however, would be reported as a separate component of owners' equity, not as part of earnings. Unlike the unrealized gain or loss account for a trading security, the unrealized gain/loss account for an available-for-sale security is *not* closed at the end of each accounting period. Therefore, when an available-for-sale security is sold, debit cash for the sales proceeds, debit or credit unrealized gain/loss for the balance in the account to close it, credit investment for its carrying amount at the last reporting date, and balance the entry with a debit (credit) to realized loss (gain) on the sale of securities for the difference between the sales proceeds and the acquisition cost.

16. Equity securities must be reevaluated at each reporting date. If the original classification is no longer applicable, the investment must be reclassified. Any transfer between categories must be made at fair value. If there is a transfer *from* the trading to the available-for-sale category, no adjustment is needed because all unrealized gains and losses have been recognized previously in earnings. On the other hand, when there is a transfer *to* the trading category, any previously recorded unrealized holding gain/loss must be recognized in earnings immediately. For example, if an available-for-sale security has had a net increase in its fair value since acquisition, its transfer to the trading category would be recorded by debiting unrealized holding gain/loss and crediting realized gain on reclassification of equity securities for the amount of the net holding gain.

17. Though very unlikely for a trading security, it is possible that an available-for-sale security might not have a readily determinable market value. In these situations the cost method is the appropriate accounting method.

18. Cost method. An investment in an equity seucrity accounted for under the *cost method,* which is only appropriate if the security does not have a readily determinable fair value, is normally carried at its acquisition cost, including brokerage fees and incidental expenses. Cash dividends received on the investment are recorded as dividend revenue: debit cash and credit dividend revenue for the amount of the dividend received.

19. The cost method reports the investment account at cost unless there is a *liquidating dividend,* a dividend that represents a return *of* the investor's original investment rather than a return *on* the investment. A liquidating dividend is actually a distribution of assets representing earnings before the investor became a shareholder of the company. An investor can determine whether a dividend is a liquidating dividend by comparing the company's cumulative earnings since acquisition with cumulative dividends since acquisition. If cumulative dividends exceed cumulative earnings, a liquidating dividend has been received by the investor. The portion of the dividend that is a liquidating dividend is credited to the investment account, whereas an ordinary dividend is credited to the dividend revenue account.

20. *Financial statement presentation and disclosures* for equity securities are numerous. Trading securities must be classified as a current asset. Available-for-sale securities are classified as a current asset if they are to be converted into cash within the next year or operating cycle, whichever is longer; if not, they should be classified as noncurrent assets. On the statement of cash flows, trading securities' transactions should be reported as operating activities and available-for-sale securities' transactions should be reported as investing activities. *Statement No. 115* has other extensive disclosure requirements for equity securities affecting the balance sheet, income statement, and notes to the financial statements.

21. Equity method. The *equity method* of valuing an investment in common stock must be used if the investor exercises significant influence over the financial and operating policies of the investee. Significant influence normally is evidenced by the ownership of 20 percent or more of the investee's outstanding voting common stock.

22. The general guideline used to determine whether an investor has significant influence over an investee was established by *APB Opinion No. 18,* which set a percentage of ownership test. If an investor has less than 20 percent of an investee's outstanding voting stock, it is presumed that the investor does not exercise significant influence over the investee. It should be noted, however, that the 20 percent figure is only a guideline, and the facts and circumstances surrounding the investment must be considered. An investor may hold less than 20 percent of an investee's outstanding stock but still have significant influence over the investee. The investor may, for example, be represented on the investee's board of directors, have material intercompany transactions, interchange managerial personnel with the investee, or have a concentration of ownership relative to the other shareholdings. When one or more of these and similar situations exist, the investment should be valued by the equity method.

23. On the other hand, an investment of 20 percent or more does not always indicate that an investor can exercise significant influence over the investee. Even if an investor held 20 percent or more of an investee's outstanding common stock, such evidence as the investor's failure in an attempt to gain a seat on the investee's board of directors could indicate that the investor does not exercise significant influence over the investee. If it is determined that significant influence of the investor over the investee does not exist, then the stock should be valued by the cost method or the fair value method if the security has a determinable fair value. It should be remembered that the 20 percent cutoff is only a guideline, and professional judgment must be exercised to evaluate the circumstances surrounding the investment.

24. Under the equity method, the investor's investment account moves in tandem with the changes of the investee's net assets. That is, the investor recognizes increases and decreases in the investee's net assets as they occur. If the investee records a periodic profit (or periodic loss or dividend distribution), for example, the investor company correspondingly increases (or decreases) its investment account.

25. The five steps to apply the equity method are discussed with illustrative journal entries where appropriate.

a. The initial investment is valued at its acquisition cost and recorded as a debit to investment and a credit to (usually) cash for the acquisition cost of the stock.

b. When the investee reports a profit (loss), the investor debits investment (investment loss) and credits investment revenue (investment) for an amount equal to the investor's share of the investee's net income (net loss) (investee's net profit or net loss multiplied by the percentage of the investee's outstanding common stock held by the investor).

c. The investor records the receipt of a cash dividend by debiting cash and crediting investment for an amount equal to the investor's share of the investee's declared dividend (total declared dividend multiplied by the percentage of the investee's outstanding common stock held by the investor).

d. When the acquisition price of the investment is greater (or less) than the underlying proportional share of the investee's net assets on the date of acquisition, the investor must adjust recorded earnings by amortizing the excess of cost over book value (or book value over cost). Cost will exceed book value if the investee's assets are undervalued in terms of the price paid by the investor or if the investor pays a premium because of unrecorded goodwill applicable to the investee. On the other hand, book value will exceed cost if the investee's assets are overvalued in terms of the price paid by the investor. As a result, the investee's reported earnings may be overstated or understated because its assets (recorded and unrecorded) do not reflect their fair value. Consequently, the investor must adjust the amount of reported earnings as if the investee had used these fair values to calculate its net income.

To illustrate the recognition of the difference between the acquisition price and underlying proportional share of the investee's net assets, assume that an investor acquires enough shares of common stock to exercise significant influence over the investee's operating and financing policies. If the price paid is in excess of the book value of the underlying interest in the investee's net assets, the investor should amortize the excess of cost over book value over the remaining estimated lives of the assets with which the excess can be identified. Assume further that a portion of the excess amount can be attributed to an undervalued depreciable asset and the remainder to unrecorded goodwill. The investor would amortize each amount over its remaining life by debiting investment revenue and crediting investment for the amount of the excess attributable to each asset divided by the estimated remaining life of the asset. It should be noted that the book value of the investment is affected by the amortization as well as by the recording of the investee's dividends, profits, and losses.

e. The investor's share of the investee's extraordinary items and the cumulative effect of a change in accounting principle should be reported in a similar fashion in the investor's income statement, if they are material to the investor.

26. *Opinion No. 18* establishes detailed disclosure guidelines for those companies that use the equity method.

27. Consolidated financial statements. An investor with more than 50 percent of an investee's outstanding voting stock has control, rather than a significant influence, over the investee. This is referred to as a parent-subsidiary relationship. Although the investor continues to maintain investee accounts under the equity method, it is preferable to report the combined entities in *consolidated financial statements*. Essentially, in a consolidated balance sheet (income statement), the investor's-parent's investment (investment revenue) account is replaced by the investee's-subsidiary's assets and liabilities (revenues and expenses) and combined with those of the investor-parent. Consolidated financial statements permit the user to view the combined entities as one economic entity.

28. International practices. The International Accounting Standards Committee (IASC) has issued two standards focusing on investments, and currently both are consistent with U.S. GAAP. The IASC, however, has considered revising *International Accounting Standard (IAS) 25,* "Accounting for Investments," to require investments classified as current to be reported at market value, with noncurrent investments continuing to be reported at cost. The proposed reporting of current investments would be in conflict with U.S. GAAP.

29. *IAS 28,* "Accounting for Investments in Associates," recommends that the equity method be used when an investor exerts significant influence over (owns 20 percent or more of an investee's stock) an investee or "associate." The equity method with a 20 percent cutoff is also required by the European Community's *Seventh Directive.* Though not followed by all countries, the equity method is gaining popularity internationally.

Other Security Investments

30. This section discusses accounting and reporting requirements for investments in preferred stock and stock rights and stock warrants.

31. Preferred stock. The accounting and reporting of nonredeemable preferred stock, an equity security, follows *SFAS No. 115*. If the nonredeemable preferred stock has a readily determinable fair value, it must be reported at its fair value and classified as a trading or available-for-sale security as appropriate. If a nonredeemable preferred stock does not have a readily determinable fair value or the security is redeemable, at the option of the investor or under mandatory redemption terms by the issuer, the cost method should be used. The balance sheet disclosure for an investment in preferred stock is based on its classification, that is, if it is classified as (*a*) a trading security it is a current asset, or (*b*) an available-for-sale security it is either a current or noncurrent asset depending on the intent of management. Since preferred stock does not give the investor influence over the investee's operations, the equity method is inappropriate to use for such investments.

32. Stock rights and stock warrants. A *stock right* gives owners of common or preferred stock a *preemptive right* to purchase additional shares from a pending new issue of stock in proportion to their present holdings. A *stock warrant* is the certificate evidencing the stock right. Stock rights are equity securities and are classified as either current or noncurrent, depending on the investor's intent. In addition, stock rights contain information that indicates (*a*) the purchase price or exercise price of a share of stock, (*b*) the number of shares of stock that may be acquired for each right, and (*c*) the expiration date.

33. Stock contracts that include a preemptive clause require a company that attempts to sell additional shares of stock to distribute one stock right for each share held by an investor. The terms of the preemptive contract may stipulate that more than one stock right is needed to acquire an additional share of stock at the exercise price. Since an investor receives stock rights without making a sacrifice, the book value of the original investment must be allocated between the shares of stock held and the stock rights in accordance with the relative fair value method. The fair value of the stock investment is considered to be the market value of the stock *ex-rights*, that is, the market price of the stock after the date at which the rights have been issued.

34. During the period between the announcement of the distribution of the stock right and its issuance, the stock is said to sell *rights on,* which means that the value of the stock right is included in the price of the stock. The portion of the carrying value of the stock investment allocated to the stock rights is calculated by multiplying the carrying value of the stock investment by the ratio of the total market price of the rights received over the sum of the market price of the rights received plus the total market value of the stock (ex-rights). The cost per right is found by dividing the portion of the carrying value of the investment allocated to the rights by the number of rights received. Because the stock rights represent a new form of investment, the entry to record the receipt of the stock rights is a debit to investment in rights and a credit to investment in stock for the amount calculated as the cost of the rights. Obviously, the total cost of the stock investment is reduced, and the book value per share of each share of stock is reduced.

35. Investments in stock rights are considered an equity security and must be accounted for according to *Statement No. 115*. If they have a readily determinable fair value, they must be classified as trading or available-for-sale securities and reported at their fair value; otherwise, the cost method is appropriate. Accordingly, if the fair value of a stock right changes, the unrealized gain or loss must be recognized consistent with the stock rights' *Statement No. 115* classification and the appropriate reporting requirements need to be observed.

36. If the stock rights are *exercised,* the acquisition of the new shares of stock is recorded by a debit to investment in stock for the sum of the cash paid for the stock plus the book value of the rights surrendered to acquire the stock, and a credit to cash (exercise price per share multiplied by number of shares acquired) and to investment in rights (book value per right multiplied by number of rights surrendered). Stock rights may also be *sold.* If the consideration received is greater or less than the book value of the rights sold, the result is a gain or loss on the sale of the rights. Stock rights that are allowed to *expire* require the book value of the rights to be written off as a loss; loss on expiration of stock rights is debited, and investments in rights is credited for the book value of the rights expired.

37. Stock warrants may be purchased separately from the issuing company; from another investor; or as a part of a unit with bonds or preferred stock, as a sweetener. In any case the warrants may be exercised, sold, or allowed to expire unless no expiration date is specified ("perpetual" warrants). The cost of a warrant is the purchase price if it is acquired separately, or an allocated portion (under the relative fair market value method) of the purchase price if the warrant is acquired with another security. Warrants are accounted for by the fair value method, if the warrants have a readily determinable market value.

38. Warrants that are acquired separately are recorded by a debit to investment in warrants and a credit to cash for the purchase price of the warrants. The cost of stock acquired with warrants is equal to the sum of the cash paid (exercise price) plus the cost of the warrants exercised. Like a stock right, a stock warrant may also be (*a*) sold, with a gain or loss recognized on the sale if the sale price is greater or less than the book value of the warrant sold; or (b) allowed to expire, with a loss being recognized equal to the book value of the warrants that expired.

Stock Splits and Stock Dividends

39. Stock splits and stock dividends have the same effect on the investor: an increase in the number of shares held on a pro rata basis, that is, in proportion to the investor's current holding. Although for the issuing company the accounting for stock splits differs from the accounting for stock dividends, both are accounted for in the same way by the investor. The investor makes no sacrifice when the additional shares are received, and the same type of security is received as the kind previously held. Accordingly, no entry is made when the stock dividend or stock split is received. The investor must, however, make a notation that the book value per share has changed [Book value of investment ÷ (Original shares held + Shares received through stock dividend or stock split)]. This new book value is used for all subsequent accounting purposes. If the investor does not have enough shares to receive a whole number of shares from the stock dividend or split, the investor may receive part of the stock dividend or split in cash equal to the market value of the fractional shares or in *fractional share warrants,* which the investor can sell. The investor may also acquire other fractional share warrants in the marketplace.

Special-Purpose Funds

40. Some special-purpose funds, such as funds established for dividends, payroll, and interest payments, require a segregation of a company's cash for such specific purposes and are classified as current assets. Other special-purpose funds are established either by contractual agreement or voluntarily for the purpose of systematically accumulating resources to meet specific future obligations. These are normally long-term funds and are classified on the balance sheet between current assets and property, plant, and equipment. Special-purpose funds required by contract and normally administered by an outside trustee include (a) a bond sinking fund to retire long-term debt, (b) a stock redemption fund to retire capital stock, and (c) a pension fund to meet pension obligations. Voluntarily established funds administered by an outside trustee or by the company include funds for plant expansion and for environmental improvements.

41. The accounting for a special-purpose long-term fund is basically straightforward. Each fund is involved in similar transactions and should be accounted for separately, with separate accounts maintained for each type of transaction that affects the fund. Typical special-purpose fund transactions and related journal entries are now presented in relation to a bond sinking fund.

a. Cash contributions are normally made to the fund in equal amounts at equal intervals. Sinking fund cash is debited, and cash is credited for the amount of the payment or contribution. The dollar amount of the payment is generally computed by dividing the desired fund balance in the future (the maturity value of the bond) by the amount of an ordinary annuity factor for the number of rents to be paid into the fund at the assumed rate of interest the fund will earn.

b. When cash from the fund is invested in some form of securities, sinking fund investment is debited and sinking fund cash is credited for the purchase price of the securities acquired.

c. When income from the securities is received, sinking fund cash is debited and sinking fund revenue is credited for the amount of revenue received.

d. When expenses are incurred in the operation of the fund, sinking fund expense is debited and sinking fund cash is credited for the amount of the expense paid.

e. When cash is needed to fulfill the purpose of the fund and the investment securities are sold (let us presume at a gain), sinking fund cash is debited for the amount of the selling price of the securities, sinking fund investment is credited for the carrying value of the securities, and gain on sale of sinking fund investment is credited for the excess of the sales price over the carrying value of the investment.

f. When the fund is used for the purpose for which it was established, bond payable is debited and sinking fund cash is credited for the amount of the bond.

g. If the fund has a cash balance remaining after all securities are sold, its purpose is fulfilled, and expenses are paid, the remaining cash should be returned to the company by a debit to cash and a credit to sinking fund cash for the balance remaining in the fund.

42. All nominal accounts pertaining to the fund will appear on the company's income statement and will be closed at the end of each period. The sinking fund cash balance and sinking fund investment balance will appear in the investment section of the company's balance sheet.

Cash Surrender Value of Life Insurance

43. Many companies take out insurance policies on the lives of their executives, naming the company itself as beneficiary. A company may acquire either a term or a whole-life insurance policy. A *whole-life insurance* policy provides benefits in the event of the insured's death and a *cash surrender value* that provides the owner of the policy with an amount of cash if the policy is canceled or expires. The cash surrender value increases each period in which premiums are paid and is classified as a long-term investment under investments and funds in the balance sheet.

44. The insurance company determines how much of each premium payment on a whole-life insurance policy represents the increase in the cash surrender value of the insurance policy. The remainder of the premium is recognized as insurance expense. To record the payment on a whole-life insurance policy, debit insurance expense for the difference between the premium payment and the determined amount of the increase in the cash surrender value, debit cash surrender value of life insurance for the amount of the increase as stipulated by the insurance company, and credit cash for the amount of the insurance premium. It should be noted that insurance expense can be reduced by the amount of any dividends received on the policy. If the insured dies, the beneficiary debits cash for the face value of the insurance policy, credits cash surrender value of life insurance for the carrying value of the investment, and credits gain on life insurance for the difference between the face value and the accumulated cash surrender value of the insurance policy. The periodic premiums on whole-life policies are not tax-deductible, and the proceeds from the policy are not taxable as income.

Appendix 13-1: Additional Issues Related to the Equity Method

45. Appendix 13-1 covers two technical accounting issues related to the equity method of accounting for long-term investments: (*a*) a change to or from the equity method, and (*b*) cases when the investor's share of investee losses exceeds the carrying value of the investment.

46. Changes to and from the equity method. An investor's interest in an investee can change over time as a result, for example, of acquisition of additional shares of stock or disposal of part of the investment. As these changes occur, the investor may gain or lose significant influence over the investee and, therefore, must change the way it accounts for the investment. If an investor that uses either the cost or the fair value method acquires additional shares that permit the investor to exercise

significant influence over the investee, the investor must *change to* the equity method. The objective of recording the change to the equity method is to make prior period financial statements appear as if the equity method had been applied during the prior periods. This retroactive treatment of the change makes the prior period financial statement comparable to the current and future statements that will reflect the equity method and requires an adjustment to the investment account and retained earnings.

47. When a *change* is made *to* the equity method, the amount of the adjustment is calculated by adjusting the investor's share of the investee's earnings for all periods in which the investment was held. Adjustments are made for (*a*) any amortization of the difference between the cost of the investment and the underlying interest in the investee's net assets at the date of acquisition, and (*b*) the investor's share of the dividends paid by the investee. In other words, the investor must determine the value of the investment account as if the investment had been accounted for by the equity method since its acquisition. Assuming that the adjustment calculation resulted in a net increase in the investment account, the change to the equity method would be recorded as a debit to investment and a credit to retained earnings for the amount calculated. In addition, if financial statements for periods before the equity method is adopted are presented, they must be restated to reflect the retroactive application of the equity method. The equity method is applied in the period of change and in subsequent periods. Amortization of any difference between the cost and underlying book value from the date of the original acquisition is continued.

48. An investor may lose significant influence over the investee because of a reduction in the number of shares held, for example, and *must change from* the equity method to either the cost or the fair value method. The accounting recognition of this change requires only that the carrying value of the investment at the time of the change become the cost basis for the new method and subsequent accounting. No retroactive calculations or future amortizations of undervalued or overvalued assets are required.

49. Losses in excess of investment. An investee may sustain an operating loss or losses that, when recognized by an investor, would cause the investment account to have a credit balance. If the investor's share of the investee's losses is greater than the balance in the investment account, the investor normally should not record additional losses after the investment account reaches zero. The equity method should be resumed only after the investee has had profitable operations and the investor's share of the profits exceeds the investor's unrecorded share of the investee's losses incurred while the application of the equity method was suspended. Under special circumstances, such as the identification of an isolated nonrecurring cause for the operating loss, the equity method should continue to be used even though its application results in a credit balance for the investment account.

SELF-STUDY LEARNING   Items marked with an asterisk (*) refer to the Appendix.

Key Terms and Concepts

Provide the appropriate term or terms to complete each of the following statements:

1. When a company reports an investment security at its fair value or market value, this accounting practice is often referred to as _____ or _____ accounting.

2. _____ receivables represent instruments to receive cash or another financial asset on demand or on or before a specified date.

3. On the date of acquisition, the valuation of an investment is governed by the _____ principle.

4. A(n) _____ security is an equity investment bought and held principally for the purpose of selling it in the near term.

5. If the fair value of an equity security investment accounted for under the fair value method increases in the period since its acquisition, the increase is referred to as a(n) _____ gain.

6. When an investor receives a dividend from an investee in excess of the investee's earnings since the investor's date of acquisition of the investment, the dividend is referred to as a(n) _____ dividend.

7. If a company has acquired enough shares of another company to influence significantly its financial and operating policies, the _____ method is the appropriate accounting method to use.

8. When an investor acquires more than 50 percent of an investee's stock, it should use the _____ method to account for the investment and prepare _____ financial statements for external reporting purposes.

9. A company that receives shares of stock through a(n) _____ or a(n) _____ does not make a sacrifice to receive the additional shares.

10. A(n) _____ insurance policy normally provides an amount of cash, referred to as the _____, which increases with each insurance premium payment.

True-False

Indicate by circling the appropriate response whether each of the following statements is true (T) or false (F):

T F   1. Equity securities are represented only by common, preferred, and other capital stock.

T F   2. When cash is paid for shares of stock, the amount of cash paid is normally considered the fair value of the stock at the date of acquisition.

T F   3. An equity security is considered to have a fair value if the security is traded on a national security exchange or on the over-the-counter market.

T F 4. The fair value accounting method applies only to equity securities that are common stock.

T F 5. Equity and debt securities can be classified as held-to-maturity securities.

T F 6. Dividends received on equity securities classified as trading securities are recorded as dividend revenue.

T F 7. When an investor uses the cost method to account for an investment in common stock, the carrying value of the investment always remains equal to the acquisition cost of the common stock.

T F 8. The cost method must be used to value a common stock investment if the stock does not have a readily determinable market value.

T F 9. As a general guideline, the APB stated that if an investor has less than 20 percent of an investee's outstanding voting stock, the investor usually cannot exercise significant influence over the investee.

T F 10. The equity method must be used to account for an investment in common stock if the investor can exercise significant influence over the financial and operating policies of the investee.

T F 11. If an investee reports a material extraordinary gain, the investor should also report its proportional share of the extraordinary gain in a similar manner in its income statement.

T F 12. An investor holding 35 percent of an investee's preferred stock should use the equity method to account for the preferred stock investment.

T F 13. A stock right with a readily determinable market value should be classified as either a trading or held-for-sale security.

T F 14. Stock rights must be either exercised or allowed to lapse.

T F 15. Since an investor makes no sacrifice to receive stock rights, no amount is recorded as a cost of the stock rights.

T F 16. If an investor does not own enough shares to receive a whole number of shares from a company issuing a stock dividend, the investor normally will receive part of the dividend as cash or fractional share warrants.

T F 17. The purpose of special-purpose funds is to accumulate resources systematically to meet specific future obligations.

T F 18. The cash surrender value of a whole-life insurance policy is normally classified as a temporary investment.

T F *19. The objective in accounting for a change from either the cost or the fair value method to the equity method of accounting for an investment is to make prior period financial statements appear as if the equity method had been applied during the prior periods.

T F *20. If an investor is using the equity method to account for an investment and the recognition of the investee's operating loss would result in a credit balance in the investment account, the loss recognized is normally limited to an amount that would make the investment account balance zero.

Multiple Choice

Select the best response for each of the following items, and circle the corresponding letter:

1. A fundamental financial instrument that represents an ownership interest in an entity is a(n):

   a. Unconditional receivable.
   b. Forward contract.
   c. Equity instrument.
   d. Option.

2. When a company acquires a common stock and a sweetener consisting of another security, the cost of the lump-sum purchase is:

   a. Recorded in the common stock investment account.
   b. Allocated between the common stock and other security on the basis of the relative fair value approach.
   c. Allocated between the common stock and the other security on the basis of the number of shares or units of each security acquired.
   d. Allocated between an investment account (the common stock) and an expense account (the other security).

3. Depending on an equity security's characteristics, all but which one of the following

accounting methods could be used to account for the investment?

a. Cost.
b. Equity.
c. Fair value.
d. Lower of cost or market.

4. The unrealized loss account from recognizing the change in the fair value of an *available-for-sale* equity investment should be reported as a:

a. Loss on the income statement.
b. Deferred charge on the balance sheet.
c. Negative element (debit) balance in owners' equity.
d. Prior period adjustment in retained earnings.

5. The unrealized loss account from recognizing the change in the fair value of a *trading* equity investment should be reported as a:

a. Loss on the income statement.
b. Deferred charge on the blance sheet.
c. Negative element (debit) balance in owners' equity.
d. Prior period adjustment in retained earnings.

6. An investor receiving a liquidating dividend should recognize it by:

a. Decreasing the cash account.
b. Decreasing the investment revenue account.
c. Decreasing the investment account.
d. Increasing the investment revenue account.

7. The investment account under the equity method is debited or credited for each of the following events and transactions:

	Purchase of Investment	Recognition of Investee Profit	Receipt of Dividend	Amortization of the Excess Cost over Book Value
a.	Debit	Debit	Debit	Debit
b.	Debit	Debit	Credit	Credit
c.	Debit	Debit	Credit	Debit
d.	Debit	Credit	Credit	Credit

8. The valuation of a share of stock acquired by exercise of a stock right is equal to:

a. The market value of the stock on the exercise date.
b. The book value of the stock right(s) surrendered.
c. The exercise price for the stock.
d. The book value of the stock right(s) surrendered plus the exercise price of the stock.

9. The cash account for a special-purpose fund designed to provide future funds for plant expansion will be debited to record:

a. Periodic contributions to the fund.
b. Purchase of securities for the fund.
c. Payment to acquire the new plant facility.
d. Expenses of operating the fund.

10. When a company is the beneficiary of a whole-life insurance policy on one of its officers or executives, the company:

a. Treats the insurance premium as an expense for book and tax purposes.
b. Recognizes an increasing amount of cash surrender value each period in which a premium is paid.
c. Recognizes as taxable income the proceeds from the policy upon the death of the insured.
d. Receives the cash surrender value of the insurance policy upon the death of the insured.

Extended Problem

Togliatti Inc. acquired three equity investments on January 1, 1995. Data about these investments follows:

	Red Co.	White Co.	Blue Co.
Cost of investment 1/1/95	$ 90,000	$ 140,000	$ 120,000
Number of shares acquired	10,000	20,000	1,500
Percentage of interest in investee	10%	30%	5%
Significant influence over investee operations	No	Yes	No
Book value of investee at date of acquisition	$ 800,000	$1,300,000	$1,800,000
Purpose of investment	Growth	Control	Growth
Net profit for 1995	$ 70,000	$ 84,000	$ 150,000
Dividend paid in 1995	$ 40,000	$ 25,000	$ 80,000
Market value per share on 12/31/95	$14	$8.50	none
Assumed life of all depreciable tangible and intangible assets	10 years	10 years	10 years

On June 30, 1995, Togliatti Inc. acquired 2,000 stock rights of Lada Co. for $2.50 per stock right. The rights expire on March 31, 1996.

REQUIRED

a. For each of the three companies, give the proper accounting method to use for the investment.
b. Complete the following table using the data for Red Co. on the preceding page. Indicate the proper dollar amount for each of the accounts as of December 31, 1995, assuming Red Co. had used each of the three methods listed (even though the method may not be correct given your answer to step a above). If the amount is zero, enter "-0-." Support your answers.

	Cost Method	Equity Method	Market Value Method[a]
Investment	$_____	$_____	$_____
Income on/from investment	$_____	$_____	$_____
Unrealized holding gain/(loss)	$_____	$_____	$_____

[a]Assume the security is a held-for-sale security.

c. Assume that on January 4, 1996, all of the shares of Red Co. are sold for $142,000. Using the answers from step b above, prepare the journal entry to record the sale of the Red Co.

investment assuming each of the following accounting methods: cost; equity; fair value, trading security; and fair value, available-for-sale security.
d. Assume that for 1995 the proper accounting method for Blue Co. is the cost method and that Togliatti Inc. purchases an additional 6,000 shares on January 4, 1996, for $400,000 when Blue Co.'s net assets are valued at $1,920,000. This purchase increases the percentage of Togliatti's holding to 25 percent and gives it the ability to exercise significant influence over the financial and operating policies of Blue Co. Assume further that during 1996 Blue Co. has profits of $130,000 and distributes a dividend of $1.20 per share. Prepare all appropriate 1996 journal entries for Togliatti Inc. related to its investment in Blue Co.
e. Assume that the fair value of the stock rights on December 31, 1995, was $2.15 per stock right. On March 1, 1996, Togliatti exercises 1,500 rights and acquires 1,500 shares of Lada Co. for 1,500 rights and $19 per share. The remainder of the stock rights are allowed to lapse on March 31, 1996. Prepare the appropriate entry (or entries) for December 31, 1995, March 1, 1996, and March 31, 1996.

COMMON ERRORS

The first statement in each of the "common errors" listed here is *incorrect*. Each incorrect statement is followed by a corrected statement and an explanation.

1. An investment in common stock acquired by exchange of a nonmonetary asset for the stock is recorded at the book value of the asset surrendered. *Wrong*

An investment in common stock acquired by exchange of a nonmonetary asset for the stock is recorded at the fair value of the asset surrendered or stock received, whichever is more readily determinable. *Right*

Whether the exchange involves only plant assets, as discussed in Chapter 11, or investments in common stock, the accounting for the exchange involving nonmonetary assets is the same. That is, the exchange of common stock for a dissimilar nonmonetary asset represents the culmination of the earnings process of the asset surrendered and the beginning of the earnings process of the common

stock received. Accordingly, the common stock investment should be recorded at the fair value of the asset surrendered or its fair value, whichever is more readily available. If the recorded book value is greater or less than the fair value of the non-monetary asset surrendered, a gain or loss must be recognized. Normally the fair value of the stock received is used if the stock is actively traded, because its fair value is readily available from the organized stock market. When the stock's fair value is not known, the fair value of the asset surrendered is used as the value at which the acquired shares of stock are recorded. In either case, the common stock investment is recorded at a fair value, not at the book value of the asset surrendered (unless neither of the fair values can be determined).

2. If an investor acquires 20 percent or more of the investee's outstanding voting stock, the equity method must be used to account for the stock investment. *Wrong*

If an investor acquires a sufficient number of shares of an investee's outstanding voting stock to exercise significant influence over the operating and financing policies of the investee, the equity method must be used to account for the investment. *Right*

It is very easy to use the 20 percent guideline as a hard and fast rule for determining when the equity method should be used. In *Opinion No. 18,* however, the APB set the 20 percent guideline as a numerical benchmark to indicate the number of shares whose ownership may be presumed to permit the investor to exercise *significant influence* over the investee's operating and financing policies. Significant influence is the real test, and the ownership of 20 percent or more of the investee's outstanding voting stock is not necessary to demonstrate it. Significant influence can be demonstrated, for example, by representation on the investee's board of directors, material intercompany transactions, or a concentration of ownership relative to other shareholders, regardless of the number of shares owned. Nor does ownership of more than 20 percent of the investee's stock always establish significant influence. Therefore, the equity method is appropriate for any investment when the investor exercises significant influence over the investee, which may be achieved with more or less than 20 percent of the investee's outstanding voting shares. All facts and circumstances surrounding the situation must be considered to determine if the equity method should be applied.

3. Only transfers of equity securities from the available-for-sale security classification to the trading security classification require the transfer to be accounted for at fair value. *Wrong*

Transfers of equity securities from any category of equity security to another category of equity security require the transfer to be accounted for at fair value. *Right*

Statement No. 115 requires that the transfer of any equity security from one category to another be accounted for at fair value. There is a difference, however, in whether or not an adjustment is necessary to recognize previously unrealized holding gains or losses.

When a security in the available-for-sale category is transferred to the trading category, the amount in the unrealized holding gain/loss account must be closed and realized immediately at the time of the transfer. Since any unrealized holding gains or losses have been deferred as an element of stockholders' equity, they must be realized in income just as the unrealized gains or losses on any other equity security in the trading category. On the other hand, securities in the trading category always have had any changes in fair value reflected in earnings

in the period of the change. Accordingly, when securities are transferred from the trading category, no adjustment is needed to recognize previously unrealized gains or losses.

All transfers of equity securities between the trading and available-for-sale categories are accounted for at fair value. Some transfers require an adjustment of previously unrecognized unrealized holding gains or losses; this is the case of transfers from the available-for-sale category to the trading category.

4. If the acquisition cost of an investment accounted for under the equity method is greater than the underlying proportional share of the investee's net assets on the date of acquisition, the excess of cost over book value is amortized by a debit to amortization expense—investment and a credit to investment. *Wrong*

If the acquisition cost of an investment accounted for under the equity method is greater than the underlying proportional share of the investee's net assets on the date of acquisition, the excess of cost over book value is amortized by a debit to investment revenue and a credit to investment. *Right*

Normally, an asset is not amortized or reduced in value by a debit to a revenue account, but the excess of cost over the underlying book value of an investee's net assets is handled in this special way. The excess cost of the investor's investment over the investee's underlying net assets arises because the price paid for the investment is greater than the investee's recorded cost of its assets; that is, some assets are valued at less than their fair values or the investee has unrecorded goodwill. Since the investor records its share of the investee's net income, which includes depreciation based on the understated or unrecorded asset values, the investor must adjust or reduce the reported income to an amount that reflects depreciation based on the fair values of the investee's assets at the date of the stock acquisition. Thus the investor recognizes the amortization of the excess of cost over underlying book value as a reduction in the reported income of the investee, not as an operating expense. In essence, the investor's earnings from the investee after adjustment are equal to an amount that the investee would report *if* the fair value of the assets were depreciated to calculate net income. The excess of cost over book value should be amortized over the remaining estimated useful life of the assets to which the excess is attributed, that is, undervalued asset or assets and/or unrecorded goodwill.

It should be noted that if an investee's assets are overvalued in terms of the price paid by an investor, the book value of this investee's assets will exceed the cost of the investment. In this situation the investor must adjust reported earnings by debiting investment and crediting investment revenue. The rationale for this entry is similar to the explanation given for the treatment of excess cost over book value, except that the amortization is adjusting reported net income to reflect the investee's overstated and hence overdepreciated assets.

5. An investor records the receipt of a stock dividend by debiting investment and crediting dividend revenue for the current market value of the stock. *Wrong*

An investor makes no entry to record the receipt of a stock dividend. *Right*

When an investor receives a stock dividend, *no* amount is recorded to recognize the stock dividend. Admittedly, the investor receives additional shares (number of shares held before the issuance of the stock dividend times the stock dividend rate). However, the investor makes no sacrifice to acquire the additional shares; they are, in effect, "free." Therefore, no entry is made, but the investor must calculate a new book value or cost basis for the investment shares [Carrying value of investment ÷ (Shares held before stock dividend + Shares received through stock dividend)]. For subsequent accounting purposes, this new cost basis is used. For example, if after receiving a stock dividend an investor were to sell 100 shares for an amount that exceeded the cost of the shares, the investor would debit cash for the market value of the 100 shares and credit investment for the *new* cost basis of the shares and gain on sale of investment for the difference between the market value and the *new* cost basis of the shares sold. Because an investor receives "free" shares when a stock split occurs, the investor's accounting treatment for a stock split is similar to that of a stock dividend.

ANSWERS

Items marked with an asterisk (*) refer to the Appendix.

Key Terms and Concepts

1. fair value, mark-to-market
2. unconditional
3. cost
4. trading
5. unrealized
6. liquidating
7. equity
8. equity, consolidated
9. stock dividend, stock split
10. whole-life, cash surrender value

True-False

1. F   Common, preferred, and other classes of stock are considered equity securities. In addition, the right to acquire the stock (for example, through warrants, rights, and call options) and the right to dispose of the stock (for example, through put options), both at fixed or determinable prices, are also considered equity securities.
2. T
3. T
4. F   *Statement No. 115* requires that equity securities be accounted for under the fair value method if the security's fair value is readily available. Moreover, *Statement No. 115* interprets equity securities broadly. Besides common stock, it includes stock rights, nonredeemable preferred stock, and stock warrants.

5. F   Only debt securities, such as bonds, can be classified as held-to-maturity securities. Equity securities, such as common stock, can be classified as either trading or available-for-sale securities, but not as held-to-maturity securities.
6. T
7. F   Normally the carrying value of an investment accounted for by the cost method is equal to the acquisition cost of the investment. When the investee, however, distributes a *liquidating dividend,* that is, a dividend in excess of the investor's cumulative share of the investee's earnings since the shares were acquired, the investment account must be reduced by the amount of the liquidating dividend.
8. F   A stock may not have a readily determinable fair or market value, but the investor may have a sufficient number of shares to exercise influence over the financial and operating policies of the investee. If this is the case, then the equity method should be used to account for the investment. In most situations, however, the cost method should be used if the equity investment did not have a readily determinable market value.
9. T
10. T
11. T
12. F   Normally, an investor with a 35 percent holding of common stock would use the equity method. Regardless of the percent-

age holding of preferred stock, however, an investor will never use the equity method because preferred stock does not give the investor the ability to exercise significant influence over the financial and operating policies of the investee.

13. T

14. F Stock rights may be exercised or allowed to lapse, but they may also be sold. After the stock rights are issued, they can be bought and sold in the marketplace. Accordingly, if an investor does not exercise the stock rights, it is normally better to sell them than to let them lapse and receive nothing for them. If the market price is greater or less than the cost of the stock right when it is sold, a gain or loss must be recognized.

15. F An investor makes no sacrifice to receive stock rights, but an amount is recorded as the cost of the rights received. The amount

assigned to the stock rights is determined by allocating a portion of the carrying value of the investment in common stock (for which the stock rights were issued) in accordance with the relative fair value method.

16. T
17. T
18. F The cash surrender value of a whole-life insurance policy is normally classified as a long-term investment under investments and funds in the balance sheet.

*19. T
*20. T

Multiple Choice

1. c	6. c
2. b	7. b
3. d	8. d
4. c	9. a
5. a	10. b

Extended Problem

a. Proper accounting method for the each of the investment securities:
Red Co.: fair value method because there is a determinable fair value and sufficient shares are not acquired to use the equity method.
White Co.: equity method because the acquisition of 20,000 shares gives Togliatti Inc. 30 percent interest, which is more than the benchmark of 20 percent, in White Co. and Togliatti Inc. has significant influence over the financial and operating policies of White Co.
Blue Co.: cost method because the stock does not have a determinable fair value. No market value is available on December 31, 1995.

b. Account values as of December 31, 1995, assuming the three accounting methods were applied to Red Co.:

	Cost Method	Equity Method	Market Value Method[a]
Investment	$90,000	$92,000[c]	$140,000[e]
Income on/from investment	$4,000[b]	$6,000[d]	$4,000[b]
Unrealized holding gain/(loss)	$-0-	$-0-	$50,000[f]

[a]Assume the security is a held-for-sale security.

[b]$40,000 × 10% = $4,000.

[c]Original cost of investment	$90,000
Profit ($70,000 × 10%)	7,000
Dividend ($40,000 × 10%)	(4,000)
Amortization of cost in excess of book value*	(1,000)
	$92,000

*Cost of 10% interest	$90,000
Book value of 10% interest ($800,000 × 10%)	80,000
Excess cost over book value	$10,000

Excess cost over book value amortized over 10 years: $10,000/10 years = $1,000 per year.

dProfit ($70,000 × 10%) .... $ 7,000
Amortization of cost in excess of book value ...   (1,000)
                                                   $ 6,000

eOriginal cost of investment .... $ 90,000
Increase in fair value
[($14 − $9) = $5 × 10,000]   50,000
                                                   $140,000

fSince the investment is a held-for-sale security, the unrealized gain of $50,000 [($14 − $9) = $5 × 10,000] is reported in ownership equity.

c. Journal entry to record sale of Red Co. investment on January 4, 1996:

Cost method:
Cash.. 142,000
    Investment..   90,000
    Realized gain on sale of security   52,000

Equity method:
Cash.. 142,000
    Investment..   92,000
    Realized gain on sale of security   48,000

Fair value method (trading security):
Cash.. 142,000
    Investment..   140,000
    Realized gain on sale of security   2,000

Fair value method (available-for-sale security):
Cash.. 142,000
Unrealized holding gain... 50,000
    Investment..   140,000
    Realized gain on sale of security   52,000

d. Journal entries for 1996 for investment in Blue Co.:

Jan. 2
Investment—Blue Co. ($123,000a − $120,000)..................................... 3,000
    Retained earnings...   3,000

To adjust investment account and retained earnings to reflect equity method applied retroactively.

aOriginal cost of investment $120,000
Profit ($150,000 × 5%).................................   7,500
Dividend ($30,000 × 5%) ....   (1,500)
Amortization of cost in excess of book valueb ....   (3,000)
                                                     $123,000

bCost of 5% interest...................................... $120,000
Book value of 5% interest ($1,800,000 × 5%)   90,000
Excess cost over book value......................... $ 30,000

Excess cost over book value amortized over 10 years: $30,000/10 years = $3,000 per year.

Investment—Blue Co.	400,000	
Cash..		400,000

Dec. 31

Investment—Blue Co. ($130,000 × 25%)...............................	32,500	
Investment revenue...		32,500

Cash ($1.20 × 7,500 shares)	9,000	
Investment—Blue Co.		9,000

Investment revenue ($1,000 + $1,600)...................................	4,600^c	
Investment—Blue Co.		4,600

^{c}Cost of additional 20% interest.........................	$400,000
Book value of 20% interest ($1,920,000 × 20%)	384,000
Excess cost over book value.............................	$ 16,000

Excess cost over book value amortized over 10 years: $16,000/10 years = $1,600 per year.

Amortization of 5% interest............................	$3,000
Amortization of 20% interest	1,600
Total amortization..	$4,600

e. Journal entries for stock rights in Lada Co.:

Dec. 31, 1995

Unrealized holding loss	700	
Investment—Lada Co. stock rights.................................		700

($2.50 – $2.15) = $.35 × 2,000 shares = $700.

March 1, 1996

Investment—Lada Co. stock	31,725	
Cash (1,500 shares × $19)...		28,500
Investment—Lada Co. stock rights.................................		3,225

($5,000 – $700) = $4,300 × 75% = $3,225.

March 31, 1996

Loss on lapse of stock rights...	1,075	
Investment—Lada Co. stock rights.................................		1,075

$4,300 – $3,225 = $1,075.

14 FINANCIAL INSTRUMENTS: DEBT SECURITIES

CHAPTER OBJECTIVES

After reading Chapter 14 and completing the questions, cases, exercises, and problems from the text chapter, you should be able to:

1. Distinguish the various types of debt securities.
2. Calculate the issue (market) price of a debt security both on the contract date and between interest dates.
3. Describe the relationship between the issue price and face value of a debt security and the stated rate of interest and market rate of interest at the issue date, and the nature of the premium or discount on a debt security.
4. Prepare the journal entry required to record debt securities issued on the contract date or between interest dates for both the issuer and the investor.
5. Describe the rationale for amortizing the premium or discount on debt as an adjustment to interest expense or interest revenue over the term of the debt securities.
6. Calculate and prepare the journal entries required to record interest expense or interest revenue and the decrease or increase in the book value

of debt securities (the premium or discount amortization) by the effective interest method at various dates, including the first interest payment date after debt securities are issued between interest dates and the end of an accounting period that does not coincide with the interest date.

7. Prepare the journal entries related to debt issued for cash, for noncash assets, and for cash and some other right or obligation for both the debtor and the creditor.
8. Prepare the journal entries required to report investments in certain debt securities at their fair value and to record transfers of such securities between categories.
9. Prepare the journal entries related to an early extinguishment or retirement of debt.
10. Prepare the journal entries related to convertible debt.
11. Prepare the journal entries related to debt issued with detachable warrants and to the exercise of warrants.
12. Prepare the journal entries related to troubled debt restructurings for both the debtor and the creditor.

CHAPTER REVIEW

Introduction

1. The two types of fundamental debt securities are bonds and notes. A *bond* or *note* is a written agreement whereby the issuing company generally promises to pay a specified amount of cash (called the *maturity value, face value, par value,* or *principal*) on a designated maturity date plus periodic cash interest at a specified rate (called the *stated rate, nominal rate,* or *coupon rate*) of the face value. The

terms of bonds, which often are traded in security markets, are specified in an *indenture*; whereas the terms of notes, which are negotiable instruments transferable by endorsement, usually are specified directly on the note. Other terms associated with bonds and notes (referred to simply as debt) follow:

a. *Term debt*. Debt securities that become due or mature on a single date.

b. *Serial debt*. Debt securities that become due or mature in installments.

c. *Deep discount* or *zero-coupon debt*. Non-interest-bearing debt securities.

d. *Debenture debt*. Unsecured debt securities that have no security other than the general financial strength of the issuing company.

e. *Senior debt*. Secured debt securities that have first claim among debt holders.

f. *Subordinate* or *junior debt*. Secured debt securities that have priority after another class of creditors.

g. *Guaranty debt*. Debt securities on which a third party guarantees payment of principal and interest in the event the issuing company defaults.

h. *Registered debt*. Debt securities for which the issuing company maintains a record of ownership and all changes in ownership for purposes of paying interest and principal.

i. *Bearer* or *coupon debt*. Debt securities on which interest and principal are paid to whoever presents evidence of ownership.

j. *Revenue debt*. Debt securities on which interest and principal are paid from a specified revenue source.

k. *Callable debt*. Debt securities that contain a call provision allowing the issuing company to retire the debt by paying a specified amount to debt holders.

l. *Convertible debt*. Debt securities that contain a conversion option allowing the debt holders to convert or exchange the debt for shares of capital stock of the issuing company.

2. The market price of a bond or note is equal to the present value of the face value (an amount for term debt or an ordinary annuity for serial debt) and the periodic interest payments (an ordinary annuity for term debt) discounted at the *market rate of interest* for financial instruments of similar risk at that date. Likewise, the market price of a non-interest-bearing bond or note is equal to the present value of the face amount discounted at the market rate of interest. Bonds and notes are not risk-free. The issuing company may be unable to pay interest or the face value when these amounts become due. This type of risk is called *credit risk*. Moreover, because the market value of bonds and notes varies inversely with the market rate of interest, investors incur a risk, called *market risk,* that the market value of bonds and notes will decline due to an increase in interest rates. When the market rate of interest is equal to the stated rate of interest, bonds are issued at *par,* since the issue price of the bonds is equal to their face value. When the market rate of interest is lower than the stated rate of interest, bonds are issued at a *premium,* since the issue price of the bonds is greater than their face value. When the market rate of interest is higher than the stated rate of interest, bonds are issued at a *discount,* since the issue price of the bonds is less than their face value. The market rate of interest may differ from the stated rate of interest for various reasons, including the time elapsing between the printing and issuing of bonds.

3. Accounting for and reporting of debt securities, such as bonds and notes, and some compound financial instruments from the perspective of both the issuer and the investor are described in this chapter review.

Unconditional Debt Securities

4. Unconditional debt securities, such as bonds and notes, are recognized by the issuer and investor at the exchange date on the basis of the cash or cash equivalent price on that date and are measured, subsequent to the exchange date, at their present value by the effective interest method. These concepts apply equally to bonds and notes. Thus, unless stated otherwise in this chapter review, the word *notes* can be substituted for the word *bonds,* and vice versa, without any loss of generality.

5. **Debt issued for cash.** When bonds are issued for cash on the contract date specified in the debenture, the issuer should debit cash and credit bonds payable for the issue price of the bonds. Coincidentally, the investor should debit investment in bonds and credit cash for the cost (issue price) of the bonds. Alternatively, the issuer and the investor may record the bonds payable and investment in bonds at the face value of the bonds and any difference between the issue price (cost) and the face value in separate discount or premium accounts. Hereinafter, for simplicity, it is assumed that the bonds are recorded by the issuer and investor in one account, net of any discount or premium. Bonds payable should be reported by the issuer on the balance sheet as a noncurrent or long-term liability. Investment in bonds should be reported on the balance sheet as a current or noncurrent asset on the basis of the criteria described in Chapter 5.

6. The issuer and investor should amortize a discount or premium as an adjustment to interest expense and interest revenue over the term of the

bonds. The reasons for amortizing the discount or premium are twofold. First, the discount or premium is amortized so that at the maturity date the book value of the bonds is equal to the face value. Second, interest is a payment for the use of money. Interest over the term of bonds, therefore, is equal to the sum of the face value and the total cash interest paid less the issue price. When bonds are issued at par, the issue price is equal to the face value, and thus total interest expense/revenue over the term of the bonds is equal to the cash interest paid. Conversely, when bonds are issued at a discount, the issue price is less than the face value, and thus total interest expense/revenue over the term of the bonds is equal to the cash interest paid plus the discount. Alternatively, when bonds are issued at a premium, the issue price is greater than the face value, and thus total interest expense/revenue over the term of the bonds is equal to the cash interest paid less the premium. Finally, because the effect is immaterial, premiums or discounts on investments in trading debt securities customarily are not amortized by the investor.

7. There are two methods of amortizing premiums and discounts on unconditional debt securities, the effective interest method and the straight-line method. *APB Opinion No. 21,* however, states that the straight-line method may be used only if the results obtained are not materially different from those that would result from the effective interest method.

8. Under the *effective interest method,* the issuer's periodic interest expense and the investor's periodic interest revenue are determined directly by multiplying the book value of the bonds at the beginning of each interest period by the effective (historical/market) rate of interest at which the bonds were issued. The decrease or increase in the book value of the bonds (the premium or discount amortization) for each interest period is determined indirectly as the difference between the cash interest paid, calculated at the stated rate, and the interest expense or interest revenue, calculated at the effective rate. Specifically, when the premium or discount is amortized by the effective interest method, on the interest payment date the issuer should (*a*) credit cash for the face value of the bonds multiplied by the stated rate of interest, (*b*) debit interest expense for the book value of the bonds at the beginning of the interest period multiplied by the effective rate of interest, and (*c*) either credit or debit bonds payable for the difference between the cash interest paid and the interest expense. Coincidentally, under the effective interest method, the investor should record a parallel journal entry on the interest payment date: (*a*) a debit to cash for the face value of the bonds multiplied by the stated rate of interest, (*b*) a credit to interest revenue for the

book value of the bonds at the beginning of the interest period multiplied by the effective rate of interest, and (*c*) either a debit or a credit to investment in bonds for the difference between the cash interest paid and the interest revenue.

9. Under the *straight-line method,* the periodic premium or discount amortization is determined directly by dividing the premium or discount by the number of interest periods over the term of the bonds. The issuer's periodic interest expense and the investor's periodic interest revenue are determined indirectly on an interest payment date as the cash interest paid (face value of the bonds multiplied by the stated rate of interest) plus the discount amortization or minus the premium amortization.

10. The straight-line method results in a constant amount of interest expense/revenue each period over the term of the bonds, since the cash interest paid and premium or discount amortization are constant amounts each period. Because the premium or discount amortization causes the book value of the bonds to change each period, the periodic interest expense/revenue as a percentage of the book value of the bonds at the beginning of each period is not a constant rate over the term of the bonds. In contrast, the effective interest method results in a constant rate of periodic interest expense/revenue as a percentage of the book value of the bonds at the beginning of each period. Since this constant rate is the effective (historical) rate at which the bonds were issued and since the book value of the bonds at any point in time is equal to the present value of the remaining cash flows discount at the historical rate, the effective interest method is considered to be conceptually preferable.

11. Debt issued for noncash assets. When a debt security, such as a note, is issued or received for a noncash asset, the present value of the note is presumed to be equal to either the fair value of the noncash asset or the discounted present value of the note, calculated at the current market rate of interest, whichever is more clearly determinable. Thus, in this circumstance, the issuing company should debit the appropriate noncash asset account and credit notes payable for either the fair value of the noncash asset or the discounted present value of the note. Coincidentally, the investor should (*a*) debit notes receivable for either the fair value of the noncash asset or the discounted present value of the note, (*b*) credit the appropriate noncash asset account for the book value of the noncash asset, and (*c*) recognize a gain or loss or sales revenue and cost of goods sold on the transfer of the noncash asset or merchandise. When the note has a stated rate of interest equal to the current market rate of interest, the face value of the note equals its present value, and thus there is no discount. Conversely, when the note either is non-interest-bearing or has a stated rate of interest that is below the current market rate of interest, the face value of the note exceeds its present value, and thus there is a discount. In such circumstances, the issuer and investor should amortize the discount as interest expense and interest revenue over the term of the note, using the effective interest method. If the note is interest-bearing, the increase in the book value of the note (the periodic discount amortization) should be equal to the interest expense or interest revenue, calculated at the effective rate, minus the cash interest paid or payable, calculated at the stated rate. If the note is non-interest-bearing, the increase in the book value of the note (the periodic discount amortization) should be equal to the interest expense or interest revenue calculated at the effective rate.

12. Debt issued for cash and other rights or obligations. When a debt security, such as a note, and some other right or obligation (such as a right or commitment to buy or sell goods at a discount in the future) are issued for cash, the present value of the note is imputed by calculating the discounted present value of the note at the current market rate of interest. Specifically, in this circumstance, the issuing company should (*a*) debit cash for the amount received, (*b*) credit notes payable for the present value of the note, and (*c*) credit unearned revenue for the discount (the excess of the face value over the discounted present value of the note). Coincidentally, the investor should (*a*) credit cash for the amount advanced, (*b*) debit notes receivable for the present value of the note, and (*c*) debit an asset account (such as prepaid purchases) for the discount (the excess of the face value over the discounted present value of the note). Subsequently, the issuer and investor should amortize the discount as interest expense and interest revenue over the term of the note, using the effective interest method. In addition, as the goods are sold to the customer (investor), the issuer should debit unearned revenue and credit sales revenue, and the investor should debit purchases or inventory and credit prepaid purchases for the discount multiplied by the ratio of the discounted goods sold or purchased during the period to the total goods committed to be sold or purchased at a discount.

13. Debt issue costs. The issuing company incurs various expenditures in connection with a bond issue, including the cost of printing the bonds, attorneys' fees, and the cost of preparing the *prospectus*, a brochure that sets forth details of the bond issue. There are two methods of accounting for such *debt issue costs*. Under one method, the debt issue costs are viewed as providing economic benefit to the issuer over the period the debt is outstanding, and thus these costs are recorded as an asset, deferred debt issue costs, and amortized to expense over the period of time from the issue date to the maturity date. Under the other method, the debt issue costs are recorded as a reduction of the bonds payable, thereby either increasing the discount or decreasing the premium and increasing interest expense over the period the bonds are outstanding.

14. Accrued debt interest. When a debt security's interest payment date does not coincide with the end of the accounting period, an adjusting journal entry should be recorded to accrue interest for the period since the most recent interest payment date. Specifically, in this circumstance, the issuer (or investor) should record an adjusting journal entry at the end of the accounting period similar to the journal entry recorded on the interest payment date, except that (*a*) interest payable should be credited (or interest receivable debited) instead of cash, and (*b*) the amounts recorded in each of the accounts should be equal to the amounts that would otherwise be recorded on the next interest payment date multiplied by a ratio of the period since the most recent interest payment date to the full interest period. Likewise, when the interest is paid during the next accounting period, the issuer (or investor) should record a journal entry for the interest payment similar to the normal journal entry, except that (*a*) interest payable should be debited (or interest receivable credited) for the amount accrued at the end of the previous accounting period and (*b*) the amounts recorded for interest expense (or interest revenue) and the decrease or increase in the book value of the debt (the premium or discount amortization) should be equal to the amounts that would otherwise be recorded on the interest payment date multiplied by a ratio of the period since the end of the previous accounting period to the full interest period. Alternatively, the adjusting journal entry may be reversed by the issuer and investor at the beginning of the next accounting period, and the normal journal entry for the full interest period may be recorded on the interest payment date. Likewise, interest accruing on non-interest-bearing notes should be recorded by the issuer (or investor) at the end of each accounting period over the term of the notes by debiting interest expense (or crediting interest revenue) and crediting notes payable (or debiting notes receivable).

15. Debt issued between interest dates. When debt securities, such as bonds, are issued between interest dates, a portion of the proceeds represents interest accrued on the bonds from the date of the bond contract up to the issue date. In this circumstance, the issuer's (or investor's) journal entry to record the bonds should be modified to credit interest payable (or to debit interest receivable) for the amount of accrued interest. Additionally, under the effective interest method, the issuer (or investor) should record a journal entry for the first interest payment similar to the normal journal entry, except that (*a*) interest payable should be debited (or interest receivable credited) for the amount accrued on the date the bonds were issued, and (*b*) the amounts recorded for interest expense (or interest revenue) and for the decrease or increase in the book value of the bonds (the premium or discount amortization) should be equal to the amounts that would otherwise be recorded if the bonds had been issued on the contract date (or previous interest date) multiplied by a ratio of the period since the bonds were issued (or purchased) to the full interest period.

16. Debt paid at maturity. When term or serial bonds or notes are paid at the maturity date, the issuer should debit bonds or notes payable and credit cash for the face value of the debt. Coincidentally, the investor should debit cash and credit investment in bonds or notes receivable for the face value.

Reporting Investments in Debt Securities at Fair Value

17. At the purchase date, debt securities are recognized at the present value of their future cash flows, discounted at the market interest rate (called the *effective* or *historical* rate) for instruments of similar risk on that date. Moreover, under the effective interest method, the book value (called *amortized cost*) of debt securities subsequent to the purchase date is equal to the present value of their remaining cash flows discounted at the historical effective rate. The market price (or fair value) of debt securities, however, varies inversely with the market rate of interest. Thus a decrease in the current market interest rate (relative to a debt security's historical effective rate) will cause the market price (fair value) of the debt security to increase to an amount that exceeds its book value under the effective interest method. Conversely, an increase in the current market interest (relative to a debt security's historical effective rate) will cause the market price (fair value) of the debt security to decrease to an amount that is below its book value under the effective interest method.

18. *Statement No. 115* requires that investments in debt securities be classified into one of three categories: held-to-maturity, available-for-sale, and trading. It also requires that investments in available-for-sale and trading debt securities be reported at their fair values (called *mark-to-market*) to provide reliable information that is relevant for predicting, assessing, and evaluating future cash flows related to those securities.

19. An investment in debt securities must be classified as *held-to-maturity securities* only if the investor has the positive intent and ability to hold those securities to maturity. Because such securities will be held to maturity, information about their fair values is not relevant for predicting, assessing, and evaluating the cash flows (face value and periodic interest) associated with those securities. Accordingly, *Statement No. 115* specifies that investments in held-to-maturity debt securities be reported in the balance sheet at their amortized cost under the effective interest method (that is, the present value of the future cash flows calculated at the security's historical effective rate). Furthermore, such investments should be classified on the balance sheet as current or noncurrent on the basis of the criteria described in Chapter 5.

20. An investment in debt securities that are bought and held principally for the purpose of selling them in the near term must be classified as *trading securities*. Because such securities will be sold in the near term, information about their fair values is relevant for predicting, assessing, and evaluating the cash flows (near-term selling price) associated with those securities. *Statement No. 115* therefore requires that investments in trading debt securities be reported at their fair value in the current asset section of the balance sheet and that the unrealized gains and losses be reported on the income statement. The FASB specified that changes in the fair value of trading securities should be included in earnings because such securities are generally used to generate profits on short-term differences in prices.

21. Investments in debt securities that are not classified as trading securities or as held-to-maturity securities must be classified as *available-for-sale securities*. Because such securities may be sold rather than held to maturity, information about their fair values is relevant for predicting, assessing, and evaluating the cash flows (future selling price) associated with those securities. Thus *Statement No. 115* requires that investments in available-for-sale debt securities be reported at their fair value in the current or noncurrent section of the balance sheet, as appropriate, and that the unrealized holding gain or loss be reported as a separate component of stockholders' equity. The FASB specified that the changes in the fair value of available-for-sale debt securities should not be reported on the income statement in order to alleviate the potential for volatility in reported earnings that would be created by requiring companies, which consider both their investments in securities and their liabilities in managing interest rate risk, to report their investments in debt securities at fair value without permitting fair value accounting for the related liabilities.

22. Under the mark-to-market procedures specified by *Statement No. 115* for trading and available-for-sale debt securities, periodic interest revenue and the increase or decrease in the book value of a security (the discount or premium amortization) should still be recognized by the effective interest method on the basis of the security's amortized cost (not fair value) at the beginning of the period and its historical effective rate. However, for reporting purposes, investments in trading debt securities and investments in available-for-sale securities must be adjusted to their fair values at the date of the financial statements. The amount of this adjustment may be calculated for a security in two steps: (*a*) the security's book value (amortized cost) is compared to its fair value to calculate the unrealized holding gain or loss at the date of the financial statements and (*b*) this amount is compared to the unrealized holding gain or loss at the date of the previous period's financial statements to calculate the increase or decrease in the unrealized holding gain or loss for the current period that should be recorded as an adjustment of the investment account. Specifically, when there is an increase (decrease) in an unrealized holding gain on trading securities, the investor should debit (credit) investment in debt securities and credit (debit) unrealized holding gain (loss). Conversely, when there is an increase (decrease) in an unrealized loss on trading securities, the investor should credit (debit) investment in debt securities and debit (credit) unrealized holding loss (gain). Alternatively, because the net amount of an unrealized holding gain or loss on available-for-sale securities should be reported as a separate component of stockholders' equity, the increase or decrease in the unrealized holding gain or loss may be debited or credited to a single account, unrealized holding gain/loss, instead of separate gain or loss accounts. The unrealized holding gain/loss account for available-for-sale securities is a real account that is reported on the balance sheet, and thus its balance should be equal to the amount of the unrealized holding gain or loss at the date of the financial statements, not the amount of the increase or decrease for the current period. In contrast, the unrealized holding gain and unrealized holding loss accounts for trading securities are nominal accounts that are reported on the income statement, and thus their balances should be equal to the amount of increase or decrease in the holding gain or loss for the current period, not the amount of the holding gain or loss at the date of the financial statements.

23. Upon the sale of an investment in debt securities, the investor should first record interest revenue, interest receivable, and the increase or decrease in the book value (the discount or premium amortization) on the securities sold for the period since the most recent interest date or since the end of the previous accounting period, whichever is later, up to the sale date. Second, when the securities are classified as trading securities, the

investor should debit cash for the selling price, credit investment in debt securities for the carrying value (that is, fair value at the end of the previous accounting period plus or minus any discount or premium amortization for the current period), and debit (or credit) realized loss (or gain) on the sale of debt securities for any difference between the selling price and carrying value of the securities. In addition, when the securities are classified as available-for-sale securities, this journal entry should include a debit or credit to unrealized holding gain/loss, a real account, for the balance at the end of the previous accounting period, to report this gain or loss, which was previously excluded from earnings, as part of the realized gain or loss on the income statement for the current period. Similarly, when the fair value of an available-for-sale or held-to-maturity debt security falls below the security's amortized cost and the decline in value is judged to be nontemporary, the investor should write down the investment to its fair value (which becomes the security's new cost basis) and recognize a realized loss for the excess of the security's carrying value over its fair value.

24. *Statement No. 115* requires that the transfer of a debt security between categories of investments be accounted for at the security's fair value at the date of the transfer. In addition:

a. When a security is transferred from or to the trading category, the unrealized holding gain or loss at that date must be recognized in earnings, and interest revenue in the future should be determined by the effective interest method using a new yield rate (the rate that equates the security's discounted future cash flows with its current fair value).

b. When a security is transferred into the available-for-sale category from the held-to-maturity category, the unrealized holding gain or loss at that date should be recognized as a separate component of stockholders' equity and interest revenue in the future should continue to be determined by the effective interest method using the historical effective rate.

c. When a security is transferred into the held-to-maturity category from the available-for-sale category, the unrealized holding gain or loss at that date should continue to be recognized as a separate component of stockholders' equity, and interest revenue in the future should continue to be determined by the effective interest method using the historical effective rate. Moreover, the unrealized holding gain or loss at the date of transfer should be amortized over the remaining term of the security as increase or decrease in the book value of the security. Thus, the book value of the security will be increased and/or decreased each period by the amortization of the security's original premium or discount (calculated using its amortized cost and historical effective rate) and by the difference between this amount and the amortization of the security's new premium or discount (calculated using the security's fair value and a yield rate that equates its discounted future cash flows with its fair value at the date of the transfer).

For transfers from the trading category, the amount of the unrealized holding gain or loss recognized at the date of transfer should be the change in the security's fair value from the end of the previous accounting period to the date of the transfer. Conversely, for transfers into the trading category and for transfers between the available-for-sale category and the held-to-maturity category, the amount of the unrealized holding gain or loss recognized at the date of the transfer should be the difference between the security's amortized cost and its fair value at the date of the transfer.

Extinguishment of Debt

25. Unconditional debt securities, such as bonds and notes, are considered to be retired or extinguished in the following circumstances:
   a. The debtor pays the creditor and thus is relieved of all the obligations related to the debt, such as by paying the face value on the maturity date, by purchasing the debt on the securities market at the current market price, by exercising a call privilege, or by substituting a new debt issue for the original issue through a process called *refunding*.
   b. The debtor is legally released from being the primary obligor for the debt, and it is probable that the debtor will not be required to make future payments related to that debt under any guarantees, such as by a third party's agreeing to become the primary obligor for the debt in conjunction with the sale of an asset that serves as the sole collateral for that debt or by a parent company's agreeing to become the primary obligor for the debt of a subsidiary. As the debtor is released from legal liability, this process is called *defeasance*.
   c. The debtor places sufficient risk-free assets (such as cash or U.S. government securities) in an irrevocable trust solely for the purpose of servicing the debt, and the pos-

sibility that the debtor will be required to make future payments related to that debt is remote. As the debtor may not be released from legal liability, this process is called *in-substance defeasance*.

In addition to these circumstances, debt may be extinguished when a creditor makes a concession that is favorable to a financially troubled debtor. Accounting for such troubled debt restructurings is discussed in Appendix 14-1.

26. When debt securities are extinguished or retired before maturity, the issuer (debtor) and the investor (creditor) should first record interest expense/revenue, interest payable/receivable, and decrease or increase in the book value (premium or discount amortization) on the debt retired for the period since the most recent interest payment date or since the end of the previous accounting period, whichever is later, up to the retirement date. Notice that this journal entry is equivalent to the accrual adjusting journal entry that is recorded when the interest payment date does not coincide with the end of the accounting period. Second, the issuer and the investor should remove from the real accounts all the balances related to the debt retired and recognize a gain or loss for any difference between the reacquisition price and the book value of the debt. *Statement No. 4* requires that the issuer report such gains or losses as extraordinary items in the income statement. In addition, it should be noted that the investor (creditor) records no journal entries for an extinguishment of debt when it is affected by a defeasance or in-substance defeasance, since the debt has not yet been formally retired but rather only transferred, legally or in-substance, from the issuer (debtor) to another entity such as a parent company or an irrevocable trust.

27. The reacquisition price of debt that is extinguished before maturity is (a) the amount of cash paid when the debt is retired by purchasing it on the securities market, (b) the amount of cash paid when the debt is retired by exercising a call privilege, (c) the present value of the debt issued when the debt is retired by a refunding, (d) zero when a parent company agrees to become the primary obligor for the debt of a subsidiary company in a defeasance, (e) the present value of the debt when a third party agrees to become the primary obligor for the debt in conjunction with the sale of a related collateralized asset in a defeasance, and (f) the amount of cash or the fair value (usually cost) of the risk-free noncash asset that is irrevocably transferred to a trust in an in-substance defeasance. Under the effective interest method, the book value of debt that is extinguished before maturity can be determined by discounting the remaining cash flows for that debt at its effective (historical) rate.

Loan Impairments

28. *Statement No. 114* requires creditors to measure impairments in the value of certain loans on the basis of the present value of the expected future cash flows discounted at the loan's historical effective interest rate or, as a practical expedient, at the loan's observable market price or the fair value of the collateral if the loan is collateral dependent. In such circumstances, the creditor should record a journal entry to debit uncollectible accounts expense or a loss and credit the loan receivable or an allowance for uncollectible accounts by the excess of the book value of the loan over its impaired value. *Statement No. 114* is applicable to loans such as accounts receivable (with terms exceeding one year) and notes receivable and all loans that are restructured in a troubled debt restructuring involving a modification of terms (discussed in Appendix 14-1), whereas *Statement No. 115,* discussed earlier, covers impairments (nontemporary declines in the value) of available-for-sale and held-to-maturity debt securities that are measured at fair value.

Compound Financial Instruments with Debt and Equity Characteristics

29. Convertible debt and debt issued with detachable stock warrants are compound financial instruments that combine both debt and equity characteristics, namely, an unconditional receivable or payable and a financial option contract. An unconditional receivable or payable is a right to receive or an obligation to pay cash or another financial asset on demand or on or before a specified date. A financial option contract is a right or an obligation to exchange other financial instruments on potentially favorable or unfavorable terms that is conditional on the occurrence of an event within the control of one party to the contract. In addition, if these securities are callable by the issuer or if the holder can request the issuer to extinguish the securities, there is a *call option* or *put option*, respectively.

30. Convertible debt. The investor who buys *convertible debt* has an option to convert or exchange that debt for a specified number of shares of stock of the issuer within a specified time period. Conceptually, because the investor has paid for the option to become a shareholder, it may be argued that the issuer should record a portion of the proceeds received for convertible debt as contributed capital. *APB Opinion No. 14,* however, requires that no portion of the proceeds be recorded as contributed capital, under the rationale that the conversion option is inseparable from the debt securities. Thus, upon the issuance of convertible bonds or notes, the issuer should record bonds or notes payable at the issue price. No portion of the proceeds should be recorded as contributed capital. Subsequently, the issuer should amortize the premium or discount over the term of the bonds or notes, even though conversion may occur at some (unpredictable) time before maturity. And if bonds or notes are converted before maturity, the issuer should remove from the real accounts all the balances related to the bonds or notes converted and record the capital shares issued at the book value of the bonds or notes. Under this method (called the *book value method*), the issuer records no gain or loss when bonds or notes are converted in accordance with the accounting convention of not recognizing gains or losses on capital transactions between the corporation and its shareholders. However, when the issuer induces conversion by offering creditors (investors) additional consideration, such as cash, warrants, or a more favorable conversion ratio, the issuer must record an expense equal to the market value of the additional securities or other consideration issued to induce conversion.

31. Accounting for convertible debt by the investor parallels the accounting by the issuer. The investor should record the investment in bonds or notes receivable at cost and amortize the premium or discount over the term of the bonds or notes. And, upon conversion, investment in stock is recorded at the book value of the bonds or notes converted, with no gain or loss recognized.

32. Debt issued with detachable warrants. Debt securities may be issued with *detachable warrants,* certificates that give the investor the right to purchase stock of the issuing company at a specified price within a specified time period. Since detachable warrants are separable from the debt, *Opinion No. 14* requires that the proceeds be allocated between the debt and the detachable warrants. Accordingly, upon the issuance of bonds or notes with detachable warrants, the issuer should (*a*) debit cash for the total amount received, (*b*) credit bonds or notes payable for the portion of the proceeds allocated to the bonds or notes, and (*c*) credit contributed capital—stock warrants outstanding for the portion of the proceeds allocated to the detachable warrants. The allocation of the total proceeds between bonds or notes and detachable warrants may be based on the relative market value of the two securities. Or, if the market value of only one of the securities is determinable, the amount allocated to the other security may be calculated by subtracting the determinable market value of the one security from the total proceeds. Subsequently, the issuer should amortize the premium or discount over the term of the bonds or notes. And upon the exercise of detachable warrants, the issuer should record the capital shares issued at the sum of the cash exercise price and the book value of the warrants exercised. Alternatively, if warrants expire without being exercised, the contributed capital originally recorded for the now expired warrants should be reclassified as contributed capital from expired warrants.

33. Accounting for debt issued with detachable warrants by the investor parallels the accounting by the issuer. The investor should use the procedures just described to allocate the total purchase price between the investment in bonds or notes receivable and the investment in stock warrants. The discount or premium on the bond investment or notes receivable should be amortized over the term of the bonds or notes. And upon the exercise of detachable warrants, the investment in stock should be recorded at the sum of the cash exercise price and the book value of the warrants exercised. Alternatively, if warrants are sold, a gain or loss should be recognized for the difference between the net proceeds and the book value of the warrants. Or, if warrants expire without being exercised, the book value of the now expired warrants should be written off as a loss.

Emerging Financial Instruments

34. There are various types of debt instruments that are designed to avoid obligating debtors to high interest rates over long periods of time and to protect creditors against loss of purchasing power as a result of holding debt that specifies fixed cash flows for interest and principal. Among these inflation-hedging debt instruments are (*a*) *variable interest rate debt*—debt on which the interest rate each period is tied to the current market rate of interest, such as the prime rate plus a specified percent; (*b*) *price-indexed debt*—debt on which the face value is tied to a specified general or specific price-level index; and (*c*) *commodity bonds* or *notes*—debt on which the face value is payable in terms of a specified commodity or its cash equivalent at the maturity date. In addition, financial transactions in which two companies agree to exchange (swap) interest obligations on an equal amount of their outstanding debt (called *interest swaps*) have become a popular means of managing interest rate risk. Such debt instruments and transactions raise many controversial and complex accounting issues. Furthermore, because authoritative pronouncements do not yet contain specific guidance for most of these issues, proposed solutions have been developed by practicing accountants by deduction from the financial reporting objectives and other theoretical concepts and by analogy from authoritative guidance and accounting practices for similar circumstances.

35. In 1986 the FASB added to its agenda a "miniconceptual framework" project on financial instruments and off-balance-sheet financing. Pending completion of the recognition and measurement phases of this project, the Board issued *Statement No. 105* in March 1990 to require disclosure of information about the off-balance-sheet risk and concentrations of credit risk arising from financial instruments. Off-balance-sheet risk refers to the risk of accounting loss in an amount that exceeds the amount reported for financial instruments as assets and liabilities in the balance sheet. Credit risk refers to the risk that the amounts will not be paid. The FASB also issued in August 1990 a discussion memorandum identifying 12 broad issues related to the distinction between liability and equity instruments and accounting for instruments that have characteristics of both. More recently, the FASB issued (*a*) *Statement No. 107,* which specifies fair value disclosure requirements for certain financial instruments, whether or not recognized as assets and liabilities under GAAP; and (*b*) *Statement No. 115,* which, as described earlier in this chapter and in Chapter 13, specifies accounting and reporting standards for certain investment in debt and equity securities.

Appendix: Troubled Debt Restructurings

36. A *troubled debt restructuring* occurs when a creditor makes a concession that is favorable to the debtor. The creditor may, for example, accept assets or equity securities in full settlement of the debt even though the value of the consideration received is less than the amount of the debt. Alternatively, the terms of the debt agreement may be modified by deferral or partial forgiveness of the amounts due or by reduction of the stated rate of interest.

37. Accounting for a troubled debt restructuring that is consummated by the transfer of assets or the issuance of equity securities is conceptually equivalent to accounting for an extinguishment of debt. The debtor should remove from the real accounts all the balances related to the restructured debt and recognize an extraordinary gain for the excess of the book value of the debt over the fair value of the assets transferred or equity securities issued. Additionally, when assets are transferred to the creditor, the debtor should remove from the real accounts all the balances related to the assets transferred and recognize a gain or loss for the difference between their book value and fair value. Alternatively, when equity securities are issued to the creditor, the debtor should record contributed capital at the fair value of the equity securities issued. Coincidentally, the creditor should remove from the real accounts all the balances related to the restructured receivable and recognize a loss for (or reduce allowance for uncollectible accounts by) the excess of the recorded value of the receivable over the fair value of the assets or equity securities received. Additionally, the creditor should record the assets or equity securities received at their fair value.

38. Accounting for a troubled debt restructuring that involves a modification of terms is somewhat more complex. In such circumstances, the creditor must recognize a loss for the excess of the book value of the receivable over the present value of the restructured cash flows discounted at the historical effective interest rate. By comparison, whether the debtor recognizes a gain depends on the relationship between the book value of the debt before restructuring and the restructured cash flows.

39. If the book value of the debt before restructuring is greater than the restructured cash flows, the debtor should (a) remove from the real accounts all the balances related to the restructured debt, (b) record a debt equal to the restructured cash flows, and (c) record a gain for the excess of the book value of the restructured debt over the restructured cash flows. Subsequently, the debtor should record all subsequent cash payments as a reduction of the debt recorded at the date of the restructuring.

40. Alternatively, if the book value of the debt before restructuring is less than the restructured cash flows, the debtor should remove from the real accounts all the balances related to the restructured debt and record a debt at the book value of the restructured debt. No gain should be recognized at the date of the restructuring. Instead, the excess of the restructured cash flows over the book value of the debt should be recognized prospectively as interest expense over the new term of the debt by the effective interest method. That is, at the subsequent cash payment dates, the debtor should record interest expense calculated at the new effective interest rate and a reduction of the debt at the residual amount paid. The new effective interest rate used to calculate the debtor's interest expense is the rate that discounts the restructured cash flows to an amount equal to the book value of the restructured debt.

SELF-STUDY LEARNING
Items marked with an asterisk (*) refer to the Appendix.

Key Terms and Concepts

Provide the appropriate term or terms to complete each of the following statements:

1. The specified amount of cash that the issuing company promises to pay on the designated maturity date of bonds or notes is called the _____, _____, _____, or _____.

2. The specified percentage of the face value that the issuing company promises to pay as periodic cash interest on bonds or notes is called the _____, _____, or _____.

3. Debt securities that become due or mature on a single date are _____, whereas debt securities that become due or mature in installments are _____.

4. Debt securities that contain an option allowing the investor to exchange them for a specified number of shares of stock of the issuing company within a specified time period are _____.

5. Certificates issued as a sweetener with debt securities, giving the investor the right to purchase shares of stock of the issuing company at a specified price within a specified time period, are called _____.

6. The excess of the issue price over the face value of bonds is called a(n) _____, whereas the excess of the face value over the issue price of bonds is called a(n) _____.

7. For financial reporting purposes, investments in debt securities are classified as _____ only if the investor has the positive intent and ability to hold those securities to the due date, as _____ if the investor intends to sell those securities in the near term, or as _____ if those securities are not classified into either of the other two categories.

8. A(n) _____ occurs, for example, when the issuing company purchases bonds on the securities market at the current market price or exercises a call privilege before the maturity date of the bond issue.

9. Debt may be extinguished by the debtor's substituting a new debt issue for the original issue through a process called _____, by the debtor's being legally released from being the primary obligor for the debt through a process called _____, or by the debtor's placing sufficient risk-free assets in an irrevocable trust solely for the purpose of servicing the debt through a process called _____.

*10. A(n) _____ occurs when a creditor makes a concession through a restructuring agreement that is favorable to the debtor.

True-False

Indicate by circling the appropriate response whether each of the following statements is true (T) or false (F):

T F 1. Bonds are always issued at an amount equal to their face value.

T F 2. When bonds are issued on the contract date specified in the indenture, the issuing company should credit bonds payable for the issue price of the bond.

T F 3. When bonds are issued between interest dates, the portion of the proceeds that represents interest accrued from the date of the bond contract up to the issue date should be recorded by the issuer as interest payable.

T F 4. Investment in trading debt securities should be reported on the balance sheet as a noncurrent asset.

T F 5. Interest expense over the term of bonds is always equal to the total cash interest paid.

T F 6. The straight-line method and the effective interest method of amortizing discounts or premiums on bonds provide the same amount of total interest expense over the term of the bonds.

T F 7. When bonds are sold on the contract date, the decrease or increase in the book value of the bonds (the premium or discount amortization) for each interest period under the straight-line method is equal to the premium or discount divided by the number of interest periods over the term of the bonds.

T F 8. Under the effective interest method, the decrease or increase in the book value of the bonds (the premium or discount amortization) for each interest period is equal to the difference between the cash interest paid calculated at the stated rate and the interest expense calculated at the effective rate.

T F 9. The straight-line method of amortization is considered to be conceptually preferable to the effective interest method because it results in a constant amount of interest expense each period over the term of the bonds.

T F 10. The amount of cash interest paid is determined by multiplying the book value of the bonds at the beginning of the period by the stated rate of interest.

T F 11. Debt issue costs may be deferred and amortized to expense over the period of time from the issue date to the maturity date.

T F 12. Investors are required to report investments in debt securities at their fair values.

T F 13. Unrealized holding gains and losses on investments in debt securities must be reported on the income statement.

T F 14. Before recording an early extinguishment of debt, the issuing company should accrue interest expense, interest payable, and premium or discount amortization for the period since the most recent interest payment date or since the end of the previous accounting period, whichever is later, up to the retirement date.

T F 15. The issuing company may record a portion of the proceeds received for convertible debt as contributed capital because the investor has acquired the right to become a shareholder.

T F 16. The issuing company should record a portion of the proceeds received for debt issued with detachable warrants as contributed capital because the detachable warrants are separable from the debt securities.

T F 17. There is no discount when a non-interest-bearing note is issued solely for cash.

T F 18. When a note and some other obligation are issued for cash, a liability such as unearned revenue should be recorded at an amount equal to the difference between the face value and discounted present value of the note.

T F 19. The issuer should record periodic discount amortization as an increase in the book value of notes payable.

T F *20. The debtor should always recognize a gain at the date of a troubled debt restructuring.

Multiple Choice

Select the best response for each of the following items, and circle the corresponding letter:

1. The issue price of a bond is equal to:

    a. The face value of the bond.

    b. The face value of the bond and the present value of the periodic interest payments discounted at the market rate of interest at the issue date.

    c. The present value of the face value of the bond and the periodic interest payments discounted at the market rate of interest at the issue date.

    d. The present value of the face value of the bond and the periodic interest payments discounted at the stated rate of interest.

2. When the market rate of interest is lower than the stated rate of interest, bonds are issued:

    a. At a premium, since the issue price is greater than the face value of the bonds.

    b. At a premium, since the issue price is less than the face value of the bonds.

    c. At a discount, since the issue price is greater than the face value of the bonds.

    d. At a discount, since the issue price is less than the face value of the bonds.

3. Which of the following is a characteristic of the effective interest method of amortizing a premium or discount on term bonds?

    a. The premium or discount amortization is a constant amount each period over the term of the bonds.

    b. Periodic interest expense is a constant amount each period over the term of the bonds.

    c. Periodic interest expense is determined indirectly as the cash interest paid plus the discount amortization or minus the premium amortization.

    d. Periodic interest expense as a percentage of the book value of the bonds at the beginning of each period is a constant rate over the term of the bonds.

4. Under the effective interest method of amortizing a premium or discount on bonds, periodic interest expense is equal to:

    a. The face value of the bonds multiplied by the stated rate of interest.

    b. The face value of the bonds multiplied by the effective rate of interest at which the bonds were issued.

    c. The book value of the bonds at the beginning of each period multiplied by the stated rate of interest.

    d. The book value of the bonds at the beginning of each period multiplied by the effective rate of interest at which the bonds were issued.

5. When the interest payment date does not coincide with the end of the accounting period, the bond issuer should accrue under the effective interest method:

   a. Interest expense and interest payable calculated at the stated rate of interest for the fraction of the period since the most recent interest payment date.
   b. Interest expense and interest payable calculated at the effective rate of interest for the fraction of the period since the most recent interest payment date.
   c. Interest expense calculated at the effective rate of interest and interest payable calculated at the stated rate of interest for the fraction of the period since the most recent interest payment date.
   d. Interest expense calculated at the stated rate of interest and interest payable calculated at the effective rate of interest for the fraction of the period since the most recent interest payment date.

6. When bonds are extinguished or retired before maturity, the difference between the reacquisition price and the book value of the bonds retired should be:

   a. Deferred and amortized to interest expense over the remaining term of the now retired bonds.
   b. Recognized currently as an extraordinary gain or loss.
   c. Reported in the financial statements as a prior period adjustment of beginning retained earnings.
   d. Recorded as contributed capital from retirement of bonds.

7. When convertible bonds are converted or exchanged for shares of stock, the issuing company should record the stock issued:

   a. At the face value of the bonds.
   b. At the cash exercise price plus the amount originally allocated to contributed capital at the date the convertible bonds were issued.
   c. At the book value of the bonds plus the amount originally allocated to contributed capital at the date the convertible bonds were issued.
   d. At the book value of the bonds at the date of conversion.

8. When bonds are issued with detachable warrants, the issuing company should record:

   a. The difference between the total proceeds and the face value of the bonds as contributed capital—stock warrants outstanding.
   b. The difference between the face value of the bonds and the portion of the proceeds allocated to the bonds as contributed capital—stock warrants outstanding.
   c. The difference between the total proceeds and the portion of the proceeds allocated to the bonds as contributed capital—stock warrants outstanding.
   d. The portion of the proceeds allocated to the detachable warrants as a liability such as detachable warrants payable.

9. When a noncash asset with a determinable fair value is acquired by issuance of a non-interest-bearing note:

   a. The noncash asset should be recorded at the face value of the note, and no gain or loss should be recognized.
   b. The noncash asset should be recorded at the face value of the note, and a gain or loss should be recognized equal to the difference between the fair value of the noncash asset and the face value of the note.
   c. The noncash asset should be recorded at its fair value, and a gain or loss should be recognized equal to the difference between the fair value of the noncash asset and the face value of the note.
   d. The noncash asset should be recorded at its fair value, and a discount equal to the difference between the fair value of the noncash asset and the face value of the note should be amortized to interest expense over the term of the note.

*10. In a troubled debt restructuring involving a modification of terms, the debtor should:

   a. Always recognize a gain at the date of the restructuring.
   b. Recognize a gain only if the book value of the debt before restructuring is greater than the restructured cash flows.
   c. Recognize a gain or loss equal to the difference between the book value of the debt before restructuring and the restructured cash flows.
   d. Amortize the excess of the book value of the debt over the restructured cash flows prospectively as interest expense over the new term of the restructured debt.

Extended Problem

Presented here are data concerning two prospective debt securities:

	TERM BONDS	NOTE
Face value	$100,000	$50,000
Contract date	1/1/95	1/1/95
Stated rate of interest	10%	None
Interest payment date(s)	Semiannual (6/30, 12/31)	None
Maturity date(s)	12/31/04	12/31/96

These data apply to the following independent situations.

REQUIRED

a. Assume that the term bonds are sold to an investor on January 1, 1995, for $88,530 at an effective rate of interest of 12 percent. The investor has the positive intent and ability to hold the bonds to maturity. The annual accounting periods of the issuer and the investor end on December 31, and both companies use the effective interest method of amortization. Prepare the journal entries related to the bonds for both the issuer and the investor as of January 1, 1995, June 30, 1995, and December 31, 1995.

b. Assume the same facts described in situation a, except that the annual accounting periods of the issuer and the investor end on September 30 instead of December 31. Prepare the journal entries related to the bonds for both the issuer and the investor as of September 30, 1995, and December 31, 1995.

c. Assume the same facts described in situation a, except that the term bonds are sold on April 1, 1995, for $113,363 plus accrued interest at an effective rate of interest of 8 percent. Prepare the journal entries related to the bonds for both the issuer and the investor as of April 1, 1995, and June 30, 1995.

d. Assume the same facts described in situation a, except that the investor does not intend to hold the term bonds to maturity and the bonds are classified as available-for-sale securities. Assume further that the amortized cost and fair value of the investor's investment in bonds were $89,173 and $90,500, respectively, at December 31, 1995, and $89,894 and $90,250, respectively, at December 31, 1996. Prepare the journal entries required (1) to report the investor's investment in bonds at their fair value at December 31, 1995 and 1996, and (2) to record the transfer of the securities to the trading category on January 15, 1997, when their fair value was $90,300.

e. Assume the same facts described in situation a, and assume further that $50,000 of the term bonds are retired on March 1, 1997, for $44,000 exclusive of accrued interest. On January 1, 1997, the book values of the issuer's bonds payable account and the investor's investment in bonds account were each $89,890. Prepare the journal entries related to the bonds retired for both the issuer and the investor as of March 1, 1997.

f. Assume the same facts described in situation a, and assume further that on January 1, 1998, the issuer purchased $50,000 of 10 percent, seven-year U.S. government bonds for $44,207 and placed them in an irrevocable trust to extinguish $50,000 of the term bonds. On this date, the bonds payable account balance was $90,705. Prepare the journal entries related to the in-substance defeasance extinguishment for the issuer.

g. Assume the same facts described in situation a, except that in accordance with the bond indenture each $1,000 term bond is convertible into 20 shares of the issuer's $10 par value common stock. Assume further that on January 1, 1998, the issuer offered the investor a more favorable conversion ratio of 25 common shares, instead of 20 common shares, for each $1,000 bond converted by January 1, 1999. Ten (10) bonds were converted on January 1, 1999, when the market price of the common stock was $35 per share. On this date, the book values of the issuer's bonds payable account and the investor's investment in bonds account were each $91,619. Prepare the journal entry required to record the induced conversion for both the issuer and the investor using the book value method.

h. Assume that on January 1, 1995, the term bonds are sold for $106,050, and assume further that attached to each $1,000 bond is a detachable warrant containing rights to purchase 10 shares of the issuer's $10 par value common stock for $30 per share by December 31, 1997. Prepare the journal entry required to record the issuance of the bonds and detachable warrants for the issuer for each of the following alternative circumstances: (1) the market price of the bonds and the detachable warrants immediately after the issue date is $1,010 and $40, respectively; and (2) the market price of the detachable warrants immediately after the issue date is $40, but there is no objectively determinable market value of the bonds.

i. Assume the same facts described in situation h(*1*), and assume further that all of the detachable warrants are exercised on December 21, 1997, when the market price of the issuer's common stock is $35 per share. Prepare the journal entry required to record the exercise of the detachable warrants for the issuer.

j. Assume that the non-interest-bearing note is issued on January 1, 1995, for land that had a determinable fair value of $39,860. The land was acquired several years ago by the investor for $20,000. The annual accounting periods of both the issuer and the investor end on December 31. Prepare the journal entries related to the note for both the issuer and the investor as of January 1, 1995, December 31, 1995, and December 31, 1996.

k. Assume that the non-interest-bearing note is issued on January 1, 1995, for $50,000 cash. Assume further that the issuer agrees to sell 10,000 units of its product to the investor over the next two years at a discount from its regular selling price. The market rate of interest for the issuer and the investor on January 1, 1995, is 12 percent. The investor purchased the 10,000 units from the issuer in two lots at a discounted price of $12.90 per unit, on account: 6,000 units on May 14, 1995, and 4,000 units on July 22, 1996. Both companies use the periodic inventory system. Prepare the journal entries related to the note and the sales or purchases of the product for both the issuer and the investor on January 1, 1995, and May 14, 1995.

*l. Assume that the term bonds are sold to an investor on January 1, 1995, for $100,000. The investor has the positive intent and ability to hold the bonds to maturity. The annual accounting periods of both the issuer and the investor end on December 31. During 2002, the issuer began to have cash flow problems and was unable to pay the interest accruing on the bonds at June 30 and December 31, 2002. Nevertheless, the investor had not yet recognized any loss on its bond investment. Eventually, the issuer and the investor agreed to restructure the troubled debt as of January 1, 2003. Prepare the journal entries related to the troubled debt restructuring for both the issuer and the investor for each of the following alternative circumstances: (*1*) the investor agreed to accept land (issuer's cost, $75,000; current market value, $95,000) in full settlement of the bonds and unpaid interest; (*2*) the investor agreed to accept 5,000 shares of the issuer's common stock (par value, $10; current market value, $19) in full settlement of the bonds and unpaid interest; (*3*) the investor agreed to forgive the unpaid interest and to reduce the maturity value of the bonds to $90,000 and the stated interest rate to 4 percent payable annually on December 31; and (*4*) the investor agreed to accept a $112,211 non-interest-bearing note due on December 31, 2004, in full settlement of the bonds and unpaid interest.

COMMON ERRORS

The first statement in each "common error" listed here is *incorrect*. Each incorrect statement is followed by a corrected statement and an explanation.

1. The issue price of semiannual interest bonds is equal to the present value of the face value discounted at the annual market rate of interest for the number of years of the term of the bonds plus the present value of the semiannual interest payments discounted at the semiannual market rate of interest for the number of semiannual interest periods during the term of the bonds. *Wrong*

The issue price of semiannual interest bonds is equal to the present value of the face value and semiannual interest payments discounted at the semiannual market rate of interest for the number of semiannual interest periods during the term of the bonds. *Right*

To determine the issue price of bonds, the present value of the interest payments is calculated by multiplying the periodic interest payment by the present value of an ordinary annuity of $1 at a specified compound interest rate (i) for a specified period (n). The present value of the face value is calculated by multiplying the face value by the present value of $1 at a specified compound interest rate (i) for a specified period (n). Since both these present value factors are at a compound interest rate, the periodic interest payments and face value of semiannual interest bonds should be discounted for the same time interval (number of semiannual interest periods during the term of the bonds) at the same compound interest rate (semiannual market rate of interest).

2. The proceeds for a bond always should be recorded as bonds payable. *Wrong*

The proceeds for a bond should be recorded as bonds payable except that a portion of the proceeds should be recorded as interest payable when bonds are sold between interest periods. *Right*

When bonds are issued between interest periods, the cash interest paid at the first interest payment date is for the full interest period, even though the bonds have been outstanding for only a portion of the period. The portion of the proceeds that represents interest accrued on the bonds from the contract date up to the issue date accordingly should be recorded as interest payable. And the remaining portion of the proceeds should be recorded as bonds payable. Later, at the first interest payment date, the cash interest paid should be recorded partly as a reduction of interest payable, and the interest expense and premium or discount amortization should be recognized only for the period the bonds have been outstanding.

3. Either the straight-line method or the effective interest method may be used to amortize a premium or discount on bonds. *Wrong*

The straight-line method may be used to amortize a premium or discount on bonds only if the results obtained are not materially different from those that would result from the effective interest method. *Right*

APB Opinion No. 21 applies to receivables and payables, such as debentures, bonds, and notes, which represent contractual rights to receive money or contractual obligations to pay money on fixed or determinable dates. It specifies that a discount or premium should be amortized over the term of the note or bond in such a way as to result in a constant rate of interest when applied to the amount outstanding at the beginning of any given period. This is the effective interest method. *Opinion No. 21* also states that other methods may be used, but only if the results obtained are not materially different from those that would result from the effective interest method.

4. Under the effective interest method, periodic interest expense on semiannual interest bonds may be calculated by dividing by 2 the product of the book value of the bonds at the beginning of each year multiplied by the annual effective rate of interest. *Wrong*

Under the effective interest method, periodic interest expense on semiannual interest bonds should be calculated by multiplying the book value of the bonds at the beginning of each interest period by the semiannual effective rate of interest (that is, the annual effective rate of interest divided by 2). *Right*

Normally, interest rates that are quoted in connection with bonds are annual rates, even though interest may be payable semiannually. Bonds that pay interest semiannually at a stated rate of interest of 10 percent, for example, may be quoted at a market price to yield an effective rate of interest of 12 percent. The interest rates quoted in this example are annual rates. Nonetheless, the issue price of such bonds is calculated by discounting the semiannual interest payments and the face value at the semiannual market rate of interest for the number of semiannual interest periods during the term of the bonds. Since the issue price of semiannual interest bonds is based on the semiannual market rate of interest, the difference between the issue price and the face value of the bonds should be amortized using the semiannual effective rate of interest.

5. When the interest period does not coincide with the end of the accounting period, the bond issuer should accrue interest expense and interest payable calculated at the stated rate for the fraction of the period since the most recent interest payment date. *Wrong*

When the interest period does not coincide with the end of the accounting period, the bond issuer should accrue interest expense and premium or discount amortization calculated at the effective rate for the fraction of the period since the most recent interest payment date and interest payable calculated at the stated rate for the fraction of the period since the most recent interest payment date. *Right*

The premium or discount on bonds should be amortized as an adjustment to interest expense for each period during the term of the bonds, including the period from the most recent interest payment date through the end of the accounting period. Specifically, under the effective interest method, interest expense accrued at the end of the accounting period should be calculated by multiplying the book value of the bonds at the beginning of the interest period by the effective rate for the fraction of the period from the most recent interest payment date to the full interest period. And the difference between this amount and the accrued interest payable should be the amount of the premium or discount amortization for the period. Likewise, the accrued interest payable should be calculated by multiplying the face value of the bonds by the stated rate for the fraction of the period from the most recent interest payment date to the full interest period.

6. When bonds are extinguished or retired before maturity, the difference between the reacquisition price and the book value of the bonds immediately after the most recent interest payment date (or as of the end of the previous accounting period, if later) should be recognized as an extraordinary gain or loss. *Wrong*

When bonds are extinguished or retired before maturity, the difference between the reacquisition price and the book value of the bonds updated to the date of retirement should be recognized as an extra-ordinary gain or loss. *Right*

Interest expense and premium or discount amortization should be recognized for each period in which bonds are outstanding. Thus when bonds are extinguished or retired between interest dates, the issuer should accrue interest expense, premium or discount amortization, and interest payable on the bonds retired for the period since the most recent interest payment date or since the end of the previous accounting period, if later, up to the retirement date. Next, the issuer should recognize an extraordinary gain or loss equal to the difference between the reacquisition price and the book value of the bonds retired at the date of retirement.

7. A noncash asset acquired in exchange for a non-interest-bearing note should be recorded at the face value of the note. *Wrong*

A noncash asset acquired in exchange for a non-interest-bearing note should be recorded at either the fair value of the noncash asset or the discounted present value of the note, whichever is more clearly determinable. *Right*

When a noncash asset is acquired in exchange for a non-interest-bearing note, the issuing company receives the noncash asset as well as the use of funds over the term of the note. Accordingly, in this circumstance, the issuer should record the non-cash asset received at the cash equivalent price, that is, either its fair value or the discounted present value of the note. Since the difference between the cash equivalent price of the noncash asset and the face value of the note represents a payment for the use of funds, it should be amortized to interest expense over the term of the note.

ANSWERS

Items marked with an asterisk (*) refer to the Appendix.

Key Terms and Concepts

1. maturity value, face value, par value, principal
2. stated rate, nominal rate, coupon rate
3. term debt, serial debt
4. convertible debt
5. detachable warrants
6. premium, discount
7. held-to-maturity debt securities, trading debt securities, available-for-sale debt securities
8. early extinguishment or retirement of debt
9. refunding, defeasance, in-substance defeasance
*10. troubled debt restructuring

True-False

1. F Bonds are issued at an amount equal to the present value of the face value (an amount or, if serial bonds, an annuity) and periodic interest payments (an ordinary annuity, if term bonds) discounted at the market rate of interest for financial instruments of similar risk at the issue date. Accordingly, bonds are issued at an amount equal to their face value only if the stated rate of interest is equal to the market rate of interest.

2. T

3. T

4. F Investment in trading debt securities should be reported on the balance sheet as a current asset, because such securities are bought and held principally for the purpose of selling them in the near term.

5. F Interest expense over the term of bonds is equal to the sum of the face value and the total cash interest paid less the issue price. Interest expense over the term of bonds, therefore, is equal to the total cash interest paid only if the issue price is equal to the face value. In contrast, if the issue price is greater than the face value, interest expense over the term of bonds is equal to the total cash interest paid minus the premium. Alternatively, if the issue price is less than the face value, interest expense over the term of bonds is equal to the total cash interest paid plus the discount.

6. T

7. T

8. T

9. F The straight-line method of amortization results in a constant amount of interest expense each period over the term of the bonds, but the effective interest method is considered to be conceptually preferable to the straight-line method principally because it results in a constant rate of periodic interest expense as a percentage of the book value of the bonds at the beginning of each period.

10. F The amount of cash interest paid is determined by multiplying the face value of the bonds outstanding during the period by the stated rate of interest.

11. T

12. F Investors are required to report investments in trading debt securities and investments in available-for-sale debt securities at their fair values. Investments in held-to-maturity debt securities, however, should be reported at their amortized cost.

13. F Unrealized holding gains and losses on investments in trading debt securities must be reported on the income statement, whereas unrealized holding gains and losses on investments in available-for-sale debt securities must be reported as a separate component of stockholders' equity.

14. T

15. F Conceptually, because the investor has acquired the right to become a shareholder, it may be argued that the issuing company should record a portion of the proceeds received for convertible debt as contributed capital. *APB Opinion No. 14*, however, requires that no portion of the proceeds be recorded as contributed capital, under the rationale that the conversion option is inseparable from the debt securities.

16. T

17. F When a noninterest-bearing note is issued solely for cash, there is a discount equal to the excess of the face value of the note over the amount of cash received. Because this difference represents a payment for the use of money, the discount should be amortized to interest expense over the term of the note.

18. T

19. T

*20. F The debtor should recognize a gain at the date of a troubled debt restructuring except when the restructured cash flows exceed the book value of the debt in a restructuring involving a modification of terms. In this circumstance, the debtor should recognize the difference between the restructured cash flows and the book value of the debt prospectively as interest expense over the new term of the restructured debt by the effective interest method.

Multiple Choice

1.	c	6.	b
2.	a	7.	d
3.	d	8.	c
4.	d	9.	d
5.	c	*10.	b

Extended Problem

a. Journal entries related to bonds issued on contract date:

Journal entries by issuer.

1/1/95	Cash	88,530	
	Bonds payable		88,530
6/30/95	Interest expense ($88,530 × 6%)	5,312	
	Cash ($100,000 × 5%)		5,000
	Bonds payable ($5,312 − $5,000)		312
12/31/95	Interest expense [($88,530 + $312) × 6%]	5,331	
	Cash ($100,000 × 5%)		5,000
	Bonds payable ($5,331 − $5,000)		331

Journal entries by investor.

1/1/95	Investment in bonds	88,530	
	Cash		88,530
6/30/95	Cash ($100,000 × 5%)	5,000	
	Investment in bonds ($5,312 − $5,000)	312	
	Interest revenue ($88,530 × 6%)		5,312
12/31/95	Cash ($100,000 × 5%)	5,000	
	Investment in bonds ($5,331 − $5,000)	331	
	Interest revenue [($88,530 + $312) × 6%]		5,331

b. Journal entries related to bonds when interest date does not coincide with year-end:

Journal entries by issuer.

9/30/95	Interest expense [($88,530 + $312) × 6% × 3/6]	2,665	
	Interest payable ($100,000 × 5% × 3/6)		2,500
	Bonds payable ($2,665 − $2,500)		165
12/31/95[a]	Interest expense [($88,530 + $312) × 6% × 3/6]	2,665	
	Interest payable ($100,000 × 5% × 3/6)	2,500	
	Cash ($100,000 × 5%)		5,000
	Bonds payable ($2,665 − $2,500)		165

Journal entries by investor.

9/30/95	Interest receivable ($100,000 × 5% × 3/6)	2,500	
	Investment in bonds ($2,665 − $2,500)	165	
	Interest revenue [($88,530 + $312) × 6% × 3/6]		2,665
12/31/95[a]	Cash ($100,000 × 5%)	5,000	
	Investment in bonds ($2,665 − $2,500)	165	
	Interest revenue [($88,530 + $312) × 6% × 3/6]		2,665
	Interest receivable ($100,000 × 5% × 3/6)		2,500

[a]Alternatively, the adjusting journal entry recorded on 9/30/95 may be reversed on 10/1/95; if so, this journal entry should be the same as the entry recorded on 12/31/95 in response to situation a.

c. Journal entries related to bonds issued between interest dates:

Journal entries by issuer.

4/1/95	Cash ($113,363 + $2,500)	115,863	
	Bonds payable		113,363
	Interest payable ($100,000 × 5% × 3/6)		2,500
6/30/95	Interest expense	2,272[a]	
	Bonds payable ($2,500 − $2,272)	228	
	Interest payable ($100,000 × 5% × 3/6)	2,500	
	Cash ($100,000 × 5%)		5,000

Journal entries by investor.

4/1/95	Investment in bonds	113,363	
	Interest receivable ($100,000 × 5% × 3/6)	2,500	
	Cash ($113,363 + $2,500)		115,863
6/30/95	Cash ($100,000 × 5%)	5,000	
	Interest revenue		2,272[a]
	Investment in bonds ($2,500 − $2,272)		228
	Interest receivable ($100,000 × 5% × 3/6)		2,500

[a]Issue price if bonds had been issued on 1/1/95 at an effective rate of interest of 8% multiplied by semiannual effective rate of interest for fraction of period bonds were outstanding during the first interest period: ($100,000 × .4564) + ($5,000 × 13.5903) = $113,592; $113,592 × 4% × 3/6 = $2,272.

d. Journal entries to report investment in debt securities at fair value:

(1). Year-end adjustments.

12/31/95	Investment in bonds ($90,500 − $89,173)	1,327	
	Unrealized holding gain/loss		1,327
12/31/96	Unrealized holding gain/loss	971	
	Investment in bonds [$1,327 − ($90,250 − $89,894)]		971

(2). Transfer.

1/15/97	Investment in bonds	90,300	
	Unrealized holding gain/loss ($1,327 − $971)	356	
	Investment in bonds		90,250
	Unrealized holding gain [$90,300 − ($90,250 − $356)]		406

e.   Journal entries related to early extinguishment of debt:

Journal entries by issuer.

3/1/97	Interest expense [($89,890 × 1/2) × 6% × 2/6]	899	
	Interest payable ($50,000 × 5% × 2/6)		833
	Bonds payable ($899 − $833)		66
3/1/97	Bonds payable [($89,890 × 1/2) + $66]	45,011	
	Interest payable ($50,000 × 5% × 2/6)	833	
	Cash ($44,000 + $833)		44,833
	Extraordinary gain on retirement of bonds ($45,011 − $44,000)		1,011

Journal entries by investor.

3/1/97	Interest receivable ($50,000 × 5% × 2/6)	833	
	Investment in bonds ($899 − $833)	66	
	Interest revenue [($89,890 × 1/2) × 6% × 2/6]		899
3/1/97	Cash ($44,000 + $833)	44,833	
	Loss on sale of investment in bonds ($45,011 − $44,000)	1,011	
	Investment in bonds [($89,890 × 1/2) + $66]		45,011
	Interest receivable ($50,000 × 5% × 2/6)		833

f.   Journal entries by issuer for in-substance defeasance extinguishment:

1/1/98	Investment in U.S. government bonds	44,207	
	Cash		44,207
1/1/98	Bonds payable ($90,705 × 1/2)	45,352	
	Investment in U.S. government bonds		44,207
	Extraordinary gain on extinguishment of bonds ($45,352 − $44,207)		1,145

g.   Journal entries related to induced conversion of bonds into common stock:

Journal entry by issuer.

1/1/99	Bonds payable ($91,619 × 1/10)	9,162	
	Conversion expense [10 × (25 − 20) × $35]	1,750	
	Common stock (10 × 25 × $10)		2,500
	Contributed capital in excess of par—common ($9,162 + $1,750 − $2,500)		8,412

Journal entry by investor.

1/1/99	Investment in stock	9,162	
	Investment in bonds ($91,619 × 1/10)		9,162

h.   Journal entry by issuer for bonds issued with detachable warrants:

(1). Both bonds and warrants have determinable market values.[a]

1/1/95	Cash	106,050	
	Bonds payable		102,010
	Contributed capital—stock warrants outstanding		4,040

[a]The total proceeds are allocated between the bonds and detachable warrants on the basis of their relative market values as follows: [$106,050 × (100 × $1,010) + ($101,000 + $4,000)] = $102,010 and [$106,050 × (100 × $40) + ($101,000 + $4,000)] = $4,040.

(2). Only warrants have a determinable market value.

1/1/95	Cash	106,050	
	Bonds payable		102,050
	Contributed capital—stock warrants outstanding (100 × $40)		4,000

i. Journal entry by issuer for exercise of detachable warrants:

12/21/97	Cash (100 × 10 × $30)..	30,000	
	Contributed capital—stock warrants outstanding	4,040	
	Common stock (100 × 10 × $10)...		10,000
	Contributed capital in excess of par—common ($30,000 + $4,040 − $10,000)		24,040

j. Journal entries related to note issued for noncash assets:

Journal entries by issuer.

1/1/95	Land..	39,860	
	Notes payable..		39,860
12/31/95	Interest expense..	4,783	
	Notes payable..		4,783[a]
12/31/96	Interest expense..	5,357	
	Notes payable..		5,357[a]
12/31/96	Notes payable..	50,000	
	Cash		50,000

Journal entries by investor.

1/1/95	Notes receivable...	39,860	
	Land..		20,000
	Gain on sale of land...		19,860
12/31/95	Notes receivable...	4,783	
	Interest revenue..		4,783[a]
12/31/96	Notes receivable...	5,357	
	Interest revenue..		5,357[a]
12/31/96	Cash	50,000	
	Notes receivable...		50,000

[a]Book value of note at beginning of period multiplied by the imputed effective rate of interest: ($39,860 × 12%) = $4,783 and [($39,860 + $4,783) × 12%] = $5,357. The effective rate of interest is imputed by finding the rate that discounts the face value of the note to an amount equal to the fair value of the land: $39,860 ÷ $50,000 = .7972 or $\overline{p_2}$ 12%.

k. Journal entries related to note issued for cash and other rights or obligations:

Journal entries by issuer.

1/1/95	Cash	50,000	
	Notes payable..		39,860[a]
	Unearned revenue ($50,000 − $39,860)...		10,140
5/14/95	Accounts receivable (6,000 × $12.90)...	77,400	
	Unearned revenue ($10,140 × 60%)...	6,084	
	Sales revenue ($77,400 + $6,084)...		83,484

Journal entries by investor:

1/1/95	Notes receivable...	39,860[a]	
	Prepaid purchases ($50,000 − $39,860)..	10,140	
	Cash		50,000
5/14/95	Purchases ($77,400 + $6,084)...	83,484	
	Accounts payable (6,000 × $12.90)..		77,400
	Prepaid purchases ($10,140 × 60%)..		6,084

[a]Present value of note discounted at market rate of interest: $50,000 × .7972 = $39,860. Notice also that if the issuer and the investor are calendar year companies, the journal entries related to the note on December 31, 1995 and 1996, would be the same as the response to situation j.

*1. Journal entries related to troubled debt restructuring:

(1). Debt restructured by transfer of asset.

Journal entry by issuer (debtor).

1/1/03	Bonds payable..	100,000	
	Interest payable ($100,000 × 5% × 2)	10,000	
	Land..		75,000
	Extraordinary gain on debt restructuring [($100,000 + $10,000) − $95,000]		15,000
	Gain on transfer of land ($95,000 − $75,000)		20,000

Journal entry by investor (creditor).

1/1/03	Land..	95,000	
	Loss on restructuring [($100,000 + $10,000) − $95,000]...........................	15,000	
	Investment in bonds...		100,000
	Interest receivable ($100,000 × 5% × 2)		10,000

(2). Debt restructured by transfer of equity securities.

Journal entry by issuer (debtor).

1/1/03	Bonds payable..	100,000	
	Interest payable ($100,000 × 5% × 2)	10,000	
	Common stock (5,000 × $10)..		50,000
	Contributed capital in excess of par—common [(5,000 × $19) − $50,000]...		45,000
	Extraordinary gain on debt restructuring [($100,000 + $10,000) − ($5,000 × $19)]		15,000

Journal entry by investor (creditor).

1/1/03	Investment in stock (5,000 × $19)...	95,000	
	Loss on restructuring ($100,000 + $10,000) − $95,000]..........................	15,000	
	Investment in bonds...		100,000
	Interest receivable ($100,000 × 5% × 2)		10,000

(3). Debt restructured by modification of terms and book value of debt greater than restructured cash flows.

Journal entries by issuer (debtor).[a]

1/1/03	Bonds payable..	100,000	
	Interest payable ($100,000 × 5% × 2)	10,000	
	Bonds payable..		97,200
	Extraordinary gain on debt restructuring ($110,000 − $97,200)................		12,800
12/31/03	Bonds payable..	3,600	
	Cash ($90,000 × 4%)..		3,600
12/31/04	Bonds payable..	93,600	
	Cash [$90,000 + ($90,000 × 4%)]...		93,600

[a]The book value of the restructured debt ($100,000 + $10,000 = $110,000) is greater than the restructured cash flows {[$90,000 + ($90,000 × 4% × 2)] = $97,200}. Thus the modified debt is recorded at an amount equal to the restructured cash flows, the excess of the book value of the restructured debt over the restructured cash flows ($110,000 − $97,200 = $12,800) is recorded as a gain by the debtor, and all subsequent cash payments are recorded as a reduction of the modified debt.

Journal entries by investor (creditor).[b]

1/1/03	Investment in bonds..	80,624	
	Loss on restructuring ($110,000 − $80,624)...	29,376	
	Investment in bonds...		100,000
	Interest receivable ($100,000 × 5% × 2)		10,000
12/31/03	Cash ($90,000 × 4%)..	3,600	
	Investment in bonds ($8,063 − $3,600)	4,463	
	Interest revenue ($80,624 × 10%)		8,063
12/31/04	Cash ($90,000 × 4%)..	3,600	
	Investment in bonds ($8,509 − $3,600)	4,909	
	Interest revenue [($80,624 + $4,463) × 10%].......................................		8,509
	Cash	90,000	
	Investment in bonds (rounded up by $4)...		90,000

[b]The present value of the restructured cash flows discounted over two years at the historical effective interest rate of 10 percent (which is equal to the stated interest because the bonds were issued at their face value) is $80,624 [($90,000 × .8264) + ($3,600 × 1.7355)].

Thus the modified debt is recorded at its impairment value, and a loss is recognized for the excess of the book value of the restructured debt over the impairment value. Subsequently, interest revenue is recognized at the historical effective interest rate of 10 percent by the effective interest method, such that at maturity date the book value of the modified debt is equal to the maturity value of $90,000.

(4). Debt restructured by modification of terms and restructured cash flows greater than book value of debt.

Journal entries by issuer (debtor).[a]

1/1/03	Bonds payable..	100,000	
	Interest payable ($100,000 × 5% × 2)......................................	10,000	
	Notes payable ($100,000 + $10,000)		110,000
12/31/03	Interest expense ($110,000 × 1%)......................................	1,100	
	Notes payable..		1,100
12/31/04	Interest expense [($110,000 + $1,100) × 1%]	1,111	
	Notes payable..		1,111
12/31/04	Notes payable..	112,211	
	Cash..		112,211

[a]The restructured cash flows ($112,211) are greater than the book value of the restructured debt ($100,000 + $10,000 = $110,000). Thus the modified debt is recorded at an amount equal to the book value of the restructured debt ($110,000), and the excess of the restructured cash flows over the book value of restructured debt ($112,211 − $110,000 = $2,211) is amortized as interest expense by the effective interest method using the interest rate (1%) that discounts the restructured cash flows to an amount equal to the book value of the restructured debt ($110,000 ÷ $112,211 = .9803 or $p_{\overline{2}|1\%}$).

Journal entries by investor (creditor).[b]

1/1/03	Note receivable	92,732	
	Loss on restructuring ($110,000 − $92,732)...........................	17,268	
	Investment in bonds..		100,000
	Interest receivable ($100,000 × 5% × 2)		10,000
12/31/03	Note receivable..	9,273	
	Interest revenue ($92,732 × 10%)......................................		9,273
12/31/04	Note receivable..	10,201	
	Interest revenue [($92,732 + $9,273) × 10%]...........................		10,201
	Cash..	112,211	
	Note receivable (rounded up by $5)...................................		112,211

[b]The present value of the restructured cash flows discounted over two years at the historical effective interest rate of 10 percent (which is equal to the stated interest because the bonds were issued at their face value) is $92,732 [$112,211 × .8264]. Thus, the modified debt is recorded at its impairment value and a loss is recognized for the excess of the book value of the restructured debt over the impairment value. Subsequently, interest revenue is recognized at the historical effective interest rate of 10 percent by the effective interest method, such that at maturity date the book value of the modified debt is equal to the maturity value of $112,211.

15 LEASES

CHAPTER OBJECTIVES

After reading Chapter 15 and completing the questions, cases, exercises, and problems from the text chapter, you should be able to:

1. Distinguish conceptually between a lease that is a rental of property (operating lease) and a lease that is an acquisition and sale and/or financing of property (capital lease and direct-financing or sales-type lease).
2. Determine the minimum lease payments related to a lease.
3. Distinguish between the interest rate implicit in the lease and the lessee's incremental borrowing rate.
4. Distinguish between guaranteed and unguaranteed residual value.

5. Identify and apply the criteria for classifying a lease as either a capital lease or an operating lease from the standpoint of the lessee.
6. Prepare the journal entries required to account for a capital lease and an operating lease from the standpoint of the lessee.
7. Identify and apply the criteria for classifying a lease as a direct-financing lease, a sales-type lease, or an operating lease from the standpoint of the lessor.
8. Prepare the journal entries required to account for a direct-financing lease, a sales-type lease, and an operating lease from the standpoint of the lessor.
9. Prepare the journal entries required to account for a sale-leaseback transaction and a sale-partial leaseback transaction.

CHAPTER REVIEW

Introduction

1. A *lease* is a contractual agreement whereby one party, called the *lessor,* conveys the right to use property to another party, called the *lessee,* usually for a stated period of time in return for cash or periodic lease payments. Leasing rather than purchasing property may offer several advantages to the lessee, including financing without substantial down payment, reduction of risk due to property obsolescence, greater tax deductions, and increased borrowing capability.

2. A lease that transfers substantially all the rights, risks, and rewards associated with the ownership of property from the lessor to the lessee can be viewed conceptually as the acquisition of an asset and the incurrence of a liability by the lessee and as a sale and/or financing of an asset by the lessor. Otherwise, a lease can be viewed as a rental of property by the lessor to the lessee.

3. The lessee accounts for a lease that transfers substantially all ownership rights, risks, and rewards from the lessor to the lessee (called a *capital lease*) the same as for any other exchange transaction in

which an entity acquires an asset and incurs a liability. The lessor accounts for such a lease as either a financing of the property acquisition by the lessee (*direct-financing lease*) or a sale and financing of the property acquisition by the lessee (*sales-type lease*). A lease that does not transfer ownership rights, risks, and rewards from the lessor to the lessee is called an *operating lease*. Both the lessor and the lessee account for an operating lease as a rental of property.

4 . The effects on earnings of accounting for a lease as a capital lease and a direct-financing or sales-type lease and as an operating lease are identical over the lease term or life of the leased property. The difference in earnings between the methods has to do with when revenues and expenses are reported on the income statement of the lessor and the lessee. The effects on the balance sheet of the methods are more pronounced. Under a capital lease and a direct-financing or sales-type lease, the lessor reports the lease receivable as an asset, whereas the lessee reports the leased property as an asset and the lease obligation as a liability. Under an operating lease, the lessor reports the leased property as an asset, whereas the lessee reports neither an asset nor a liability.

5. The guidelines for the practical application of these conceptual aspects of accounting for and reporting of leases are contained in *FASB Statement No. 13*, the major provisions of which are described in the remainder of this chapter review. Although *Statement No. 13* is consistent with *International Accounting Standard 17*, U.S. requirements are the most detailed and prescriptive in the world. Indeed, in countries where accounting emphasizes legal form rather than economic substance, all leases are accounted for as operating leases. Moreover, because the European Community has no specific requirements regarding accounting for leases, there is likely to be diversity in this area within Europe and internationally for the foreseeable future.

Accounting by Lessee

6 . The lessee should classify and account for a lease as a *capital lease* if one or more of the following criteria are met at the date of the lease agreement; conversely, the lessee should classify and account for a lease as an *operating lease* if none of these criteria is met:

a. The lease transfers ownership of the property to the lessee by the end of the lease term.
b. The lease contains a *bargain purchase option,* a provision allowing the lessee to purchase the leased property for a price that is sufficiently lower than its expected fair value that

exercise of the option appears to be reasonably assured.
c. The *lease term,* the fixed noncancelable term of the lease plus certain other periods such as those covered by bargain renewal options, is equal to 75 percent or more of the estimated economic life of the leased property.
d. The present value of the minimum lease payments at the beginning of the lease term, excluding payments representing executory costs to be paid by the lessor, equals or exceeds 90 percent of the excess of the fair value of the leased property at the date of the lease agreement over any investment tax credit retained and expected to be realized by the lessor.

These four criteria represent the FASB's implementation of the conceptual criterion of whether the lease transfers substantially all the rights, risks, and rewards associated with the ownership of the leased property from the lessor to the lessee. Such transfers can be evidenced by the transfer or reasonably assured transfer of title to the leased property from the lessor to the lessee (criterion a or b), by a lease term that is substantially equal to the economic life of the leased property (criterion c), or by lease payments that are approximately equal to the fair value of the leased property plus interest over the lease term (criterion d). The latter two criteria, however, are not applicable if the beginning of the lease term falls within the last 25 percent of the estimated economic life of the leased property.

7. When a lease is a capital lease, the lessee should record at the date of the lease agreement an asset (leased property) and a liability (lease liability) at the lower of the present value of the minimum lease payments (excluding payments representing executory costs to be paid by the lessor) or the fair value of the leased property. Additionally, a lease payment (excluding executory costs) that occurs at the date of the lease agreement should be recorded by the lessee as a reduction of the lease liability.

8. *Minimum lease payments* are the payments that the lessee is obligated to make under the terms of the lease agreement excluding any contingent rental payments. If the lease agreement contains no bargain purchase option, the minimum lease payments include (*a*) the periodic lease payments over the lease term, (*b*) the amount of any guarantee by the lessee or a related third party of the residual value of the leased property at the end of the lease term, and (*c*) any payment required by the lessee for failure to renew or extend the lease at the end of the lease term. If the lease agreement contains a bargain purchase option, the minimum lease payments include the periodic lease payments up to the date the

bargain purchase option becomes exercisable and the payment called for by the bargain purchase option.

9. *Executory costs,* such as insurance, maintenance, and taxes, related to leased property may be paid by the lessee or the lessor, depending on the terms of the lease agreement. Any portion of the minimum lease payments that represents executory costs to be paid by the lessor should be excluded from the determination of the present value of the minimum lease payments, since these costs are not part of the payment for property rights. Hereinafter, for simplicity, it is assumed that the minimum lease payments exclude any payments that represent executory costs to be paid by the lessor; that is, the executory costs are paid by the lessee directly.

10. The discount rate used by the lessee to determine the present value of the minimum lease payments should be the lower of the lessee's incremental borrowing rate or the interest rate implicit in the lease (if known). The *interest rate implicit in the lease* is the rate that causes the aggregate present value of the minimum lease payments and the unguaranteed residual value accruing to the lessor to be equal to the fair value of the leased property less any investment tax credit retained and expected to be realized by the lessor. The *lessee's incremental borrowing rate* is the interest rate that the lessee would have incurred to borrow the funds necessary to purchase the leased property. The interest rate implicit in the lease should be used when it is less than the incremental borrowing rate, because the lower present value of the minimum lease payments that would result from the use of the higher incremental borrowing rate could cause the lessee to fail to meet the fourth (90 percent of fair value) criterion for a capital lease. Conversely, the incremental borrowing rate should be used when it is less than the implicit interest rate or when it is not practicable for the lessee to learn the implicit rate, subject to the limitation that the leased property should not be recorded by the lessee at an amount in excess of its fair value at the date of the lease agreement.

11. In accounting for a capital lease during the lease term, the lessee should record the periodic lease payments as a reduction of the lease liability and any contingent rental payments as an expense. Coincidentally, the lessee also should recognize interest expense on the lease liability over the lease term by the effective interest method. Specifically, whether the periodic lease payments are payable at the beginning or the end of each period, the lessee should record at the end of each period the interest accrued on the lease liability by debiting interest expense and crediting lease liability for the balance of the lease liability at the beginning of the period multiplied by the appropriate interest rate.

12. The interest rate that should be used by the lessee to determine the periodic interest expense depends on the amount at which the lease liability is recorded at the date of the lease agreement. When the lease liability is recorded at the present value of the minimum lease payments, the appropriate interest rate is either the lessee's incremental borrowing rate or the interest rate implicit in the lease, depending on which rate is used to determine the recorded present value amount. When the lease liability is recorded at the fair value of the leased property, the appropriate interest rate is the rate that causes the present value of the minimum lease payments to be equal to the recorded fair value amount.

13. In accounting for a capital lease, the lessee also should record at the end of each period depreciation on the leased property, in accordance with its normal depreciation policy, by debiting depreciation expense and crediting accumulated depreciation. If the lease either transfers ownership of the property to the lessee by the end of the lease term or contains a bargain purchase option, the period of depreciation should be the estimated economic life of the leased property and the salvage value should be the expected value of the property at the end of its useful life. Conversely, if the lease neither transfers ownership of the property to the lessee by the end of the lease term nor contains a bargain purchase option, the period of depreciation should be the lease term and the salvage value normally should be the amount of any guaranteed residual value.

14. In a classified balance sheet, the lessee should report the leased property less the accumulated depreciation as a noncurrent asset and the lease liability partly as a current liability and partly as a noncurrent liability. The portion of the lease liability that typically is reported as a current liability is the amount of the minimum lease payments that will be made during the next 12 months or the operating cycle, if longer, less the amount of interest expense that will be accrued during that period.

15. The lease liability at the end of the lease term should have a balance equal to the amount of any guaranteed residual value or the amount called for by the bargain purchase option, if one is contained in the lease agreement. If the actual residual value is less than the guaranteed amount, the lessee must pay the deficiency to the lessor and record a gain or loss for the difference between the net carrying value of the leased property and lease liability and the amount of the residual value deficiency. When the estimated salvage value of the leased property equals the guaranteed residual value, for example, the lessee should record the return of the leased property and the payment of the residual value deficiency to the lessor by (*a*) debiting loss on residual value guarantee for the excess of the guaranteed residual value over the actual amount, (*b*) debiting lease liability for the amount of the guaranteed residual value, (*c*) debiting accumulated depreciation for the recorded value of the leased property less the guaranteed residual value, (*d*) crediting leased property for its recorded value, and (*e*) crediting cash for the excess of the guaranteed residual value over the actual amount. Alternatively, when the bargain purchase option contained in a lease agreement is exercised, the lessee should debit lease liability and credit cash for the amount called for by the bargain purchase option.

16. When a lease is an operating lease, the lessee should record the rental payments as an expense of the period in which use benefit is derived from the rental property. The lessee should record neither an asset nor a liability for the rental property.

Accounting by Lessor

17. The lessor should classify and account for a lease as a direct-financing lease or a sales-type lease if all of the following criteria are met at the date of the lease agreement; otherwise the lessor should classify and account for a lease as an *operating lease*.

a. One or more of the four criteria for a capital lease, described earlier for the lessee, are met.
b. Collectibility of the lease payments is reasonably predictable.
c. There is no significant uncertainty related to the amount of unreimbursable costs yet to be incurred by the lessor under the lease.

It should be observed that the latter two criteria simply are applications of the revenue recognition criteria discussed in Chapters 2 and 7, namely, reasonable predictability of the amounts to be collected and virtual completion of the earnings process.

18. The lessor should account for a lease that meets all the preceding criteria as a *direct-financing lease* if the only source of earnings is interest over the lease term (that is, the fair value of the leased property at the date of the lease agreement equals the cost of the property to the lessor); as a *sales-type lease* if a profit arises as a result of the transfer of the property (that is, the fair value of the leased property at the date of the lease agreement exceeds the cost of the property to the lessor); or as a *leveraged lease* if the transaction also involves a third party that provides financing for the lessor's initial purchase of the leased property. Because of their technical complexity, accounting for leveraged leases is not discussed in the text chapter.

19. When a lease is a direct-financing lease, the lessor should record the following journal entry at the date of the lease agreement: (*a*) a debit to lease receivable for the present value of the minimum lease payments (including any residual value guaranteed by an unrelated third party) and any unguaranteed residual value accruing to the benefit of the lessor and (*b*) a credit to the appropriate asset account for the cost of the leased property to the lessor. Additionally, a lease payment that occurs at the date of the lease agreement should be recorded by the lessor as a reduction of the lease receivable. Also, *initial direct costs,* such as commissions and legal fees, incurred by the lessor in negotiating and consummating the lease transaction should be recorded as a debit to lease receivable, to be implicitly matched with the interest revenue over the lease term.

20. In accounting for a direct-financing lease during the lease term, the lessor should record the periodic lease payments as a reduction of the lease receivable and any contingent rental payments as revenue. Coincidentally, the lessor also should recognize interest revenue on the lease receivable over the lease term by the effective interest method. Specifically, whether the periodic lease payments are payable at the beginning or the end of each period, the lessor should record at the end of each period the interest accrued on the lease receivable by debiting lease receivable and crediting interest revenue. When there are no initial direct costs, the periodic interest revenue should be calculated by multiplying the lease receivable at the beginning of the period by the interest rate implicit in the lease. When there are initial direct costs, the periodic interest revenue should be calculated by multiplying the lease receivable at the beginning of the period by the interest rate that causes the present value of the minimum lease payments and the unguaranteed residual value accruing to the lessor to be equal to the lease receivable (including the initial direct costs) at the date of the lease agreement.

21. When a lease is a sales-type lease, at the date of the lease agreement the lessor should (*a*) debit lease receivable for the present value of the minimum lease payments (including any residual value guaranteed by an unrelated third party) and any unguaranteed residual value accruing to the benefit of the lessor, (*b*) debit cost of goods sold for the cost of the leased property to the lessor less the present value of the unguaranteed residual value accruing to the lessor, (*c*) credit sales revenue for the present value of the minimum lease payments, and (*d*) credit inventory for the cost of the leased property to the lessor. The present value amounts recorded as part of this journal entry should be determined by the interest rate implicit in the lease. Additionally, a lease payment that occurs at the date of the lease agreement should be recorded by the lessor as a reduction of the lease receivable. Also, initial direct costs incurred by the lessor in nego- tiating and consummating the lease transaction should be recorded as an expense to be matched with the gross profit recognized at the date of the lease agreement.

22. After the date of the lease agreement, the lessor should account for a sales-type lease the same as for a direct-financing lease; that is, the periodic lease payments should be recorded as a reduction of the lease receivable, and the interest revenue should be accrued over the lease term by the effective interest method at the interest rate implicit in the lease.

23. In a classified balance sheet, the lessor should report the lease receivable in a direct-financ- ing lease or a sales-type lease partly as a current asset and partly as a noncurrent asset. The portion of the lease receivable that typically is reported as a current asset is the minimum lease payments that will be received during the next 12 months or the operating cycle, if longer, less the amount of interest revenue that will be accrued during that period.

24. The lease receivable at the end of the lease term should have a balance equal to the amount of the guaranteed residual value and/or the unguaran- teed residual value accruing to the lessor or the amount called for by the bargain purchase option, if any. If the actual residual value is less than the guaranteed amount, the lessor should record the return of the leased property and the payment of the residual value deficiency by the lessee by (*a*) debit- ing cash for the excess of the guaranteed residual value over the actual amount, (*b*) debiting the appropriate asset account for the actual residual value of the leased property, and (*c*) crediting lease receivable for the amount of the guaranteed residual value. If the actual residual value is equal to or greater than the guaranteed amount, the lessor should debit the appropriate asset account and credit lease receivable for the amount of the guaranteed residual value. No gain for the excess of the actual residual value over the guaranteed amount should be recognized by the lessor until it is realized. Simi- larly, if the residual value is not guaranteed, when the leased property is sold, the lessor should record a gain or loss equal to the difference between the actual residual value and the estimated residual value at the date of the lease agreement. Alternatively, when the bargain purchase option contained in a lease agreement is exercised by the lessee, the lessor should debit cash and credit lease receivable for the amount called for by the bargain purchase option.

25. When a lease is an operating lease, the lessor should record the rental receipts as revenue of the period in which they are earned. The rental property should be reported as a noncurrent asset and depreciated in accordance with the lessor's normal depreciation policy. And initial direct costs should be recorded as an asset to be amortized over the lease term in proportion to the recognition of rental revenue.

Sale-Leaseback Transactions

26. A *sale-leaseback* transaction occurs when one party, called the *seller-lessee*, sells property to and immediately leases it back from another party, called the *purchaser-lessor*. A gain on a sale- leaseback transaction should be deferred by the seller-lessee because the transaction does not represent the culmination of the earnings process. A loss on a sale-leaseback transaction, however, should be included in the determination of current net income rather than deferred. Specifically, the seller-lessee should record the sale of the property to the purchaser-lessor by (*a*) debiting cash for the amount received, (*b*) crediting the appropriate asset account for the cost of the property to the seller- lessee, and (*c*) either crediting deferred gain on sale- leaseback, if the selling price exceeds the cost of the property, or debiting loss on sale-leaseback, if the cost exceeds the selling price of the property.

27. Subsequently, if the lease is a capital lease, the seller-lessee should amortize the deferred gain as a reduction of depreciation expense over the period the leased property is being depreciated by debiting deferred gain on sale-leaseback and crediting depreci- ation expense. Furthermore, the seller-lessee should report the unamortized deferred gain on the balance sheet as a contra asset to the leased property. The effect of these procedures is to reduce depreciation expense and the lease property to the seller-lessee's original cost basis. In all other respects, the seller- lessee should account for a capital lease arising from a sale-leaseback transaction the same as for any other capital lease.

28. Alternatively, if the lease is an operating lease, the seller-lessee should amortize the deferred gain as a reduction of rent expense over the lease term. And because the rental property under an operating lease is not recorded as an asset by the lessee, the seller-lessee reports the unamortized deferred gain on the balance sheet as a deferred credit rather than as a contra asset.

29. A *sale-partial leaseback* transaction occurs when only a portion of the property is leased back or the property is leased back for only a portion of its useful life. When only a minor portion of the use of the property sold is leased back (that is, the present value of the lease payments equals or is less than 10 percent of the fair value of the property), any gain on the sale should be included by the seller-lessee in current net income rather than deferred and amortized. Conversely, when more than a minor portion but less than substantially all of the use of the property sold is leased back, the seller-lessee should include in current net income only that portion of any gain that is in excess of (*a*) the present value of the lease payments, if the lease-back is an operating lease, or (*b*) the recorded value of the leased property, if the leaseback is a capital lease. In this circumstance, the remainder of any gain should be deferred and amortized. Finally, when substantially all of the use of the property sold is leased back, the total amount of any gain on the sale should be deferred and amortized by the seller-lessee. In all other respects, the seller-lessee should account for a sale-partial leaseback the same as another sale-leaseback transaction.

30. The purchaser-lessor should record the purchase of the property from the seller-lessee by debiting the appropriate asset account and crediting cash for the amount paid. Subsequently, the purchaser-lessor should account for a lease arising from a sale-leaseback transaction, whether or not partial, the same as another lease, except that such leases cannot be accounted for as a sales-type lease.

Appendix: Real Estate Leases

31. There are several technical issues related to the classification of and accounting for real estate leases. First, in a lease of land only, both the lessee and the lessor should classify the lease on the basis of the first (transfers title) and second (bargain purchase option) criteria for a capital lease; that is, the third (75 percent of economic life) and fourth (90 percent of fair market value) criteria for a capital lease are not applicable to leases of land. Second, when a lease covers land and buildings and either the first or the second criterion for a capital

lease is met, the lessee should record the land and buildings separately (by allocating the present value of the minimum lease payments between the land and buildings in proporation to their fair values) and the lessor should classify and account for the land and building as a single unit. Conversely, if neither the first nor the second criterion is met and the fair value of the land is less than 25 percent of the total fair value of the leased property, both the lessee and the lessor should classify and account for the land and buildings as a single unit. Alternatively, if neither the first nor the second criterion for a capital lease is met and the fair value of the land is 25 percent or more of the total fair value of the leased property, both the lessee and the lessor should first allocate the minimum lease payments between the land and buildings (by applying the lessee's incremental borrowing rate to the fair value of the land to determine the annual minimum lease payments applicable to the land) and then classify and account for the land and buildings separately. Third, when a lease covers equipment and real estate, both the lessee and the lessor should first estimate the portion of the minimum lease payments applicable to the equipment and then classify and account for the equipment and real estate separately. Finally, when a lease covers only part of a building and the cost and fair value of the leased property are objectively determinable, both the lessee and the lessor should classify and account for the lease the same as for a lease of land and buildings. Conversely, if the fair value of the leased property is not objectively determinable, the lessee should classify the lease on the basis of the third criterion for a capital lease. And if either the cost or the fair value of the leased property is not objectively determinable, the lessor should classify the lease as an operating lease.

SELF-STUDY LEARNING   Items marked with an asterisk (*) refer to the Appendix.

Key Terms and Concepts

Provide the appropriate term or terms to complete each of the following statements:

1. From the standpoint of the lessee, a lease that transfers substantially all the rights, risks, and rewards associated with the ownership of property from the lessor to the lessee is a(n) _____;
   otherwise, it is a(n) _____.

2. The lessor recognizes a profit at the date of the lease agreement and interest revenue over the lease term when the lease is a(n) _____, whereas the lessor recognizes only interest revenue over the lease term when the lease is a(n) _____.

3. A provision allowing the lessee to purchase the leased property for a price that is sufficiently lower than its expected fair value so that exercise of the option appears to be reasonably assured is called a(n) _____.

4. When a lease contains no bargain purchase option, the _____ include the periodic lease payments over the lease term, the amount of any guaranteed residual value at the end of the lease term, and any payments required by the lessee for failure to renew or extend the lease at the end of the lease term.

5. The rate that causes the aggregate present value of the minimum lease payments and the unguaranteed residual value accruing to the lessor to be equal to the fair value of the leased property less any investment tax credit retained and expected to be realized by the lessor is called the _____.

6. The rate that the lessee would have had to pay to borrow over a similar term the funds necessary to purchase the leased property is called the _____.

7. Insurance, maintenance, taxes, and other costs that are incidental to the ownership of leased property are called _____.

8. The portion of the leased property's residual value at the end of the lease term that is not guaranteed by the lessee or another party is called the _____.

9. The costs incurred by the lessor that are directly associated with negotiation and consummation of the lease transaction are called _____.

10. A transaction whereby one party, called the seller-lessee, sells property to and immediately leases it back from another party, called the purchaser-lessor, is a(n) _____ , or if only a portion of the property is leased back or the property is leased back for only a portion of its useful life, the transaction is a(n) _____.

True-False

Indicate by circling the appropriate response whether each of the following statements is true (T) or false (F):

T F 1. A lease should be classified and accounted for as a capital lease by the lessee only if the lease either contains a bargain purchase option or transfers ownership of the property to the lessee by the end of the lease term.

T F 2. A lease generally must be noncancelable in order to be classified and accounted for as a capital lease.

T F 3. A lease should be classified and accounted for as an operating lease when the beginning of the lease term falls within the last 25 percent of the estimated economic life of the property.

T F 4. The leased property and lease liability in a capital lease must be recorded by the lessee at the present value of the minimum lease payments determined by the incremental borrowing rate.

T F 5. When a lease is a capital lease, the lessee should record the leased property and lease liability at the present value of the minimum lease payments or the fair value of the property, if lower.

T F   6. The interest rate implicit in the lease is the rate that causes the present value of the minimum lease payments to be equal to the fair value of the leased property.

T F   7. Any portion of the minimum lease payments that represents executory costs to be paid by the lessor should be excluded from the computation of the recorded value of leased property, because these amounts do not represent payments for property rights.

T F   8. Under a capital lease, the leased property should be depreciated by the lessee in accordance with its normal depreciation policy, except that no salvage value should be deducted to determine the depreciation base of the property.

T F   9. When a lease is a capital lease, the lessee should report the minimum lease payments that will be made over the lease term as a current liability on the balance sheet.

T F   10. At the end of the term of a capital lease, the balance in the lease liability should equal any guaranteed residual value or bargain purchase option price.

T F   11. The lease receivable recorded by the lessor for a direct-financing lease or a sales-type lease should include the present value of the guaranteed residual value and any unguaranteed residual value accruing to the lessor.

T F   12. In accounting for a sales-type lease, the lessor should record the lease receivable at the cost of the leased property.

T F   13. Interest revenue from both a direct-financing lease and a sales-type lease should be accrued over the lease term by the effective interest method.

T F   14. Sales revenue recognized by the lessor from a sales-type lease should be recorded at the present value of the minimum lease payments determined by the interest rate implicit in the lease.

T F   15. After the date of the lease agreement, a sales-type lease is accounted for the same as a direct-financing lease.

T F   16. The initial direct costs incurred by the lessor in negotiating and consummating lease transactions should be expensed as they are incurred, regardless of the type of lease.

T F   17. Accounting for a lease by the purchaser-lessor is not affected by a sale-leaseback transaction, except that the lease cannot be accounted for as a sales-type lease.

T F   18. Any gain on a sale-leaseback transaction should be deferred by the seller-lessee only if the lease is a capital lease.

T F   19. The lessor should report the leased property as an asset when the lease is an operating lease.

T F *20. Only two of the four criteria for a capital lease are applicable to leases of land.

Multiple Choice

Select the best response for each of the following items, and circle the corresponding letter:

1. Which of the following is *not* one of the criteria for classifying a lease as a capital lease?

   a. The lease transfers ownership of the property to the lessee by the end of the lease term.
   b. The lease contains a bargain purchase option.
   c. The lessee is responsible for insurance, maintenance, taxes, and other costs that are incidental to the ownership of the leased property.
   d. The lease term is equal to 75 percent or more of the estimated economic life of the leased property.

2. When a lease is a capital lease, the lessee should record the leased property and lease liability at:

   a. The aggregate amount of the minimum lease payments.
   b. The present value of the minimum lease payments determined by the incremental borrowing rate.
   c. The present value of the minimum lease payments determined by the interest rate implicit in the lease if it is practicable for the lessee to learn the implicit rate and if the implicit rate is less than the incremental borrowing rate.
   d. The cost of the leased property to the lessor.

3. Leased property acquired under a capital lease should be depreciated by the lessee over:

   a. The lease term.
   b. The estimated economic life of the property.
   c. The estimated economic life of the property only if the lease transfers ownership of the property to the lessee by the end of the lease term.
   d. The lease term unless the lease either transfers ownership of the property to the lessee by the end of the lease term or contains a bargain purchase option.

4. The periodic interest expense recorded by the lessee for a capital lease should be determined by the effective interest method, with the appropriate interest rate being:

   a. The lessee's incremental borrowing rate.
   b. The interest rate implicit in the lease.
   c. Either the lessee's incremental borrowing rate or the interest rate implicit in the lease, depending on which rate is used to determine the recorded present value of the minimum lease payments.
   d. The prime interest rate.

5. In a lease that is appropriately accounted for as a sales-type lease, the lease receivable and the sales revenue should be recorded at the same amount except when there is (are):

   a. Initial direct costs.
   b. Unguaranteed residual value accruing to the lessor.
   c. Both a and b.
   d. Neither a nor b.

6. The unguaranteed residual value that accrues to the benefit of the lessor in a sales-type lease is not part of the computation of the amount debited or credited, at the date of the lease agreement, to:

   a. Inventory.
   b. Cost of goods sold.
   c. Lease receivable.
   d. Sales.

7. In a sales-type lease, the lessor should record cost of goods sold at:

   a. The cost of the leased property.
   b. The cost of the leased property less the guaranteed residual value.
   c. The cost of the leased property less the unguaranteed residual value accruing to the lessor.
   d. The cost of the leased property less the present value of the unguaranteed residual value accruing to the lessor.

8. In a lease that is appropriately recorded as a direct-financing lease, interest revenue:

   a. Should be accrued over the lease term by the effective interest method.
   b. Should be accrued over the lease term by the straight-line method.
   c. Does not arise.
   d. Should be accrued at the date of the lease agreement.

9. In a lease that is appropriately recorded as an operating lease by the lessee, the equal annual rental payments should be recorded as:

   a. Depreciation expense.
   b. Interest expense.
   c. A reduction of the lease liability.
   d. Rental expense.

10. Any gain on a sale-leaseback transaction that is a capital lease from the standpoint of the seller-lessee should be:

   a. Included in the determination of income currently except when the transaction is a sale-partial leaseback.
   b. Deferred and amortized as an adjustment of depreciation expense, with the unamortized balance reported on the balance sheet as a deferred credit.
   c. Deferred and amortized as an adjustment of depreciation expense, with the unamortized balance reported on the balance sheet as a contra asset to the leased property.
   d. Deferred currently and recognized at the end of the lease term.

Extended Problem

The two independent cases presented here involve leases that meet the criteria for capital leases from the standpoint of the lessee. In each case, the date of the lease agreement is January 1, 1995, and the equal annual lease payments are payable over the lease term on December 31 except for the first lease payment, which is due on the date of the lease agreement. Additional details for each case are shown in the table on the following page.

	CASE 1	CASE 2
Cancelability	Noncancelable	Noncancelable
Lease transfers ownership	No	No
Lease contains bargain purchase option	No	No
Lease term	10 years	10 years
Estimated economic life of leased property	10 years	12 years
Annual lease payments	$10,000	$12,000
Residual value of leased property		
Guaranteed by lessee	-0-	$5,000
Unguaranteed by lessee	-0-	-0-
Fair value of leased property	$67,590	$83,036
Cost of leased property to lessor	$67,590	$67,590
Responsibility for maintenance, insurance, and taxes	Lessee	Lessee
Lessee's incremental borrowing rate	10%	10%
Interest rate implicit in lease	10%	10%
Initial direct costs incurred by lessor	-0-	$500

REQUIRED

a. Explain why the leases in Cases 1 and 2 are capital leases from the standpoint of the lessee.

b. Describe what additional information would need to be obtained in order to determine whether the leases in Cases 1 and 2 are sales-type leases or direct-financing leases from the standpoint of the lessor.

c. Assuming that all the criteria are met, describe how it can be determined whether each lease is a sales-type lease or a direct-financing lease from the standpoint of the lessor.

d. Prepare the journal entries related to the lease in Case 1 for both the lessee and the lessor at the date of the lease agreement and on December 31, 1995, and show how the account balances should be reported in the classified balance sheet of the lessee and the lessor as of December 31, 1995.

e. Assume that the lessee's incremental borrowing rate in Case 1 is 12 percent (rather than 10 percent) and that it is not practicable for the lessee to learn the interest rate implicit in the lease. Calculate the amount at which the lessee should record the leased property and lease liability on January 1, 1995.

f. Assume that the lessee's incremental borrowing rate in Case 1 is 8 percent (rather than 10 percent). Calculate the amount at which the lessee should record the leased property and lease liability on January 1, 1995.

g. Assume that the lessor in Case 1 incurred initial direct costs of $1,162 (rather than none), which, when added to the cost of the leased property, reduced the rate of return on the lease to 9.5 percent. Prepare the journal entries required at the date of the lease agreement and on December 31, 1995, for the lessor.

h. Assume that the leased property in Case 1 had been originally acquired by the lessee at a cost of $60,000 and then sold to the lessor for $67,590. Prepare the journal entry required to record the sale of the property by the seller-lessee.

i. Prepare the journal entries related to the lease in Case 2 for both the lessee and the lessor at the date of the lease agreement and on December 31, 1995.

j. Prepare the journal entries related to the lease in Case 2 for both the lessee and the lessor at the end of the lease term (1) assuming the actual residual value of the leased property is $5,500, and (2) assuming the actual residual value of the leased property is $2,000 and the lessee pays the amount of the deficiency to the lessor.

k. Assume that the estimated residual value of the leased property in Case 2 is unguaranteed, with the benefits accruing to the lessor, rather than guaranteed. Prepare the journal entries related to the lease for both the lessee and the lessor at the date of the lease agreement and on December 31, 1995.

l. Assume the same facts described in situation k. Prepare the journal entries required at the end of the lease term for both the lessee and the lessor (1) assuming that the actual residual value of the leased property is $5,500, and (2) assuming that the actual residual value of the leased property is $2,000.

COMMON ERRORS

The first statement in each "common error" listed here is *incorrect*. Each incorrect statement is followed by a corrected statement and an explanation.

1. A lease that is a capital lease from the standpoint of the lessee is always a direct-financing lease or a sales-type lease from the standpoint of the lessor. *Wrong*

A lease that is a capital lease from the standpoint of the lessee is usually, but not necessarily, a direct-financing lease or a sales-type lease from the standpoint of the lessor. *Right*

A lease is a capital lease from the standpoint of the lessee if one or more of four criteria are met at the date of the lease agreement. These same four criteria plus two additional criteria are applied to determine whether a lease is a direct-financing lease or a sales-type lease from the standpoint of the lessor. A lease may meet one or more of the four criteria for a capital lease from the standpoint of both the lessee and the lessor but fail to meet the two additional criteria concerning the predictability of the collection of lease payments and the uncertainty of unreimbursable costs yet to be incurred by the lessor. Consequently, a lease may be a capital lease from the standpoint of the lessee and an operating lease from the standpoint of the lessor.

2. When the initial lease payment for a capital lease is made on the date of the lease agreement, the present value of the equal annual lease payments is calculated by the present value of an ordinary annuity factor for a period equal to the lease term. *Wrong*

When the initial lease payment for a capital lease is made on the date of the lease agreement, the present value of the equal annual lease payments should be calculated by the present value of an annuity due factor for a period equal to the lease term. *Right*

Equal annual lease payments that are payable at the beginning of each period over the lease term represent an annuity due rather than an ordinary annuity. The present value factor for the lease payment made on the date of the lease agreement is 1. The present value factor for the remaining annual lease payments is equal to the present value of an ordinary annuity factor for a period equal to the lease term minus 1. The sum of these two factors is the present value of an annuity due factor for a period equal to the lease term. This factor also can be determined from a table of the present value

of annuity due factors or by multiplying the present value of an ordinary annuity factor for a period equal to the lease term by 1 plus the interest rate.

3. The lessee should depreciate all leased property acquired in a capital lease over the lease term. *Wrong*

The lessee should depreciate the leased property acquired in a capital lease over the estimated economic life of the property if the lease either transfers ownership of the property to the lessee by the end of the lease term or contains a bargain purchase option; otherwise, the lessee should depreciate the leased property over the lease term. *Right*

Depreciation is the process of allocating the net cost of a depreciable asset over the period to be benefited by its use. If a lease either transfers ownership of the leased property to the lessee by the end of the lease term or contains a bargain purchase option, the lessee will have the use of the property over its entire estimated economic life. Otherwise the lessee will have the use of the property only over the lease term.

4. The amount recorded as the lease receivable in a direct-financing lease or a sales-type lease that contains no bargain purchase option should be based on the periodic lease payments over the lease term and the amount of any guaranteed residual value at the end of the lease term. *Wrong*

The amount recorded as the lease receivable in a direct-financing lease or a sales-type lease that contains no bargain purchase option should be based on the minimum lease payments over the lease term and the amount of any unguaranteed residual value accruing to the lessor at the end of the lease term. *Right*

When a lease contains no bargain purchase option, the minimum lease payments include the periodic lease payments over the lease term and the amount of any guaranteed residual value at the end of the lease term. When the terms of the lease agreement state that the unguaranteed residual value accrues to the lessor, the lessor's investment (receivable) in the lease includes the periodic lease payments over the lease term as well as both the guaranteed residual value and any unguaranteed residual value at the end of the lease term.

5. In accounting for a sales-type lease, the lessor always should record sales revenue at the normal selling price (fair market value) of the leased property and cost of goods sold at the cost of the leased property. *Wrong*

In accounting for a sales-type lease, the lessor should record sales revenue at the present value of the minimum lease payments and cost of goods sold at the cost of the leased property less the present value of the unguaranteed residual value accruing to the lessor. *Right*

The interest rate implicit in the lease is the rate that causes the aggregate present value of the minimum lease payments and the unguaranteed residual value accruing to the lessor to be equal to the fair value of the leased property less any investment tax credit retained and expected to be realized by the lessor. Accordingly, in the absence of an investment tax credit and an unguaranteed residual value, the present value of the minimum

lease payments (the recorded sales revenue) will be equal to the fair value (normal selling price) of the leased property. In contrast, when there is an unguaranteed residual value accruing to the lessor, the present value of the minimum lease payments (the recorded sales revenue) will be less than the fair value (normal selling price) of the leased property by an amount equal to the present value of the unguaranteed residual value. In effect, the present value of the unguaranteed residual value is deducted from both sales revenue and cost of goods sold, because this portion of the property has not been transferred from the lessor to the lessee. Notice that this treatment of the unguaranteed residual value has no effect on the gross profit recognized by the lessor, since both sales revenue and cost of goods sold are reduced by an equal amount.

ANSWERS   Items marked with an asterisk (*) refer to the Appendix.

Key Terms and Concepts

1. capital lease, operating lease
2. sales-type lease, direct-financing lease
3. bargain purchase option
4. minimum lease payments
5. interest rate implicit in the lease
6. incremental borrowing rate
7. executory costs
8. unguaranteed residual value
9. initial direct costs
10. sale-leaseback transaction, sale-partial leaseback transaction

True-False

1. F   A lease should be classified and accounted for as a capital lease by the lessee if one or more of four criteria are met at the date of the lease agreement. Two of the criteria are mentioned in the question. The other two criteria are that (*a*) the lease term is equal to 75 percent or more of the estimated economic life of the leased property, and (*b*) the present value of the minimum lease payments equals or exceeds 90 percent of the excess of the fair value of the property over any investment tax credit retained and expected to be realized by the lessor.
2. T
3. F   Only the third and fourth criteria for a capital lease are not applicable if the beginning of the lease term falls within

the last 25 percent of the estimated economic life of the property. The first and second criteria are still applicable. Thus if either of these criteria is met, the lease should be classified and accounted for as a capital lease by the lessee.

4. F   The interest rate implicit in the lease should be used by the lessee to determine the present value of the minimum lease payments if it is practicable for the lessee to learn the implicit rate and if the implicit rate is less than the lessee's incremental borrowing rate. Conversely, the lessee's incremental borrowing rate should be used to determine the present value of the minimum lease payments when it is less than the implicit rate or when it is not practicable for the lessee to learn the implicit rate, subject to the limitation that the leased property should not be recorded at an amount in excess of its fair value at the date of the lease agreement.

5. T
6. F   The interest rate implicit in the lease is the rate that causes the aggregate present value of the minimum lease payments and the unguaranteed residual value accruing to the lessor to be equal to the fair value of the leased property less any investment tax credit retained and expected to be realized by the lessor.

7. T
8. F   Under a capital lease, the leased property should be depreciated by the lessee in

accordance with its normal depreciation policy. If the lease either transfers ownership of the property to the lessee by the end of the lease term or contains a bargain purchase option, the period of depreciation should be the estimated economic life of the leased property and the salvage value should be the expected value of the property at the end of its useful life. If the lease neither transfers ownership of the property to the lessee by the end of the lease term nor contains a bargain purchase option, the period of depreciation should be the lease term and the salvage value normally should be the guaranteed residual value.

9. F   When a lease is a capital lease, the lessee should report the minimum lease payments that will be made during the next 12 months or the operating cycle, if longer, less the interest expense that will be accrued during that period as a current liability on the balance sheet.

10. T

11. T

12. F   When a lease is a direct-financing lease, the lessor should record the lease receivable at the cost of the leased property.

13. T

14. T

15. T

16. F   The initial direct costs incurred by the lessor in negotiating and consummating lease transactions should be expensed as they are incurred if the lease is a sales-type lease. The initial direct costs incurred by the lessor in connection with either a direct-financing lease or an operating lease, however, should be recorded as an asset and amortized over the lease term.

17. T

18. F   Any gain on a sale-leaseback transaction should be deferred by the seller-lessee regardless of the type of lease. If the lease is a capital lease, the seller-lessee should amortize the deferred gain as a reduction of depreciation expense over the period the leased property is being depreciated. If the lease is an operating lease, the seller-lessee should amortize the deferred gain as a reduction of rent expense over the lease term. All or a portion of any gain on a sale-partial leaseback transaction, however, should be included by the seller-lessee in current net income rather than deferred and amortized, if specific conditions are met.

19. T

*20. T

Multiple Choice

1. c		6. a
2. c		7. d
3. d		8. a
4. c		9. d
5. b		10. c

Extended Problem

a. The lease term in each case is equal to 75 percent or more of the estimated economic life of the leased property; in Case 1 the lease term (10 years) is equal to 100 percent of the estimated economic life of the property (10 years), and in Case 2 the lease term (10 years) is equal to 83 1/3 percent of the estimated economic life of the property (12 years). Moreover, as shown in the answers to questions d and i that follow, in each case the present value of the minimum lease payments equals the excess of the fair value of the leased property over any investment tax credit retained and expected to be realized by the lessor.

b. Additional information would need to be obtained to determine whether the collectibility of the lease payments is reasonably predictable and whether there is any significant uncertainty related to the amount of unreimbursable costs yet to be incurred by the lessor under the lease.

c. The lease in Case 1 is a direct-financing lease, because the fair value of the leased property at the date of the lease agreement equals the cost of the property to the lessor. The lease in Case 2 is a sales-type lease, because the fair value of the leased property at the date of the lease agreement exceeds the cost of the property to the lessor.

d. Journal entries and balance sheet presentation related to capital lease and direct-financing lease:

Journal entries by lessee.

1/1/95	Leased property...	67,590[a]	
	Lease liability...		67,590
1/1/95	Lease liability..	10,000	
	Cash..		10,000

[a]Present value of minimum lease payments at beginning of lease term: $10,000(P_{D\overline{10}|10\%})$, or $10,000(6.7590)$.

12/31/95	Interest expense [($67,590 − $10,000) × 10%].......................................	5,759	
	Lease liability...		5,759
12/31/95	Lease liability..	10,000	
	Cash..		10,000
12/31/95	Depreciation expense ($67,590 ÷ 10)...	6,759	
	Accumulated depreciation..		6,759

Balance sheet presentation by lessee as of December 31, 1995.

Assets
Leased property..	$67,590
Less: Accumulated depreciation	6,759
	$60,831

Liabilities
Current: Lease liability..	$ 4,665[a]
Noncurrent: Lease liability..	$48,684[b]

[a]Minimum lease payments that will be made during the next 12 months less the interest expense that will be accrued during that period: $10,000 − [($67,590 − $10,000 + $5,759 − $10,000) × 10%].
[b]Total lease liability less current portion: ($67,590 − $10,000 + $5,759 − $10,000) − $4,665.

Journal entries by lessor.

1/1/95	Lease receivable...	67,590	
	Equipment		67,590
1/1/95	Cash...	10,000	
	Lease receivable...		10,000
12/31/95	Lease receivable...	5,759	
	Interest revenue [($67,590 − $10,000) × 10%]		5,759
12/31/95	Cash...	10,000	
	Lease receivable...		10,000

Balance sheet presentation by lessor as of December 31, 1995.

Assets
Current: Lease receivable...	$ 4,665[a]
Noncurrent: Lease receivable	$48,684[b]

[a]Minimum lease payments that will be received during the next 12 months less the interest revenue that will be accrued during that period: $10,000 − [($67,590 − $10,000 + $5,759 − $10,000) × 10%].
[b]Total lease receivable less current portion: ($67,590 − $10,000 + $5,759 − $10,000) − $4,665.

e. Since it is not practicable for the lessee to learn the interest rate implicit in the lease, the leased property and lease liability should be recorded at the present value of the minimum lease payments determined by the lessee's incremental borrowing rate (12%), as follows: $10,000(P_{D\overline{10}|12\%})$, or $10,000(6.3283) = $63,283.

f. Since the lessee's incremental borrowing rate is less than the interest rate implicit in the lease, the lessee should use the incremental borrowing rate to calculate the present value of the minimum lease payments, as follows: $10,000(P_{D\overline{10}8\%})$, or $10,000(7.2469) = \$72,469$. However, since the present value of the minimum lease payments exceeds the fair value of the leased property, the lessee should record the leased property and lease liability at the fair value of the property, \$67,590.

g. Journal entries by lessor related to initial direct costs incurred in direct-financing lease:

1/1/95	Lease receivable ($67,590 + $1,162).....................................	68,752	
	Equipment		67,590
	Cash		1,162
1/1/95	Cash	10,000	
	Lease receivable..		10,000
12/31/95	Lease receivable..	5,581[a]	
	Interest revenue..		5,581
12/31/95	Cash	10,000	
	Lease receivable..		10,000

[a]Lease receivable at the beginning of the period multiplied by the rate of return on the lease, which is less than the implicit interest rate (10%) due to the initial direct costs: $(\$68,752 - \$10,000) \times 9.5\%$.

h. Journal entry by seller-lessee related to sale-leaseback transaction:

1/1/95	Cash	67,590	
	Equipment		60,000
	Deferred gain on sale-leaseback......................................		7,590

i. Journal entries related to capital lease and sales-type lease when residual value guaranteed:

Journal entries by lessee.

1/1/95	Leased property..	83,036[a]	
	Lease liability		83,036
1/1/95	Lease liability	12,000	
	Cash		12,000

[a]Present value of minimum lease payments at beginning of lease term: $12,000 ($P_{D\overline{10}10\%}$) + $5,000 ($p_{D\overline{10}10\%}$), or $12,000 (6.7590) + $5,000(.3855)$.

12/31/95	Interest expense [$(\$83,036 - \$12,000) \times 10\%$]......................................	7,104	
	Lease liability		7,104
12/31/95	Lease liability	12,000	
	Cash		12,000
12/31/95	Depreciation expense [$(\$83,036 - \$5,000) \div 10$]....................................	7,804	
	Accumulated depreciation..		7,804

Journal entries by lessor.

1/1/95	Lease receivable..	83,036[a]	
	Cost of goods sold...	67,590	
	Sales revenue..		83,036
	Inventory..		67,590
1/1/95	Cash	12,000	
	Lease receivable..		12,000
1/1/95	Expenses (direct costs)...	500	
	Cash		500

[a]Present value of minimum lease payments at beginning of lease term: $12,000 ($P_{D\overline{10}10\%}$) + $5,000 ($p_{D\overline{10}10\%}$), or $12,000 (6.7590) + $5,000(.3855)$.

12/31/95	Lease receivable...	7,104	
	Interest revenue [$(\$83,036 - \$12,000) \times 10\%$]		7,104
12/31/95	Cash	12,000	
	Lease receivable..		12,000

j. Journal entries at the end of the lease term related to guaranteed residual value:

(1). Actual residual value greater than guaranteed amount.

Journal entry by lessee.

12/31/04	Lease liability	5,000[a]	
	Accumulated depreciation ($83,036 – $5,000)...	78,036	
	Leased property..		83,036

Journal entry by lessor.

12/31/04	Equipment	5,000	
	Lease receivable..		5,000[a]

[a]The lessee's lease liability and the lessor's lease receivable should have balances at the end of the lease term equal to the amount of the guaranteed residual value. Notice further that the lessor should not recognize a gain for the excess of the actual residual value ($5,500) over the guaranteed amount ($5,000) until it is realized.

(2). Actual residual value less than guaranteed amount.

Journal entry by lessee.

12/31/04	Lease liability	5,000	
	Loss on residual value guarantee ($5,000 – $2,000)...............................	3,000	
	Accumulated depreciation ($83,036 – $5,000)...	78,036	
	Leased property..		83,036
	Cash ($5,000 – $2,000)..		3,000

Journal entry by lessor.

12/31/04	Cash ($5,000 – $2,000)...	3,000	
	Equipment	2,000	
	Lease receivable..		5,000

k. Journal entries related to capital lease and sales-type lease when residual value unguaranteed:

Journal entries by lessee.

1/1/95	Leased property..	81,108[a]	
	Lease liability		81,108
1/1/95	Lease liability	12,000	
	Cash..		12,000

[a]Present value of minimum lease payments at beginning of lease term: $12,000 ($P_{D\overline{10}10\%}$), or $12,000(6.7590)$.

12/31/95	Interest expense [($81,108 – $12,000) × 10%]......................................	6,911	
	Lease liability		6,911
12/31/95	Lease liability	12,000	
	Cash..		12,000
12/31/95	Depreciation expense ($81,108 + 10)...	8,111	
	Accumulated depreciation...		8,111

Journal entries by lessor.

1/1/95	Lease receivable...	83,036[a]	
	Cost of goods sold..	65,662[b]	
	Sales revenue...		81,108[c]
	Inventory...		67,590
1/1/95	Cash	12,000	
	Lease receivable..		12,000
1/1/95	Expenses (direct costs)	500	
	Cash..		500

[a]Present value of the minimum lease payments and unguaranteed residual value at the beginning of the lease term: $12,000 ($P_{D\overline{10}10\%}$) + $5,000 ($P_{D\overline{10}10\%}$), or $12,000 (6.7590) + $5,000(.3855)$.
[b]Cost of leased property less present value of unguaranteed residual value: $67,590 – $5,000 ($P_{D\overline{10}10\%}$), or $67,590 – $5,000 (.3855)$.
[c]Present value of minimum lease payments at beginning of lease terms: $12,000 ($P_{D\overline{10}10\%}$) or $12,000 (6.7590)$.

12/31/95	Lease receivable..	7,104	
	Interest revenue [($83,036 − $12,000) × 10%]...................................		7,104[a]
12/31/95	Cash...	12,000	
	Lease receivable...		12,000

[a]Notice that when any unguaranteed residual value accrues to the lessor, the periodic interest revenue recognized by the lessor ($7,104) differs from the periodic interest expense recognized by the lessee ($6,911).

1. Journal entries at the end of the lease term related to unguaranteed residual value:

   (1). Actual residual value greater than estimated amount.

   Journal entry by lessee.

12/31/04	Accumulated depreciation..	81,108	
	Leased property...		81,108

   Journal entry by lessor.

12/31/04	Equipment..	5,000	
	Lease receivable..		5,000

   (2). Actual residual value less than estimated amount.

   Journal entry by lessee.

12/31/04	Accumulated depreciation..	81,108	
	Leased property...		81,108

   Journal entry by lessor.

12/31/04	Equipment..	2,000	
	Loss on unguaranteed residual value ($5,000 − $2,000)............................	3,000	
	Lease receivable..		5,000

16 PENSIONS AND OTHER POSTRETIREMENT BENEFITS

CHAPTER OBJECTIVES

After reading Chapter 16 and completing the questions, cases, exercises, and problems from the text chapter, you should be able to:

1. Distinguish between various types of postretirement benefit plans, including public and private plans, funded and unfunded plans, contributory and noncontributory plans, fully vested and partially vested pension plans, defined contribution and defined benefit plans, and pay-related and nonpay-related plans.

2. Compute the service cost for a particular year, the projected benefit obligation as of a particular date, the accumulated benefit obligation as of a particular date, the prior service cost arising from a plan adoption or amendment, and gains or losses arising from changes in the value of either the projected benefit obligation or the plan assets as a result of changes in actuarial assumptions or experience different from that expected for an individual employee under a noncontributory, pay-related, defined benefit pension plan.

3. Identify and describe the rationale for the components of net periodic pension cost—namely, service cost, interest on projected benefit obligation, expected return on plan assets, amortization of unrecognized prior service cost, amortization of an unrecognized net gain or loss, and amortization of the unrecognized net asset

or net obligation existing at the date of initial application of *Statement No. 87.*

4. Compute net periodic pension cost under a defined benefit plan.

5. Prepare the journal entry required under a defined benefit pension plan to record net periodic pension cost and the contribution of cash by the employer to an independently controlled pension fund.

6. Prepare the journal entry required under a defined benefit plan to record an additional pension liability when the accumulated benefit obligation exceeds the fair value of plan assets.

7. Prepare a schedule that reconciles the funded status of a defined benefit plan with the pension amounts reported on the employer's balance sheet.

8. Compute net periodic postretirement benefit cost under a single-employer defined benefit plan.

9. Prepare the journal entry required to record net periodic postretirement benefit cost and cash benefit payments.

10. Prepare a schedule that reconciles the funded status of a defined benefit plan with the postretirement benefit amount reported on the employer's balance sheet.

11. Identify the information about a defined benefit pension and other postretirement plans that the sponsoring employer is required to disclose in its financial statements.

CHAPTER REVIEW

Introduction

1. A *postretirement benefit plan* is an arrangement under which a governmental unit or a private company provides for pension and other postretirement benefits for retired employees. *Public plans* are established by law and are sponsored by federal, state, and local governments. *Private plans* exist largely at the discretion of the employers who sponsor the plans and are established by agreement between employers and employees. Employers' accounting for and reporting of private pension plans and other postretirement benefit plans are described in this chapter review.

Characteristics of Private Postretirement Benefit Plans

2. A postretirement benefit plan may be funded or unfunded. In a *funded retirement plan,* the employer makes contributions to a fund controlled by an independent funding agent, such as a bank or an insurance company, for future payment of benefits to retired employees. The act of making cash contributions to an independently controlled fund is called *funding* of the retirement plan. In an *unfunded retirement plan,* the fund is controlled by the employer rather than by an independent funding agent. In the United States, most pension plans are funded, whereas most retirement health care plans are not funded.

3. A postretirement benefit plan may be contributory or noncontributory. A *contributory plan* is a plan under which both the employer and the employees make contributions to the postretirement benefit fund. A *noncontributory plan* is a plan under which employees do not contribute to the postretirement benefit fund. With respect to pension plans, employees retain a claim to their own contributions in nearly all contributory plans. Employees' rights to the employer's contributions to the fund are prescribed by the vesting provisions of the plan. The right is *fully vested* if an employee's right to receive earned (or accumulated) benefits that are funded by the employer's contributions to the fund is not contingent on continued employment with that employer; the right is *partially vested* if an employee's right to receive earned (or accumulated) benefits that are funded by the employer's contributions to the fund would be reduced should employment with that employer cease. Other postretirement benefit plans, such as health care plans, ordinarily do not contain vesting provisions.

4. There are essentially two types of private postretirement benefit plans, defined contribution plans and defined benefit plans. In a *defined contribution plan,* the employer promises to make specified contributions to the retirement fund, but the amount of benefits that will be paid to retired employees is not specified. The employer's net postretirement cost for a period is the contribution called for in that period, and the amount of benefits ultimately paid to retired employees is limited to the contributions to the retirement fund plus earnings on the fund's assets. In a *defined benefit plan,* the employer promises to make benefit payments to or on behalf of employees in specified amounts during their retirement years, but the amount that the employer will contribute to the retirement fund is not specified. The annual benefits, for example, may be determined at retirement by multiplying a specified percentage for each year of employee service that qualifies for postretirement credit by the simple average of the employee's highest annual salaries for a specified number of years.

5. The Employee Retirement Income Security Act (ERISA), passed by Congress in 1974, established several pension plan requirements, including minimum funding, participation, and vesting requirements. It also created the Pension Benefit Guaranty Corporation (PBGC), which is responsible for ensuring payment of minimum benefits by defined benefit pension plans and for administering defined benefit plans that have been terminated. ERISA applies to virtually all private pension plans in the United States.

6. Because there are substantial similarities between the accounting and reporting standards related to pension plans and other postretirement benefit plans, the remainder of this chapter review first focuses on the employer's accounting for and reporting of funded, noncontributory, defined benefit pension plans in accordance with the requirements specified by *Statement No. 87,* which was issued by the FASB in 1985. Such pension plans involve three parties: (*a*) the sponsoring employer, who recognizes net periodic pension cost (pension expense) and makes cash contributions to an independently controlled pension fund; (*b*) the funding agent, who receives the cash contributions to the pension fund, manages the pension fund's assets, and pays pension benefits to retired employees covered by the pension plan; and (*c*) the employees, who upon retirement receive pension benefits as specified by the terms of the pension plan. This chapter review then highlights the similarities and differences between the accounting and reporting standards for pension benefits and those for other postretirement benefits.

Accounting for Pension Benefits

7. Net periodic pension cost. The calculation of the employer's cost of providing pension benefits to employees is based on present value techniques and actuarial assumptions about factors such as interest rates, mortality rates, employee turnover, future compensation levels, and inflationary trends. Pension benefit costs usually are calculated by *actuaries*, individuals who are trained in the use of present value techniques and in making reasonable assumptions about future events such as those just cited. The calculation of pension amounts based on present value techniques and reasonable assumptions about the future is called an *actuarial valuation*, and the amounts so calculated are called *actuarial present values*. Because actual future events may not correspond to the assumptions incorporated in an actuarial valuation, an actuarial present value calculated at any point in time is only an estimate.

8. The pension benefits that retired employees are entitled to receive under a pension plan are calculated in accordance with a *pension benefit formula*. Plans for which the pension benefit formula is based on future compensation levels are called *pay-related plans*. In pay-related plans, pension benefit cost may be calculated on the basis of either compensation levels to date or estimated future compensation levels. Calculation of pension benefit cost on the basis of compensation levels to date is called calculation of *accumulated pension benefits*, whereas calculation of pension benefit cost on the basis of estimated future compensation levels is called calculation of *projected pension benefits*. Plans for which the pension benefit formula is not based on future compensation levels are called *nonpay-related plans*. In nonpay-related plans, the accumulated pension benefits and projected pension benefits are the same. With the exception of a balance sheet adjustment that is applicable only under certain conditions, *Statement No. 87* requires that pension benefit cost be based on projected pension benefits if the pension benefit formula incorporates future compensation levels.

9. There are two general approaches for allocating (attributing) pension benefit cost to periods of employee service: a benefit approach and a cost approach. A *benefit approach* determines an amount of pension benefits attributed to employee service rendered in a period and then calculates the pension (service) cost for the period as the actuarial present value of those pension benefits. A *cost approach* projects an estimated total pension benefit at retire-

ment and then calculates the level contribution (annuity) that, together with return on plan assets expected to accumulate at the assumed rates, would be sufficient to provide that pension benefit at retirement. *Statement No. 87* requires that net periodic pension cost be based on a benefit approach.

10. The application of the matching objective to pension plans requires that pension benefit cost be recognized in the period in which economic benefits are received by the employer (employee services are rendered). To accomplish this objective, *Statement No. 87* requires that the following components be included in the calculation of net periodic pension cost (pension expense) under defined benefit pension plans: (*a*) service cost for the period; (*b*) interest on projected benefit obligation; (*c*) expected return on plan assets, if any; (*d*) amortization of unrecognized prior service cost, if any; and (*e*) amortization of an unrecognized net gain or loss, if material. Each of these components of net periodic pension cost is discussed in the remainder of this section. An additional component, temporarily, is the amortization of the unrecognized net obligation or net asset existing at the date of initial application of the *Statement*. This component of net periodic pension cost is discussed in a separate section later.

11. Service cost. The cost of pension benefits attributed to a particular period is called the *service cost* for that period The service cost for a period is the present value of pension benefits attributed by the pension benefit formula to employee services rendered during that period, calculated on the basis of estimated future compensation levels if the pension benefit formula incorporates those future compensation levels. As a simplified example, the service cost of a noncontributory, pay-related, defined benefit plan under which the future pension benefits are to be paid annually to an individual employee at the end of each retirement year can be calculated for a particular service year as follows: (*a*) the amount of the estimated annual pension benefits to be paid to the employee for the service year is calculated in accordance with the pension benefit formula on the basis of estimated future compensation levels; (*b*) the present value of the estimated annual pension benefits attributed to the service year as of the employee's projected retirement date is calculated by multiplying the estimated annual pension benefits attributed to the service year by the present value factor of an ordinary annuity, where n is the employee's projected retirement period and i is the discount rate; and (*c*) the service cost for the year is calculated by multiplying the present value of the estimated annual pension benefits attributed to the service year as of the employee's projected retirement date by the present value factor of an amount, where n is the employee's projected remaining service period and i is the discount rate. *Statement No. 87* requires that service cost for a period be included as a component of the net periodic pension cost for that period.

12. Interest on projected benefit obligation. The cost of pension benefits attributed to years of service prior to a particular date is called the *projected benefit obligation* at that date. The projected benefit obligation as of a particular date is the present value of all pension benefits attributed by the pension benefit formula to employee services rendered prior to that date, calculated on the basis of estimated future compensation levels if the pension benefit formula incorporates those future compensation levels. The projected benefit obligation for an individual employee can be calculated by the procedures described earlier for service cost, except that the amount of the estimated annual pension benefits is based on the employee's services rendered to date rather than on the employee's services rendered during a particular year only. *Statement No. 87* requires that interest on the projected benefit obligation be added to service cost in the calculation of net periodic pension cost. It requires further that the interest cost for a period, which is identical to interest expense that accrues with the passage of time on other monetary liabilities, be calculated by multiplying the projected benefit obligation at the beginning of the period by the discount rate. The *discount rate* is defined as that rate at which the employer's pension obligation could be effectively settled, such as by purchasing *annuity contracts* from an insurance company (that is, contracts in which an insurance company unconditionally undertakes a legal obligation to provide specified pension benefits to specific individuals in return for a fixed consideration or premium).

13. Expected return on plan assets. *Plan assets* are assets, such as stocks, bonds, and other income-yielding investments, that have been segregated and restricted in an independently controlled pension fund to provide for the payment of pension benefits to retired employees as set forth in the pension plan agreement. Plan assets include amounts contributed by the employer (and by employees for a contributory plan) and amounts earned from investing the contributions, less pension benefits paid to retired employees. Because earnings on plan assets increase the net assets of the pension fund and decrease the employer's required contributions, *Statement No. 87* requires that the expected return on plan assets be deducted from service cost and interest cost in the calculation of net periodic pension cost. It requires further that the expected return on plan assets for a period be calculated by multiplying the expected long-term rate of return on plan

assets by the market-related value of plan assets at the beginning of the period, measured at either fair value or a calculated value that recognizes changes in fair value in a systematic and rational manner over not more than five years.

14. Amortization of unrecognized prior service cost. The cost of retroactive pension benefits attributed by the pension benefit formula to employee services rendered in periods prior to a plan adoption or amendment is called *prior service cost*. Prior service cost can arise from the initial adoption of a pension plan or from a subsequent amendment to an existing plan only if retroactive pension credit is granted for employee services rendered in periods prior to the adoption or amendment date.

15. The prior service cost arising from the adoption of a pension plan is the present value of all pension benefits attributed by the pension benefit formula to employee services rendered in periods prior to the inception date. The prior service cost arising from a plan adoption can be calculated for an individual employee by the procedures described earlier for service cost, except that the amount of the estimated annual pension benefits is based on the employee's services rendered in periods prior to the plan inception date rather than on the employee's services rendered during a particular year only. Thus the prior service cost arising from the adoption of a pension plan is the projected benefit obligation at the plan inception date. Likewise, the prior service cost arising from an amendment to a pension plan is the increase in the projected benefit obligation as a result of the amendment. The prior service cost arising from a plan amendment can be calculated as the difference between the projected benefit obligation immediately before and after the amendment.

16. As retroactive pension benefits are granted with the expectation that the employer will realize economic benefits in the future, *Statement No. 87* requires that prior service cost be amortized as a component of net periodic pension cost over the future service periods of those active employees, at the adoption or amendment date, who are expected to receive benefits under the plan. It states further that prior service cost should be amortized by assigning an equal amount to each future service period of each employee active at the adoption or amendment date who is expected to receive benefits under the plan. Under this method (called the *service-years-outstanding method*), amortization of prior service cost for a particular year is calculated by multiplying the prior service cost by a ratio that has the number of employee years of service rendered during that year in the numerator and the total expected future years of employee service subsequent to the adoption or amendment date in the denominator. This method results in a declining pattern of amortization over time as employees' remaining service years decline through attrition, retirement, or termination. Alternatively, to reduce the complexity and detail of the computations required, *Statement No. 87* permits prior service cost to be amortized on a straight-line basis over the average remaining service period of active employees, at the adoption or amendment date, who are expected to receive benefits under the plan. Under this method, the periodic amortization of prior service cost is calculated by dividing the prior service cost by the average remaining service period of the active employees (that is, the total expected future years of employee service subsequent to the adoption or amendment date divided by the number of those employees).

17. **Amortization of unrecognized net gain or loss.** *Gains* and *losses,* sometimes called actuarial gains and losses, are changes in the value of either the projected benefit obligation or the plan assets arising from changes in actuarial assumptions (such as a change in the discount rate) or from experience different from that incorporated in the assumptions (such as a difference between expected and actual rates of return on plan assets). Gains reduce pension benefit cost by increasing the value of plan assets, decreasing the projected benefit obligation, or a combination of both; losses increase pension benefit cost by decreasing the value of plan assets, increasing the projected benefit obligation, or a combination of both. However, because of the long-term nature of pension plan agreements and because gains or losses in one period may be offset by losses or gains in subsequent periods, *Statement No. 87* requires recognition of gains and losses as a part of net periodic pension cost only if the *unrecognized net gain or loss* (the cumulative net gain or loss that has not yet been recognized as a part of net periodic pension cost) is material. Specifically, it requires that amortization of an unrecognized net gain or loss be included as a component of net pension cost for a year if, as of the beginning of the year, that unrecognized net gain or loss exceeds 10 percent (called the *corridor*) of the greater of the projected benefit obligation or the market-related value of plan assets. If amortization is required, it requires further that the minimum amortization be that excess divided by the average remaining service period of active employees who are expected to receive pension benefits under the plan. Net periodic pension cost is decreased by amortization of an unrecognized net gain; it is increased by amortization of an unrecognized net loss.

18. **Prepaid/accrued pension cost.** As summarized earlier, net periodic pension cost for a period under a defined benefit plan is equal to:

a. Service cost for the period, plus

b. Interest on the projected benefit obligation at the beginning of the period, minus
c. Expected return on plan assets at the beginning of the period, plus
d. Amortization of unrecognized prior service cost arising from a plan adoption or amendment, minus or plus
e. Amortization of an unrecognized net gain or loss arising from changes in actuarial assumptions or from experience different from that assumed.

When there is no unrecognized net obligation or net asset existing at the date of initial application of *Statement No. 87* (discussed later), the summation of these five components is the amount that should be debited to pension expense for the period.

19. In a funded pension plan, the employer makes periodic cash contributions to an independent funding agent, such as a bank or insurance company, that invests the cash contributions in stocks, bonds, and other income-yielding assets and pays pension benefits to retired employees as specified by the terms of the pension plan. The amount of cash contributed by the employer to the pension fund during a period is a function of many considerations, such as working capital requirements, the availability of attractive alternative investments, ERISA's minimum funding requirements, and tax regulations. Moreover, the employer must use a benefit approach to determine service cost and other components of net periodic pension cost but may use a cost approach to determine the amount of cash contributed to the pension fund each year. Additionally, the discount rate (or borrowing rate) that must be used to determine service cost and other components of net periodic pension cost may not be equal to the expected long-term rate of return on plan assets (or lending rate) that is used to determine the amount of cash that the employer should contribute to the pension fund each year. As a result of these factors, the amount of net periodic pension cost for a period may be, but is not necessarily, equal to the amount of cash contributed by the employer to the pension fund during that period. Assuming for simplicity that the employer's periodic cash contribution to an independently controlled pension fund and recognition of net periodic pension cost (pension expense) are recorded at the end of the year, there are three categories of possible circumstances as follows:

a. *Cash contribution equals net periodic pension cost.* In this circumstance, net periodic pension cost and the employer's cash contribution to the pension fund should be recorded by debiting pension expense and crediting cash at the amount of the net periodic pension cost for the year.

b. *Cash contribution is greater than net periodic pension cost.* In this circumstance, the net periodic pension cost for the year should be debited to pension expense, the amount contributed by the employer to the pension fund for the year should be credited to cash, and the excess of the employer's cash contribution over the net periodic pension cost should be debited to accrued/prepaid pension cost.

c. *Cash contribution is less than net periodic pension cost.* In this circumstance, the net periodic pension cost for the year should be debited to pension expense, the amount contributed by the employer to the pension fund for the year should be credited to cash, and the excess of the net periodic pension cost over the employer's cash contribution should be credited to accrued/prepaid pension cost.

It should be noted that, in the long run, the total net periodic pension cost must equal the employer's total cash contributions to the pension fund. However, if as of a particular date the cumulative amount of cash contributed by the employer is not equal to the cumulative amount of its net periodic pension cost, there should be as of that date either a prepaid pension cost (asset) debit balance equal to the excess of the cumulative amount funded by the employer over the cumulative amount of net periodic pension cost to date or an accrued pension cost (liability) credit balance equal to the excess of the cumulative amount of net periodic pension cost over the cumulative amount funded by the employer to date. Conversely, if as of a particular date the cumulative amount of cash contributed by the employer is equal to the cumulative amount of net periodic pension cost, there should be as of that date neither a prepaid pension cost debit balance nor an accrued pension cost credit balance.

20. Minimum liability. As just described, any difference between the cumulative amount recorded as pension expense and the cumulative amount funded by the employer must be reported on the balance sheet as either prepaid pension cost, if the cumulative funding exceeds the cumulative pension expense, or accrued pension cost, if the cumulative pension expense exceeds the cumulative funding. In addition, *Statement No. 87* requires recognition of a *minimum liability,* at each balance sheet date, at least equal to the employer's *unfunded accumulated benefit obligation* (that is, the excess of the accumulated benefit obligation over the fair value of plan assets). The *accumulated benefit obligation* as of a particular date is the present value of all pension benefits attributed by the pension benefit formula to employee services rendered prior to

that date, calculated on the basis of compensation levels to date, if appropriate. The accumulated benefit obligation differs from the projected benefit obligation in that it includes no assumption about future compensation levels. The accumulated benefit obligation therefore can be calculated for an individual employee by the procedures described earlier for the projected benefit obligation, except that the estimated annual pension benefits are based on compensation levels to date rather on estimated future compensation levels. For plans with nonpay-related pension benefit formulas, the accumulated benefit obligation and projected benefit obligation are the same.

21. *Statement No. 87* requires that the additional pension liability required to recognize a minimum liability be combined with any accrued pension cost or prepaid pension cost that has been recognized for the difference between the cumulative amount recorded as pension expense and the cumulative amount funded. Coincidentally, it requires that an intangible asset be recognized at an amount equal to the lower of the additional pension liability or unrecognized prior service cost and that, if the additional pension liability exceeds the unrecognized prior service cost, the excess be reported as a contra account in the stockholders' equity section of the balance sheet. Thus, assuming that the fair value of plan assets exceeded the accumulated benefit obligation at the preceding balance sheet date but the reverse is true at the current balance sheet date, the journal entry to recognize a minimum liability should include (*a*) a credit to the additional pension liability account at an amount equal to the unfunded accumulated benefit obligation minus any accrued pension cost credit balance or plus any prepaid pension cost debit balance; (*b*) a debit to an intangible asset account (which is not amortized) at the lower of the amount credited to the additional pension liability account or any unrecognized prior service cost (including an unrecognized net obligation existing at the transition date, as discussed in the next section); and (*c*) a debit to excess of additional pension liability over unrecognized prior service cost, a stockholders' equity contra account, at the excess, if any, of the amount credited to the additional pension liability account over the amount debited to the intangible asset account. At each subsequent balance sheet date, the unfunded accumulated benefit obligation and unrecognized prior service cost should be determined, and a journal entry should be recorded to increase, decrease, or totally eliminate these account balances, as appropriate.

22. Transaction requirements. Prior to the issuance of *Statement No. 87,* generally accepted accounting principles applicable to employers' accounting for pension plans were contained in

APB Opinion No. 8. Even though there are substantial differences in the requirements of the two pronouncements, there are some common requirements. *Opinion No. 8,* for example, required that the difference between the cumulative amount recognized as pension expense and the cumulative amount funded be recognized as an accrued pension cost or prepaid pension cost, but it did not require recognition of an additional pension liability for any unfunded accumulated benefit obligation.

23. Under the transition requirements of *Statement No. 87,* the employer is required to determine, as of the beginning of the fiscal year in which it is first applied, the difference between (*a*) the projected benefit obligation and (*b*) the fair value of plan assets plus any previously recognized accrued pension cost or minus any previously recognized prepaid pension cost. The difference between these two amounts is called the *unrecognized net obligation* if the projected benefit obligation exceeds the fair value of plan assets, as adjusted; it is called the *unrecognized net asset* if the fair value of plan assets, as adjusted, exceeds the projected benefit obligation. Because retroactive restatement would not have been practicable for some employers and to be consistent with the delayed recognition approach adopted for other components, *Statement No. 87* requires that the unrecognized net obligation or net asset existing at the date of its initial application (which was no later than December 31, 1988) be amortized as a component of net periodic pension cost on a straight-line basis over the average remaining service period of employees expected to receive benefits under the plan. Net periodic pension cost is increased by amortization of an unrecognized net obligation; it is decreased by amortization of an unrecognized net asset.

24. Disclosure requirements. *Statement No. 87* requires that an employer sponsoring a defined benefit pension plan disclose the following:

a. A description of the plan including employee groups covered; type of benefit formula; funding policy; types of assets held and significant nonbenefit liabilities, if any; and the nature and effect of significant matters affecting comparability of information for all periods presented.

b. The amount of net periodic pension cost for the period showing separately the service cost component, the interest cost component, the *actual return on plan assets* for the period (that is, the expected return on plan assets plus or minus the net asset gain or loss for the period) and the net total of other components.

c. A schedule reconciling the *funded status* of the plan (that is, the difference between the projected benefit obligation and the fair value of plan assets) with amounts reported in the employer's statement of financial position, showing separately (*1*) the fair value of plan assets, minus (*2*) the projected benefit obligation, identifying the accumulated benefit obligation and the vested benefit obligation, plus (*3*) the amount of unrecognized prior service cost, plus or minus (*4*) the amount of unrecognized net loss or net gain, plus or minus (*5*) the amount of any remaining unrecognized net obligation or net asset existing at the date of initial application of the *Statement,* minus (*6*) the amount of any additional pension liability recognized pursuant to the minimum liability requirement, equals (*7*) the amount of the net pension asset or liability recognized in the statement of financial position.

It should be noted that the schedule reconciling the funded status of the plan with amounts reported in the statement of financial position discloses, in off-balance-sheet form, the same information that would be reported in the financial statements directly under the theoretically preferable immediate recognition approach of accounting for prior service cost and gains and losses, which is compared in the text with the delayed recognition requirements of *Statement No. 87.*

Accounting for Other Postretirement Benefits

25. In December 1990, after considering the issue for more than a decade, the FASB issued *Statement No. 106,* "Employers' Accounting for Postretirement Benefits Other Than Pensions." Postretirement benefits other than pensions include health care, life insurance that is provided outside a pension plan, tuition assistance, legal and tax services, day care, and housing subsidies. The predominant practice before the issuance of *Statement No. 106* was for employers to delay recognition of the cost of such postretirement benefits by the pay-as-you-go (cash) basis, until those benefits were paid to or on behalf of retired employees. In contrast, *Statement No. 106* is based on the same accrual concept as *Statement No. 87;* namely, (*a*) an employer's promise to provide retirees with postretirement benefits represents a form of deferred compensation to employees in return for their current services, and (*b*) the cost of promised postretirement benefits should be recognized systematically over the service periods for which employees earn postretirement benefit credit.

26. To parallel the standards specified by *Statement No. 87, Statement No. 106* requires that the following six components be included in the calculation of net periodic postretirement benefit cost for a single-employer defined benefit postretirement plan:

a. Service cost for the period, plus
b. Interest cost on the accumulated postretirement benefit obligation at the beginning of the period, minus
c. Actual or expected return on plan assets for the period, plus
d. Amortization of unrecognized prior service cost arising from plan amendments or initiation, minus or plus
e. Amortization of an unrecognized net gain or loss arising from changes in actuarial assumptions or from experience different from that assumed, plus or minus
f. Amortization of transition obligation or asset.

Each of these components of net periodic postretirement benefits cost is discussed in the remainder of this section.

27. Service cost. The *service cost* for an employee for a period is that portion of the expected postretirement benefit obligation that is attributed to the employee's service during that period. The *expected postretirement benefit obligation* (EPBO) for an employee as of a particular date is the present value of the postretirement benefits expected to be paid by the employer's plan to or on behalf of the employee, the employee's beneficiaries, or any covered dependents. The EPBO is conceptually identical to the expected projected benefit obligation under a pension plan. The *discount rate* required to be used to determine the EPBO is the current rate of return on high-quality, fixed-income investments currently available and expected to be available during the expected benefit payment period. As a general rule, *Statement No. 106* requires that an equal amount of the EPBO for an employee be included in net postretirement benefit cost in each year of service in the employee's attribution period. As a simplified example, the service cost for an employee for a period can be calculated by multiplying the EPBO at the end of that period by 1 divided by the employee's total attribution period. The *attribution period* begins with the employee's date of hire (or from a later credited service start date, if specified by the plan's benefit formula) and ends on the employee's full eligibility date (such as the employee's expected retirement date or an earlier date), as specified by

the plan. After an employee's full eligibility date, there is no service cost for that employee.

28. Interest cost on accumulated postretirement benefit obligation. The *accumulated postretirement benefit obligation* (APBO) for an employee as of a particular date is that portion of the EPBO that is attributed to the employee's service rendered to that date. The APBO is conceptually identical to the projected benefit obligation under a pension plan. Interest cost for a period is the increase in the APBO during that period due to the passage of time; it can be calculated by multiplying the APBO at the beginning of the period by the discount rate. Prior to an employee's full eligibility date, the APBO can be calculated by multiplying the EPBO on that date by the employee's credited service years to date divided by the attribution period. Alternatively, under simplified assumptions, the APBO, as of the end of a period, for an unfunded plan can be calculated as the sum of the APBO at the beginning of that period, plus the interest cost for that period, plus the service cost for that period, minus the employer's benefit payments at the end of that period. On or after the full eligibility date, the APBO and EPBO (as well as the employer's cumulative net postretirement benefit cost) for an employee are the same.

29. Actual or expected return on plan assets. The *actual return on plan assets* is the change in the fair value of the plan assets for a period, adjusted for the contributions and benefit payments during that period. The *expected return on plan assets* is the long-term rate of return on plan assets based on the market-related value of plan assets at the beginning of the period. *Statement No. 106* permits employers to include as a component of net periodic postretirement benefit cost either the actual return on plan assets or the expected return on plan assets for the period. However, under the latter option, the difference between the expected and actual return on plan assets is required to be included as part of the amortization of an unrecognized net gain or loss (discussed later). Because postretirement benefit plans ordinarily are not funded, many of the text's illustrations are based on the assumption that there are no plan assets, and thus there is no actual or expected return on plan assets.

30. Amortization of unrecognized prior service cost. *Prior service cost* is the cost of benefit improvements, attributable to plan participants' prior service, from a plan amendment or initiation that provides benefits in exchange for plan participants' prior service. Prior service cost can be calculated as the increase in the APBO on the plan amendment date or initiation date. *Statement No. 106* requires that prior service cost be amortized as a component of net periodic postretirement benefit cost by assigning an equal amount to each remaining service year to the full eligibility date of each active plan participant who is not yet fully eligible for benefits at the amendment or initiation date. Alternatively, it permits prior service cost to be amortized on a straight-line basis over the average remaining years of service to full eligibility for benefits of active plan participants. A decrease in the APBO arising from a plan amendment that reduces postretirement benefits, however, is required to be accounted for, first, as a reduction in any existing unrecognized prior service cost and, then, as a reduction of any unrecognized transition obligation (discussed later), before being amortized as a reduction of net periodic postretirement benefit cost.

31. Amortization of unrecognized net gain or loss. *Gains* and *losses* are changes in either the APBO or the fair value of plan assets arising from changes in assumptions or from actual experience different from that assumed. *Statement No. 106* requires, at a minimum, that the excess of an unrecognized net gain or loss over 10 percent of the greater of the APBO or the market-related value of plan assets as of the beginning of the period be amortized on a straight-line basis over the average remaining service period through the expected retirement date of active plan participants.

32. Amortization of transition obligation or asset. *Statement No. 106* requires that the *transition obligation* or *asset* be determined, at the beginning of the fiscal year in which it is first applied, as the difference between the APBO and the fair value of the plan assets plus or minus any previously recognized accrued or prepaid postretirement benefit cost. It requires further that a transition obligation or asset be either recognized immediately in net income as the cumulative effect of a change in accounting principle or amortized, as a component of net periodic postretirement benefit cost, on a straight-line basis over the average remaining service period ending with the expected retirement date of active plan participants or, if longer, an optional 20-year period. However, if cumulative net periodic postretirement benefit cost as of the end of a fiscal year is less than the cumulative benefit payments since the transition date, an additional amount of the transition obligation, equal to the excess cumulative benefit payments, must be amortized for that year.

33. Accrued/prepaid postretirement benefit cost and disclosure requirements. Assuming for simplicity that an employer's periodic cash payments after the transition date are limited to postretirement benefit payments at the end of the year, the employer should record the net periodic postretirement benefit cost and the benefit payments by (*a*) debiting postretirement benefit cost (expense)

for the sum of the six components specified by *Statement No. 106,* (*b*) crediting cash for the amount of the benefit payments, and (*c*) either crediting accrued postretirement benefit cost for the excess of the net periodic postretirement benefit cost over the benefit payments or debiting accrued postretirement benefit cost for the excess of the benefit payments over the net periodic postretirement benefit cost. In this circumstance, the accrued postretirement benefit cost account will be a credit balance, which should be reported on the balance sheet as a liability. Furthermore, *Statement No. 106* does not require employers to recognize a minimum liability on the balance sheet for the unfunded APBO. Employers, though, are required to disclose a schedule reconciling the plan's funded status (that is, the difference between the APBO and the fair value of plan assets) with the amount reported in the employer's statement of financial position, as well as other extensive disclosures similar in many respects to those required for pensions.

International Standards

34. There is substantial diversity internationally in accounting for and reporting on pension and other postretirement benefit costs and obligations. U.S. GAAP, as specified by *Statements No. 87* and *106,* are the most detailed and comprehensive rules covering the subject. The International Accounting Standards Committee, however, has proposed revisions to *International Accounting Standard 19* to recommend standards similar to those specified by U.S. GAAP. These standards specifically prohibit recognition of periodic postretirement benefit cost as benefits are paid to retired employees (called *pay-as-you-go accounting*), as cash is contributed by the employer to a retirement fund, and at the employee retirement date. Nevertheless, these methods (especially pay-as-you-go accounting) are common around the world. Furthermore, in some countries, postretirement benefit costs are recognized to the extent that they are deductible for income tax purposes.

Appendixes

35. Multiemployer retirement plans. A multiemployer retirement plan is a plan to which two or more unrelated employers contribute. A characteristic of multiemployer plans is that assets contributed by one participating employer may be used to provide benefits to employees of other participating employers. Both *Statements No. 87* and *106* require that an employer participating in a multiemployer plan recognize as net periodic pension or postretirement benefit cost the required contribution for the period and recognize as a liability any contributions due and unpaid. They both require further that an employer participating in one or more multiemployer plans disclose the following separately from disclosures for a single-employer plan: (*a*) a description of the multi-employer plan, including the employee groups covered, the type of benefits provided (defined benefit or defined contribution), and the nature and effect of significant matters affecting comparability of information for all periods presented, and (*b*) the amount of cost recognized during the period.

36. Settlements and curtailments and termination benefits. A *settlement* is an irrevocable action that relieves the employer (or the plan) of primary responsibility for a pension or other postretirement benefit obligation and eliminates significant risks related to the obligation and the assets used to effect the settlement. An employer, for example, may settle a pension or other postretirement obligation under a defined benefit plan by making lump-sum cash payments to plan participants in exchange for their rights to receive specified pension or other postretirement benefits or by purchasing nonparticipating annuity contracts to cover vested or accumulated benefits. In such circumstances, *Statement No. 88* requires the employer to recognize in the income statement a gain or loss equal to the unrecognized net pension gain or loss plus any remaining unrecognized net asset existing at the date of initial application of *Statement No. 87* multiplied by the percentage reduction in the projected benefit obligation. A *curtailment* is an event that significantly reduces the expected years of future service of active plan participants or eliminates for a significant number of active plan participants the accrual of defined benefits for some or all of their future services. Curtailments include termination of employees' services earlier than expected and termination or suspension of a plan so that employees do not earn additional defined benefits for future services. In these circumstances, *Statement No. 88* requires the employer to recognize in the income statement a net gain or net loss equal to the sum of the following: (*a*) a loss equal to the unrecognized prior service cost plus any remaining unrecognized net obligation existing at the date of initial application of *Statement No. 87* multiplied by the percentage reduction (or elimination) of the estimated remain

ing future years of employee service, and (*b*) if the projected benefit obligation is decreased or increased by the curtailment, a gain (or loss) equal to the excess of the decrease (or increase) in the projected benefit obligation over any unrecognized net pension loss (or net pension gain), including any remaining unrecognized net asset existing at the transition date. Finally, *Statement No. 88* requires an employer that provides *termination benefits* to employees in connection with their termination of employment to recognize a loss and a liability equal to the amount of any lump-sum payments and the present value of any expected future payments. *Statement No. 106* specifies essentially the same standards for settlements, curtailments, and termination benefits related to other postretirement benefits.

37. Accounting and reporting by the pension plan. The pension plan is an accounting entity separate from the employer sponsoring the plan. *Statement No. 35,* which applies to both private pension plans and state and local governmental public pension plans, contains the financial accounting and reporting standards for defined benefit pension plans. Among these standards are the following: (*a*) the annual financial statements of a pension plan should include a statement that includes information regarding the net assets available for benefits as of the end of the plan year, including plan investments (other than contracts with insurance companies) reported at their fair market value, a statement that includes information regarding the changes during the year in the net assets available for benefits, information regarding the actuarial present value of accumulated plan benefits as of either the beginning or the end of the plan year, and information regarding the effects (if significant) of factors affecting the year-to-year change in the actuarial present value of accumulated plan benefits; (*b*) the disclosures of a plan's accounting policies should include a description of the methods and significant assumptions used to determine the fair market value of investments, the reported value of contracts with insurance companies, and the actuarial present value of accumulated plan benefits; and (c) the financial statements should contain several additional disclosures (if applicable) including a description of the plan agreement, a description of significant plan amendments adopted during the current year, the funding policy and any changes in that policy during the current year, and the federal income tax status of the plan.

SELF-STUDY LEARNING   Items marked with an asterisk (*) refer to the Appendixes.

Key Terms and Concepts

Provide the appropriate term or terms to complete each of the following statements:

1. An arrangement under which an employer provides for pension and other retirement benefits for retired employees is called a(n) _____.

2. A postretirement benefit plan under which both the employer and the employees make contributions to the retirement fund is a(n) _____, whereas a postretirement benefit plan under which the employees do not contribute to the retirement fund is a(n) _____.

3. An employee's right to receive earned (or accumulated) benefits that are funded by the employer's contributions to the postretirement benefit fund is _____ if the right is not contingent on continued employment with that employer, whereas it is _____ if the right would be reduced should employment with that employer cease before retirement.

4. A postretirement benefit plan under which the employer makes contributions to a fund controlled by an independent funding agent, such as a bank or insurance company, is called a(n) _____, whereas a postretirement benefit plan under which the fund is controlled by the employer rather than by an independent funding agent is called a(n) _____.

5. A postretirement benefit plan under which the employer promises to make specified contributions to a fund but which does not specify the amount of benefits that will be paid to retired employees is called a(n) _____; a postretirement benefit plan under which the employer promises to make benefit payments to employees in specified amounts during their retirement years but which does not specify the amount that the employer will contribute to the fund is called a(n) _____.

6. Assets, such as stocks, bonds, and other income-yielding investments, that have been segregated and restricted in an independently controlled fund to provide for the payment of the benefits to retired employees as set forth in the postretirement benefit agreement are called _____.

7. The present value of pension benefits attributed by the pension benefit formula to employee services rendered during a particular period is called the _____ for that period, whereas the present value as of a particular date of all pension benefits attributed by the pension benefit formula to employee services rendered prior to that date is called the _____, if calculated on the basis of estimated future compensation levels, or the _____, if calculated on the basis of compensation levels to that date.

8. The cost of retroactive postretirement benefits attributed to employee services rendered in periods prior to a plan adoption or amendment is called _____.

9. Changes in the value of either the projected benefit obligation (or accumulated postretirement benefit obligation) or the plan assets arising from changes in actuarial assumptions or from experience different from that incorporated in the assumptions are called _____.

10. The difference between the projected benefit obligation (or accumulated postretirement benefit obligation) and the fair value of plan assets, adjusted by any previously recognized accrued or prepaid postretirement benefit cost, as of the beginning of the fiscal year in which *Statements No. 87* and *106* are first applied, is called the _____.

True-False

Indicate by circling the appropriate response whether each of the following statements is true (T) or false (F):

T F 1. Net periodic pension cost should be recognized by the employer only as pension benefits are actually paid to retired employees.

T F 2. When the compensation levels of active employees are expected to increase and the pension benefit formula is based on those future compensation levels, the accumulated benefit obligation will be greater than the projected benefit obligation.

T F 3. The interest cost component of net periodic pension cost under a defined benefit plan must be calculated by multiplying the accumulated benefit obligation at the end of the period by the expected long-term rate of return on plan assets.

T F 4. The expected return on the plan assets component of net periodic pension cost under a defined benefit plan must be calculated by multiplying the discount rate by the market-related value of plan assets at the beginning of the period, measured at either fair value or a calculated value that recognizes changes in fair value in a systematic and rational manner over not more than five years.

T F 5. Prior service cost under a defined benefit pension plan can arise only if retroactive pension credit is granted for employee services rendered in periods prior to the plan adoption or amendment.

T F 6. The prior service cost arising from an amendment to a defined benefit pension plan is measured as the increase in the projected benefit obligation as a result of the amendment.

T F 7. Prior service cost is not required to be recognized as an asset or a liability.

T F 8. Prior service cost must be amortized as a component of net periodic pension cost on a straight-line basis over the average remaining service period of active employees who are expected to receive benefits under the plan.

T F 9. Changes in the value of either the projected benefit obligation or the pension plan assets arising from changes in actuarial assumptions or from experience different from that assumed must be reported on the income statement as gains or losses.

T F 10. Net periodic pension cost under a defined benefit plan is decreased by amortization of an unrecognized net gain arising from changes in the value of either the projected benefit obligation or the plan assets as a result of changes in actuarial assumptions or experience different from that assumed.

T F 11. In accounting for a defined benefit pension plan, the employer must report either a liability at the excess of the accumulated benefit obligation over the fair value of plan assets or an asset at the excess of the fair value of plan assets over the accumulated benefit obligation.

T F 12. An intangible asset arising from the recognition of a minimum pension liability for an unfunded accumulated benefit obligation must be amortized on a straight-line basis over the average remaining service period of employees expected to receive benefits under the plan.

T F 13. When a minimum liability is recognized under a defined benefit pension plan, any excess of the additional pension liability over the unrecognized prior service cost must be reported as a contra account in the stockholders' equity section of the balance sheet.

T F 14. When there is no minimum liability, the difference between the cumulative amount of net periodic pension cost and the cumulative amount funded by the employer to an independently controlled pension fund must be reported on the balance sheet.

T F 15. When the cumulative amount funded by the employer under a defined benefit plan is equal to the cumulative amount of its net periodic pension cost, there should be no pension amounts reported on the balance sheet.

T F 16. Net periodic pension cost under a defined benefit plan is decreased by amortization of an unrecognized net asset existing at the date of initial application of *Statement No. 87*.

T F 17. In a schedule reconciling the funded status of a defined benefit plan with the pension amounts reported on the balance sheet, an unrecognized net gain arising from changes in the value of either the projected benefit obligation or the plan assets as a result of changes in actuarial assumptions or experience different from that assumed should be deducted from the difference between the projected benefit obligation and the fair value of plan assets.

T F 18. When an employer's cash payments for other postretirement benefits are limited to benefit payments, there should be no actual or expected return on plan assets included in the calculation of net periodic postretirement benefit cost.

T F 19. *Statement No. 87* requires employers to report a minimum liability at least equal to any unfunded accumulated benefit obligation, whereas *Statement No. 106* does not require employers to

report a minimum liability for an unfunded accumulated postretirement benefit obligation.

T F *20. In the annual financial statements of a defined benefit pension plan, investments (excluding contracts with insurance companies) must be reported at the lower of their cost or fair market value.

Multiple Choice

Select the best response for each of the following items, and circle the corresponding letter:

1. Net periodic pension cost under a defined benefit plan is increased by:

   a. Expected return on plan assets.
   b. Amortization of an unrecognized net loss arising from changes in the value of either the projected benefit obligation or the plan assets as a result of changes in actuarial assumptions or experience different from that assumed.
   c. Amortization of the excess of a decrease in the projected benefit obligation arising from a plan amendment over the unrecognized prior service cost.
   d. Amortization of an intangible asset arising from recognition of a minimum liability for an unfunded accumulated benefit obligation.

2. Net periodic pension cost under a defined benefit plan is decreased by:

   a. Interest on projected benefit obligation.
   b. Expected return on plan assets.
   c. Amortization of unrecognized prior service cost.
   d. Amortization of the unrecognized net obligation existing at the date of initial application of *Statement No. 87*.

3. Which of the following is required to be included in the determination of net periodic pension cost under a defined benefit plan only if the plan is funded?

   a. Service cost.
   b. Interest on projected benefit obligation.
   c. Expected return on plan assets.
   d. Amortization of an unrecognized net gain or loss arising from changes in the projected benefit obligation as a result of changes in actuarial assumptions or experience different from that assumed.

4. Which of the following is required to be included in the determination of net periodic pension cost under a defined benefit plan only if retroactive pension benefits are granted for employee services rendered in periods before a plan adoption or amendment?

   a. Amortization of the unrecognized net obligation existing at the date of initial application of *Statement No. 87*.
   b. Amortization of an unrecognized net loss rising from an increase in the projected benefit obligation or a decrease in the value of plan assets as a result of changes in actuarial assumptions or experience different from that assumed.
   c. Interest on projected benefit obligation.
   d. Amortization of unrecognized prior service cost.

5. Which of the following amounts is required to be amortized as a component of net periodic pension cost under a defined benefit plan only if, as of the beginning of the year, it is material in relationship to the larger of the projected benefit obligation or the market-related value of plan assets?

   a. Unrecognized prior service cost.
   b. An intangible asset arising from recognition of a minimum liability for an unfunded accumulated benefit obligation.
   c. Unrecognized net gain or loss arising from changes in the value of either the projected benefit obligation or the plan assets as a result of changes in actuarial assumptions or experience different from that assumed.
   d. Unrecognized net asset or net obligation existing at the date of the initial application of *Statement No. 87*.

6. Which of the following may be amortized on other than a straight-line basis in the calculation of net periodic pension cost under a defined benefit plan?

   a. Unrecognized prior service cost.
   b. Unrecognized net gain or loss arising from changes in the value of either the projected benefit obligation or the plan assets as a result of changes in actuarial assumptions or experience different from that assumed.
   c. Unrecognized net asset or net obligation existing at the date of the initial application of *Statement No. 87*.
   d. An intangible asset arising from recognition of a minimum liability for an unfunded accumulated benefit obligation.

7. When the cumulative amount of net periodic pension cost under a defined benefit plan is equal to the cumulative amount funded by the employer, the journal entry to record the recognition of a minimum liability for the first time should include:

   a. A credit to additional pension liability and a debit to intangible asset at the excess of the projected benefit obligation over the fair value of plan assets.
   b. A credit to additional pension liability and a debit to intangible asset at the excess of the accumulated benefit obligation over the fair value of plan assets.
   c. A credit to additional pension liability at the excess of the accumulated benefit obligation over the fair value of plan assets and a debit to intangible asset at the lower of the unfunded accumulated benefit obligation or unrecognized prior service cost.
   d. A credit to additional pension liability and a debit to intangible asset at the excess of the unrecognized prior service cost over the fair value of plan assets.

8. Under the transition requirements of *Statement No. 87*, the difference between the projected benefit obligation and the fair value of plan assets, adjusted by any previously recognized prepaid pension cost or accrued pension cost, as of the beginning of the fiscal year in which it is first applied is required to be:

   a. Amortized as a component of net periodic pension cost over the average remaining service period of active employees expected to receive benefits under the plan.
   b. Reported on the income statement as the cumulative effect of the change in accounting principle.
   c. Reported in the statement of retained earnings as a prior period adjustment to beginning retained earnings, with retroactive restatement of prior year financial statements that are presented for comparative purposes.
   d. Carried forward to be applied as a reduction of any net gain or loss arising from changes in the value of either the projected benefit obligation or the plan assets as a result of changes in actuarial assumptions or experience different from that assumed.

9. A decrease in the accumulated postretirement benefit obligation that reduces postretirement benefits is required to be:

a. Accounted for as a reduction of net periodic postretirement benefit cost for the year of the plan amendment.
b. Amortized as a reduction of net periodic postretirement benefit cost on a declining basis.
c. Amortized as a reduction of net periodic postretirement benefit cost on a straight-line basis.
d. Accounted for as a reduction of any existing unrecognized prior service cost and any unrecognized transition obligation before being amortized as a component of net periodic postretirement benefit cost.

*10. When a pension obligation under a defined benefit pension plan is fully settled by purchasing nonparticipating annuity contracts, the employer must recognize in the income statement a gain or loss equal to:

a. The unrecognized net pension gain or loss.
b. The unrecognized prior service cost.
c. The unrecognized net pension gain or loss plus any remaining unrecognized net asset existing at the date of initial application of *Statement No. 87.*
d. The unrecognized prior service cost plus any remaining unrecognized net obligation existing at the date of initial application of *Statement No. 87.*

Extended Problem

This problem concerns the funded, noncontributory, defined benefit pension plans of three companies—Amend Corporation, Adopt Corporation, and Transition Corporation. Data related to two of the companies for the years 1995 through 1998 are presented here; data related to the pension and other postretirement benefit costs of the third company are given later. Unless otherwise indicated, assume that the projected benefit obligation and the fair value of plan assets amounts that follow are both the projected and actual values (that is, there were no gains or losses).

	AMEND CORPORATION				ADOPT CORPORATION			
	1995	1996	1997	1998	1995	1996	1997	1998
Service cost for year	$40,000	$ 45,000	$ 50,000	$ 55,000	$ 40,000	$ 45,000	$ 50,000	$ 60,000
Prior service cost arising from adoption of plan at beginning of year	-0-	-0-	-0-	-0-	150,000	-0-	-0-	-0-
Prior service cost arising from amendment to plan at beginning of year	-0-	20,000	-0-	-0-	-0-	-0-	-0-	-0-
Projected benefit obligation at end of year	40,000	111,000	172,100	244,310	205,000	270,500	389,778[b]	488,756
Accumulated benefit obligation at end of year	24,000	66,000	103,260	146,586	123,000	162,300	233,867	293,254
Fair value of plan assets at end of year	40,000	91,630	174,470[a]	249,547	64,412	140,265	228,704	335,986
Employer's cash contribution to pension fund at end of year	40,000	47,630	52,630	57,630	64,412	69,412	74,412	84,412
Discount rate and expected long-term rate of return on plan assets	10%	10%	10%	10%	10%	10%	10%	10%

[a]The actual fair value of plan assets at the end of 1997 ($174,470) was greater than the projected fair value of plan assets at that date [$91,630 + ($91,630 × 10%) + $52,630 = $153,423]; that is, there was a gain of $21,047 during 1997. At the end of 1997, the average remaining service period of active employees expected to receive benefits under the plan was 18 years.

[b]The actual value of the projected benefit obligation at the end of 1997 ($389,778) was greater than the projected value of the projected benefit obligation at that date [$270,500 + ($270,500 × 10%) + $50,000 = $347,550]; that is, there was a loss of $42,228 during 1997. At the end of 1997, the average remaining service period of active employees expected to receive benefits under the plan was 13 years.

REQUIRED

a. Amend Corporation was organized and adopted its pension plan on January 1, 1995. The prior service cost arising from the amendment to the plan as of January 1, 1996, when the average remaining service period of active employees expected to receive benefits under the plan was 20 years, is being funded in 15 equal year-end payments of $2,630 (the prior service cost, $20,000, divided by the present value factor of an ordinary annuity for 15 years at 10 percent, 7.6061). The service cost is being funded in full at the end of each year.

(1). Calculate the net periodic pension cost for each of the years 1995 through 1998.
(2). Prepare the journal entry required to record net periodic pension cost and the employer's cash contribution to the pension fund for each of the years 1995 through 1998.
(3). Calculate the prepaid pension cost or accrued pension cost balance as of December 31 for each of the years 1995 through 1998.
(4). Prepare the journal entry required, if any, to record or adjust the minimum pension liability at December 31 for each of the years 1995 through 1998.
(5). Prepare a schedule that reconciles the funded status of the plan with the pension amounts reported on the employer's balance sheet as of December 31, for each of the years 1995 through 1998.

b. Adopt Corporation, which was organized several years ago, adopted its pension plan as of January 1, 1995, when the average remaining service period of active employees expected to receive benefits under the plan was 16 years. The service cost is being funded in full at the end of each year. The prior service cost arising from the adoption of the plan is being funded in 10 equal year-end payments of $24,412 (the prior service cost, $150,000, divided by the present value factor of an ordinary annuity for 10 years at 10 percent, 6.1446).

(1). Calculate the net periodic pension cost for each of the years 1995 through 1998.
(2). Prepare the journal entry required to record net periodic pension cost and the employer's cash contribution to the pension fund for each of the years 1995 through 1998.
(3). Prepare the journal entry required, if any, to record or adjust the minimum pension liability at December 31 for each of the years 1995 through 1998.

(4). Prepare a schedule that reconciles the funded status of the plan with the pension amounts reported on the employer's balance sheet as of December 31 for each of the years 1995 through 1998.

c. Transition Corporation, which was organized and adopted its pension plan several years ago, began applying the provisions of *Statement No. 87* at the beginning of 1988, when the average remaining service period of active employees expected to receive benefits under the plan was 15 years. For the current year 1995, net pension cost before amortization of the unrecognized net asset or net obligation existing at the date of initial application of *Statement No. 87* is $60,000. Calculate the total net periodic pension cost for 1995 in each of the following alternative circumstances:

(1). As of the beginning of 1988, the projected benefit obligation was $500,000, the fair value of plan assets was $400,000, and the accrued pension cost credit balance was $25,000.
(2). As of the beginning of 1988, the projected benefit obligation was $500,000, the fair value of plan assets was $600,000, and the prepaid pension cost debit balance was $40,000.

d. Assume that Transition Corporation (described in situation c) began applying *Statement No. 106* to its postretirement health care plan as of January 1, 1993, when the accumulated postretirement benefit obligation was $150,000 and the average remaining service period of the active plan participants was 12 years. Since the company had recognized this postretirement benefit cost on a pay-as-you-go (cash) basis in prior years, there were no plan assets or accrued or prepaid postretirement benefit cost balance on the transition date. Assume further that the company's accumulated postretirement benefit obligation and accrued postretirement benefit cost account balance at December 31, 1994, are $180,000 and $55,000, respectively; that the company's service costs for 1995 and 1996 are $22,500 and $23,200, respectively; that the company's cash benefit payments for 1995 and 1996 are $21,700 and $24,600, respectively; that the benefit payments are made by the company at the end of each year; that the discount rate for both years is 10 percent; that there are no gains or losses in both years; and that the company is amortizing its transition obligation over the average remaining service period of the active plan participants.

(1). Calculate the net periodic postretirement benefit cost for 1995 and 1996.

(2). Prepare the journal entry required to record net periodic postretirement benefit cost and the cash benefit payments.

(3). Prepare a schedule that reconciles the funded status of the plan with the postretirement benefit cost amount reported on the company's balance sheet at December 31, 1995 and 1996.

(4). Without prejudice to your earlier answers, assume that as of December 31, 1996, the "actual value" of the accumulated postretirement benefit obligation was deter-mined to be $248,000, instead of the "projected value" of $217,280. Assume further that on January 1, 1997, the average remaining service period of the active plan participant was 10 years and that the company's service cost and cash benefit payments for 1997 were $25,400 and $29,200, respectively. Calculate the amount of the loss that should be amortized, if any, as a component of net periodic postretirement benefit cost for each of the years 1997 and 1998, using the corridor approach.

COMMON ERRORS

The first statement in each "common error" listed here is *incorrect*. Each incorrect statement is followed by a corrected statement and an explanation.

1. The amount of net periodic pension cost recognized under a defined benefit plan should equal the amount of cash contributed by the employer to the pension fund during the period. *Wrong*

The amount of net periodic pension cost recognized under a defined benefit plan may be, but is not necessarily, equal to the amount of cash contributed by the employer to the pension fund during the period. *Right*

The amount of net periodic pension cost recognized under a defined benefit plan must be calculated by the employer in accordance with the requirements specified in *Statement No. 87*. These requirements state that the amount recognized for a period must include the following components: service cost, interest on projected benefit obligation, expected return on plan assets, amortization of unrecognized prior service cost, amortization of an unrecognized net pension gain or loss, and amortization of the unrecognized net asset or net obligation existing at the date of initial application of the *Statement*. In contrast, the amount of cash contributed by the employer to the pension fund during a period is a function of a combination of factors, including working capital requirements, the availability of attractive alternative investments, ERISA's minimum funding requirements, and tax regulations. An employer, for example, may decide to fund pension cost over a shorter period in order to maximize tax deductions currently and to maximize tax-exempt earnings accumulating on plan assets. Alternatively, an employer may decide to fund pension cost over a longer period in order to retain funds for working capital requirements or for attractive alternative investments. Consequently, the amount of net periodic pension cost recognized under a defined benefit plan may be, but is not necessarily, equal to the amount of cash contributed by the employer to the pension fund during the period.

2. The rates used to compute the interest cost and expected return on plan assets components of net periodic pension cost under a defined benefit plan are the same. *Wrong*

The rates used to compute the interest cost and expected return on plan assets components of net periodic pension cost under a defined benefit plan are different. *Right*

Statement No. 87 requires that the interest cost component of net periodic pension cost under a defined benefit plan be computed by multiplying the projected benefit obligation at the beginning of the period by the discount rate used to measure the projected benefit obligation. The discount rate is defined as that rate at which the pension benefit obligation could be effectively settled, such as by purchasing annuity contracts from an insurance company. Because the projected benefit obligation is measured on the basis of the discount rate, the interest cost accruing on the projected benefit obligation with the passage of time must be computed using that same rate. Conversely, *Statement No. 87* requires that the expected return on plan assets component of net periodic pension cost be computed by multiplying the market-related value of plan assets at the beginning of the period by the expected long-term rate of return on plan assets. The expected long-term rate of return on plan assets is defined as the average rate of earnings expected on funds invested or to be invested to provide for the benefits included in the projected benefit obligation. Thus the rates that must be used to compute the interest cost and expected return on plan assets components of net periodic pension cost are different. One is a borrowing rate, whereas the other is a lending rate. These rates, however, may be equal during a particular period.

3. The minimum amortization of an unrecognized net gain or loss that is required to be included as a component of net periodic pension cost is the unrecognized net gain or loss divided by the average remaining service period of active employees expected to receive pension benefits under the plan. *Wrong*

The minimum amortization of an unrecognized net gain or loss that is required to be included as a component of net periodic pension cost is the excess of the unrecognized net gain or loss over 10 percent of the larger of the projected benefit obligation or market-related value of plan assets divided by the average remaining service period of active employees expected to receive pension benefits under the plan. *Right*

Gains and losses are changes in the value of either the projected benefit obligation or the plan assets arising from changes in actuarial assumptions or from experience different from that assumed. Because gains or losses in one period may be offset by losses or gains in subsequent periods, *Statement No. 87* requires that gains or losses be amortized as a component of net periodic pension cost only if, as of the beginning of the year, the unrecognized net gain or loss exceeds 10 percent of the greater of the projected benefit obligation or the market-related value of plan assets. And if amortization is required, *Statement No. 87* requires that the minimum amortization be that excess divided by the average remaining service period of active employees expected to receive pension benefits under the plan.

4. Amortization of an unrecognized net gain results in an increase in net periodic pension cost; amortization of an unrecognized net loss results in a decrease in net periodic pension cost. *Wrong*

Amortization of an unrecognized net gain results in a decrease in net periodic pension cost; amortization of an unrecognized net loss results in an increase in net periodic pension cost. *Right*

Gains are either decreases in the projected benefit obligation or increases in the value of plan assets arising from changes in actuarial assumptions or from experience different from that assumed; losses are either increases in the projected benefit obligation or decreases in the value of plan assets arising from changes in actuarial assumptions or from experience different from that assumed. Because gains result in a reduction of the total pension benefit cost over time, amortization of an unrecognized net gain results in a decrease in net periodic pension cost. Conversely, because losses result in an increase in the total pension benefit cost over time, amortization of an unrecognized net loss results in an increase in net periodic pension cost.

5. Amortization of an unrecognized net asset results in an increase in net periodic pension cost; amortization of an unrecognized net obligation results in a decrease in net periodic pension cost. *Wrong*

Amortization of an unrecognized net asset results in a decrease in net periodic pension cost; amortization of an unrecognized net obligation results in an increase in net periodic pension cost. *Right*

The unrecognized net asset, as of the beginning of the fiscal year in which *Statement No. 87* is first applied, is the excess of the fair value of plan assets, adjusted for any previously recognized accrued pension cost or prepaid pension cost, over the projected benefit obligation. Because the unrecognized net asset represents primarily an unrecognized net gain from previous periods and because gains result in a reduction of the total pension benefit cost over time, amortization of an unrecognized net asset results in a decrease in net periodic pension cost. Conversely, the unrecognized net obligation existing as of the transition date is the excess of the projected benefit obligation over the fair value of plan assets, adjusted for any previously recognized accrued pension cost or prepaid pension cost. Because the unrecognized net obligation represents primarily either an unrecognized prior service cost or unrecognized net loss from previous periods, and because prior service cost and losses result in an increase in total pension benefit cost over time, amortization of an unrecognized net obligation results in an increase in net periodic pension cost.

6. The journal entry to recognize a minimum liability for the first time always should include a credit to additional pension liability at the excess of the accumulated benefit obligation over the fair value of plan assets. *Wrong*

The journal entry to recognize a minimum liability for the first time should include a credit to additional pension liability at the excess of the accumulated benefit obligation over the fair value of plan assets plus any recognized prepaid pension cost or minus any recognized accrued pension cost. *Right*

If the accumulated benefit obligation exceeds the fair value of plan assets, *Statement No. 87* requires that a net pension liability at least equal to that unfunded accumulated benefit obligation (called a minimum liability) be reported on the balance sheet. When there is neither a prepaid pension cost debit balance nor an accrued pension cost credit balance, the journal entry to recognize a minimum liability for the first time should include a credit to additional pension liability at the excess of the accumulated benefit obligation over the fair value of plan assets. Conversely, when there is an accrued pension cost credit balance, the journal entry to recognize a minimum liability for the first time should include a credit to additional pension liability at the excess of the accumulated benefit obligation over the fair value of plan assets minus the accrued pension cost credit balance. Alternatively, when there is prepaid pension cost debit balance, the journal entry to recognize a minimum liability for the first time should include a credit to additional pension liability at the excess of the accumulated benefit obligation over the fair value of plan assets plus the prepaid pension cost debit balance.

7. In a schedule reconciling the funded status of a defined benefit plan with the net pension amount reported on the balance sheet, unrecognized prior service cost, an unrecognized net loss (net gain), and the unrecognized net obligation (net asset) should be deducted from (added to) the funded status. *Wrong*

In a schedule reconciling the funded status of a defined benefit plan with the net pension amount reported on the balance sheet, unrecognized prior service cost, an unrecognized net loss (net gain), and the unrecognized net obligation (net asset) should be added to (deducted from) the funded status. *Right*

A reconciliation is a schedule that explains the causes of the difference between two amounts by indicating those items that are included in one of the amounts but not yet included in the other amount, or vice versa. In the reconciliation required by *Statement No. 87,* the two amounts to be reconciled are the funded status of the plan and the net pension amount reported on the balance sheet. The funded status is the fair value of plan assets minus the projected benefit obligation. The net pension amount reported on the balance sheet is either an accrued pension cost or a prepaid pension cost equal to the difference between the cumulative amount of net periodic pension cost and the cumulative amount funded by the employer or, if a minimum liability has been recognized, a net pension liability equal to the excess of the accumulated benefit obligation over the fair value of plan assets. When no minimum liability has been recognized, the funded status should be reconciled with the accrued

pension cost or prepaid pension cost reported on the balance sheet as follows:

a. Unrecognized prior service cost should be added to the funded status because it represents a decrease in the funded status (an increase in the projected benefit obligation) that has not yet been recognized in net periodic pension cost.
b. An unrecognized net loss should be added to the funded status because it represents a decrease in the funded status (either an increase in the projected benefit obligation or a decrease in the value of plan assets) that has not yet been recognized in net periodic pension cost. Conversely, an unrecognized net gain should be deducted from the funded status because it represents an increase in the funded status (either a decrease in the projected benefit obligation or an increase in the value of plan assets) that has not yet been recognized in net periodic pension cost.
c. The unrecognized net obligation existing at the transition date should be added to the funded status because it represents a decrease in the funded status, arising primarily from either unrecognized prior service cost (an increase in the projected benefit obligation) or an unrecognized net loss (either an increase in the projected benefit obligation or a decrease in the value of plan assets) from previous periods, that has not yet been recognized in net periodic pension cost. Conversely, the unrecognized net asset existing at the transition date should be deducted from the funded status because it represents an increase in the funded status, arising primarily from an unrecognized net gain (either a decrease in the projected benefit obligation or an increase in the value of plan assets) from previous periods, that has not yet been recognized in net periodic pension cost.

In addition, when a minimum liability has been recognized, the adjustment required to recognize the additional pension liability (the excess of the accumulated benefit obligation over the fair value of plan assets plus any recognized prepaid pension cost or minus any recognized accrued pension cost) should be deducted from the funded status because it represents a portion of the unfunded status (the excess of the accumulated benefit obligation over the fair value of plan assets) that has been recognized in the net pension amount reported on the balance sheet.

ANSWERS
Items marked with an asterisk (*) refer to the Appendixes.

Key Terms and Concepts

1. postretirement benefit plan
2. contributory plan, noncontributory plan
3. fully vested, partially vested
4. funded plan, unfunded plan
5. defined contribution plan, defined benefit plan
6. plan assets
7. service cost, projected benefit obligation, accumulated benefit obligation
8. prior service cost
9. gains and losses (or sometimes actuarial gains and losses)
10. unrecognized net obligation or net asset at the transition date

True-False

1. F Net periodic pension cost should be recognized by the employer in the period in which pension benefits are earned by employees. Employees who are covered by a pension plan receive a portion of their compensation currently in the form of salaries and wages and another portion of their compensation during retirement years in the form of pension benefits. Both forms of compensation should be recognized by the employer as an expense in the period in which the employee services are rendered.

2. F The projected benefit obligation is measured using assumptions as to future compensation levels if the pension benefit formula is based on those future compensation levels; the accumulated benefit obligation is measured using no assumptions about future compensation levels. Thus when the compensation levels of active employees are expected to increase and the pension benefit formula is based on those future compensation levels, the projected benefit obligation will be greater than the accumulated benefit obligation.

3. F The interest cost component of net periodic pension cost under a defined benefit plan must be calculated by multiplying the projected benefit obligation at the beginning of the period by the discount rate (that is, that rate at which the pension obligation could be effectively settled, such as by purchasing annuity contracts from an insurance company).

4. F The expected return on plan assets components of net periodic pension cost under a defined benefit plan must be calculated by multiplying the expected long-term rate of return on plan assets by the market-related value of plan assets at the beginning of the period, measured at either fair value or a calculated value that recognizes changes in fair value in a systematic and rational manner over not more than five years.

5. T
6. T
7. T

8. F Prior service cost must be amortized as a component of net periodic pension cost over the future service period of those active employees, at the adoption or amendment date, who are expected to receive benefits under the plan. *Statement No. 87* specifies that prior service cost should be amortized on a declining basis by assigning an equal amount to each future service period of each employee active at the adoption or amendment date who is expected to receive benefits under the plan. Alternatively, to reduce the complexity and detail of the computations required, *Statement No. 87* permits prior service cost to be amortized on a straight-line basis over the average remaining service period of active employees who are expected to receive benefits under the plan.

9. F Changes in the value of either the projected benefit obligation or the pension plan assets arising from changes in actuarial assumptions or from experience different from that assumed must be amortized as a component of net pension cost for a year if, as of the beginning of the year, that unrecognized net gain or loss exceeds 10 percent of the greater of the projected benefit obligation or the market-related value of plan assets. And, if amortization is required, the amount to be amortized, as a minimum, must be the amount of that excess divided by the average remaining service period of active employees expected to receive benefits under the plan.

10. T
11. F In accounting for a defined benefit pension plan, the employer must report a liability (called the minimum liability) at least

equal to the excess of the accumulated benefit obligation over the fair value of plan assets. The employer, however, may not report an asset at the excess of the fair value of plan assets over the accumulated benefit obligation.

12. F An intangible asset arising from the recognition of a minimum liability for an unfunded accumulated benefit obligation should not be amortized, because the minimum liability and related intangible asset, in essence, represent amounts that will be recognized in the future as components of net periodic pension cost through, for example, amortization of unrecognized prior service cost.

13. T

14. T

15. F When the cumulative amount funded by the employer under a defined benefit plan is equal to the cumulative amount of its net periodic pension cost, there should be neither a prepaid pension cost nor an ac-

crued pension cost reported on the balance sheet. Nevertheless, if the accumulated benefit obligation exceeds the fair value of plan assets, a minimum liability at least equal to that excess must be reported on the balance sheet.

16. T
17. T
18. T
19. T
*20. F In the annual financial statements of a defined benefit pension plan, investments (excluding contracts with insurance companies) must be reported at their fair market value.

Multiple Choice

1. b
2. b
3. c
4. d
5. c

6. a
7. c
8. a
9. d
*10. c

Extended Problem

a. Amend Corporation:

(1). Calculation of net periodic pension cost.

	1995	1996	1997	1998
Service cost	$40,000	$45,000	$50,000	$55,000
Interest on projected benefit obligation at beginning of year				
$0 × 10%	-0-			
($40,000 + $20,000) × 10%		6,000		
$111,000 × 10%			11,100	
$172,100 × 10%				17,210
Expected return on plan assets at beginning of year				
$0 × 10%	-0-			
$40,000 × 10%		(4,000)		
$91,630 × 10%			(9,163)	
$174,470 × 10%				(17,447)
Amortization of unrecognized prior service cost arising from amendment to plan				
($20,000 ÷ 20 years)	-0-	1,000	1,000	1,000
Amortization of unrecognized net gain				
{[$21,047 − ($174,470 × 10%)] ÷ 18 years}	-0-	-0-	-0-	(200)
Total net periodic pension cost	$40,000	$48,000	$52,937	$55,563

(2). Journal entry to record net periodic pension cost and cash contribution.

12/31/95	Pension expense	40,000	
	Cash		40,000
12/31/96	Pension expense	48,000	
	Accrued/prepaid pension cost ($48,000 − $47,630)		370
	Cash		47,630
12/31/97	Pension expense	52,937	
	Accrued/prepaid pension cost ($52,937 − $52,630)		307
	Cash		52,630
12/31/98	Pension expense	55,563	
	Accrued/prepaid pension cost ($57,630 − $55,563)	2,067	
	Cash		57,630

(3). Calculation of prepaid/accrued pension cost balance.

	1995	1996	1997	1998
Prepaid/(accrued) pension cost at beginning of year......................	$ -0-	$ -0-	$(370)	$ (677)
Debit (credit) to record difference between net periodic pension cost and cash contribution	-0-	(370)	(307)	2,067
Prepaid/(accrued) pension cost at end of year.............................	$ -0-	$(370)	$(677)	$1,390

(4). No journal entry is required to record or adjust a minimum pension liability in any of the years because, as shown here, at the end of each year the fair value of plan assets exceeded the accumulated benefit obligation; that is, there was no unfunded accumulated benefit obligation.

	1995	1996	1997	1998
Accumulated benefit obligation	$ 24,000	$ 66,000	$ 103,260	$ 146,586
Fair value of plan assets	(40,000)	(91,630)	(174,470)	(249,547)
Unfunded (overfunded) accumulated benefit obligation...................	$(16,000)	$(25,630)	$ (71,210)	$(102,961)

(5). Schedule reconciling funded status with pension amounts reported on balance sheet.

	1995	1996	1997	1998
Projected benefit obligation	$(40,000)	$(111,000)	$(172,100)	$(244,310)
Plan assets at fair value...	40,000	91,630	174,470	249,547
Funded status..	$ -0-	$ (19,370)	$ 2,370	$ 5,237
Unrecognized prior service cost...	-0-			
$20,000 − $1,000		19,000		
$20,000 − ($1,000 × 2)..			18,000	
$20,000 − ($1,000 × 3)..				17,000
Unrecognized net gain	-0-	-0-		
$21,047 − $0			(21,047)	
$21,047 − $200..				(20,847)
Prepaid/(accrued) pension cost	$ -0-	$ (370)	$ (677)	$ 1,390

b. Adopt Corporation:

(1). Calculation of net periodic pension cost.

	1995	1996	1997	1998
Service cost	$40,000	$45,000	$50,000	$60,000
Interest on projected benefit obligation at beginning of year				
$150,000 × 10%...	15,000			
$205,000 × 10%...		20,500		
$270,500 × 10%...			27,050	
$389,778 × 10%...				38,978
Expected return on plan assets at beginning of year				
$0 × 10%..	-0-			
$64,412 × 10%		(6,441)		
$140,265 × 10%			(14,027)	
$228,704 × 10%				(22,870)
Amortization of unrecognized prior service cost arising from adoption of plan				
($150,000 ÷ 16 years)..	9,375	9,375	9,375	9,375
Amortization of unrecognized net loss				
{[$42,228 − ($389,778 × 10%)] ÷ 13 years}...........................	-0-	-0-	-0-	250
Total net periodic pension cost...	$64,375	$68,434	$72,398	$85,733

(2). Journal entry to record net periodic pension cost and cash contribution.

12/31/95	Pension expense..	64,375	
	Accrued/prepaid pension cost ($64,412 − $64,375)................................	37	
	Cash...		64,412
12/31/96	Pension expense..	68,434	
	Accrued/prepaid pension cost ($69,412 − $68,434)................................	978	
	Cash...		69,412
12/31/97	Pension expense..	72,398	
	Accrued/prepaid pension cost ($74,412 − $72,398)................................	2,014	
	Cash...		74,412
12/31/98	Pension expense..	85,733	
	Accrued/prepaid pension cost ($85,733 − $84,412)................................		1,321
	Cash...		84,412

(3). Journal entry to record or adjust minimum pension liability. (Calculation of adjustments shown in following schedule.)

12/31/95	Intangible asset..	58,625	
	Additional pension liability...		58,625
12/31/96	Additional pension liability..	35,575	
	Intangible asset...		35,575
12/31/97	Additional pension liability..	14,858	
	Intangible asset...		14,858
12/31/98	Additional pension liability..	8,192	
	Intangible asset...		8,192

Calculation of adjustments related to minimum pension liability.

	1995	1996	1997	1998
Accumulated benefit obligation................................	$123,000	$162,300	$233,867	$293,254
Fair value of plan assets	(64,412)	(140,265)	(228,704)	(335,986)
Unfunded (overfunded) accumulated benefit obligation............	$ 58,588	$ 22,035	$ 5,163	$ (42,732)
(Accrued)/prepaid pension cost at beginning of year..............	$ -0-	$ 37	$ 1,015	$ 3,029
Debit (credit) to record difference between net periodic pension cost and cash contribution..............................	37	978	2,014	(1,321)
(Accrued)/prepaid pension cost at end of year...................	$ 37	$ 1,015	$ 3,029	$ 1,708
Additional pension liability at end of year....................	$ 58,625	$ 23,050	$ 8,192	$ -0-
Additional pension liability at beginning of year..............	-0-	(58,625)	(23,050)	(8,192)
Credit (debit) to record or adjust additional pension liability[a]	$ 58,625	$(35,575)	$(14,858)	$ (8,192)

[a]For each of the years 1995 through 1998, the amount to record or adjust the minimum pension liability is the unfunded accumulated benefit obligation minus or plus the accrued/prepaid pension cost credit or debit balance. At the end of 1998, however, the minimum liability is reduced to zero ($58,625 − $35,575 − $14,858 − $8,192 = $0), because the fair value of the plan assets exceeds the accumulated benefit obligation at that date.

(4). Schedule reconciling funded status with pension amounts reported on balance sheet.

	1995	1996	1997	1998
Projected benefit obligation....................................	$(205,000)	$(270,500)	$(389,778)	$(488,756)
Plan assets at fair value	64,412	140,265	228,704	335,986
Funded status..	$(140,588)	$(130,235)	$(161,074)	$(152,770)
Unrecognized prior service cost				
$150,000 − $9,375...................................	140,625			
$150,000 − ($9,375 × 2).............................		131,250		
$150,000 − ($9,375 × 3).............................			121,875	
$150,000 − ($9,375 × 4).............................				112,500
Unrecognized net loss..	-0-	-0-		
$42,228 − $0.......................................			42,228	
$42,228 − $250.....................................				41,978
Additional pension liability...................................	(58,625)	(23,050)	(8,192)	-0-
Net pension asset (liability)[a]..............................	$ (58,588)	$ (22,035)	$ (5,163)	$ 1,708

[a]The sum of the additional pension liability balance at the end of the year, if any, plus or minus the accrued/prepaid pension cost at that date. For example, the net pension liability of $58,588 at December 31, 1995, is equal to the additional pension liability of $58,625 minus the prepaid pension cost of $37. Notice that the net pension liability at this date also is equal to the unfunded accumulated benefit obligation (the minimum liability), if any.

c. Transition Corporation:

	CIRCUMSTANCE	
	(1)	(2)
Net periodic pension cost before amortization of unrecognized net asset or net obligation existing at transition date..	$60,000	$60,000
Amortization of unrecognized net obligation (net asset) existing at transition date		
[$500,000 − ($400,000 + $25,000)] ÷ 15 years...	5,000	
[($600,000 − $40,000) − $500,000] ÷ 15 years...		(4,000)
Total net periodic pension cost	$65,000	$56,000

d. Transition Corporation:

(1). Calculation of net periodic postretirement benefit cost.

	1995	1996
Service cost	$22,500	$23,200
Interest on accumulated postretirement benefit obligation at beginning of year		
$180,000 × 10%	18,000	
($180,000 + $18,000 + $22,500 − $21,700) × 10%		19,880
Amortization of transition obligation ($150,000 ÷ 12)..	12,500	12,500
Net periodic postretirement benefit cost	$53,000	$55,580

(2). Journal entry to record net periodic postretirement benefit cost and cash benefit payment.

12/31/95	Postretirement benefit expense	53,000	
	Cash		21,700
	Accrued postretirement benefit cost..		31,300
12/31/96	Postretirement benefit expense	55,580	
	Cash		24,600
	Accrued postretirement benefit cost..		30,980

(3). Schedule reconciling funded status with postretirement amount reported on balance sheet.

	1995	1996
Accumulated postretirement benefit obligation[a]	$198,800	$217,280
Plan assets at fair value	-0-	-0-
Funded status...	$198,800	$217,280
Unrecognized transition obligation	(112,500)	(100,000)
Accrued postretirement benefit cost[b]...	$ 86,300	$117,280

[a]The accumulated postretirement benefit obligation at the end of the year is equal to the accumulated postretirement benefit obligation at the beginning of the year, plus the interest cost for the year, plus the service cost for the year, minus the cash benefit payments at the end of the year, as follows: $180,000 + $18,000 + $22,500 − $21,700 = $198,800, and $198,880 + $19,880 + $23,200 − $24,600 = $217,280.

[b]The accrued postretirement benefit cost account balance at the end of the year is the balance at the beginning of the year plus the amount credited to the account during the year, as follows: $55,000 + $31,300 = $86,300, and $86,300 + $30,980 = $117,280.

(4). Calculation of amortization of unrecognized net loss.

	1997	1998
Unrecognized net loss at beginning of year		
$248,000 − $217,280	$30,720	
$30,720 − $740		$29,980
10% of greater of accumulated postretirement benefit obligation or fair value of plan assets at beginning of year (i.e., corridor)		
$248,000 × 10%	24,800	
[$248,000 + ($248,000 × 10%) + $25,400 − $29,200] × 10%		26,900
Excess of unrecognized net loss over "corridor"...	$ 5,920	$ 3,080
Amortization of unrecognized net loss		
$5,920 ÷ 10..	$ 592	
$3,080 ÷ 9		$ 342

17 ACCOUNTING FOR INCOME TAXES

CHAPTER OBJECTIVES

After reading Chapter 17 and completing the questions, cases, exercises, and problems from the text chapter, you should be able to:

1. Identify the principal causes of differences between pretax financial income and taxable income.
2. Define and identify common examples of temporary differences.
3. Describe the reasoning underlying the recognition of the deferred tax consequences of temporary differences.
4. Distinguish between partial recognition and comprehensive recognition of deferred tax consequences, and describe the principal arguments for each.
5. Distinguish between the asset/liability method and the deferred method, and describe the rationale for each.
6. Identify the temporary differences existing as of the date of the financial statements, calculate the expected future taxable and deductible amounts from existing temporary differences and loss carryforwards, and calculate the deferred tax consequences of the existing temporary differences and loss carryforwards by applying

the enacted marginal tax rate to the expected future taxable and deductible amounts.
7. Determine whether deferred tax assets should be reduced by a valuation allowance, and, if so, calculate the amount of the valuation allowance required.
8. Prepare the journal entry or entries to record income taxes for the year when there are temporary differences.
9. Define and identify common examples of events that do not have tax consequences.
10. Prepare the journal entry or entries required to record income taxes for the year when there are events that do not have tax consequences.
11. Distinguish between loss carrybacks and loss carryforwards.
12. Prepare the journal entries required to record loss carrybacks and loss carryforwards.
13. Present the deferred tax liability and asset accounts in the balance sheet.
14. Allocate total income tax expense or benefits for a period among, for example, continuing operations, discontinued operations, extraordinary items, cumulative effect of accounting changes, and prior period adjustments by the process of intraperiod tax allocation.

CHAPTER REVIEW

Introduction

1. *Taxable income* is the excess of taxable revenues over tax deductible expenses and exemptions for a period that is calculated in

accordance with prescribed tax rules and regulations. Income taxes based on taxable income are levied against corporations by governmental units to obtain revenues to finance their operations and programs.

2. *Pretax financial income* is income, exclusive of income tax expense, for a period that is calculated in accordance with generally accepted accounting principles. Income is reported in the financial statements to provide information that is useful for assessing a corporation's cash flow prospects.

3. Pretax financial income reported in a corporation's financial statements generally differs from taxable income reported in its income tax return. There are three principal causes of these differences: (*a*) tax rules and regulations provide for the exclusion of certain revenues and expenses from the determination of taxable income, (*b*) tax rules and regulations differ from generally accepted accounting principles as to the recognition and measurement of certain revenues and expenses, and (*c*) corporations often select different methods of accounting for tax purposes and financial reporting purposes. Accounting for and reporting of differences between taxable income and pretax financial income are described in this chapter review. Such differences arise in most of the English-speaking world and the Netherlands, where accounting for financial reporting purposes is distinct from tax accounting. These complexities, however, do not arise where there is no such distinction, including Japan and most of continental Europe.

Conceptual Issues

4. Temporary differences. A *temporary difference* is a difference, at a financial reporting date, between the tax basis of an asset or a liability and its reported amount in the statement of financial position that is expected to result in taxable or deductible amounts in future years when the reported amount of the asset or liability is recovered or settled, respectively. Differences between the tax basis of an asset or a liability and its reported amount in the financial statements often result from the recognition of revenues and expenses in different periods for tax purposes and financial reporting purposes (called *timing differences*). The gross profit on an installment sale, for example, may be included in pretax financial income in the period of sale but included in taxable income in the period or periods of cash collection. In this example, the gross profit that has been recognized for financial reporting purposes would be included in the gross amount of the installment receivable reported in the balance sheet, whereas the gross profit that has not yet been recognized for tax purposes would be deducted from the gross amount of the installment receivable to determine its tax basis.

5. Deferred tax consequences. There are two basic accounting alternatives for the expected tax consequences of temporary differences. Under one alternative, the deferred tax consequences of temporary differences are ignored, and thus income tax expense reported on the income statement equals income taxes payable for the period. Advocates of this alternative argue that the legal liability for income taxes is determined by the tax return, and taxes payable in future years will be determined by taxable income in those years. Under the other alternative, the deferred tax consequences of temporary differences are recognized by including the tax consequences in income tax expense on the income statement and as a liability or an asset in the balance sheet. Advocates of this alternative argue that the accrual basis of accounting focuses on transactions and events that have cash consequences rather than strictly on cash receipts and cash disbursements and that the deferred tax (or future cash) consequences of temporary differences should be recognized in the financial statements.

6. Partial vs. comprehensive recognition. There are two basic views about the extent to which the deferred tax consequences of temporary differences should be recognized: partial recognition and comprehensive recognition. Proponents of *partial recognition* believe that deferred tax consequences should not be recognized for recurring temporary differences that give rise to an indefinite postponement or prepayment of taxes, since the tax consequences of such temporary differences will not have cash flow consequences in the foreseeable future and thus are remote contingencies rather than liabilities or assets. It is further argued that deferred tax consequences should only be recognized for nonrecurring temporary differences that are expected to be reversed within a relatively short period of time, since the tax consequences of these temporary differences are reasonably certain to affect cash flows in the foreseeable future. In contrast, proponents of *comprehensive recognition* believe that deferred tax consequences should be recognized for all temporary differences. The principal argument for this view is that the reported amounts of assets and liabilities will have tax consequences in the future as those amounts are recovered and settled, respectively, and thus the future tax consequences related to recognized assets and liabilities should likewise be recognized. Furthermore, although new temporary differences may arise in the future to offset taxable or deductible amounts related to existing temporary differences, it is argued that individual temporary differences, whether recurring or nonrecurring, are expected to have tax consequences in the future.

7. Asset/liability vs. deferred method. There are two fundamental methods of measuring the deferred tax consequences of temporary differences: the asset/liability method and the deferred method. Under the *asset/liability method,* the tax consequences of temporary differences are measured at the tax rates that have been enacted for those years when the temporary differences are expected to give rise to taxable or deductible amounts. Additionally, a deferred tax liability or asset recognized under this method theoretically should be determined on a discounted present value basis to reflect the time value of money. Because of its emphasis on measurement of the deferred tax liability or asset resulting from temporary differences, the asset/liability method may be perceived as a balance sheet approach. Under the *deferred method,* the tax consequences of temporary differences are measured at the tax rates in effect in the years when the temporary differences originate and are not adjusted for subsequent changes in tax rates or to reflect the enactment of new taxes. Because of its emphasis on matching the current-period tax savings or prepayment resulting from temporary differences with reported revenues and expenses, the deferred method may be perceived as an income statement approach. Some theorists also argue that the tax consequences of temporary differences (calculated by either the asset/liability or deferred method) should be accounted for as reductions of the reported amounts of the related assets and liabilities based on the rationale that taxability and tax deductibility are relevant factors in the valuation of assets and liabilities. In summary, the objective of providing measurements of assets and liabilities that are useful in assessing future cash flows is best met under the asset/liability method. The deferred method ignores future tax rates, and net-of-tax reporting denies the separate existence of a deferred tax liability or asset.

Accounting for Temporary Differences

8. For 20 years, the accounting and reporting requirements for income taxes were specified by *APB Opinion No. 11,* which required comprehensive recognition of deferred tax consequences by the deferred method. However, as a result of increasing concern with the complexity and relevance of these requirements, the FASB added accounting for income taxes to its agenda in January 1982. After six years of research and deliberation on the topic, in December 1987 the FASB issued *Statement No. 96,* which superseded *Opinion No. 11. Statement No. 96* was to be effective for fiscal years beginning after December 15, 1988, with earlier adoption encouraged. However, because of criticism about its complexity and restrictions on recognizing deferred tax assets, the FASB deferred the effective date of *Statement No. 96* three times and ultimately issued in February 1992 *Statement No. 109* to supersede

Statement No. 96. Statement No. 109 requires comprehensive recognition of deferred tax consequences by the asset/liability method.

9. The basic steps for recognizing deferred tax consequences by the asset/liability method under *Statement No. 109* are:

a. Identify existing temporary differences between the book and tax basis of assets and liabilities.
b. Calculate the taxable and deductible amounts expected to arise in future years from the existing temporary differences.
c. Calculate the tax consequences of the existing temporary differences on the basis of the enacted marginal tax rates.

These steps and the standards specified by the *Statement* relating to temporary differences are discussed in the remainder of this section in more detail.

10. Identify temporary differences. As indicated earlier, a temporary difference is a difference, at a financial reporting date, between the tax basis of an asset or a liability and its reported amount in the statement of financial position that is expected to result in taxable or deductible amounts in future years when the reported amount of the asset or liability is recovered or settled, respectively. The categories of transactions and events that give rise to temporary differences include:

a. Revenues or gains that are taxable in periods after they are recognized in pretax financial income, such as a receivable from an installment sale that will result in future taxable amounts when the asset is recovered.
b. Expenses or losses that are deductible for tax purposes in periods after they are recognized in pretax financial income, such as a product warranty accrual that will result in future tax deductible amounts when the liability is settled.
c. Revenues or gains that are taxable in periods before they are recognized in pretax financial income, such as rent received in advance that will result in future tax deductible amounts when the liability is settled.
d. Expenses or losses that are deductible for tax purposes in periods before they are recognized in pretax financial income, such as greater depreciation for tax purposes than for financial reporting purposes in the early periods of an asset's life that will result in future taxable amounts when the excess of the book basis over the tax basis of the asset is recovered.

e. A reduction in the tax basis of depreciable assets because of tax credits that will result in future taxable amounts when the excess of the book basis over the tax basis of the asset is recovered.

f. An investment tax credit accounted for by the deferred method that will result in future tax deductible amounts when the excess of the tax basis over the book basis of the asset is recovered.

g. An increase in the tax basis of assets because of indexing for inflation that will result in future tax deductible amounts when the excess of the tax basis over the book basis is recovered.

Categories *a* to *d*, which are the focus of the text's chapter, pertain to revenues, expenses, gains, or losses that are included in taxable income of an earlier or later year than the year in which they are recognized in pretax financial income. These temporary (timing) differences may arise from discretionary decisions to use different methods of accounting for tax purposes and financial reporting purposes, or from nondiscretionary compliance with tax rules and regulations that differ from generally accepted accounting principles as to the timing of recognition of certain revenues, expenses, gains, and losses. Differences between taxable income and pretax financial income arising from timing differences also create differences between the tax basis of an asset or liability and its reported amount in the financial statements. Categories *e* to *g* pertain to other events that create differences between the tax basis of an asset or liability and its reported amount in the financial statements. For all categories, the temporary difference is expected to result in taxable or deductible amounts in future years when the reported amount of the related asset or liability is recovered or settled, respectively.

11. Calculate future taxable and deductible amounts. After the temporary differences existing at the balance sheet date have been identified, a schedule should be prepared as of the end of that year to calculate the taxable and deductible amounts that are expected to result in future years from existing temporary differences and from existing loss carryforwards for tax purposes. This schedule can be prepared in three steps.

12. The first step in preparing the schedule is to calculate the future taxable or deductible amount that is expected to result from each of the existing temporary differences. The scheduling of the four categories of temporary differences that result from timing differences, for example, is as follows:

a. Revenues or gains that are taxable in periods after they are recognized in pretax financial income are shown as future taxable amounts, because those revenues or gains will be recognized for tax purposes when the related asset is recovered in future years.

b. Expenses or losses that are deductible for tax purposes in periods after they are recognized in pretax financial income are shown as future deductible amounts, because those expenses or losses will be recognized for tax purposes when the related liability is settled in future years.

c. Revenues or gains that are taxable in periods before they are recognized in pretax financial income are shown as future deductible amounts, because those revenues or gains will be recognized for financial reporting purposes when the related liability is settled in future years.

d. Expenses or losses that are deductible for tax purposes in periods before they are recognized in pretax financial income are shown as future taxable amounts, because those expenses or losses will be recognized for financial reporting purposes when the related asset or excess of the asset's book basis over tax basis is recovered in future years.

It is important to note that the future taxable or deductible amount shown in the schedule for each temporary difference should equal the cumulative amount of that timing difference or the difference between the tax basis and book basis of the related asset or liability as of the balance sheet date.

13. The second step in preparing the schedule is to determine whether a taxable loss for the current year is to be carried back or forward. Federal tax regulations permit *net operating losses* (an excess of deductions over revenues for tax purposes) to be offset against taxable income of other years to reduce taxes otherwise payable in those years. There are two options, a loss carryback election and a loss carryforward election. Under the *loss carryback* election, the loss is carried back to the 3 years preceding the loss year, starting with the third year, to offset the taxable income of those years and to provide a basis for a claim for a refund for taxes paid in those years; the remainder of the loss, if any, is then carried forward to offset the taxable income of the next 15 years and to reduce taxes that would otherwise be payable in those years. Under the *loss carryforward* election, the loss is carried forward only to offset the taxable income of the next 15 years and to reduce taxes that would otherwise be payable in those years. Thus, for the purposes of scheduling, a loss carryback should be deducted from taxable income of the preceding three years, starting with the third year, and a loss carryforward existing as of the balance sheet date should be shown as a future deductible amount.

14. The third step is to calculate the total of the future taxable amounts and the total of the future deductible amounts as of the balance sheet date by summing the expected future taxable and deductible amounts shown in the schedule for the temporary differences and loss carryforwards.

15. Calculate deferred tax consequences. Finally, referring to the schedule, the current and deferred tax consequences of events recognized in pretax financial income or loss should be calculated and recorded, under the regular tax system, by applying the enacted marginal tax rates to the total future taxable and deductible amounts shown in the schedule. Specifically:

a. Income taxes currently payable should be calculated by multiplying taxable income, after deduction of any loss carryforwards for tax purposes from prior years, by the current tax rate. This is the amount that should be credited to the income taxes payable account, which should be reported as a current liability in the balance sheet. Alternatively, the tax benefits realized from a loss carryback for tax purposes, if any, should be calculated by multiplying the portion of the taxable loss that can be offset against taxable income of the three years preceding the loss year, starting with the third year, by the tax rate in effect during those years. This is the amount that should be debited to the income refund receivable account, which should be reported as a current asset in the balance sheet.

b. The tax consequences of future taxable or deductible amounts should be calculated by multiplying the total future taxable or deductible amounts by the enacted marginal tax rates. This is the amount to which the deferred tax liability or asset account should be adjusted. If there is no deferred tax liability (asset) balance at the end of the preceding year, the deferred tax liability (asset) account should be credited (debited) at this amount. If there is a deferred tax liability (asset) balance at the end of the preceding year, the deferred tax liability (asset) account should be either credited (debited) for the excess of this amount over the balance in the account or debited (credited) for the excess of the balance in the account over this amount.

c. Total income tax expense or benefit for the period should be calculated (in the absence of a valuation allowance) as the amount credited to income taxes payable (or debited to income tax refund receivable) plus or minus the amount or amounts credited or debited to deferred tax liability or deferred tax asset. This is the amount that should be debited to the income tax expense account or credited to the income tax benefit account.

Furthermore, because the tax consequences of expected future taxable and deductible amounts are calculated at each balance sheet date on the basis of the enacted marginal tax rate as of that date, tax rate changes enacted in subsequent years must be recognized as an adjustment to the deferred tax liability and asset accounts as of the enactment date. The *enacted marginal tax rate* is the enacted rate expected to apply to the last dollars of taxable income in future periods in which deferred tax liabilities or assets are expected to be settled or recovered.

Valuation Allowance for Deferred Tax Assets

16. Deferred tax assets are required to be recognized for future deductible amounts expected to result from temporary differences and from loss carryforwards. However, if the weight of the evidence indicates that some portion or all of the tax benefits associated with deferred tax assets will not be realized, the deferred tax assets must be reduced, by a valuation allowance, to the amount that is more likely than not to be realized.

17. Examples of sources of taxable income and other positive evidence that would support a conclusion that no valuation allowance is required include:

a. Future reversals of existing taxable temporary differences.
b. Future taxable income exclusive of reversing temporary differences and carryforwards.
c. Taxable income in prior carryback year or years if carryback is permitted under the tax law.
d. Tax planning strategies.
e. Existing contracts or firm sales backlog that will produce more than enough taxable income to realize the deferred tax asset.
f. An excess of appreciated asset value over the tax basis of the company's net assets in an amount sufficient to realize the deferred tax asset.
g. A strong earnings history exclusive of the loss that created the future deductible amount, coupled with evidence that the loss is an aberration rather than a continuing condition.

The latter three examples might support a conclusion that a valuation allowance is not required, even when there is tangible, negative evidence, such as:

a. Cumulative losses in recent years.

b. A history of operating loss or tax credit carryforwards expiring unused.

c. Losses expected in early future years by a presently profitable company.

d. Unsettled circumstances that, if unfavorably resolved, would adversely affect future profit levels on a continuing basis.

e. A carryback, carryforward period that is so brief that it might limit realization of tax benefits.

Judgment must be used to determine whether such negative evidence is outweighed by positive evidence.

18. If the tangible, negative evidence outweighs the positive evidence, the deferred tax assets must be reduced by that portion of the future deductible amounts that is expected will not be realized multiplied by the enacted marginal tax rate. This is the amount to which the valuation allowance account should be adjusted. If there is no valuation allowance balance at the end of the preceding year, allowance for reduction of deferred tax asset (a contra asset account) should be credited and income tax expense or benefits should be debited at this amount. If there is a valuation allowance balance at the end of the preceding year, allowance for reduction of deferred tax asset should be either credited for the excess of this amount over the balance in the account or debited for the excess of the balance in the account over this amount, and income tax expense or benefit should be debited or credited, respectively, for the same amount.

Accounting for No-Tax-Consequence Events

19. Differences between taxable income and pretax financial income may arise from certain revenues and expenses that are recognized for financial reporting purposes but not for tax purposes. Such differences result from specific tax rules and regulations that permit the exclusion of certain revenues (called *tax-exempt revenues*) from taxable income and prohibit the deduction of certain expenses (called *not tax-deductible expenses*) in the computation of taxable income. Sources of common tax-exempt revenues and not tax-deductible expenses include interest received on state and local government obligations, interest expense on debt incurred to acquire tax-exempt securities, life insurance proceeds received by a company as beneficiary of a policy on officers or employees, premiums paid for life insurance on officers and employees when the company is the beneficiary, and fines and expenses resulting from violations of the law.

20. Because tax-exempt revenues and not tax-deductible expenses do not have tax consequences, deferred tax liabilities and assets should not be recognized for such events. Thus, when there are tax-exempt revenues and/or not tax-deductible expenses but no temporary differences or special tax deductions and credits, income tax expense can be calculated by multiplying pretax financial income plus not tax-deductible expenses minus tax-exempt revenues by the current tax rate. In contrast, when there are temporary differences, income tax expense should be calculated as the amount credited to income taxes payable plus or minus the amount or amounts credited or debited to deferred tax liability or deferred tax asset.

Financial Statement Presentation

21. Deferred tax assets (and related valuation allowances) and deferred tax liabilities must be classified as current or noncurrent on the basis of the classification of the related assets or liabilities or, if there are no related assets or liabilities, on the basis of the expected reversal dates of the temporary differences or loss carryforwards. All current amounts and noncurrent amounts related to the same tax jurisdiction must then be offset to report a net current deferred tax liability or asset and a net noncurrent deferred tax liability or asset in the balance sheet. In addition, the components of a net deferred tax liability or asset must be disclosed, namely, (a) the total of all deferred tax liabilities, (b) the total of all deferred tax assets, and (c) the total valuation allowance recognized for deferred tax assets. Corporations also must disclose the net change in a valuation allowance during the year and the dollar amounts of temporary differences, carryforwards, or carrybacks that cause significant portions of deferred tax assets and liabilities.

22. The total income tax expense or benefit for a period must be allocated among continuing operations, discontinued operations, extraordinary items, cumulative effect of accounting changes, prior period adjustments, gains and losses included in comprehensive income but excluded from net income, and capital transactions by a process referred to as *intraperiod tax allocation*. The amount of income tax expense or benefits allocated to continuing operations is the tax consequences of items included in pretax income or loss from continuing operations for the period, and the amount allocated to the other items is in proportion to their individual effects on income tax expense or benefits for the year. In addition, income tax expense allocated to continuing operations must be reconciled to the amount of income tax expense that would result from applying the regular statutory tax rates to pretax income from continuing operations.

Additional Issues

23. Tax-planning strategies. *Tax-planning strategies* refer to management actions that (*a*) are prudent and feasible, (*b*) a company ordinarily might not take but would take to prevent an operating loss or a tax credit carryforward from expiring unused, and (*c*) would result in realization of deferred tax assets. Tax-planning strategies must be considered in determining the required amount of a valuation allowance. However, if there is sufficient positive evidence to support a conclusion that a valuation allowance is not required, tax-planning strategies need not be considered. Examples of tax-planning strategies that may be used are sale-leaseback of assets, shift of estimated future taxable income between years, election to waive the carry-back option for a net operating loss deduction, and shift of estimated pattern and timing of future reversals of temporary differences.

24. Alternative minimum tax. Because U.S. tax regulations require corporations to determine their federal income taxes as the greater of the regular tax or an alternative minimum tax (AMT), the calculation of future taxable and deductible amounts and the calculation of the deferred tax consequences of temporary difference must be performed under both systems. Thus the AMT is another potential complexity in determining the deferred tax consequences of temporary differences. The actual calculations under the AMT system, however, are beyond the scope of the text's chapter.

SELF-STUDY LEARNING

Key Terms and Concepts

Provide the appropriate term or terms to complete each of the following statements:

1. An excess of taxable revenues over deductible expenses and exemptions for a period calculated in accordance with prescribed tax rules and regulations is called _____, whereas income exclusive of income tax expense for a period calculated in accordance with generally accepted accounting principles is called _____.

2. A difference, at a financial reporting date, between the tax basis of an asset or a liability and its reported amount in the financial statements that is expected to result in taxable or deductible amounts in future years when the reported amount of the asset or liability is recovered or settled, respectively, is called a(n) _____.

3. There are two basic views about the extent to which deferred tax consequences should be recognized: _____, which is based on the belief that deferred tax consequences should not be recognized for recurring temporary differences that give rise to an indefinite postponement or prepayment of taxes, and _____, which is based on the belief that deferred tax consequences should be recognized for all temporary differences.

4. There are two fundamental methods of measuring deferred tax consequences: the _____, which requires that the future tax consequences of temporary differences be measured at the tax rates that have been enacted for those years when the temporary differences are expected to give rise to taxable or deductible amounts, and the _____, which requires that the future tax consequences of temporary differences be measured at the tax rates in effect in the year when the temporary differences originate.

5. The legally established rate expected to apply to the last dollars of taxable income in future periods in which deferred tax liabilities or assets are expected to be settled or recovered, respectively, is called the _____.

6. An excess of deductible expenses and exemptions over taxable revenues when taxable income is computed is called a(n) _____.

7. Two federal tax elections are permitted for net operating losses: _____, under which the loss is offset against the taxable income of the 3 years preceding the loss year to provide a basis for a claim for a refund for taxes paid in those years, and any remaining loss is offset against the taxable income of the next 15 years to reduce taxes that would otherwise be payable in those years; and _____, under which the loss is offset only against the taxable income of the next 15 years to reduce taxes that would otherwise be payable in those years.

8. Revenues that are permitted to be excluded from taxable income are called _____, whereas expenses that are prohibited from deduction in the computation of taxable income are called _____.

9. The process of allocating total income tax expense or benefits for a period among, for example, continuing operations, discontinued operations, extraordinary items, cumulative effect of accounting changes, and prior period adjustments is referred to as _____.

10. AMT is an acronym for _____, one of the two systems for computing federal income taxes for a period.

True-False

Indicate by circling the appropriate response whether each of the following statements is true (T) or false (F):

T F 1. All temporary differences result from timing differences.

T F 2. One of the objectives of accounting for income taxes is to recognize deferred tax liabilities and assets for the future tax consequences of events that have been recognized in the financial statements or tax return.

T F 3. *APB Opinion No. 11* required comprehensive recognition of deferred tax consequences by the asset/liability method, whereas *Statement No. 109* requires comprehensive recognition of deferred tax consequences by the deferred method.

T F 4. A deferred tax liability is not required to be recognized for recurring temporary differences that give rise to an indefinite postponement of taxes.

T F 5. In the absence of temporary differences, income tax expense should equal income taxes payable for the year.

T F 6. In the absence of temporary differences, special tax deductions and credits, and events that do not have tax consequences, income tax expense can be calculated by multiplying pretax financial income by the current tax rate.

T F 7. When there are tax-exempt revenues but no temporary differences or special tax deductions and credits, income tax expense can be calculated by multiplying pretax financial income minus the tax-exempt revenues by the current tax rate.

T F 8. Rent collected in advance is a temporary difference that will result in deductible amounts in future years when the liability is settled.

T F   9. In calculating future taxable and deductible amounts, a loss carryforward for tax purposes must be deducted from taxable amounts occurring in the carryforward period.

T F 10. The tax consequences of existing temporary differences that will result in taxable amounts in future years must be measured at the enacted marginal tax rate for those future years.

T F 11. In the year in which an expense is recognized earlier for tax purposes than for financial reporting purposes, income tax expense should be less than income taxes payable and deferred tax asset should be debited.

T F 12. The deferred tax consequences of a receivable from an installment sale should be recognized as a deferred tax liability, because it will result in taxable amounts in future years when the asset is recovered.

T F 13. In the year in which a temporary difference that resulted in taxable amounts is fully reversed, deferred tax liability should be debited for the balance in the account at the end of the preceding year.

T F 14. A deferred tax liability or asset is not required to be adjusted for tax rate changes enacted in subsequent years.

T F 15. Deferred tax assets must be reduced by a valuation allowance if, based on the weight of available evidence, it is more likely than not that some portion or all of the deferred tax assets will not be realized.

T F 16. The deferred tax consequences of temporary differences that will result in taxable amounts must be reported as current amounts in a classified balance sheet, whereas the deferred tax consequences of temporary differences that will result in deductible amounts must be reported as noncurrent amounts.

T F 17. Deferred tax assets and liabilities related to the same tax jurisdiction must be reported in the balance sheet as a net current amount and a net noncurrent amount.

T F 18. A net operating loss must be carried back to offset the taxable income of the 3 years preceding the loss year before it is carried forward to offset the taxable income of the next 15 years.

T F 19. Intraperiod tax allocation is required only when a corporation presents a classified balance sheet.

T F 20. Tax-planning strategies that meet specified criteria may, but are not required to, be considered in determining the required amount of a valuation allowance for deferred tax assets.

Multiple Choice

Select the best response for each of the following items, and circle the corresponding letter:

1. Which of the following items causes a temporary difference between the tax basis of an asset or a liability and its reported amount in the financial statements?

   a. Fines and expenses resulting from violations of the law.
   b. Interest received on state and local government obligations.
   c. Premiums paid for life insurance on officers and employees when the company is the beneficiary.
   d. Greater depreciation for tax purposes than for financial reporting purposes in the early period of an asset's life.

2. Which of the following temporary differences will result in taxable amounts in future years?

   a. An officer's or employee's bonus accrual.
   b. Rent received in advance.
   c. A receivable from an installment sale.
   d. An increase in the tax basis of an asset because of indexing for inflation.

3. Which of the following temporary differences will result in deductible amounts in future years?

   a. Greater depreciation for tax purposes than for financial reporting purposes in the early period of an asset's life.
   b. A product warranty accrual.
   c. Rent paid in advance.
   d. A reduction in the tax basis of a depreciable asset because of tax credits.

4. The expected future taxable or deductible amount for a temporary difference caused by a timing difference should be equal to:

   a. The cumulative amount of that timing difference as of the balance sheet date.
   b. The difference between the tax basis and book basis of the related asset or liability as of the balance sheet date.
   c. Both a and b.
   d. Neither a nor b.

5. A deferred tax liability is required to be recognized for:

   a. Events that do not have tax consequences.
   b. Recurring temporary differences that will result in taxable amounts in future years.
   c. Nonrecurring temporary differences that will result in taxable amounts in future years.
   d. All temporary differences that will result in taxable amounts in future years.

6. A deferred tax asset is required to be recognized for:

   a. Events that do not have tax consequences.
   b. Recurring temporary differences that will result in deductible amounts in future years.
   c. Nonrecurring temporary differences that will result in deductible amounts in future years.
   d. All temporary differences that will result in deductible amounts in future years.

7. The tax consequences of taxable or deductible amounts that will occur in future years from existing temporary differences must be measured at the:

   a. Tax rate for the current year.
   b. Enacted marginal tax rate for those future years.
   c. Higher of the tax rate for the current year or the enacted marginal tax rate for those future years.
   d. Lower of the tax rate for the current year or the enacted marginal tax rate for those future years.

8. When there is an existing temporary difference from the preceding year that will result in taxable amounts in the current and future years, the journal entry to record income taxes for the current year should include:

   a. A debit to deferred tax asset at the future taxable amounts multiplied by the tax rate.
   b. A credit to deferred tax liability at the future taxable amounts multiplied by the tax rate.

   c. A debit or credit to deferred tax asset for the difference between the balance at the end of the preceding year and the future taxable amounts multiplied by the tax rate.
   d. A debit or credit to deferred tax liability for the difference between the balance at the end of the preceding year and the future taxable amounts multiplied by the tax rate.

9. Which of the following items may cause a difference between pretax financial income and taxable income but has no tax consequences?

   a. Interest expense on debt incurred to acquire tax-exempt securities.
   b. A receivable from an installment sale.
   c. A product warranty accrual.
   d. Rent received in advance.

10. When there are changes in the enacted marginal tax rate over time and temporary differences, income tax expense should equal:

    a. Income taxes payable plus or minus the amount or amounts credited or debited to the deferred tax liability or deferred tax asset accounts.
    b. Taxable income multiplied by the current tax rate.
    c. Pretax financial income multiplied by the current tax rate.
    d. Pretax financial income adjusted for the temporary differences multiplied by the current tax rate.

Extended Problem

A reconciliation of pretax financial income (loss) and taxable income (loss) of TD Corporation for the calendar years 1995 through 1999 is presented here. The differences shown in this reconciliation were caused by the following transactions and events:

a. Plant assets, which were acquired on January 1, 1995, for $210,000, were depreciated on a straight-line basis over five years for financial reporting purposes and on an MACRS basis in amounts of $70,000 in 1995, $92,000 in 1996, $32,000 in 1997, and $16,000 in 1998 for tax purposes. The plant assets were scrapped at the end of 1999 for a zero net salvage value.
b. During 1995 only, product sales included a three-year warranty against defects. For financial reporting purposes, accrued warranty costs were $50,000 for 1995; for tax

purposes, warranty costs deductions were $5,000 in 1995, $15,000 in 1996, and $30,000 in 1997.

c. On December 31, 1996, land, which originally cost $56,000, was sold for an $80,000, 10 percent, two-year note receivable, with the face value due in two equal annual payments on December 31, 1997 and 1998. The gain was recognized for financial reporting purposes at the date of sale but was deferred and recognized for tax purposes proportionally as the note was collected.

d. A $20,000 rental payment for the two-year period January 1, 1998, to December 31, 1999, was collected in advance on December 31, 1997. The rent was recognized for tax purposes when the advance was received but was deferred and recognized for financial reporting purposes equally over the two-year rental period as it was earned.

e. Tax-exempt interest revenue of $2,000 was recognized for financial reporting purposes in 1996 and 1997.

TD Corporation was incorporated on January 1, 1995, was not required to remit estimated tax payments during any of the years, selected the loss carryback election in 1997, and determined (except where stated otherwise later) that no valuation allowance was required for deferred tax assets.

	1995	1996	1997	1998	1999
Pretax financial income (loss)............	$53,000	$131,000	$(30,000)	$22,000	$48,000
Temporary differences:					
Depreciation............................	(28,000)	(50,000)	10,000	26,000	42,000
Warranty costs........................	45,000	(15,000)	(30,000)		
Gain.......................................		(24,000)	12,000	12,000	
Rent.......................................			20,000	(10,000)	(10,000)
Other difference:					
Tax-exempt revenue..................		(2,000)	(2,000)		
Taxable income (loss).................	$70,000	$40,000	$(20,000)	$50,000	$80,000
Enacted marginal tax rates............	40%	30%	30%	30%	30%

REQUIRED

a. Identify the temporary differences existing at December 31 for each of the years 1995 through 1999.

b. Calculate the expected future taxable and deductible amounts at December 31 for each of the years 1995 through 1999, and prepare the journal entries required to record income taxes for each of the years 1995 through 1999.

c. Assuming that the enacted tax rate for 1999, and thereafter was increased from 30 percent to 40 percent during 1998, prepare the journal entries required to record income taxes for 1998 and 1999.

d. Assuming that TD Corporation was incorporated on January 1, 1994 (rather than 1995) and reported a pretax financial loss and taxable loss of $40,000 for that year, prepare the journal entries required, if any, to record income taxes for 1994 (when the current and enacted marginal tax rate was 40 percent) and 1995.

e. Assuming the same facts described in situation d except that, after reviewing all available evidence at the end of 1994, TD Corporation determined that it was more likely than not that $30,000 of the future deductible amounts related to deferred tax assets would not produce future tax benefits, prepare the journal entry related to the valuation allowance at the end of 1994.

f. Assuming the same facts described in situation e and assuming further that TD Corporation determined at the end of 1995 that it was now more likely than not that only $8,000 of the future deductible amounts related to the deferred tax assets would not produce future tax benefits, prepare the journal entry related to the valuation allowance at the end of 1995.

COMMON ERRORS

The first statement in each "common error" listed here is *incorrect*. Each incorrect statement is followed by a corrected statement and an explanation.

1. Income tax expense is always equal to pretax financial income multiplied by the current tax rate. *Wrong*

Income tax expense may be, but is not necessarily, equal to pretax financial income multiplied by the current tax rate. *Right*

Because the current and deferred tax consequences of events recognized in pretax financial income for a year must be recognized in income tax expense for that year, it is sometimes thought that income tax expense may always be computed directly by multiplying pretax financial income by the current tax rate. This approach, however, is appropriate only in simple situations. In complex situations, other approaches must be used to compute income tax expense. First, when there are tax-exempt revenues and/or not tax-deductible expenses but no temporary differences or special tax deductions and credits, income tax expense may be computed by multiplying pretax financial income plus the not tax-deductible expenses minus the tax-exempt revenues by the current tax rate. Second, when there are temporary differences and changes in the enacted marginal tax rate over time, income tax expense must be computed as the amount credited to income taxes payable plus or minus the amount or amounts credited or debited to deferred tax liability or deferred tax asset.

2. When there are tax-exempt revenues and/or not tax-deductible expenses, income tax expense is always equal to pretax financial income adjusted for these events multiplied by the current tax rate. *Wrong*

When there are tax-exempt revenues and/or not tax-deductible expenses, income tax expense may be, but is not necessarily, equal to pretax financial income adjusted for these events multiplied by the current tax rate. *Right*

Tax-exempt revenues and not tax-deductible expenses do not have tax consequences. Consequently, when there are such events but no temporary differences or special tax deductions and credits, income tax expense may be computed directly by multiplying pretax financial income plus the not tax-deductible expenses minus the tax-exempt revenues by the current tax rate. As just explained, however, when there are temporary differences and changes in the enacted marginal tax rate over time, income tax expense must be computed indirectly as

the amount credited to income taxes payable plus or minus the amount or amounts credited or debited to deferred tax liability or deferred tax asset.

3. A deferred tax liability or asset is computed by multiplying the expected future taxable or deductible amounts by the current year's tax rate. *Wrong*

A deferred tax liability or asset is computed by multiplying the expected future taxable or deductible amounts by the enacted marginal tax rate for those years. *Right*

Because a deferred tax liability or asset is recognized for the taxes payable or tax benefits realizable in future years on taxable or deductible amounts that will result from existing temporary differences, the tax consequences of taxable or deductible amounts must be measured at the enacted marginal tax rate for those future years rather than at the current year's tax rate. Of course, in the absence of present changes in the enacted marginal tax rate, the current year's marginal tax rate is the enacted marginal tax rate for future years for purposes of measuring a deferred tax liability or asset at the current balance sheet date.

4. A deferred tax liability should always be credited at the expected future taxable amounts multiplied by the enacted marginal tax rate. *Wrong*

A deferred tax liability should be debited or credited for the difference between the expected future taxable amounts multiplied by the enacted marginal tax rate and the balance in the account at the end of the preceding year. *Right*

The tax consequences of taxable amounts that will result in future years from existing temporary differences must be calculated as of the end of the current year by multiplying the taxable amounts by the enacted marginal tax rate for those future years. This is the amount at which the deferred tax liability should be reported in the balance sheet for the current year. Thus, as part of the journal entry required to record income taxes for the current year, deferred tax liability should be either credited at the excess of this amount over the balance in the account at the end of the preceding year or debited at the excess of the balance in the account at the end of the preceding year over this amount. This principle applies to deferred tax assets, too.

5. The tax benefit of a loss carryback for tax purposes is calculated by multiplying the loss carryback by the tax rate in effect in the loss year. *Wrong*

The tax benefit of a loss carryback for tax purposes should be computed by multiplying the loss carryback by the tax rate that was in effect in the loss carryback year or years. *Right*

Under the loss carryback election, a net operating loss is carried back to the 3 years preceding the loss year, starting with the third year, to offset taxable income in those years and to provide a basis for a claim for a refund for taxes paid in those years. Because the refund claim is for the taxes previously paid in the loss carryback period, the tax benefit of a loss carryback for tax purposes should be computed by multiplying the loss carryback by the tax rate that was in effect in the various years of the loss carryback period.

ANSWERS

Key Terms and Concepts

1. taxable income, pretax financial income
2. temporary difference
3. partial recognition, comprehensive recognition
4. asset/liability method, deferred method
5. enacted marginal tax rate
6. net operating loss
7. loss carryback, loss carryforward
8. tax-exempt revenues, not tax-deductible expenses
9. intraperiod tax allocation
10. alternative minimum tax

True-False

1. F   Most, but not all, temporary differences result from timing differences. A reduction in the tax basis of depreciable assets because of tax credits, for example, is a temporary difference that does not result from a timing difference.
2. T
3. F   *APB Opinion No. 11* required comprehensive recognition of deferred tax consequences by the deferred method, whereas *Statement No. 109* requires comprehensive recognition of deferred tax consequences by the asset/liability method.
4. F   A deferred tax liability is required to be recognized for all temporary differences that are expected to result in taxable amounts in future years.
5. T
6. T
7. T
8. T
9. F   In calculating future taxable and deductible amounts, a loss carryforward for tax purposes should be treated as a future deductible amount.
10. T

11. F   In the year in which an expense is recognized earlier for tax purposes than for financial reporting purposes, income tax expense should be greater than income taxes payable and deferred tax liability should be credited.
12. T
13. T
14. F   The tax consequences of taxable and deductible amounts expected to arise from temporary differences must be calculated at each balance sheet date on the basis of the enacted marginal tax rate as of that date. Consequently, a deferred tax liability or asset is required to be adjusted for tax rate changes enacted in subsequent years.
15. T
16. F   The deferred tax consequences of temporary differences must be reported as current or noncurrent in a classified balance sheet on the basis of the classification of the related assets or liabilities or, if there are no related assets or liabilities, on the basis of the expected reversal dates of the temporary differences.
17. T
18. F   A net operating loss may be carried back to offset the taxable income of the 3 years preceding the loss year before it is carried forward to offset the taxable income of the next 15 years. Alternatively, a net operating loss may just be carried forward to offset the taxable income of the next 15 years.
19. F   Intraperiod tax allocation is the process of allocating total income tax expense or benefits for a period among continuing operations, discontinued operations, extraordinary items, cumulative effect of accounting changes, prior period adjustments, gains and losses included in comprehensive income but excluded from net income, and capital transactions. Thus intraperiod tax allocation is required regard-

less of whether a corporation presents a classified or an unclassified balance sheet.

20. F Tax-planning strategies that meet specified criteria must be considered in determining the required amount of a valuation allowance for deferred tax assets.

Multiple Choice

1. d	6. d
2. c	7. b
3. b	8. d
4. c	9. a
5. d	10. a

Extended Problem

a. Identification of temporary differences:[a]

TEMPORARY DIFFERENCES	1995	1996	1997	1998	1999
Depreciation	✔	✔	✔	✔	
Warranty costs	✔	✔			
Gain			✔	✔	
Rent				✔	✔

[a] A check mark (✔) denotes the temporary differences existing at December 31, of that particular year.

b. Calculation of future taxable and deductible amounts and journal entry to record income taxes:

(1). For the year ended December 31, 1995.

	END OF CURRENT YEAR 1995	FUTURE TAXABLE AMOUNTS	FUTURE DEDUCTIBLE AMOUNTS
Temporary differences:			
Depreciation	$ 28,000	$28,000	
Warranty costs	(45,000)		$45,000
Net temporary difference	$(17,000)		
Taxable income (loss)	$ 70,000		
Total		$28,000	$45,000
Enacted marginal tax rate		.30	.30
Deferred tax liability		$ 8,400	
Deferred tax asset			$13,500

Income tax expense ($28,000 + $8,400 − $13,500)	22,900	
Deferred tax asset	13,500	
Income taxes payable ($70,000 × .40)		28,000
Deferred tax liability		8,400

(2). For the year ended December 31, 1996.

	PRIOR YEAR 1995	END OF CURRENT YEAR 1996	FUTURE TAXABLE AMOUNTS	FUTURE DEDUCTIBLE AMOUNTS
Temporary differences:				
Depreciation		$78,000	$ 78,000	
Warranty costs		(30,000)		$30,000
Gain		24,000	24,000	
Net temporary difference		$72,000		
Taxable income (loss)	$70,000	$40,000		
Total			$102,000	$30,000
Enacted marginal tax rate			.30	.30
Deferred tax liability			$ 30,600	
Deferred tax asset				$ 9,000

Income tax expense ($12,000 + $4,500 + $22,200)	38,700	
Income taxes payable ($40,000 × .30)		12,000
Deferred tax asset ($13,500 − $9,000)		4,500
Deferred tax liability ($30,600 − $8,400)		22,200

(3). For the year ended December 31, 1997.

	PRIOR YEARS 1995	1996	END OF CURRENT YEAR 1997	FUTURE TAXABLE AMOUNTS	FUTURE DEDUCTIBLE AMOUNTS
Temporary differences:					
Depreciation			$ 68,000	$68,000	
Gain..........................			12,000	12,000	
Rent...........................			(20,000)		$20,000
Net temporary difference..			$ 60,000		
Taxable income (loss)........	$70,000	$40,000	$(20,000)		
Loss carryback.................	(20,000)	-0-	20,000		
Total............................	$50,000	$40,000	$ -0-	$80,000	$20,000
Enacted marginal tax rate....				.30	.30
Deferred tax liability				$24,000	
Deferred tax asset.............					$ 6,000

Income tax refund receivable ($20,000 × .40)................................	8,000	
Deferred tax liability ($30,600 − $24,000)...................................	6,600	
Deferred tax asset ($9,000 − $6,000)		3,000
Income tax benefits ($8,000 + $6,600 − $3,000)...........................		11,600

(4). For the year ended December 31, 1998.

	PRIOR YEARS 1995	1996	1997	END OF CURRENT YEAR 1998	FUTURE TAXABLE AMOUNTS	FUTURE DEDUCTIBLE AMOUNTS
Temporary differences:						
Depreciation				$42,000	$42,000	
Rent............................				(10,000)		$10,000
Net temporary difference..				$32,000		
Taxable income (loss)........	$70,000	$40,000	$(20,000)	$50,000		
Loss carryback.................	(20,000)	-0-	20,000	-0-		
Total............................	$50,000	$40,000	$ -0-	$50,000	$42,000	$10,000
Enacted marginal tax rate....					.30	.30
Deferred tax liability					$12,600	
Deferred tax asset.............						$ 3,000

Income tax expense ($15,000 + $3,000 − $11,400)..........................	6,600	
Deferred tax liability ($24,000 − $12,600)..................................	11,400	
Income taxes payable ($50,000 × .30)		15,000
Deferred tax asset ($6,000 − $3,000)		3,000

(5). For the year ended December 31, 1999.

	PRIOR YEARS 1995	1996	1997	1998	END OF CURRENT YEAR 1999	FUTURE TAXABLE AMOUNTS	FUTURE DEDUCTIBLE AMOUNTS
Temporary differences:					$ -0-	$ -0-	$ -0-
Taxable income (loss)........	$70,000	$40,000	$(20,000)	$50,000	$80,000		
Loss carryback.................	(20,000)	-0-	20,000	-0-	-0-		
Total............................	$50,000	$40,000	$ -0-	$50,000	$80,000	$ -0-	$ -0-
Enacted marginal tax rate....						.30	.30
Deferred tax liability						$ -0-	
Deferred tax asset.............							$ -0-

Income tax expense ($24,000 + $3,000 − $12,600)...........................	14,400	
Deferred tax liability ($12,600 − $0)	12,600	
Income taxes payable ($80,000 × .30)		24,000
Deferred tax asset ($3,000 − $0)		3,000

c.   Journal entries to record income taxes when change in enacted marginal tax rate:

   (1). For the year ended December 31, 1998.

Income tax expense ($15,000 + $2,000 − $7,200)	9,800	
Deferred tax liability [$24,000 − ($42,000 × .40)]	7,200	
Income taxes payable ($50,000 × .30)		15,000
Deferred tax asset [$6,000 − ($10,000 × .40)]		2,000

   (2). For the year ended December 31, 1999.

Income tax expense ($32,000 + $4,000 − $16,800)	19,200	
Deferred tax liability ($42,000 × .40)	16,800	
Income taxes payable ($80,000 × .40)		32,000
Deferred tax asset ($10,000 × .40)		4,000

d.   Journal entries to record tax loss carryforward:

   (1). For the year ended December 31, 1994.

Deferred tax asset ($40,000 × .40)	16,000	
Income tax benefits		16,000

   (2). For the year ended December 31, 1995.

Income tax expense ($12,000 + $8,400 + $2,500)	22,900	
Income taxes payable [($70,000 − $40,000) × .40]		12,000
Deferred tax liability ($28,000 × .30)		8,400
Deferred tax asset [($40,000 × .40) − ($45,000 × .30)]		2,500

e.   Journal entry to record valuation allowance:

Income tax benefits	12,000	
Allowance for reduction of deferred tax asset ($30,000 × .40)		12,000

f.   Journal entry to adjust valuation allowance:

Allowance for reduction of deferred tax asset [$12,000 − ($8,000 × .30)]	9,600	
Income tax expense		9,600

18 STOCKHOLDERS' EQUITY

CHAPTER OBJECTIVES

After reading Chapter 18 and completing the questions, cases, exercises, and problems from the text chapter, you should be able to:

1. Define stockholders' equity and distinguish between contributed capital and retained earnings.
2. Describe the unique characteristics of the corporate form of business organization.
3. Prepare the journal entry required to record the issuance of capital stock for cash, for noncash assets or services, on a subscription basis, and through the exercise of a conversion privilege and the issuance of two or more classes of capital stock as a unit.
4. Prepare the journal entries related to stock rights issued to existing shareholders in connection with the preemptive right or granted to employees in connection with a stock-based compensation plan.
5. Prepare the journal entry required to record the receipt of assets by the corporation as donations from shareholders or others.
6. Prepare the journal entry required to record the acquisition and formal retirement of shares of capital stock by the issuing corporation.

7. Prepare the journal entries required to record the acquisition and subsequent reissuance or retirement of treasury shares by the issuing corporation under both the cost method and the par value method.
8. Identify the types of transactions and other events that increase or decrease retained earnings.
9. Describe the nature of dividends, including cash dividends, scrip dividends, property dividends, liquidating dividends, and stock dividends.
10. Prepare the journal entries required to record the declaration and payment or distribution of cash dividends, scrip dividends, property dividends, liquidating dividends, and stock dividends.
11. Describe the nature of stock splits.
12. Calculate the appropriate distribution of dividends among preferred shareholders and common shareholders.
13. Disclose in the financial statements restrictions on retained earnings by appropriation of retained earnings or by parenthetical or footnote disclosure, and prepare the journal entries related to formal retained earnings appropriations.

CHAPTER REVIEW

Introduction

1. The generally accepted accounting principles related to assets and liabilities discussed in the previous chapters are applicable to the three legal forms of business organizations, namely, sole proprietorships, partnerships, and corporations. But because of the legal requirements and unique terminology associated with corporations, the accounting and reporting principles related to the owners' equity of corporations differ significantly from the accounting and reporting principles related to the owners' equity of sole proprietorships and partnerships.

2. Owners' equity is defined as the residual interest in the assets of the entity that remains after its liabilities are deducted. The owners' equity of corporations, normally called *stockholders' equity* or *shareholders' equity*, consists of two elements: contributed capital and retained earnings. *Contributed capital* represents that portion of the corporate net assets that has been obtained from shareholder investments and other capital transactions. *Retained earnings* represents that portion of the corporate net assets that has been generated by profitable operating activities and retained in the business. The accounting for and reporting of transactions and events that affect stockholders' equity are discussed in this chapter review.

Corporate Form of Organization

3. Each state has its own laws governing the incorporation of businesses. A business may become incorporated by applying to the appropriate governmental unit in the state in which the applicants wish to incorporate. Upon approving the application, the state grants a *corporate charter*. The charter, also called the *articles of incorporation*, is an agreement between the state and the corporation that grants to the corporation the right to operate and to raise capital according to the terms of the charter. The state recognizes the corporation as a legal entity that is separate from its owners.

4. Capital stock. Corporations obtain assets by borrowing money, by issuing capital stock, and by profitable operations. Of these three sources of assets, only the issuance of ownership units in the form of *capital stock* is unique to corporations. The transfer of capital stock between investors, however, affects neither the corporation's assets nor the continuity of its operations. In contrast, an ownership change in a sole proprietorship or partnership generally terminates the entity's legal existence.

5. The capital stock of a corporation conveys certain rights and privileges to the shareholders. In the absence of specific provisions to the contrary, capital stock generally conveys the following rights:

a. The right to share in profits, as declared and distributed as dividends, in proportion to the number of shares held.
b. The right to vote for directors and on management policy issues.
c. The right to maintain proportionate ownership interest by sharing proportionately in new issues of the same class of stock. This right is referred to as the *preemptive right*.

d. The right to share proportionately in corporate assets in the event of liquidation.

A *stock contract* governs each class of capital stock issued by the corporation. The preceding four rights are presumed to exist unless the stock contract specifically states that one or more of these rights do not exist.

6. A corporation may create two or more classes of capital stock with different rights and privileges in order to appeal to a broader spectrum of investors. The class of capital stock that controls the management of the corporation and assumes the ultimate rewards and risks associated with corporate operations is called *common stock*. This class of capital stock generally has the four aforementioned rights, except perhaps the preemptive right. The special classes of capital stock that exclude selected rights and convey additional privileges are called *preferred stock*. This class of capital stock generally has no voting right, but in exchange for this right preferred stock typically has a preference (priority) over common shareholders in the distribution of dividends at a specified rate per share and of assets upon liquidation at a stated value per share. Additionally, preferred stock may possess one or more of the following features:

a. *Cumulative feature.* Preferred stock is cumulative if preferred dividends that are not declared in any year (called *passed dividends* or *dividends in arrears*) must be paid to the preferred shareholders in following years before any dividends are paid to the common shareholders. Dividends in arrears do not represent a liability of the corporation until the board of directors formally declares them. Nonetheless, the amount of any dividends in arrears should be disclosed in the financial statements, since it represents a probable future cash outflow.
b. *Participation feature.* Preferred stock is *participating* if the preferred shareholders may share with the common shareholders in dividends beyond the stated dividend rate. Preferred stock may be fully participating or partially participating. Preferred stock is *fully participating* if the preferred shareholders may share proportionately with the common shareholders beyond the stated dividend rate on the basis of the relative total par value of the outstanding shares of each class of capital stock. Preferred stock is *partially participating* if the preferred shareholders may share proportionately with the common shareholders only up to a stated maximum amount per share.

c. *Call* or *redemption feature*. Preferred stock is *callable* if the issuing corporation, at its option, may call or redeem the stock at a specified price. Preferred stock is *redeemable* if the issuing corporation is required to redeem the stock at a specified price and date.

d. *Conversion feature*. Preferred stock is *convertible* if the preferred shareholders, at their option, may exchange the preferred shares for common shares according to a specified ratio.

The stock contract must specify whether these features apply to a particular preferred stock issue. Additionally, information about the rights and privileges of the various classes of capital stock issued by the corporation should be disclosed in the financial statements, since this information may be relevant to users in assessing future cash flows.

7. Limited liability. Another unique characteristic of corporations is that the shareholders have no responsibility for corporate debt. The corporation, as a separate legal entity, has the responsibility for repayment of any debt it incurs. The creditors of the corporation have recourse to the corporate assets only. The personal assets of the shareholders are not available to the creditors for the satisfaction of corporate debt. Thus the maximum loss that can be incurred by a shareholder generally is the amount invested. In contrast, when the business organization is a sole proprietorship or partnership, the creditors have the legal right to go beyond the business assets to the personal assets of the owners to satisfy business debt.

8. The creditors have a priority claim to corporate assets over the shareholders. In order to protect the priority claim of the creditors, state laws require that corporations not voluntarily distribute assets to the shareholders if prior claims exist and if the dollar amount of contributed capital would be reduced below an amount called *legal capital* as a result of the distribution. The definition of legal capital is not uniform in all states. At a minimum, legal capital includes the total par value of the shares issued. *Par value* is an arbitrary dollar amount assigned by the corporation to each share of a capital stock issue. There is no necessary relationship between either the issue or trading price of capital stock and its par value. Capital stock that is issued at a price in excess of par value is said to have been issued at a *premium*. In some states, legal capital also includes the premium paid for shares issued. Capital stock that is issued at a price below par value is said to have been issued at a *discount*. A contingent liability exists for shareholders who acquire capital stock from the corporation at a discount, because the corporate creditors may recover from these shareholders the amount of the discount in the event that their claims exceed the corporate assets. Thus shareholders who acquire shares at a discount may lose their original investment plus an amount equal to the discount. Most states now prohibit the issuance of capital stock at a discount.

9. Dividend policies. A corporation's periodic dividends are usually less than its periodic earnings, for one or more of the following reasons:

a. The corporation may desire to retain assets generated by profitable operations for internal expansion or growth.

b. An agreement between the corporation and its creditors may require that the corporation retain assets generated by profitable operations in order to provide additional protection for the creditors.

c. The corporation may wish to smooth periodic dividends over time by retaining assets generated by earnings in profitable years for dividend distributions in less profitable years.

d. State laws may require that retained earnings equal to the cost of treasury stock purchased be restricted from dividends to prevent a distribution of assets that could impair legal capital.

The annual dividends divided by earnings is called the *dividend payout ratio*.

10. The maximum amount that the corporation can legally distribute to its shareholders is equal to stockholders' equity less legal capital and any other amount legally restricted, such as the cost of treasury stock purchased. When the dividend distribution exceeds the credit balance in retained earnings, the excess is considered to be a liquidating dividend (a return of capital). Only that portion of the dividend that is equal to or less than the credit balance in retained earnings is considered to be a distribution of earnings (a return on capital). Additionally, since dividends (other than stock dividends) ultimately result in a distribution of assets, the corporation's financial position also influences its ability to distribute dividends. Dividend distributions may be affected by financial factors such as the amount of existing cash, the amount and composition of other assets, the amount of liabilities that require settlement in cash, and the need for cash to finance the acquisition of assets in the future.

Issuance of Capital Stock

11. Three general principles govern the accounting for the issuance of capital stock. First, contributed capital should be recorded at the fair value of the consideration received by the corporation for the capital stock issued. Second, the contributed capital recorded upon the issuance of capital stock should distinguish between the portion that represents legal capital and the portion, if any, that represents amounts paid in excess of legal capital. Third, contributed capital should be distinguished as to the source.

12. Issuance for cash. Corporations may issue par value capital stock either by choice or to comply with state laws requiring that a par value be specified. Par value is an arbitrary dollar amount assigned by the corporation to each share of a capital stock issue to distinguish between legal capital and amounts paid in excess of legal capital. The issuing corporation should record the issuance of par value common stock for cash by (a) debiting cash for the amount received, (b) crediting common stock for the par value of the shares issued, and (c) crediting contributed capital in excess of par—common for the excess of the total proceeds over the par value of the shares issued. The journal entry to record the issuance of par value preferred stock for cash is similar, except that preferred stock should be credited for the par value of the shares issued and contributed capital in excess of par—preferred should be credited for the excess of the total proceeds over the par value of the shares issued. Hereinafter, for simplicity, it is assumed that the capital stock involved is common stock.

13. Many states permit corporations to issue capital stock without par value but require the issuing corporation to assign an arbitrary value per share (called *stated value*) to distinguish between legal capital and amounts paid in excess of legal capital. Since stated value serves the same purpose as par value, the journal entry to record the issuance of no-par capital stock with a stated value is equivalent to the journal entry to record the issuance of par value capital stock, except that the amount paid in excess of legal capital should be credited to an account that refers to stated value rather than to par value, such as contributed capital in excess of stated value—common.

14. Many states also permit corporations to issue no-par capital stock with no stated value (also called *true no-par stock*). The total proceeds received for such stock represent legal capital. Accordingly, upon the issuance of no-par common stock with no stated value, common stock should be credited for the total proceeds. Hereinafter, for simplicity, it is assumed that the capital stock involved is par value stock.

15. Issuance for noncash consideration. Corporations may issue capital stock in exchange for property, goods, or services. In this circumstance, the issuing corporation should record the assets or services received and the contributed capital (common stock plus contributed capital in excess of par—common) at either the fair value of the property, goods, or services received or the fair value of the capital stock issued, whichever is more readily determinable. If neither fair value is readily determinable, the issuing corporation's board of directors must assign a value to record the transaction. Independent appraisal values usually are used in such circumstances.

16. Issuance by subscriptions. Corporations also may issue capital stock on a subscription basis. In such circumstances, the purchasers of the stock (subscribers) make a cash down payment, with the remainder of the purchase (subscription) price payable later according to the terms of the subscription agreement. In most states, subscribers have the same status as fully paid shareholders with respect to voting and other rights. The corporation does not issue the capital stock to the subscribers, however, until it receives full payment for the shares.

17. The corporation should record the issuance of capital stock on a subscription basis by (a) debiting cash for the amount received as the subscription down payment, (b) debiting subscriptions receivable for the amount due in the future, (c) crediting common stock subscribed for the par value of the subscribed shares, and (d) crediting contributed capital in excess of par—common for the excess of the subscription price over the par value of the subscribed shares. Common stock subscribed should be reported in the stockholders' equity section of the balance sheet immediately below common stock. In practice, most corporations report subscriptions receivable in the current asset section of the balance sheet separately from trade receivables. Some corporations, however, report subscriptions receivable in the stockholders' equity section of the balance sheet as a deduction from the related contributed capital, since it represents amounts that have not yet been paid. As the remaining subscription payments are received, the corporation should debit cash and credit subscriptions receivable for the amount received. And when the shares are fully paid, the corporation should debit common stock subscribed and credit common stock for the par value of the shares issued.

18. When a subscriber to capital stock is unable or unwilling to pay the full subscription price, the treatment of the amount already paid by the defaulting subscriber is governed by the laws of the state in which the corporation is incorporated. The following treatments are possible:

a. The corporation returns to the defaulting subscriber the amount previously paid. In this circumstance, the corporation should (1) debit common stock subscribed for the par value of the defaulted shares, (2) debit contributed capital in excess of par—common for the excess of the subscription price over the par value of the defaulted shares, (3) credit subscriptions receivable for the uncollected portion of the subscription price, and (4) credit cash for the amount previously paid by the defaulting subscriber.

b. The corporation keeps the amount previously paid by the defaulting subscriber. In this circumstance, the corporation should record a journal entry similar to the journal entry just described, except that contributed capital from defaulted stock subscriptions rather than cash should be credited for the amount previously paid by the defaulting subscriber.

c. The corporation returns to the defaulting subscriber the amount previously paid less any deficiency realized by the corporation upon the reissuance of the shares. In this circumstance, the corporation first should record a journal entry similar to the one described earlier, except that payable to defaulting subscriber rather than cash should be credited for the amount previously paid by the defaulting subscriber. Later, upon the reissuance of the defaulted shares, the corporation should record a journal entry similar to the normal entry for the issuance of capital stock. Finally, upon the remittance of the net amount payable to the defaulting subscriber, the corporation should (1) debit payable to defaulting subscriber for the amount previously paid by the defaulting subscriber, (2) credit contributed capital in excess of par—common for any excess of the subscription price over the reissue price of the defaulted shares, and (3) credit cash for the difference between these two amounts.

d. The corporation issues to the defaulting subscriber a number of shares based on the amount previously paid. In this circumstance, the amount previously paid by the defaulting subscriber is divided by the subscription price to determine the equivalent number of fully paid shares that are to be issued by the corporation to the defaulting subscriber. Upon the issuance of the shares to the defaulting subscriber, the corporation should (1) debit common stock subscribed for the par value of the defaulted shares, (2) debit contributed capital in excess of par—common for the product of the number of defaulted shares minus the number of shares issued multiplied by the excess of the subscription price over the par value of the stock, (3) credit common stock for the par value of the shares issued, and (4) credit

subscriptions receivable for the uncollected portion of the subscription price.

It should be remembered that the laws of the state of incorporation determine which of these possible treatments is required in a particular situation.

19. Lump-sum issuances. Corporations sometimes issue two or more classes of capital stock as a unit. In this circumstance, the corporation must allocate the total proceeds between the classes of capital stock. If the fair values of both classes of stock are determinable, the total proceeds should be allocated on the basis of the relative fair values of the two classes of stock at the date of issuance. Alternatively, if the fair value of one of the classes of stock is not determinable, the class of stock that has a determinable fair value should be recorded at its fair value and the class of stock that has no determinable fair value should be recorded at the remainder of the total proceeds. The amount allocated to each class of stock should be credited partly to common stock (or preferred stock) for the par value of the shares issued and partly to contributed capital in excess of par—common (or preferred) for the excess of the allocated amount over the par value of the related shares.

20. Issue costs. Corporations incur legal, accounting, administrative, and promotional costs in connection with the issuance of capital stock. These *stock issue costs* should be recorded as a reduction of the contributed capital associated with the shares issued, since they are related to capital transactions rather than to earnings activities.

21. Issuance through conversions. Corporations also issue shares of common stock through the exercise by the investor of a conversion privilege contained in a bond indenture or preferred stock issue. As described in Chapter 14, when bonds are converted into common stock, the corporation should remove from the real accounts all the balances related to the bonds converted, record the contributed capital for the common shares issued at the book value of the bonds converted, and recognize no gain or loss (called the *book value method*). Likewise, when preferred stock is converted into common stock, the corporation should (a) debit preferred stock for the par value of the shares converted, (b) debit contributed capital in excess of par—preferred for the excess of the original contributed capital over the par value of the shares converted, (c) credit common stock for the par value of the shares issued, and (d) credit contributed capital in excess of par—common for the excess of the book value of the shares converted over the par value of the shares issued. No gain or loss is recognized in accordance with the accounting convention of not recognizing gains or losses on capital transactions between the corporation and its shareholders.

Stock Rights

22. *Stock rights* convey to the holders of the rights the opportunity to acquire shares of capital stock of the issuing corporation according to specified terms. Corporations usually issue stock rights:

a. To satisfy the preemptive right of existing shareholders in connection with the issuance of additional shares of capital stock.
b. To enhance the marketability of another type of security, such as bonds or preferred stock.
c. To provide executives and employees with an opportunity to acquire shares of capital stock in connection with stock option plans adopted by the corporation.

The accounting for and reporting of stock rights issued with bonds are described in Chapter 14, whereas the accounting for and reporting of stock rights issued in connection with the preemptive right and stock-based compensation plans are described in the remainder of this section.

23. Rights to existing stockholders. The preemptive right provides the existing shareholders with an opportunity to maintain their proportion of ownership interest in the corporation whenever additional shares are issued. The stock rights are issued to existing shareholders in proportion to their ownership interest in the form of *warrants,* certificates that give the holders the right to acquire capital stock of the issuing corporation at a specified price within a specified time period. No formal journal entry is required when warrants are issued in connection with a preemptive right, since the corporation receives no consideration from its shareholders for the stock rights. Later, if the stock rights are exercised, the issuing corporation should record the normal journal entry for the issuance of capital stock for cash. Alternatively, if the stock rights are permitted to expire, no formal journal entry is required, since the issuing corporation received no consideration for the now expired stock rights.

24. Stock-based compensation plans. Corporations frequently grant stock rights to executives and employees in connection with stock-based compensation plans to compensate executives and employees, to raise capital, and to spread ownership of their capital stock among employees. Since 1972, accounting for these plans has been governed by *APB Opinion No. 25.* However, because of widespread dissatisfaction with this *Opinion,* the FASB recently issued an *Exposure Draft* of a proposed *Statement* to supersede *Opinion No. 25.* The text's chapter and this chapter review are based

on the assumption that this *Exposure Draft* will be issued as a *Statement* in late 1994 or early 1995.

25. A *stock-based compensation plan* is a compensation arrangement under which employees receive shares of stock, stock options, or other equity instruments, or under which the employer incurs liabilities to employees in amounts based on the price of the employer's stock. The FASB's *Exposure Draft* on accounting for stock-based compensation plans is based on the following conceptual foundation:

a. Employees provide services for employers and, in exchange, the employees receive compensation from their employers.
b. Stock-based compensation is a component of employee compensation.
c. Stock options are equity instruments.
d. Equity instruments are recorded at the fair value of the consideration received (employee services) or at the fair value of the equity instruments (stock options), whichever is more reasonably determinable.
e. The fair value of stock options is more reasonably determinable than the fair value of the employee services rendered in exchange for the stock-based compensation.

On the basis of this conceptual foundation, the *Exposure Draft* requires that the total compensation cost for stock-based compensation plans be measured at the fair value of the stock options at the *grant date* (the date at which the employer and employee agree to the terms of a stock-based compensation award) using an option-pricing model. It requires further that the total compensation cost be recognized as expense over the *service period* (the period or periods during which the employee performs the service in exchange for stock options and similar awards) or, if the award is for past services, at the grant date.

26. In accounting for a stock-based compensation plan in accordance with the *Exposure Draft,* the employer should record a journal entry on the grant date to debit prepaid compensation (an asset account) and credit options outstanding (an equity account) for the total compensation cost. The total compensation cost should be determined by multiplying the fair value of the stock options at the grant date by the estimated number of options expected to vest (that is, the number of options granted under a fixed stock option plan or the estimated number of options to be earned under a performance-based stock option plan minus the estimated number of options expected to be forfeited due to employee turnover, and so forth). In addition, when recognition of prepaid compensation as an asset creates a temporary difference for tax purposes, the employer should record another journal entry on the grant date to debit options outstanding and credit deferred tax liability for the total compensation cost multiplied by the enacted marginal tax rate. Subsequently, the compensation cost and related tax consequences should be allocated ratably over the service period of the employees, usually the period from the grant date to the *vesting date* (the date that the employee's right to receive or retain shares of stock or cash under the aware is no longer contingent on remaining in the service of the employer), (*a*) by a debit to compensation expense and a credit to prepaid compensation for the total compensation cost divided by the service period, and (*b*) by a debit to deferred tax liability and a credit to income (deferred) tax expense for the compensation expense multiplied by the enacted marginal tax rate. Moreover, if the stock options eventually are exercised, the employer should record a journal entry for the issuance of the stock by (*a*) debiting cash for the number of shares issued multiplied by the exercise price, if any, (*b*) debiting options outstanding for the number of shares issued multiplied by the fair value of the options at the grant date multiplied by 1.0 minus the enacted marginal tax rate, (*c*) crediting common stock for the number of shares issued multiplied by the par value of the stock, and (*d*) crediting contributed capital in excess of par—common for the number of shares issued multiplied by the sum of the exercise price, if any, and the net-of-tax value of the options at the grant date minus the par value of the stock. Additionally, when the difference between the market price of the stock on the exercise date and the exercise price is deductible for tax purposes, the employer should record another journal entry to debit income tax expense and credit a contributed capital account for the product of the number of shares issued multiplied by the excess of the market price over the exercise price multiplied by the tax rate. Alternatively, if the options are permitted to expire, the employer should reclassify the options outstanding balance that is related to the expired options as contributed capital—expired stock options. Finally, the estimate of the total compensation cost may change due to such factors as revisions in the estimated forfeiture rate, differences between the estimated and actual forfeiture rates, and revisions in the estimated number of options to be earned under a performance-based stock option plan. In such circumstances, the employer should record journal entries to adjust compensation expense, options outstanding, and deferred tax liability on a year-to-date basis.

27. Some stock-based compensation awards specify that employees can compel the employer to settle the award by transferring cash or other assets to employees rather than by issuing equity instru-ments. The employer should recognize a liability for such stock-based compensation. For example, when stock appreciation rights (SARs) are granted to employees, the employer should record a journal entry at the end of that year to (*a*) credit liability under stock option plan for the estimated number of SARs expected to vest multiplied by the excess of the year-end market price over the predetermined price of the stock, (*b*) debit compensation expense for the estimated total compensation cost divided by the service period, and (*c*) debit prepaid compensation for the residual amount of the estimated total compensation cost. Subsequently, the amount of the liability under stock options should be adjusted at the end of each period on the basis of the current market price of the stock, and any increase or decrease in the liability should be recognized as an adjustment of compensation expense for that period. In addition, when the liability is settled, the employer should record a journal entry to debit liability under stock option plan and to either credit cash or common stock and contributed capital in excess of par—common, depending upon whether the employee elects to receive cash or stock, respectively.

28. The *Exposure Draft's* required disclosures include a description of the plan or plans and, for each year of which an income statement is presented, information about such items as the number of outstanding and exercisable options; the number of options granted, exercised, forfeited, or expired during the year; the methods and assumptions used to estimate the fair value of options; and the total compensation expense for stock-based compensation plans. These disclosure requirements are effective for fiscal years beginning after December 31, 1993, whereas the recognition and measurement requirements will be effective for awards granted after December 31, 1996, with earlier application encouraged.

Donated Capital

29. Corporations occasionally receive assets from shareholders or others as donations. A good example is the donation of land by a city to a corporation as an inducement to locate a new plant in the region. When assets are received as a donation, the corporation should debit the appropriate asset account or accounts and credit donated capital for the fair value of the donated assets. Donated capital should be reported in the stockholders' equity section of the balance sheet as either additional contributed capital or a separate category between contributed capital from investments by stockholders and retained earnings.

Acquired Capital Stock

30. Corporations may acquire and formally retire shares of their own capital stock. Such transactions represent a return of previously contributed capital by the issuing corporation to the shareholders. In such circumstances, the issuing corporation accordingly should record a journal entry that includes (*a*) a debit to common stock for the par value of the retired shares, (*b*) a debit to contributed capital in excess of par—common for the excess of the original or average contributed capital over the par value of the retired shares, and (*c*) a credit to cash for the amount paid. Additionally, if the amount paid is less than the original or average contributed capital of the retired shares, the difference should be credited to contributed capital from retirement of stock—common. Conversely, if the amount paid is greater than the original or average contributed capital of the retired shares, the difference should be debited, first, to any contributed capital arising from prior treasury stock transactions or retirements of the same class of capital stock and, second, to retained earnings for the remainder of the excess.

31. Corporations also may acquire shares of their own capital stock and hold them for subsequent reissuance. Capital shares that are acquired by the issuing corporation but not formally retired or canceled are called *treasury stock* or *treasury shares*. There are two generally accepted methods of accounting for treasury stock: the cost method and the par value method.

32. Under the *cost method* of accounting for treasury shares, the corporation should record the acquisition of its own shares by debiting treasury stock and crediting cash for the amount paid. Later, if the treasury shares are reissued, the corporation should record a journal entry that includes (*a*) a debit to cash for the amount received and (*b*) a credit to treasury stock for the cost of the reissued shares determined by either specific identification or an average cost or FIFO cost flow assumption. Additionally, if the amount received is greater than the cost of the reissued shares, the difference should be credited to contributed capital from treasury stock transactions—common. Conversely, if the amount received is less than the cost of the reissued shares, the difference should be debited, first, to any contributed capital arising from prior treasury stock transactions or retirements of the same class of capital stock and, second, to retained earnings for the remainder of the excess. Alternatively, if the treasury shares are formally retired rather than reissued, the corporation should record a journal entry equivalent to the normal journal entry for the retirement of capital stock, except that treasury stock rather than cash should be credited for the cost

of the retired shares. U.S. GAAP requires that treasury stock recorded at cost be reported on the balance sheet as a deduction from total stockholders' equity, whereas the Fourth Directive of the European Community requires that treasury stock be reported as an asset.

33. Under the *par value method* of accounting for treasury shares, the corporation should record a journal entry for the acquisition of its own shares similar to the journal entry for the formal retirement of capital stock, except that treasury stock rather than common stock should be debited for the par value of the acquired shares. Later, if the treasury shares are reissued, the corporation should record a journal entry similar to the normal journal entry for the issuance of capital stock, except that treasury stock rather than common stock should be credited for the par value of the reissued shares. Alternatively, if the treasury shares are formally retired rather than reissued, the corporation should debit common stock and credit treasury stock for the par value of the retired shares. U.S. GAAP requires that treasury stock recorded at par value be reported in the stockholders' equity section of the balance sheet as a deduction from the par value of the issued shares of the same class of stock.

34. Stockholders occasionally donate to the issuing corporation shares of its own capital stock. Under the cost method of accounting for treasury stock, the corporation should record no formal journal entry when it receives donated shares, since the shares are acquired at no cost to the corporation. When the donated shares subsequently are reissued, however, the corporation should record a journal entry to debit cash and credit donated capital from treasury stock for the amount received. In contrast, under the par value method of accounting for treasury stock, the corporation should record the receipt of donated shares by (*a*) debiting treasury stock for the par value of the donated shares, (*b*) debiting contributed capital in excess of par—common for the excess of the original or average contributed capital over the par value of the donated shares, and (*c*) crediting donated capital from treasury stock for the original or average contributed capital of the donated shares. When the donated shares subsequently are reissued, the corporation should record a journal entry similar to the normal journal entry for the issuance of capital stock, except that treasury stock rather than common stock should be credited for the par value of the reissued shares.

35. One or more of the amounts recorded as part of the journal entries related to the corporation's acquisition or retirement of its own capital stock often are based on the contributed capital associated with the shares. In such circumstances, the amount of the contributed capital associated with the shares may be determined on the basis of either the original contributed capital recorded at the date the shares were issued or the average contributed capital of the shares at the date of the transaction. Although both bases are acceptable, the average contributed capital basis typically is used since the amount of the original contributed capital usually is not readily determinable, especially when the corporation's shares are issued over time at various prices and transferred among investors. Of course, if the original contributed capital is readily determinable, it may be used to measure the amount of the contributed capital associated with the acquired or retired shares.

36. It should be noted that corporations cannot "create earnings" from transactions in their own capital stock. Such transactions generally increase or decrease contributed capital. Furthermore, a corporation's acquisition or reissuance of its own capital stock occasionally may reduce retained earnings, but such transactions cannot increase retained earnings.

Nature of Retained Earnings

37. *Retained earnings* represents that portion of the corporate net assets that has been generated by profitable operating activities and retained in business. Other terms used to describe retained earnings include *earnings retained in the business, accumulated earnings, earnings employed in the business,* and *retained income.* The use of the terms *earned surplus* to describe retained earnings and *capital surplus* to describe contributed capital in excess of par is discouraged because they intimate that the corporation has something it does not need. The transactions and other events that increase or decrease retained earnings are:

a. Net income or loss.
b. Prior period adjustments, such as error corrections that affect the financial statements of prior periods (discussed in Chapters 4 and 19).
c. Certain changes in accounting principles that are reported by retroactive restatement of the financial statements of prior periods (discussed in Chapters 4 and 19).
d. Dividends.
e. Certain treasury stock transactions (discussed earlier in this chapter).
f. Quasi-reorganizations.

This chapter describes the accounting for and reporting of dividends, stock splits, retained earnings restrictions (appropriations), and quasi-reorganizations.

Dividends

38. Dividends, other than stock dividends, are distributions (*nonreciprocal transfers*) of assets by a corporation to its shareholders on a pro rata basis. Cash dividends are the most frequent type of dividend distribution. Other types of dividends include scrip dividends, property dividends, liquidating dividends, and stock dividends.

39. Cash dividends. *Cash dividends* are distributions of cash by the corporation to its shareholders on a pro rata basis. Three important dates are associated with dividends: the declaration date, the date of record, and the payment date. The *declaration date* is the date on which the corporation's board of directors formally announces (declares) that a dividend is to be paid. This is the date on which the corporation incurs an obligation to pay the dividend. Accordingly, upon the declaration of a cash dividend, the corporation should debit retained earnings (or a temporary account, dividends declared, which is subsequently closed to retained earnings) and credit dividends payable for the number of shares outstanding multiplied by the cash dividend declared per share. Dividends should be reported in the statement of retained earnings (or statement of stockholders' equity) as a reduction of retained earnings, whereas dividends payable should be reported as a current liability on the balance sheet. It should be noted that dividends are not declared on treasury shares. The *date of record* is a date chosen by the corporation's board of directors in order to establish to whom the dividend will be paid on the payment date. No journal entry is required on the date of record, since this date simply serves as a date to establish stock ownership. The *payment date* is the date on which the dividend is paid and the liability is settled. On the payment date, the corporation should debit dividends payable and credit cash for the amount paid.

40. Scrip dividends. *Scrip* (or *liability*) *dividends* are distributions of cash by the corporation to its shareholders on a pro rata basis, but because several months may elapse between the declaration date and the payment date, the corporation issues promissory notes (pieces of paper, or "scrip") as evidence of its intention to pay the dividend. A scrip dividend may be declared when the corporation is temporarily short of cash, and the promissory notes issued usually bear interest. Upon the declaration of a scrip dividend, the corporation should debit retained earnings and credit scrip dividends payable for the number of shares outstanding multiplied by the dividend declared per share. When the dividend and the interest on the promissory notes subsequently are paid, the corporation should (*a*) debit scrip dividends payable for the amount of the dividend, (*b*) debit interest expense for the amount of interest accrued on the promissory notes, and (*c*) credit cash for the sum of these two amounts.

41. Property dividends. *Property dividends* are distributions of assets other than cash by the corporation to its shareholders on a pro rata basis. A property dividend may be any asset or group of assets other than cash. Because the assets are distributed among the shareholders in proportion to their holdings, however, property dividends usually are securities of other corporations that are held as an investment by the corporation declaring the dividend. Upon the declaration of a property dividend, the corporation should record two journal entries: (*a*) the assets that are to be distributed to the shareholders as the property dividend should be adjusted to their fair value at the declaration date, and a gain or loss should be recognized for the difference between the book value and fair value of the assets; and (*b*) retained earnings should be debited and property dividend payable should be credited for the fair value of the assets at the declaration date. Later, on the payment date, the corporation should debit property dividend payable and credit the appropriate asset account for the fair value of the assets at the declaration date.

42. Liquidating dividends. *Liquidating dividends* are pro rata distributions of assets by the corporation to its shareholders for amounts in excess of the credit balance in retained earnings. Only the portion of the dividend that exceeds the credit balance in retained earnings is considered to be a liquidating dividend (a *return of capital*); the portion of the dividend that is equal to the credit balance in retained earnings is considered to be a distribution of earnings (a *return on capital*). Shareholders should be informed when any portion of a dividend is liquidating. When a portion of a dividend is liquidating, the corporation should record the following journal entry on the declaration date: (*a*) a debit to retained earnings for the portion of the dividend that equals the credit balance in retained earnings, (*b*) a debit to other contributed capital (including contributed capital in excess of par and from treasury stock transactions or retirements of stock) for the portion of the dividend that exceeds the credit balance in retained earnings, and (*c*) a credit to the appropriate dividends payable account for the total amount of the dividend. On the payment date, the corporation should debit the appropriate dividends payable account and credit the appropriate asset account for the total amount of the dividend.

43. Stock dividends. *Stock dividends* are distributions of additional shares of the corporation's own stock to its shareholders on a pro rata basis with no change in the par or stated value per share. Corporations may issue stock dividends for one or more of the following reasons:

a. Since a stock dividend increases the number of shares outstanding without decreasing the corporation's assets, the stock dividend may cause the market price of stock to decline to a trading range accessible to a greater number of investors.

b. The corporation may wish to retain assets for internal expansion or growth but may wish to distribute something to shareholders in lieu of cash or other assets. And since the shares may be sold for cash, shareholders may be willing to accept stock in lieu of cash or other assets.

c. The corporation may wish to reduce the retained earnings available for future dividends.

Stock dividends are stated as a percentage of the shares outstanding. Accordingly, the number of additional shares to be distributed in connection with a stock dividend is determined by multiplying the number of shares outstanding by the declared stock dividend rate.

44. *Small stock dividends,* which are defined as less than approximately 20 to 25 percent of the shares outstanding, are recorded at the fair market value of the stock on the declaration date. *Large stock dividends,* which are defined as greater than 20 to 25 percent of the shares outstanding, are recorded at either the legal requirement of the state of incorporation (usually par or stated value) or the average contributed capital per share on the declaration date. The rationale for the different methods of accounting for small and large stock dividends is based on the shareholders' perceptions regarding the value of the additional shares distributed. Small stock dividends may produce "extra value" to the shareholders, since the market price of the stock per share may not be affected by the distribution of the additional shares. Small stock dividends are recorded accordingly at the fair market value of the shares distributed. Conversely, large stock dividends do not produce "extra value" to the shareholders because the market price of the stock per share declines proportionately. Large stock dividends therefore are required to be recorded, at a minimum, only to the extent of legal requirements.

45. When a small stock dividend is both declared and distributed on the same date, the corporation should record the following journal entry: (*a*) a debit to retained earnings for the number of shares distributed multiplied by the fair value of the stock on the declaration date, (*b*) a credit to common stock for the number of shares distributed multiplied by the par value of the stock, and (*c*) a credit to contributed capital in excess of par—common for the number of shares distributed multiplied by the excess of the fair value over the par value of the stock. In contrast, the journal entry to record the declaration and distribution of a large stock dividend when par value is used as the basis of measurement consists of a debit to retained earnings and a credit to common stock for the number of shares distributed multiplied by the par value of the stock. And the journal entry to record the declaration and distribution of a large stock dividend when average contributed capital per share is used as the basis of measurement consists of (*a*) a debit to retained earnings for the number of shares distributed multiplied by the average contributed capital per share on the declaration date, (*b*) a credit to common stock for the number of shares distributed multiplied by the par value of the stock, and (*c*) a credit to contributed capital in excess of par—common for the number of shares distributed multiplied by the excess of the average contributed capital over the par value of the stock. Alternatively, when the issue date follows the declaration date, the journal entry to record the declaration of a stock dividend (small or large) should be modified to credit stock dividends distributable rather than common stock for the number of shares to be distributed multiplied by the par value of the stock. If financial statements are issued between the declaration date and issue date, stock dividends distributable should be reported in the stockholders' equity section of the balance sheet, immediately below common stock. Stock dividends distributable is not a liability, since the corporation has no obligation to transfer assets to its shareholders as a result of the stock dividend. Later, when the additional shares are distributed to the shareholders, the corporation should debit stock dividends distributable and credit common stock for the number of shares distributed multiplied by the par value of the stock. Finally, it should be noted that stock dividends have no effect on total stockholders' equity. A stock dividend merely results in a reclassification of amounts within the stockholders' equity section of the balance sheet, a transfer (or capitalization) of retained earnings to contributed capital.

46. Stock splits. *Stock splits* are distributions of additional shares of the corporation's own stock to its shareholders on a pro rata basis with a proportional reduction in the par or stated value per share. Stock dividends, discussed earlier, also are distributions of additional shares, but with no change in the par or stated value per share. The primary purpose of a stock split is to reduce the market price of the stock per share to a trading range accessible to a greater number of investors. No formal journal entry is required to record a stock split, since the total dollar amount of the capital stock at its par or stated value is unchanged. All that is required is a memorandum entry to indicate the new number of shares outstanding with a lower par or stated value per share.

47. Dividend preferences. When the corporation has both preferred stock and common stock issued and outstanding, the claims of preferred shareholders to dividends must be satisfied before those of common shareholders. Additionally, preferred stock may be cumulative and/or participating. Assuming that the preferred stock dividend rate is stated as a percent of par value, the amount of dividends to be distributed to each class of stockholders may be determined as follows:

a. If preferred stock is noncumulative and nonparticipating, the preferred shareholders should receive dividends equal to the total par value of the preferred shares outstanding multiplied by the stated dividend rate and the common shareholders should receive the remainder of the total dividend distribution.

b. If preferred stock is cumulative and nonparticipating, the preferred shareholders should receive dividends equal to the sum of any preferred dividends in arrears plus preferred dividends for the current year and the common shareholders should receive the remainder of the total dividend distribution.

c. If preferred stock is noncumulative and fully participating, first, the preferred shareholders should receive the preferred dividends for the current year; next, the common shareholders should receive dividends equal to the total par value of the common shares outstanding multiplied by the stated dividend rate of the preferred stock; and finally, both the preferred shareholders and the common shareholders should receive dividends equal to the remainder of the total dividend distribution allocated proportionately on the basis of the relative total par value of the outstanding shares in each class of stock.

d. If preferred stock is cumulative and fully participating, first, the preferred shareholders should receive any preferred dividends in arrears and preferred dividends for the current year; next, the common shareholders should receive dividends equal to the total par value of the common shares outstanding multiplied by the stated dividend rate of the preferred stock; and finally, both the preferred shareholders and the common shareholders should receive dividends equal to the remainder of the total dividend distribution allocated proportionately on the basis of the relative total par value of the outstanding shares in each class of stock.

It should be noted that if preferred stock is partially rather than fully participating, the preferred shareholders should share in the remainder of the total dividend distribution only up to the stated maximum total rate. Any residual amount of the total dividend distribution should be paid to the common shareholders only.

Restrictions on Retained Earnings

48. Corporations may be required or may desire to restrict a portion of retained earnings from dividend availability because of one or more of the following conditions:

a. Legal restrictions, such as state laws that require that retained earnings equal to the cost of treasury stock purchased be restricted from dividend distributions.
b. Contractual restrictions, such as a bond indenture requirement that restricts a portion of retained earnings from dividend availability during the life of the bond issue.
c. Discretionary restrictions, such as a desire to retain assets for internal expansion or for expected or possible losses arising from inventory price declines, lawsuits, and other contingencies.

The existence of restrictions on the amount of retained earnings available for dividend distributions should be disclosed in the financial statements in order to communicate to shareholders that there are dividend restrictions. Such restrictions may be disclosed by appropriation of retained earnings or by parenthetical or footnote disclosure.

49. The formal journal entry to record a *retained earnings appropriation* includes a debit to retained earnings and a credit to the specific retained earnings appropriated account, which is reported in the stockholders' equity section of the balance sheet as part of the total retained earnings balance. Subsequently, when the retained earnings appropriation is no longer required, the appropriation is reversed by a debit to the retained earnings appropriated account and a credit to retained earnings. No losses or other events should be debited to a retained earnings appropriated account, even if the appropriation was initially established for a loss contingency that subsequently is confirmed by future events. Instead, such losses should be reported on the income statement. Moreover, the retained earnings appropriation does not set aside or earmark assets for the designated purpose. Nonetheless, assets coincidentally may be transferred to a special fund such as a building fund or bond sinking fund. If so, the fund should be accounted for separately from the retained earnings appropriation. A retained earnings appropriation, however, does not necessarily imply that such a fund has been established. Alternatively, restrictions on retained earnings may be disclosed in the financial statements merely by a parenthetical notation following retained earnings in the stockholders' equity section of the balance sheet and/or by a footnote accompanying the financial statements. These methods of disclosing restrictions on

retained earnings are generally considered to be less confusing than formal retained earnings appropriations. Some countries, however, require corporations to appropriate "legal reserves" at a specified percentage of stockholders' equity to protect creditors from overpayment of dividends.

Appendixes

50. Quasi-reorganizations. When there is a debit balance in retained earnings, the corporation may have difficulty obtaining additional capital from potential investors, even though the prospects of improved profitability are favorable, because the retained earnings deficit may prevent the corporation from paying dividends in the foreseeable future. The inability to obtain additional capital eventually may result in insolvency or bankruptcy. Many states allow a corporation that faces such economic circumstances to revalue its assets, eliminate the retained earnings deficit against contributed capital, and proceed as a going concern without legally reorganizing. This arrangement is called a *quasi-reorganization,* which consists of the following steps:

a. All assets are adjusted (written up or written down) to their current fair values. This revaluation generally increases the deficit in retained earnings.
b. The retained earnings deficit is eliminated by a debit to other contributed capital and a credit to retained earnings for the deficit balance after the revaluation of the assets. If the amount of other contributed capital is insufficient to absorb the retained earnings deficit, it may be increased before the deficit is eliminated by shareholder donations of capital stock and/or by reduction of the par or stated value of the shares outstanding.
c. For a reasonable number of years following the quasi-reorganization, retained earnings is "dated" in subsequent financial statements to disclose that a quasi-reorganization has been effected.

The shareholders must approve the quasi-reorganization agreement.

51. The use of option-pricing models to determine the fair value of stock-based compensation. The FASB's *Exposure Draft* specifies that the fair value of stock options should be determined using mathematical models, such as the Black-Scholes option-pricing and binomial models. The two principal components of these models are a minimum value and a volatility value.

The *minimum value* of a stock option is the current price of the stock minus the sum of the present value of the exercise price and the present value of the expected dividends on the stock during the term of the option, both discounted at the risk-free interest rate. The *volatility value* is a measure of the amount by which the price of the stock is expected to fluctuate during the term of the option. The volatility component recognizes that options may result in gains equal to the difference between the exercise price and market price of stock on the exercise date or losses equal to the amount paid for the option. Because the amount of the upside gain of an option is greater than the amount of its potential downside fixed loss, the value of stock options increases proportionately with the volatility of the stock. Application of these option-pricing models is beyond the scope of the text.

SELF-STUDY LEARNING
Items marked with an asterisk (*) refer to the Appendixes.

Key Terms and Concepts

Provide the appropriate term or terms to complete each of the following statements:

1. The owners' equity of corporations generally is called _____, and it consists of two elements: _____, which represents that portion of the corporate net assets that has been obtained from shareholder investments and other capital transactions, and _____, which represents that portion of the corporate net assets that has been generated by profitable operating activities and retained in the business.

2. Corporations may create two or more classes of capital stock with different rights and privileges: _____, the class of capital stock that controls the management of the corporation and assumes the ultimate rewards and risks associated with corporate operations, and _____, the special class of capital stock that generally has no voting rights but has a priority right to dividends and to assets upon liquidation.

3. In order to protect the priority claim of creditors to corporate assets, state laws require that corporations do not voluntarily distribute assets to the shareholders if prior claims exist and if the distribution would reduce the dollar amount of contributed capital below an amount called _____.

4. An arbitrary dollar amount assigned by the corporation to each share of a capital stock issue to distinguish between legal capital and amounts paid in excess of legal capital is called _____ or _____.

5. The right of existing shareholders to maintain their proportionate ownership interest by sharing proportionately in new issues of the same class of capital stock is called the _____.

6. A _____ is an arrangement under which employees receive shares of stock, stock options, or other equity instruments in exchange for services, or the employer incurs liabilities to employees in amounts based on the price of the employer's stock.

7. The total compensation cost for a stock-based compensation plan should be allocated over the employee's _____, which usually is the period from the _____,

which is the date at which the employer and employee agree to the terms of the award, to the _____, which is the date that the employee's right to receive or retain shares of stock or cash under the award is no longer contingent on remaining in the service of the employer.

8. Shares of capital stock that are acquired by the issuing corporation but not formally retired or canceled are called _____.

9. Distributions of assets by the corporation to its shareholders on a pro rata basis are _____.

10. There are various types of dividends, including _____, which are distributions of cash; _____, which are distributions of cash but because of a temporary shortage of cash the intention to pay the dividend is evidenced by the issuance of promissory notes; and _____, which are distributions of assets other than cash.

11. Three important dates are associated with dividends: the _____, which is the date on which the corporation's board of directors formally announces that a dividend is to be paid; the _____, which is the date chosen by the corporation's board of directors in order to establish stock ownership; and the _____, which is the date on which the dividend is distributed and the liability is settled.

12. When the dividend distribution exceeds the credit balance in retained earnings, the excess is considered to be a(n) _____.

13. Distributions of additional shares of the corporation's own stock to its shareholders on a pro rata basis with no change in the par or stated value per share are _____; distributions of additional shares of the corporation's own stock to its shareholders on a pro rata basis with a proportional reduction in the par or stated value per share are _____.

14. When preferred stock is _____, preferred dividends not declared in any year are said to be in arrears and must be paid to the preferred shareholders in following years before any dividends are paid to common shareholders; when preferred stock is _____, the preferred shareholders may share proportionately in dividends with common shareholders over and above the stated dividend rate of the preferred stock.

*15. An arrangement that allows the corporation to revalue its assets, eliminate a retained earnings deficit against contributed capital, and proceed as a going concern without legally reorganizing is called a(n) _____.

True-False

Indicate by circling the appropriate response whether each of the following statements is true (T) or false (F):

T F 1. Dividends in arrears on cumulative preferred stock should be reported on the balance sheet as a current liability.

T F 2. When capital stock is issued for non-cash assets, the contributed capital should be recorded at either the book value of the noncash assets received or the par value of the shares issued, whichever is more readily determinable.

T F 3. Subscriptions receivable arising from the issuance of capital stock on a subscription basis may be reported on the balance sheet as either a current asset or a deduction from contributed capital.

T F 4. Common stock subscribed should be reported as a liability on the balance sheet, since the corporation has an obligation to issue shares of capital stock in the future upon the receipt of full payment.

T F 5. Stock issue costs should be recorded as a reduction of the contributed capital associated with the shares issued.

T F 6. No formal journal entry is required when warrants are issued in connection with the preemptive right, since the corporation receives no consideration from its shareholders for the stock rights.

T F 7. The total compensation cost for stock-based compensation plans should be measured at the fair value of the options at the exercise date.

T F 8. A deferred tax liability should be recognized at the grant date of a fixed stock option plan, when recognition of the compensation cost as an asset on that date creates a temporary difference for tax purposes.

T F 9. Total compensation cost for a stock-based compensation plan should be recognized as expense at the grant date.

T F *10. The minimum value of a stock option is less than the fair value of a stock option because of the stock's potential price volatility.

T F 11. No formal journal entry should be recorded when assets are received by the corporation as a donation from shareholders or others, since the assets are acquired at no cost to the corporation.

T F 12. The journal entry to record the acquisition or retirement of shares of capital stock by the issuing corporation may include a debit, but should never include a credit, to retained earnings.

T F 13. The journal entry to record the acquisition of treasury stock in accordance with the par value method of accounting is equivalent to the journal entry to record the acquisition and formal retirement of capital stock, except that

treasury stock rather than common stock is debited for the par value of the acquired shares.

T F 14. The journal entry to record the reissuance of treasury stock accounted for by the cost method is equivalent to the journal entry to record the original issuance of capital stock, except that treasury stock rather than common stock is credited for the cost of the reissued shares.

T F 15. U.S. GAAP requires that treasury stock be reported as an asset on the balance sheet, since the corporation may reissue the shares for cash.

T F 16. The maximum amount that the corporation legally can distribute to its shareholders is stockholders' equity less legal capital and any other amount legally restricted, such as the cost of treasury stock purchased, but the portion of a dividend that exceeds the credit balance in retained earnings is considered to be a liquidating dividend rather than a distribution of earnings.

T F 17. All dividends except stock dividends should be reported in the statement of retained earnings (or the statement of stockholders' equity) as a reduction of retained earnings.

T F 18. Dividends are not declared on treasury shares, since it is illogical for the corporation to pay a dividend to itself.

T F 19. Dividends may be recorded either as a reduction of retained earnings directly or in a temporary account, such as dividends declared, which is subsequently closed to retained earnings.

T F 20. Interest paid on promissory notes issued in connection with a scrip dividend should be recorded as a reduction of retained earnings, since the shareholders receive the face value of the notes plus interest.

T F 21. Property dividends should be recorded at the fair value of the related assets on the payment date.

T F 22. Small stock dividends should be recorded at the fair value of the shares on the issue date.

T F 23. The journal entry to record the declaration of a large stock dividend, when par value is used as the basis of measurement, includes a debit to retained earnings and a credit to stock dividends distributable for the number of shares to be distributed multiplied by the par value of the stock.

T   F   24. Contributed capital in excess of par—common stock should not be credited to record a large stock dividend when average contributed capital per share is used as the basis of measurement.

T   F   25. Stock dividends distributable should be reported as a liability on the balance sheet, because the corporation has an obligation to distribute additional shares of stock to its shareholders.

T   F   26. Neither stock dividends nor stock splits have an effect on total stockholders' equity.

T   F   27. No formal journal entry is required to record a stock split, since the total dollar amount of the capital stock at its par or stated value is unchanged.

T   F   28. When preferred stock is cumulative and nonparticipating, the preferred shareholders should receive dividends equal only to any dividends in arrears and the common shareholders should receive the remainder of the total dividend distribution.

T   F   29. Disclosure of restrictions on retained earnings is optional.

T   F   *30. In a quasi-reorganization, the retained earnings deficit is eliminated by a debit to other contributed capital and a credit to retained earnings for the deficit balance after the revaluation of the assets.

Multiple Choice

Select the best response for each of the following items, and circle the corresponding letter:

1. The journal entry to record the original issuance of par value common stock for cash should include:

   a. A debit to cash for the par value of the shares issued.
   b. A credit to common stock for the total amount paid for the shares issued.
   c. A credit to contributed capital in excess of par—common for any excess of the total amount paid for the shares issued over the par value of the shares.
   d. A debit to retained earnings for any excess of the par value of the shares issued over the total amount paid for the shares.

2. When common stock is issued for noncash assets, the noncash assets received and the contributed capital for the shares issued should be recorded at:

   a. The book value of the noncash assets received.
   b. The par value of the shares issued.
   c. Either the fair value of the noncash assets received or the fair value of the shares issued, whichever is more readily determinable.
   d. A value that the corporation's board of directors arbitrarily assigns to the transaction.

3. The journal entry to record the sale of par value common stock on a subscription basis should include:

   a. A credit to common stock for the subscription price of the subscribed shares.
   b. A credit to common stock for the par value of the subscribed shares.
   c. A credit to common stock subscribed for the subscription price of the subscribed shares.
   d. A credit to common stock subscribed for the par value of the subscribed shares.

4. When the corporation is required by state laws to return to a defaulting subscriber the amount previously paid for par value common stock sold on a subscription basis:

   a. Common stock subscribed should be debited for the subscription price of the defaulted shares.
   b. Contributed capital in excess of par—common should be debited for the excess of the subscription price of the defaulted shares over the amount paid by the defaulting subscriber.
   c. Subscriptions receivable should be credited for the excess of the subscription price of the defaulted shares over the amount paid by the defaulting subscriber.
   d. Cash should be credited for the par value of the defaulted shares.

5. When par value common stock is issued in connection with a fixed stock option plan, options outstanding should be debited for the number of shares issued multiplied by:

a. The fair value of the stock options at the grant date.
b. 1.0 minus the enacted marginal tax rate.
c. Neither a nor b.
d. Both a and b.

6. The journal entry to record the acquisition and formal retirement of shares of par value preferred stock by the issuing corporation should *not* include:

   a. A debit to preferred stock for the par value of the retired shares.
   b. A debit to contributed capital in excess of par—preferred for the average contributed capital of the retired shares.
   c. A debit to retained earnings for the excess of the amount paid over the average contributed capital of the retired shares.
   d. A credit to contributed capital from retirement of stock—preferred for the excess of the average contributed capital of the retired shares over the amount paid.

7. When treasury stock that is accounted for by the cost method subsequently is reissued:

   a. Treasury stock should be credited for the par value of the reissued shares.
   b. Contributed capital from treasury stock transactions should be credited for the excess of the amount received over the par value of the reissued shares.
   c. Retained earnings should be credited for the excess of the amount received over the cost of the reissued shares.
   d. Any recorded contributed capital from treasury stock transactions should be debited for the excess of the cost of the reissued shares over the amount received.

8. When the par value method is used by the issuing corporation to account for the acquisition of shares of par value common stock:

   a. Common stock should be debited for the par value of the acquired shares.
   b. Treasury stock should be debited for the cost of the acquired shares.
   c. Contributed capital in excess of par—common should be debited for the excess of the average contributed capital over the par value of the acquired shares.
   d. Retained earnings should be credited for the excess of the average contributed capital over the cost of the acquired shares.

9. Which of the following transactions or events should *not* be recorded as an increase or a decrease in retained earnings?

   a. Stock splits.
   b. Dividends.
   c. Quasi-reorganizations.
   d. Prior period adjustments.

10. The maximum amount that the corporation legally can distribute to its shareholders is equal to:

    a. Retained earnings.
    b. Stockholders' equity.
    c. Stockholders' equity less legal capital.
    d. Stockholders' equity less legal capital and any other amount legally restricted, such as the cost of treasury stock purchased.

11. Which of the following is *not* an authoritative guideline regarding the accounting for property dividends?

    a. The book value of the assets to be distributed should be adjusted to their fair value at the declaration date.
    b. A gain or loss should be recognized for the difference between the book value and fair value of the assets at the declaration date.
    c. A gain or loss should be recognized for the change in the fair value of the assets between the declaration date and the payment date.
    d. The dividend and the related liability should be recorded at the fair value of the assets at the declaration date.

12. When a dividend is partly a distribution of earnings and partly a liquidating dividend, the journal entry to record the dividend declaration should include:

    a. A debit to retained earnings for the total dividend distribution.
    b. A debit to other contributed capital for the total dividend distribution.
    c. A debit to other contributed capital for the portion of the dividend distribution that exceeds the credit balance in retained earnings.
    d. A credit to dividends payable only for the portion of the dividend distribution that equals the credit balance in retained earnings.

13. When preferred stock is cumulative and fully participating, the dividends distributed to the preferred shareholders and the common shareholders as a percentage of the total par or stated value of the outstanding shares in each class of stock should be equal if:
    a. There are no dividends in arrears.

b. The total dividend is not greater than the credit balance in retained earnings.

c. There are no dividends in arrears and the total dividend is at least equal to the total par or stated value of the preferred and common shares outstanding multiplied by the stated dividend rate of the preferred stock.

d. There are dividends in arrears but the total dividend is at least equal to the dividends in arrears plus the total par or stated value of the preferred and common shares outstanding multiplied by the stated dividend rate of the preferred stock.

14. Which of the following is a common misconception regarding the accounting for retained earnings appropriations?

a. A retained earnings appropriation should be recorded only when assets are transferred to a special fund.

b. Assets that coincidentally are transferred to a special fund should be accounted for separately from the retained earnings appropriation.

c. Retained earnings appropriations should be reported in the stockholders' equity section of the balance sheet as part of the total retained earnings balance.

d. The formal journal entry to record an increase or decrease in a retained earnings appropriated account should also include a corresponding decrease or increase in retained earnings.

*15. In a quasi-reorganization:

a. Assets should be revalued to the lower of their book values or current fair values.

b. The retained earnings deficit should be eliminated by a debit to retained earnings and a credit to other contributed capital for the deficit balance before the revaluation of the assets.

c. Assets may be written up to their current fair values only if the amount of other contributed capital is insufficient to absorb the retained earnings deficit.

d. Retained earnings should be "dated" in subsequent financial statements for a reasonable number of years to disclose that a quasi-reorganization has been effected.

Extended Problems

1. The stockholders' equity section of the balance sheet of the Capital Corporation as of December 31, 1994, follows:

9% preferred stock, $100 par (authorized, 10,000 shares; issued and outstanding, 2,000 shares)	$ 200,000
Common stock, $5 par (authorized, 500,000 shares; issued and outstanding, 100,000 shares)	500,000
Additional contributed capital:	
Contributed capital in excess of par—preferred	10,000
Contributed capital in excess of par—common	700,000
Total contributed capital	$1,410,000
Retained earnings	390,000
Total stockholders' equity	$1,800,000

These data are to be used in responding to the following independent situations. In other words, assume that no transactions other than those described in each of the situations occurred after December 31, 1994.

REQUIRED

a. Assume that on March 16, 1995, Capital Corporation issued 1,000 shares of preferred stock for $105 cash per share. Prepare the journal entry required to record the issuance of the preferred stock.

b. Assume that on March 16, 1995, Capital Corporation issued 20,000 shares of common stock in exchange for a tract of land. Prepare the journal entry required to record the issuance of the common stock for the land for each of the following alternative circumstances: (1) the land had a determinable fair value of $290,000, but the common stock had no determinable fair value; (2) the common stock had a determinable fair value of $15 per share, but the land had no determinable fair value; and (3) neither the land nor the common stock had a determinable fair value, but the board of directors accepted an appraisal value of $295,000 as the value of the land.

c. Assume that on March 16, 1995, Capital Corporation sold 20,000 shares of common stock on a subscription basis at $15 per share, with a required down payment of 20 percent and the remainder payable in two equal installments on May 15, 1995, and July 15, 1995. Prepare the journal entries required to record the subscription and the receipt of the down payment, the collection of the first installment, the collection of the second installment, and the issuance of the subscribed shares.

d. Assume the same facts described in situation c, except that a subscriber to 1,000 shares defaulted on the second (last) installment of the subscription. Prepare the journal entries required to account for the defaulted subscription for each of the following alternative circumstances: (1)

Capital Corporation returned to the defaulting subscriber the amount paid, (2) Capital Corporation kept the amount paid by the defaulting subscriber, (3) Capital Corporation returned to the defaulting subscriber the amount paid less the excess of the subscription price ($15) over the reissue price ($14), and (4) Capital Corporation issued shares to the defaulting subscriber on the basis of the amount paid.

e. Assume that on March 16, 1995, Capital Corporation issued 1,000 shares of preferred stock and 13,000 shares of common stock for $296,000 cash. Prepare the journal entry required to record the issuance of the shares in each of the following alternative circumstances: (1) the preferred stock and common stock had determinable fair values of $105 and $15 per share, respectively; and (2) the common stock had a determinable fair value of $15 per share, but the preferred stock had no determinable fair value.

f. Assume that Capital Corporation adopted a stock option plan for its employees at the beginning of 1995. Under the plan, options are exercisable beginning 3 years after the date of grant for a maximum of 10 years. On January 1, 1995, Capital Corporation granted 12,000 stock options at an exercise price of $15 per share. At that date, Capital Corporation calculated the fair value of each option at $4 and estimated that 9,000 of the options would vest. At the end of 1997, 9,500 options actually vested and, on January 2, 1998, 4,000 options were exercised, when the market price of the common stock was $22 per share. Assume further that the corporate tax rate is 34 percent, the difference between the exercise price and the market price of the stock on the exercise date is deductible for tax purposes, and Capital Corporation elects to adopt the *Exposure Draft's* requirements on accounting for stock-based compensation. Prepare the journal entries required to account for the stock options for each of the years 1995 through 1998.

g. Assume that on January 10, 1995, Capital Corporation acquired and formally retired 500 shares of its preferred stock for $102 cash per share. Prepare the journal entry required to record the acquisition and retirement of the preferred stock.

h. Assume that on January 10, 1995, 500 shares of Capital Corporation's preferred stock that were originally issued for $105 per share were converted into common stock in accordance with the stock contract at a conversion rate of 8 common shares for each preferred share. Prepare the journal entry required to record the conversion of the preferred stock into common stock.

i. Assume that on January 10, 1995, Capital Corporation acquired 3,000 shares of its common stock for $14 cash per share. On March 16,

1995, 1,000 of the treasury shares were reissued for $15 cash per share; on May 14, 1995, 1,000 of the shares were reissued for $12 cash per share; and on September 11, 1995, the remaining 1,000 shares were formally retired. Prepare the journal entries required to record the acquisition, reissuance, and retirement of the treasury shares by (1) the cost method and (2) the par value method.

2. The stockholders' equity section of the balance sheet of the Redivo Corporation as of December 31, 1994, follows:

Common stock, $5 par value (authorized, 400,000 shares; issued and outstanding, 100,000 shares)	$ 500,000
Contributed capital in excess of par—common	160,000
Total contributed capital	$ 660,000
Retained earnings	390,000
Total stockholders' equity	$1,050,000

These data apply to each of the following independent situations. It may be assumed that no transactions or events other than those described in each situation occurred after December 31, 1994.

REQUIRED

a. On January 3, 1995, the board of directors declared a cash dividend of $1 per share of common stock, payable on February 7, 1995, to shareholders of record on January 31, 1995. Prepare the journal entries required to record the declaration and payment of the cash dividend.

b. On January 2, 1995, the corporation purchased 2,000 shares of its own common stock at a total cost of $24,000. On January 3, 1995, the board of directors authorized a formal appropriation of retained earnings for the cost of the treasury stock purchased and declared a cash dividend of $1 per share of common stock, payable on February 7, 1995, to shareholders of record on January 31, 1995.

(1). Prepare the journal entry required to record the appropriation of retained earnings.
(2). Calculate the amount the corporation legally could distribute to its shareholders immediately after the purchase of the treasury stock.
(3). Calculate the total amount of the cash dividend.
(4). Prepare the journal entry required to reverse the retained earnings appropriation if the treasury stock is sold for $25,000 on February 2, 1995.

c. On January 3, 1995, the board of directors declared a scrip dividend of $1 per share of common stock, payable on July 3, 1995, to shareholders of record on January 31, 1995. The promissory notes (scrip) have a stated rate of interest of 10 percent. Prepare the journal entries required to record the declaration and payment of the scrip dividend.

d. On January 3, 1995, the board of directors declared a property dividend on the common stock, payable on February 7, 1995, to shareholders of record on January 31, 1995. The dividend was paid in shares of stock of another corporation that had been acquired as an investment at a cost of $75,000. The cost method has been used to account for the investment. On January 3, 1995, the fair value of the stock was $90,000; on February 7, 1995, the fair value of the stock was $92,000. Prepare the journal entries required to record the declaration and payment of the property dividend.

e. Assume that the retained earnings balance as of December 31, 1994, was $80,000 instead of $390,000. On January 3, 1995, the board of directors declared a cash dividend of $1 per share of common stock, payable on February 7, 1995, to shareholders of record on January 31, 1995. Prepare the journal entries required to record the declaration and payment of the cash dividend.

f. On January 3, 1995, the board of directors declared a 10 percent stock dividend on the common stock, distributable on February 7, 1995, to shareholders of record on January 31, 1995. On January 3, 1995, the fair value of the stock was $12.00 per share; on February 7, 1995, the fair value of the stock was $12.50 per share. Prepare the journal entries required to record the declaration and distribution of the stock dividend.

g. On January 3, 1995, the board of directors declared a 50 percent stock dividend on the common stock, distributable on February 7, 1995, to shareholders of record on January 31, 1995. On January 3, 1995, the fair value of the stock was $12.00 per share; on February 7, 1995, the fair value of the stock was $8.25 per share.

(1). Prepare the journal entries required to record the declaration and distribution of the stock dividend, using par value as the basis of measurement.

(2). Prepare the journal entries required to record the declaration and distribution of the stock dividend, using average contributed capital per share as the basis of measurement.

h. On January 3, 1995, the board of directors declared a two-for-one stock split on the common stock. Prepare a memorandum entry to record the stock split.

i. Assume that on December 31, 1994, the corporation also had 1,000 shares of 6 percent $100 par value preferred stock issued and outstanding. On January 3, 1995, the board of directors declared a total cash dividend of $60,000. Calculate the amount of the dividend that should be paid to the preferred shareholders and the common shareholders for each of the following alternative circumstances:

(1). The preferred stock is noncumulative and nonparticipating.

(2). The preferred stock is cumulative, with two years' dividends in arrears, and nonparticipating.

(3). The preferred stock is cumulative, with two years' dividends in arrears, and fully participating.

(4). The preferred stock is cumulative, with no dividends in arrears, and partially participating to a stated maximum total rate of 8 percent.

*j. Assume that the retained earnings balance as of December 31, 1995, was a deficit of $280,000. On that date the shareholders approved an arrangement consisting of the following steps: (1) the plant and equipment was revalued from a book value of $490,000 to its current fair value of $400,000, (2) the par value of the common stock was changed from $5.00 to $2.50, and (3) the deficit in retained earnings was eliminated against contributed capital. Prepare the journal entries required to record the quasi-reorganization.

COMMON ERRORS

The first statement in each "common error" listed here is *incorrect*. Each incorrect statement is followed by a corrected statement and an explanation.

1. When par value common stock is issued on a subscription basis, common stock subscribed may be credited for the subscription price of the subscribed shares. *Wrong*

When par value common stock is issued on a subscription basis, common stock subscribed should be credited for the par value of the subscribed shares and contributed capital in excess of par—common should be credited for the excess of the subscription price over the par value of the subscribed shares. *Right*

Par value is an arbitrary dollar amount assigned by the corporation to each share of a capital stock issue to distinguish between legal capital and amounts paid in excess of legal capital. Although shares are not issued by the corporation to the subscribers until they are fully paid, state laws specify that the par value of subscribed shares constitutes part of the legal capital of the corporation. Accordingly, on the subscription date, common stock subscribed should be credited for the par value of the subscribed shares and contributed capital in excess of par—common should be credited for the excess of the subscription price over the par value of the subscribed shares.

2. In accounting for the acquisition, retirement, or reissuance of shares of its own capital stock, the corporation may debit or credit retained earnings. *Wrong*

In accounting for the acquisition, retirement, or reissuance of shares of its own capital stock, the corporation may debit but not credit retained earnings. *Right*

Retained earnings represents that portion of the corporation's net assets that has been generated by profitable operating activities and retained in the business. Since the corporation's acquisition, retirement, or reissuance of shares of its own capital stock does not constitute an operating activity, retained earnings should not be credited (increased) as a result of such a transaction. Retained earnings, however, may be debited (decreased) as a result of such a transaction under the rationale that the excess of the reduction in corporate assets over the related reduction in contributed capital represents an additional dividend paid to the previous shareholders. Amounts resulting from capital transactions that may be debited to retained earnings include the excess of the cost over the average contributed capital of shares formally retired or of treasury shares accounted for by the par value method, and the excess of the cost over the reissue price of treasury shares accounted for by the cost method.

3. Retained earnings is an asset. *Wrong*

Retained earnings represents the portion of the corporation's net asset (assets less liabilities) or stockholders' equity that has been generated by profitable operating activities and retained in the business. *Right*

Various transactions and other events cause an increase or decrease in retained earnings, but the principal items that affect retained earnings are net income or loss and dividends. Broadly speaking, net income equals revenues less expenses. When revenue is recorded, an increase in an asset (such as cash or accounts receivable) or a decrease in a liability (such as unearned revenue) also is recorded. Similarly, when an expense is recorded, a decrease in an asset (such as cash, inventory, plant and equipment, or prepaid expenditure) or an increase in a liability (such as accounts payable) also is recorded. Net income, which is closed to retained earnings, is therefore the recorded net effect of operating activities on the corporation's net assets or stockholders' equity during the period. Likewise, when a dividend (other than a stock dividend) is declared, both a decrease in retained earnings or stockholders' equity and a decrease in assets ultimately are recorded. Consequently, retained earnings represents the portion of the corporation's net assets (asset less liabilities) or stockholders' equity that has been generated by profitable operating activities and retained in the business.

4. Property dividends may be recorded at the book value of the assets that are to be distributed by the corporation to its shareholders. *Wrong*

Property dividends should be recorded at the fair value of the assets that are to be distributed by the corporation to its shareholders, and a gain or loss should be recognized for the difference between the fair value and the book value of the assets at the declaration date. *Right*

It is a generally accepted accounting convention that corporations should not recognize gains or losses on capital transactions with their own shareholders. Because of this convention, some people argue that property dividends should be recorded at the book value of the related assets, and no gain or loss should be recognized. *APB Opinion No. 29,* however, requires that property dividends be recorded at the fair value of the related assets and that a gain or loss be recognized for the difference between the fair value and the book value of the assets at the declaration date. The rationale cited for this requirement is that the dividend would otherwise be misstated, and the gain or loss that has already been earned or incurred by the corporation would not be recognized.

5. When a small stock dividend is declared, stock dividends distributable should be credited for an amount equal to the number of shares to be distributed multiplied by the fair value of the stock at the declaration date. *Wrong*

When a small stock dividend is declared, stock dividends distributable should be credited for the number of shares to be distributed multiplied by the par value of the stock and contributed capital in excess of par—common should be credited for the number of shares to be distributed multiplied by the excess of the fair value over the par value of the stock. *Right*

Small stock dividends are required to be recorded as a reduction of retained earnings at the fair value of the stock, because it is presumed that the shareholders perceive the shares received to have a value equal to their current market price. However, because stock dividends result in the issuance of additional shares with no change in the par value per share, a stock dividend also creates an increase in the legal capital of the corporation on the declaration date. For this reason, stock dividends distributable should be recorded at the par value of the shares distributable. In addition, contributed capital in excess of par—common should be credited on the declaration date for the difference between the amount debited to retained earnings and the amount credited to stock dividends distributable.

6. When the corporation formally appropriates retained earnings, assets are always set aside or earmarked for the purpose specified in the appropriation. *Wrong*

When the corporation formally appropriates retained earnings, assets may be but are not necessarily set aside or earmarked for the purpose specified in the appropriation. *Right*

Retained earnings appropriations are formally disclosed in the financial statements by disaggregation of total retained earnings in the stockholders' equity section of the balance sheet into an appropriated amount and an unappropriated amount. The single purpose of the retained earnings appropriation is to communicate to the shareholders that there is a restriction on the availability of existing assets for future dividend distributions equal to the appropriated amount. In some circumstances, the corporation may coincidentally set aside or earmark assets for the purpose specified in the appropriation. Cash may be transferred to a building fund, for example, when the corporation desires to retain assets for internal expansion or growth. Alternatively, cash may be transferred to a bond sinking fund so that the corporation can meet the requirements of a bond indenture. Such special funds should be accounted for apart from the retained earnings appropriation, and the fund balances should be reported as investments on the balance sheet. In other circumstances, assets may not be set aside or earmarked for the purpose specified in the appropriation. Retained earnings appropriations for the cost of treasury stock purchased is a good example of such a circumstance. Thus assets may be but are not necessarily set aside or earmarked when the corporation formally appropriates retained earnings.

ANSWERS

Items marked with an asterisk (*) refer to the Appendixes.

Key Terms and Concepts

1. stockholders' equity or shareholders' equity, contributed capital, retained earnings
2. common stock, preferred stock
3. legal capital
4. par value, stated value
5. preemptive right
6. stock-based compensation plan
7. service period, grant date, vesting date
8. treasury stock or treasury shares
9. dividends
10. cash dividends, scrip dividends, property dividends
11. declaration date, date of record, payment date
12. liquidating dividend
13. stock dividends, stock splits
14. cumulative, participating
15. quasi-reorganization

True-False

1. F Dividends in arrears on cumulative preferred stock should not be reported as a liability on the balance sheet, since dividends do not represent a liability of the corporation until they are formally declared by the board of directors. The amount of any dividends in arrears, however, should be disclosed in the financial statements, since it represents a probable future cash outflow.

2. F When capital stock is issued for noncash assets, the contributed capital should be recorded at either the fair value of the noncash assets received or the fair value of the shares issued, whichever is more readily determinable.

3. T

4. F Common stock subscribed should not be reported as a liability on the balance sheet,

since the corporation has no obligation to transfer assets or provide services in the future upon the receipt of full payment for the subscribed shares. Instead, common stock subscribed must be reported in the stockholders' equity section of the balance sheet immediately below common stock.

5. T
6. T
7. F The total compensation cost for stock-based compensation plans should be measured at the fair value of the options at the grant date.
8. T
9. F Total compensation cost for a stock-based compensation plan should be recognized as expense over the period or periods during which the employee performs the service in exchange for stock options or, if the award is for past service, at the grant date.
10. T
11. F When assets are received by the corporation as a donation from shareholders or others, the corporation should record a journal entry to debit the appropriate asset account or accounts and credit donated capital for the fair value of the donated assets. This journal entry is recorded in order to establish an appropriate basis of corporate accountability for the donated assets.
12. T
13. T
14. F The journal entry to record the reissuance of treasury stock accounted for by the par value method is equivalent to the journal entry to record the original issuance of capital stock, except that treasury stock rather than common stock is credited for the par value of the reissued shares. In contrast, the journal entry to record the reissuance of treasury stock accounted for by the cost method includes a debit to cash for the amount received and a credit to treasury stock for the cost of the reissued shares. Additionally, if the amount received is greater than the cost of the reissued shares, the difference is credited to contributed capital from treasury stock transactions—common. Conversely, if the amount received is less than the cost of the reissued shares, the difference is debited, first, to any contributed capital arising from prior treasury stock transactions or retirements of the same class of capital stock and, second, to retained earnings.
15. F U.S. GAAP requires that treasury stock be reported in the stockholders' equity section of the balance sheet as a deduction from either total stockholders' equity (cost method) or the par value of the issued shares of the same class of stock (par value method). Treasury shares as well as authorized but unissued shares are not an asset under U.S. GAAP.
16. T
17. F All dividends except liquidating dividends should be reported in the statement of retained earnings (or the statement of stockholders' equity) as a reduction of retained earnings. The portion of a dividend distribution that is considered to be a liquidating dividend should be reported in the statement of stockholders' equity as a reduction of other contributed capital. A stock dividend should be reported in the statement of retained earnings as a reduction of retained earnings or in the statement of stockholders' equity as both a reduction of retained earnings and an increase in contributed capital.
18. T
19. T
20. F Interest paid on promissory notes issued in connection with a scrip dividend should be recorded as interest expense, since the interest has accrued on a liability.
21. F Property dividends should be recorded at the fair value of the related assets on the declaration date, since this is the date on which the corporation forgoes the opportunity to sell the assets at their current market value.
22. F Small stock dividends should be recorded at the fair value of the shares on the declaration date, because this is the date on which the corporation forgoes the opportunity to issue the shares at the current market price.
23. T
24. F Contributed capital in excess of par—common stock should not be credited to record a large stock dividend when par value is used as the basis of measurement. Conversely, to record a large stock dividend when average contributed capital per share is used as the basis of measurement, contributed capital in excess of par—common should be credited for the number of shares to be distributed multiplied by the excess of the average contributed capital over the par value of the stock. Additionally, retained earnings should be debited for the number of shares to be distributed multiplied by the average contributed capital per share on the declaration date, and stock dividends distributable

should be credited for the number of shares to be distributed multiplied by the par value of the stock.

25. F   Stock dividends distributable should not be reported as a liability on the balance sheet, since the corporation has no obligation to transfer assets to its shareholders as a result of the stock dividend. Instead, stock dividends distributable should be reported in the stockholders' equity section of the balance sheet, immediately below common stock.

26. T

27. T

28. F   When preferred stock is cumulative and nonparticipating, the preferred shareholders should be paid both the dividends in arrears and the dividends for the current year before any dividends are paid to the common shareholders.

29. F   Restrictions on retained earnings should be disclosed in the financial statements to communicate to shareholders that there are dividend restrictions. The existence of such restrictions may be disclosed by appropriation of retained earnings or by a parenthetical or footnote disclosure.

30. T

Multiple Choice

1.	c	9.	a
2.	c	10.	d
3.	d	11.	c
4.	c	12.	c
5.	d	13.	c
6.	b	14.	a
7.	d	15.	d
8.	c		

Extended Problems

1. a. Journal entry to record issuance of preferred stock for cash:

3/16/95	Cash (1,000 × $105)..	105,000	
	Preferred stock (1,000 × $100).......................................		100,000
	Contributed capital in excess of par—preferred ($105,000 − $100,000).......		5,000

   b. Journal entry to record issuance of common stock for land:

   (1). Land had a determinable fair value

3/16/95	Land..	290,000	
	Common stock (20,000 × $5)..		100,000
	Contributed capital in excess of par—common ($290,000 − $100,000).......		190,000

   (2). Common stock had a determinable fair value.

3/16/95	Land (20,000 × $15)..	300,000	
	Common stock (20,000 × $5)..		100,000
	Contributed capital in excess of par—common ($300,000 − $100,000).......		200,000

   (3). Neither land nor common stock had a determinable fair value.

3/16/95	Land..	295,000	
	Common stock (20,000 × $5)..		100,000
	Contributed capital in excess of par—common ($295,000 − $100,000).......		195,000

   c. Journal entries related to sale of common stock on a subscription basis:

3/16/95	Cash (20,000 × $3)...	60,000	
	Subscriptions receivable (20,000 × $12)...............................	240,000	
	Common stock subscribed (20,000 × $5)........................		100,000
	Contributed capital in excess of par—common [20,000 × ($15 − $5)]..........		200,000
5/15/95	Cash (20,000 × $6)...	120,000	
	Subscriptions receivable		120,000
7/15/95	Cash (20,000 × $6)...	120,000	
	Subscriptions receivable		120,000
7/15/95	Common stock subscribed (20,000 × $5)............................	100,000	
	Common stock		100,000

d. Journal entries related to defaulted subscription:

(1). Corporation returned the amount paid.

7/15/95	Common stock subscribed (1,000 × $5)...	5,000	
	Contributed capital in excess of par—common [1,000 × ($15 – $5)]	10,000	
	Subscriptions receivable (1,000 × $6)..		6,000
	Cash (1,000 × $9)..		9,000

(2). Corporation kept the amount paid.

7/15/95	Common stock subscribed (1,000 × $5)...	5,000	
	Contributed capital in excess of par—common [1,000 × ($15 – $5)]	10,000	
	Subscriptions receivable (1,000 × $6)..		6,000
	Contributed capital from defaulted stock subscriptions—common (1,000 × $9)		9,000

(3). Corporation returned the amount paid less the excess of the subscription price over the reissue price.

7/15/95	Common stock subscribed (1,000 × $5)...	5,000	
	Contributed capital in excess of par—common [1,000 × ($15 – $5)]	10,000	
	Subscriptions receivable (1,000 × $6)..		6,000
	Payable to defaulting subscriber (1,000 × $9)...............................		9,000
7/15/95	Cash (1,000 × $14)..	14,000	
	Common stock (1,000 × $5)...		5,000
	Contributed capital in excess of par—common ($14,000 – $5,000)............		9,000
7/15/95	Payable to defaulting subscriber	9,000	
	Cash ($9,000 – $1,000)..		8,000
	Contributed capital in excess of par—common [1,000 × ($15 – $14)].........		1,000

(4). Corporation issued shares on the basis of the amount paid.

7/15/95	Common stock subscribed (1,000 × $5)...	5,000	
	Contributed capital in excess of par—common [(1,000 – 600) × ($15 – $5)]	4,000	
	Subscriptions receivable (1,000 × $6)..		6,000
	Common stock (600 × $5)[a]		3,000

[a]The equivalent number of fully paid shares issued (600) is determined by dividing the amount paid (1,000 × $9 = $9,000) by the subscription price ($15).

e. Journal entry to record issuance of preferred stock and common stock as a unit:

(1). Both preferred stock and common stock had determinable fair values.[a]

3/16/95	Cash	296,000	
	Preferred stock (1,000 × $100)...		100,000
	Contributed capital in excess of par—preferred ($103,600 – $100,000).......		3,600
	Common stock (13,000 × $5)..		65,000
	Contributed capital in excess of par—common ($192,400 – $65,000).........		127,400

[a]The total contributed capital is allocated between the two classes of stock according to the relative fair values of the shares as follows: [$296,000 × $105,000 ÷ ($105,000 + $195,000)] = $103,600 and [$296,000 × $195,000 ÷ ($105,000 + $195,000)] = $192,400.

(2). Only common stock had a determinable fair value.

3/16/95	Cash	296,000	
	Preferred stock (1,000 × $100)...		100,000
	Contributed capital in excess of par—preferred		
	[($296,000 – $195,000) – $100,000]		1,000
	Common stock (13,000 × $5)..		65,000
	Contributed capital in excess of par—common [(13,000 × $15) – $65,000]..		130,000

f. Journal entries related to stock-base compensation:

1/1/95	Prepaid compensation (9,000 × $4)...	36,000	
	Options outstanding..		36,000
	Options outstanding...	12,240	
	Deferred tax liability ($36,000 × .34)..		12,240
12/31/95	Compensation expense ($36,000 ÷ 3)...	12,000	
	Prepaid compensation...		12,000
	Deferred tax liability ($12,000 × .34)..	4,080	
	Income tax expense...		4,080
12/31/96	Compensation expense ($36,000 ÷ 3)...	12,000	
	Prepaid compensation...		12,000
	Deferred tax liability ($12,000 × .34)..	4,080	
	Income tax expense...		4,080
12/31/97	Prepaid compensation [(9,500 − 9,000) × $4]	2,000	
	Options outstanding..		2,000
	Options outstanding...	680	
	Deferred tax liability ($2,000 × .34)..		680
	Compensation expense [($36,000 + $2,000) − ($12,000 × 2)]	14,000	
	Prepaid compensation...		14,000
	Deferred tax liability ($14,000 × .34)	4,760	
	Income tax expense...		4,760
1/2/98	Cash (4,000 × $15)...	60,000	
	Options outstanding [4,000 × $4 × (1.00 − .34)]...............................	10,560	
	Common stock (4,000 × $5)...		20,000
	Contributed capital in excess of par—common ($60,000 + $10,560 − $20,000)		50,560
	Income tax expense...	9,520	
	Contributed capital from tax benefits of exercised stock options {[4,000 × ($22 − $15)] × .34}...		9,520

g. Journal entry to record acquisition and formal retirement of preferred stock:

1/10/95	Preferred stock (500 × $100)...	50,000	
	Contributed capital in excess of par—preferred [500 × ($105 − $100)][a]	2,500	
	Cash (500 × $102)..		51,000
	Contributed capital from retirement of stock—preferred ($52,500 − $51,000)		1,500

[a] Average contributed capital per share ($105) is determined by dividing preferred stock ($200,000) plus contributed capital in excess of par—preferred ($10,000) by the number of preferred shares issued and outstanding (2,000).

h. Journal entry to record conversion of preferred stock into common stock:

1/10/95	Preferred stock (500 × $100)...	50,000	
	Contributed capital in excess of par—preferred [500 × ($105 − $100)]............	2,500	
	Common stock [(500 × 8) × $5]...		20,000
	Contributed capital in excess of par—common ($52,500 − $20,000)		32,500

i. Journal entries to record acquisition, reissuance, and retirement of treasury shares:

(1). Cost method.

1/10/95	Treasury stock (3,000 × $14)...	42,000	
	Cash...		42,000
3/16/95	Cash (1,000 × $15)..	15,000	
	Treasury stock (1,000 × $14)...		14,000
	Contributed capital from treasury stock transactions—common ($15,000 − $14,000)..		1,000

5/14/95	Cash (1,000 × $12)..	12,000	
	Contributed capital from treasury stock transactions—common...................	1,000	
	Retained earnings ($14,000 − $13,000)................................	1,000	
	Treasury stock (1,000 × $14).....................................		14,000
9/11/95	Common stock (1,000 × $5).....................................	5,000	
	Contributed capital in excess of par—common [1,000 × ($12 − $5)][a]............	7,000	
	Retained earnings [$14,000 − (1,000 × $12)]............................	2,000	
	Treasury stock (1,000 × $14).....................................		14,000

(2). Par value method.

1/10/95	Treasury stock (3,000 × $5).....................................	15,000	
	Contributed capital in excess of par—common [3,000 × ($12 − $5)][a]...........	21,000	
	Retained earnings [$42,000 − (3,000 × $12)]............................	6,000	
	Cash (3,000 × $14)...		42,000
3/16/95	Cash (1,000 × $15)...	15,000	
	Treasury stock (1,000 × $5).....................................		5,000
	Contributed capital in excess of par—common ($15,000 − $5,000)...........		10,000
5/14/95	Cash (1,000 × $12)...	12,000	
	Treasury stock (1,000 × $5).....................................		5,000
	Contributed capital in excess of par—common ($12,000 − $5,000)...........		7,000
9/11/95	Common stock (1,000 × $5).....................................	5,000	
	Treasury stock...		5,000

[a]Average contributed capital per share ($12) is determined by dividing common stock ($500,000) plus contributed capital in excess of par—common ($700,000) by the number of common shares issued and outstanding (100,000).

2. a. Journal entries related to cash dividend:

1/3/95	Retained earnings (100,000 × $1)................................	100,000	
	Dividends payable...		100,000
2/7/95	Dividends payable...	100,000	
	Cash...		100,000

b. (1). Journal entry to record appropriation of retained earnings:

1/3/95	Retained earnings...	24,000	
	Retained earnings appropriated for cost of treasury stock........................		24,000

(2). Amount corporation legally could distribute to its shareholders:

Total stockholders' equity................................		$1,050,000
Less: Legal capital................................	$500,000	
Cost of treasury stock................................	24,000	524,000
Amount legally distributable................................		$ 526,000

(3). Total amount of cash dividend: [(100,000 − 2,000) × $1] = $98,000.

(4). Journal entry to record reversal of retained earnings appropriation:

2/2/95	Retained earnings appropriated for cost of treasury stock........................	24,000	
	Retained earnings...		24,000

c. Journal entries related to scrip dividend:

1/3/95	Retained earnings (100,000 × $1)................................	100,000	
	Scrip dividends payable...		100,000
7/3/95	Scrip dividends payable...	100,000	
	Interest expense ($100,000 × 10% × 6/12)................................	5,000	
	Cash ($100,000 + $5,000)...		105,000

d. Journal entries related to property dividend:

1/3/95	Investment in stock ($90,000 – $75,000)	15,000	
	Gain on disposition of investment		15,000
1/3/95	Retained earnings	90,000	
	Property dividend payable		90,000
2/7/95	Property dividend payable	90,000	
	Investment in stock		90,000

e. Journal entries related to liquidating dividend:

1/3/95	Retained earnings	80,000	
	Contributed capital in excess of par–common ($100,000 – $80,000)	20,000	
	Dividends payable (100,000 × $1)		100,000
2/7/95	Dividends payable	100,000	
	Cash		100,000

f. Journal entries to record declaration and distribution of small stock dividend:

1/3/95	Retained earnings (100,000 × 10% × $12)	120,000	
	Stock dividends distributable (100,000 × 10% × $5)		50,000
	Contributed capital in excess of par—common ($120,000 – $50,000)		70,000
2/7/95	Stock dividends distributable	50,000	
	Common stock		50,000

g. (1). Journal entries to record declaration and distribution of large stock dividend, par value used as basis of measurement:

1/3/95	Retained earnings (100,000 × 50% × $5)	250,000	
	Stock dividends distributable		250,000
2/7/95	Stock dividends distributable	250,000	
	Common stock		250,000

(2). Journal entries to record declaration and distribution of large stock dividend, average contributed capital per share used as a basis of measurement:

1/3/95	Retained earnings (100,000 × 50% × $6.60)[a]	330,000	
	Stock dividends distributable (100,000 × 50% × $5)		250,000
	Contributed capital in excess of par—common ($330,000 – $250,000)		80,000

[a] Average contributed capital per share ($6.60) is determined by dividing common stock ($500,000) plus contributed capital in excess of par—common ($160,000) by the number of common shares issued and outstanding (100,000).

| 2/7/95 | Stock dividends distributable | 250,000 | |
| | Common stock | | 250,000 |

h. Memorandum entry to record stock split:

| 1/3/95 | Common stock (100,000 shares, $5 par) | 500,000 | |
| | Common stock (200,000 shares, $2.50 par) | | 500,000 |

i. Calculation of dividend payment to preferred shareholders and common shareholders:

(1). Preferred stock noncumulative and nonparticipating.

	PREFERRED	COMMON	TOTAL
Dividend for current year ($100,000 × 6%)	$6,000		$ 6,000
Remainder ($60,000 – $6,000)		$54,000	54,000
Total	$6,000	$54,000	$60,000

(2). Preferred stock cumulative and nonparticipating.

	PREFERRED	COMMON	TOTAL
Dividends in arrears ($100,000 × 6% × 2)	$12,000		$12,000
Dividend for current year ($100,000 × 6%)	6,000		6,000
Remainder ($60,000 – $18,000)		$42,000	42,000
Total	$18,000	$42,000	$60,000

(3). Preferred stock cumulative and fully participating.

	PREFERRED	COMMON	TOTAL
Dividends in arrears ($100,000 × 6% × 2)	$12,000		$12,000
Dividends for current year			
$100,000 × 6%	6,000		6,000
$500,000 × 6%		$30,000	30,000
Remainder ($12,000 ÷ $600,000 = 2%)			
$100,000 × 2%	2,000		2,000
$500,000 × 2%		10,000	10,000
Total	$20,000	$40,000	$60,000

(4). Preferred stock cumulative and partially participating.

	PREFERRED	COMMON	TOTAL
Dividends for current year			
$100,000 × 6%	$6,000		$ 6,000
$500,000 × 6%		$30,000	30,000
Remainder ($24,000 ÷ $600,000 = 4%)			
$100,000 × 2%	2,000		2,000
$24,000 – $2,000		22,000	22,000
Total	$8,000	$52,000	$60,000

*j. Journal entries related to quasi-reorganization:

12/31/95	Retained earnings ($490,000 – $400,000)	90,000	
	Plant and equipment		90,000
12/31/95	Common stock (100,000 × $2.50)	250,000	
	Contributed capital in excess of par—common		250,000
12/31/95	Contributed capital in excess of par—common	370,000	
	Retained earnings ($280,000 + $90,000)		370,000

19 ACCOUNTING CHANGES AND ERROR ANALYSIS

CHAPTER OBJECTIVES

After reading Chapter 19 and completing the questions, cases, exercises, and problems from the text chapter, you should be able to:

1. Distinguish a change in accounting principle, a change in accounting estimate, a change in the reporting entity, and an accounting error.
2. Calculate the cumulative effect of a change in accounting principle on prior periods.
3. Prepare the journal entry required to record a change in accounting principle.
4. Report the effects of a change in accounting principle in the financial statements of the period of the change and in the financial statements of prior periods presented for comparative purposes under both the current period approach (general requirement) and the retroactive approach (if specifically required).
5. Prepare the journal entry required to account for

the effects of a change in accounting estimate prospectively in the current period or in the current and future periods.
6. Distinguish a classification error that does not affect income, a counterbalancing error, and a noncounterbalancing error.
7. Analyze the effects of an error on the financial statements, both the statements of the current period in which an error is discovered and those of prior periods affected by an error.
8. Prepare the correcting journal entry (or entries) required, if any, to adjust the accounts for the effects of an error discovered both before and after the books have been closed.
9. Report the effects of an error in both the financial statements of the current period in which an error is discovered and the affected financial statements of prior periods presented for comparative purposes.

CHAPTER OBJECTIVES

Introduction

1. Accounting changes, such as changes in accounting principle, changes in accounting estimates, and changes in the reporting entity, as well as accounting errors can affect the interperiod comparability of financial statements. There are three approaches for reporting accounting changes: (a) the *current period* (or *catch-up*) *approach* under which the effect of the change is reported in the current period only, (b) the *retroactive approach*

under which the effect of the change is reported retroactively by restating the financial statements of prior years, and (c) the *prospective approach* under which the effect of the change is reported prospectively in the current period or in the current and future periods. The current period approach and the prospective approach are based on the rationale that if financial statements of prior periods are continually restated for comparative purposes, the reliability and credibility of financial reporting may be questioned. The retroactive approach is based on the rationale that when the financial statements of prior periods are restated, they will be comparable to those of the current and future periods. These three approaches were considered by the APB in *Opinion No. 20,* which is described in the remainder of this chapter review.

Change in Accounting Principle

2. A *change in accounting principle* is a change from one generally accepted accounting principle to another generally accepted accounting principle. Examples of changes in accounting principle include a change in the method of inventory pricing, as from the FIFO method to the LIFO method; a change in the method of depreciating previously recorded assets, as from the straight-line method to the double-declining-balance method; and a change in the method of accounting for long-term construction contracts, as from the completed-contract method to the percentage-of-completion method. A change in accounting principle also includes a change in the method of applying a principle. A change from an accounting principle that is not generally accepted to one that is generally accepted, however, is a correction of an error rather than a change in accounting principle.

3. There is a presumption that once an accounting principle has been adopted, it should not be changed, since the consistent application of accounting principles from one accounting period to another enhances the comparability of accounting data. This presumption may be overcome only if an alternative acceptable principle is judged to be preferable by management.

4. A change in accounting principle should be recorded as of the beginning of the period of the change. The journal entry to record a change in accounting principle normally should include the following three elements: (*a*) the asset or liability account (or related contra account) affected by the change in accounting principle should be adjusted to the amount it would have been at the beginning of the period if the new accounting principle had been applied in all prior periods; (*b*) the appropriate income tax real account, such as income taxes payable or deferred tax liability, should be adjusted by the tax effect of the change in accounting principle on all prior periods; and (*c*) the difference between these two amounts, representing the difference between the amount of retained earnings at the beginning of the period of the change and the amount of retained earnings that would have been reported if the new accounting principle had been applied in all prior periods, should be recorded either as cumulative effect of change in accounting principle, if the current period approach is required,

or as an adjustment to retained earnings, if the retroactive approach is required. Thereafter, the normal journal entries for the application of the new accounting principle should be recorded during the period of the change and future periods.

5. General requirement. The *cumulative effect of a change in accounting principle* is the difference between the amount of retained earnings at the beginning of the period of the change and the amount of retained earnings that would have been reported if the new accounting principle had been applied in all prior periods. As a general requirement, *Opinion No. 20* specifies that the cumulative effect of a change in accounting principle should be reported in the income statement between extraordinary items and net income. Additionally, the financial statements of prior periods included for comparative purposes should be presented as they were previously reported, not retroactively restated. Retroactive restatement of the financial statements of prior periods to disclose the effects of a change in accounting principle could dilute the public confidence in financial statements. However, in order to make the income statements more comparable, retroactively restated *pro forma amounts* of income before extraordinary items, net income, and earnings per share must be reported on the face of the income statement for all periods presented *as if* the new accounting principle had been applied during those periods.

6. Exceptions to general requirement. There are two classes of exceptions to the general requirement that the cumulative effect of a change in accounting principle should be reported in the income statement of the period of the change: changes in accounting principle whose cumulative effect is not determinable and special changes in accounting principle, which must be reported by restatement of the financial statements of prior periods with the new accounting principle applied retroactively.

7. The cumulative effect of a change in accounting principle may not be determinable in some circumstances. When an entity changes to the LIFO method of inventory pricing, for example, information may not be available to permit the computation of the layers that would have existed had the LIFO method been applied in all prior periods. In this situation, the inventory carrying value under the previously applied pricing method is designated as the initial LIFO layer. No adjusting entry is recorded and no cumulative effect is computed or reported. Disclosure is limited to showing the effect of the change in accounting principle on the results of operations of the period of the change and to explaining the reason for the omission of accounting for the cumulative effect and of disclosure of pro forma amounts for prior periods.

8. When certain changes in accounting principle are made, the advantages of applying the new accounting principle retroactively to the financial statements of prior periods are judged to outweigh the disadvantages. In these special situations, the cumulative effect of the change in accounting principle should be reported as an adjustment of beginning retained earnings, and the financial statements of all prior periods presented for comparative purposes should be *retroactively restated* to reflect the effects of the change. The cumulative effect of the change and pro forma amounts should not be reported in the income statement of the period of the change. *Opinion No. 20* specifies that the following changes in accounting principle should be reported retroactively:

a. A change from the LIFO method of inventory pricing to another method.
b. A change in the method of accounting for long-term construction contracts, as from the completed-contract method to the percentage-of-completion method, or vice versa.
c. A change to or from the full-cost method of accounting for exploration costs incurred in the extractive industries.
d. Changes made at the time a company's financial statements are first used to obtain additional equity capital from investors, to effect a business combination, or to register securities.

Other authoritative pronouncements also require retroactive restatement when special changes in accounting principle are made. *Opinion No. 18,* for example, requires retroactive restatement for a change from the cost method to the equity method of accounting for investments. Additionally, the FASB generally had required retroactive restatement for the transition from previously acceptable accounting principles to the promulgated standard.

Change in Accounting Estimate

9. Estimates are an inherent part of the accounting process. Estimates are required, for example, in the case of uncollectible receivables, salvage values and useful lives of depreciable assets, number of periods to be benefited by a deferred expenditure, and inventory obsolescence. Occasionally estimates may change as more experience is acquired, as circumstances change, or as additional information is obtained. An accounting change that results from new information or subsequent developments, and accordingly from better insight or improved judgment, is a *change in accounting estimate*. A new accounting method adopted in partial or complete recognition of a change in estimated future benefits also is a change in estimate.

10. The effect of a change in accounting estimate should be accounted for *prospectively* in the period of the change, if the change affects that period only, or in the period of the change and future periods, if the change affects both periods. Financial statements of prior periods should not be restated, and pro forma amounts for prior periods should not be reported. A change in the estimated useful life of a depreciable asset, for example, should be accounted for by depreciating the undepreciated cost of the asset (cost less accumulated depreciation) less the estimated salvage value, if any, over the estimated remaining useful life. The depreciation reported in the financial statements of prior periods presented for comparative purposes should be based on the original estimated useful life.

Change in Reporting Entity

11. A *change in the reporting entity* is a special type of accounting change that involves the preparation of financial statements for a new accounting entity. Accounting changes of this type include the presentation of consolidated or combined financial statements in place of statements of individual companies, a change in the specific subsidiaries that comprise the group of companies for which consolidated financial statements are presented, and a change in the companies included in combined financial statements. In such situations, the reporting entity is composed of a different group of companies after the change.

12. A change in the reporting entity should be reported by restating the financial statement of all prior periods presented in order to disclose financial information of the new reporting entity for all periods.

Error Analysis and Correction

13. *Accounting errors* generally arise as a result of (*a*) mathematical mistakes, such as in the computation of depreciation; (*b*) use of an accounting method that is not appropriate in a given set of economic circumstances, such as the use of the direct write-off method of accounting for uncollectible accounts when estimates of the collectibility of receivables are clearly available; (*c*) oversight or misuse of available facts, such as failure to accrue an expense or a revenue; and (*d*) incorrect classification of items in the income statement or balance sheet.

14. Two principles govern the reporting of error corrections. First, when an error that affects the financial statements of the current period is discovered before the statements are issued, the corrected amounts should be reported. Second, when an error affects the financial statements of prior periods, the effect of the error on prior periods should be reported as a *prior period adjustment* of beginning retained earnings and the financial statements of the prior periods presented for comparative purposes should be retroactively restated to correct the effects of the error. These two reporting principles apply to all errors, whether or not a correcting journal entry is required to adjust the accounts for the effects of an error.

15. Although the potential uniqueness of errors makes it difficult to formulate any specific procedures that can be applied to correct all errors, the following four steps are helpful in situations involving errors:

a. Determine the journal entry that was recorded incorrectly or omitted erroneously.
b. Determine the journal entry that should have been recorded.
c. Determine the effects of the error on the current financial statements and those of any prior periods.
d. Determine what journal entry (if any) is required to correct the accounts for the effects of the error and determine how the financial statements of prior periods should be restated, if necessary.

The specific journal entry that may be required to correct the accounts for the effects of an error typically depends on whether the error is discovered in the period in which it is made or in a subsequent period; whether the accounting entity is subject to income taxes and, if so, whether or not income taxes for the period have been recorded; whether the error is discovered before or after the books have been closed; and the type of error. When an error that affects income is discovered in the period in which it is made, for example, the expense or revenue account and the asset or liability account (and/or related contra account) affected by the error should be adjusted by the full amount of the error. In addition, if the accounting entity is subject to income taxes and income taxes have been recorded for the current period, income tax expense and the appropriate income tax real account, such as income taxes payable or deferred tax liability, should be adjusted by the tax effect of the error. No adjustment of retained earnings or retroactive restatement of the financial statements of prior periods is required, since the error affects the current period only. Nonetheless, the corrected amounts

should be reported in the financial statements of the current period. Accounting for and reporting of other common types of errors are described in the remainder of this section. For the purpose of discussion, errors are grouped into three categories: classification errors that do not affect income, counterbalancing errors, and noncounterbalancing errors.

16. Classification errors with no effect on income. *A classification error that does not affect income* involves an error in the classification of an item on either the balance sheet or the income statement. If a classification error is discovered before the financial statements are issued, the statements should be corrected to show the proper classification. Similarly, if a classification error relates to financial statements of prior periods, those statements should be corrected to show the proper classification when they are presented for comparative purposes. No correcting journal entry is required for a classification error that does not affect income unless the error relates to an item that is incorrectly classified in real accounts or in nominal accounts that have not yet been closed.

17. Counterbalancing errors. *Counterbalancing errors* are errors that are automatically corrected in the accounts through the recording process over a two-year period. The understatement or overstatement of net income caused by a counterbalancing error in one year is automatically offset by an understatement or overstatement of the following year's net income in the opposite direction. Counterbalancing errors usually involve such accounts as inventories, prepayments, and accruals. Examples of counterbalancing errors include an understatement or overstatement of inventory, failure to allocate prepaid expenditures or unearned revenues to the period or periods in which the expense is incurred or the revenue is earned, and failure to accrue expenses incurred or revenues earned.

18. As a general rule, no correcting journal entry is required for a counterbalancing error that is discovered in the following period after the books have been closed, since the error has been automatically corrected in the accounts through the recording process over the two-year period. Nonetheless, the correct amounts should be reported in the financial statements of the current period. Furthermore, the effect of the error on the financial statements of the previous period should be reported as a prior period adjustment of beginning retained earnings, and the financial statements of the previous period presented for comparative purposes should be retroactively restated to correct the effects of the error.

19. Conversely, a correcting journal entry is required for a counterbalancing error that is discovered in the following period before the books have been closed, since the error has not yet been automatically corrected in the accounts through the recording process over the two-year period. In this circumstance, if the accounting entity is not subject to income taxes, the correcting journal entry should normally include the following two elements: (*a*) either the expense or revenue account affected by the error during the current period or the asset or liability account (and/or related contra account) affected by the error in the preceding period should be adjusted by the full amount of the error, depending on whether or not the counterbalancing effect of the error had been recorded during the current period, respectively; and (*b*) the effect of the error should be recorded as either an adjustment directly to retained earnings or a prior period adjustment—error correction, which is subsequently closed to retained earnings. In addition, if the accounting entity is subject to income taxes, this correcting journal entry should be modified as follows: (*a*) retained earnings or prior period adjustment—error correction should be adjusted by the net-of-tax effect, rather than the full amount, of the error, and (*b*) either income tax expense or the appropriate income tax real account, such as income taxes payable or deferred tax liability, should be adjusted by the tax effect of the error, depending on whether or not income taxes have been recorded during the current period, respectively. Finally, in all of these cases, the corrected account balances should be reported in the financial statements of the current period, the effect of the error on the financial statements of the previous period should be reported as a prior period adjustment of beginning retained earnings, and the financial statements of the previous period presented for comparative purposes should be retroactively restated to correct the effects of the error.

20. Occasionally, a counterbalancing error has no effect on net income. An overstatement or understatement of inventory accompanied by a corresponding overstatement or understatement of purchases is such an error. Since this error has no effect on net income, the correcting journal entry, if required, normally does not include an adjustment to retained earnings. A correcting journal entry to adjust the beginning inventory and purchases of the current period may be necessary, however, if the books have not been closed. Moreover, the corrected amounts should be reported in the financial statements of the current period, and the financial statements of the previous period presented for comparative purposes should be retroactively restated to correct the effects of the error.

21. Noncounterbalancing errors. *Noncounterbalancing errors* are errors that are not automatically corrected in the accounts through the recording process over a two-year period. Errors of this type typically involve long-lived assets and long-term liabilities.

22. When a noncounterbalancing error is discovered in a subsequent period after the books have been closed and the accounting entity is not subject to income taxes, the correcting journal entry normally should include adjustments of (*a*) the asset or liability account (and/or related contra account) affected by the error and (*b*) retained earnings, by the effect of the error through the end of the current period. In addition, if the accounting entry is subject to income taxes, this correcting journal entry should be modified as follows: (*a*) retained earnings should be adjusted by the net-of-tax effect, rather than the full effect, of the error through the end of the current period, and (*b*) the appropriate income tax real account, such as income taxes payable or deferred tax liability, should be adjusted by the full tax effect of the error through the end of the current period. In both circumstances, the correcting journal entry does not include any adjustments to nominal accounts, since the books have been closed. Nonetheless, the correct amounts should be reported in the financial statements of the current period. Furthermore, the effect of the error on the financial statements of prior periods should be reported as a prior period adjustment of beginning retained earnings, and the financial statements of prior periods presented for comparative purposes should be retroactively restated to correct the effects of the error.

23. When a noncounterbalancing error is discovered in a subsequent period before the books have been closed and the accounting entity is not subject to income taxes, the correcting journal entry should normally include the following three elements: (*a*) the asset or liability account (and/or related contra account) affected by the error should be adjusted by the full effect of the error through the end of the current period, (*b*) the effect of the error through the end of the previous period should be recorded as either an adjustment directly to retained earnings or a prior period adjustment—error correction, and (*c*) the expense or revenue account affected by the error should be adjusted by the full effect of the error on the current period. The first two elements of this correcting journal entry are equivalent to those for a noncounterbalancing error that is discovered after the books have been closed, since the accounts involved are real accounts. However, since the books have not been closed, retained earnings is adjusted only for the effect of the error through the end of the previous period and the appropriate nominal accounts are adjusted for the effects of the error on the current period. In addition, if the accounting entity is subject to income taxes and income taxes have been recorded for the current period, this correcting entry should be modified as follows: (*a*) retained earnings or prior period adjustment—error correction should be adjusted by the net-of-tax effect, rather than the full effect, of the error through the end of the previous period; (b) the appropriate income tax real account, such as income taxes payable or deferred tax liability, should be adjusted by the full tax effect of the error through the end of the current period; and (c) income tax expense should be adjusted by the tax effect of the error on the current period. Alternatively, if income taxes have not yet been recorded for the current period, the appropriate income tax real account, such as income taxes payable or deferred tax liability, should be adjusted only by the full tax effect of the error through the end of the previous period and income tax expense should not be adjusted, since the account currently has a zero balance. In this situation, income tax expense and income taxes payable for the current period are calculated and recorded later on the basis of income before taxes after correction for the effects of the error. Finally, as with all errors, the corrected amounts should be reported in the financial statements of the current period, the effect of the error on the financial statements of prior periods should be reported as a prior period adjustment of beginning retained earnings, and the financial statements of prior periods presented for comparative purposes should be retroactively restated to correct the effects of the error.

Appendix: Worksheet Analysis for Errors

24. When a company has made numerous errors, a worksheet may facilitate the analysis of the effects of the errors. The worksheet illustrated in the text's appendix contains a column for each year affected by the errors and a column for the correcting journal entries. The effect of each error on income before taxes is placed in the column or columns for the year or years affected by the error. The correcting journal entry for each error then is placed in the right-hand column next to the analysis of the effects of the error on income before taxes. The adjustments included in the correcting journal entries are determined by means of the analytical procedures described earlier for counterbalancing and noncounterbalancing errors, except that there are no adjustments of income tax accounts and the adjustments to retained earnings are not net of the related tax effects. The tax effects of all errors are considered after the analysis of the errors has been completed. The correcting journal entry to record the tax effects of the errors also is placed in the right-hand column of the worksheet. Finally, the net income adjustments are added to or deducted from the previously reported net income amounts to arrive at the corrected net income amounts.

SELF-STUDY LEARNING

Key Terms and Concepts

Provide the appropriate term or terms to complete each of the following statements:

1. A change from one generally accepted accounting principle to another generally accepted accounting principle is a(n) _____.

2. The difference between the amount of retained earnings at the beginning of the period in which there is a change in accounting principle and the amount of retained earnings that would have been reported if the new accounting principle had been applied in all prior periods is called the _____.

3. Amounts reported on the income statement for a change in accounting principle as if the new accounting principle had been applied in all periods presented are called _____.

4. An accounting change that results from new information or subsequent developments, and accordingly from better insight or improved judgment, is a(n) _____.

5. The effect of a change in accounting estimate should be accounted for in the current period or in the current and future periods, that is, _____.

6. A special type of accounting change that involves the presentation of financial statements for a new accounting entity is a(n) _____ .

7. A mathematical mistake, use of an incorrect accounting principle, or oversight or misuse of available facts that has an effect on the financial statements is a(n) _____.

8. Financial statements of prior periods presented for comparative purposes should be _____ to correct the effects of errors and to reflect special changes in accounting principle.

9. The cumulative effect of an error on financial statements of prior periods is called a(n) _____.

10. An error that is automatically corrected in the accounts through the recording process over a two-year period is called a(n) _____; an error that is not automatically corrected in the accounts through the recording process over a two-year period is called a(n) _____.

True-False

Indicate by circling the appropriate response whether each of the following statements is true (T) or false (F):

T F 1. A change in the method of applying an accounting principle is a change in accounting principle.

T F 2. A change from an accounting principle that is not generally accepted to one that is generally accepted is a change in accounting principle.

T F 3. The cumulative effect of a change in accounting principle, if determinable, should be reported either in the income statement of the period of the change or as an adjustment of beginning retained earnings, depending on the type of change.

T F 4. As a general requirement, the cumulative effect of a change in accounting principle must be reported in the income statement of the period of the change, because the restatement of financial statements of prior periods to reflect the effects of the change could cause financial statement users to question the reliability and credibility of financial reporting.

T F 5. When the cumulative effect of a change in accounting principle is not determinable, the financial statements of prior periods presented for comparative purposes should be retroactively restated to reflect the effects of the change.

T F 6. The cumulative effect of certain changes in accounting principle should be reported as an adjustment of beginning retained earnings, and the financial statements of all prior periods presented for comparative purposes should be retroactively restated to reflect the effects of the change.

T F 7. Pro forma amounts—amounts reported as if the new accounting principle had been applied in all periods presented—should be reported on the income statement whenever a change in accounting principle has been made.

T F 8. The pro forma amounts that should be reported on the income statement when a change in accounting principle has been made are essentially equivalent to the income amounts that would otherwise be reported if the financial statements of prior periods were retroactively restated to reflect the effects of the change.

T F 9. The manner of reporting the effects of a change in accounting principle does not necessarily affect the substance of the journal entry required to record the change.

T F 10. When a change in accounting estimate has been made, the amounts reported in the financial statements of prior periods presented for comparative purposes should be based on the original estimate.

T F 11. The effect of a change in accounting estimate on financial statements of prior periods should be reported in the income statement between extraordinary items and net income.

T F 12. A change in the reporting entity should be reported by restating the financial statements of all prior periods presented for comparative purposes.

T F 13. When an error that affects the financial statements of the current period is discovered before the statements are issued, the corrected amounts should be reported even if the books have been closed.

T F 14. The effect of an error on financial statements of prior periods should be reported as a prior period adjustment of beginning retained earnings, but the financial statements of the prior periods presented for comparative purposes should be presented as they were previously reported.

T F 15. No correcting journal entry is required when an error is discovered after the books have been closed.

T F 16. A correcting journal entry is required for a counterbalancing error that is discovered in the following period before the books have been closed, since the error has not yet been automatically corrected in the accounts.

T F 17. The correcting journal entry for an error involving an overstatement or understatement of inventory accompanied by a corresponding overstatement or understatement of purchases normally does not include an adjustment to retained earnings, since the error has no effect on net income.

T F 18. The journal entry to correct a non-counterbalancing error that is discovered after the books have been closed does not include any adjustment of nominal accounts.

T F 19. In a journal entry to correct a non-counterbalancing error, retained earnings always should be adjusted for the effect of the error through the end of the previous period.

T F 20. When a counterbalancing error is discovered in the following period before the books have been closed but after the counterbalancing effect of the error has been recorded, the correcting journal entry should include an adjustment of the asset or liability affected by the error in the preceding period.

Multiple Choice

Select the best response for each of the following items, and circle the corresponding letter:

1. Which of the following is the general requirement for reporting the effect of a change in accounting principle?

   a. The cumulative effect of the change on prior periods should be reported prospectively in the period of the change and future periods.
   b. The cumulative effect of the change on prior periods should be reported as a prior period adjustment of beginning retained earnings.
   c. The cumulative effect of the change on prior periods should be reported in the income statement between extraordinary items and net income.
   d. The financial statements of prior periods presented for comparative purposes should be retroactively restated to reflect the effects of the change.

2. The cumulative effect of which of the following changes in accounting principle should be reported in the income statement?

   a. A change in accounting principle whose cumulative effect is not determinable, such as a change to the LIFO method of inventory pricing.
   b. A change from the LIFO method of inventory pricing to another method.
   c. A change from the completed-contract method to the percentage-of-completion method of accounting for long-term construction contracts.
   d. A change from the straight-line method to an accelerated method of depreciating previously recorded assets.

3. The journal entry to record a change in accounting principle generally should *not* include:

   a. An adjustment of the asset or liability account affected by the change to the amount it would have been at the beginning of the period if the new accounting principle had been applied in all prior periods.
   b. A debit or credit to cumulative effect of change in accounting principle for the difference between the amount of retained earnings at the beginning of the period of the change and the amount of retained earnings that would have been reported if the new accounting principle had been applied in all prior periods.
   c. An adjustment of retained earnings to the amount it would have been if the new accounting principle had been applied in all prior periods.
   d. An adjustment of the appropriate income tax real account, such as deferred tax liability or income taxes payable, to reflect the tax effect of the change on all prior periods.

4. Which of the following is *not* part of the general requirement for reporting the effects of a change in accounting principle in the financial statements?

   a. The amounts reported in the financial statements of prior periods presented for comparative purposes should be based on the accounting principle that was previously applied.
   b. The cumulative effect of the change on all prior periods should be included in the determination of the net income of the period of the change.
   c. With the exception of the cumulative effect of the change, the amounts reported in the financial statements of the period of the change should be the amounts that would have been reported if the new accounting principle had been applied in all prior periods.
   d. The amounts reported in the financial statements of prior periods presented for comparative purposes should be the amounts that would have been reported if the new accounting principle had been applied in those periods.

5. When a change in accounting principle is appropriately reported by retroactively restating the financial statements of prior periods:

   a. The cumulative effect of the change on prior periods should be reported in the income statement of the period of the change.
   b. The cumulative effect of the change on prior periods should be reported as an adjustment of beginning retained earnings.
   c. Pro forma amounts—amounts presented as if the new accounting principle had been applied in all prior periods—should be reported on the income statement of the period of the change.
   d. The financial statements of prior periods included for comparative purposes should be presented as they were previously reported.

6. The financial statements of prior periods presented for comparative purposes should be retroactively restated to reflect:

   a. A change in accounting principle.
   b. A change in accounting estimate.
   c. A correction of an error in previous financial statements.
   d. A correction of an error that affects the financial statements of the current period only.

7. When an error that was made in the preceding period is discovered in the following period after the books have been closed, a correcting journal entry is required for:

   a. A classification error involving nominal accounts that does not affect income.
   b. A counterbalancing error.
   c. A noncounterbalancing error.
   d. All types of errors.

8. No correcting journal entry is required for:

   a. A counterbalancing error that is discovered in the following period before the books have been closed.
   b. A counterbalancing error that is discovered in the following period after the books have been closed.
   c. A noncounterbalancing error that is discovered in a subsequent period before the books have been closed.
   d. A noncounterbalancing error that is discovered in a subsequent period after the books have been closed.

9. Assuming the books of the current year have not been closed, the correcting journal entry required to adjust the accounts for an error involving interest paid during the current year that was erroneously not accrued in the previous year should include:

   a. A debit to interest payable and a credit to interest expense.
   b. A debit to interest payable and a credit to retained earnings.

c. A debit to retained earnings and a credit to cash.

d. A debit to retained earnings and a credit to interest expense.

10. Assuming the books of the current year have been closed, the correcting journal entry required to adjust the accounts for an error involving an expenditure that was incorrectly expensed when

it was incurred in the preceding year rather than capitalized and depreciated should *not* include:

a. A debit to the appropriate asset account and a credit to the accumulated depreciation.

b. A credit to retained earnings.

c. A credit to income taxes payable or deferred tax liability.

d. A debit to depreciation expense and a credit to income tax expense.

Extended Problem

Standard Corporation, a wholesaler of office supplies, was organized in 1992. Presented here are the company's income statement and statement of retained earnings as previously reported for the year ended December 31, 1994, and a partially completed income statement and statement of retained earnings for the year ended December 31, 1995.

Standard Corporation

INCOME STATEMENT
FOR THE YEARS ENDED
DECEMBER 31, 1995 AND 1994

	1995	1994
Sales	$600,000	$500,000
Cost of goods sold	$295,000	$255,000
Salaries and wages expense	92,000	78,000
Depreciation expense—building		16,000
Depreciation expense—equipment		15,000
Insurance expense		12,000
Other operating expenses	33,140	22,000
Income tax expense		40,800
Total expenses	$	$438,800
Income before extraordinary item	$	$ 61,200
Extraordinary item—gain on retirement of debt before applicable income taxes	5,000	-0-
Net income	$	$ 61,200

Standard Corporation

STATEMENT OF RETAINED EARNINGS
FOR THE YEARS ENDED
DECEMBER 31, 1995 AND 1994

	1995	1994
Retained earnings, 1/1	$136,200	$ 95,000
Net income		61,200
Dividends	(30,000)	(20,000)
Retained earnings, 12/31	$	$136,200

Additional information:

a. At the beginning of 1995, the company changed from the straight-line method to the

double-declining-balance method of depreciating all its equipment. The double-declining-balance method has been used for tax purposes in prior years. Data regarding the depreciation under the two methods follow:

YEAR	STRAIGHT-LINE	DOUBLE-DECLINING-BALANCE	DIFFERENCE
1992	$15,000	$30,000	$15,000
1993	15,000	24,000	9,000
1994	15,000	19,200	4,200
1995	15,000	15,360	360
Total	$60,000	$88,560	$28,560

b. The company has one building, which was acquired at the beginning of 1992 at a cost of $400,000. The company has been depreciating the building by the straight-line method on the basis of an estimated useful life of 25 years with no salvage value. At the beginning of 1995, the estimated useful life of the building is changed to 30 total years (or 27 remaining years) with a salvage value of $14,500.

c. An examination of the company's records discloses three errors that have not yet been corrected in the accounts: salaries and wages payable of $2,000 as of December 31, 1994, were not accrued at the end of 1994, but rather they were recorded as salaries and wages expense when they were paid in 1995; the physical inventory as of December 31, 1994, was understated by $5,000; and an insurance premium of $12,000 covering the three years starting January 1, 1994, was recorded as an expense when it was paid at the beginning of 1994. The company uses the periodic system of accounting for inventory.

d. The income tax rate for all years is 40 percent, and there are no permanent differences between pretax financial income and taxable income.

REQUIRED

a. Prepare the journal entry required to record the change from the straight-line method to the double-declining-balance method of depreciating the equipment.

b. Prepare the journal entries required to record depreciation on the equipment and building for 1995.

c. Prepare the correcting journal entry required, if any, to adjust the accounts for the effects of the error related to salaries and wages for each of the following alternative circumstances: (*1*) assuming that income taxes have not been recorded and the books have not been closed for 1995, (*2*) assuming that income taxes have been recorded but the books have not been closed for 1995, and (*3*) assuming that the books have been closed for 1995.

d. Prepare the correcting journal entry required, if any, to adjust the accounts for the effects of the error related to inventory for each of the following alternative circumstances: (*1*) assuming that income taxes have not been recorded and the books have not been closed for 1995, (*2*) assuming that income taxes have been recorded but the books have not been closed for 1995, and (*3*) assuming that the books have been closed for 1995.

e. Prepare the correcting journal entry required, if any, to adjust the accounts for the effects of the error related to insurance for each of the following alternative circumstances: (*1*) assuming that income taxes have not been recorded and the books have not been closed for 1995, (*2*) assuming that income taxes have been recorded but the books have not been closed for 1995, and (*3*) assuming that the books have been closed for 1995.

f. Prepare a comparative income statement including pro forma amounts and a comparative statement of retained earnings for the years ended December 31, 1995 and 1994. Ignore earnings per share and all other required supplementary disclosures.

COMMON ERRORS

The first statement in each "common error" listed here is *incorrect*. Each incorrect statement is followed by a corrected statement and an explanation.

1. The cumulative effect of a change in accounting principle may be measured as the difference between the recorded amount of the asset or liability affected by the change and the amount it would have been if the new accounting principle had been applied in all prior periods. *Wrong*

The cumulative effect of a change in accounting principle may be measured as the difference between the recorded amount of the asset or liability affected by the change and the amount it would have been if the new accounting principle had been applied in all prior periods minus the tax effect of the change on all prior periods. *Right*

There are two methods of determining the cumulative effect of a change in accounting principle. Under one method, the cumulative effect is calculated indirectly as the residual amount of the journal entry to record the change in accounting principle, as follows: (*a*) the asset or liability account (or related contra account) affected by the change is adjusted to the amount it would have been if the

new accounting principle had been applied in all prior periods; (*b*) the appropriate income tax real account, such as income taxes payable or deferred tax liability, is adjusted by the tax effect of the change on all prior periods; and (c) the cumulative effect of change in accounting principle account is debited or credited for the difference between these two amounts. In other words, the cumulative effect of the change is measured as the difference between the recorded amount of the asset or liability affected by the change and the amount it would have been if the new accounting principle had been applied in all prior periods minus the tax effect of the change on all prior periods. In contrast, under the other method, the cumulative effect of the change is calculated directly rather than as a residual amount. Specifically, because the cumulative effect of a change in accounting principle conceptually is the cumulative effect of the change on prior years' income, it is equal to the difference between prior years' reported income and the prior years' income that would have been reported if the new accounting principle had been applied in all prior periods. Consequently, the cumulative effect of a change in accounting principle may also be measured as the difference between the recorded amount of retained earnings and the amount it would have been if the new accounting principle had been applied in all prior periods. Both methods of measuring the cumulative effect of a change in accounting principle yield the same amount. Notice further that the cumulative effect should be recorded and reported net of the applicable tax effect of the change on all prior periods.

2. A change in accounting principle may be recorded as of the end of the period of the change. If so, the amounts reported in the income statement for the period of the change should be based on the accounting principle that was previously applied, and the cumulative effect of the change should be measured as of the end of the period. *Wrong*

A change in accounting principle must be recorded as of the beginning of the period of the change. Thus the amounts reported in the income statement for the period of the change should be based on the new accounting principle, and the cumulative effect of the change should be measured as of the beginning of the period. *Right*

Opinion No. 20 requires that a change in accounting principle be recorded as of the beginning of the period of the change. Accordingly, the cumulative effect of the change should be measured as of that date, and the other amounts reported in the income statement for the period of the change should be based on the new accounting principle.

3. Pro forma net income for the period in which there is a change in accounting principle is equal to the reported net income for that period. *Wrong*

Pro forma net income for the period in which there is a change in accounting principle should be equal to the reported net income for that period exclusive of the cumulative effect of the change. *Right*

As a general requirement, net income for the period in which there is a change in accounting principle is equal to income before the cumulative effect of the change, determined on the basis of the new accounting principle, plus or minus the cumulative effect of the change on prior years' income. In contrast, the pro forma amounts are the amounts of income that would have been reported for each period presented if the new accounting principle had been applied during those periods. Since income before the cumulative effect of the change and the pro forma amounts both are based on the new accounting principle, the reported net income for the period of the change exclusive of the cumulative effect of the change should be the pro forma amount of net income disclosed for that period.

4. When the corrected amounts are appropriately reported in the income statement of the period in which an error is discovered, no amount should be reported as a prior period adjustment of beginning retained earnings. *Wrong*

When the corrected amounts are appropriately reported in the income statement of the period in which an error is discovered, no amount should be reported as a prior period adjustment of beginning retained earnings if the error had no effect on reported net income of prior periods. Otherwise, the reporting of the corrected amounts in the income statement of the period in which an error is discovered does not supplant the requirement to report the effect of the error on prior periods as an adjustment of beginning retained earnings. *Right*

When an error that affects the financial statements of the current period is discovered before the statements are issued, the corrected amounts should be reported. An error may affect the financial statements of the current period only. A counterbalancing or noncounterbalancing error, for example, may be discovered before the financial statements of the period in which the error originates are issued. If so, the corrected amounts should be reported in the financial statements. Furthermore, because the error is discovered before the statements are issued, it has no effect on the financial statements of prior periods and thus no prior period adjustment of beginning retained earnings should be reported. In contrast, if a counterbalancing or noncounterbalancing error is discovered after the period in which it originates, the error has an effect on the financial statements of prior periods and thus a prior period adjustment of beginning retained earnings should be reported. Additionally, the corrected amounts should be reported in the financial statements of the current period, and the financial statements of prior periods presented for comparative purposes should be retroactively restated to correct the effects of the error.

5. The amount recorded as an adjustment to retained earnings for the effect of an error is always the same amount that should be reported in the financial statements as a prior period adjustment of beginning retained earnings. *Wrong*

The amount recorded as an adjustment to retained earnings for the effect of an error is the same amount that should be reported in the financial statements as a prior period adjustment of beginning retained earnings only if the error is discovered and corrected before the books have been closed. *Right*

When an error is discovered after the books have been closed, the effects of the error through the end of the period in which it is discovered have been closed to retained earnings. In this circumstance, the amount recorded as an adjustment to retained earnings accordingly should include the effects of the error on both the prior periods and the current period. The amount reported in the financial statements as a prior period adjustment of beginning retained earnings, however, should be the effect of the error on the financial statements of prior periods only. Thus when an error is discovered after the books have been closed, the amount recorded as an adjustment to retained earnings usually differs from the amount that should be reported in the financial statements as a prior period adjustment of beginning retained earnings. In contrast, when an error is discovered before the books have been closed, the effects of the error on the current period have not been closed to retained earnings. In this circumstance, the correcting journal entry accordingly should include an adjustment to a revenue or expense account for the effect of the error on the current period and an adjustment to retained earnings for the effect of the error on prior periods. Thus when an error is discovered and corrected before the books have been closed, the amount recorded as an adjustment to retained earnings is the same amount that should be reported in the financial statements as a prior period adjustment of beginning retained earnings.

6. The amount reported in the financial statements as a prior period adjustment of beginning retained earnings should be the full amount of the error in prior periods. *Wrong*

The amount reported in the financial statements as a prior period adjustment of beginning retained earnings should be the full amount of the error in prior periods minus the tax effect of the error. *Right*

An error in the amount of revenue or expense reported in the financial statements of a prior period normally causes an error in the amount of income tax expense reported for that period. Specifically, because an overstatement of revenue or an understatement of expense causes income before taxes to be overstated, income tax expense of that period will be overstated. Alternatively, because an understatement of revenue or an overstatement of expense causes income before taxes to be understated, income tax expense of that period will be understated. Thus the effect of an error on income before taxes is partially offset by an error in income tax expense in the same direction. Since the effects of both errors in prior periods are closed to retained earnings, the amount reported in the financial statements as a prior period adjustment of beginning retained earnings should be net of the applicable income taxes.

ANSWERS

Key Terms and Concepts

1. change in accounting principle
2. cumulative effect of change in accounting principle
3. pro forma amounts
4. change in accounting estimate
5. prospectively
6. change in reporting entity
7. accounting error
8. retroactively restated
9. prior period adjustment
10. counterbalancing error, noncounterbalancing error

True-False

1. T
2. F The use of an accounting principle that is not generally accepted is an error. Thus a change from an accounting principle that is not generally accepted to one that is generally accepted is a correction of an error rather than a change in accounting principle.
3. T
4. T
5. F When the cumulative effect of a change in accounting principle is not determinable, no cumulative effect is computed or reported and the financial statements of prior periods included for comparative purposes should be presented as they were previously reported. In this circumstance, the required disclosure is limited to a description of the effect of the change on the results of operations during the period of the change and to an explanation of the reason for the omission of accounting for the cumulative effect and of disclosure of pro forma amounts for prior periods.
6. T
7. F Pro forma amounts are required to be reported on the income statement only when the cumulative effect of a change in accounting principle is included in the determination of net income of the period of the change. No pro forma amounts

should be reported when the financial statements of prior periods presented for comparative purposes are retroactively restated to reflect the effects of a change in accounting principle, since the restated amounts are equivalent to the pro forma amounts that would otherwise be reported.

8. T
9. T
10. T
11. F   The cumulative effect of a change in accounting principle on financial statements of prior periods generally should be reported in the income statement between extraordinary items and net income. The effect of a change in accounting estimate, however, should be accounted for prospectively in the current period or in the current and future periods, and thus it should be reflected in the amounts reported in those periods for the revenue or expense affected by the change.

12. T
13. T
14. F   The effect of an error on financial statements of prior periods should be reported as a prior period adjustment of beginning retained earnings, and the financial statements of the prior periods presented for comparative purposes should be retroactively restated to correct the effects of the error.

15. F   No correcting journal entry normally is required for a counterbalancing error that is discovered in the following period after the books have been closed, since the error has been automatically corrected in the accounts through the recording process over the two-year period. A correcting journal entry, however, is required for a noncounterbalancing error that is discovered after the books have been closed, since the error has not been automatically corrected in the accounts through the recording process.

16. T
17. T

18. T
19. F   In a journal entry to correct a noncounterbalancing error, retained earnings should be adjusted for the effect of the error through the end of the previous period if the error is discovered in a subsequent period before the books have been closed. If a noncounterbalancing error is discovered in a subsequent period after the books have been closed, the effects of the error on the current period have been closed to retained earnings, and thus retained earnings should be adjusted for the effect of the error through the end of the current period.

20. F   The understatement or overstatement of expense or revenue in the period in which a counterbalancing error originates is automatically offset through the recording process in the following period by an understatement or overstatement of the same expense or revenue in the opposite direction. Thus if a counterbalancing error is discovered in the following period before the books have been closed but after the counterbalancing effect of the error has been recorded, the correcting journal entry should include an adjustment of the revenue or expense of the current period rather than the asset or liability affected by the error in the preceding period. Alternatively, if the counterbalancing effect of the error has not yet been recorded, the correcting journal entry should include an adjustment of the asset or liability affected by the error in the preceding period rather than the revenue or expense of the current period that would otherwise have been affected by the error.

Multiple Choice

1.	c	6.	c
2.	d	7.	c
3.	c	8.	b
4.	d	9.	d
5.	b	10.	d

Extended Problem

a.   Journal entry to record change in method of depreciation:[a]

1/1/95			
	Cumulative effect of change in accounting principle ($28,200 – $11,280)..........	16,920	
	Deferred tax liability ($28,200 × 40%)..	11,280	
	Accumulated depreciation—equipment ($15,000 + $9,000 + $4,200)...........		28,200

[a]Accumulated depreciation—equipment is adjusted at the beginning of the year to the amount it would have been if the double-declining-balance method had been applied in all prior periods; deferred tax liability, representing the tax effect of the temporary difference recognized in prior periods, is eliminated, since the temporary difference has been reversed by the change in accounting principle; and the difference between these two amounts, representing the effect of the change net of tax on all prior periods, is recorded as a cumulative effect of change in accounting principle.

b.   Journal entries to record depreciation:

12/31/95	Depreciation expense—equipment	15,360	
	Accumulated depreciation—equipment		15,360
12/31/95	Depreciation expense—building	12,500[a]	
	Accumulated depreciation—building		12,500

[a]Depreciation recorded each year has been $16,000 ($400,000 ÷ 25). Thus the accumulated depreciation at the beginning of 1995 is $48,000 ($16,000 × 3). To account for the change in estimates, the undepreciated cost less the estimated salvage value is depreciated over the estimated remaining useful life of the building as follows: ($400,000 – $48,000 – $14,500) ÷ 27 = $12,500.

c.   Correcting journal entry to adjust accounts for error related to salaries and wages:

(1). Income taxes not recorded and books not closed.[a]

12/31/95	Retained earnings (or prior adjustment—error correction) ($2,000 – $800).........	1,200	
	Income taxes payable ($2,000 × 40%)..	800	
	Salaries and wages expense..		2,000

[a]Salaries and wages expense for 1994 was understated by $2,000. Thus income before taxes was overstated by $2,000, income tax expense and income taxes payable were overstated by $800 ($2,000 × 40%), and retained earnings as of December 31, 1994, was overstated by $1,200 ($2,000 – $800). Furthermore, salaries and wages expense for 1995 is overstated by $2,000. Notice that if the error had been discovered before the salaries and wages had been paid in 1995, salaries and wages payable rather than expense would be credited for $2,000.

(2). Income taxes recorded but books not closed.[a]

12/31/95	Retained earnings (or prior period adjustment—error correction) ($2,000 – $800)	1,200	
	Income tax expense ($2,000 × 40%)...	800	
	Salaries and wages expense..		2,000

[a]Salaries and wages expense for 1995 is overstated by $2,000. Thus income before taxes is understated by $2,000, and income tax expense is understated by $800 ($2,000 × 40%). No adjustment of income taxes payable is required, since the net effect of the error on income before taxes over the two-year period is zero.

(3). Books closed.[a]

[a]The failure to accrue the salaries and wages payable as of December 31, 1994, is a counterbalancing error, which, after the books have been closed for 1995, has been automatically corrected in the accounts through the recording process over the two-year period. Thus no correcting journal entry is required.

d.   Correcting journal entry to adjust accounts for error related to inventory:

(1). Income taxes not recorded and books not closed.[a]

12/31/95	Inventory—beginning (or cost of goods sold)...	5,000	
	Retained earnings (or prior period adjustment—error correction)($5,000–$2,000)		3,000
	Income taxes payable ($5,000 × 40%)		2,000

[a]The physical inventory as of December 31, 1994, was understated by $5,000. Thus cost of goods sold was overstated by $5,000, income before taxes was understated by $5,000, income tax expense and income taxes payable were understated by $2,000 ($5,000 × 40%), and retained earnings as of December 31, 1994, was understated by $3,000 ($5,000 – $2,000). Furthermore, since the physical inventory as of December 31, 1994, was understated by $5,000, the beginning inventory or cost of goods sold for 1995 is understated by $5,000. The account debited depends on whether the beginning inventory has been transferred to cost of goods sold yet.

(2). Income taxes recorded but books not closed.[a]

12/31/95	Cost of goods sold..	5,000	
	Retained earnings (or prior period adjustment—error correction) ($5,000–$2,000)		3,000
	Income tax expense ($5,000 × 40%)...		2,000

[a]The beginning inventory as of January 1, 1995, was understated by $5,000. Thus cost of goods sold is understated by $5,000, income before taxes is overstated by $5,000, and income tax expense is overstated by $2,000 ($5,000 × 40%). No adjustment of income taxes payable is required, since the net effect of the error on income before taxes over the two-year period is zero.

(3). Books closed.[a]

[a]The understatement of the physical inventory as of December 31, 1994, is a counterbalancing error, which, after the books have been closed for 1995, has been automatically corrected in the accounts through the recording process over the two-year period. Thus no correcting journal entry is required.

e. Correcting journal entry to adjust accounts for error related to insurance:

(1). Income taxes not recorded and books not closed.[a]

12/31/95			
	Unexpired insurance [$12,000 – ($4,000 × 2)]	4,000	
	Insurance expense ($12,000 ÷ 3)	4,000	
	Retained earnings (or prior period adjustment—error correction)($8,000–$3,200)		4,800
	Income taxes payable ($8,000 × 40%)		3,200

[a]Insurance expense for 1994 was overstated by $8,000 [$12,000 – ($12,000 ÷ 3)]. Thus income before taxes was understated by $8,000, income tax expense and income taxes payable were understated by $3,200 ($8,000 × 40%), and retained earnings as of December 31, 1994, was understated by $4,800 ($8,000 – $3,200). Furthermore, as of December 31, 1995, the company has a right to one more year of insurance coverage [$12,000 – ($4,000 × 2)], and for 1995 one-third of the total premium is recorded as an expense.

(2). Income taxes recorded but books not closed.[a]

12/31/95			
	Unexpired insurance [$12,000 – ($4,000 × 2)]	4,000	
	Insurance expense ($12,000 ÷ 3)	4,000	
	Retained earnings (or prior period adjustment—error correction)($8,000–$3,200)		4,800
	Income tax expense ($4,000 × 40%)		1,600
	Income taxes payable ($4,000 × 40%)		1,600

[a]Insurance expense for 1995 is understated by $4,000. Thus income before taxes is overstated by $4,000, and income tax expense is overstated by $1,600 ($4,000 × 40%). Furthermore, since income before taxes over the two-year period is understated by $4,000 ($8,000 – $4,000), income taxes payable as of December 31, 1995, is understated by $1,600 ($4,000 × 40%).

(3). Books closed.[a]

12/31/95			
	Unexpired insurance [$12,000 – ($4,000 × 2)]	4,000	
	Retained earnings ($4,000 – $1,600)		2,400
	Income taxes payable ($4,000 × 40%)		1,600

[a]Insurance expense was overstated by $8,000 in 1994 and understated by $4,000 in 1995, income before taxes was understated by $8,000 in 1994 and overstated by $4,000 in 1995, and income tax expense was understated by $3,200 ($8,000 × 40%) in 1995 and overstated by $1,600 ($4,000 × 40%) in 1995. Collectively, the effect of the error on retained earnings as of December 31, 1995, is an understatement of $2,400 [$8,000 – $3,200) – ($4,000 – $1,600), or $4,000 – $1,600].

f. Comparative income statement and statement of retained earnings:

Standard Corporation

INCOME STATEMENT
FOR THE YEARS ENDED DECEMBER 31, 1995 AND 1994

	1995	1994
Sales	$600,000	$500,000
Cost of goods sold[a]	$300,000	$250,000
Salaries and wages expense[a]	90,000	80,000
Depreciation expense—building[b]	12,500	16,000
Depreciation expense—equipment[c]	15,360	15,000
Insurance expense[a]	4,000	4,000
Other operating expenses	33,140	22,000
	$455,000	$387,000
Income before taxes, extraordinary item, and cumulative effect of change in accounting principle	$145,000	$113,000
Income tax expense[a]	58,000	45,200
Income before extraordinary item and cumulative effect of change in accounting principle	$ 87,000	$ 67,800
Extraordinary item—gain on retirement of debt, net of applicable income taxes	3,000	-0-
Cumulative effect of change in accounting principle, net of applicable income taxes[c]	(16,920)	-0-
Net income	$ 73,080	$ 67,800
Pro forma amounts when new accounting principle is applied retroactively:[c]		
Income before extraordinary item	$ 87,000	$ 65,280
Net income	$ 90,000	$ 65,280

[a]The amounts reported for 1994 have been retroactively restated to correct the effects of the errors, and the corrected amounts are reported for 1995.
[b]The amount reported for 1994 is the amount that was previously reported, and the amount reported for 1995 is based on the revised estimates.
[c]The amount reported for 1994 is the amount that was previously reported, and the amount reported for 1995 is based on the new accounting principle. The cumulative effect of the change on prior years is reported between the extraordinary item and net income. The pro forma amounts are presented at the bottom of the statement. For 1995, pro forma net income is larger than reported net income by the amount of the cumulative effect of the change ($73,080 + $16,920); for 1994, pro forma net income is less than reported net income by the difference net of tax between the depreciation under the two methods [$4,200 – ($4,200 × 40%) = $2,520].

Standard Corporation

STATEMENT OF RETAINED EARNINGS
FOR THE YEARS ENDED DECEMBER 31, 1995 AND 1994

	1995	1994
Retained earnings, 1/1, as previously reported	$136,200	$ 95,000
Prior period adjustment for correction of errors, net of applicable income taxes[a]	6,600	-0-
Retained earnings, 1/1, as restated	$142,800	$ 95,000
Net income	73,080	67,800
Dividends	(30,000)	(20,000)
Retained earnings, 12/31[b]	$185,880	$142,800

[a]The amount reported as a prior period adjustment is the sum of the three adjustments to retained earnings in the correcting journal entries required when the books have not been closed ($3,000 + $4,800 − $1,200 = $6,600).

[b]Retained earnings as of December 31, 1994, is equal to the retained earnings as of January 1, 1995, as restated, because net income for 1994 has been restated to correct the effects of the errors.

20 EARNINGS PER SHARE

CHAPTER OBJECTIVES

After reading Chapter 20 and completing the questions, cases, exercises, and problems from the text chapter, you should be able to:

1. Calculate earnings per share (EPS) strictly on the basis of the weighted average number of shares of common stock actually outstanding during the period.
2. Describe the characteristics of potentially dilutive securities and the rationale for their inclusion in EPS calculations.
3. Determine whether a potentially dilutive security is dilutive or antidilutive.
4. Determine whether a corporation has a simple capital structure that requires a single presentation of earnings per common share or a complex capital structure that requires a dual presentation consisting of primary EPS and fully diluted EPS.
5. Distinguish among EPS based strictly on the weighted average number of shares of common stock actually outstanding during the period, primary EPS, and fully diluted EPS.
6. Classify potentially dilutive securities as either common stock equivalents that are included in both primary EPS and fully diluted EPS or other potentially dilutive securities that are included only in fully diluted EPS.
7. Adjust EPS calculations for the dilutive effect of stock options and warrants and their equivalents by the treasury stock method or, if the 20 percent test is met, by the modified treasury stock method.
8. Adjust EPS calculations for the dilutive effect of contingently issuable shares of common stock.
9. Adjust EPS calculations for the dilutive effect of convertible securities by the if-converted method.
10. Calculate primary EPS and fully diluted EPS.
11. Identify the per share amounts and related disclosures that are required to be presented in the financial statements.

CHAPTER REVIEW

Introduction

1. *Earnings per share* (EPS) of outstanding common stock probably is the most often mentioned and reported measure of a company's performance. Because of the importance placed on EPS by investors and creditors, the APB in *Opinion No. 15* established detailed guidelines for the uniform calculation and financial statement presentation of EPS amounts. Indeed, *Opinion No. 15* requires that certain EPS amounts be presented on the face of the income statement. Subsequently, however, the FASB suspended these EPS requirements for non-public companies. Moreover, because banks and national governments, instead of security markets, provide most of the capital for companies in many countries, there are only a few countries, such as the United States, Great Britain, and Japan, where disclosure of EPS amounts is required. EPS disclosures are also not required by the Directives of the European Community or by any *International Accounting Standard*. The complex standards that govern the calculation and financial statement presentation of EPS amounts by U.S. companies are described in this chapter review.

Basic EPS

2. EPS is the amount of income earned on each share of common stock outstanding during the period. The basic formulation of the EPS calculation (often called *basic EPS, earnings per common share,* or *EPS based strictly on weighted average common shares outstanding*) is as follows: income (or loss) for the period minus (or plus) income applicable to senior securities divided by the weighted average number of shares of common stock outstanding during the period.

3. Because EPS relates only to the residual claim of common stockholders on income, income applicable to senior securities must be deducted from income or added to a loss for the period in the numerator of EPS calculations in order to determine the income or loss applicable to common stock. Income applicable to senior securities is the claims on income that must be paid before the claims of the common shareholders. Among senior claims are dividends declared during the period on noncumulative preferred stock and dividends accumulating during the period on cumulative preferred stock.

4. The number of shares of common stock outstanding during the period, in the denominator of EPS calculations, must be weighted for the length of time those shares were outstanding in order to reflect the portion of the period during which the related capital or net assets were available to generate income. There are two methods of determining the weighted average number of shares of common stock outstanding during the period. Under one method, (*a*) the number of shares of common stock issued or acquired in each stock transaction during the period is multiplied by a weighting factor consisting of the number of months (or days) from the date of the transaction through the end of the period divided by the total number of months (or days) in the period, and (*b*) the products of these computations are added to or deducted from the number of shares of common stock outstanding at the beginning of the period. Under the other method, (*a*) the number of shares of common stock outstanding continuously for any interval of time during the period is multiplied by a weighting factor consisting of the number of months (or days) those shares were outstanding divided by the total number

of months (or days) in the period, and (*b*) the products of these computations are added together.

5. Several other technical aspects of the determination of the weighted average number of shares of common stock outstanding during the period should be noted. First, acquisition of treasury stock is treated the same as retirement of shares, and reissuance of treasury stock is treated the same as issuance of new shares. Second, conversion of convertible preferred stock or convertible bonds increases the number of shares of common stock outstanding from the date of conversion through the end of the period. Third, exercise of stock options, stock purchase rights, or stock warrants increases the number of shares of common stock outstanding from the date of exercise through the end of the period. Finally, shares issued in connection with stock dividends or stock splits must be treated retroactively as outstanding from the beginning of the period (or from the date the stock was issued, if later), both for the current period and for all prior periods that are presented for comparative purposes, even if the distribution occurs between the date of the financial statements and the date the financial statements are issued.

The Concept of Dilution

6. A *potentially dilutive security* is a security that is not a common stock but that usually contains provisions that enable the holder of the security to obtain shares of common stock through exercise or conversion of the security. Potentially dilutive securities include convertible preferred stock, convertible bonds, stock purchase rights, stock warrants, and contingent shares.

7. Potentially dilutive securities can be either dilutive or antidilutive. A potentially dilutive security is *dilutive* if assumed exercise or conversion of the security would decrease the amount that would otherwise be reported as earnings per share or increase the amount that would otherwise be reported as net loss per share. Conversely, a potentially dilutive security is *antidilutive* if assumed exercise or conversion of the security would increase the amount that would otherwise be reported as earnings per share or decrease the amount that would otherwise be reported as net loss per share. Potentially dilutive securities that are dilutive are included in EPS calculations in order to provide relevant and timely information about the effect that exercise or conversion of the securities could have on earnings per common share, whereas potentially dilutive securities that are antidilutive are excluded from EPS calculations.

8. There are two methods of determining whether a potentially dilutive security is dilutive or

antidilutive. Under one method, the numerator and denominator of the EPS calculations are adjusted for the effects of the assumed exercise or conversion of the potentially dilutive security, and the EPS after the security is included is compared with the EPS before the security is included. This method, for example, can be applied to determine whether a convertible bond is dilutive or antidilutive as follows: (*a*) income applicable to common stock (the numerator) is increased by the after-tax interest expense (interest expense multiplied by 1 minus the tax rate) that would not have been recognized during the period if the bond had been converted into common stock, (*b*) the weighted average number of shares of common stock outstanding during the period (the denominator) is increased by the weighted average number of additional shares that would have been outstanding during the period if the bond had been converted into common stock, (*c*) the adjusted income applicable to common stock for the period is divided by the adjusted weighted average number of shares of common stock outstanding during the period, and (*d*) the EPS after the convertible bond is included is compared with the EPS before the convertible bond is included. If the adjusted EPS is lower, the security is dilutive; if it is higher, the security is antidilutive. Under the other method, the EPS effect resulting from the assumed exercise or conversion of the potentially dilutive security is compared with the EPS before the security is included. This method can be applied to determine whether a convertible bond is dilutive or antidilutive as follows: (*a*) the additional after-tax income applicable to common stock (interest expense multiplied by 1 minus the tax rate) that would have been reported for the period if the bond had been converted into common stock is divided by the weighted average number of additional shares that would have been outstanding during the period if the bond had been converted into common stock, and (*b*) this amount (called *income per incremental common share effect*) is compared with the EPS before the convertible bond is included. If the income per incremental common share effect is lower, the security is dilutive; if it is higher, the security is antidilutive.

Simple Versus Complex Capital Structures

9. For the purposes of EPS calculations, *Opinion No. 15* requires that a corporation's capital structure be classified as either a simple capital structure or a complex capital structure. A *simple capital structure* is defined as a capital structure that either consists solely of common stock or includes no potentially dilutive securities that in the aggre-

gate could dilute EPS based strictly on the weighted average number of common shares actually outstanding during the period by 3 percent or more. Thus a corporation has a simple capital structure if during the period it either has no potentially dilutive securities or has potentially dilutive securities with less than a 3 percent (immaterial) aggregate dilutive effect on earnings per common share. In contrast, a *complex capital structure* is defined as a capital structure that includes common stock and potentially dilutive securities that in the aggregate could dilute EPS based strictly on the weighted average number of common shares actually outstanding during the period by 3 percent or more. Thus a corporation has a complex capital structure if during the period it has potentially dilutive securities with a 3 percent or more (material) aggregate dilutive effect on earnings per common share. It should be noted that (*a*) only potentially dilutive securities that individually are dilutive are included in the 3 percent test (that is, antidilutive securities are excluded), (*b*) the 3 percent test is an aggregate test that is applied to the combination of all potentially dilutive securities that individually are dilutive, and (*c*) a corporation may have a simple capital structure one period and a complex capital structure the next period, or vice versa.

10. A corporation with a simple capital structure is required to present only earnings per common share (basic EPS) on the face of the income statement, whereas a corporation with a complex capital structure is required to present two types of EPS data with equal prominence on the face of the income statement. These two types of EPS data are referred to as primary EPS and fully diluted EPS.

Primary EPS

11. The *primary EPS* calculation is equivalent to the basic EPS calculation except that the numerator and denominator are adjusted for the dilutive effects of assumed exercise or conversion of potentially dilutive securities classified as common stock equivalents. The difference between basic EPS and primary EPS is the dilution that results from the inclusion of common stock equivalents in the primary EPS calculation.

12. Common stock equivalents. A *common stock equivalent* is a security that in form is not a common stock but that usually contains provisions that enable the holder of the security to become a common stockholder, and thus its market value tends to change with changes in the market value of the common stock for which it can be exchanged. Common stock equivalents include:

a. Stock options and warrants and their equivalents, such as stock purchase contracts, stock subscriptions not fully paid, deferred compensation plans providing for the issuance of common stock, and convertible securities allowing or requiring the payment of cash at conversion.
b. Contingently issuable shares of common stock.
c. Convertible securities for which the effective yield rate is less than two-thirds of the average Aa corporate bond yield at the time the securities are issued.

Potentially dilutive securities that are not common stock equivalents are classified as *other potentially dilutive securities*. Other potentially dilutive securities are excluded from the primary EPS calculation, but are included in the fully diluted EPS calculation. That is, only potentially dilutive securities that are classified as common stock equivalents are included in the primary EPS calculation.

13. Stock options and warrants. *Stock options and warrants and their equivalents* are always classified as common stock equivalents. The dilutive effect of stock options and warrants and their equivalents is included in EPS calculations by means of a procedure called the treasury stock method. Under the *treasury stock method* in the primary EPS calculation, if the market price of the common stock has been greater than the exercise price of the stock options or warrants for *substantially all* (at least 11 weeks) of a quarter preceding the end of the period for which EPS data are being calculated, then (*a*) the stock options or warrants are assumed to have been exercised at the beginning of the period or at the date the stock options or warrants were issued, if later, and (*b*) any cash that would be received therefrom is assumed to have been used to purchase (buy back) shares of the corporation's common stock at the average market price during the period. And, if the result is dilutive, the weighted average number of incremental shares (shares assumed issued less shares assumed purchased) is added to the weighted average number of shares of common stock outstanding during the period in the denominator of the primary EPS calculation.

14. Several other technical aspects of the application of the treasury stock method in the primary EPS calculation should be noted. First, when stock options or warrants have been issued during the period, the assumed incremental shares of common stock outstanding must be weighted for the length of time from the issue date of the stock options or warrants through the end of the period. Second, when stock options or warrants have actually been exercised during the period, the assumed incremen-

tal shares of common stock outstanding must be weighted for the length of time from the beginning of the period (or the date the stock options or warrants were issued, if later) through the exercise date. Third, once the "substantially all" test is met, the treasury stock method should be applied only during those periods in which the average market price of the common stock is greater than the exercise price of the stock options or warrants. Conversely, if the average market price of the common stock for a period is less than the exercise price of the stock options or warrants, the application of the treasury stock method is antidilutive, and thus the stock options or warrants should be excluded from the primary EPS calculation for that period. Finally, if the number of common shares that are issuable under the exercise provisions of all stock options and warrants and their equivalents (including both dilutive and antidilutive securities) in the aggregate exceeds 20 percent of the number of common shares outstanding at the end of the period, then the treasury stock method is modified as follows: (*a*) all the stock options and warrants are assumed to have been exercised, and (*b*) the aggregate proceeds that would be received therefrom are assumed to have been used, in the following order, to purchase up to 20 percent of the outstanding shares of common stock at the average market price during the period, to reduce any short-term or long-term debt of the corporation, and to acquire U.S. government securities or commercial paper. Additionally, under the *modified treasury stock method,* income applicable to common stock in the numerator of the EPS calculation is increased by the after-tax interest on any assumed reduction of debt or assumed acquisition of U.S. government securities or commercial paper, and the weighted average number of shares of common stock outstanding in the denominator of the EPS calculation is increased by the incremental shares assumed to be outstanding. If the net effect is dilutive, all the stock options and warrants are included in the EPS calculation; if the net effect is antidilutive, they are excluded from the calculation.

15. Contingently issuable shares. *Contingently issuable shares of common stock* are shares of common stock that will be issued in the future upon the occurrence of some specified event. Contingently issuable shares of common stock are classified as common stock equivalents and are added to the weighted average number of shares of common stock outstanding during the period in the denominator of the primary EPS calculation if (*a*) the shares are to be issued upon the mere passage of time or (*b*) the shares are to be issued upon the attainment or maintenance of a specified level of income and that level is currently being attained.

16. Convertible securities. A *convertible security* is classified as a common stock equivalent if, at the time of issuance, it has an effective yield rate of less than two-thirds of the average Aa corporate bond yield for a brief period of time, such as one week, that includes or immediately precedes the date of issuance. The effective yield of a convertible security that has a stated maturity date (typically convertible bonds) is defined as the lowest of the rates, to maturity and to all call dates, that equate the aggregate present value of the stated annual interest or dividend payments and stated maturity or call values with the market price of the security at the time of issuance. The effective yield of a convertible security that has no stated maturity date (typically convertible preferred stock) is defined as the ratio of the stated annual interest or dividend payments to the market price of the security at the time of issuance. Furthermore, when the stated annual interest or dividend payments on the security are scheduled to change within the first five years after issuance, the lowest scheduled payments during those five years are used to determine the effective yield at the time of issuance.

17. The dilutive effect of convertible securities that are classified as common stock equivalents is included in the primary EPS calculation by means of a procedure called the if-converted method. Under the *if-converted method,* convertible securities are assumed to have been converted into common stock at the beginning of the period or the date the convertible securities were issued, if later. Specifically, if the result is dilutive, the numerator and denominator of the EPS calculation are adjusted for the assumed conversion of convertible securities as follows: (*a*) income applicable to common stock (the numerator) is increased by the after-tax interest expense on convertible bonds or by the dividends declared or accumulating on convertible preferred stock, which would not have occurred during the period if the bonds or preferred stock had been converted into common stock, and (*b*) the weighted average number of shares of common stock outstanding during the period (the denominator) is increased by the weighted average number of additional shares that would have been outstanding during the period if the bonds or preferred stock had been converted into common stock.

18. Several other technical aspects of the application of the if-converted method in the primary EPS calculation should be noted. First, when convertible securities have been issued during the period, the assumed new shares of common stock outstanding must be weighted for the length of time from the issue date of the convertible securities through the end of the period. Second, when convertible securities have actually been converted into shares of common stock during the period, the assumed new shares of common stock outstanding must be weighted for the length of time from the beginning of the period (or the date the convertible securities were issued, if later) through the conversion date. Finally, when the conversion privilege is not effective during the period, conversion is assumed in the primary EPS calculation only if the conversion privilege is effective within five years from the end of the period.

19. Order of entry into EPS calculation. When several common stock equivalent securities are to be considered at the same time for inclusion in the primary EPS calculation, the following steps should be applied in order to determine which of the securities are dilutive and thus should be included in the primary EPS calculation, and which securities are antidilutive and so should be excluded from the calculation: (*a*) the *income per incremental common share effect* (that is, the add-back adjustment of income applicable to common stock for dividends or after-tax interest expense, if any, divided by the weighted average number of incremental or additional common shares from assumed exercise or conversion) is calculated for each potentially dilutive security that is classified as a common stock equivalent; (*b*) the securities are ranked from the smallest income per incremental share effect to the largest income per incremental share effect; (*c*) the smallest income per incremental share effect is compared with the EPS before inclusion of the security under consideration, and if that EPS amount is larger, the security is included in the primary EPS calculation because it is dilutive; (*d*) a new EPS amount is calculated, with the dilutive effect of the security just tested included by means of the procedures described earlier for stock options and warrants, contingently issuable shares, and convertible securities; (*e*) the next smallest income per incremental share effect is compared with the new EPS amount, and if the new EPS amount is larger, the security is included in the primary EPS calculation because it is dilutive; (*f*) this process is continued, each increasing income per incremental share effect being tested in turn and the security under consideration being included in a new EPS amount, until an income per incremental share effect exceeds the previous EPS amount; and (*g*) the security just tested and those remaining on the list are excluded from the primary EPS calculation because these securities are antidilutive.

Fully Diluted EPS

20. The *fully diluted EPS* calculation is equivalent to the basic EPS calculation except that the numerator and denominator are adjusted for the dilutive effects of assumed exercise or conversion of both common stock equivalents and other potentially dilutive securities. The difference between primary EPS and fully diluted EPS is the additional dilution that results from slightly different treatment of some common stock equivalents when fully diluted EPS is calculated and from the inclusion of other potentially dilutive securities in the fully diluted EPS calculation. Thus fully diluted EPS is a more conservative measure than primary EPS because it reflects the maximum dilution effect of common stock equivalents as well as of all other potentially dilutive securities.

21. Other potentially dilutive securities. *Other potentially dilutive securities* are securities that usually contain provisions that enable their holders to become common shareholders by exercising or converting the securities, but that are not classified as common stock equivalents. Common stock equivalents are included in both the primary EPS calculation and the fully diluted EPS calculation, whereas other potentially dilutive securities are included only in the fully diluted EPS calculation.

22. Stock options and warrants. *Stock options and warrants and their equivalents* are included in both the primary EPS and the fully diluted EPS calculation by means of the treasury stock method or, if the 20 percent test is met, the modified treasury stock method. When the treasury stock method is applied in the fully diluted EPS calculation, however, the higher of the end-of-the-period market price or the average market price during the period is used as the assumed buy-back price to determine the number of shares of common stock assumed to have been purchased. Consequently, a stock option or warrant is included in fully diluted EPS when it is included in the primary EPS calculation or when the end-of-the-period market price of the common stock is greater than the exercise price of the stock option or warrant. Furthermore, it is possible that a stock option or warrant may be included in fully diluted EPS because the end-of-the-period market price of the common stock is greater than the exercise price of the stock option or warrant, but it may be excluded from the primary EPS calculation because the average market price of the common stock during the period is less than the exercise price. In all other respects, the application of the treasury stock method in the fully diluted EPS calculation is equivalent to its application in the primary EPS calculation.

23. Contingently issuable shares. *Contingently issuable shares of common stock* are included in both the primary EPS calculation and the fully diluted EPS calculation if (*a*) the shares are to be issued upon the mere passage of time or (*b*) the shares are to be issued upon the attainment or maintenance of a specified level of income and that level is currently being attained. However, when shares are to be issued upon the attainment or maintenance of a specified level of income but that level is not currently being attained, the contingent shares are included only in the fully diluted EPS calculation. Specifically, if such contingent shares are dilutive, the numerator and denominator of the EPS calculation are adjusted as follows: (*a*) income applicable to common stock (the numerator) is increased by the increased income that is required in order to reach the higher specified level, and (*b*) the weighted average number of shares of common stock outstanding during the period (the denominator) is increased by the new shares to be issued. In all other respects, the inclusion of contingently issuable shares of common stock in the fully diluted EPS calculation is equivalent to their inclusion in the primary EPS calculation.

24. Convertible securities. *Convertible securities* that are classified as common stock equivalents are included in both the primary EPS calculation and the fully diluted EPS calculation. However, convertible securities that are not classified as common stock equivalents (that is, those that either have an effective yield rate of two-thirds or more of the average Aa corporate bond yield at the time of issuance or are otherwise not classified as common stock equivalents) are included only in the fully diluted EPS calculation. The dilutive effect of convertible securities is included in the fully diluted EPS calculation by the if-converted method. When the conversion privilege is not effective during the period, conversion is assumed in the fully diluted EPS calculation if the conversion privilege is effective within 10 years of the end of the period. Furthermore, when convertible securities have actually been converted into shares of common stock during the period, the securities are assumed to have been converted at the beginning of the period or the date the convertible securities were issued, if later, in the fully diluted EPS calculation, whether the result is dilutive or antidilutive. In all other respects, the application of the if-converted method in the fully diluted EPS calculation is equivalent to its application in the primary EPS calculation.

25. Order of entry into EPS calculation. When several potentially dilutive securities are to be considered at the same time for inclusion in the fully diluted EPS calculation, the order of entry steps described earlier in regard to the primary EPS calculation should be applied to all potentially dilutive securities (that is, both common stock equivalents and other potentially dilutive securities) to determine which of the securities is dilutive (and thus should be included in the fully diluted EPS calculation), and which securities are antidilutive (and so should be excluded from the calculation).

Consequently, it is possible that a security may be included in primary EPS because it is a common stock equivalent and dilutes the primary EPS calculation, but it may be excluded from fully diluted EPS because it does not dilute the fully diluted EPS calculation. Thus fully diluted EPS should be calculated by adjusting the numerator and denominator of basic EPS, not primary EPS.

Financial Statement Presentation and Disclosure

26. A corporation with a simple capital structure is required to report a *single presentation* of earnings per common share (basic EPS) only, whereas a corporation with a complex capital structure is required to report a *dual presentation*, consisting of primary EPS and fully diluted EPS. Moreover, whether a single or dual presentation is required, per share amounts are required to be presented on the face of the income statement for (*a*) income or loss from continuing operations,

(*b*) income or loss before extraordinary items, (*c*) the cumulative effect of a change in accounting principle, and (*d*) net income or loss.

27. In addition, *Opinion No. 15* requires the following disclosures concerning the EPS data presented in the financial statements: (*a*) a summary explanation of the pertinent rights and privileges that accompany the various securities outstanding; (*b*) a schedule or footnote explaining the bases on which both primary EPS and fully diluted EPS are calculated, including identification of any securities regarded as common stock equivalents, identification of securities included in the calculation of fully diluted EPS, descriptions of all assumptions and resulting adjustments made to arrive at the EPS figures, and the number of shares issued upon conversion, exercise, or satisfaction of required conditions; (*c*) calculations and/or reconciliations, if necessary, to provide a clear understanding of how the EPS figures were derived; and (*d*) supplementary information about the effects of conversions after the balance sheet date but before issuance of the financial statements.

SELF-STUDY LEARNING

Key Terms and Concepts

Provide the appropriate term or terms to complete each of the following statements:

1. EPS is an acronym for _____.

2. In the basic formulation of the EPS calculation, the numerator is the _____ and the denominator is the _____.

3. Convertible preferred stock, convertible bonds, stock options and warrants, and contingent shares are examples of _____.

4. A security whose assumed exercise or conversion would cause a decrease in the amount that would otherwise be reported as earnings per share or an increase in the amount that would otherwise be reported as net loss per share is called a(n) _____; a security whose assumed exercise or conversion would cause an increase in the amount that would otherwise be reported as earnings per share or a decrease in the amount that would otherwise be reported as net loss per share is called a(n) _____.

5. A capital structure that either consists solely of common stock or includes no securities that upon exercise or conversion could, in the aggregate, dilute EPS based strictly on the weighted average number of common shares actually outstanding during the period by 3 percent or more is called a(n) _____;

a capital structure that includes common stock and other securities that upon exercise or conversion could, in the aggregate, dilute EPS based strictly on the weighted average number of common shares actually outstanding during the period by 3 percent or more is called a(n) _____.

6. A corporation whose capital structure consists solely of common stock is required to report a single presentation of _____ on the face of the income statement, whereas a corporation whose capital structure includes potentially dilutive securities with a 3 percent or more aggregate dilutive effect is required to report a dual presentation consisting of _____ and _____ on the face of the income statement.

7. The dilutive effect of stock options and warrants and their equivalents is included in EPS calculations by means of a procedure called the _____.

8. Shares of common stock that will be issued in the future upon the occurrence of some specified event, such as the passage of time or the attainment of a specified level of income, are called _____.

9. The dilutive effect of convertible securities is included in EPS calculations by means of a procedure called the _____.

10. Potentially dilutive securities that are included in both primary EPS and fully diluted EPS are called _____, whereas potentially dilutive securities that are included only in fully diluted EPS are called _____.

True-False

Indicate by circling the appropriate response whether each of the following statements is true (T) or false (F):

T F 1. Income for the period, in the numerator of EPS calculations, should be reduced by dividends declared on nonconvertible, noncumulative preferred stock during the period.

T F 2. The number of shares of common stock outstanding, in the denominator of EPS calculations, should be weighted for the length of time those shares were outstanding during the period.

T F 3. In the determination of the weighted average number of shares of common stock outstanding during the period, shares issued in connection with stock dividends or stock splits should be treated as outstanding from the beginning of the period or from the date the stock was issued, if later.

T F 4. All bonds and preferred stock are potentially dilutive securities.

T F 5. A potentially dilutive security is dilutive if EPS after inclusion of the security is less than EPS before inclusion of the security.

T F 6. EPS based strictly on the weighted average number of common shares actually outstanding during the period must always be presented on the face of the income statement.

T F 7. A corporation must present both primary EPS and fully diluted EPS on the face of the income statement if it has convertible securities outstanding during the period.

T F 8. A corporation may have a simple capital structure one period and a complex capital structure the next period, or vice versa.

T F 9. When all the potentially dilutive securities of a corporation are classified as common stock equivalents, fully diluted EPS should equal primary EPS.

T F 10. Potentially dilutive securities that are classified as common stock equivalents should always be included in primary EPS.

T F 11. A potentially dilutive security may be included in EPS calculations in one period because it is dilutive but not in the next period because it is anti-dilutive, or vice versa.

T F 12. A potentially dilutive security should be included in EPS calculations only if the rights associated with the security have actually been exercised or if the security has actually been converted into common stock during the period.

T F 13. Stock options and warrants and their equivalents should always be included in EPS calculations.

T F 14. Stock options and warrants should be included in primary EPS if the average market price of the common stock during the period exceeds the exercise price of the stock options or warrants.

T F 15. When the treasury stock method is used to calculate fully diluted EPS, stock options or warrants are assumed to have been exercised at the beginning of the period or at the date of issuance, if later, and any cash that would be received therefrom is assumed to have been used to purchase shares of the corporation's common stock at the higher of the end-of-the-period market price or the average market price for the period.

T F 16. It is possible that stock options and warrants may be included in fully diluted EPS but excluded from primary EPS.

T F 17. Convertible securities should be classified as common stock equivalents if the stated annual interest or dividend rate is less than two-thirds of the average Aa corporate bond yield at the time the securities are issued.

T F 18. In the common stock equivalency test for a convertible security that has no stated maturity date, the effective yield rate is the stated annual interest or dividend payments divided by the market price of the security at the end of the period.

T F 19. Convertible securities that are classified as common stock equivalents should be included in the primary EPS calculation only if the add-back adjustment of income applicable to common stock from assumed conversion of the security divided by the weighted average number of equivalent common shares from assumed conversion is less than EPS before inclusion of the security.

T F 20. When convertible securities are outstanding but the conversion privilege is not effective during the period, conversion should be assumed for neither primary EPS nor fully diluted EPS.

Multiple Choice

Select the best response for each of the following items, and circle the corresponding letter:

1. When nonconvertible, cumulative preferred stock is outstanding, income for the period in the numerator of EPS calculations should be reduced by:

   a. Dividends paid on the preferred stock during the period.
   b. Dividends declared on the preferred stock during the period.
   c. Dividends accumulating on the preferred stock during the period.
   d. Dividends in arrears on the preferred stock at the end of the period.

2. In the determination of the weighted average number of shares of common stock actually outstanding during the period for the purposes of EPS calculations:

   a. Treasury shares acquired should be treated as outstanding from the date of acquisition through the date of reissuance.
   b. Treasury shares reissued should be treated as outstanding from the date of acquisition through the date of reissuance.
   c. Shares issued upon conversion of convertible preferred stock or convertible bonds should be treated as outstanding from the date of conversion through the end of the period.
   d. Shares issued upon exercise of stock options or warrants should be treated as outstanding from the beginning of the period or from the date the stock options or warrants were issued, if later, through the end of the period.

3. A corporation is required to report a dual presentation consisting of primary EPS and fully diluted EPS if during the period it has:

   a. Common stock only.
   b. No potentially dilutive securities.
   c. Potentially dilutive securities with less than a 3 percent aggregate dilutive effect on earnings per common share.
   d. Potentially dilutive securities with a 3 percent or more aggregate dilutive effect on earnings per common share.

4. Potentially dilutive securities that are classified as common stock equivalents, if dilutive, should be included in:

   a. Primary EPS only.
   b. Fully diluted EPS only.
   c. Both primary EPS and fully diluted EPS.
   d. Neither primary EPS nor fully diluted EPS.

5. Potentially dilutive securities that are *not* classified as common stock equivalents, if dilutive, should be included in:

   a. Primary EPS only.
   b. Fully diluted EPS only.
   c. Both primary EPS and fully diluted EPS.
   d. Neither primary EPS nor fully diluted EPS.

6. When the treasury stock method is applied to calculate primary EPS, any cash hypothetically received upon the assumed exercise of the stock options or warrants is assumed to have been used to purchase the corporation's common stock at:

   a. The exercise price of the stock options or warrants.
   b. The average market price of the common stock during the period.
   c. The end-of-the-period market price of the common stock.
   d. The higher of the end-of-the-period market price of the common stock or the average market price of the common stock during the period.

7. Contingently issuable shares of common stock should be excluded from primary EPS but included in fully diluted EPS if the shares are to be issued:

   a. Upon the mere passage of time.
   b. Upon the attainment or maintenance of a specified level of income and that level is currently being attained.
   c. Upon the attainment or maintenance of a specified level of income, but that level is not currently being attained.
   d. Between five and ten years of the end of the period.

8. Convertible bonds should be classified as common stock equivalents for the purposes of EPS calculations if:

   a. The effective yield rate is less than two-thirds of the average Aa corporate bond yield at the time the securities are issued.
   b. The effective yield rate is less than two-thirds of the average Aa corporate bond yield at the end of the period.
   c. The stated annual interest rate is less than two-thirds of the average Aa corporate bond yield at the time the securities are issued.
   d. The stated annual interest rate is less than two-thirds of the average Aa corporate bond yield at the end of the period.

9. Under the if-converted method, the amount of the add-back adjustment of income applicable to common stock for convertible bonds should be:

   a. The interest paid or payable on the bonds for the period.
   b. The interest paid or payable on the bonds for the period multiplied by 1 minus the tax rate.
   c. The interest expense on the bonds for the period.
   d. The interest expense on the bonds for the period multiplied by 1 minus the tax rate.

10. For which of the following items is a per share amount *not* required to be presented on the face of the income statement?

   a. Income or loss from continuing operations.
   b. Income or loss from discontinued operations.
   c. Income or loss before extraordinary items.
   d. Net income or loss.

Extended Problem

Presented here are the long-term debt and stockholders' equity sections of the SPE Corporation's balance sheet as of December 31, 1995:

Long-term debt

7% convertible debentures, including unamortized premium of $112,500	$ 2,112,500
Other long-term debt, less current portion	1,000,000
Total long-term debt	$ 3,112,500

Stockholders' equity

$4 cumulative convertible preferred stock, par value $50 per share (authorized, 20,000 shares; issued, 10,000 shares; outstanding, 9,000 shares; liquidation preference $60 per share, aggregating $540,000)	$ 450,000
Common stock, par value $1 per share (authorized, 1,000,000 shares; issued, 500,000 shares, including 8,000 shares held in treasury)	500,000
Additional contributed capital	10,580,000
Retained earnings	2,820,000
Total	$14,350,000
Less cost of 8,000 shares of common stock held in treasury	200,000
Total stockholders' equity	$14,150,000
Total long-term debt and stockholders' equity	$17,262,500

Additional information:

a. The 7 percent convertible debentures were issued for $2,147,000 on January 1, 1993, at an effective yield of 6 percent, when the average Aa corporate bond yield was 10 percent. The bond interest is payable annually on January 1, and the bonds are scheduled to mature on January 1, 2003. The bond premium is being amortized by the effective interest method, and the unamortized balance at January 1, 1995, was $125,000. Each bond has a face value of $1,000 and is convertible into 40 shares of common stock. None of the bonds has been converted.

b. The $4 cumulative convertible preferred stock was issued at $52 per share on July 1, 1994, when the average Aa corporate bond yield was 11 percent. Each share of preferred stock is convertible into two shares of common stock. On April 1, 1995, 1,000 shares of preferred stock were converted into common stock. Quarterly dividends of $1 per share were declared and paid on the preferred stock during 1995.

c. On October 1, 1994, SPE Corporation granted options to its officers to purchase 50,000 shares of common stock at a price of $24 per share. None of the options has been exercised.

d. On January 1, 1995, SPE Corporation had 498,000 shares of common stock issued and outstanding. During 1995, SPE Corporation issued 2,000 shares of common stock on April 1 upon conversion of 1,000 shares of preferred stock; acquired 20,000 treasury shares of common stock on July 1 at a cost of $25 per share; and reissued 12,000 treasury shares of common stock on November 1 at $27 per share. Quarterly dividends of $.50 per share were declared and paid on the common stock during 1995.

e. The average and end-of-the-period market prices of SPE Corporation's common stock for 1995 were $25 and $30, respectively.

f. SPE Corporation's net income for the year ended December 31, 1995, was $1,511,500. The provision for income taxes was computed at a rate of 40 percent.

REQUIRED

a. Prepare a schedule that shows the evaluation of the common stock equivalency status of:
    (1). The convertible debentures.
    (2). The convertible preferred stock.
    (3). The stock options.

b. Prepare a schedule that shows for the year 1995 the calculation of:
    (1). EPS based strictly on the weighted average number of common shares actually outstanding during the period (basic EPS).
    (2). Primary EPS.
    (3). Fully diluted EPS.

COMMON ERRORS

The first statement in each "common error" listed here is *incorrect*. Each incorrect statement is followed by a corrected statement and an explanation.

1. The numerator of the basic EPS calculation is income for the period minus dividends paid on preferred stock during the period. *Wrong*

The numerator of the basic EPS calculation is income for the period minus dividends accumulating on cumulative preferred stock during the period or dividends declared on noncumulative preferred stock during the period. *Right*

Dividends other than stock dividends are distributions of assets by the corporation to its shareholders on a pro rata basis. Because the claims of preferred shareholders to dividends must be satisfied before those of common shareholders, dividends on preferred stock should be deducted from income for the period in order to determine income applicable to common stock. Preferred stock may be either cumulative or noncumulative. When preferred stock is cumulative, preferred dividends that accumulate during the period should be deducted from income, because the claims of the preferred shareholders to dividends accumulate even if they are not actually declared. In contrast, when preferred stock is noncumulative, only preferred dividends declared during the period should be deducted from income, because the claims of the preferred shareholders to dividends are limited to those actually declared.

2. Only potentially dilutive securities that have a dilutive effect of 3 percent or more are included in primary and/or fully diluted EPS calculations. *Wrong*

All potentially dilutive securities that have a dilutive effect should be included in primary and/or fully diluted EPS calculations. *Right*

A corporation with a complex capital structure is required to report a dual presentation consisting of primary EPS and fully diluted EPS. Because a complex capital structure is defined as one that includes potentially dilutive securities that could in the aggregate dilute earnings per common share by 3 percent or more, it is sometimes thought that a potentially dilutive security must have a dilutive effect of 3 percent or more in order to be included in primary and/or fully diluted EPS. The 3 percent test, however, is an aggregate (materiality) test that is applied to the combination of all potentially dilutive securities that individually have a dilutive effect. Thus when a corporation has a complex capital structure, all potentially dilutive securities that individually have a dilutive effect should be included in primary and/or fully diluted EPS.

3. The incremental shares added to the weighted average number of common shares actually outstanding during the period to include shares hypothetically issued on the assumed exercise of stock options or warrants is the weighted average number of shares issuable under the exercise provisions of the stock options or warrants. *Wrong*

The incremental shares added to the weighted average number of common shares actually outstanding during the period to include shares hypothetically issued on the assumed exercise of stock options or warrants should be the weighted average excess of the number of shares issuable under the exercise provisions of the stock options or warrants minus the number of shares assumed to have been purchased with any cash that would be received on the exercise of the stock options or warrants. *Right*

The dilutive effect of stock options and warrants is included in EPS calculations by means of a procedure called the treasury stock method. Under the treasury stock method, the stock options or warrants are assumed to have been exercised at the beginning of the period or at the date the stock options or warrants were issued, if later, and any cash that would be received therefrom is assumed to have been used to purchase (buy back) shares of the corporation's common stock. Thus, the weighted average excess of the number of shares assumed to have been issued minus the number of shares assumed to have been purchased is added to the weighted average number of common shares actually outstanding during the period in the denominator of the EPS calculations.

4. The treasury stock method is modified whenever the number of shares assumed to have been purchased in the aggregate exceeds 20 percent of the number of common shares outstanding at the end of the period. *Wrong*

The treasury stock method should be modified whenever the number of shares issuable under the exercise provisions of all stock options and warrants and their equivalents in the aggregate exceeds 20 percent of the number of common shares outstanding at the end of the period. *Right*

Under the modified treasury stock method, all stock options and warrants are assumed to have been exercised and the aggregate proceeds that would be received therefrom are assumed to have been used, in the following order, to purchase up to

20 percent of the outstanding shares of common stock, to reduce any short-term or long-term debt of the corporation and to acquire U.S. government securities or commercial paper. The treasury stock method should be modified, however, only if the number of shares issuable under the exercise provisions of all stock options and warrants and their equivalents in the aggregate exceeds 20 percent of the number of common shares outstanding. That is, a 20 percent test is applied to the number of shares issuable to determine whether the treasury stock method should be modified. And if the 20 percent test is met, a 20 percent limitation is applied to the number of shares assumed to have been purchased under the treasury stock method.

5. Convertible securities are classified as common stock equivalents if the stated annual interest or dividend rate is less than two-thirds of the average Aa corporate bond yield at the time the securities are issued. *Wrong*

Convertible securities should be classified as common stock equivalents if the effective yield rate is less than two-thirds of the average Aa corporate bond yield at the time the securities are issued. *Right*

APB Opinion No. 15, as amended, requires that the effective yield rate, at the time of issuance, be used to test the common stock equivalency status of convertible securities. The effective yield of a convertible security that has a stated maturity date (typically convertible bonds) is defined as the lowest of the rates, to maturity and to all call dates, that equate the aggregate present value of the stated annual interest or dividend payments and stated maturity or call values with the market price of the security at the time of issuance. The effective yield of a convertible security that has no stated maturity date (typically convertible preferred stock) is defined as the ratio of the stated annual interest or dividend payments to the market price of the security at the time of issuance. Consequently, when a noncallable convertible security is issued at its face or par value, the security's effective yield rate will equal its stated annual interest or dividend rate. Conversely, when a convertible security is issued at a premium or discount or when a convertible security is callable at a premium or discount, the security's effective yield rate will not equal its stated annual interest or dividend rate. In such circumstances, the convertible security's effective yield rate must be determined in accordance with the guidelines just described.

6. The add-back adjustment of income applicable to common stock on the assumed conversion of convertible bonds is the interest expense recognized on the bonds for the period. *Wrong*

The add-back adjustment of income applicable to common stock on the assumed conversion of convertible bonds should be the excess of the interest expense recognized on the bonds for the period minus the increased income taxes that would otherwise have been recognized for the period. *Right*

Under the if-converted method, income applicable to common stock in the numerator of EPS calculations is increased by the interest expense that would not have been recognized for the period if convertible bonds had been converted into common stock. Moreover, because interest is a tax-deductible expense, income applicable to common stock is also reduced by the increased income taxes that would have been recognized for the period if convertible bonds had been converted into common stock. Thus the add-back adjustment of income applicable to common stock on the assumed conversion of convertible bonds should be the excess of the interest expense recognized on the bonds for the period minus the increased income taxes that would otherwise have been recognized for the period. Incidentally, there are two methods of determining the after-tax interest adjustment of income applicable to common stock on the assumed conversion of convertible bonds. Under one method, interest expense is reduced by interest expense multiplied by the tax rate; under the other method, interest expense is multiplied by 1 minus the tax rate.

7. The after-tax interest adjustment of income applicable to common stock on the assumed conversion of convertible bonds is always the interest paid or payable on the bonds for the period multiplied by 1 minus the tax rate. *Wrong*

The after-tax interest adjustment of income applicable to common stock on the assumed conversion of convertible bonds should be the interest paid or payable on the bonds for the period plus any bond discount amortization or minus any bond premium amortization multiplied by 1 minus the tax rate. *Right*

When bonds are issued at their face value, interest expense is the interest paid or payable on the bonds for the period. Thus the after-tax interest adjustment of income applicable to common stock on the assumed conversion of convertible bonds that are issued at their face value is the interest paid or payable on the bonds for the period multiplied by 1 minus the tax rate. Conversely, when bonds are issued at an amount in excess of their face value, the difference (called a premium) is amortized as a reduction of interest expense over the life of the bonds. Alternatively, when bonds are issued at an amount less than their face value, the difference (called a discount) is amortized as an addition to interest expense over the life of the bonds. That is, when bonds are issued at an amount different from their face value, interest expense is interest paid or payable on the bonds for the period plus bond discount amortization or minus bond premium amortization. Consequently, the after-tax interest adjustment of income applicable to common stock on the assumed conversion of convertible bonds that are issued at an amount different from their face value should be the interest paid or payable on the bonds for the period plus bond discount amortization or minus bond premium amortization (determined by either the effective interest method or the straight-line method) multiplied by 1 minus the tax rate.

8. The amount added to the weighted average number of common shares actually outstanding during the period to include shares hypothetically issued on the assumed conversion of convertible securities always is the number of convertible securities multiplied by the conversion ratio. *Wrong*

The amount added to the weighted average number of common shares actually outstanding during the period to include shares hypothetically issued on the assumed conversion of convertible securities should be the number of convertible securities multiplied by the conversion ratio multiplied by the weighting factor for the length of time the convertible securities were outstanding during the period. *Right*

When convertible securities are outstanding at the beginning of the period and there are no conversions during the period, the amount added to the denominator for EPS calculations on the assumed conversion of the securities should be the number of convertible securities multiplied by the conversion ratio. Conversely, when convertible securities are issued during the period and there are no conversions, the amount added to the denominator for EPS calculations on the assumed conversion of the securities should be the number of convertible securities multiplied by the conversion ratio multiplied by the weighting factor for the length of time from the issue date through the end of the period. Moreover, when convertible securities actually are converted during the period, the amount added to the denominator for EPS calculations on the assumed conversion of the securities should be the number of convertible securities multiplied by the conversion ratio multiplied by the weighting factor for the length of time from the beginning of the period (or date of issuance, if later) through the conversion date. Thus when convertible securities are issued and/or converted during the period, the number of new shares added to the denominator for EPS calculations on the assumed conversion of the securities should be weighted for the length of time the convertible securities were outstanding during the period. Incidentally, it should be remembered that shares actually issued upon the conversion of convertible securities are included in the weighted average number of common shares actually outstanding during the period from the date of conversion through the end of the period.

ANSWERS

Key Terms and Concepts

1. earnings per share
2. income (or loss) for the period minus (or plus) income applicable to senior securities, weighted average number of shares of common stock outstanding during the period
3. potentially dilutive security
4. dilutive security, antidilutive security
5. simple capital structure, complex capital structure
6. earnings per common share (also called basic EPS or EPS based strictly on the weighted average number of common shares actually outstanding during the period), primary EPS, fully diluted EPS
7. treasury stock method
8. contingently issuable shares of common stock
9. if-converted method
10. common stock equivalents, other potentially dilutive securities

True-False

1. T
2. T
3. T
4. F Convertible bonds and convertible preferred stock are potentially dilutive securities, because they enable the holder to obtain shares of common stock through conversion of the security. Nonconvertible bonds and nonconvertible preferred stock, however, are not potentially dilutive securities.

5. T
6. F EPS based strictly on the weighted average number of common shares actually outstanding during the period must be presented on the face of the income statement if the corporation has a simple capital structure during the period or if the corporation has a complex capital structure during the period but has no common stock equivalent securities with a 3 percent or more aggregate dilutive effect.
7. F A corporation must present both primary EPS and fully diluted EPS on the face of the income statement if during the period it has potentially dilutive securities with a 3 percent or more aggregate dilutive effect on EPS based strictly on the weighted average number of common shares actually outstanding during the period. Potentially dilutive securities include convertible bonds, convertible preferred stock, stock purchase rights, stock warrants, and contingent shares.
8. T
9. F Even though all the potentially dilutive securities of a corporation are classified as common stock equivalents, fully diluted EPS may not equal primary EPS because of the additional dilution that results from sightly different treatment of some common stock equivalents when fully diluted EPS is calculated. When the treasury stock method is applied in the calculation of fully diluted EPS, for example, the higher of the end-of-the-period market price or the average market price during the period is used as the assumed buy-back price to determine the number of shares of common stock assumed to have been purchased. Furthermore, when shares of common stock are to be issued upon the attainment or maintenance of a specified level of income but that level is not currently being attained, the contingent shares, if dilutive, are included only in the fully diluted EPS calculation. Additionally, when the conversion privilege associated with convertible securities is not effective during the period, conversion is assumed in the primary EPS calculation if the conversion privilege is effective within 5 years of the end of the period, whereas conversion is assumed in the fully diluted EPS calculation if the conversion privilege is effective within 10 years of the end of the period. Finally, when convertible securities have actually been converted into shares of common stock during the

period, the securities are assumed to have been converted at the beginning of the period or the date the convertible securities were issued, if later, in the fully diluted EPS calculation, whether the result is dilutive or antidiutive, whereas such conversion is assumed in the primary EPS calculation only if the result is dilutive.
10. F A potentially dilutive security that is classified as a common stock equivalent should be included in primary EPS only if the security has a dilutive effect, that is, only if assumed exercise or conversion of the security would cause a decrease in the amount that would otherwise be reported as earnings per share or an increase in the amount that would otherwise be reported as net loss per share.
11. T
12. F When a corporation has a complex capital structure, a potentially dilutive security should be included in EPS calculations if assumed exercise or conversion of the security would cause a decrease in the amount that would otherwise be reported as earnings per share or an increase in the amount that would otherwise be reported as net loss per share. Actual exercise or conversion of the security during the period is not a necessary condition for the inclusion of a potentially dilutive security in EPS calculations.
13. F Stock options and warrants and their equivalents should be included in EPS calculations only if (a) the corporation has a complex capital structure during the period, (b) the market price of the common stock has been greater than the exercise price of the stock options or warrants for substantially all (at least 11 weeks) of a quarter preceding the end of the period, and (c) the application of the treasury stock method during the period has a dilutive effect; that is, either the average market price of the common stock during the period, in primary EPS calculations, or the higher end-of-the-period market price of the common stock, in fully diluted EPS calculations, exceeds the exercise price of the stock options or warrants.
14. T
15. T
16. T
17. F Convertible securities should be classified as common stock equivalents if the effective yield rate is less than two-thirds of the average Aa corporate bond yield at the time the securities are issued.

18. F   In the common stock equivalency test for a convertible security that has no stated maturity date, the effective yield rate is the stated annual interest or dividend payments divided by the market price of the security at the time of issuance.

19. T

20. F   When convertible securities are outstanding but the conversion privilege is not effective during the period, conversion should be assumed (a) for primary EPS if the conversion privilege is effective within 5 years from the end of the period, (b) for fully diluted EPS if the conversion privi-lege is effective within 10 years from the end of the period, and (c) for neither primary EPS nor fully diluted EPS if the conversion privilege is effective beyond 10 years from the end of the period.

Multiple Choice

1.	c	6.	b
2.	c	7.	c
3.	d	8.	a
4.	c	9.	d
5.	b	10.	b

Extended Problem

a.   Schedule of evaluation of common stock equivalency status:

	7% CONVERTIBLE DEBENTURES	$4 CONVERTIBLE PREFERRED STOCK	STOCK OPTIONS
Effective yield rate			
Debentures................................	6.00%		NA[a]
Preferred stock ($4 ÷ $52)..............		7.69%	
Two-thirds of average Aa corporate bond yield at issuance date			NA[a]
Debentures ($2/3 \times 10\%$)	6.67%		
Preferred stock ($2/3 \times 11\%$)................		7.33%	
Common stock equivalent, that is, effective yield rate less than two-thirds of average Aa corporate bond yield?.........	Yes	No	Yes (at all times)
Thus if dilutive, include in			
Primary EPS.............................	Yes	No	Yes
Fully diluted EPS.........................	Yes	Yes	Yes

[a]NA = not applicable

b.   Schedule of 1995 EPS calculations:

	BASIC EPS	PRIMARY EPS[a]	FULLY DILUTED EPS[b]
Numerator			
Net income for period	$1,511,500	$1,511,500	$1,511,500
Deduct dividends accumulating on cumulative preferred stock during period:[c]			
9,000 × $1 × 4 = $36,000			
1,000 × $1 × 1 = 1,000			
Total $37,000.....................................	(37,000)	(37,000)	(37,000)
Add after-tax interest expense on convertible debentures during period:			
[($2,000,000 + $125,000) × 6%] × (1.00 − .40)..........		76,500	76,500
Add dividends on convertible preferred stock during period:			
9,000 × $1 × 4 = $36,000			
1,000 × $1 × 1 = 1,000			
Total $37,000.....................................			37,000
Total numerator.......................................	$1,474,500	$1,551,000	$1,588,000

Denominator
  Weighted average number of common shares actually
    outstanding during period:

$498,000 \times {}^3/_{12} = 124,500$			
$500,000 \times {}^3/_{12} = 125,000$			
$480,000 \times {}^4/_{12} = 160,000$			
$492,000 \times {}^2/_{12} = \underline{82,000}$			
Total $\underline{491,500}$	491,500	491,500	491,500

Add incremental shares on assumed exercise of stock options
less assumed purchase of common stock at average market
price for primary EPS and at higher of average or end-of-
the-period market price for fully diluted EPS:

$\{50,000 - [(50,000 \times \$24) \div \$25]\} \times {}^{12}/_{12}$		2,000	
$\{50,000 - [(50,000 \times \$24) \div \$30]\} \times {}^{12}/_{12}$			10,000

Add new shares on assumed conversion of convertible debentures:

$(\$2,000,000 \div \$1,000) \times 40 \times {}^{12}/_{12}$		80,000	80,000

Add new shares on assumed conversion of convertible preferred
stock:[d]

$9,000 \times 2 \times {}^{12}/_{12} = 18,000$			
$1,000 \times 2 \times {}^3/_{12} = \underline{500}$			
Total $\underline{18,500}$			$\underline{18,500}$
Total denominator	$\underline{\underline{491,500}}$	$\underline{\underline{573,500}}$	$\underline{\underline{600,000}}$

Earnings per share (numerator ÷ denominator):

Basic EPS ($1,474,500 ÷ 491,500)...............................	$\underline{\$3.00}$		
Primary EPS ($1,551,000 ÷ 573,500)...........................		$\underline{\$2.70}$	
Fully diluted EPS ($1,588,000 ÷ 600,000)....................			$\underline{\$2.65}$

[a]The order of entry of the common stock equivalents (stock options and convertible debentures) in the calculation of primary EPS starts with the security that has the smallest income per incremental common share effect. First, because the income per incremental share effect of the stock options ($0 ÷ 2,000 = $0) is less than EPS before inclusion of the security [($1,511,500 − $37,000) ÷ 491,500 = $3.00], the stock options are dilutive, and so their dilutive effect is included in primary EPS. Second, because the after-tax interest expense on the convertible debentures divided by the new shares hypothetically issued on the assumed conversion of the convertible debentures ($76,500 ÷ 80,000 = $.96) is less than EPS before inclusion of the security [($1,511,500 − $37,000) ÷ (491,500 + 2,000) = $2.99], the convertible debentures are dilutive, and so their dilutive effect is included in primary EPS.

[b]The order of entry of the common stock equivalents (stock options and convertible debentures) and other potentially dilutive securities (convertible preferred stock) in the calculation of fully diluted EPS starts with the security that has the smallest income per incremental common share effect. First, because the income per incremental share effect of the stock options ($0 ÷ 10,000 = $0) is less than EPS before inclusion of the security [($1,511,500 − $37,000) ÷ 491,500 = $3.00], the stock options are dilutive, and so their dilutive effect is included in fully diluted EPS. Second, because the after-tax interest expense on the convertible debentures divided by the new shares hypothetically issued on the assumed conversion of the convertible debentures ($76,500 ÷ 80,000 = $.96) is less than EPS before inclusion of the security [($1,511,500 − $37,000) ÷ (491,500 + 10,000) = $2.94], the convertible debentures are dilutive, and so their dilutive effect is included in fully diluted EPS. Finally, because the add-back adjustment for dividends on the convertible preferred stock divided by the new shares hypothetically issued on the assumed conversion of the preferred stock ($37,000 ÷ 18,500 = $2.00) is less than EPS before inclusion of the security [($1,511,500 − $37,000 + $76,500) ÷ (491,500 + 10,000 + 80,000) = $2.67], the convertible preferred stock is dilutive, and so its dilutive effect is included in fully diluted EPS. Incidentally, it should be noted that even if the convertible preferred stock had been antidilutive, the 1,000 shares of preferred stock that were actually converted on April 1, 1995, would be assumed to have been converted into 2,000 shares of common stock at the beginning of the year in the fully diluted EPS calculation. Specifically, in this circumstance, the add-back adjustment to the numerator for dividends on the convertible preferred stock would be $1,000 (1,000 × $1) instead of $37,000, and the weighted average number of new shares that would be added to the denominator for the assumed conversion of the convertible preferred stock would be 500 (1,000 × 2 × ³/₁₂), instead of 18,500.

[c]One thousand shares of the preferred stock were converted into common stock on April 1, 1995, and thus dividends accumulated on these shares for only one quarter.

[d]Because 1,000 shares of the convertible preferred stock were actually converted into 2,000 shares of common stock on April 1, 1995, these shares (1,000 × 2) were potentially dilutive securities only from the beginning of the year to the date of conversion (three months, or three-twelfths of the year).

21

A: REVISITING THE STATEMENT OF CASH FLOWS
B: ADDITIONAL DISCLOSURE TOPICS

CHAPTER OBJECTIVES

After reading Chapter 21 and completing the questions, cases, exercises, and problems from the text chapter, you should be able to:

1. Prepare a statement of cash flows, at an intermediate level, in accordance with standards specified by *Statement No. 95*.
2. Use a worksheet to prepare a statement of cash flows.
3. Identify the modifications in the application of generally accepted accounting principles that are permitted for the preparation of interim financial reports.
4. Describe the minimum information that is required to be disclosed in interim financial reports.
5. Identify and apply the materiality tests to determine when public companies are required to report financial information about their industry segments, their foreign operations, their export sales, and the extent of their reliance on major customers.
6. Describe the financial information that public companies are required to report concerning their industry segments, their foreign and domestic operations, and the extent of their reliance on major customers.

CHAPTER REVIEW

Part A: Revisiting the Statement of Cash Flows

Introduction

1. Chapter 6 discusses the historical background and usefulness of the statement of cash flows and illustrates the preparation of the statement at the principles level. Part A of this chapter extends the presentation in Chapter 6 to include intermediate-level transactions (such as those related to available-for-sales securities, pensions, deferred taxes, and leases) and to illustrate the use of a worksheet (and, in the appendix, the use of T-accounts).

2. *Statement No. 95* states that the primary purpose of the statement of cash flows is to provide information about a company's cash receipts and cash payments during a period. It states further that cash receipts and cash payments must be classified in the statement by operating, investing, and financing activities. Under this reporting format (called an *activity format*), the statement of cash flows consists of three sections—operating, investing, and financing—each reporting the cash receipts, cash payments, and net cash provided or used by

that activity during the period. Furthermore, although it permits cash flows from operating activities to be determined and reported by either a direct approach or an indirect approach, *Statement No. 95* encourages companies to report cash flows from operating activities by the direct approach within the statement of cash flows and to disclose a reconciliation of net income and net cash provided by operating activities by the indirect approach in a supplementary schedule to the statement. In addition, *Statement No. 95* requires that the gross amounts of cash inflows and cash outflows resulting from investing and financing activities be reported separately in the corresponding section of the statement of cash flows. It also requires that investing and financing activities not involving cash receipts or cash payments in the period be disclosed separately in either a narrative or a supplementary schedule to the statement of cash flows, so that information is provided about all investing and financing activities. Finally, *Statement No. 95* requires that the net increase or decrease in cash and cash equivalents during the period be reported at the bottom of the statement of cash flows, as an addition to or deduction from the beginning balance to reconcile to the ending balance.

3. Chapter 6 of this guide summarizes the fundamental procedures for preparing the statement of cash flows in accordance with *Statement No. 95*, whereas Part A of this chapter review focuses on the procedures for reporting selected intermediate-level transactions in the statement of cash flows. Thus, for a comprehensive summary of the procedures for preparing the statement of cash flows, a student should first read the chapter review section of Chapter 6 and then read the remainder of this chapter review.

Selected Intermediate-Level Transactions

4. **Uncollectible accounts.** Allowance for uncollectible accounts is a contra asset account that should be reported on the balance sheet as a deduction from accounts receivable. This contra account is increased each period by uncollectible accounts expense, which is reported on the income statement; it is decreased when specific accounts receivable that are judged to be uncollectible are written off against the allowance. Because uncollectible accounts expense does not involve a cash outflow, it should be excluded from the determination of net cash provided by operating activities under the direct approach or added to net income to determine net cash provided by operating activities under the indirect approach. In addition, the amount of accounts receivable written off as uncollectible during the period should be added to the ending balance of accounts receivable, and then the difference between this amount and the beginning balance of accounts receivable should be added to or deducted from sales revenue, to determine cash collections from customers under the direct approach, or added to or deducted from net income, to determine net cash provided by operating activities under the indirect approach.

5. **Debt discount/premium amortization.** Issuers of debt securities (and investors in debt securities) should amortize the difference between the issue price (cost) and face value as an adjustment to periodic interest expense (revenue). Specifically, when the issue price (cost) of a debt security is greater than the face value, the premium should be amortized by the issuer (investor) as a reduction of periodic interest expense (revenue). Conversely, when the issue price (cost) of a debt security is less than the face value, the discount should be amortized by the issuer (investor) as an addition to periodic interest expense (revenue). Thus, when net cash provided by operating activities is determined by the direct approach, the periodic discount (premium) amortization on debt securities should be deducted from (added to) interest expense and interest revenue by the issuer and investor, respectively. Alternatively, under the indirect approach, the periodic discount (premium) amortization on debt securities should be added to (deducted from) net income by the issuer and deducted from (added to) net income by the investor, to determine net cash provided by operating activities.

6. **Investments.** Cash flows from purchases, sales, and maturities of investments in debt and equity securities should be reported in the statement of cash flows (*a*) as part of the net increase or decrease in cash and cash equivalents when the securities are classified as cash equivalents, (*b*) as investing activities when the securities are classified as available-for-sale securities or held-to-maturity securities or when the securities are accounted for under the equity method, or (*c*) as operating activities when the securities are classified as trading securities. Furthermore, unrealized gains and losses recognized on trading securities should be either excluded from the determination of net cash provided by operating activities under the direct approach or deducted from or added to net income to determine net cash provided by operating activities under the indirect approach. In addition, cash dividends that are recorded as a reduction of an investment accounted for by the equity method (rather than the noncash investment revenue that is recorded as an increase in the investment) should be included as a cash inflow in the determination of net cash provided by operating activities under the

direct approach. Alternatively, under the indirect approach, the net increase or decrease in an investment accounted for by the equity method should be deducted from or added to net income to determine net cash provided by operating activities.

7. Capital leases. When a lease is a capital lease, the lessee should record at the date of the lease agreement an asset and a liability at the present value of the minimum lease payments. Subsequently, the lessee should accrue periodic interest expense on the lease liability, record the periodic lease payments as a reduction of the lease liability, and depreciate the leased asset. At the date of the lease agreement, a capital lease is a noncash investing and financing activity that should be disclosed separately in either a narrative or a supplementary schedule to the statement of cash flows for that period. Furthermore, over the term of the lease, the excess of the periodic lease payments over the periodic interest expense (that is, the amount of the net reduction in the lease liability) should be reported as a cash outflow in the financing activities section of the statement. Finally, the depreciation expense on the leased asset should be excluded from the determination of net cash provided by operating activities under the direct approach or added to net income to determine net cash provided by operating activities under the direct approach.

8. Pension cost. *Statement No. 87* requires that the difference between the cumulative amount recorded as pension expense and the cumulative amount funded by the employer be reported on the balance sheet as either an asset, if the cumulative funding exceeds the cumulative expense, or a liability, if the cumulative expense exceeds the cumulative funding. Thus, an increase in a pension asset or decrease in a pension liability resulting from an excess of the amount funded over pension expense for a period should be either added to pension expense under the direct approach or deducted from net income under the indirect approach, to determine net cash provided by operating activities. Conversely, a decrease in a pension asset or increase in a pension liability resulting from an excess of pension expense over the amount funded for a period should be either deducted from pension expense under the direct approach or added to net income under the indirect approach, to determine net cash provided by operating activities.

9. Deferred taxes. *Statement No. 109* requires that income tax expense for a period be the sum of current income taxes payable or receivable plus or minus any increase or decrease in a deferred tax asset or liability and in a valuation allowance for a deferred tax asset. Thus, when net cash provided by operating activities is determined by the direct approach, income taxes paid for the period should be determined by adjusting income tax expense as follows: deduct (add) an increase (decrease) in income taxes payable, deduct (add) an increase (decrease) in a deferred tax liability, add (deduct) an increase (decrease) in a deferred tax asset, and deduct (add) an increase (decrease) in a valuation allowance for a deferred tax asset. Alternatively, because income tax expense reduces net income, the additions to (deductions from) income tax expense under the direct approach are deductions from (additions to) net income under the indirect approach of determining net cash provided by operating activities.

10. Reclassifications within stockholders' equity. Transactions and other events that represent reclassifications within the stockholders' equity section of the balance sheet should not be reported in or otherwise disclosed as part of the statement of cash flows, because such reclassifications have no effect on cash and are not investing or financing activities. Such transactions include stock dividends, stock splits, retained earnings appropriations, and reversals of retained earnings appropriations. A conversion of preferred stock into common stock, however, is a noncash financing activity that should be disclosed in either a narrative or a supplementary schedule to the statement.

11. Noncash accounts not related to operating activities. Net changes in noncash accounts that are related to the company's operating activities should be added to or deducted from the related revenues and expenses (under the direct approach) or net income (under the indirect approach) to determine net cash provided by operating activities during the period. Conversely, the transactions and other events that caused the changes in noncash accounts that are not related to the company's operating activities should be reported in the statement of cash flows as investing or financing activities. Proceeds from issuance and outlays for repayment of short-term debt in a period, for example, should be reported in the cash flows from financing activities section of the statement.

12. Extraordinary items. Cash flows from transactions and other events whose effects are included in net income but which are not related to operating activities, should be reported as investing or financing activities. An extraordinary gain on extinguishment of debt, for example, should be excluded from cash flows from operating activities (under the direct approach) or deducted from net income (under the indirect approach), and the cash outflow for the extinguishment should be reported in the cash flows from financing activities section of the statement.

Using a Worksheet

13. A worksheet may be used to prepare the statement of cash flows in a well-organized and efficient manner. The worksheet illustrated in the text chapter for the direct approach has three sections and four columns. The upper section of the worksheet contains the balance sheet account titles; the middle section contains the income statement account titles; and the lower section, as completed, contains major headings that are identical to those presented in the statement of cash flows and the supplementary schedule. The worksheet is completed in two stages.

14. During the first stage, the balance sheet account balances at the beginning and end of the period are entered in the upper section of the worksheet in the first and fourth columns, respectively, and the income statement account balances are entered in the middle section of the worksheet in the first column.

15. During the second stage, the transactions and other events that caused the changes in noncash balance sheet accounts that are related to investing and financing activities and the income statement account balances plus or minus the net changes in noncash balance sheet accounts that are related to operating activities are entered, in summary form, in the middle two columns in the upper, middle, and lower sections of the worksheet, until all the noncash balance sheet accounts have been reconciled and all the income statement accounts have been re-created. As general rules, (a) the debits and credits entered in the upper section in noncash balance sheet accounts that are related to investing and financing activities are identical to the debits and credits that were recorded in the formal journal entries; (b) the debits entered in noncash balance sheet accounts in the upper section are associated with credits entered in the middle and lower sections, and vice versa; (c) the debits entered in income statement accounts in the middle section plus or minus the debits or credits entered in the upper section in noncash balance sheet accounts that are related to operating activities are associated with credits entered in the lower section, and vice versa; and (d) the debits and credits entered in the lower section correspond to cash inflows and cash outflows, respectively. A cash issuance of no-par common stock, for example, is entered as a credit to common stock in the upper section and as a debit to issuance of common stock under cash flows from financing activities in the lower section; a cash purchase of equipment is entered as a debit to equipment in the upper section and as a credit to purchase of equipment under cash flows from investing activities in the lower section; a cash sale of land at a gain is entered as a credit to land in the

upper section, as a credit to gain on sale of land in the middle section, and as a debit to sale of land under cash flows from investing activities in the lower section; and salaries expense and a net decrease in salaries payable are entered as a debit to salaries expense in the middle section, as a debit to salaries payable in the upper section, and as a credit to payments to employees for salaries under cash flows from operating activities in the lower section.

16. After the worksheet is completed, the data entered in the lower section are used to prepare the formal statement of cash flows and the supplementary schedule.

Part B: Additional Disclosure Topics

Interim Reporting

17. *Interim financial reports* are financial reports covering periods of less than one year. These reports normally are issued externally on a quarterly basis in the United States and on a semiannual basis internationally, to provide more timely financial information about the company.

18. *APB Opinion No. 28* contains the general guidelines for preparing interim financial reports. It states that each interim period should be viewed as an integral part of the annual period rather than as a basic (discrete) accounting period. Accordingly, although the results of operations for each interim period generally should be based on the accounting principles used by the company for its most recent annual financial statements, *Opinion No. 28* specifies certain modifications in the application of generally accepted accounting principles that are permitted for the preparation of interim financial reports. These modifications as well as other significant guidelines regarding the preparation of interim financial reports are summarized here.

a. The revenue of interim periods should be recognized on the same basis as the revenue of the annual period.
b. Expenses that are associated directly with revenue should be matched against revenue on the same basis as expenses of the annual period, except that (1) an estimation method may be used to determine cost of goods sold and the cost of inventory for interim period reports; (2) temporary declines in market prices related to inventory need not be recognized as a loss at the interim period date, but if they are recognized, subsequent increases in market prices in later interim periods of the same annual period should be recognized as a gain to the extent of the previously recognized loss; and (3) planned

variances from standard cost related to inventory that are expected to be absorbed by the end of the annual period should not be recognized at the interim period date, but unplanned variances should be recognized by means of the same procedures as those used at the end of the annual period.

c. Expenses that are not associated directly with revenue should be allocated among the interim periods on the basis of estimated time expired, benefit received, or activity associated with the periods. Those expenses that cannot be readily identified with the activities or benefits of other interim periods, however, should be deducted in calculating income in the interim period in which they are incurred.

d. Gains and losses that are not deferred for annual reporting purposes should not be deferred at the interim period date.

e. The estimated effective annual tax rate (estimated annual income tax expense divided by estimated annual pretax income from continuing operations) should be used to determine income tax expense for each interim period on a current year-to-date basis.

f. The materiality of extraordinary items, discontinued segments of a business, and other items that are reported separately on the income statement net of applicable income taxes should be determined at the interim period date on the basis of the estimated income for the annual period.

g. The cumulative effect of a change in accounting principle that qualifies for the current period approach should be included in net income of the first interim period of the annual period in which the change is made. When the change is made in an interim period other than the first, financial information of the prechange interim periods of the current annual period should be retroactively restated to show the effects of the change, and the cumulative effect of the change on retained earnings at the beginning of the current annual period should be included in the restated net income of the first interim period of the annual period.

Interim financial reports must disclose, as a minimum, the following summarized information: sales or gross revenues, income tax expense, extraordinary items, cumulative effect of a change in accounting principle, and net income; earnings per share figures determined in accordance with *APB Opinion No. 15,* discussed in Chapter 20; seasonal revenue, costs, or expenses; significant changes in estimated or actual income tax expense; disposal of

a segment of a business and extraordinary, unusual, or infrequent items; contingent items; changes in accounting principles or estimates; and significant cash flows. This interim financial information should be reported for the current interim period and for either the current year to date or the last 12 months to date, together with comparable data for the preceding year. Publicly traded companies also are encouraged, but not required, to present a balance sheet and statement of cash flows at interim reporting dates. When these statements are not presented, such companies must disclose at each interim reporting date material changes in liquid assets, net working capital, long-term liabilities, and stockholders' equity since the most recent reporting date.

Segment Reporting

19. Many companies operate in more than one industry or geographic area. These diverse activities are required to be reported as aggregated (or consolidated) amounts in the company's financial statements. As the rate of profitability, rate of return, levels and types of risk, and opportunities for growth may vary among the industries and geographic areas of a company's operations, *Statement No. 14* requires that public companies report certain disaggregated financial information as supplementary disclosures in conjunction with the annual financial statements.

20. Industry segments. Public companies are required to disclose certain information about their operations in different industry segments. An *industry segment* is a component of a company that is engaged in providing a product or service or a group of related products and services primarily to customers outside the company (called *unaffiliated customers*) for a profit. Information must be disclosed for those industry segments that meet one or more of the following materiality tests for classification as a *reportable segment:*

a. *Revenue test.* The revenue, including both sales to unaffiliated customers and intersegment sales or transfers, of the industry segment is 10 percent or more of the combined revenue of all industry segments.

b. *Operating profit or loss test.* The operating profit or loss of the industry segment is 10 percent or more of the greater, in absolute amount, of either the combined operating profit of all industry segments with operating profits or the combined operating loss of all industry segments with operating losses. The operating profit or loss of an industry segment is its revenue minus operating expenses, excluding general corporate expenses, interest expense, income taxes, investment revenue or loss under the equity method, gain or loss on discontinued operations, extraordinary items, noncontrolling or minority interest, and the cumulative effect of a change in accounting principle.

c. *Identifiable assets test.* The identifiable assets of the industry segment are 10 percent or more of the combined identifiable assets of all industry segments. *Identifiable assets* are those tangible and intangible assets that are used exclusively by the industry segment plus an allocated portion of those assets that are used jointly by two or more industry segments. Assets maintained for general corporate purposes and intersegment loans and advances (unless the segment is a financial segment) are not identifiable assets.

Moreover, if the combined revenues from sales of all reportable segments to unaffiliated customers is less than 75 percent of the combined revenue from sales of all industry segments to unaffiliated customers, additional industry segments must be classified as reportable segments until the 75 percent test is met.

21. Companies are required to disclose the following information for each reportable segment and, in the aggregate, for the remainder of the industry segments that are not classified as reportable segments: (*a*) revenue from sales to unaffiliated customers and from intersegment sales or transfers; (*b*) operating profit or loss; (*c*) aggregate book value of identifiable assets; and (*d*) other related disclosures, including such amounts as aggregate depreciation, depletion, and amortization expense and capital expenditures. This information must be reconciled to the related amounts reported in the company's financial statements, and it may be reported within the body of the financial statements with supporting footnote disclosures, entirely in the footnotes to the financial statements, or in a separate schedule that is included as an integral part of the financial statements. This information need not be reported, however, if the company is dominated by a single industry segment with revenue, operating profit or loss, and identifiable assets each constituting more than 90 percent of the related combined totals for all industry segments, and if no other industry segment meets any of the 10 percent tests for a reportable segment.

22. Foreign operations and export sales. Public companies also are required to disclose certain information about their foreign operations and export sales. *Foreign operations* include any revenue-producing operations located outside the company's home country that are generating revenue from either sales to unaffiliated customers

or intracompany sales or transfers between geographic areas. *Domestic operations,* on the other hand, include those revenue-producing operations located in the company's home country that are generating revenue from either sales to unaffiliated customers or intracompany sales or transfers between geographic areas. Information about revenue, operating profit or loss, and identifiable assets is required to be reported for foreign operations and domestic operations separately if either of the following materiality tests is met: (*a*) revenue generated by foreign operations from sales to unaffiliated customers is 10 percent or more of the total revenue reported in the company's income statement, or (*b*) identifiable assets of foreign operations are 10 percent or more of the total assets reported in the company's balance sheet. Additionally, the information related to foreign operations must be reported separately for each *foreign geographic area* that has revenue from sales to unaffiliated customers or identifiable assets of 10 percent or more of the related totals reported in the company's financial statements and, in the aggregate, for all other foreign operations. The amount of revenue generated by domestic operations from sales to unaffiliated customers in foreign countries (called *export sales*) also must be reported if it is 10 percent or more of the total revenue reported in the company's income statement. This disclosure is required even if the company operates only in one industry or has no foreign operations.

23. Major customers. In addition, public companies are required to disclose information about the extent of their reliance on major customers. Specifically, if 10 percent or more of the company's revenue is derived from sales to any single customer, including a government unit, that fact and the amount of revenue attributable to each such customer must be disclosed. The disclosure is required even if the company operates only in one industry or has no foreign operations.

24. International reporting practices. These U.S. segment reporting requirements are the most comprehensive in the world. The most common international requirement is only for disclosure of sales by line of business and geographic area. Companies that operate in global capital markets, though, voluntarily present extensive product line and geographic segment information.

Appendix: Using T-accounts to Prepare a Statement of Cash Flows

25. T-accounts also may be used to prepare the statement of cash flows. The T-account approach is analytically equivalent to the worksheet approach, except that the entries to determine data for preparing the formal statement of cash flows are entered in T-accounts instead of a columnar worksheet. Under the T-account approach using the direct approach, T-accounts are first established for each of the balance sheet accounts, an income summary account and a noncash investing and financing activities account. Second, the net change in each of the balance sheet accounts is entered in the appropriate T-account. Third, the transactions and other events that caused the changes in noncash balance sheet accounts that are related to investing and financing activities and the income statement account balances plus or minus the net changes in noncash balance sheet accounts that are related to operating activities are entered, in summary form, in the appropriate T-accounts, until all the net changes in noncash balance sheet accounts have been reconciled and all the income statement accounts have been re-created within the income summary T-account. As general rules, (*a*) the debits and credits entered in noncash balance sheet T-accounts that are related to investing and financing activities are identical to the debits and credits that were recorded in the formal journal entries; (*b*) the debits entered in noncash balance sheet T-accounts are associated with credits entered in the cash T-account, the income summary T-account, and the noncash investing and financing activities T-

account, and vice versa; (*c*) the debits entered in the income summary T-account plus or minus the debits or credits entered in the noncash balance sheet T-accounts that are related to operating activities are associated with credits entered in the cash T-account, and vice versa; and (*d*) the debits and credits entered in the cash T-account correspond to cash inflows and cash outflows, respectively. A cash issuance of no-par common stock, for example, is entered as a credit to the common stock T-account and as a debit to the cash T-account under financing activities; a cash purchase of equipment is entered as a debit to the equipment T-account and as a credit to the cash T-account under investing activities; a cash sale of land at a gain is entered as a credit to the land T-account, as a credit to the income summary T-account, and as a debit to the cash T-account under investing activities; and salaries expense and a net decrease in salaries payable are entered as a debit to the income summary T-account, as a debit to the salaries payable T-account, and as a credit to the cash T-account under operating activities. Finally, the amounts entered in the cash T-account and the noncash investing and financing activities T-account are used to prepare the formal statement of cash flows and the supplementary schedule, respectively.

SELF-STUDY LEARNING

Items marked with an asterisk (*) refer to the Appendix.

Note: Chapter 6's Self-Study Learning section also contains key terms and concepts, true-false and multiple-choice questions, and extended problems on the statement of cash flows. For a comprehensive review, you should first complete Chapter 6's Self-Study Learning section before proceeding with this section.

Key Terms and Concepts

Provide the appropriate term or terms to complete each of the following statements:

*1. A statement of cash flows may be prepared in a well-organized and efficient manner from a(n) _____ and by using _____.

2. Financial reports covering periods of less than one year are called _____.

3. Disclosure of disaggregated financial information about a company's operations in different industries and countries is referred to as _____.

4. Customers outside the company are called _____ .

5. A component of a company that is engaged in providing a product or service or a group of related products and services primarily to unaffiliated customers for a profit is a(n)_____.

6. The tangible and intangible assets that are used exclusively by an industry segment plus an allocated portion of the assets that are used jointly by two or more industry segments are called _____.

7. Those industry segments that meet one or more of the 10 percent materiality tests concerning revenue, operating profit or loss, and identifiable assets are called _____.

8. Revenue-producing operations that are located outside the company's home country are called _____.

9. Revenue-producing operations that are located in the company's home country are called _____.

10. Sales by the domestic operations of a company to unaffiliated customers in foreign countries are called

_____.

True-False

Indicate by circling the appropriate response whether each of the following statements is true (T) or false (F):

T F 1. When interest expense has been increased by long-term debt discount amortization, an amount equal to the accrual-basis interest expense less the discount amortization should be included in the determination of net cash provided by operating activities under the direct approach.

T F 2. Lease payments on a capital lease should be reported as a cash outflow in the financing activities section of the statement cash flows.

T F 3. Cash dividends declared but not paid during the period should not be reported in or otherwise disclosed as part of the statement of cash flows, because they do not affect cash.

T F 4. Conversion of preferred stock into common stock should be reported in neither the statement of cash flows nor a supplementary schedule, since it represents a reclassification within the stockholders' equity section of the balance sheet.

T F 5. Stock dividends should be reported in the statement of cash flows, since this transaction causes changes in noncash balance sheet accounts.

T F 6. Cash flows from investing and financing transactions whose effects are included in net income should be included in the determination of net cash provided by operating activities.

T F 7. When interim financial reports are prepared, each interim period should be viewed as a basic or discrete accounting period.

T F 8. The results of operations for each interim period should be based solely on the accounting principles used by a company for its most recent annual financial statements.

T F 9. Modifications in the application of generally accepted accounting principles are permitted for the preparation of interim financial reports because each interim period is viewed as an integral part of the annual period.

T F 10. The revenue of interim periods should be recognized on the same basis as revenue of the annual period.

T F 11. The materiality of extraordinary items and other items that are reported separately on the income statement net of applicable income taxes should be determined at the interim period date on the basis of the income for that interim period.

T F 12. The cumulative effect of a change in accounting principle that qualifies for the current period approach should be included in net income of the interim period in which the change is made.

T F 13. Interim financial information should be reported for the current interim period and for either the current year to date or the last 12 months to date, together with comparable data for the preceding year.

T F 14. Public companies are required to report certain disaggregated financial information as supplementary disclosures in conjunction with the annual financial statements because the rate of profitability, rate of return, levels and types of risk, and opportunities for growth may vary among the industries and geographic areas of a company's operations.

T F 15. Information must be reported separately for each industry segment of a public company.

T F 16. An industry segment should be classified as a reportable segment if its revenue, including both sales to unaffiliated customers and intersegment sales or transfers, is 10 percent or more of the combined revenue of all industry segments.

T F 17. If the combined revenue of all reportable segments from sales to unaffiliated customers is less than 75 percent of the combined revenue from sales of all industry segments to unaffiliated customers, additional industry segments must be classified as reportable segments until the 75 percent test is met.

T F 18. The combined totals of the information reported for each reportable segment and, in the aggregate, for the remainder of the industry segments that are not classified as reportable segments should equal the related amounts reported in a company's financial statements.

T F 19. Information about foreign operations is required to be reported by public companies if revenue generated by foreign operations from sales to unaffiliated customers and identifiable assets of foreign operations are each 10 percent or more of the related totals reported in a company's financial statements.

T F 20. The amount of revenue generated by domestic operations from sales to unaffiliated customers in foreign countries must be reported by public companies.

Multiple Choice

Select the best response for each of the following items, and circle the corresponding letter:

1. Which of the following should be deducted from the sales revenue reported on the income statement to determine the amount of cash collections from customers during the period?

   a. A net increase in accounts receivable.
   b. A net decrease in accounts receivable.
   c. A net increase in accounts receivable before deduction of accounts receivable written off during the period.
   d. A net decrease in accounts receivable before deduction of accounts receivable written off during the period.

2. When net cash provided by operating activities is determined and reported under the indirect approach, the additions to net income should include:

   a. A net increase in accounts receivable.
   b. Gains on sales of property, plant, and equipment.
   c. A net increase in short-term bank loans.
   d. Discount amortization on long-term debt.

3. Cash flows from purchases, sales, and maturities of investments in debt and equity securities that are classified as trading securities should be reported in the statement of cash flows as:

   a. Operating activities.
   b. Investing activities.
   c. Financing activities.
   d. Part of the net increase or decrease in cash and cash equivalents.

4. Which of the following transactions or events should be reported in neither the body of the statement of cash flows nor a supplementary schedule?

   a. The acquisition of plant assets by the issuance of long-term debt.
   b. The conversion of long-term debt into equity securities.
   c. A stock split.
   d. The conversion of preferred stock into common stock.

5. Which of the following is *not* one of the modifications in the application of generally accepted accounting principles that are permitted for the preparation of interim financial reports?

   a. Standard cost inventory variances that are expected to be absorbed by the end of the annual period should not be recognized at the interim period date.

b. An estimation method may be used to determine cost of goods sold and the cost of inventory for interim period reports.

c. Subsequent increases in the market prices of inventory in later interim periods of the same annual period should be recognized as a gain to the extent of a previously recognized loss.

d. Expenses that are not associated directly with revenue should be allocated arbitrarily among the interim periods.

6. Income tax expense for each interim period should be determined as follows:

a. Pretax income from continuing operations for the current interim period is multiplied by the estimated effective annual tax rate.

b. Pretax income from continuing operations for the current interim period is multiplied by the applicable statutory tax rate.

c. Pretax income from continuing operations for the current year to date is multiplied by the estimated effective annual tax rate, and from this amount the cumulative income tax expense recognized for all previous interim periods of the current annual period is subtracted.

d. Pretax income from continuing operations for the current year to date is multiplied by the applicable statutory tax rate, and from this amount the cumulative income tax expense recognized for all previous interim periods of the current annual period is subtracted.

7. An industry segment should be classified as a reportable segment if:

a. Its net income or loss is 10 percent or more of the net income or loss reported in the company's income statement.

b. Its operating profit or loss is 10 percent or more of the net income or loss reported in the company's income statement.

c. Its operating profit or loss is 10 percent or more of the greater of either the combined operating profit of all industry segments with operating profits or the combined operating loss of all industry segments with operating losses.

d. Its operating profit is 10 percent or more of the combined operating profit of all industry segments with operating profits or its operating loss is 10 percent or more of the combined operating loss of all industry segments with operating losses.

8. Which of the following is *not* required to be reported for each reportable segment and, in the aggregate, for the remainder of the industry segments that are not classified as reportable segments?

a. Revenue from sales to unaffiliated customers and from intersegment sales or transfers.

b. Net income or loss.

c. Aggregate book value of identifiable assets.

d. Capital expenditures.

9. Information about foreign operations is required to be reported if:

a. Revenue generated by foreign operations from sales to unaffiliated customers and from intracompany sales or transfers between geographic areas is 10 percent or more of the combined revenue of foreign operations and domestic operations.

b. Revenue generated by foreign operations from sales to unaffiliated customers is 10 percent or more of the total revenue reported in the company's income statement.

c. Revenue generated by domestic operations from sales to unaffiliated customers in foreign countries is 10 percent or more of the total revenue of foreign operations.

d. Identifiable assets of foreign operations are 10 percent or more of the identifiable assets of domestic operations.

10. If 10 percent or more of a public company's revenue is derived from sales to any single customer, that fact and the amount of revenue attributable to each such customer must be disclosed:

a. Only if the company is required to report information about its industry segments.

b. Only if the company is required to report information about its foreign operations.

c. Only if the company is required to report information about its industry segments and foreign operations.

d. Even if the company operates only in one industry or has no foreign operations.

Extended Problems

1. Presented here are an income statement, comparative balance sheets, and additional information for SCF Company.

SCF Company

INCOME STATEMENT
FOR THE YEAR ENDED DECEMBER 31, 1995

Sales...	$680,000
Interest revenue...	3,000
Investment revenue.......................................	18,000
Realized gain on sale of investment.................	2,000
	$703,000
Cost of goods sold.......................................	$400,000
Depreciation expense	48,000
Other operating expenses	179,000
Interest expense..	23,000
Loss on sale of equipment.............................	3,000
	$653,000
Income before income taxes	$ 50,000
Income taxes..	20,000
Net income	$ 30,000

SCF Company

BALANCE SHEET
AS OF DECEMBER 31, 1995, AND DECEMBER 31, 1994

	DECEMBER 31, 1995	DECEMBER 31, 1994
Cash...	$ 16,000	$ 12,000
Temporary investments	24,000	18,000
Accounts receivable	76,000	88,000
Allowance for uncollectible accounts................	(5,000)	(6,000)
Inventories..	138,000	125,000
Prepaid expenditures	11,000	10,000
Total current assets	$260,000	$247,000
Land...	$118,000	$ 80,000
Plant and equipment	440,000	400,000
Accumulated depreciation	(150,000)	(120,000)
Leased property	120,000	120,000
Accumulated depreciation	(16,000)	(8,000)
Investment at fair value................................	-0-	14,000
Investment at equity method..........................	63,000	50,000
	$575,000	$536,000
Total assets..	$835,000	$783,000
Accounts payable	$115,000	$110,000
Salaries payable...	1,000	5,000
Short-term note payable................................	40,000	30,000
Dividends payable	4,000	-0-
Total current liabilities	$160,000	$145,000
Bonds payable (10% stated rate)	$ 97,000	$ 96,000
Deferred tax liability	20,000	18,000
Lease liability..	102,000	110,000
Pension liability...	40,000	45,000
	$259,000	$269,000
Preferred stock ($100 par)	$ 30,000	$ 60,000
Common stock ($10 par)................................	265,000	200,000
Contributed capital in excess of par—common	44,000	30,000
Retained earnings..	77,000	76,000
Unrealized holding gain	-0-	3,000
	$416,000	$369,000
Total liabilities and stockholders' equity	$835,000	$783,000

Additional information for the year ended December 31, 1995:

a. Temporary investments of idle cash in short-term highly liquid securities (cash equivalents) were acquired for $46,000, and such temporary investments were redeemed at their maturity dates for $40,000.
b. Accounts receivable of $10,000 were written off as uncollectible.
c. Land with a fair market value of $38,000 was acquired by paying $20,000 and issuing 1,500 shares of common stock.
d. Equipment, with an original cost of $20,000 and accumulated depreciation of $10,000, was sold for $7,000, and equipment was purchased for $60,000.
e. The fair value-basis investment, classified as an available-for-sale security, was sold for $13,000, resulting in a realized gain of $2,000.
f. The equity-basis investment was increased by investment revenue of $18,000 and decreased by cash dividends of $5,000.
g. A six-month note payable was issued to a bank on December 31, 1995, for $40,000, and a one-year note payable was repaid to a bank on January 1, 1995 at $30,000.
h. 300 shares of preferred stock were converted into 2,500 shares of common stock.
i. 2,000 shares of common stock were issued for $24,000.
j. A stock dividend of 1,000 shares of common stock was declared and distributed when the common stock had a market value of $12 per share.
k. 500 shares of common stock with a book value of $5,000 were purchased for $6,000 and retired, and the difference of $1,000 was debited to retained earnings.
l. Cash dividends of $16,000 were declared, with $12,000 paid and $4,000 not yet paid.
m. Other operating expenses included salaries expense, pension expense, uncollectible accounts expense, and so forth.
n. Interest expense of $23,000 consisted of $11,000 of interest on the bonds ($10,000 plus $1,000 of discount amortization) and $12,000 of interest on the lease liability. The lease payment was $20,000.

REQUIRED

a. Prepare a schedule that reconciles the income statement and net cash provided by operating activities for 1995 by the direct approach.
b. Prepare a schedule that reconciles net income and net cash provided by operating activities for 1995 by the indirect approach.
c. Prepare a statement of cash flows for 1995, reporting cash flows from operating activities by the direct approach and noncash investing and financing activities in supplementary schedule.

2. Public Corporation has five industry segments, each of which had sales revenue, operating expenses, operating profit (loss), and identifiable assets for the year ended December 31, 1995, as shown on the following page. There were no intersegment sales or transfers.

REQUIRED

a. Identify Public Corporation's reportable industry segments for 1995, and prepare a schedule reporting financial information about the operations of its industry segments for the year ended December 31, 1995.
b. On the basis of the following facts related to Public Corporation's operations for the year ended December 31, 1995, compute the amounts that should be reported in each quarterly report for 1995 for net sales, selling expenses—sales commissions, administrative expenses—property taxes, interest expense, and income tax expense.
   (1). Net sales for the first through the fourth quarter of 1995 were $200,000, $160,000, $100,000, and $140,000, respectively. All sales were subject to a sales commission of 6 percent.
   (2). Annual property taxes of $10,000 were paid on January 1, 1995.
   (3). Interest on 12%, $100,000 bonds is payable semiannually on April 30 and October 31.
   (4). Pretax income from continuing operations for the first through the fourth quarter of 1995 and the estimated effective annual tax rate as of the end of each quarter were $12,000 (25%), $8,000 (35%), $4,000 (40%), and $6,000 (40%), respectively.

	INDUSTRY SEGMENTS					CORPORATE	TOTAL
	P	U	B	L	C		
Net sales	$240,000	$180,000	$90,000	$50,000	$40,000	$ -0-	$600,000
Cost of goods sold	$125,000	$105,000	$70,000	$30,000	$30,000	$ -0-	$360,000
Administrative expenses	35,000	23,000	16,000	8,000	8,000	14,000	104,000
Selling expenses	30,000	21,000	6,000	4,000	4,000	-0-	65,000
Depreciation expense	10,000	6,000	4,000	3,000	2,000	5,000	30,000
Operating profit (loss)	$ 40,000	$ 25,000	$ (6,000)	$ 5,000	$(4,000)	$ (19,000)	$ 41,000
Interest revenue	-0-	-0-	-0-	-0-	-0-	1,000	1,000
Interest expense	-0-	-0-	-0-	-0-	-0-	(12,000)	(12,000)
Income taxes	-0-	-0-	-0-	-0-	-0-	(12,000)	(12,000)
Net income (loss)	$ 40,000	$ 25,000	$ (6,000)	$ 5,000	$ (4,000)	$ (42,000)	$ 18,000
Identifiable assets	$160,000	$110,000	$80,000	$40,000	$30,000	$ 80,000	$500,000

COMMON ERRORS

The first statement of each of the "common errors" listed here is *incorrect*. Each incorrect statement is followed by a corrected statement and an explanation.

1. All transactions and events that cause changes in noncurrent balance sheet accounts should be reported in either the statement of cash flows or a supplementry schedule. *Wrong*

Investing and financing transactions and events that cause changes in noncurrent balance sheet accounts should be reported in either the statement of cash flows or a supplementary schedule; conversely, transactions and events that cause changes in noncurrent stockholders' equity accounts but do not represent investing or financing activities should be reported in neither the statement nor a supplementary schedule. *Right*

Stock dividends, stock splits, retained earnings appropriations, and reversals of retained earnings appropriations are transactions or events that cause changes in noncurrent stockholders' equity accounts but do not represent investing or financing activities. Thus these reclassifications within the stockholders' equity section of the balance sheet should not be reported as part of the statement of cash flows.

2. Net cash provided by operating activities is determined by adjusting the revenues and expenses included in net income, under the direct approach, or net income, under the indirect approach, for the changes in all noncash current accounts. *Wrong*

Net cash provided by operating activities should be determined by adjusting the revenues and expenses included in net income, under the direct approach, or net income, under the indirect approach,

for the changes in noncash current accounts that are related to the company's operating activities; conversely, the cash receipts and cash payments that cause the changes in noncash current accounts that are not related to the company's operating activities should be reported in the statement of cash flows as cash flows from investing or financing activities. *Right*

Net cash provided by operating activities may be determined by a direct approach or an indirect approach. Under the direct approach, the income statement is converted from an accrual basis to a cash basis by adjusting the revenues and expenses reported on the income statement for the changes in the related balance sheet accounts directly; under the indirect approach, net income is converted from an accrual basis to a cash basis by adjusting the revenues and expenses included in net income for the changes in the related balance sheet accounts indirectly. An increase or a decrease in receivables related to sales of merchandise, for example, is deducted from or added to sales revenue, under the direct approach, or net income, under the indirect approach, to adjust the accrual-basis revenues included in net income to the amount of cash collections from customers during the period. Changes in some noncash current accounts, however, are not related to accrual-basis amounts reported on the income statement. A good example is an increase in short-term notes payable arising from bank loans. If this increase in notes payable were deducted from expenses, under the direct approach, or added to net income, under the indirect approach, net cash provided by operating activities would not be a representative measure of the cash generated by the company's operating activities during the period. Thus changes in noncash current accounts that are not related to the company's operating activities should not be included in the determination of net cash provided by operating activities. Instead, the cash receipts and cash payments that cause the changes in these current accounts should be reported in the statement of cash flows as cash flows from investing or financing activities. Examples of current accounts that are not related to operating activities include dividends payable, notes receivable arising from activities other than sales, and notes payable arising from activities other than merchandise purchases.

3. Expenses that are not associated directly with revenue may be allocated arbitrarily among the interim periods. *Wrong*

Expenses that are not associated directly with revenue should be either deducted in calculating income in the interim period in which they are incurred or allocated among the interim periods on the basis of estimated time expired, benefit received, or activity associated with the periods. *Right*

Expenses that are not associated directly with revenue often are deducted in calculating income in the period in which they are incurred for annual reporting purposes because there is no determinable relationship between the expense and the activities or benefits of other annual periods. However, since each interim period should be viewed as an integral part of the annual period, these expenses may be allocated among the interim periods if there is a readily identifiable relationship between the expense and the activities or benefits of other interim periods within the current annual period. Annual period expenses that may be allocated among the interim periods include major repairs and advertising costs. Expenses that are not associated directly with revenue, however, should not be allocated arbitrarily among the interim periods. Instead, these expenses should be deducted in calculating income in the interim period in which they are incurred if there is no readily identifiable relationship between the expense and the activities or benefits of other interim periods.

4. Income tax expense for each interim period may be determined by multiplying pretax income from continuing operations for the interim period by the statutory tax rate. *Wrong*

Income tax expense for each interim period should be determined by multiplying pretax income from continuing operations for the current year to date by the estimated effective annual tax rate and subtracting from this amount the cumulative income tax expense recognized in all previous interim periods of the current annual period. *Right*

APB Opinion No. 28 requires that the estimated effective annual tax rate be used to determine income tax expense for each interim period on a current year-to-date basis. There are two reasons for this requirement. First, as each interim period is viewed as an integral part of the annual period, income tax expense for each interim period should be based on the estimated effective annual tax rate rather than on the statutory tax rate. Second, because changes in the estimated effective annual tax rate represent a change in accounting estimate, income tax expense for each interim period should be determined on a current year-to-date basis.

5. All public companies are required to report information about their operations in different industry segments. *Wrong*

Public companies need not report information about their operations in different industry segments if certain materiality tests are met. *Right*

Statement No. 14 specifies that information about industry segments need not be reported if a company is dominated by a single industry segment with revenue, operating profit or loss, and identifiable assets each constituting more than 90 percent of the related combined totals for all industry segments and no other industry segment meets any of the 10 percent materiality tests for classification as a reportable segment. Otherwise, public companies are required to report information about their operations in different industry segments in the annual financial statements.

6. The amount of revenue generated by a public company from sales to each major customer must be disclosed only if the company is required to report information about industry segments or foreign operations. *Wrong*

The amount of revenue generated by a public company from sales to each major customer must be disclosed even if a company is not required to report information about industry segments or foreign operations. *Right*

Statement No. 14 requires public companies to report up to four different types of information if specific materiality tests for each type of information are met. (*a*) Information about industry segments is required to be reported unless the company is dominated by a single industry segment with revenue, operating profit or loss, and identifiable assets each constituting more than 90 percent of the related combined totals of all industry segments and no other industry segment meets any of the 10 percent materiality tests for classification as a reportable segment. (*b*) Information about foreign operations and domestic operations is required to be reported if either revenue generated by foreign operations from sales to unaffiliated customers is 10 percent or more of the total revenue reported in the company's income statement or identifiable assets of foreign operations are 10 percent or more of the total assets reported in the company's balance sheet. (*c*) The amount of revenue generated by domestic operations from export sales is required to be reported if it is 10 percent or more of the total revenue reported in the company's income statement. (*d*) The amount of revenue generated by sales to each major customer is required to be reported if it constitutes 10 percent or more of the total revenue reported in the company's income statement. Each of these four types of disclosures is required only if the corresponding materiality test is met.

7. An industry segment should be classified as a reportable segment if its operating profit or loss is 10 percent or more of the operating profit or loss reported in the company's income statement. *Wrong*

An industry segment should be classified as a reportable segment if the absolute amount of its operating profit or loss is 10 percent or more of the greater, in absolute amount, of either the combined operating profit of all industry segments with operating profits or the combined operating loss of all industry segments with operating losses. *Right*

The application of the operating profit or loss materiality test for the classification of an industry segment as a reportable segment is illustrated in *Statement No. 14* as follows. First, the absolute amount of the combined operating profit of all industry segments with operating profits and the absolute amount of the combined operating loss of all industry segments with operating losses are determined. Second, the greater of these two absolute amounts is multiplied by 10 percent. Third, all industry segments with operating profits or losses of an absolute amount equal to or greater than this product are classified as reportable segments.

ANSWERS
Items marked with an asterisk (*) refer to the Appendix.

Key Terms and Concepts

*1. worksheet, T-accounts
2. interim reports
3. segment reporting
4. unaffiliated customers
5. industry segment
6. identifiable assets
7. reportable segments
8. foreign operations
9. domestic operations
10. export sales

True-False

1. T
2. F Interest that accrues on a lease liability over the term of a capital lease is recognized as interest expense and as an increase in the lease liability. Thus, the lease payments that are recognized as a reduction of the lease liability, in effect, are partly a payment of interest and partly a payment of principal. Because interest expense should be included in the determination of net cash provided by operating activities, the excess of the lease payments over the interest expense for a period should be reported as a cash outflow in the financing activities section of the statement of cash flows.
3. F Cash dividends declared but not paid during the period are a noncash financing activity that should be reported in either a narrative or a supplementary schedule to the statement of cash flows.
4. F Conversion of preferred stock into common stock is a noncash financing activity that should be reported in either a narrative or a supplementary schedule to the statement of cash flows.
5. F Even though stock dividends cause changes in noncash balance sheet accounts, this transaction should be reported in neither the statement of cash flows nor a supplementary schedule, because it represents a reclassification within stockholders' equity rather than a financing activity.
6. F Cash flows from transactions or other events whose effects are included in net income, but which are investing or financing activities, should be classified in the statement of cash flows on the basis of the nature of the underlying transaction or event rather than included in the determination of net cash provided by operating activities. An extraordinary gain or loss on extinguishment of debt, for example, should be reported as part of a cash outflow for financing activities, and a gain or

loss from sale of plant assets should be reported as part of a cash inflow from investing activities.

7. F When interim financial reports are prepared, each interim period should be viewed as an integral part of the annual period rather than as a basic or discrete accounting period.

8. F The results of operations for each interim period generally should be based on the accounting principles used by a company for its most recent annual financial statements. However, because each interim period is viewed as an integral part of the annual period, certain modifications in the application of generally accepted accounting principles are permitted for the preparation of interim financial reports.

9. T

10. T

11. F The materiality of extraordinary items and other items that are reported separately on the income statement net of applicable income taxes should be determined at the interim period date on the basis of the estimated income for the annual period. That is, as each interim period should be viewed as an integral part of the annual period, extraordinary items and other items occurring during an interim period should be reported net of applicable income taxes in the interim report for that period only if it is expected that they will be reported in that manner in the annual financial statements.

12. F The cumulative effect of a change in accounting principle that qualifies for the current period approach should be included in net income of the first interim period even if the change is made in a later interim period of the current annual period. When the change is made in an interim period other than the first, financial information of the prechange interim periods of the current annual period should be retroactively restated to show the effects of the change and the cumulative effect of the change on retained earnings at the beginning of the current annual period should be included in the restated net income of the first interim period of the annual period.

13. T

14. T

15. F Information must be reported separately for each industry segment that meets one or more of the 10 percent materiality tests for classification as a reportable segment.

Moreover, if the combined revenue from sales of all reportable segments to unaffiliated customers is less than 75 percent of the combined revenue from sales of all industry segments to unaffiliated customers, information must be reported separately for additional industry segments until the 75 percent test is met. The required information also must be reported, in the aggregate, for the remainder of the industry segments. Information about industry segments need not be reported, however, if the company is dominated by a single industry segment with revenue, operating profit or loss, and identifiable assets each constituting more than 90 percent of the related combined totals for all industry segments and if no other industry segment meets any of the 10 percent materiality tests for a reportable segment.

16. T

17. T

18. F The combined totals of the information reported for each reportable segment and, in the aggregate, for the remainder of the industry segments normally will not equal the related amounts reported in a company's financial statements for a variety of reasons. Revenue and operating profit or loss reported for the industry segments, for example, include amounts from intersegment sales or transfers, whereas revenue and operating profit or loss reported in a company's income statement exclude these amounts. In addition, the identifiable assets reported for the industry segments exclude assets that are maintained for general corporate purposes, whereas the total assets reported in a company's balance sheet include these assets. These differences are representative of the reconciling items that are required to be reported.

19. F Information about foreign operations is required to be reported by public companies if either of the following materiality tests is met: (*a*) revenue generated by foreign operations from sales to unaffiliated customers is 10 percent or more of the total revenue reported in a company's income statement, or (*b*) identifiable assets of foreign operations are 10 percent or more of the total assets reported in a company's balance sheet.

20. F The amount of revenue generated by domestic operations from sales to unaffiliated customers in foreign countries must be reported by public companies only if it is 10 percent or more of the total revenue

reported in the company's income statement. This disclosure is required even if the company is not required to report information about industry segments or foreign operations.

Multiple Choice

1.	c	6.	c
2.	d	7.	c
3.	a	8.	b
4.	c	9.	b
5.	d	10.	d

Extended Problems

1. Statement of cash flows:

   a. Reconciliation of income statement and net cash provided by operating activities by the direct approach:

	ACCRUAL BASIS	ADJUSTMENTS AND EXCLUSIONS[a]	CASH BASIS
Sales	$680,000	$ 2,000	$682,000
Interest revenue	3,000	-0-	3,000
Investment revenue	18,000	(13,000)	5,000
Realized gain on sale of investment	2,000	(2,000)	-0-
Cost of goods sold	(400,000)	{(13,000) 5,000}	(408,000)
Depreciation expense	(48,000)	48,000	-0-
Other operating expenses	(179,000)	{9,000 (1,000) (4,000) (5,000)}	(180,000)
Interest expense	(23,000)	1,000	(22,0000
Loss on sale of equipment	(3,000)	3,000	-0-
Income taxes	(20,000)	2,000	(18,000)
Net income	$ 30,000)		
Net cash provided by operating activities			$ 62,000

[a]The decrease in accounts receivable before deduction of accounts receivable written off [$88,000 – ($76,000 + $10,000) = $2,000] is added to sales because the cash collections from customers are greater than the sales during the period. The increase in the equity-basis investment ($13,000) is deducted from investment revenue because the dividends received ($5,000) were less than the revenue during the period. The realized gain on the sale of investment ($2,000) is excluded because it is neither a measure of the cash provided by the sale nor related to operations. The increase in inventories ($13,000) is added to cost of goods sold because the purchases are greater than the cost of goods sold during the period. The increase in accounts payable ($5,000) is deducted from cost of goods sold because the cash payments to suppliers are less than the purchases during the period. Depreciation expense ($48,000) is excluded because it does not require an outlay of cash during the period. The increase in allowance for uncollectible accounts before deduction of accounts receivable written off [($5,000 + $10,000) – $6,000 = $9,000] is deducted from other operating expenses because uncollectible accounts expense does not require an outlay of cash. The increase in prepaid expenditures ($1,000) is added to other operating expenses because the cash payments are greater than the expense during the period. The decrease in salaries payable ($4,000) is added to other operating expenses because the cash payments are greater than the expense during the period. The decrease in pension liability ($5,000) is added to other operating expenses because the amount funded is greater than the expense during the period. Discount amortization on bonds payable ($1,000), loss on sale of equipment ($3,000), and increase in deferred tax liability ($2,000) are deducted from interest expense, loss on sale of equipment, and income taxes, respectively, because these items do not require an outlay of cash during the period.

b. Reconciliation of net income and net cash provided by operating activities by the indirect approach:

Net income	$ 30,000
Adjustments to reconcile net income to net cash provided by operating activities:	
Realized gain on sale of investment	(2,000)
Depreciation expense	48,000
Amortization of discount on bonds payable	1,000
Uncollectible accounts expense	9,000
Loss on sale of equipment	3,000
Increase in investment at equity method	(13,000)
Decrease in pension liability	(5,000)
Increase in deferred tax liability	2,000
Decrease in accounts receivable (before deducting accounts written off)	2,000
Increase in inventories	(13,000)
Increase in prepaid expenditures	(1,000)
Increase in accounts payable	5,000
Decrease in salaries payable	(4,000)
Net cash provided by operating activities	$ 62,000

c. Statement of cash flows and supplementary schedule for noncash investing and financing activities:

SCF Company

STATEMENT OF CASH FLOWS
FOR THE YEAR ENDED DECEMBER 31, 1995

Cash flows from operating activities:		
Cash received from customers	$682,000	
Interest received	3,000	
Dividends received	5,000	
Cash paid to suppliers of merchandise	(408,000)	
Cash paid to employees and other suppliers	(180,000)	
Interest paid	(22,000)	
Income taxes paid	(18,000)	
Net cash provided by operating activities		$ 62,000
Cash flows from investing activities:		
Purchase of land	$ (20,000)	
Purchase of equipment	(60,000)	
Sale of investment in securities	13,000	
Sale of equipment	7,000	
Net cash used by investing activities		(60,000)
Cash flows from financing activities:		
Issuance of common stock	$ 24,000	
Retirement of common stock	(6,000)	
Dividends paid	(12,000)	
Repayment of lease liability	(8,000)	
Issuance of short-term note payable	40,000	
Repayment of short-term note payable	(30,000)	
Net cash provided by financing activities		8,000
Net increase in cash and cash equivalents		$ 10,000
Cash and cash equivalents at beginning of year		30,000
Cash and cash equivalents at end of year		$ 40,000
Supplementary schedule of noncash investing and financing activities:		
Purchase of land		$ 38,000
Less: Cash paid for land		(20,000)
Purchased by issuing common stock		$ 18,000
Issuance of common stock upon conversion of preferred stock		$ 30,000
Dividends declared		$ 16,000
Less: Dividends paid		(12,000)
Dividends payable		$ 4,000

2. a. Identification of reportable industry segments:

	INDUSTRY SEGMENTS				
	P	U	B	L	C
Revenue test, that is, segment's revenue equal to or greater than $60,000 (10% × $600,000)?...	Yes	Yes	Yes	No	No
Operating profit/loss test, that is, segment's operating profit/loss equal to or greater than $7,000 (10% × $70,000)?[a]	Yes	Yes	No	No	No
Identifiable assets test, that is, segment's identifiable assets equal to or greater than $42,000 [10% × ($500,000 − $80,000)]?...........	Yes	Yes	Yes	No	No
Reportable segment, that is, one or more of preceding tests met?[b].............	Yes	Yes	Yes	No	No

[a]The combined operating profit of all industry segments with operating profits ($40,000 + $25,000 + $5,000 = $70,000) is greater than the combined operating loss of all industry segments with operating losses ($6,000 + $4,000 = $10,000), and so this amount is used in the operating profit/loss test.

[b]The combined revenue from sales of all reportable segments to unaffiliated customers ($240,000 + $180,000 + $90,000 = $510,000) is equal to or greater than 75 percent of the combined revenue from sales of all industry segments to unaffiliated customers (75% × $600,000 = $450,000), and so no additional industry segments must be classified as reportable segments.

Schedule reporting financial information about operations of industry segments:

Public Corporation
INFORMATION ABOUT OPERATIONS IN DIFFERENT INDUSTRIES
FOR THE YEAR ENDED DECEMBER 31, 1995

	INDUSTRY			OTHER INDUS-TRIES	CONSOL-IDATED
	P	U	B		
Net sales	$240,000	$180,000	$ 90,000	$ 90,000	$600,000
Operating profit (loss)............................	$ 40,000	$ 25,000	$ (6,000)	$ 1,000	$ 60,000
Interest revenue.....................................					1,000
General corporate expense					(19,000)
Interest expense.....................................					(12,000)
Income from continuing operations before taxes...					$ 30,000
Identifiable assets, 12/31/95.....................	$160,000	$110,000	$ 80,000	$ 70,000	$420,000
Corporate assets......................................					80,000
Total assets, 12/31/95.............................					$500,000

Note to schedule: Depreciation for industries P, U, and B was $10,000, $6,000, and $4,000, respectively. There were no capital expenditures by any industry segments during 1995.

b. Computation of interim financial report amounts:

	QUARTER			
	1st	2nd	3rd	4th
Net sales	$200,000	$160,000	$100,000	$140,000
Selling expenses—sales commissions (net sales × 6%)......	12,000	9,600	6,000	8,400
Administrative expenses—property taxes ($10,000 × 3/12)...	2,500	2,500	2,500	2,500
Interest expense ($100,000 × 12% × 3/12)	3,000	3,000	3,000	3,000
Income tax expense ($12,000 × 25%)............................	3,000			
[($20,000 × 35%) − $3,000]		4,000		
[($24,000 × 40%) − $7,000]			2,600	
[($30,000 × 40%) − $9,600]				2,400

APPENDIX
CONCEPTS OF PRESENT AND FUTURE VALUE

APPENDIX OBJECTIVES

After reading the Appendix and completing the questions, cases, exercises, and problems from the text, you should be able to:

1. Understand the concept of interest and the variables—amount of principal (p), rate of interest (i), and time period (n)—that affect the dollar amount of interest.
2. Differentiate between simple and compound interest.
3. Understand the concept and calculation of the future value of a single amount, a.
4. Understand the concept and calculation of the present value of a single amount, p.

5. Find the unknown variable i (or n) when a, p, and n (or i) are known.
6. Define an annuity, and distinguish between an ordinary annuity and an annuity due.
7. Understand the concepts and calculation of the future and present values of an ordinary annuity.
8. Understand the concepts and calculation of the future and present values of an annuity due.
9. Understand the concepts and calculation of the future and present values of a deferred annuity.
10. Apply the concepts of future value and present value to the accounting for long-term bonds, pension obligations, equipment replacement funds, and lease obligations.

APPENDIX REVIEW

Introduction

1. The value of money is not static; it changes over time. Thus we say that money has a time value. A dollar invested today can earn interest or a return in the future, so that the investor can receive an amount in the future greater than the amount initially invested. The concepts of present and future value are closely related to the notion of the time value of money and have influenced the development of accounting theory and practice. Accountants use these concepts to record and report some accounting information, such as that related to leases, bonds, and pensions, and in capital budgeting. The Appendix review covers the basic interest computations and fundamentals of the present and future values of both single amounts and annuities, and it discusses some applications of these concepts to accounting.

Interest and the Time Value of Money

2. Stated simply, *interest* is the cost of borrowing money or the return on money lent. In other words, interest is the difference between the amount borrowed or lent and the amount paid or received in the future. Interest rates are normally stated as an annual rate and are affected by the perceived risk or probability of nonpayment applicable to each transaction. Thus similar loan transactions may have different stated interest rates because the perceived risks of nonpayment by the borrower are different. Similarly, companies will make an investment only if the interest or return on the investment is sufficient to balance the risk of the investment. As a company decides on investment alternatives, it attempts to balance the risk of each investment against its expected return. The greater the risk is, the higher the interest or return must be to make the proposal attractive.

3. The three variables that affect the dollar amount of interest in a given situation are (*a*) the *amount* or *principal* borrowed or lent; (*b*) the *rate of interest*; and (*c*) the *time period* covered by the loan. As each of these variables increases, so does the dollar amount of the interest.

4. Simple interest. *Simple interest* represents interest that is earned on the beginning principal only. The formula for the calculation of simple interest is $I = p \times i \times n$, where I = the simple interest, p = the principal or amount borrowed or lent at the contract date, i = the interest rate per year, and n = the number of years or fractional portions thereof. For purposes of calculations in the text, a month is considered to be 1/12 of a year and a day 1/30 of a month, or 1/360 of a year.

5. Compound interest. *Compound interest* is interest that is earned on both interest *and* principal. If the time period of the principal extends beyond one interest period, interest for each subsequent period will be earned on the original principal plus the interest earned (accumulated) for the preceding period or periods. In effect, the principal increases each period by the amount of interest earned that period. Because the compounding of interest permits interest to be earned on both principal and interest, the total interest earned on an amount outstanding for more than two or more periods will be greater than the amount that would be earned if simple interest were calculated, because under the simple interest method, interest is calculated only on the initial principal each period.

6. As previously stated, interest rates are normally expressed as an annual (yearly) rate. If interest is to be calculated for a period of less than a year, the annual interest rate must be adjusted. The following formulas will be used throughout the remainder of the Appendix to adjust an annual interest rate for periods of less than a year:

a. Interest rate per compounding period = Annual rate ÷ Number of compounding periods per year.
b. Total number of interest compounding periods = Number of years involved × Number of compounding periods per year.

Present and Future Value—Single Amounts

7. To visualize the cash flows associated with a particular situation over time, a time diagram is normally prepared. As illustrated in the text, a *time diagram* divides a horizontal time line into equal time periods, called interest periods or compounding periods. The 0 (zero) point on the line represents the present; the end point represents the future.

8. Future value. The *future value of a single amount*, signified by the symbol *a*, is the total amount of money that would accumulate by the end of several interest periods from a single amount invested. A time diagram of the future value of a single amount is as follows:

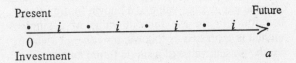

9. To determine the dollar value of *a*, the principal is multiplied by the appropriate interest rate and then the interest thus determined is added to the principal to determine the future value at the end of one period. This procedure is repeated until the future value is calculated for the desired number of periods. Another approach is to use the general formula for the future value of a single amount: $a = p(a_{\overline{n}|i})$, where a = the future value of a single sum, p = the beginning principal, $a_{\overline{n}|i}$ (read "small a angle n at i") = $(1 + i)^n$, i = the interest rate per period, and n = the number of interest periods. Although this formula can be used, it is more convenient to use tables that have been constructed for the future value factors ($a_{\overline{n}|i}$) for various interest rates and time periods. A table (Table A) of the future value factors appears in the text at the end of this Appendix, and a partial table appears at the end of the Answers section of this Appendix. To use the table illustrated to find the future value factor, first locate the appropriate number of interest compounding periods in the n column and then move across the selected n row until the appropriate interest rate (i) column is found. (Remember that interest rates are normally expressed as annual rates. If interest is compounded more frequently than once a year, the appropriate n and i must be found by means of the adjustments previously explained.) The table value at the intersection of the n row and i column is the future value factor to use in a future value calculation; that is, $a = p \times$ future value factor. Before continuing, check your understanding of the use of the table by seeing whether you agree that the future value factor for $a_{\overline{8}|5\%}$) is 1.4775.

10. Present value. *Present value* is the value today of an amount to be received or paid in the future. The concept of present value, which has many applications in accounting, is illustrated by a time diagram:

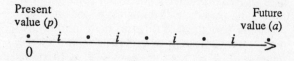

Present
value (*p*)   Future
                                              value (*a*)

11. The time diagram makes it clear that there is a relationship between the present value and future value. In fact, the present value of a future amount can be calculated by dividing the known future value by the appropriate factor in Table A. This is not, however, the most efficient way to calculate the present value of a known future value. The formula for the present value of a single amount is expressed as follows: $p = a(p_{\overline{n}|i})$, where *p* = the present value of a single future amount, *a* = the future amount, $p_{\overline{n}|i}$ read "small *p* angle *n* at *i*") $= \dfrac{1}{(1 + i)^n}$, *i* = interest rate per period, and *n* = the number of periods. Again, tables have been constructed to provide present value factors of a single amount. Table B, as found in the text and at the end of this Appendix, contains factors for the present value of 1 at various interest rates and time periods. This table is read in a manner similar to that described for Table A.

12. The present value of an amount to be received or paid in the future represents the future amount *discounted* for *n* periods at *i* rate of interest. In other words, if the present value amount were invested at *i* interest rate for *n* periods, the present value amount would increase to the future amount. The amount of periodic interest earned in each of the *n* periods increases (decreases) as the investment increases (decreases), but it is always at a constant rate of return, that is, *i*. The process of calculating periodic interest by multiplying the investment at the beginning of the period by *i* is referred to as the *effective interest method,* and it is one of the most important concepts used in accounting and finance.

13. Special single amount considerations. In situations requiring the calculation of a future value or present value, it has been assumed that the interest rate (*i*) and number of periods (*n*) are known for the present value and future value of a single amount, respectively. It should be understood, however, that if the values of any three of the four variables (*a, p, i,* and *n*) are known, the unknown variable may be determined. In some situations, for example, both *a* and *p* and *either n* or

i may be known, and the unknown variable (either *n* or *i*) needs to be determined. If *n* is the unknown variable, it may be found by an approach based on the formula for either the future value or the present value. When the present value formula [*p* = $a(p_{\overline{n}|i})$] is used, the first step is to divide *p* by *a;* this calculation results in a present value factor ($p_{\overline{n}|i}$) as found in Table B. Next, to find *n*, read down the interest column for the known *i* until the calculated present value factor is located and then read across to find the value of *n*. A similar approach can be used with the future value formula ($a = p_{\overline{n}|i}$) and Table A. Moreover, if *n* were known, but not *i, i* could be determined by the same general approaches just described, except that when Table B or Table A is used, you should read across the known *n* row until the calculated present value or future value factor is found in an interest column. Move up this interest column to find the related *i* percentage.

14. Interest rates may change over time because of inflation, fluctuations in supply and demand, investors' perception of risk, and other factors. When interest rates change, the calculations of future values and present values are adjusted accordingly. If a single sum is invested now and the interest rate changes before the sum is withdrawn, for example, the determination of its future value becomes a series of future value calculations. The future value of the initial investment is calculated for the number of periods at the beginning interest rate until the interest rate changes. The future value just calculated is now treated as a new investment, and its future value is calculated at the new interest rate for the number of periods the new interest rate stays constant. This process of using the calculated future value as a new investment is repeated each time the interest rate changes and for as long as the initial single amount remains invested.

Present and Future Value—Annuities

15. An *annuity* is a series of equal cash flows called rents (either cash payments or receipts) that occur at equal intervals over a period of time. The cash flows (*R*) can occur at the end or beginning of an interest period. When the first of the series of cash flows occurs at the end of the first interest period, the annuity is called an *ordinary annuity* or an annuity in arrears; when the cash flow occurs at the beginning of the interest period, the annuity is an *annuity due* or annuity in advance. The difference between an ordinary annuity and an annuity due is depicted in the time diagrams on the following page.

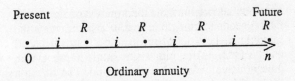

Ordinary annuity

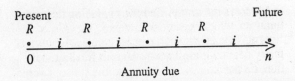

Annuity due

Ordinary Annuity

16. Future value. The *future value* of an ordinary annuity is the amount that would accumulate at the end of n periods if equal cash flows occurred at the end of each of the n periods. One method to calculate the future value of an ordinary annuity is to consider each individual cash flow as a single amount and add the calculated future values of each single amount. A less tedious and time-consuming method is to use the formula for the future value of an ordinary annuity: $A = R(A_{\overline{n}|i})$, where A = the future value of an ordinary annuity, R = the periodic cash flows (rents), A (read "capital A angle n at i") $= \dfrac{(1 + i)^n - 1}{i}$, n = the number of rents, and i = the interest rate per period. Yet another approach is to use a table (Table C), which appears at the end of this Appendix. If the amount of the rent, number of periods, and interest rate are known, the future value of the series of rents is calculated by multiplying R by the ordinary annuity factor from Table C for the appropriate i and n. It should be recalled that i and n must be determined according to the rules previously stated if the rents are received or paid at intervals of less than one year. Moreover, it should be apparent that the amount of interest increases each succeeding period because it is based on the amount accumulated at the beginning of the period, which increases each period by the amount of the rent and the interest for the preceding period.

17. Present value. The *present value of an ordinary annuity* is the value now of periodic rents that will occur over n periods at a certain interest rate (i). The present value of an ordinary annuity may be computed in three ways. First, each cash flow can be considered as a single amount, and the present value of the ordinary annuity is equal to the sum of the present values of each of the single amounts. Again, this approach can become laborious if there are many rents. Second, the formula approach may be used: $P = R(p_{\overline{n}|i})$, where P = present value of an ordinary annuity, R = the periodic annuity of rent, $P_{\overline{n}|i}$ (read "capital P angle n at i") $= \dfrac{1 - \dfrac{1}{(1 + i)^n}}{i}$, n = the number of rents, and i = the interest (discount) rate per period. Third, Table D, as illustrated in the text and at the end of this Appendix, contains the present value of an ordinary annuity factor $(P_{\overline{n}|i})$ for various values of i and n. If R, n, and i are known, P is found by multiplying R by the present value of an ordinary annuity factor for the appropriate values for n and i.

18. An interesting pattern arises when an annuity is withdrawn from an initial investment. For each period that interest is earned on the investment at the beginning of the period, the investment increases; but with each periodic cash flow or withdrawal (rent), the investment decreases. This results in a "sawtooth curve." It should be noted that if the interest earned is greater than the periodic withdrawal, the investment would continue to grow. Conversely, if the interest earned is less than the periodic withdrawal, the investment would eventually decrease to zero. This pattern has many accounting applications, such as pensions and leases.

19. Other values related to ordinary annuities. At the end of the discussion of single amounts, techniques for determining an unknown variable if three other variables are known were presented. The same basic techniques apply to ordinary annuities and are briefly reviewed. If R, P, or A, and n or i are known, it is possible to find the unknown variable, i or n. If R, A, and i are known, for example, n can be determined by the formula $A = R\ (A_{\overline{n}|i})$. Since A and R are known, A divided by R will result in a future value of an ordinary annuity factor which can be located in Table C. When you read down the known i column until the factor is located and then move across the row, the unknown n is the n that corresponds to the appropriate row. Similarly, if i is unknown and n is known, you can find i by moving across the known n row until you locate the factor and then moving up the column where the factor appeared to read the corresponding i rate.

20. When R, P, and n are known, i can be determined by the formula $P = R(P_{\overline{n}|i})$. As before, with P and R known, P divided by R will result in a present value of an ordinary annuity factor as found in Table D. Read across the known n row until the calculated factor is located and then move up the corresponding column; the i at the top of the column is the unknown i. If the same situation existed except that n rather than i were unknown, n could be found by reading down the known i column until the calculated factor was located and then across the row to find the corresponding n for that row, which is the unknown n.

21. A somewhat different situation arises when P or A, i, and n are known, but not R. Say that P, i, and n are known. In this case the present value of an ordinary annuity formula, $P = R(P_{\overline{n}|i})$, is used. Since P and $P_{\overline{n}|i}$ are known, R is found by solving for R, that is, $P \div P_{\overline{n}|i}$.

22. In summary, it should be evident from this discussion and the similar one related to single amounts that when the appropriate formula and table are used, it is possible to determine one of the variables of the formula if the other variables are known. These techniques are often used by accountants.

Annuities Due

23. Like ordinary annuities, annuities due have periodic cash flows. The cash flows occur, however, at the *beginning* of each interest period rather than at the end, as is the case with ordinary annuities. Tables C and D contain the future value and present value factors for ordinary annuities, respectively, and require adjustment to be used for annuities due.

24. Future value.

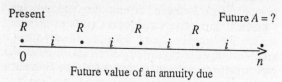
Future value of an annuity due

As the preceding time diagram indicates, the number of interest periods is equal to the number of rents in an annuity due problem. It should be recalled that Table C was derived for an ordinary annuity, which has one less interest period than the number of rents. Thus, in order to use Table C for an annuity due problem, a modification to the formula must be made *before* Table C can be used. Basically, the annuity due must be converted in such a way that it appears to be an ordinary annuity. A revised time diagram for an annuity due appears as follows:

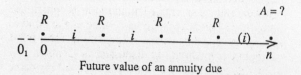
Future value of an annuity due

Notice that by moving back to 0_1, the first rent is in effect made at the end of the first period; and by eliminating the last i period, that is, (i), the diagram is like that for an ordinary annuity (one

less interest period than the number of rents). To find the future value of an annuity due, calculate the future value of an ordinary annuity (A) for the R, n, and i and then, treating A as a single amount, find the future value of A for one period. The formula for the future value of an annuity due becomes:

$$A_D = R(A_{\overline{n}|i})(1 + i)$$

25. Present value.

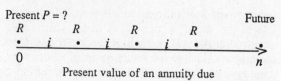
Present value of an annuity due

The preceding time diagram of the present value of an annuity due shows that the number of interest periods is one less than the number of periodic rents. Table D was compiled for the present value of an ordinary annuity, which has an equal number of interest periods and rents. Accordingly, the formula for the present value of an ordinary annuity, $P = R(P_{\overline{n}|i})$, must be modified. Similar to the adjustment made for the future value of an annuity due, a revised time diagram for the present value of an annuity due is as follows:

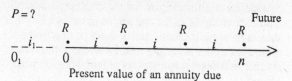
Present value of an annuity due

As before, the time diagram is extended back one period to 0_1, and it now appears as the present value of an ordinary annuity (an equal number of rents and interest periods). To calculate the present value of an annuity due, find the present value of an ordinary annuity for the given R, n, and i and then compound this amount for one period. The modified formula for the present value of an annuity due becomes:

$$P_D = R(P_{\overline{n}|i})(1 + i)$$

26. Since many of the problems accountants need to solve involve the present value of annuities due, a special table has been constructed. Table E, which appears at the end of this Appendix, provides the factors for the present value of an annuity due. To find the present value of an annuity due of n rents and i interest by means of Table E, multiply R by the present value of an annuity due factor found at the intersection of the n row and the i column. Thus no modification of the formula for the present value of an ordinary annuity is necessary when Table E is used.

Present P = ?   Future A = ?

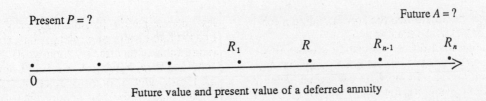

Future value and present value of a deferred annuity

Deferred Annuities

27. In another type of annuity, called a *deferred annuity,* the first rent occurs after at least two periods have elapsed. The time diagram at the top of this page illustrates the future value and present value of a deferred annuity.

28. Finding the future value of a deferred annuity, assuming the cash flow occurs at the end of the period, is relatively simple. It is found exactly as if it were an ordinary annuity of n rents at i interest rate. Since no rent or interest accrues during the deferral period, the deferral period has no effect on the calculation of the future value.

29. The calculation of the *present value of a deferred annuity,* however, is more complicated. Because no rents are made but interest does accrue during the deferral period, the usual present value calculation cannot be used. One way to find the present value of an annuity of n rents and R dollar amount at an interest rate of i deferred n^1 periods requires a two-step process. First, find the present value of an ordinary annuity $[P = R(P_{\overline{n}|i})]$ to one period before the first rent. Second, find the present value of a single amount to the present $[p = a(p_{\overline{n}|i})]$, where a is equal to P from the first step. Another approach is to consider the annuity as starting at the end of the present period for $n + n^1$ rents or periods, calculate its present value, and then deduct the present value of an annuity of R cash flows for n^1 periods or the deferral period; this is, $P = R(P_{\overline{n+n}|i}) - R(P_{\overline{n}|i})$.

Accounting Applications

30. **Long-term bonds.** The issuance of a long-term bond requires that a selling, or issue, price be established for the bond. The issue price is based on the two future cash flow streams associated with the long-term bond: the interest payments made periodically (usually paid at the end of the period) and the principal, or face value, of the bond (usually paid at maturity). Because these cash flows occur in the future, the issue price of a bond is equal to the present value of the principal (a single amount) plus the present value of the interest payments (an ordinary annuity) or bond issue price =

$a(p_{\overline{n}|i}) + R(P_{\overline{n}|i})$, where a = the principal amount due at bond's maturity, R = the periodic interest payment calculated at the stated interest rate, n = the number of interest compounding periods until the bond matures, and i = the market rate of interest for bonds of similar risk. It should be noted that the market rate of interest—the rate of interest an investor earns on the investment in the bond—directly affects the issue price.

31. If the stated interest rate equals the market rate of interest, the present value of the bond will equal the face or par value of the bond. At this purchase price, an investor would be able to receive a rate of return (Rate of return = Interest + Principal) equal to the market rate of interest. If the stated interest rate is less than the market interest rate, the present value of the bond, and thus its selling price, will be less than the face value of the bond. The difference between the face value and present value is referred to as the *bond discount*. This difference occurs because an investor is unwilling to pay the par value for a bond that permits a return of only the stated rate of interest when the market rate of interest for bonds of similar risk is higher. Thus the bond sells for its present value because at this price the bond provides an investor an *effective yield* equal to the current market rate of interest. In other words, by initially paying less than par value for a bond, an investor can earn an effective return on the investment equal to the higher market rate of interest on bonds of similar risk.

32. In contrast, if the stated interest rate is greater than the market rate of interest, the present value of the bond will be greater than its face value. The bond will sell at the higher amount because it will provide an investor an effective yield on the bond investment that equals the current market (lower) rate of interest. The amount by which the present value exceeds the face value of the bond is called the *bond premium*. (Accounting for a bond discount or premium is discussed in Chapter 14.) Thus at all times the issue price of a long-term bond is equal to the present value of the cash flows of the bond. Moreover, at no time will an investor earn more or less on an investment in a long-term bond than the market rate or effective yield rate of interest on bonds of similar risk.

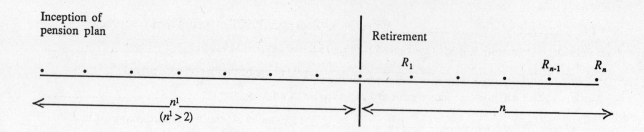

Inception of pension plan

Retirement

R_1 R_{n-1} R_n

n^1
$(n^1 > 2)$

n

33. Employee pension plans. A pension plan provides retirement benefits for a company's employees. These annual payments normally start at the date of an employee's retirement and continue until the employee's death. For financial reporting purposes, these future pension payments or pension obligations should be reported at their present value.

34. To simplify the following illustration, assume that the pension plan is initiated in the present period and pertains to only one employee. Further assume that the annual pension payments, an annuity (R), the expected number of payments (n), and the interest rate (i) are known. The problem of finding the present value of the pension plan in the present period, at least two periods before the date of retirement (n^1), is the same as that of calculating the present value of a deferred annuity. A time diagram for a typical pension plan is presented above.

35. It should be recalled that the present value of a deferred annuity is found by first calculating the present value of the annuity to one period before the first payment and then calculating the present value of this single amount to the present period:

present value of pension plan $= R(P_{\overline{n}|i})(p_{\overline{n}|i})$. The present value of the deferred annuity represents the amount that, if it were invested now by the company, would provide the employee an annuity that would commence upon retirement and continue until the employee's death. Pension plans are discussed in Chapter 16.

36. Lease obligations. As an alternative to purchasing property, many companies enter into an agreement to lease property. Because a lease requires future payments, many accountants believe that the lease obligation should be reported on the balance sheet at its present value. The present value is also thought to be the cash equivalent price of the leased asset. To calculate the present value of the lease obligation, the formula for the present value of an annuity due is used, because the lease payments normally begin at the inception of the lease: $P_D = R[(P_{\overline{n}|i})(1 + i)]$ where P = the present value of the lease payments, R = the periodic lease payment, n = the number of lease payments, and i = the discount rate. Leases are discussed in Chapter 15.

SELF-STUDY LEARNING

Key Terms and Concepts

Provide the appropriate term or terms to complete each of the following statements:

1. The cost of borrowing money or the return on money lent is called _____.

2. When interest is earned on both interest and principal, it is referred to as _____ interest.

3. If a lump-sum deposit is made now, the concept related to the amount that will accumulate by a future time period is called the _____ concept.

4. The _____ of an amount of money is the value today of the amount to be received or paid in the future.

5. When the _____ method is used, the rate of return on an investment _____ each period.

6. A(n) _____ is a series of equal cash flows that occur at equal intervals.

7. If the rent of an annuity is paid at the end of each period, it is referred to as a(n) _____.

8. The rent of a(n) _____ is paid at the beginning of each period.

9. All future value and present value cases can be depicted on a(n) _____.

10. The first rent of a(n) _____ occurs after at least two periods have expired.

True-False

Indicate by circling the appropriate response whether each of the following statements is true (T) or false (F):

T F 1. Interest is the difference between the amount borrowed and the amount paid in the future.

T F 2. Loans of the same type and for the same dollar amount normally have the same interest rate.

T F 3. In making a decision between two investment proposals, a company is most likely to select the one with the lowest return and lowest risk.

T F 4. Simple interest is computed for a period of only one year.

T F 5. When interest is deducted on an amount in advance, the interest is referred to as the discount.

T F 6. When interest is compounded, it is calculated on the principal plus any interest previously earned.

T F 7. The number of interest compounding periods is equal to the number of years involved divided by the number of compounding periods per year.

T F 8. A time diagram is a horizontal time line that is divided into equal time periods, called interest periods or compounding periods.

T F 9. If an investment were made today with interest compounded annually, its future value at the end of two years would be equal to the investment plus two years' simple interest.

T F 10. The present value of an amount to be received or paid in the future is that amount discounted for n periods at i rate of interest.

T F 11. An annuity is a series of cash flows that occur at intervals over a period of time.

T F 12. When the cash flows occur at the beginning of each period, the cash flows are referred to as an ordinary annuity.

T F 13. If the amount of the rent and the future value of an ordinary annuity factor (from the appropriate table) are known, the future value of the ordinary annuity is calculated by dividing the rent by the future value of an ordinary annuity factor.

T F 14. When a table constructed for the future value of an ordinary annuity is used to calculate the future value of an annuity due of R rents for n periods at i interest rate, R is multiplied by $(A_{\overline{n}|i})(1 + i)$.

T F 15. The number of rents for the present value of an annuity due is one more than the number of interest periods.

T F 16. A deferred annuity is an annuity whose rents are paid or received every other period.

T F 17. If the future value (a), the present value (p), and the number of periods (n) are known, the interest rate (i) can be found by dividing a by p.

T F 18. When considering the future value of an annuity due, there is an equal number of rents and interest periods.

T F 19. When the present value or selling price of a long-term bond is calculated, the principal and total interest are both considered as single amounts.

T F 20. To determine the proper balance sheet valuation of a pension plan with the anticipated date of retirement several years in the future, a present value of a deferred annuity calculation must be made.

Multiple Choice

Select the best response for each of the following items, and circle the corresponding letter:

1. The simple interest formula involves three variables: principal (*p*), interest rate per year (*i*), and number of years (*n*). The correct formula for computing simple interest (*I*) is:

   a. $I = (p \times i) + n$.
   b. $I = p \times i \times n$.
   c. $I = p + i + n$.
   d. $I = p \times (i + n)$.

2. Assuming the same interest rate, if an interest-bearing note matures in more than one year, the dollar amount of simple interest compared with the dollar amount of compound interest will be:

   a. Greater.
   b. Less.
   c. Equal.
   d. Either less or equal, depending on whether the compounding is done annually or semi-annually.

3. If interest is compounded more frequently than once a year and the stated interest is an annual percentage, the interest rate per compounding period is equal to:

   a. The stated annual rate.
   b. The stated annual rate divided by the number of years.
   c. The number of compounding periods multiplied by the annual rate.
   d. The annual rate divided by the number of compounding periods per year.

4. When an unknown interest rate (*i*) is sought, which of the following variables must be known before *i* can be found?

   a. Future value (*a*) and number of periods (*n*) only.
   b. Present value (*p*) and future value (*a*) only.
   c. Present value (*p*) and number of periods (*n*) only.
   d. Present value (*p*), future value (*a*), and number of periods (*n*).

5. The cash flows of an annuity due:

   a. Occur at the beginning of each period.
   b. Number two more than the number of interest periods.
   c. Occur at the end of each period.
   d. Number two less than the number of interest periods.

6. The present value of a deferred annuity of *R* rents for *n* periods discounted at *i* interest rate deferred n^1 periods could be found by which of the following formulas?

   a. $P = R(P_{\overline{n+n}|i})$.
   b. $P = R(P_{\overline{n}|i}) - R(P_{\overline{n}|i})$.
   c. $P = R(P_{\overline{n+n}|i}) - R(P_{\overline{n}|i})$.
   d. $P = R(P_{\overline{n}|i}) + R(P_{\overline{n}|i})$.

7. The issuing or selling price of a long-term bond is equal to:

   a. The present value of the principal.
   b. The present value of the principal plus the present value of the periodic interest.
   c. The future value of the principal.
   d. The future value of the principal plus the future value of the periodic interest.

8. The market rate of interest for a long-term bond that is sold for less than its face value or principal is:

   a. Less than the stated interest rate.
   b. Greater than the stated interest rate.
   c. Equal to the stated interest rate.
   d. Not related to the stated interest rate.

9. The concept of future or present value associated with the calculation of the present value of future pension payments to be issued to an employee for several periods starting many years in the future is the present value of:

   a. A single amount.
   b. An ordinary annuity.
   c. An annuity due.
   d. A deferred annuity.

10. Many accountants believe that a lease requiring the first of a series of periodic payments to be made at the inception of the lease and periodically at the beginning of each succeeding period should be reported on the balance sheet at an amount equal to:

    a. The present value of an ordinary annuity.
    b. The present value of an annuity due.
    c. The future value of an ordinary annuity.
    d. The future value of an annuity due.

Extended Problems

1. These simple problems are designed to provide an understanding of the concepts of future value and present value. They also provide practice in solving future value and present value problems by means of the tables in the Appendix of the text or those found at the end of this Appendix.

REQUIRED

Identify the future value or present value concept involved in each of the following problems, illustrate the problem on a time diagram (except problems 1 and m), and solve the problem. The first problem is completed as an example.

a. What is the future value of $2,000 if $n = 4$ and $i = 6$ percent compounded annually?
   Concept: Future value of a single amount.
   Time diagram:

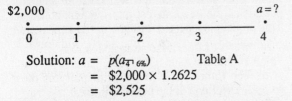

$2,000 $a = ?$

   Solution: $a = p(a_{\overline{4}\,6\%})$ Table A
   $\quad\quad\quad = \$2,000 \times 1.2625$
   $\quad\quad\quad = \$2,525$

b. What is the future value of $2,000 if $n = 4$ and $i = 6$ percent compounded semiannually?
c. What is the future value of an annuity of four rents of $2,000 each made at the end of each period if $i = 6$ percent compounded annually?
d. What is the present value of $2,000 to be received in five years if $i = 3$ percent compounded semiannually?
e. What is the present value of six rents of $2,000 if each rent is made at the end of the period and $i = 10$ percent compounded annually?
f. What is the present value of six rents of $2,000 if each rent is made at the beginning of the period and $i = 10$ percent compounded annually?
g. What is the future value of a single $10,000 amount if $n = 10$ years and $i = 6$ percent for years 1 to 4 and 8 percent for years 5 to 10?
h. What is the present value of a single $10,000 amount to be received in 10 years if $i = 6$ percent for years 1 to 4 and 8 percent for years 5 to 10?
i. What is the future value of an annuity of $3,000 to be deposited at the beginning of each of four

periods starting now if $i = 6$ percent compounded annually?
j. What is the future value of an annuity of six rents of $2,500 each starting at the end of year 4 (now is $t = 0$) if $i = 10$ percent compounded annually?
k. What is the present value of an annuity of six rents of $2,500 each if the rents begin at the end of year 4 (now is $t = 0$) and $i = 10$ percent compounded annually?
l. If the future value of six rents is $25,000, what should be the dollar amount of each of six rents made at the ends of the periods if $i = 8$ percent compounded annually?
m. How many rents of $1,500 must be made at the ends of the periods if the future value of the rents is $13,384.20 and $i = 8$ percent compounded annually?

2. On January 2, 1995, Future Corporation decided to replace a major portion of its assembly line, but the company is short of cash. Future Corporation can either (a) borrow most of the needed $500,000 by issuing a $500,000, 8 percent, four-year bond with the interest paid semiannually, or (b) lease the required new assets for $100,000 per year for six years with the payments made each January 2, starting this year.

REQUIRED

a. Compute the amount of the proceeds that Future Corporation would receive from the sale of the bonds if the market rate of interest for bonds of similar risk were 6 percent. Also assume that the market rate is 10 percent.
b. Compute the present value of the lease payments on January 2, 1995, the date of the proposed lease agreement. Assume that $i = 8$ percent.

COMMON ERRORS

The first sentence in each of the "common errors" listed here is *incorrect*. Each incorrect statement is followed by a corrected statement and an explanation.

1. The dollar amount of interest may be calculated for any loan if the principal and interest rate are known. *Wrong*
   The dollar amount of interest may be calculated for any loan if the principal, interest rate, and time period covered by the loan are known. *Right*

Interest is based on three variables: principal (p), interest rate (i), and time period (n). The dollar amount of interest (I) can be computed only if all three variables are known; that is, $I = p \times i \times n$. The time period is an important variable because interest is normally expressed as an annual rate, and if the loan is outstanding for a period of less than a year or more than a year, the calculation of the amount of interest must reflect the actual time the loan is outstanding. For purposes of this text, a year has 360 days and each month has 30 days. If, for example, a $1,000, 15 percent loan matures in three months, the dollar amount of interest on the loan is $37.50 [$1,000 × .15 × (90 ÷ 360)].

2. If two loans mature at the same time (at the end of a period of more than one year) and are for the same dollar amount and have an equal interest rate, the dollar amount of interest on each loan must be the same. *Wrong*

If two loans mature at the same time (at the end of a period of more than one year) and are for the same dollar amount and have an equal interest rate, the dollar amount of interest on each loan depends on how the interest is calculated. *Right*

Interest on a loan can be calculated as either simple interest or compound interest. Simple interest is based solely on the initial principal. A loan for more than one period would have the same dollar amount of interest each period the loan is outstanding. Compound interest is based on the initial principal plus any interest accrued on the loan. In other words, the dollar amount of compound interest increases each period because it is based on a larger amount (principal plus accumulated interest) each period.

In addition, the interest can be compounded annually or at any interval of less than a year: semiannually, quarterly, monthly, and so on. This means that as the compounding period shortens, interest is being earned more often on an increasing amount. It should be recalled that if interest is compounded more frequently than once a year, the interest rate must be adjusted. That is, the interest rate per compounding period is equal to the annual interest rate divided by the number of compounding periods per year. If the annual interest rate is 9 percent and interest is compounded quarterly, for example, the interest rate per compounding period or quarter is 2.25 percent (9% ÷ 4).

In summary, of two loans that mature in more than one year and are identical except for the method of computing interest, the dollar amount of interest will always be greater on the loan with compound interest than on the loan with simple interest. Moreover, the more frequent the compounding is, the greater will be the dollar amount of interest over the life of the loan.

3. If a single amount is deposited but the interest rate is expected to fluctuate several times before the deposit will be withdrawn, it is not possible to calculate the future value of the deposit. *Wrong*

If a single amount is deposited but the interest rate is expected to fluctuate several times before the deposit will be withdrawn, the future value of the deposit can be calculated. *Right*

Most problems concerned with present value and future value assume a single interest rate. Interest

rates do change as a result of factors such as supply and demand, investors' perceptions of risk, and inflation. Changes in interest rates are expected, especially over long periods of time, but they certainly do not preclude the calculation of future value or present value. Finding the future value of a single deposit when the interest rate is expected to change involves a series of future value calculations. The future value of the initial investment is calculated for the number of periods the initial interest rate stays constant. Then the calculated future value is treated as a new deposit for as many periods as the new interest rate remains constant. This process is repeated until the initial deposit and accumulated interest are expected to be withdrawn at the future date.

It should be noted that the present value of a single amount can be calculated if the interest rate is expected to change between the future date and the present. The calculation is similar to that discussed for future value, except that the known future value is discounted in a series of steps to the present. Present value will be calculated as many times as the interest rate changes. Future value and present value can certainly be calculated when interest rates are expected to change, but the calculations are usually more involved than they would be if the interest rate did not change.

4. The only difference between an ordinary annuity and an annuity due of *n* rents is the timing of the rents. With an ordinary annuity the cash flow occurs at the end of each period, and with an annuity due it occurs at the beginning of the period. *Wrong*

An ordinary annuity and an annuity due of *n* rents differ in two respects: the timing of the rents and the number of interest compounding periods. *Right*

Perhaps the most obvious of the distinctions between an ordinary annuity and an annuity due is the time when the rents are made: with an ordinary annuity at the end of each period, and with an annuity due at the beginning of each period. The timing of the rent also affects the number of compound interest periods. The future value of an ordinary annuity, for example, is based on one *less* interest period than rents. Since the first rent is not made until the end of the first period, no interest is earned the first period. The future value of an annuity due, however, is based on an *equal* number of interest periods and rents. Because the first rent is made at the beginning of the first period, interest is earned during the first period. Table C is constructed to provide the future value of ordinary annuity factors ($A_{\overline{n}|i}$) and cannot be used without adjustment for the calculation of the future value of an annuity due. The modified formula to calculate the future value of an annuity due is $A_D = R(A_{\overline{n}|i})$ $(1 + i)$.

Thus annuities do differ in the timing of the rents, but they also differ in the number of compound interest periods, a factor that affects the calculation of future value and present value.

5. To find the present value of a long-term bond, the stated interest rate is used to discount the principal and interest payments to the present. *Wrong*

To find the present value of a long-term bond, the current market rate of interest is used to discount the principal and interest payments to the present. *Right*

The stated rate of interest is used only to determine the dollar amount of the periodic interest payments, not to discount the future cash flows. The current market rate of interest, or the interest rate on bonds of similar risk, is used to discount

the future cash flows. The use of this rate results in a selling price for the bonds that will provide the investor with an effective yield equal to the market rate of interest. In other words, when the market rate of interest is used for discounting, the stated interest rate or return to the investor is adjusted so that the amount actually paid for the bonds permits a return or effective yield equal to the market rate of interest. If the stated rate of interest and market rate are the same, the present value or selling price of the bond is its par or face value. If, however, the stated rate of interest is higher than the market rate of interest, the present value of the bond will be greater than the face value of the bond; if the stated interest rate is lower than the market rate, the bond's present value will be less than its face value. In each case, discounting by the market rate of interest permits the effective yield on the bond to be equal to the current market rate of interest regardless of the stated interest rate.

ANSWERS

Key Terms and Concepts

1. interest
2. compound
3. future value
4. present value
5. effective interest, remains constant
6. annuity
7. ordinary annuity
8. annuity due
9. time diagram
10. deferred annuity

True-False

1. T
2. F The interest rate on a loan is not based entirely on the type of loan or its amount. Interest rates are affected by the perceived risk, or the probability of nonpayment. Therefore, loans that appear to be similar in type and amount may have different rates of interest if the risks attached to them are perceived to differ.
3. F Unless a company was extremely conservative, it would normally not select the proposal that had both the lowest return and the lowest risk. A company attempts to balance the risk and the return on the investment. Thus a company could select

the riskier of the alternatives if its expected return were sufficient to cover the risk.
4. F When interest is stated, it is usually stated on an annual basis. That does not mean, however, that interest can be calculated only annually. Interest may be calculated for a fraction of a year, such as quarterly, monthly, or daily.
5. T
6. T
7. F The number of interest compounding periods is equal to the number of years involved multiplied by the number of compounding periods per year. If interest is compounded quarterly over 5 years, for example, the number of interest compounding periods is 20 (4×5 years).
8. T
9. F The whole advantage of having interest compounded is that interest is earned on interest, not just on the initial principal. Accordingly, the future value of the investment at the end of two years is greater than the sum of the investment plus two years' simple interest. When interest is compounded annually, interest for the second year is calculated on the investment *plus* the first year's interest.
10. T
11. F This question picks on a very small but important detail. An annuity is a series of

equal cash flows that occur at *equal* intervals over a period of time. Each cash flow (either a receipt or a payment) must be of an equal dollar amount.

12. F   Just the opposite is true. The cash flows of an ordinary annuity occur at the *ends* of the periods.

13. F   To calculate the future value of an ordinary annuity, the periodic rent is *multiplied* by the future value of an ordinary annuity factor.

14. T

15. T

16. F   The periodic rents of a deferred annuity are paid or received every period, but the first rent is delayed or deferred at least two periods from the present.

17. F   When a, p, and n are known, the division of a by p results in a table factor, not an interest rate. More specifically, given the known variables, the formula for the future value of a single amount, $a = p(\overline{\,n\,}_i)$, could be used to find the table value ($a_{\overline{\,n\,}_i}$), from Table A (that is, $a \div p = a_{\overline{\,n\,}_i}$). The interest rate is found by locating the computed table value in the n row and moving up the corresponding column to find the unknown interest rate.

18. T

19. F   The present value of a long-term bond is found by adding the present value of the principal and interest payments. The principal is considered a single amount. The interest payments, however, are made periodically and are, therefore, considered an annuity.

20. T

Multiple Choice

1. b
2. b
3. d
4. d
5. a

6. c
7. b
8. b
9. d
10. b

Extended Problems

1. b. Concept: Future value of a single amount.
        Time diagram:

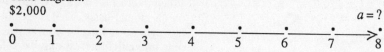

$2,000 at time 0, $a = ?$ at time 8.

Solution: $a = p(a_{\overline{8}\,3\%})$ Table A
$\quad\quad\quad = \$2,000 \times 1.2668$
$\quad\quad\quad = \$2,533.60$

c. Concept: Future value of an ordinary annuity.
    Time diagram:

$2,000 $2,000 $2,000 $2,000

0   1   2   3   4

Solution: $A = R(A_{\overline{4}\,6\%})$ Table C
$\quad\quad\quad = \$2,000 \times 4.3746$
$\quad\quad\quad = \$8,749.20$

d. Concept: Present value of a single amount.
    Time diagram:

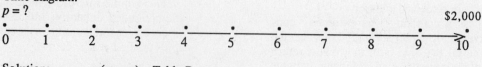

$p = ?$ at time 0, $2,000 at time 10.

Solution: $p = a(p_{\overline{10}\,1.5\%})$ Table B
$\quad\quad\quad = \$2,000 \times .8617$
$\quad\quad\quad = \$1,723.40$

e. Concept: Present value of an ordinary annuity.
   Time diagram:

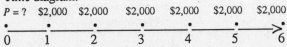

Solution: $P = R(P_{\overline{6}|10\%})$ Table D
$= \$2,000 \times 4.3553$
$= \$8,710.60$

f. Concept: Present value of an annuity due.
   Time diagram:

P = ?

$2,000 $2,000 $2,000 $2,000 $2,000 $2,000

0   1   2   3   4   5   6

Solution: $P_D = R[(P_{\overline{6}|10\%})(1 + .10)]$ Table D
$= \$2,000 \times (4.3553)(1.10)$
$= \$2,000 \times 4.7908$
$= \$9,581.60$

   or

$P_D = R(P_{\overline{6}|10\%})$ Table E
$= \$2,000 \times 4.7908$
$= \$9,581.60$

g. Concept: Future value of a single amount
   (changing interest rates).
   Time diagram:

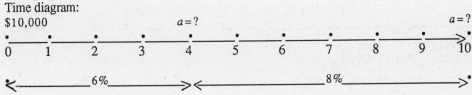

Solution: $a = p(a_{\overline{4}|6\%})$ Table A
$= \$10,000 \times 1.2625$
$= \$12,625$

   and

$a = p(a_{\overline{6}|8\%})$ Table A
$= \$12,625 \times 1.5869$
$= \$20,034.61$

h. Concept: Present value of a single amount (changing interest rates).
Time diagram:

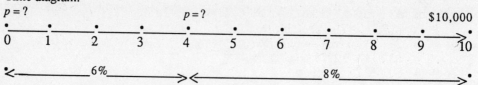

Solution: $p = a(p_{\overline{6}|8\%})$ Table B
$= \$10,000 \times .6302$
$= \$6,302$

and

$p = a(p_{\overline{4}|6\%})$ Table B
$= \$6,302 \times .7921$
$= \$4,991.81$

i. Concept: Future value of an annuity due.
Time diagram:

$3,000 \quad \$3,000 \quad \$3,000 \quad \$3,000 \quad A = ?$

Solution: $A_D = R[(A_{\overline{4}|6\%})(1 + .06)]$ Table C
$= \$3,000 \times (4.3746)(1.06)$
$= \$3,000 \times 4.6371$
$= \$13,911.30$

j. Concept: Future value of a deferred annuity.
Time diagram:

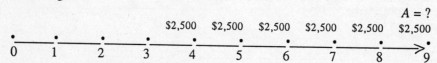

Solution: $A = R(A_{\overline{6}|10\%})$ Table C
$= \$2,500 \times 7.7156$
$= \$19,289$

k. Concept: Present value of a deferred annuity.
Time diagram:
$p = ?$

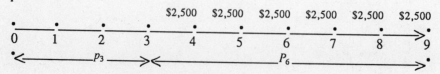

Solution: $P = R(P_{\overline{6}|10\%})$ Table D
$= \$2,500 \times 4.3553$
$= \$10,888.25$
and

$$p = a(p_{\overline{3}|10\%}) \quad \text{Table B}$$
$$= \$10,888.25 \times .7513$$
$$= \$8,180.34$$

or

$$P = R(P_{\overline{9}|10\%} - P_{\overline{3}|10\%}) \quad \text{Table D}$$
$$= \$2,500 \,[(5.7590) - (2.4869)]$$
$$= \$2,500 \times 3.2721$$
$$= \$8,180.25$$

l. Concept: Find R given n, i, and A.
Solution: $A = R(A_{\overline{6}|8\%})$ Table C
$$\$25,000 = R \times 7.3359$$
$$\$3,407.90 = R$$

m. Concept: Find n given i, R, and A.
Solution: $A = R(A_{\overline{n}|8\%})$ Table C
$$\$13,384.20 = \$1,500 \,(A_{\overline{n}|8\%})$$
$$8.9228 = A_{\overline{n}|8\%} \quad \text{(table factor)}$$

if $i = 8\%$, then $n = 7$

2. a. Proceeds from bond issue if market rate of interest is 6 percent:
Proceeds = present value of principal + present value of interest
$$= a(p_{\overline{8}|3\%}) + R(P_{\overline{8}|3\%})$$
$$= (\$500,000 \times .7894) + (\$20,000 \times 7.0197)$$
$$= \$394,700 + \$140,394$$
$$= \$535,094$$

Note: Interest is compounded semiannually; therefore, $n = 8$ (2×4 years) and $i = 3\%$ ($6\% \div 2$).

Proceeds from bond issue if market rate of interest is 10 percent:
Proceeds = $a(p_{\overline{8}|5\%}) + R(P_{\overline{8}|5\%})$
$$= (\$500,000 \times .6768) + (\$20,000 \times 6.4632)$$
$$= \$338,400 + \$129,264$$
$$= \$467,664$$

b. Present value of lease payments:
$$P_D = R(P_{\overline{6}|8\%})(1 + .08) \quad \text{Table D}$$
$$= \$100,000 \times (4.6229)(1.08)$$
$$= \$100,000 \times 4.9927$$
$$= \$499,270$$

or

$$P_D = R(P_{\overline{6}|8\%}) \quad \text{Table E}$$
$$= \$100,000 \times 4.9927$$
$$= \$499,270$$

PRESENT AND FUTURE VALUE TABLES

Table A: Future Value of 1 (a)

$$a = a\,\overline{_{n}|_i} = (1 + i)^n$$

This table shows the compound amount of $1 at various interest rates and for various time periods. The table may be used to find the future value of *any* dollar amount by multiplying the dollar amount by the factor below corresponding to the appropriate interest rate (i) and number of periods (n).

i

n	1%	1.5%	2%	2.5%	3%	4%	5%	6%	8%	10%
1	1.0100	1.0150	1.0200	1.0250	1.0300	1.0400	1.0500	1.0600	1.0800	1.1000
2	1.0201	1.0302	1.0404	1.0506	1.0609	1.0816	1.1025	1.1236	1.1664	1.2100
3	1.0303	1.0457	1.0612	1.0769	1.0927	1.1249	1.1576	1.1910	1.2597	1.3310
4	1.0406	1.0614	1.0824	1.1038	1.1255	1.1699	1.2155	1.2625	1.3605	1.4641
5	1.0510	1.0773	1.1041	1.1314	1.1593	1.2167	1.2763	1.3382	1.4693	1.6105
6	1.0615	1.0934	1.1262	1.1597	1.1941	1.2653	1.3401	1.4185	1.5869	1.7716
7	1.0721	1.1098	1.1487	1.1887	1.2299	1.3159	1.4071	1.5036	1.7138	1.9487
8	1.0829	1.1265	1.1717	1.2184	1.2668	1.3686	1.4775	1.5938	1.8509	2.1436
9	1.0937	1.1434	1.1951	1.2489	1.3048	1.4233	1.5513	1.6895	1.9990	2.3579
10	1.1046	1.1605	1.2190	1.2801	1.3439	1.4082	1.6289	1.7908	2.1589	2.5937

Table B: Present Value of 1 (p)

$$p = p\,\overline{_{n}|_i} = \frac{1}{(1 + i)^n}$$

This table shows the present value of $1 discounted at various rates of interest and for various time periods. The table may be used to find the present value of *any* future dollar amount by multiplying the future dollar amount by the table factor corresponding to the appropriate interest rate (i) and number of periods (n).

i

n	1%	1.5%	2%	2.5%	3%	4%	5%	6%	8%	10%
1	0.9901	0.9852	0.9804	0.9756	0.9709	0.9615	0.9524	0.9434	0.9259	0.9091
2	0.9803	0.9707	0.9612	0.9518	0.9426	0.9246	0.9070	0.8900	0.8573	0.8264
3	0.9706	0.9563	0.9423	0.9286	0.9151	0.8890	0.8638	0.8396	0.7938	0.7513
4	0.9610	0.9422	0.9238	0.9060	0.8885	0.8548	0.8227	0.7921	0.7350	0.6830
5	0.9515	0.9283	0.9057	0.8839	0.8626	0.8219	0.7835	0.7473	0.6806	0.6209
6	0.9420	0.9145	0.8880	0.8623	0.8375	0.7903	0.7462	0.7050	0.6302	0.5645
7	0.9327	0.9010	0.8706	0.8413	0.8131	0.7599	0.7107	0.6651	0.5835	0.5132
8	0.9235	0.8877	0.8535	0.8207	0.7894	0.7307	0.6768	0.6274	0.5403	0.4665
9	0.9143	0.8746	0.8368	0.8007	0.7664	0.7026	0.6446	0.5919	0.5002	0.4241
10	0.9053	0.8617	0.8203	0.7812	0.7441	0.6756	0.6139	0.5584	0.4632	0.3855

Table C: Future Value of an Ordinary Annuity of 1 (A)

$$A = A \, _{\overline{n}|i} = \frac{(1 + i)^n - 1}{i}$$

This table shows the future value of an ordinary annuity of $1 at various interest rates for various rents. The table may be used to find the present value of an ordinary annuity of *any* dollar amount by multiplying the dollar amount of the rents by the factor corresponding to the appropriate interest rate (*i*) and number of rents (*n*).

i

n	1%	1.5%	2%	2.5%	3%	4%	5%	6%	8%	10%
1	1.0000	1.0000	1.0000	1.0000	1.0000	1.0000	1.0000	1.0000	1.0000	1.0000
2	2.0100	2.0150	2.0200	2.0250	2.0300	2.0400	2.0500	2.0600	2.0800	2.1000
3	3.0301	3.0452	3.0604	3.0756	3.0909	3.1216	3.1525	3.1836	3.2464	3.3100
4	4.0604	4.0909	4.1216	4.1525	4.1836	4.2465	4.3101	4.3746	4.5061	4.6410
5	5.1010	5.1523	5.2040	5.2563	5.3091	5.4163	5.5256	5.6371	5.8666	6.1051
6	6.1520	6.2296	6.3081	6.3877	6.4684	6.6330	6.8019	6.9753	7.3359	7.7156
7	7.2135	7.3230	7.4343	7.5474	7.6625	7.8983	8.1420	8.3938	8.9228	9.4872
8	8.2857	8.4328	8.5830	8.7361	8.8923	9.2142	9.5491	9.8975	10.6366	11.4359
9	9.3685	9.5593	9.7546	9.9545	10.1591	10.5828	11.0266	11.4913	12.4876	13.5795
10	10.4622	10.7027	10.9497	11.2034	11.4639	12.0061	12.5779	13.1808	14.4866	15.9374

Table D: Present Value of an Ordinary Annuity of 1 (P)

$$P = P \, _{\overline{n}|i} = \frac{1 - \frac{1}{(1 + i)^n}}{i}$$

This table shows the present value of an ordinary annuity of $1 at various interest rates for various rents. The table may be used to find the present value of an ordinary annuity of *any* dollar amount by multiplying the dollar amounts of the rents by the factor corresponding to the appropriate interest rate (*i*) and number of rents (*n*).

i

n	1%	1.5%	2%	2.5%	3%	4%	5%	6%	8%	10%
1	0.9901	0.9852	0.9804	0.9756	0.9709	0.9615	0.9524	0.9434	0.9259	0.9091
2	1.9704	1.9559	1.9416	1.9274	1.9135	1.8861	1.8594	1.8334	1.7833	1.7355
3	2.9410	2.9122	2.8839	2.8560	2.8286	2.7751	2.7232	2.6730	2.5771	2.4869
4	3.9020	3.8544	3.8077	3.7620	3.7171	3.6299	3.5460	3.4651	3.3121	3.1699
5	4.8534	4.7826	4.7135	4.6458	4.5797	4.4518	4.3295	4.2124	3.9927	3.7908
6	5.7955	5.6972	5.6014	5.5081	5.4172	5.2421	5.0757	4.9173	4.6229	4.3553
7	6.7282	6.5982	6.4720	6.3494	6.2303	6.0021	5.7864	5.5824	5.2064	4.8684
8	7.6517	7.4859	7.3255	7.1701	7.0197	6.7327	6.4632	6.2098	5.7466	5.3349
9	8.5660	8.3605	8.1622	7.9709	7.7861	7.4353	7.1078	6.8017	6.2469	5.7590
10	9.4713	9.2222	8.9826	8.7521	8.5302	8.1109	7.7217	7.3601	6.7101	6.1446

Table E: Present Value of an Annuity Due of $1 ($P_D$)

$$P_D = (P\,\overline{\raise.5pt\hbox{$\scriptstyle n$}}\,_i)\,(1 + i) = \left[\frac{1 - \dfrac{1}{(1 + i)^n}}{i}\right][1 + i]$$

This table shows the present value of an annuity due of $1 at various rates of interest and for various numbers of rents. The table may be used to find the present value of an annuity due of *any* dollar amount by multiplying the dollar amount of the rents by the appropriate factors corresponding to the interest rate (i) and number of rents (n).

i

n	1%	1.5%	2%	2.5%	3%	4%	5%	6%	8%	10%
1	1.0000	1.0000	1.0000	1.0000	1.0000	1.0000	1.0000	1.0000	1.0000	1.0000
2	1.9901	1.9852	1.9804	1.9756	1.9709	1.9615	1.9524	1.9434	1.9259	1.9091
3	2.9704	2.9559	2.9416	2.9274	2.9135	2.8861	2.8594	2.8334	2.7833	2.7355
4	3.9410	3.9122	3.8839	3.8560	3.8268	3.7751	3.7232	3.6730	3.5771	3.4869
5	4.9020	4.8544	4.8077	4.7620	4.7171	4.6299	4.5460	4.4651	4.3121	4.1699
6	5.8534	5.7826	5.7135	5.6458	5.5797	5.4518	5.3295	5.2124	4.9927	4.7908
7	6.7955	6.6972	6.6014	6.5081	6.4172	6.2421	6.0757	5.9173	5.6229	5.3553
8	7.7282	7.5982	7.4720	7.3494	7.2303	7.0021	6.7864	6.5824	6.2064	5.8684
9	8.6517	8.4859	8.3255	8.1701	8.0197	7.7327	7.4632	7.2098	6.7466	6.3349
10	9.5660	9.3605	9.1622	8.9709	8.7861	8.4353	8.1078	7.8017	7.2469	6.7590